Word 2003 All-in-One Reference For Dummies

M000114779

Formatting Toolbar

Line spacing

Styles and formatting — Font Size — Italic — Align right — Increase indent
Align left — Bullets — Highlight

Style — Font — Bold — Center — Numbering — Border — Font color

Underline — Justify — Decrease indent

The Word Window

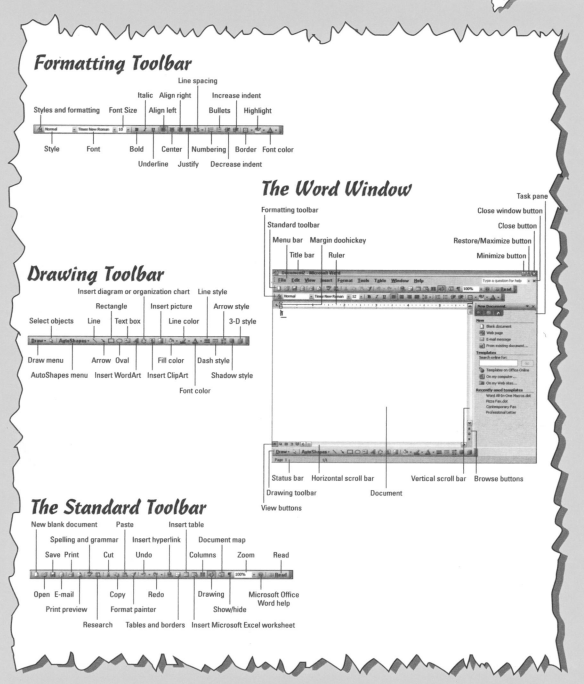

Formatting toolbar — Task pane
Standard toolbar — Close window button
Menu bar — Margin doohickey — Close button
Title bar — Ruler — Restore/Maximize button
Minimize button

Status bar — Horizontal scroll bar — Vertical scroll bar — Browse buttons
Drawing toolbar — Document
View buttons

Drawing Toolbar

Insert diagram or organization chart — Line style
Rectangle — Insert picture — Arrow style
Select objects — Line — Text box — Line color — 3-D style

Draw menu — Arrow Oval — Fill color — Dash style
AutoShapes menu — Insert WordArt — Insert ClipArt — Shadow style
Font color

The Standard Toolbar

New blank document — Paste — Insert table
Spelling and grammar — Insert hyperlink — Document map
Save Print — Cut — Undo — Columns — Zoom — Read

Open E-mail — Copy — Redo — Drawing — Microsoft Office Word help
Print preview — Format painter — Show/hide
Research — Tables and borders — Insert Microsoft Excel worksheet

For Dummies: Bestselling Book Series for Beginners

Word 2003 All-in-One Desk Reference For Dummies®

Cheat Sheet

Formatting Keyboard Commands

Command	Keys
Bold	Ctrl+B
Italic	Ctrl+I
Underline	Ctrl+U
Center	Ctrl+E
Left Align	Ctrl+L
Right Align	Ctrl+R
Justify	Ctrl+J
Normal	Ctrl+Spacebar

Editing Keyboard Commands

Undo	Ctrl+Z
Cut	Ctrl+X
Copy	Ctrl+C
Paste	Ctrl+V
Select All	Ctrl+A
Find	Ctrl+F
Replace	Ctrl+H

Commonly Used File Commands

New	Ctrl+N
Open	Ctrl+O
Save	Ctrl+S
Print	Ctrl+P

Function Key Gazetteer

Key	Plain	Shift+	Ctrl+	Alt+
F1	Help	Reveal formatting	Reveal formatting	(nothing)
F2	Copy Text	Move Text	Print Preview	(nothing)
F3	Insert AutoText	Change Case	Spike	Create AutoText
F4	Redo	Repeat Find	Close	Exit
F5	Go to	Go back	Restore doc window	Restore app window
F6	Switch panes	Switch panes	Next window	Next window
F7	Proofing	Thesaurus	Move window	Next misspelling
F8	Extend selection	Shrink selection	Size window	Macros
F9	Update fields	Toggle field	Insert field chars	Toggle all fields
F10	Menu	(nothing)	Maximize doc	Maximize app
F11	Next field	Previous field	Lock field	View macro editor
F12	Save As	Save	Open	(nothing)

Navigation Keyboard Commands

→	Right one character
←	Left one character
↑	Up one line
↓	Down one line
Ctrl+→	Right one word
Ctrl+←	Left one word
Ctrl+↑	Up one paragraph
Ctrl+↓	Down one paragraph
Page Up	Up one screen
Page Down	Down one screen
End	End of current line
Home	Start of current line
Ctrl+End	End of document
Ctrl+Home	Start of document

For Dummies: Bestselling Book Series for Beginners

Word 2003

ALL-IN-ONE DESK REFERENCE

FOR

DUMMIES®

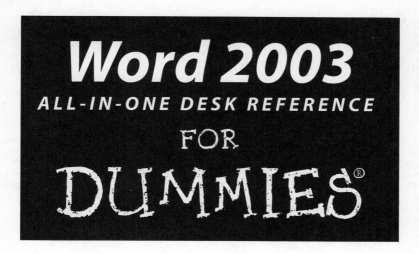

Word 2003
ALL-IN-ONE DESK REFERENCE
FOR
DUMMIES®

by Doug Lowe

WILEY

Wiley Publishing, Inc.

Word 2003 All-in-One Desk Reference For Dummies®

Published by
Wiley Publishing, Inc.
111 River Street
Hoboken, NJ 07030-5774

WILEY

About the Author

Doug Lowe has written a whole bunch of computer books, including more than 30 *For Dummies* books, such as *Networking For Dummies,* 6th Edition, *PowerPoint 2003 For Dummies*, *Internet Explorer 6 For Dummies*, *Networking All-in-One Desk Reference For Dummies,* and *Microsoft Office 2002 For Dummies Quick Reference*. He lives in that sunny All-American City, Fresno, California, where all the politicians are actors and all the actors think they're politicians. He's one of those obsessive-compulsive decorating nuts who creates computer-controlled Halloween decorations that rival Disney's Haunted Mansion and Christmas displays that can be seen from space. Maybe his next book should be *Tacky Holiday Decorations For Dummies*.

Dedication

To Debbie, Rebecca, Sarah, and Bethany.

Author's Acknowledgments

I'd like to thank project editor Nicole Sholly, who did an excellent job of managing all the details that have to fall in place just right for a book like this to come together. I'd also like to thank Sharad Kumar Saksena of Dreamtech for a thorough technical review and excellent suggestions, and copy editor Rebecca Senninger who made sure the i's were crossed and the t's dotted (oops, reverse that!). And, as always, thanks to all the behind-the-scenes people who chipped in with help I'm not even aware of.

Publisher's Acknowledgments

We're proud of this book; please send us your comments through our online registration form located at www.dummies.com/register/.

Some of the people who helped bring this book to market include the following:

Acquisitions, Editorial, and Media Development

Associate Project Editor: Nicole Sholly

Acquisitions Editor: Melody Layne

Copy Editor: Rebecca Senninger

Technical Editor:
Wiley-Dreamtech India Pvt Ltd

Editorial Manager: Kevin Kirschner

Media Development Manager:
Laura VanWinkle

Media Development Supervisor:
Richard Graves

Editorial Assistant: Amanda Foxworth

Cartoons: Rich Tennant, www.the5thwave.com

Composition

Project Coordinator: Maridee Ennis

Layout and Graphics: Karl Brandt, Amanda Carter, Lauren Goddard, Denny Hager, Stephanie D. Jumper, Michael Kruzil, Lynsey Osborn, Heather Ryan, Julie Trippetti, Melanee Wolven

Proofreaders: Andy Hollandbeck, Betty Kish, Carl William Pierce

Indexer: Tom Dinse

Publishing and Editorial for Technology Dummies

> **Richard Swadley,** Vice President and Executive Group Publisher
>
> **Andy Cummings,** Vice President and Publisher
>
> **Mary C. Corder,** Editorial Director

Publishing for Consumer Dummies

> **Diane Graves Steele,** Vice President and Publisher
>
> **Joyce Pepple,** Acquisitions Director

Composition Services

> **Gerry Fahey,** Vice President of Production Services
>
> **Debbie Stailey,** Director of Composition Services

Contents at a Glance

Table of Contents

Introduction

Welcome to *Word 2003 All-in-One Desk Reference For Dummies,* the book written especially for those of you who use Word on a daily basis and need a handy reference to all the various and sundry things this mighty program can do. This book contains all of the basic and not-so-basic information you need to know to get the most out of Word, whether you use it to compose simple letters or write 200-page government grants.

About This Book

Word 2003 All-in-One Desk Reference For Dummies is a big book that's actually made up of nine smaller books, each of which covers a specific aspect of using Word. You find minibooks on such topics as editing your documents, working with graphics, using Word to create Web pages, and customizing Word to make it work the way you want it to.

Word 2003 All-in-One Desk Reference For Dummies doesn't pretend to be a comprehensive reference for every detail of these topics. Instead, this book shows you how to get up and running fast so that you have more time to do the things you really want to do. Designed using the easy-to-follow *For Dummies* format, this book helps you get the information you need without laboring to find it.

Whenever one big thing is made up of several smaller things, confusion is always a possibility. That's why *Word 2003 All-in-One Desk Reference For Dummies* is designed to have multiple access points (I hear an acronym coming on — MAP!) to help you find what you want. At the beginning of the book is a detailed Table of Contents that covers the entire book. Then, each minibook begins with a mini Table of Contents that shows you at a glance what chapters are included in that minibook. Useful running heads appear at the top of each page to point out the topic discussed on that page. And handy thumb tabs run down the side of the pages to help you quickly find each minibook. Finally, a comprehensive index lets you find information anywhere in the entire book.

This book isn't the kind you pick up and read from start to finish, as if it were a cheap novel. If I ever see you reading it at the beach, I'll kick sand in your face. This book is more like a reference, the kind of book you can pick up, turn to just about any page, and start reading. You don't have to memorize anything in this book. It's a "need-to-know" book: You pick it up when you need to know something. Need to know how to do a mail merge? Pick up the book. Need to know how to crop an image? Pick up the book. After you find what you need, put the book down and get on with your life.

How to Use This Book

This book works like a reference. Start with the topic you want to find out about. Look for it in the Table of Contents or in the index to get going. The Table of Contents is detailed enough that you can find most of the topics you're looking for. If not, turn to the index, where you can find even more detail.

After you find your topic in the Table of Contents or the index, turn to the area of interest and read as much as you need or want. Then close the book and get on with it.

Of course, the book is loaded with information, so if you want to take a brief excursion into your topic, you're more than welcome. If you want to know everything about customizing Word, read the whole minibook on customization. But if you just want to find out how to create a simple keyboard shortcut to apply a style that you use 200 times a day, just read the section on keyboard shortcuts. You get the idea.

If you need to type something, you see the text you need to type like this: **Type this stuff**. In this example, you type **Type this stuff** at the keyboard and press Enter. An explanation usually follows, just in case you're scratching your head and grunting, "Huh?"

Whenever I describe a message or information that you see on-screen, I present it as follows:

```
A message from your friendly word processor
```

Note: The names of dialog boxes, menu commands, and options are spelled with the first letter of each main word capitalized, even though these letters may not be capitalized on-screen. This format makes sentences filled with long option names easier for you to read. (Haven't we thought of everything?)

How This Book Is Organized

Each of the nine minibooks contained in *Word 2003 All-in-One Desk Reference For Dummies* stands alone. The first minibook covers the basics of using Word. The remaining minibooks cover a variety of Word topics. Even those minibooks that cover familiar ground are packed with techniques and commands you may not know about. I think you'll find something useful in every chapter. Here is a brief description of what you find in each minibook.

Book 1: Word Basics

This minibook covers the basics you need to get going with Word. You find out how to start Word, how to create and save a document, how to work with templates, how to print your documents, and how to get help. Even if you've been using Word for years, I recommend at least skimming over these chapters, particularly the chapter on templates. Many Word users don't realize the power of the lowly template.

Book II: Formatting Text

Here is where I discuss the ins and outs of formatting your text, from simple formats such as bold and italics to complicated page and section formatting, multi-column layouts, tables, lists, and the like. The most important chapter in this minibook — and perhaps the most important chapter in the entire book — is Chapter 3, which shows you how to use styles. Styles is one of Word's best features, but most Word users don't take advantage of this powerful feature.

Book III: Editing Techniques

In this minibook, I give you the ins and outs of editing text with Word. The early chapters cover basic editing techniques you probably already know about, but then it launches into more advanced topics such as the Find and Replace commands, the AutoText feature, proofing tools, and collaboration features. The more you use Word, the more it pays to know all of the tips and shortcuts that I present in this minibook.

Book IV: Getting Graphic

The Getting Graphic chapters cover all of the powerful graphics features built into Word. I show you how to insert pictures and clip art, how to use the Drawing toolbar to draw shapes on your pages, and how to create charts and diagrams. My favorite chapter in this minibook is Chapter 6, which unlocks some of the secret techniques for fancy desktop publishing effects.

Book V: Web Publishing

The chapters in this minibook are devoted to Word's HTML editing features. You discover how to work with Web documents, how to use Word as an HTML editor, and how to use advanced HTML features, such as cascading style sheets and frames. I also briefly show you how to work with XML documents in Word.

Book VI: Advanced Document Features

This minibook is where you find out how to add advanced features to your document. The chapters in this minibook cover such diverse topics as fields, custom forms, outlines, master documents, indexes, Tables of Contents, tables of figures, and tables of authorities.

Book VII: Letters, Envelopes, and Labels

In these chapters, I tell you all about creating letters, envelopes, and labels in Word, from single letters to mass mailings using the mail merge feature. You even see how to use Word to send faxes. If you use Word to mail letters to your customers, friends, or relatives, you want to focus especially on Chapters 3 and 4.

Book VIII: Customizing Word

As powerful as Word is, one of its most powerful features is the customization features that let you tailor Word so that it works exactly the way you want it to. The chapters in this minibook show you how to do just that. You discover how to set Word's options to your liking and how to customize menus, toolbars, and keyboard shortcuts. You even find out how to teach Word to take dictation and respond to voice commands.

Book IX: Programming Word with VBA

The last minibook is devoted to those of you who want to dig deep into the depths of Word by writing your own macros using Word's powerful programming language, Visual Basic for Applications (VBA). The chapters in this minibook are not for the feint of heart, but if you're willing to take the plunge, you can make Word do things you never thought possible.

Icons Used in This Book

Like any *For Dummies* book, this book is chock-full of helpful icons that draw your attention to items of particular importance. You find the following icons throughout this book:

Did I tell you about the memory course I took?

Hold it — technical stuff is just around the corner. Read on only if you have your pocket protector.

Pay special attention to this icon; it lets you know that some particularly useful tidbit is at hand — perhaps a shortcut or a little-used command that pays off big.

Danger Will Robinson! This icon highlights information that may help you avert disaster.

Where to Go from Here

Yes, you can get there from here. With this book in hand, you're ready to plow right through the rugged networking terrain. Browse through the Table of Contents and decide where you want to start. Be bold! Be courageous! Be adventurous! And above all, have fun!

Book I

Word Basics

"A BRIEF ANNOUNCEMENT, CLASS – AN OPEN-FACED PEANUT BUTTER SANDWICH IS NOT AN APPROPRIATE REPLACEMENT FOR A MISSING MOUSEPAD."

Contents at a Glance

Chapter 1: Getting to Know Word

In This Chapter

- ✔ **Starting Word**
- ✔ **Making sense of all the stuff on-screen**
- ✔ **Entering and editing text**
- ✔ **Printing your document**
- ✔ **Saving your work**
- ✔ **Closing a document and quitting Word**

*T*his chapter is an introduction to the very basics of using Word: starting the program; using all the toolbars, task panes, and other ornaments that adorn Word's screen; typing and editing text; printing and saving a document; and perhaps most important of all, quitting Word when you're done. Have fun!

Starting Word

You can start Word in so many different ways that you can probably use a different technique every day for a fortnight. Rather than bore you with the details of every possible way to start Word, I show you the most common way first. Then, I show you a couple of shortcuts that are useful in case you use Word a lot.

Turn your computer on, and then follow these steps to start Word:

1. **Get ready.**

Light some votive candles. Take two Tylenol. Put on a pot of coffee. If you're allergic to banana slugs, take an allergy pill. Sit in the lotus position facing Redmond, Washington, and recite the Windows creed three times:

Bill Gates is my friend. Resistance is futile. No beer and no TV make Homer something something . . .

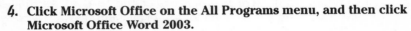

2. Click the Start button.

Find the Start button at the lower-left corner of the Windows display. When you click it, the famous Start menu appears. The Start menu works pretty much the same, no matter which version of Windows you're using.

If you can't find the Start button, try moving the mouse pointer all the way to the bottom edge of the screen and holding it there a moment. With luck on your side, you see the Start button appear. If not, try moving the mouse pointer to the other three edges of the screen: top, left, and right. Sometimes the Start button hides behind these edges. If all else fails, press the Ctrl and Esc buttons at the same time. That always brings up the Start menu.

3. Point to All Programs on the Start menu.

Move the mouse pointer up to the word *Programs* and hold it there a moment. Yet another menu appears, revealing a bevy of commands.

On older versions of Windows (prior to Windows XP), All Programs is called simply "Programs."

4. Click Microsoft Office on the All Programs menu, and then click Microsoft Office Word 2003.

Your computer whirs and clicks and possibly makes other unmentionable noises while Word comes to life.

The following paragraphs describe some shortcut ways to start Word. You'll want to look into these methods if you use Word frequently and you grow weary of trudging through the depths of the Start menu.

✦ If you use Word frequently, it may appear in an area of the Start menu called the *Frequently Used Program List,* which appears directly above the All Programs command. If so, you can start Word by clicking it directly from the Start menu, without having to click through All Programs and Microsoft Office to get to it.

✦ If you want Word to always appear at the top of the Start menu, choose Start⇨All Programs⇨Microsoft Office. Then, right-click Microsoft Office Word 2003 and choose the Pin to Start Menu command. This command "pins" Word to the Start menu, above the Frequently Used Program List.

✦ You can create an icon for Word on your desktop. Then, you can start Word by double-clicking its desktop icon. To create a desktop icon for Word, open the Start menu, navigate through All Programs and Microsoft Office, then right-click Microsoft Office Word 2003 and choose Send To⇨Desktop.

✦ My personal favorite way to start Word is to create an icon for it on the Quick Launch area of the task bar, right next to the Start button. To create a quick launch icon for Word, first create a desktop shortcut as described in the preceding paragraph. Then, drag the desktop icon to the Quick Launch bar and release the mouse button. To start Word from the Quick Launch bar, just click the Word icon once. No need to double-click in the Quick Launch bar.

✦ Yet another way to start Word is to open your My Documents folder by choosing Start⇨My Documents. Then, double-click the icon for any Word document in your My Documents folder. Windows responds by starting Word and opening the document you chose.

✦ One more trick before moving on. If you use Word every day, you can set it to start automatically every time you start your computer. To do that, navigate your way through the Start menu to the Microsoft Office Word 2003 command. Then, drag it into the Startup group under Start⇨All Programs.

What Is All This Stuff?

When you start Word, it greets you with a screen that's so cluttered with stuff that you're soon ready to dig out your grandfather's manual typewriter. The center of the screen is mercifully blank and vaguely resembles a piece of typing paper, but all around the edges and tucked into every corner are little icons and buttons, rulers and menus, and whatnot. What is all that stuff?

Figure 1-1 shows the basic Word screen in all its cluttered glory. The following list points out the more important parts of the Word screen:

✦ **Title bar:** At the very top of the Word screen is the *title bar,* which displays the name of the document you're working on. The title bar also includes the standard Minimize, Restore, and Close buttons present in every window.

✦ **Menu bar:** Just below the Microsoft Office Word title is the *menu bar.* The deepest and darkest secrets of Word are hidden on the menu bar. Wear a helmet when exploring it.

Word has an annoying "feature" that tries to simplify menus by showing only those commands that you frequently use on the menus. If this feature is enabled on your computer, the menus start out by showing only those commands that the programmers at Microsoft think you'll use most often. The less frequently used commands are hidden beneath the double down arrow that appears at the bottom of each menu. As you work with Word, the commands that you use most often show up on the menus, so you don't have to click the down arrow to access them.

Standard toolbar

Menu bar   Title bar

Formatting toolbar

Ruler   Task pane

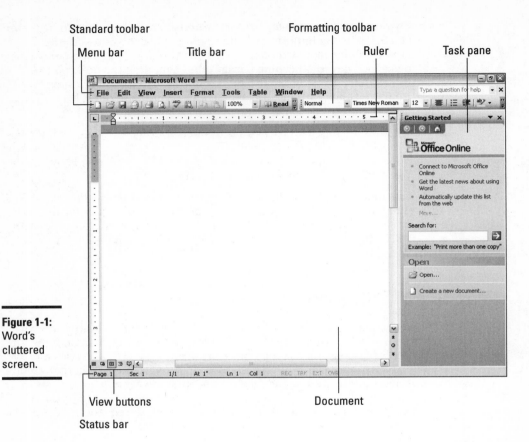

Figure 1-1:
Word's
cluttered
screen.

View buttons

Status bar

Document

As a result, don't give up if you can't find a menu command. Just click the double down arrow at the bottom of the menu. Or, just stare at the menu for a few seconds without blinking. Eventually, Word realizes that you can't find what you're looking for and blinks. The missing menu commands magically appear. (If this behavior drives you nuts, choose Tools⇨Customize, click the Options tab, select the Always Show Full Menus option, and click OK.)

✦ **Toolbars:** Just below the menu bar are two of the many *toolbars* that Word offers you in an effort to make its most commonly used features easy to use. Each toolbar consists of a bunch of buttons that you can click to perform common functions. The toolbar on the top is the Standard toolbar; immediately beneath it is the Formatting toolbar.

If you're not sure about the function of one of the billions and billions of buttons that clutter the Word screen, place the mouse pointer on the button in question. After a moment, the name of the button appears in a box just below the button.

✦ **Ruler:** Below the Formatting toolbar is the *ruler,* which you use to set margins and tab stops.

✦ **Task pane:** The right side of the Word screen is dominated by the *task pane,* which helps you complete common tasks quickly. When you first start Word, the task pane appears with the Getting Started options, which provides easy access to help information and lets you open an existing document or create a new document. After you get going, the task pane may disappear for a while. Don't worry, it returns when needed.

✦ **View buttons:** The group of five buttons located to the left of the horizontal scroll bar near the bottom of the screen lets you switch among Word's various document views. You can find out more about these views in the section "The View from Here Is Great."

✦ **Status bar:** At the very bottom of the screen is the *status bar,* which tells you a bunch of useful information, such as what page you're looking at and where the insertion point is currently positioned.

✦ **Salad bar:** The salad bar is located . . . well, actually, there is no salad bar. You have to pay extra for that.

You'll never get anything done if you feel that you have to understand every pixel of the Word screen before you can do anything. Don't worry about the stuff that you don't understand; just concentrate on what you need to know to get the job done and worry about the bells and whistles later.

Lots of stuff is crammed onto the Word screen — enough stuff that the program works best if you let it run in *maximized* mode. If Word doesn't take over your entire screen, look for the boxy-looking Maximize button on the right side of the title bar (it's the middle of the three buttons). Click it to maximize the Word screen. Click it again to restore Word to its smaller size.

The View from Here Is Great

On the bottom-left edge of the Word screen is a series of five View buttons that let you switch among various document views. If you prefer menu commands to buttons, you can also switch views using the first five commands under the View menu. The following paragraphs describe these five commands (the View button for switching to each view is shown in the margin):

✦ View⇨Normal sets Word to Normal view, which formats text as it appears on the printed page with a few exceptions. For example, headers and footers are not shown. Most people prefer this mode.

✦ View⇨Web Layout switches Word into Web Layout view, which shows how a document appears when viewed by a Web browser, such as Internet Explorer. Web Layout view is the mode you normally work in when you use Word to create HTML documents.

✦ View⇨Print Layout activates Print Layout view, which displays pages exactly as they will appear when printed, complete with columns, headers and footers, and all other formatting details. Word is noticeably slower in Print Layout view than in Normal view, especially when you format the document with headers and footers or use multiple columns. On a fast computer, you probably won't notice the difference. But if you're using a hand-me-down computer powered by hamsters, you may want to avoid Print Layout view.

✦ View⇨Outline View activates Outline view, which lets you work with outlines established via Word's standard heading styles. For more information about using outlines, consult Book VI, Chapter 3.

✦ View⇨Reading Layout activates Reading Layout view, a new feature of Word 2003 designed for easy on-screen reading.

Typing and Editing Text

I devote all of Book III to the many and sundry techniques for editing your documents. In the following paragraphs, I just highlight some very basic editing techniques to get you started. For real editing, though, you need to peruse Book III.

✦ Any text you type is inserted into the document at the location of the *insertion pointer.* You can move the insertion pointer around the screen by using the cursor movement keys (the four keys with arrows pointing up, down, left, and right), or by simply clicking the mouse at the location you want to move the insertion pointer to.

✦ If you press the Insert key, Word switches to *overtype mode.* Your typing replaces text already on-screen. You can turn overtype mode off by pressing the Insert key again.

✦ If you make a mistake (never!), press the Backspace key to back up, erasing text as you go. For more efficient ways to correct mistakes, refer to Book III.

✦ Press the Enter key at the end of each paragraph to begin a new paragraph.

Don't press the Enter key at the end of every line. Word automatically wraps your text to the next line when it reaches the margin.

✦ Press the Tab key to indent text. Don't press the spacebar repeatedly to indent text; that's a rookie mistake.

Printing Your Masterpiece

After you finish your masterpiece, you may want to print it. I have a lot more to say about printing in Chapter 4 of this minibook. But for now, here's the quick procedure for printing a document:

1. **Make sure that your printer is turned on and ready to print.**

Check the paper supply while you're at it.

2. **Click the Print button on the Standard toolbar.**

If you prefer, use the File➪Print command or press Ctrl+P or Ctrl+Shift+ F12. Whichever way you do it, you see the Print dialog box, as shown in Figure 1-2. The Print dialog box has a myriad of options you can fiddle with to print just parts of your document or to print more than one copy. But to print a single copy of the entire document, you can leave these settings alone.

3. **Click OK or press the Enter key.**

Make sure that you say "Print" in a knowing manner, pointing at your printer as you do so. The secret is to fool your printer into thinking you know what you're doing.

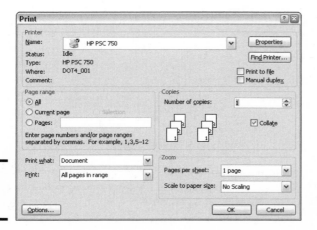

Figure 1-2: The Print dialog box.

Saving Your Work

Now that you've spent hours creating your document, you have to save your work to a file. If you make the rookie mistake of turning off your computer before you save your presentation, *poof!* Your work vanishes as if David Copperfield is in town.

Like everything else in Word, you have at least four ways to save a document:

✦ Click the Save button on the Standard toolbar.

✦ Choose File➪Save.

✦ Press Ctrl+S.

✦ Press Shift+F12.

If you haven't yet saved the file to your hard drive, the magical Save As dialog box appears, as shown in Figure 1-3. Type the name that you want to use for the file in the Save As dialog box and click the OK button to save the file. After you save the file once, subsequent saves update the disk file with any changes that you made to the document since the last time you saved it.

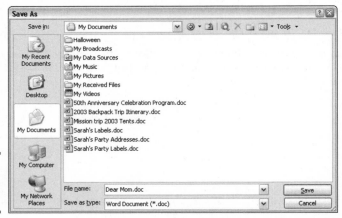

Figure 1-3:
The Save As
dialog box.

Some notes to keep in mind when saving files:

✦ Put on your Thinking Cap when assigning a name to a new file. The file-name is how you can recognize the file later on, so pick a meaningful name that suggests the file's contents.

✦ After you save a file for the first time, the name in Word's title bar changes from *Document1* to the name of your file. This name is simply proof that you saved the file.

✦ Don't work on your file for hours at a time without saving it. I learned the hard way to save my work every few minutes. After all, I live in California, so I never know when a rolling blackout will hit my neighborhood. Get into the habit of saving every few minutes, especially after making a significant change to a document. In fact, I usually save after completing every paragraph.

Opening a Document

After you save your document to your hard drive, you can retrieve it later when you want to make additional changes or to print it. As you may guess, Word gives you about 2,037 ways to accomplish the retrieval. Here are the four most common:

✦ Click the Open button on the Standard toolbar.

✦ Choose File➪Open.

✦ Press Ctrl+O.

✦ Press Ctrl+F12.

All four retrieval methods pop up the Open dialog box, which gives you a list of files to choose from, as shown in Figure 1-4. Click the file you want, and then click the Open button or press the Enter key.

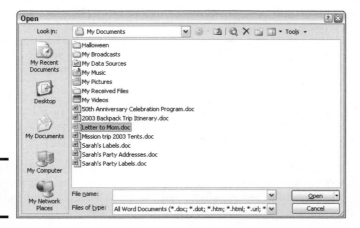

Figure 1-4:
The Open
dialog box.

The Open dialog box has controls that enable you to rummage through the various folders on your hard drive in search of your files. If you know how to open a file in any Windows application, you know how to do it in Word; the Open dialog box is pretty much the same in any Windows program.

If you seem to have lost a file, rummage around in different folders to see whether you can find it. Perhaps you saved a file in the wrong folder by accident. Also, check the spelling of the filename. Maybe your fingers weren't on the home row when you typed the filename, so instead of `River City.doc`, you saved the file as `Eucwe Xurt`.doc. I hate when that happens. If all else fails, you can use Windows' built-in search feature. Choose Start⇨Search and follow the instructions that appear in the Search Results window.

The fastest way to open a file from the Open dialog box is to double-click the file that you want to open. This action spares you from having to click the file once and then clicking Open. Double-clicking also exercises the fast-twitch muscles in your index finger.

Word keeps track of the last four files that you've opened and displays them on the File menu. To open a file you've recently opened, click the File menu and inspect the list of files at the bottom of the menu. If the file you want is in the list, click it to open it.

The last four files you opened are also listed on the Getting Started task pane, so you can open them quickly if the Getting Started task pane is visible.

Closing a Document

Having finished your document and printed it just right, you have come to the time to close it. Closing a document is kind of like gathering up your papers, putting them neatly in a file folder, and returning the folder to its proper file drawer. The document disappears from your computer screen. Don't worry: It's tucked safely away on your hard drive where you can get to it later if you need to.

To close a file, choose File⇨Close. You also can use the keyboard shortcut Ctrl+W, but you need a mind like a steel trap to remember that Ctrl+W stands for Close.

You don't have to close a file before exiting Word. If you exit Word without closing a file, Word graciously closes the file for you. The only reason you may want to close a file is that you want to work on a different file and you don't want to keep both files open at the same time.

If you made changes since the last time you saved the file, Word offers to save the changes for you. Click Yes to save the file before closing or click No to abandon any changes you've made to the file.

If you close all the open Word documents, you may discover that most of Word's commands are rendered useless (they are grayed out on the menu). Fear not. Open a document, or create a new one, and the commands return to life.

Exiting Word

Had enough excitement for one day? Use any of these techniques to shut down Word:

+ Choose File⇨Exit.
+ Click the X box at the top-right corner of the Word window.
+ Press Alt+F4.

Bam! Word is history.

You should know a few things about exiting Word (or any application):

+ Word doesn't let you abandon ship without first considering whether you want to save your work. If you made changes to any documents and haven't saved them, Word offers to save the documents for you. Lean over and plant a fat kiss right in the middle of your monitor — Word just saved you your job.

+ Never, never, never, ever, never turn off your computer while Word or any other program is running. Bad! Always properly exit Word and all other programs that are running before you turn off your computer.

Chapter 2: Managing Your Documents

In This Chapter

✔ **Retrieving documents with the File⇨Open command**

✔ **Finding files gone astray**

✔ **Retrieving files from the Internet**

✔ **Saving your documents, including how to set Word's file saving options**

✔ **Dealing with documents from different word processors, including older versions of Word**

You can't get very far in Word without knowing how to save and retrieve documents on disk. So, this chapter dives headfirst into the world of Word document management.

Creating a New Document

The easiest way to create a new document in Word is to click the New Blank Document button on the Standard toolbar. This button creates a new document using a standard template called Normal.dot. A *template* is simply a model document from which new documents are created. New documents based on the Normal.dot template have the following characteristics:

✦ The margins are set at one inch from the top and bottom and 1.25" from the left and right. If you want to change these margin settings, refer to Book II, Chapter 4.

✦ The text is formatted using 12-point Times New Roman. To change the text format, refer to Book II, Chapter 1.

✦ The document includes a few built-in styles you can use to format headings. To discover how to work with these styles or to create your own styles, refer to Book II, Chapter 3.

The Normal.dot template is adequate for generic types of documents, such as book reports and letters to your mom. For more specialized types of documents, you can use other templates that come with Word. Or, you can create your own templates. For more information about working with templates, see Chapter 3 of this minibook.

After you create a new document, you can then edit the document however you want. Then, you can choose File⇨Save, as I describe later in this chapter, to save the new document to disk.

Another way to create a new document is to choose File⇨New. When you do, the New Document task pane appears. It provides several links you can click to create various types of documents:

✦ **Blank document:** Click this link to create a blank document, the same as if you click the New Blank Document button.

✦ **Web page:** Click this link to create a new Web page. For more information, see Book V, Chapter 1.

✦ **E-mail message:** Click this link to create a new e-mail message that can then be delivered to an e-mail recipient.

✦ **From existing document:** Click this link to create a new document based on a copy of an existing document.

The New Document task pane also includes several links that let you create new documents based on templates. For more information about working with templates, see Chapter 3 of this minibook.

Using the File⇨Open Command

The most direct way to open a document is to choose File⇨Open. You can summon this command three ways:

✦ Choose File⇨Open from the menu.

✦ Click the Open button on the Standard toolbar.

✦ Press Ctrl+O or Ctrl+F12.

Ctrl+O is the more intuitive keyboard shortcut for the File⇨Open command ("O" is for "Open"), but Ctrl+F12 is left over from the early days of Windows, before Microsoft programmers decided that keyboard shortcuts make more sense. Rather than drop an antiquated and senseless keyboard shortcut in favor of one that makes sense and is consistent across all Windows applications (or at least is supposed to be), the Word developers at Microsoft decided to leave *both* keyboard shortcuts in place.

However you do it, the Open dialog box appears, as shown in Figure 2-1.

The most important control in the Open dialog box is the Look In drop-down list. The Look In control lists every location where documents may be hiding: all your disk drives, your desktop (you can store documents on the desktop by dragging them there from an Explorer window), your My Documents folder, and a few other locations, such as network drives and such.

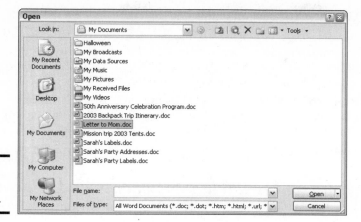

Figure 2-1:
The Open
dialog box.

Although the Look In drop-down list is the primary method of navigating through your drives and folders, you can still work your way down through the folder hierarchy by double-clicking folder icons. You can move back up the folder hierarchy by clicking the Up One Level button, which appears next to the Look In field. You can also move up one level in the hierarchy by pressing the Backspace key.

You can open more than one document at once by selecting several files and clicking the Open button. Use one of the following techniques to select several files:

✦ Hold down the Ctrl key while clicking the files you want to select.

✦ To select a range of files, click the first file in the range, hold down the Shift key, and click the last file in the range.

Changing views

The Open dialog box lets you switch among eight different views of your documents. The Views button at the top of the Open dialog box displays a menu that lets you choose your view:

✦ **Thumbnails:** Displays a large icon that represents the contents of each file. For image files, the thumbnail displays a small view of the image contained in the file. But for document files, the thumbnail simply displays the Word icon. As a result, thumbnail view isn't very useful for documents.

✦ **Tiles:** Displays each document using large icons, with descriptive information listed to the right of each icon.

✦ **Icons:** Displays each document with a medium-sized icon and descriptive information listed below each icon.

✦ **List:** Displays a list of folders and documents with small icons.

✦ **Details:** Displays a list of folders and documents with details, including the filename, type, size, and creation date. *Note:* The headers at the top of the columns are actually buttons; you can sort the list on any of the columns simply by clicking the column's button.

✦ **Properties:** Displays a panel showing various properties for the selected file, including the Title, Author, Template, Word count, and other useful information.

✦ **Preview:** Displays a preview of the selected file in a separate pane.

Deleting and renaming documents and folders

You can delete and rename files and folders from the Open dialog box. Here's how:

✦ To delete a file or folder, select the file or folder and press the Del key.

✦ To rename a file or folder, select it by clicking it once and then click the filename again. A text editing box appears around the file or folder name, allowing you to edit the name. (Don't click it too quickly, or Word thinks you double-clicked and the file or folder opens.)

Setting the default document location

When you call up the Open dialog box, Word initially displays the contents of the folder indicated by the default Document File Location option setting. When you install Word, this option is initially set to the My Documents folder on your computer's local disk drive. However, you can change that location if you want. For example, you may want to set up Word so that the default document location is on a network drive. To do so, follow these steps:

1. **Choose Tools⇨Options.**

The Options dialog box appears.

2. **Click the File Locations tab.**

3. **Click Documents.**

A Modify Location dialog box appears, as shown in Figure 2-2.

4. **In the Folder name text box, type the complete path (drive letter and folder) for the location where you want to store documents. Or, use the controls in the Modify Location dialog box to navigate to the folder.**

5. **Click OK to return to the Options dialog box.**

6. **Click Close to dismiss the Options dialog box.**

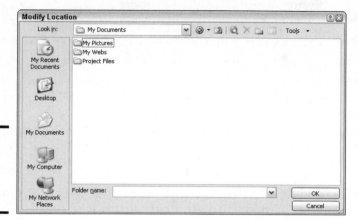

Figure 2-2:
Changing
the default
document
location.

Using the shortcut menu

You can right-click a folder or document in the Open dialog box to call up a
shortcut menu, as shown in Figure 2-3.

Figure 2-3:
The shortcut
menu for a
document in
the Open
dialog box.

The shortcut menu for a document contains the following commands:

✦ **Select:** Selects the document. This option is the same as clicking the
document with the left mouse button.

✦ **Open:** Opens the document. This option is the same as double-clicking
the document or selecting the document and clicking the Open button.

✦ **Edit:** The same as Open.

✦ **New:** Creates a new Word document.

✦ **Print:** Prints the document without actually opening it.

✦ **Open With:** Lets you open a document using another program besides Word. I don't know why you'd want to do that, but it's good to know you can.

✦ **Send To:** This option is one of the most useful commands to appear on the shortcut menu. It allows you to send the selected document to any of several destinations, such as an e-mail recipient, your floppy disk, or a recordable CD-RW drive.

✦ **Cut:** Deletes the document and places it on the Clipboard. Cutting a document allows you to paste it into another folder.

✦ **Copy:** Copies the document to the Clipboard so that you can paste it into another folder.

✦ **Create Shortcut:** Creates a shortcut to the selected document.

✦ **Delete:** Deletes the document or folder. You can achieve the same result by pressing the Del key.

✦ **Rename:** Lets you change the document's name.

✦ **Properties:** Displays the document's properties, the same as if you opened the document and chose the File⇨Properties command. I cover file properties in more detail later in this chapter.

Using the Tools menu

The Tools menu, located in the top-right corner of the Open dialog box, displays commands that manipulate the selected document or that sets options that govern how the Open dialog box works. The commands on the Tools include the following:

✦ **Search:** Brings up a File Search dialog box that lets you search for documents.

✦ **Delete:** Deletes the document or folder. You can achieve the same result by pressing the Del key.

✦ **Rename:** Lets you change the document's name.

✦ **Print:** Prints the document without actually opening it.

✦ **Add to My Places:** Adds an icon for the selected item to the list of common document locations that appears down the left edge of the

Open dialog box. For more information, see "Using My Places" later in this chapter.

✦ **Map Network Drive:** Lets you associate a drive letter with a network folder. Don't mess with this command unless you know something about networks.

✦ **Properties:** Displays the document's properties, the same as if you opened the document and chose the File⇨Properties command. I cover file properties in more detail later in this chapter.

Using My Places

My Places refers to the band of icons that runs down the left side of the Open dialog box. By default, Word provides the following icons in My Places:

✦ **My Recent Documents:** A list of recently used documents.

✦ **Desktop:** Your computer's desktop. (I don't recommend storing documents on the desktop. Unlike my real desktop, I like to keep my computer desktop uncluttered.)

✦ **My Documents:** Your My Documents folder, which is the normal location for storing documents.

✦ **My Computer:** The My Computer folder gives you access to all the disk drives on your computer.

✦ **My Network Places:** Lets you access locations available via your network.

You can quickly access any of these document locations by clicking the icon in the My Places bar.

You can add your own locations to the My Places bar. To do so, summon the Open dialog box and navigate to the folder you want to add to My Places. Then, choose Tools⇨Add to My Places. (Use the Tools menu in the Open dialog box, not the one on Word's standard menu bar.) An icon is added at the bottom of the My Places bar. You have to scroll the bar down to see it, but it's there, trust me.

Opening Recently Used Documents

Way down at the bottom of Word's File menu is a list of documents you recently used. You can quickly reopen one of these documents by selecting it from the menu.

By default, the four most recent documents you opened are listed on the File menu. You can change the number of files listed by following these steps:

1. **Choose Tools⇨Options.**

2. **On the General tab, adjust the Entries spin control (located next to the Recently Used File List check box) to indicate how many documents you want listed.**

3. **Click OK.**

Finding Lost Files

Word offers several ways to search for lost files, as described in the following sections.

Using the Search pane

You can perform simple document searches by choosing File⇨File Search. This command brings up the Basic File Search task pane, as shown in Figure 2-4.

Figure 2-4:
The Basic
File Search
task pane.

To search for a file, type some text you know is in the document you're looking for. Then, click the Go button. Word rummages through the document files on your hard disk and displays a list of any files that contain the text you specify. When you see the document you're looking for, double-click it to open it.

Word may take a while to find your documents. But fortunately, you don't have to twiddle your thumbs during the search. You can continue working on your document while the search progresses.

Improving your search

Midway down the Basic File Search task pane, you find two options that can help you refine your searches:

✦ **Search In:** This option lets you specify where you want to search for lost documents. The default setting is to search all the disk drives on your computer, but not to search any network places that are at your disposal. If you think the missing document might be tucked away on a network drive, you can include network places in your search.

✦ **Results Should Be:** This option lets you specify what types of files to look for. The default is to look for all Office documents, including Word, Excel, and PowerPoint documents. You can further refine your search by including other types of Office documents, or Outlook items and Web pages.

Enabling fast searching

Office 2003 includes a feature called *fast searching* that's designed to improve the speed with which Office finds lost documents. Fast searching generates an index of all the documents on your computer. Unfortunately, the act of creating this index can noticeably slow down your computer. As a result, Office 2003 initially disables the fast searching feature. If you have a super-fast computer and lose documents a lot, you may want to enable this feature.

To do so, click the <u>Search options</u> link midway down the Basic File Search task pane to bring up the Indexing Service Settings dialog box, shown in Figure 2-5. Select the Yes radio button, and then click OK.

Figure 2-5:
Enabling
fast
searching.

Indexing Service Settings

When Indexing Service is enabled, the files on your computer are indexed and maintained so you can perform faster searches. Indexing Service also provides greater search capabilities.

Status: Fast searching is currently disabled

Do you want to enable Indexing Service?

○ <u>Y</u>es, enable Indexing Service and run when my computer is idle.

⊙ <u>N</u>o, do not enable Indexing Service.

[OK]
[Cancel]
[Advanced...]
[Help]

Note that when you enable fast searching, you enable it for all Office applications — not just Word.

If your computer suddenly slows to a crawl when you enable fast searching, call up the Indexing Service Settings dialog box again and select the No radio button to disable the fast search feature.

Advanced searches

For more advanced searches, you can click the <u>Advanced File Search</u> link in the Basic File Search task pane to call up the Advanced File Search task pane, shown in Figure 2-6.

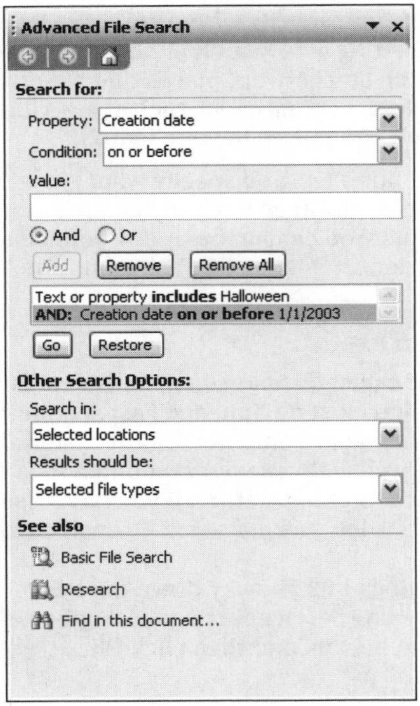

Figure 2-6:
The
Advanced
File Search
task pane.

This task pane lets you search for files based on complicated criteria. For example, the criteria for the search shown is:

```
Text or property includes Halloween
AND: Creation date on or before 1/1/2003
```

Most search criteria lines include three items: a property, a condition, and a value. In the previous example, the property for the first criterion is **Text or property**, the condition is **includes**, and the value is **Halloween**.

To add additional lines to the search criteria, follow these steps:

1. **If the criteria list contains more than one line, click the line after which you want to add the new line.**

2. **Select the property you want to match from the Property drop-down list box or, to search for a property that isn't in the list (such as a custom property), just type the property name.**

Table 2-1 lists the properties you can search for. (***Note:*** Many of these properties do not apply to Word documents. For example, the Number of Slides property searches for PowerPoint documents, not Word documents.)

3. **Select the condition from the Condition drop-down list box.**

The conditions available in this list box vary depending on which property you selected in Step 2. Table 2-2 lists the condition settings available for various Property types.

4. **Type a value in the Value field, if appropriate.**

Some property/condition combinations do not require values.

5. **Select the And or Or radio button.**

If you select And, both the criteria you are adding and the previous criteria must be met for the file to be selected. If you select Or, either the criteria you are adding or the previous criteria must be met.

6. **Click the Add button.**

The criteria is added to the list.

Table 2-1		Properties for Advanced Searches	
Address	Email	Number of characters	Resources
All day event	End	Number of characters + spaces	Revision
Application name	Fax	Number of hidden slides	Sent
Attendees	Filename	Number of lines	Size
Author	Format	Number of multimedia clips	Start
Category	From	Number of notes	Status
CC	Importance	Number of pages	Subject
Comments	Job title	Number of paragraphs	Template

(continued)

Table 2-1 *(continued)*

Company	Keywords	Number of slides	Text or property
Contents	Last modified	Number of words	Title
Creation date	Last printed	Owner	Total edit time
Date completed	Last saved by	Phone	Web page
Date due	Location	Priority	
Description	Manager Name	Received	

Table 2-2	**Conditions for Advanced Searches**
Condition	*Explanation*
Text fields	
Is (exactly)	The field must match the text specified in the value field exactly.
Includes	The field must contain the text specified in the Value field. This condition is equivalent to placing an asterisk (*) wildcard before and after the value.
Begins with	The field must begin with the text specified in the Value field. This condition is equivalent to placing an asterisk (*) wildcard after the value.
Ends with	The field must end with the text. This condition is equivalent to placing an asterisk (*) wild card before the value.
Numeric fields	
Equals	The field must match the value exactly.
Does not equal	Any value other than the specified value is accepted.
Any number between	Lets you specify a range of values. In the Value field, specify the low and high values separated by the word and. For example, 10 and 100.
At most	The same as the familiar Less Than Or Equal To (<=) operator.
At least	The same as the familiar Greater Than Or Equal To (>=) operator.
More than	The same as the familiar Greater Than (>) operator.
Less than	The same as the familiar Less Than (<) operator.
Date fields	
On	The date matches a specific date value.
On or after	The date matches or follows a specific date value.
On or before	The date matches or precedes a specific date value.
Yesterday	The date matches yesterday's date.
Today	The date matches today's date.
Tomorrow	The date matches tomorrow's date. (Try using this condition to search for documents you haven't written yet.)
This Week	The date is from the current week.

Condition	Explanation
Date fields	
Next Week	The date is from the following week.
Last Week	The date is from the previous week.
This Month	The date is from the current month.
Next Month	The date is from next month.

To remove a line from the search criteria, click the line to select it and then click the Remove button. Notice that the settings for the line you deleted are placed in the Property, Condition, and Value fields so that you can use them as the starting point for a new line. Although you can't edit a criteria line directly, you can edit a line by deleting it, making whatever changes you want, and then clicking the Add button to add the line back.

After you set up the search, you must click the Go button to perform the search.

Using the Save As Command

The Save As command saves a new file or an existing file under a different name. You can summon this command in two ways:

✦ Choose File➪Save As from the menu.

✦ Press F12.

You can also invoke the Save As command by using the Save command for any document that is not yet saved to disk:

✦ Choose File➪Save from the menu.

✦ Click the Save button on the Standard toolbar.

✦ Press Ctrl+S or Shift+F12. Ctrl+S is easy to remember because "S" stands for Save.

Figure 2-7 shows the Save As dialog box, displayed when you invoke the Save As command. As you can see, this dialog box shares many features and controls with the Open dialog box.

To save a document, call up the Save As command, navigate to the folder where you want to save the document, type a new name for the document, and click the Save button.

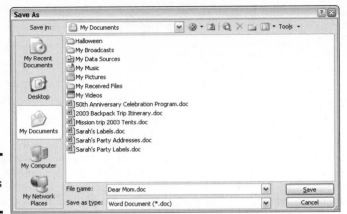

Figure 2-7:
The Save As
dialog box.

If you want to replace an existing document with the current document, double-click the document you want replaced. Word displays a dialog box asking whether you really want to replace the document. If you click Yes, the existing document is overwritten by the document you are editing.

When you first call up the Save As dialog box, Word takes a wild guess that you want the text in the first paragraph of the document to be the filename. This guess makes sense if the first paragraph is the title of the document, but in most cases, you want to type a more sensible document name.

Like the File Open dialog box, the Save As dialog box contains several buttons. The following list describes the function of each of these buttons:

✦ **Up One Level:** Moves up the folder hierarchy one level, to the current folder's parent folder.

✦ **Search the Web:** Calls up Internet Explorer so that you can waste time on the Web rather than save your document.

✦ **Delete:** Deletes the selected file or folder.

✦ **Create New Folder:** Creates a new folder as a subfolder of the current folder. You are prompted to type a name for the new folder.

✦ **Views:** Lets you switch views. For more information, see the section "Changing views" earlier in this chapter.

✦ **Tools:** Brings up the ever handy Tools menu. For more information, see the section "Using the Tools menu" earlier in this chapter.

Notice that the Save As dialog box also includes a Save As Type list box. Normally, this field is set to Word Document (*.doc) so that documents are stored in Word format. You can change this setting to save a document in another format.

Not all file types support all Word's formatting features. Any special formatting not supported by the file type is lost when you save the file. So if you're going to save your masterpiece in one of these formats, you may want to keep a version in Word format, too.

Save Options

If you choose Tools⇨Save Options from the Save As dialog box or if you use Word's regular Tools⇨Options command and click the Save tab, you see the dialog box shown in Figure 2-8. This dialog box controls the settings for several options that affect how documents are saved.

The following paragraphs describe the effect each of these options has:

✦ **Always Create Backup Copy:** If you select this option, Word always saves the previous version of the document as a backup copy each time it saves the document. The backup copy uses the extension BAK.

Do not rely on the Always Create Backup Copy option as your only backup of important documents. The backup copy created by this option resides on the same drive and in the same folder as the document itself. As a result, if a disk failure or other problem renders the drive or folder inaccessible, the backup copy is inaccessible as well. Always back up important documents to a separate disk drive or to tape.

✦ **Allow Fast Saves:** If you work with large documents that take a long time to save, you can select the Allow Fast Saves option to speed things up. This option tells Word to save only those parts of the document that have changed since the last time you saved the document. The changes are written to the end of the document file.

The disadvantages of Fast Saves are twofold. First, although the Fast Saves feature saves files faster, opening files becomes correspondingly slower. Second, the size of the document increases each time you save it with Fast Saves enabled because changes to the document are written to the end of the file.

✦ **Allow Background Saves:** Saves documents while allowing you to continue working.

✦ **Embed TrueType Fonts:** Saves TrueType fonts in the document file. This option increases the size of the document file but enables you to copy the file to another system without worrying about whether the other system has the fonts used in the document. If your document uses only the basic Times New Roman and Arial fonts, if you don't plan on using the document on another system, or if you're sure the other system has all the fonts used in the document, don't bother with this option.

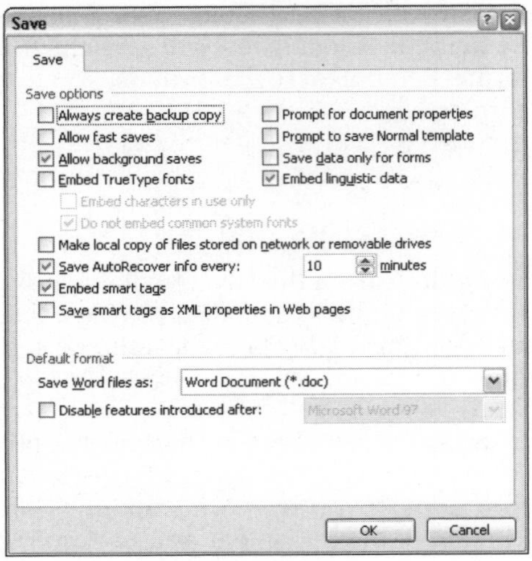

Figure 2-8:
The Save options.

✦ **Prompt for Document Properties:** If you want to use document properties, such as summary and keyword information, enable this option. Then when you save a file for the first time, Word prompts you for the summary information.

✦ **Prompt to Save Normal Template:** This option forces Word to ask for your permission before saving changes to the Normal.dot template. If you're concerned about proliferating changes to this template, enable this option.

✦ **Save Data Only for Forms:** Saves just the data for a form. This option is useful if you create a new document based on a template that includes a form, and then you want to save just the data, not the form itself.

✦ **Embed Linguistic Data:** Saves speech and handwritten text along with the document.

✦ **Make Local Copy of Files Stored on Network or Removable Drives:** Creates a local copy of documents stored on network or removable drives so that they can be recovered in case you lose access to the network or removable drive.

✦ **Save AutoRecovery Info Every *n* Minutes:** This option automatically saves recovery information at regular intervals. The default setting is to save the recovery information every 10 minutes, but you can change the time interval if you want.

✦ **Embed Smart Tags:** Saves smart tag information with your document.

✦ **Save Smart Tags as XML Properties in Web Pages:** Saves all of the smart tags in a document to an HTML file.

✦ **Save Word Files As:** Lets you specify the default format for saving files.

✦ **Disable Features Introduced After:** Lets you disable recent features of Word to increase compatibility with users stuck with older versions.

Password Protecting Your Files

Word allows you to protect your sensitive files from snooping eyes by using passwords. You can apply two types of passwords to your documents:

✦ A *Password to Open* password prevents users who do not know the password from opening the file. Use this password for files you don't want unauthorized users to examine.

✦ A *Password to Modify* password prevents users who do not know the password from saving the file. Use this password for files you don't want unauthorized users to modify.

To password protect a document, follow these steps:

1. **Open the document.**

2. **Call up Tools⇨Options and click the Security tab.**

   The Security options appear, as shown in Figure 2-9.

3. **Type a password in the Password to Open field or the Password to Modify field (or both, if you want to provide a different password for each type of access).**

   Word displays asterisks as you type the password, which prevents Looky-Lous from seeing your password as you type it.

4. **Click OK.**

5. **When Word prompts you to re-enter the password, type it again, exactly as you did the first time.**

6. **Click OK.**

7. **Save the file.**

After the file is password protected, Word prompts you (or anyone else) to enter the password before allowing you to open the document with the dialog box shown in Figure 2-10.

Figure 2-9:
The Security
options.

Figure 2-10:
The
Password
dialog box.

Here are some tips for working with passwords:

✦ Do not forget your password! If you forget, you can't access your document.

✦ Don't use different passwords for every document. You'll never remember them all. Instead, use the same password for all your documents.

✦ Do not write your password down on a sticky note and stick it on your computer monitor.

✦ Don't use obvious passwords, such as your kids' names, your spouse's name, your dog's name, or the name of your boat.

To remove password protection from a file, open the file (you have to supply the password to do it), choose Tools⇨Options, click the Security tab, and then highlight and delete the password. Click OK and save the file.

Chapter 3: Working with Templates

In This Chapter

✔ Discovering templates

✔ Enabling default settings for Word documents

✔ Creating documents based on a template

✔ Building your own templates

✔ Using global templates properly

✔ Working with the Organizer

✔ Utilizing Word's wizards

An entire chapter on templates this early in the book may seem premature, but I want to impress upon you right from the start that understanding templates is one of the keys to using Word as efficiently as possible. You can use Word for years without even knowing what a template is, but either your documents all look the same or you spend way too much time fiddling with the same formatting options over and over again. Besides, the proper use of templates comes up again and again throughout this book, so I may as well get the subject of templates out in the open.

What Is a Template?

A *template* is a special type of document file used as the basis for formatting your documents. Whenever you create a new document, a template file is the starting point for the new document. The following items are copied from the template into the new document:

✦ Styles, used to apply paragraph and character formatting quickly. For more information about working with styles, see Book II, Chapter 3.

✦ Margins and other page layout information, such as the paper size, orientation, headers, footers, and so on.

✦ Text and graphics, often referred to as boilerplate text.

✦ AutoText entries, which are sections of text you can quickly insert into your documents simply by typing a few keystrokes.

✦ Keyboard, toolbar, and menu customizations made via Tools⇨ Customize.

✦ Macros, which allow you to automate routine chores.

Each document has one and only one template attached to it. If you don't specify a template to attach to a new document, Word attaches the generic Normal.dot template, which contains the standard styles such as Normal, Heading 1, Heading 2, and Heading 3, plus default margins, keyboard short-cuts, toolbars, and so on. You can attach a different template to a document later, and you can copy the styles from the new template into the existing document, if you want. Then you have access to the styles from the new template as well as the existing document.

A template is basically the same thing as a normal document, except that it is given the extension DOT rather than DOC, as normal documents are. Word permits you to open and edit templates as if they are documents, and you can easily convert a document to a template by saving it as a template rather than as a document. The real difference between documents and templates lies in how you use them.

The Normal.dot Template

If you don't specify a template when you create a document, Word attaches the Normal.dot template to it. Word obtains the default document format, margins, page orientation, and the standard styles such as Normal, Heading 1, Heading 2, and Heading 3 from the Normal.dot template. In other words, Normal.dot is where Word stores its default settings for any feature controlled by templates.

Computer nerds call Normal.dot a *global template,* which means it is always available in Word, whether the document you're working with is attached to it or not. (We computer nerds love to use the term *global* because we dream of dominating the world someday.) Even if you attach a different template to a document, the settings in Normal.dot are still available because Normal.dot is a global template.

Any changes you make to Normal.dot effectively change Word's default behavior. For example, if you don't like Word's default style for Heading 1 paragraphs, you can change the Heading 1 style in Normal.dot. Or, you can customize the toolbars or add keyboard shortcuts to Normal.dot. By making careful changes to Normal.dot, you can change Word's behavior to suit your own working style. In effect, you can create your own individualized version of Word.

You can restore your Normal.dot template to its pristine condition by deleting the Normal.dot template. You can find the template in the c:\Program Files\ Microsoft Office\Templates folder. If Word discovers that Normal.dot is missing, it reverts to its original default settings and creates a new Normal.dot. Be aware that when you do delete the template, you lose everything you added to Normal.dot.

To create a new document based on the Normal template, call up File⇨New, and then click New Blank Document in the New Document task pane. Or, just click the New Blank Document button on the Standard toolbar.

Creating a New Document Based on a Template

To create a document based on a template other than Normal.dot, you must choose File⇨New. It displays the New Document task pane. From the Templates section of the New Document task pane, click the <u>On My Computer</u> link to bring up the Templates dialog box, shown in Figure 3-1. From this dialog box, you pick the template on which you want to base the new document, and then click OK to create the document.

Figure 3-1:
The
Templates
dialog box.

The New dialog box has a series of tabs that lead to different categories of document templates. The default tab, General, shows three templates: Blank Document, which is in reality the Normal.dot template; Web Page; and E-Mail message. Other tabs display other templates that come with Word.

Both the Ctrl+N keyboard shortcut and the New Blank Document button on the Standard toolbar completely bypass the New dialog box, automatically using the Normal.dot template for the new document. The only way to create a document based on a template other than Normal.dot is to use the File⇨ New command.

When you create a new document based on a template, any text and graphics contained in the template automatically copy into the new document. Templates are often used for this purpose to supply text or graphics that always appear in certain types of documents. For example, a Memo template would contain a standard memo header. A Letter template would contain your letterhead. If you attach a template to an existing document, the text and graphics contained in the template do not copy into the document. For information about the formatting provided by each of the Word templates, see the section, "A Gallery of Word's Templates" later in this chapter.

If you pick a wizard rather than a template from the New dialog box, the wizard leads you through a series of prompts to gather information about the document that you want to create. It then creates the document for you. When the wizard finishes, the document is fully formatted and loaded with styles, but it is based on the Normal.dot template. In this case, the wizard creates the formatting and styles; they are not drawn from a template.

Creating a Document from an Online Template

Microsoft maintains an Office Web site that has additional templates you can use for your documents. To create a document using one of these online templates, choose File⇨New, and then click the <u>Templates on Office Online</u> link in the New Document task pane. The Templates page of the Office online site comes up, as shown in Figure 3-2.

After you find a template you want to use, click the template's Download Now button. The template downloads to your computer and automatically creates a new document based on it.

You can also access the online templates by clicking the Templates on Office Online button in the Templates dialog box shown in Figure 3-1.

Figure 3-2:
The
Templates
page at the
Microsoft
Office Web
site.

Changing the Template Attached to a Document

You can change the template attached to a document at any time. When you do, all the macros, custom toolbars, menus, and keyboard shortcuts, as well as AutoText entries from the new template, automatically copy into the document. Any boilerplate text or graphics in the template do not copy into the document. Styles from the template are copied into the document only if you select the Automatically Update Document Styles option when you attach the template.

To change the template attached to a document, choose Tools⇨Templates and Add-Ins to summon the Templates and Add-Ins dialog box, shown in Figure 3-3. Click the Attach button to bring up an Explorer-style dialog box that takes you to your template files. In this dialog box, select the template you want to attach to the document, and then click Open. (You may have to look in various folders to find the template you want to attach.) If you want the styles from the template you're attaching to replace the styles in your document, make sure that the Automatically Update Document Styles box is checked. Then, click OK to attach the template.

Figure 3-3:
The
Templates
and Add-Ins
dialog box.

If you update styles and your document uses styles to control its formatting, the effects of the new template are immediately visible.

You can't go back

Changing the template attached to a document is one of the few Word actions that you cannot undo with the Edit⇨Undo command. As a result, if you inadvertently attach the wrong template to a document, correcting your error can be difficult. That's because when you attach a new template, Word copies elements from the new template into the document, but does not remove elements from the document derived from the previous template.

To illustrate the type of problem this situation can cause, suppose that you're working on a document that has a handful of custom styles, and you mistakenly attach a template that has 50 custom styles. Because you used the

Automatically Update Document Styles option, those 50 styles are copied into your document. The problem arises: How can you get rid of them? You can choose File⇨Templates to attach the correct template, but the 50 styles copied in from the incorrect template remain in your document! And you can't remove them easily.

To avoid this type of problem, save your document immediately before changing templates. Then, if you're not satisfied with the results after attaching the new template, you can revert to the previously saved version of the document if necessary by closing the document without saving changes and reopening the previously saved copy of the document.

Creating Your Own Templates

Word comes with a collection of templates that let you create a wide variety of document types, but sooner or later you'll almost certainly want to create your own templates. The sections that follow explain everything you need to know about creating and using your own templates.

Converting a document to a template

Suppose that you've been working on a document for hours, toiling with its formats until they're just the way you want them, and you realize that you might want to create other documents using the same formats. Creating a template from this document is a simple matter.

Open the document you want to use to create the template and call up File⇨ Save As. Down at the bottom of the Save As dialog box is a Save As Type Drop-down list box, which is set to Word Document. Change this field to Document Template. Type a name for your template, navigate over to the folder where you want to save the template, and click OK to save the document as a template.

Now that you saved your document as a template, take a few moments to improve the template's usefulness. Begin by removing any unnecessary text. ***Remember:*** Any text you leave in the template appears in any new documents you create using the template, so you want to leave only true boilerplate text that you want to appear in every document based on the template.

To delete all of the text from the document, press Ctrl+A to select the entire document and press the Del key.

You might also want to remove any unnecessary styles, macros, AutoText, or anything else that isn't template-worthy. When the template is just right, save it again.

You might be tempted to open the document, delete text and other unnecessary elements, and then choose File⇨Save As. I caution you against this, though, because deleting an entire document's worth of text and accidentally using File⇨Save rather than File⇨Save As is easy! To avert this disaster, save the document as a template before you begin deleting massive amounts of text.

Creating a new template from scratch

To create a new template from scratch, choose File⇨New, and then click the On My Computer link in the Templates section of the New Documents task pane to bring up the Templates dialog box. Select the existing template on which you want to base the new template. Then, select the Template radio button (found at the bottom right of the dialog box) and click OK.

Your new template inherits whatever styles, text, and other elements contained in the template you based it on. Now is the time to add any additional styles, macros, or other new elements to the template or to change existing template elements. In addition, you can add boilerplate text and graphics. When you're ready, use the Save command to save the template, assigning it an appropriate name and placing it in the correct folder.

Modifying an existing template

To modify an existing template, use File⇨Open to call up the Open dialog box. Change the Files of Type list box from Word Documents to Document Templates, and locate and select the template you want to modify. Click Open to open the template, make any changes you want to make, and use File⇨Save to save the changes. That's all there is to it.

Another way to modify an existing template is to open a document based on the template and change those elements of the document stored in the template rather than in the document. This method is a bit confusing, however: Some elements of a document are stored only in the template, while other elements are copied from the template at the time the template is attached and subsequently stored in the document.

The following list indicates how changes to various elements of a document affect the template attached to the document:

✦ **Text:** Any text you add to the document does not affect the template. The only way to change boilerplate text in a template is to edit the template directly.

✦ **Direct formatting:** Any direct formatting you apply to the document affects the document only and is not copied back to the template.

✦ **Styles:** Changes to a document's styles do not affect the template. Although styles are copied from the template to the document when you attach the template, subsequent changes to the styles are stored in the document and not copied back to the template. However, you can use the Organizer to copy styles back to the template. (I explain the Organizer later in this chapter, in the section "Using the Organizer.")

Boring details about where to store templates

By default, Word stores its templates in the \Documents and Settings*user name*\Microsoft Office\Templates folder. But you can change the location where templates are stored by choosing Tools⇨Options command, clicking the File Locations tab, and then double-clicking the User Templates option.

You can also specify a location for Workgroup Templates, which are templates you access via a network. Workgroup Templates come in handy if you and other network users need to share a set of common templates. In that case,

place the common templates on a network file server, and then use the Workgroup Templates option under the File Locations tab to indicate the location of the shared templates.

When you create your own templates, you usually store them in the User Templates folder. However, if you create a new folder within the User Templates folder, the new folder appears as a separate tab in the Templates dialog box. You can use this little trick to organize your templates if you create a lot of them.

+ **Macros:** Macros are always stored in a template, so any macros you create or modify are stored in the template, not in the document itself. When you create a macro, you must indicate whether you want the macro stored in Normal.dot, the attached template, or another global template.

+ **Customizations:** Changes to custom keyboard shortcuts, toolbars, or menus are stored in the template. You must specify whether you want the change stored in Normal.dot, the attached template, or a global template.

+ **AutoText:** Changes to AutoText entries are also stored in the template, either Normal.dot, the attached template, or a global template.

Using Global Templates

A *global template* is a template with macros, AutoText entries, and customization (keyboard, toolbar, and menu) elements available to all open documents regardless of which template is attached to the document. Normal.dot is a global template, which means that its elements are available even in documents attached to some other template. You can add your own templates to the list of global templates if you want, so that their elements also are available globally.

Note that only the macros, AutoText entries, and customization settings in a global template are available to other documents. Styles and boilerplate text contained in global templates are not available (unless the document happens to be attached to the template).

A global template is a great way to create a library of customized macros. You could place all your macros in the Normal.dot template, but placing them in a separate template for global macros gives you some added flexibility. For example, you can exchange your global macro template with other users without worrying about overwriting their Normal.dot templates. And you can quickly remove all of your custom macros by removing the global macro template without losing other custom items in your Normal.dot.

Follow these steps to activate a global template:

1. **Summon Tools⇨Templates and Add-Ins.**

   The Templates and Add-Ins dialog box appears. (Refer to Figure 3-3.)

2. **Locate the Global Templates and Add-Ins list box.**

   It contains a list of all the currently available global templates, along with buttons to add or remove global templates.

3. **Click the Add button.**

   An Add Templates dialog box appears.

4. **Choose the template that you want to make global, and then click OK.**

   When you return to the Templates and Add-Ins dialog box, the template you chose appears in the Global Templates and Add-Ins list box.

Stop me before I tell you about the startup directory

When you add a template to the Global Templates and Add-Ins list, the template remains in the list each time you start Word. However, you must use Tools⇨Templates and Add-Ins and select the check box next to the template in the list to make the template global. If you don't want to do that each time you start Word, follow these steps:

1. Exit Word using the File⇨Exit command.

2. Double-click the My Computer icon on your desktop. Navigate to the folder that contains the template you want to make global.

3. Double-click My Computer again to open a second My Computer window. Double-click the C drive, and then navigate to the \Program Files\Microsoft Office\Office\ Startup folder.

4. Drag any templates you want to be global ones from the template folder to the Startup folder. Use the right mouse button to drag the template. When you release the right mouse button, a pop-up menu appears; choose the Create Shortcut Here command.

5. Close both My Computer windows and then start Word.

Any template files in the \Program Files\ Microsoft Office\Office\Winword\Startup folder automatically load and are made global. If you previously added the template to the Global Templates and Add-Ins list, remove it before following the preceding procedure.

5. **Click OK.**

   You're done.

Some tidbits about global templates follow:

✦ To disable a global template temporarily, conjure up File⇨Templates and uncheck the template's check box in the Global Templates and Add-Ins list box. To remove the template from the list, choose it and click the Remove button.

✦ After you make a template global, it remains global until you quit Word. The next time you start Word, the template is included in the Global Templates and Add-Ins list box, but its check box is unchecked so that it is not active. To activate the template to make it global, use File⇨Templates and check the template's check box. See the sidebar, "Stop me before I tell you about the startup directory," to find out how to set up a global template that's active each time you start Word.

How Word Resolves Duplicate Template Elements

When you use global templates, the possibility of duplicate template elements is very real. For example, what happens if a global template has a macro named CopyStyle and the template attached to the document also has a macro named CopyStyle? Which one takes precedence?

The following order of precedence determines which template elements to use when name conflicts occur:

1. The template attached to the document always has first priority. Any element defined in the attached template supersedes any like-named elements in Normal.dot or a global template.

2. The Normal.dot template is next. Any element that exists in Normal.dot takes precedence over a like-named element in another global template.

3. Global templates are last. Elements from global templates are used only if the attached template and Normal.dot do not have a like-named element.

4. If two or more global templates have identically named elements, Word uses the one that comes first in alphabetical order. For example, if Global Template and My Global Macros are both loaded as global templates and both contain a macro named CopyStyle, the one from Global Template is used.

Using the Organizer

If you want to move styles en masse from one document or template to another, the easiest way is to use the Organizer — Word's tenacious tool for taming templates. The organizer is especially useful when you create several new styles in a document and you want to copy those files to the document's template.

To copy styles from your document to a template, follow these steps:

1. **Choose Tools⇨Templates and Add-Ins.**

The Templates and Add-Ins dialog box appears.

2. **Click the Organizer button.**

The Organizer dialog box, shown in Figure 3-4, appears.

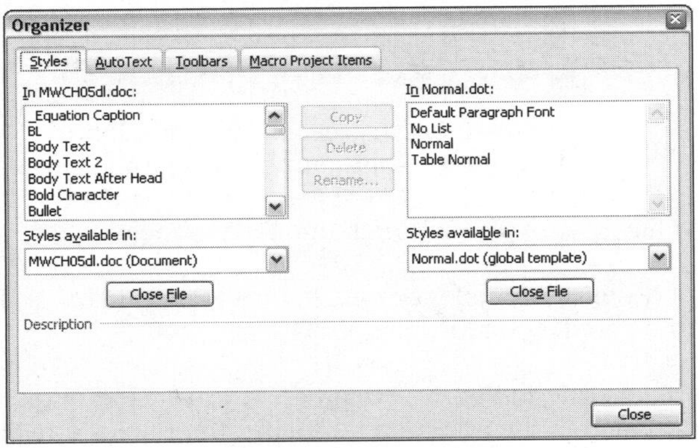

Figure 3-4:
The
Organizer
dialog box.

3. **If you want to copy styles to a template other than Normal.dot, click the right Close File button, click the Open File button, select the template file, and click Open.**

4. **Choose the styles you want to copy in the left style list (the In list box).**

To choose several styles, hold down the Ctrl key while clicking style names. To choose a block of styles, click the first style in the block; then hold down the Shift key and click the last style.

5. **Click the Copy button.**

The styles copy from the document to the template.

6. **Click the Close button.**

The Organizer is a helpful beast:

✦ You can copy styles from either list in the Organizer dialog box. If you choose styles in the right box, the In and To designations switch and the arrows on the Copy button change to indicate that styles copy from the right list to the left list.

✦ To move styles from the current document to Normal.dot, skip Step 3 in the preceding steps.

✦ Click the down arrow next to the Styles Available In list box on the left side of the Organizer dialog box to reveal a list of style sources that includes the current document, the currently attached style, and Normal.dot. To move styles from the attached template to Normal.dot, choose the template in the Styles Available In list.

✦ You can also use the Organizer to delete or rename styles. To delete styles, choose them in either the left or right list; then click the Delete button. If you've been good, Word asks for confirmation before it deletes the styles. To rename a style, choose it and click the Rename button. When Word asks for a new name, start typing. (Notice that you can rename only one style at a time.)

✦ The Organizer is also handy for copying AutoText, toolbars, and macros from one template to another. Just click the appropriate Organizer tab and have at it.

A Gallery of Word's Templates

Word comes with a large collection of templates that you can use to format several common types of documents. The following sections illustrate the various templates included with Word.

Many of Word's templates come in three families: Contemporary, Elegant, and Professional. You can use these template families together to create a unified design for your correspondence. You should pick one of these styles and use it whenever possible.

Letters

You find three templates for letters on the Letters & Faxes tab of the Templates dialog box: Contemporary Letter.dot, Elegant Letter.dot, and Professional Letter.dot. In each case, the template provides for your company name and return address, the recipient's address, and the recipient's name, in addition to your name and title. The Contemporary Letter also provides a slogan printed at the bottom of the page. To get the most from these templates, customize them so that your name and company information is permanently stored in the template.

Each template includes an envelope icon in the letter body that you can double-click. When you do, the template runs a macro that creates a separate document filled with tips for customizing the letter template. Before you use any of these templates, double-click the envelope and read the resulting document.

Note: Word also includes a Letter Wizard that you can use to create a letter formatted according to the Contemporary, Elegant, or Professional Letter templates. The wizard gives you more precise control over which of the various elements common to most letters are included, and it can supply you with several prewritten letters. For more information about using wizards, see the section "Using Wizards" later in this chapter.

Figures 3-5, 3-6, and 3-7 illustrate the letter templates.

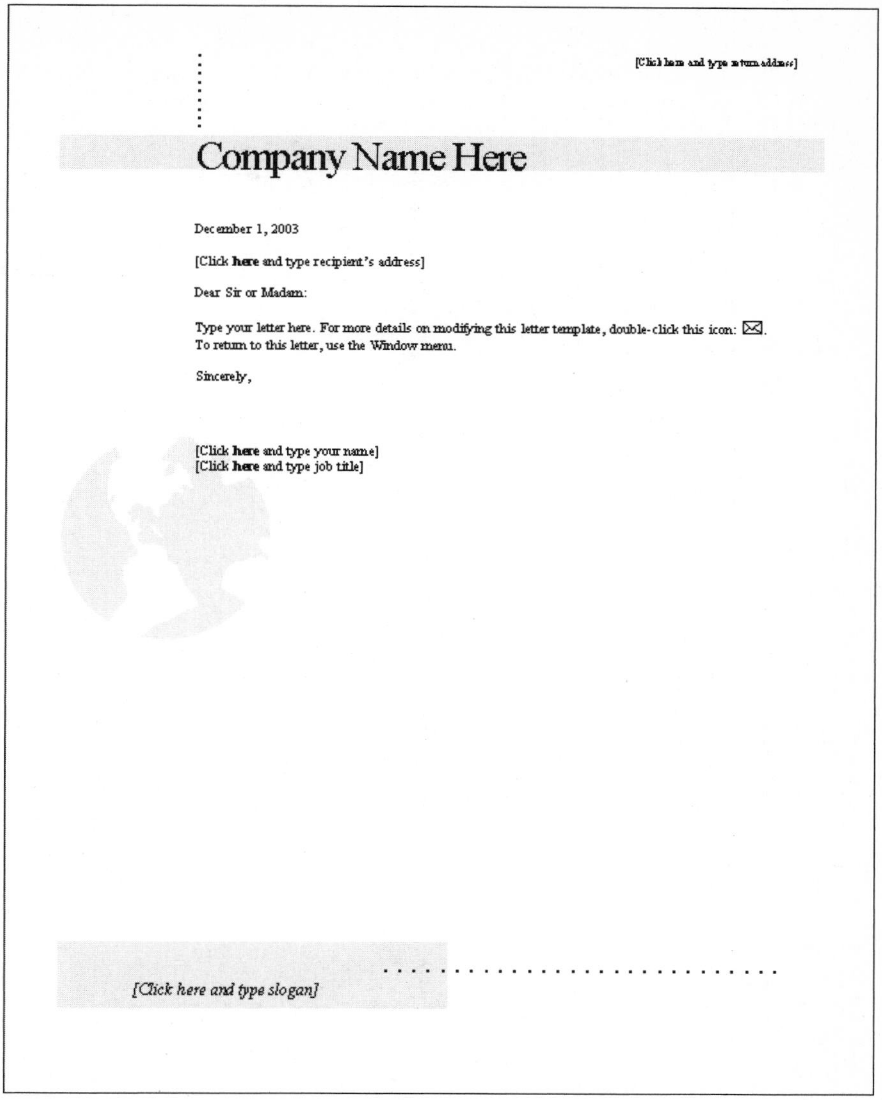

[Click here and type return address]

Company Name Here

December 1, 2003

[Click **here** and type recipient's address]

Dear Sir or Madam:

Type your letter here. For more details on modifying this letter template, double-click this icon: ✉.
To return to this letter, use the Window menu.

Sincerely,

[Click **here** and type your name]
[Click **here** and type job title]

[Click here and type slogan]

Figure 3-5:
The Contemporary Letter.dot template.

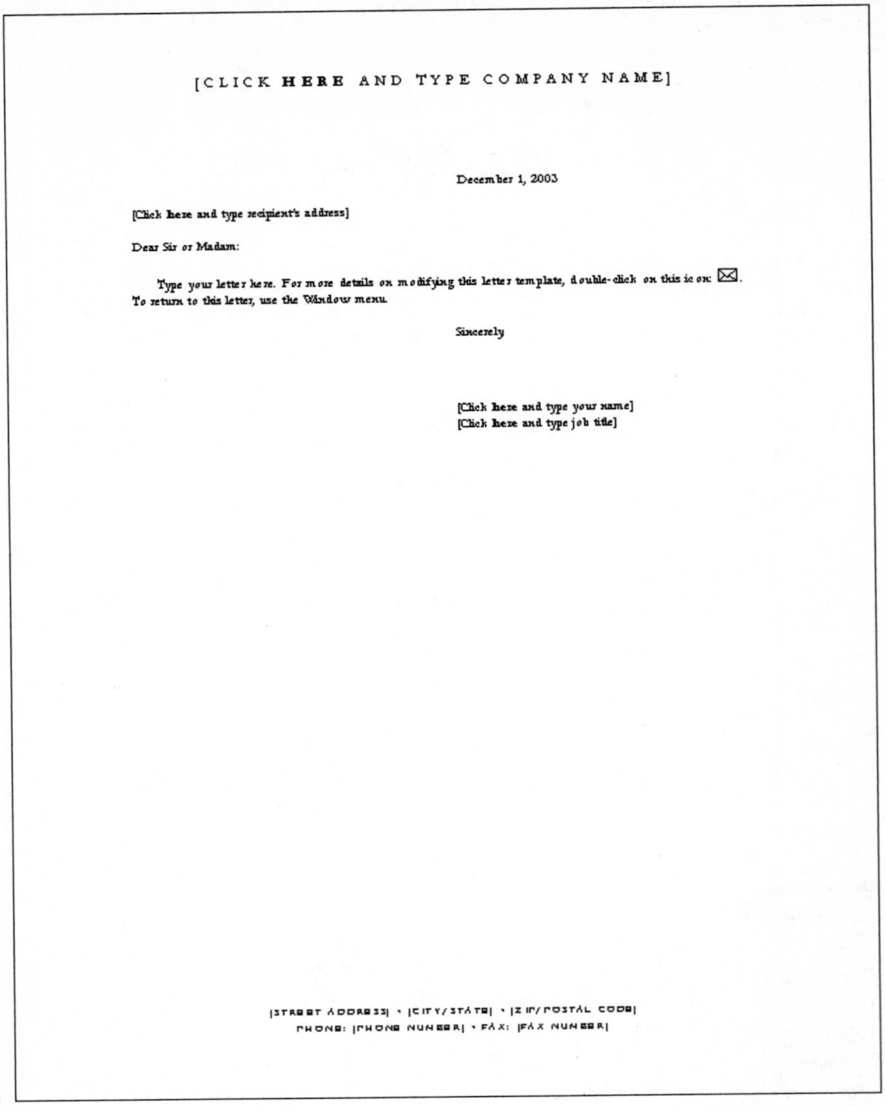

[CLICK **HERE** AND TYPE COMPANY NAME]

December 1, 2003

[Click here and type recipient's address]

Dear Sir or Madam:

Type your letter here. For more details on modifying this letter template, double-click on this icon: ✉.
To return to this letter, use the Window menu.

Sincerely

[Click here and type your name]
[Click here and type job title]

|STREET ADDRESS| • |CITY/STATE| • |ZIP/POSTAL CODE|
PHONE: |PHONE NUMBER| • FAX: |FAX NUMBER|

Figure 3-6:
The Elegant
Letter.dot
template.

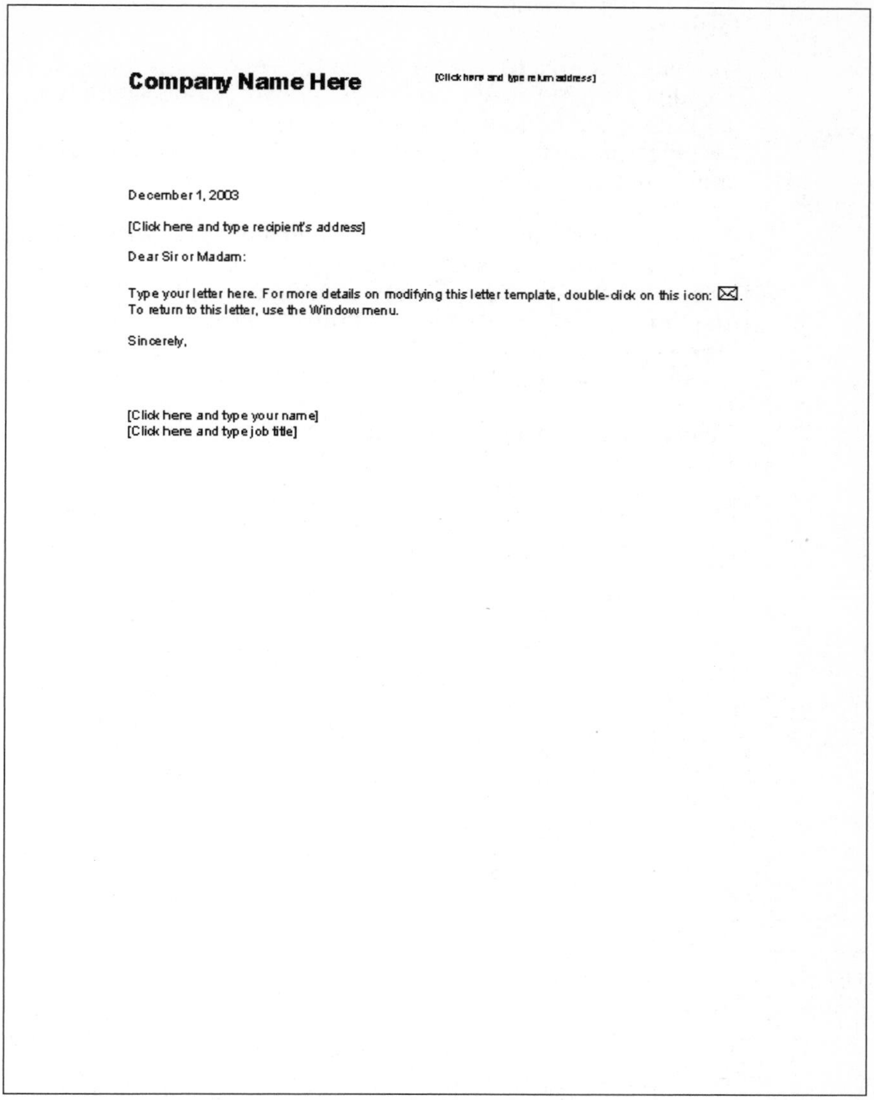

Company Name Here [Click here and type return address]

December 1, 2003

[Click here and type recipient's address]

Dear Sir or Madam:

Type your letter here. For more details on modifying this letter template, double-click on this icon: ✉.
To return to this letter, use the Window menu.

Sincerely,

[Click here and type your name]
[Click here and type job title]

Figure 3-7:
The
Professional
Letter.dot
template.

Faxes

You find three fax templates on the Letters & Faxes tab: Contemporary Fax.dot, Elegant Fax.dot, and Professional Fax.dot. These templates create a Fax Transmittal form you can use to accompany your faxes. The form includes space for your name, the recipient's name, the fax number, the number of pages, and the priority.

Word also includes a Fax Wizard, found alongside the Fax templates on the Letters & Faxes tab of the New dialog box. It constructs a fax document that includes whatever elements you want. Rather than use the Contemporary, Elegant, and Professional templates, the Fax Wizard uses its own Contemporary, Modern, and Jazzy styles. For more information about using wizards, see the section "Using Wizards" later in this chapter.

Figures 3-8, 3-9, and 3-10 illustrate the fax templates.

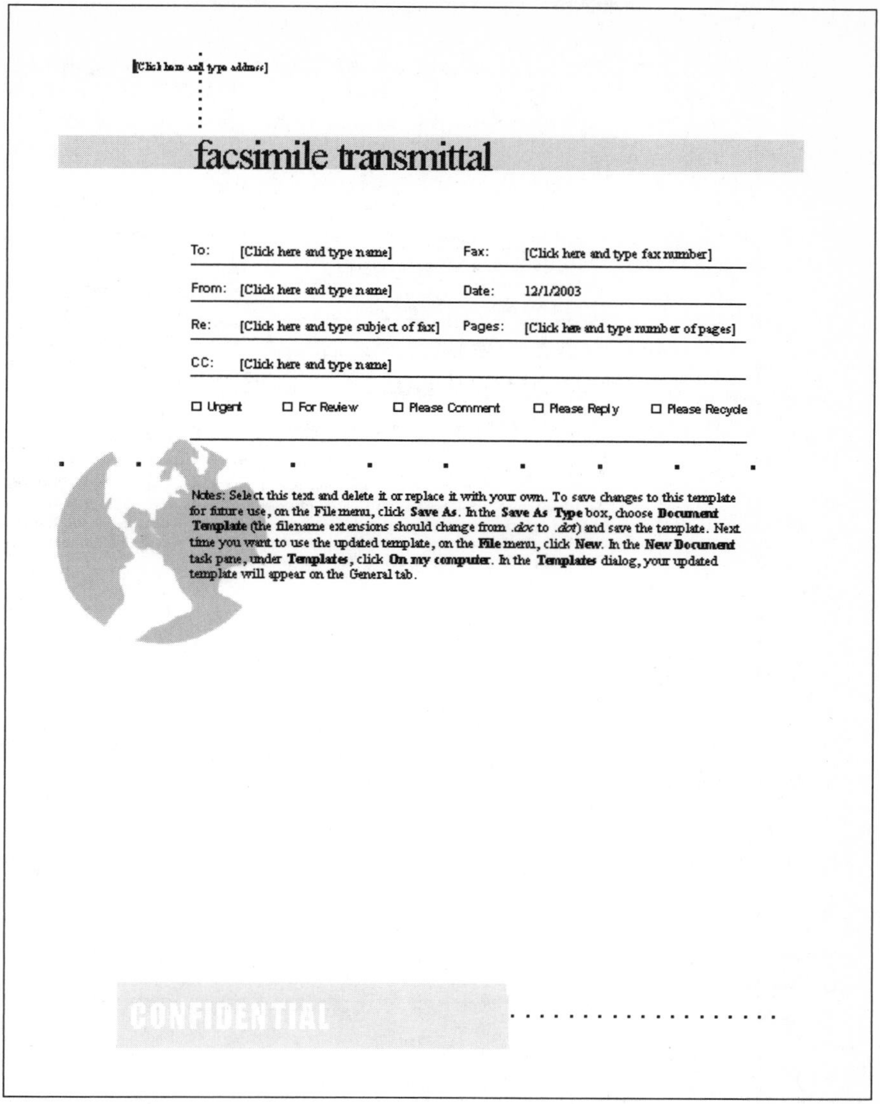

[Click here and type address]

facsimile transmittal

To:	[Click here and type name]	Fax:	[Click here and type fax number]
From:	[Click here and type name]	Date:	12/1/2003
Re:	[Click here and type subject of fax]	Pages:	[Click here and type number of pages]
CC:	[Click here and type name]		

☐ Urgent   ☐ For Review   ☐ Please Comment   ☐ Please Reply   ☐ Please Recycle

Notes: Select this text and delete it or replace it with your own. To save changes to this template for future use, on the File menu, click **Save As**. In the **Save As Type** box, choose **Document Template** (the filename extensions should change from *.doc* to *.dot*) and save the template. Next time you want to use the updated template, on the **File** menu, click **New**. In the **New Document** task pane, under **Templates**, click **On my computer**. In the **Templates** dialog, your updated template will appear on the General tab.

CONFIDENTIAL

Figure 3-8:
The Contemporary Fax.dot template.

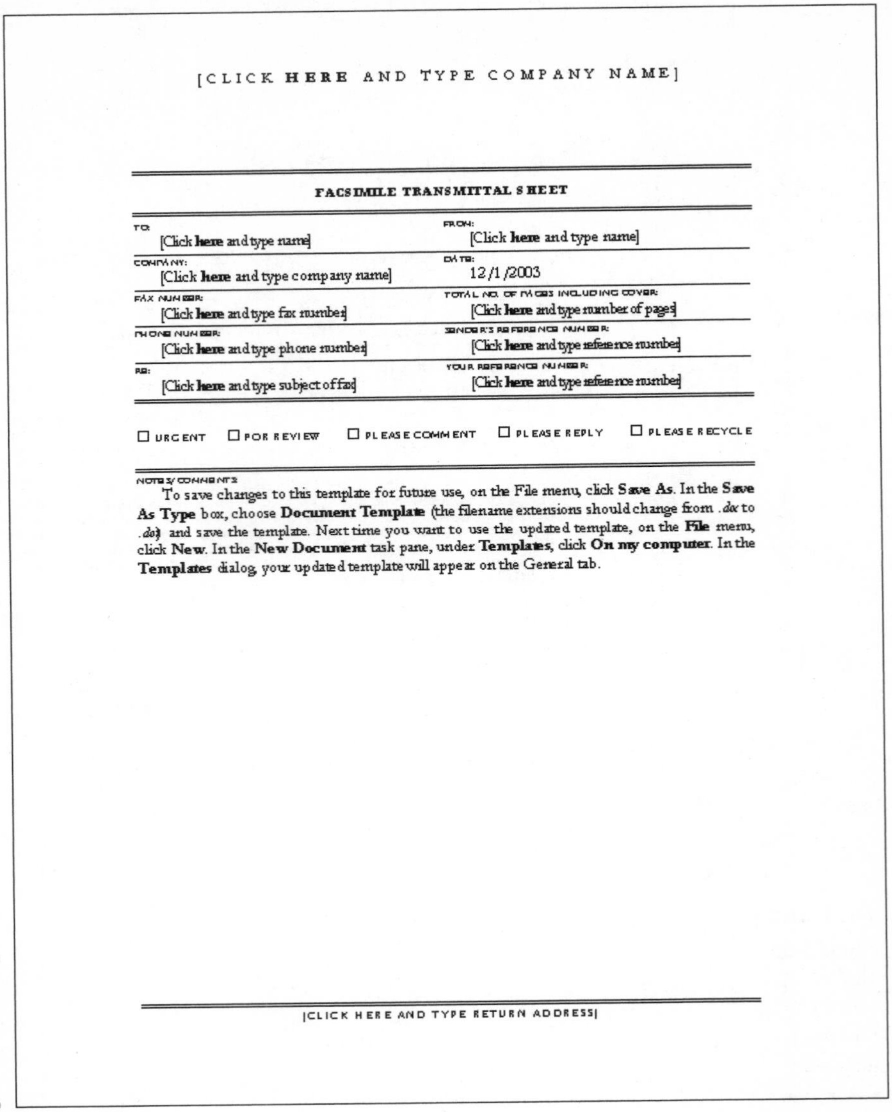

[CLICK HERE AND TYPE COMPANY NAME]

FACSIMILE TRANSMITTAL SHEET

TO:	FROM:
[Click here and type name]	[Click here and type name]
COMPANY:	DATE:
[Click here and type company name]	12/1/2003
FAX NUMBER:	TOTAL NO. OF PAGES INCLUDING COVER:
[Click here and type fax number]	[Click here and type number of pages]
PHONE NUMBER:	SENDER'S REFERENCE NUMBER:
[Click here and type phone number]	[Click here and type reference number]
RE:	YOUR REFERENCE NUMBER:
[Click here and type subject of fax]	[Click here and type reference number]

☐ URGENT   ☐ FOR REVIEW   ☐ PLEASE COMMENT   ☐ PLEASE REPLY   ☐ PLEASE RECYCLE

NOTES/COMMENTS:

To save changes to this template for future use, on the File menu, click **Save As**. In the **Save As Type** box, choose **Document Template** (the filename extensions should change from *.doc* to *.dot*) and save the template. Next time you want to use the updated template, on the **File** menu, click **New**. In the **New Document** task pane, under **Templates**, click **On my computer**. In the **Templates** dialog, your updated template will appear on the General tab.

[CLICK HERE AND TYPE RETURN ADDRESS]

Figure 3-9:
The Elegant
Fax.dot
template.

[Click here and type return address and phone and fax number]

Company Name Here

To:	[Click here and type name]	**From:**	[Click here and type name]
Fax:	[Click here and type fax number]	**Pages:**	[Click here and type # of pages]
Phone:	[Click here and type phone number]	**Date:**	12/1/2003
Re:	[Click here and type subject of fax]	**CC:**	[Click here and type name]

☐ **Urgent**   ☐ **For Review**   ☐ **Please Comment**   ☐ **Please Reply**   ☐ **Please Recycle**

● **Comments:** To save changes to this template for future use, on the File menu, click Save As. In the Save As Type box, choose Document Template (the filename extensions should change from .doc to .dot) and save the template. Next time you want to use the updated template, on the File menu, click New. In the New Document task pane, under Templates, click On my computer. In the Templates dialog, your updated template will appear on the General tab.

Figure 3-10:
The
Professional
Fax.dot
template.

Memos

You find three templates for creating memos on the Memos tab in the Templates dialog box: Contemporary Memo.dot, Elegant Memo.dot, and Professional Memo.dot. Boilerplate text in these templates provides for standard Memorandum heading information such as From, To, CC, Date, and Re. In addition, the body of the Memo is filled with tips for using and customizing the memo templates.

A Memo Wizard is also located on the Memos tab in the Templates dialog box. The Memo Wizard automatically creates a memo based on the Contemporary Memo.dot, Elegant Memo.dot, or Professional Memo.dot templates and lets you select various elements of the memo. For more information about using wizards, see the section "Using Wizards" later in this chapter.

Figures 3-11, 3-12, and 3-13 illustrate the memo templates.

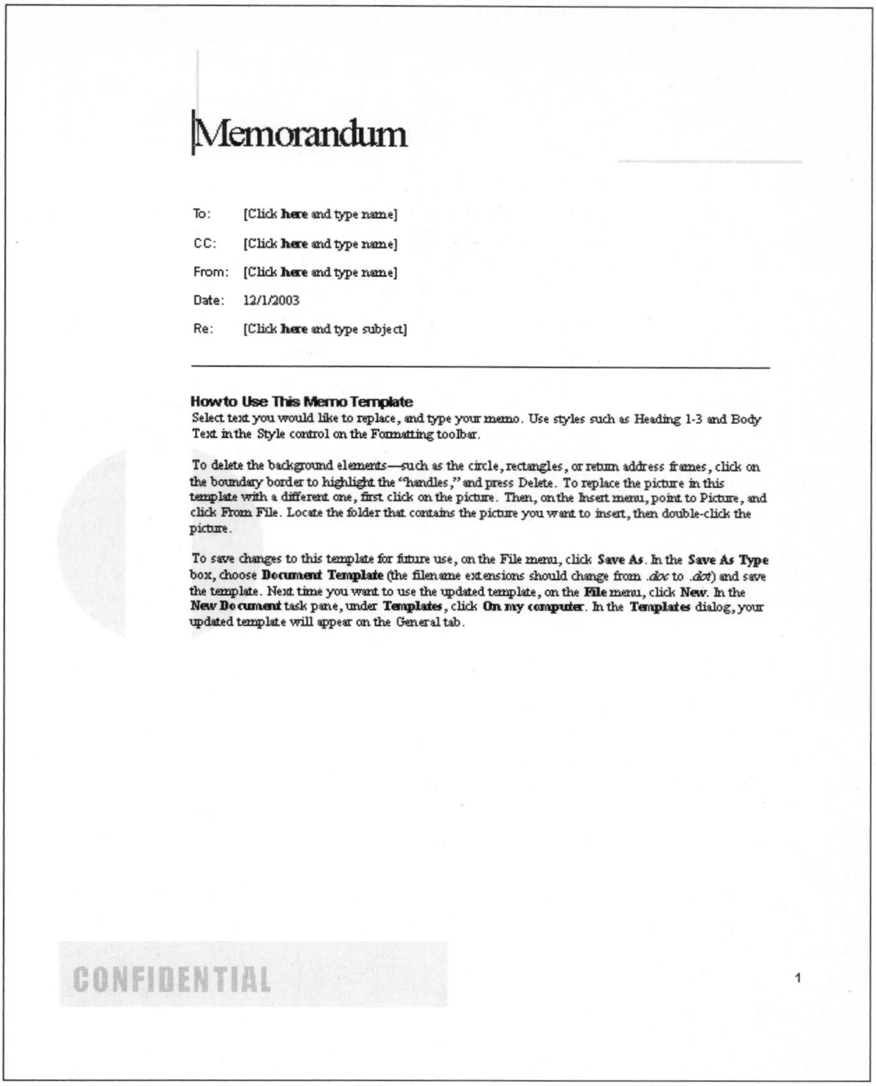

Memorandum

To: [Click **here** and type name]

CC: [Click **here** and type name]

From: [Click **here** and type name]

Date: 12/1/2003

Re: [Click **here** and type subject]

How to Use This Memo Template

Select text you would like to replace, and type your memo. Use styles such as Heading 1-3 and Body Text in the Style control on the Formatting toolbar.

To delete the background elements—such as the circle, rectangles, or return address frames, click on the boundary border to highlight the "handles," and press Delete. To replace the picture in this template with a different one, first click on the picture. Then, on the Insert menu, point to Picture, and click From File. Locate the folder that contains the picture you want to insert, then double-click the picture.

To save changes to this template for future use, on the File menu, click **Save As**. In the **Save As Type** box, choose **Document Template** (the filename extensions should change from .doc to .dot) and save the template. Next time you want to use the updated template, on the **File** menu, click New. In the **New Document** task pane, under **Templates**, click **On my computer**. In the **Templates** dialog, your updated template will appear on the General tab.

CONFIDENTIAL

1

Figure 3-11:
The
Contempo-
rary
Memo.dot
template.

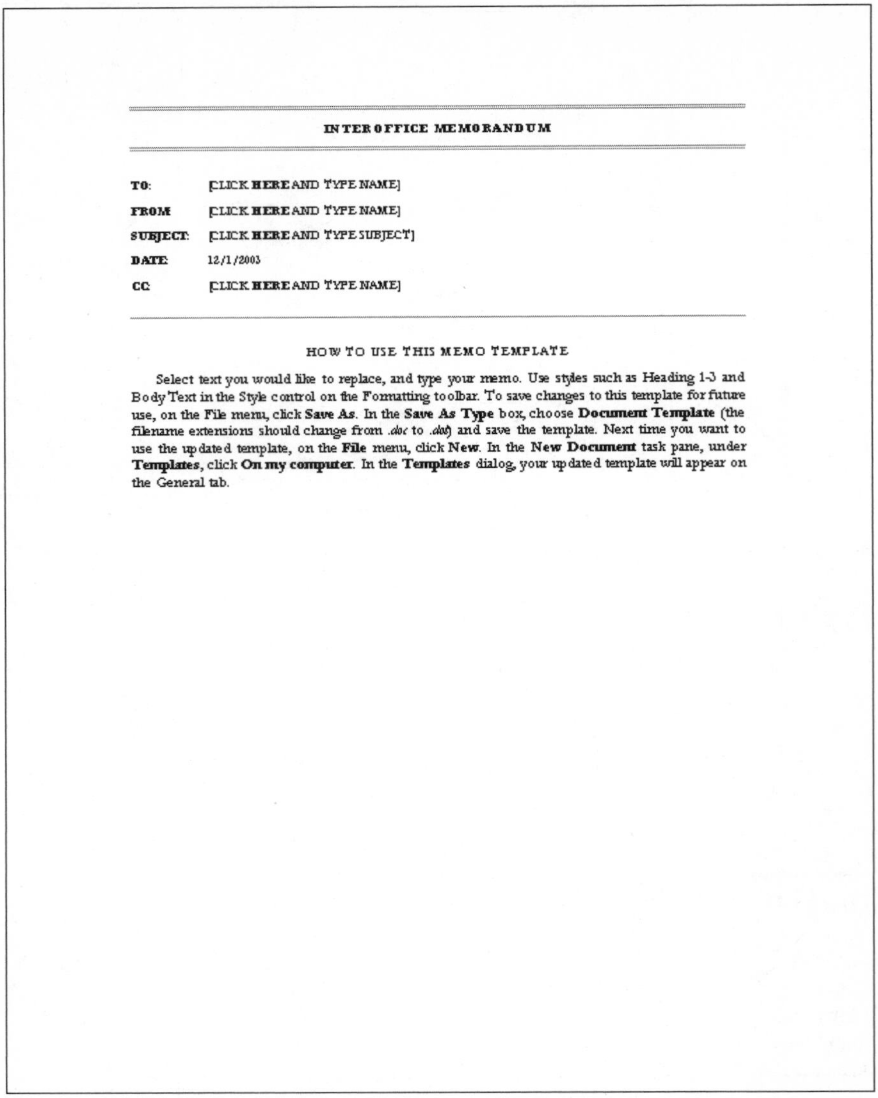

INTER OFFICE MEMORANDUM

TO: [CLICK HERE AND TYPE NAME]

FROM: [CLICK HERE AND TYPE NAME]

SUBJECT: [CLICK HERE AND TYPE SUBJECT]

DATE: 12/1/2003

CC: [CLICK HERE AND TYPE NAME]

HOW TO USE THIS MEMO TEMPLATE

Select text you would like to replace, and type your memo. Use styles such as Heading 1-3 and Body Text in the Style control on the Formatting toolbar. To save changes to this template for future use, on the **File** menu, click **Save As**. In the **Save As Type** box, choose **Document Template** (the filename extensions should change from *.doc* to *.dot*) and save the template. Next time you want to use the updated template, on the **File** menu, click **New**. In the **New Document** task pane, under **Templates**, click **On my computer**. In the **Templates** dialog, your updated template will appear on the General tab.

Figure 3-12:
The Elegant
Memo.dot
template.

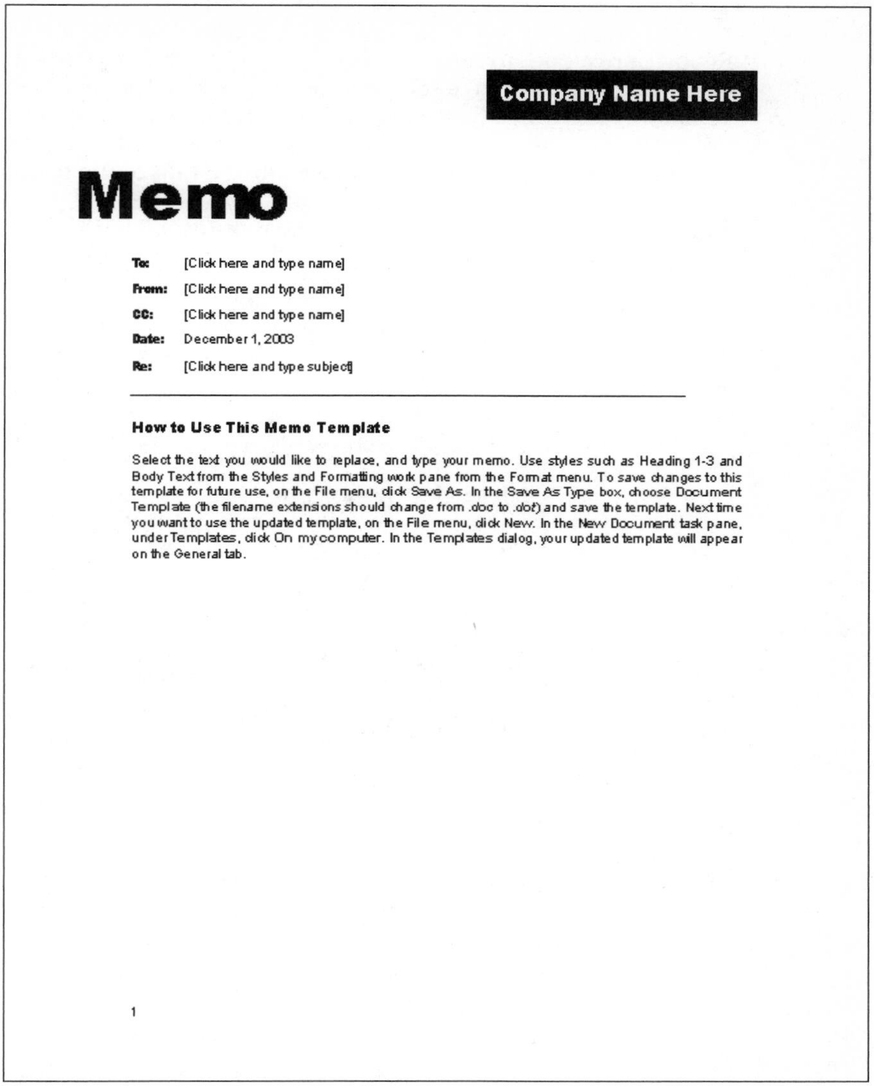

Company Name Here

Memo

To: [Click here and type name]

From: [Click here and type name]

CC: [Click here and type name]

Date: December 1, 2003

Re: [Click here and type subject]

How to Use This Memo Template

Select the text you would like to replace, and type your memo. Use styles such as Heading 1-3 and Body Text from the Styles and Formatting work pane from the Format menu. To save changes to this template for future use, on the File menu, click Save As. In the Save As Type box, choose Document Template (the filename extensions should change from .doc to .dot) and save the template. Next time you want to use the updated template, on the File menu, click New. In the New Document task pane, under Templates, click On my computer. In the Templates dialog, your updated template will appear on the General tab.

1

Figure 3-13:
The
Professional
Memo.dot
template.

Reports

Reports are a bore to read, but with Word's report templates, at least they look good. You find three templates for reports on the Reports tab of the Template dialog box: Contemporary Report.dot, Elegant Report.dot, and Professional Report.dot. These templates include a title page and a few pages of text that describe how to use and customize the templates.

Figures 3-14, 3-15, and 3-16 illustrate the report templates.

Type Address Here

blue sky associates

FilmWatch Division Marketing Plan

Trey's Best Opportunity to Dominate Market Research for the Film Industry

Figure 3-14a: The Contemporary Report.dot template (first page).

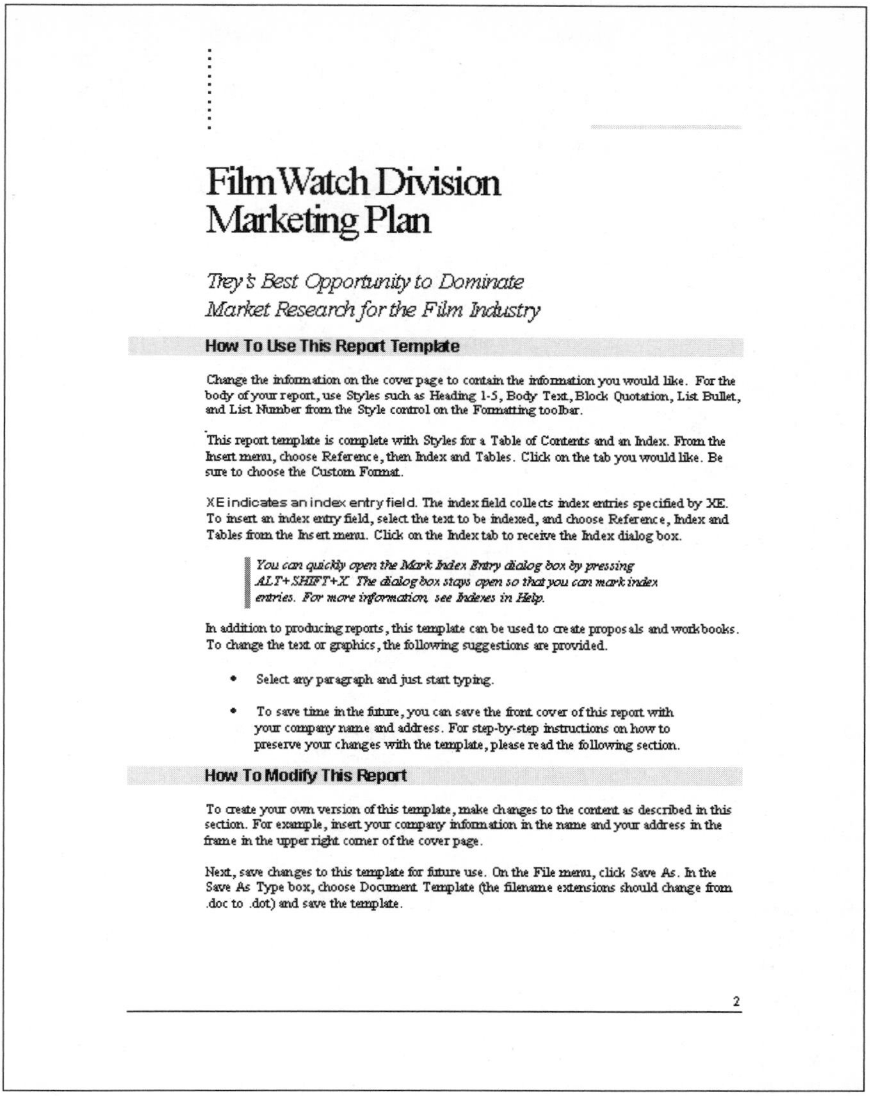

Film Watch Division
Marketing Plan

Trey's Best Opportunity to Dominate
Market Research for the Film Industry

How To Use This Report Template

Change the information on the cover page to contain the information you would like. For the body of your report, use Styles such as Heading 1-5, Body Text, Block Quotation, List Bullet, and List Number from the Style control on the Formatting toolbar.

This report template is complete with Styles for a Table of Contents and an Index. From the Insert menu, choose Reference, then Index and Tables. Click on the tab you would like. Be sure to choose the Custom Format.

XE indicates an index entry field. The index field collects index entries specified by XE. To insert an index entry field, select the text to be indexed, and choose Reference, Index and Tables from the Insert menu. Click on the Index tab to receive the Index dialog box.

> You can quickly open the Mark Index Entry dialog box by pressing ALT+SHIFT+X. The dialog box stays open so that you can mark index entries. For more information, see Indexes in Help.

In addition to producing reports, this template can be used to create proposals and workbooks. To change the text or graphics, the following suggestions are provided.

- Select any paragraph and just start typing.

- To save time in the future, you can save the front cover of this report with your company name and address. For step-by-step instructions on how to preserve your changes with the template, please read the following section.

How To Modify This Report

To create your own version of this template, make changes to the content as described in this section. For example, insert your company information in the name and your address in the frame in the upper right corner of the cover page.

Next, save changes to this template for future use. On the File menu, click Save As. In the Save As Type box, choose Document Template (the filename extensions should change from .doc to .dot) and save the template.

2

Figure 3-14b:
The Contemporary Report.dot template (second page).

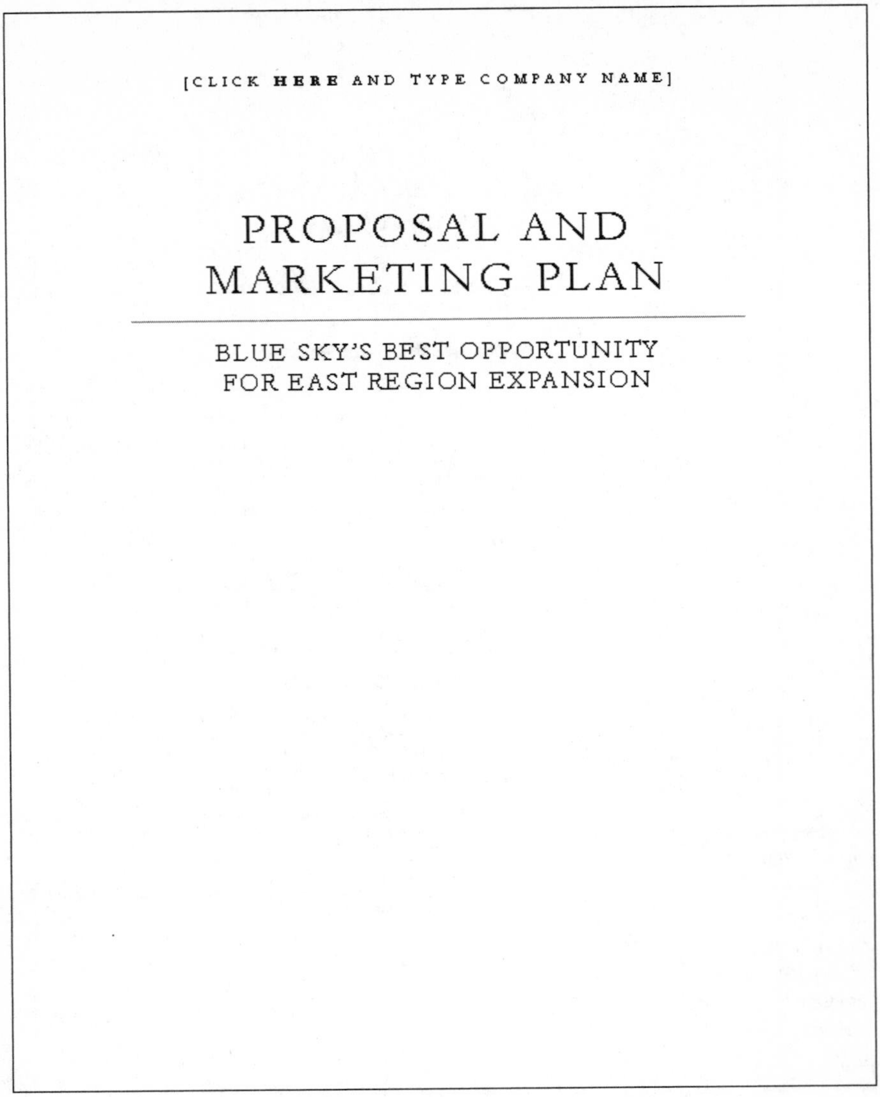

[CLICK **HERE** AND TYPE COMPANY NAME]

PROPOSAL AND MARKETING PLAN

BLUE SKY'S BEST OPPORTUNITY
FOR EAST REGION EXPANSION

Figure 3-15a:
The Elegant
Report.dot
template
(first page).

PROPOSAL AND MARKETING PLAN

BLUE SKY'S BEST OPPORTUNITY FOR EAST REGION EXPANSION

HOW TO USE THIS REPORT TEMPLATE

Change the information on the cover page to contain the information you would like. For the body of your report, use Styles such as Heading 1-5, Body Text, Block Quotation, List Bullet, and List Number from the Style control on the Formatting toolbar.

This report template is complete with Styles for a Table of Contents and an Index. From the Insert menu, choose Reference and then Index and Tables. Click on the tab you would like to use.

HOW TO CUSTOMIZE THIS REPORT

TO CREATE YOUR OWN CUSTOMIZED VERSION OF THIS TEMPLATE:

1. Insert your company name and address in place of the text on the cover page by clicking once and typing. The address should be typed in the frame in upper right corner of the title page.

2. Make any other edits to the document that you want to have as part of the template.

3. To save changes to this template for future use, on the File menu, click **Save As**. In the **Save As Type** box, choose **Document Template** (the filename extensions should change from *.doc* to *.dot*) and save the template.

HOW TO CREATE A DOCUMENT

To create a report from your newly saved template, on the **File** menu, click **New**. In the **New Document** task pane, under **Templates**, click **On my computer**. In the **Templates** dialog, your updated template will appear on the General tab.. Your company information should appear in place. Now, type your report using Styles as needed.

HOW TO CREATE BULLETS AND NUMBERED LISTS

To create a bulleted list like this, select one or more paragraphs and choose the List Bullet style from the Style drop-down list on the Format toolbar, or from the Styles and Formatting work pane located under the Format menu.

To create a numbered list like the numbered paragraphs above, select one or more paragraphs and choose the List Number style from the Style drop-down list — Word will automatically number the paragraphs for you.

Figure 3-15b:
The Elegant
Report.dot
template
(second
page).

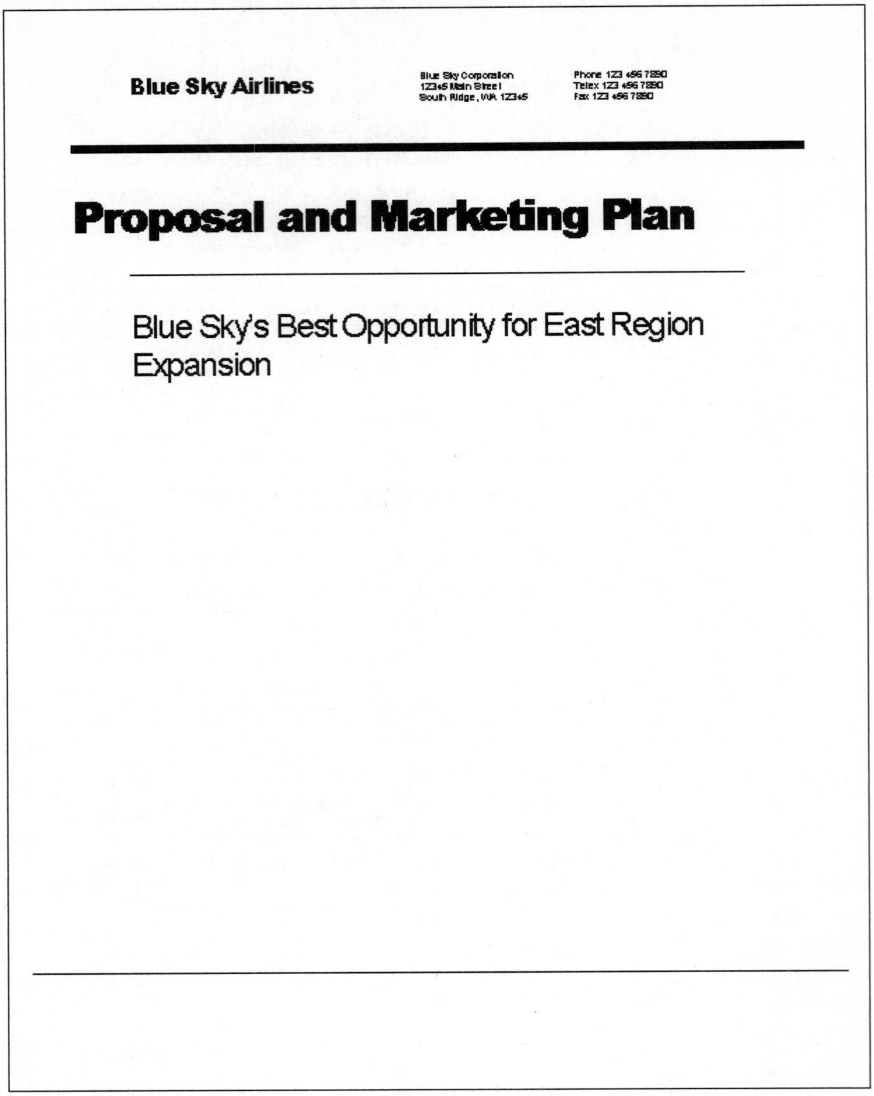

Blue Sky Airlines

Blue Sky Corporation
12345 Main Street
South Ridge, WA 12345

Phone 123 456 7890
Telex 123 456 7890
Fax 123 456 7890

Proposal and Marketing Plan

Blue Sky's Best Opportunity for East Region Expansion

Figure 3-16a: The Professional Report.dot template (first page).

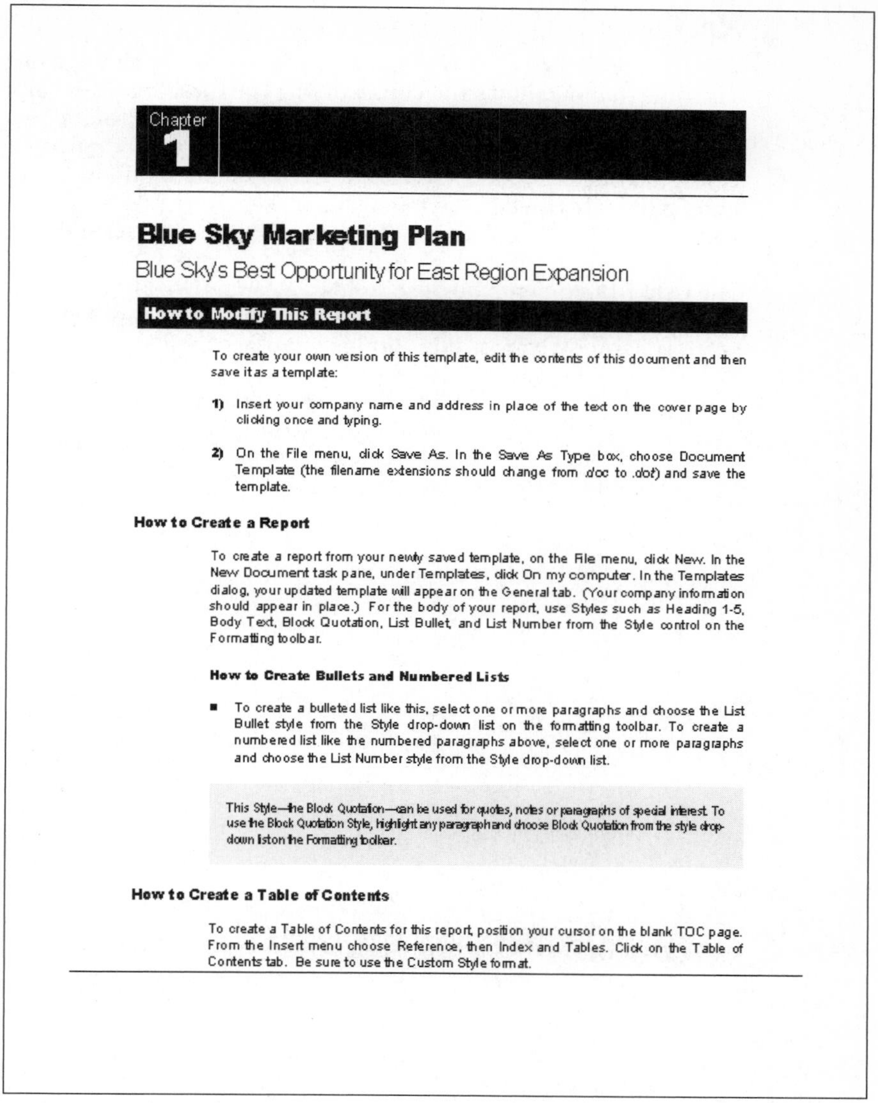

Chapter
1

Blue Sky Marketing Plan
Blue Sky's Best Opportunity for East Region Expansion

How to Modify This Report

To create your own version of this template, edit the contents of this document and then save it as a template:

1) Insert your company name and address in place of the text on the cover page by clicking once and typing.

2) On the File menu, click Save As. In the Save As Type box, choose Document Template (the filename extensions should change from .doc to .dot) and save the template.

How to Create a Report

To create a report from your newly saved template, on the File menu, click New. In the New Document task pane, under Templates, click On my computer. In the Templates dialog, your updated template will appear on the General tab. (Your company information should appear in place.) For the body of your report, use Styles such as Heading 1-5, Body Text, Block Quotation, List Bullet, and List Number from the Style control on the Formatting toolbar.

How to Create Bullets and Numbered Lists

■ To create a bulleted list like this, select one or more paragraphs and choose the List Bullet style from the Style drop-down list on the formatting toolbar. To create a numbered list like the numbered paragraphs above, select one or more paragraphs and choose the List Number style from the Style drop-down list.

> This Style—the Block Quotation—can be used for quotes, notes or paragraphs of special interest. To use the Block Quotation Style, highlight any paragraph and choose Block Quotation from the style drop-down list on the Formatting toolbar.

How to Create a Table of Contents

To create a Table of Contents for this report, position your cursor on the blank TOC page. From the Insert menu choose Reference, then Index and Tables. Click on the Table of Contents tab. Be sure to use the Custom Style format.

Figure 3-16b: The Professional Report.dot template (second page).

Resumes

Word won't land you a new job, but the resume templates can help you craft a resume that outshines the competition. The three resume templates — Contemporary Resume.dot, Elegant Resume.dot, and Professional Resume.dot — are located on the Other Documents tab of the Templates dialog box. These templates contain several standard resume sections, but note that the sample text provided in the templates makes some pretty outrageous claims. You'd better tone it down a bit if you expect to be taken seriously.

The Other Documents tab also holds a Resume Wizard that helps you further customize your resume. For more information about wizards, see the section "Using Wizards" later in this chapter.

Figures 3-17, 3-18, and 3-19 illustrate the three resume templates.

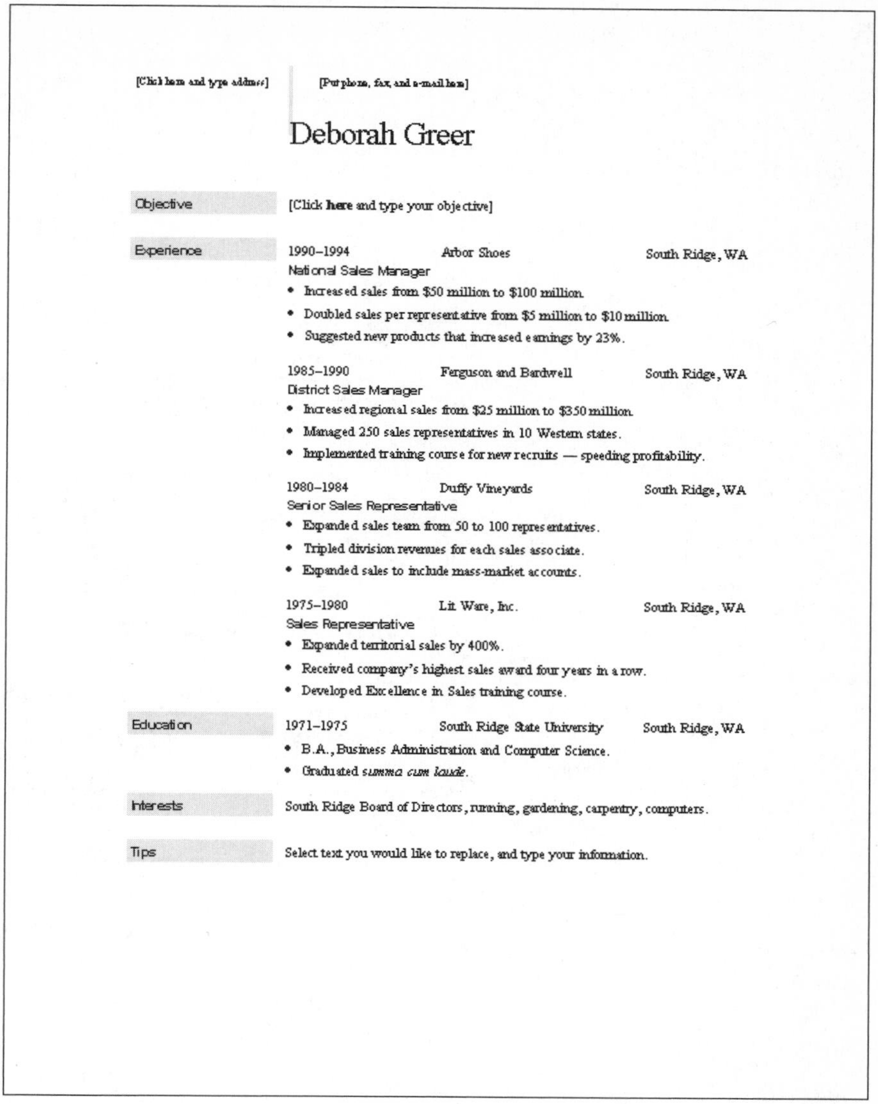

[Click here and type address]   [Put phone, fax, and e-mail here]

Deborah Greer

Objective   [Click here and type your objective]

Experience   1990–1994   Arbor Shoes   South Ridge, WA
National Sales Manager
* Increased sales from $50 million to $100 million.
* Doubled sales per representative from $5 million to $10 million.
* Suggested new products that increased earnings by 23%.

1985–1990   Ferguson and Bardwell   South Ridge, WA
District Sales Manager
* Increased regional sales from $25 million to $350 million.
* Managed 250 sales representatives in 10 Western states.
* Implemented training course for new recruits — speeding profitability.

1980–1984   Duffy Vineyards   South Ridge, WA
Senior Sales Representative
* Expanded sales team from 50 to 100 representatives.
* Tripled division revenues for each sales associate.
* Expanded sales to include mass-market accounts.

1975–1980   Lit Ware, Inc.   South Ridge, WA
Sales Representative
* Expanded territorial sales by 400%.
* Received company's highest sales award four years in a row.
* Developed Excellence in Sales training course.

Education   1971–1975   South Ridge State University   South Ridge, WA
* B.A., Business Administration and Computer Science.
* Graduated *summa cum laude*.

Interests   South Ridge Board of Directors, running, gardening, carpentry, computers.

Tips   Select text you would like to replace, and type your information.

Figure 3-17:
The
Contempo-
rary
Resume.dot
template.

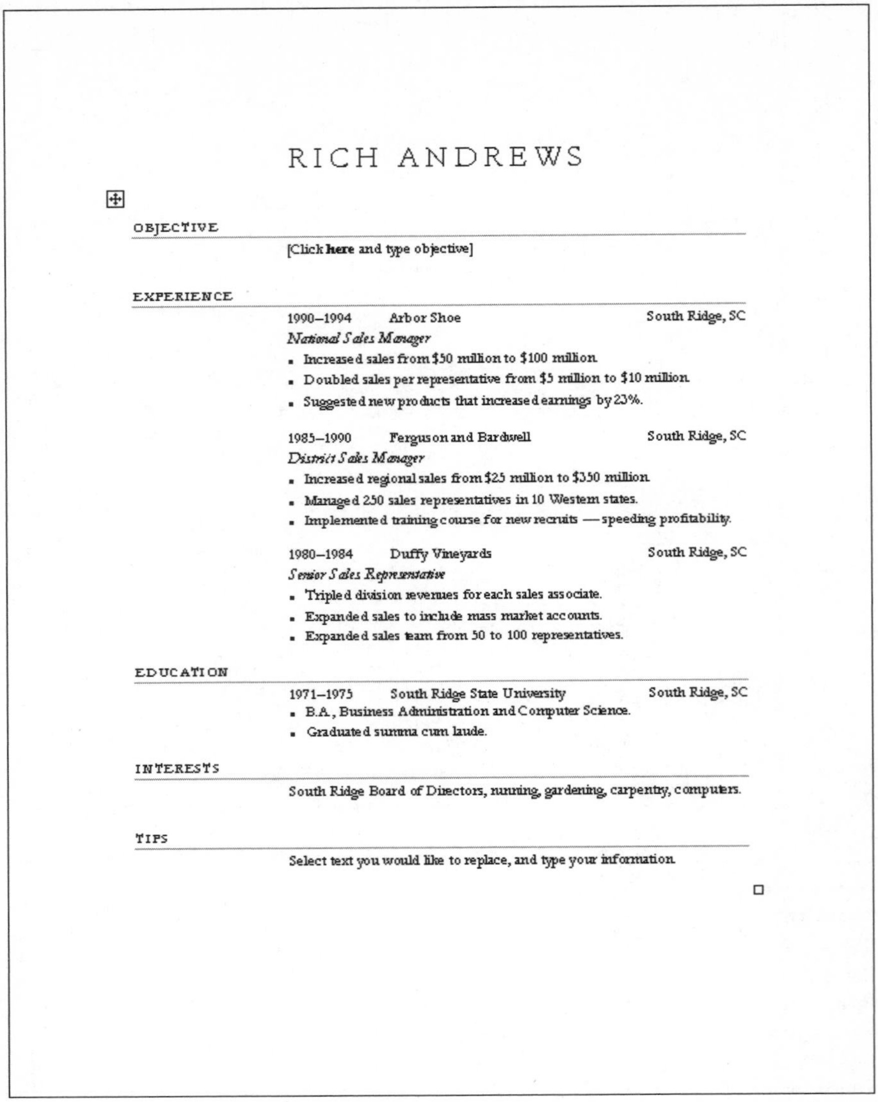

RICH ANDREWS

OBJECTIVE

[Click **here** and type objective]

EXPERIENCE

| 1990–1994 | Arbor Shoe | South Ridge, SC |

National Sales Manager
- Increased sales from $50 million to $100 million.
- Doubled sales per representative from $5 million to $10 million.
- Suggested new products that increased earnings by 23%.

| 1985–1990 | Ferguson and Bardwell | South Ridge, SC |

District Sales Manager
- Increased regional sales from $25 million to $350 million.
- Managed 250 sales representatives in 10 Western states.
- Implemented training course for new recruits — speeding profitability.

| 1980–1984 | Duffy Vineyards | South Ridge, SC |

Senior Sales Representative
- Tripled division revenues for each sales associate.
- Expanded sales to include mass market accounts.
- Expanded sales team from 50 to 100 representatives.

EDUCATION

| 1971–1975 | South Ridge State University | South Ridge, SC |
- B.A., Business Administration and Computer Science.
- Graduated summa cum laude.

INTERESTS

South Ridge Board of Directors, running, gardening, carpentry, computers.

TIPS

Select text you would like to replace, and type your information.

Figure 3-18:
The Elegant
Resume.dot
template.

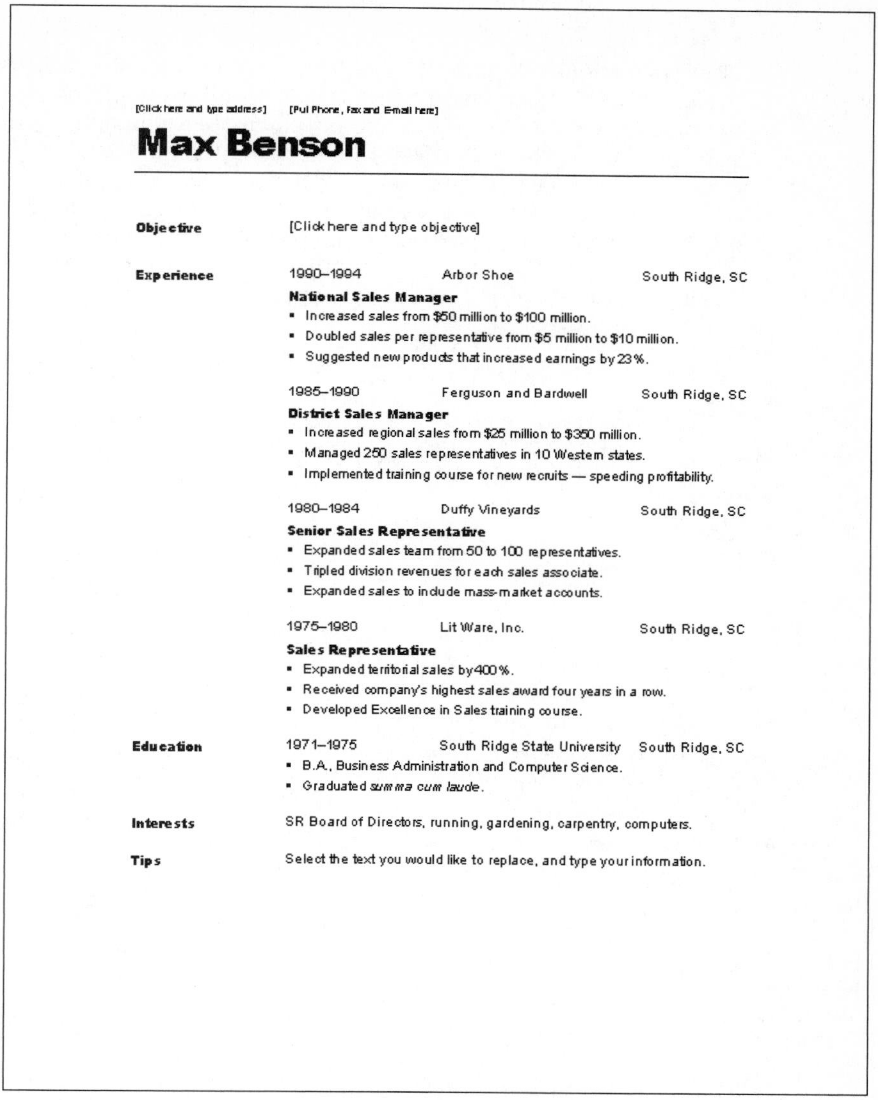

[Click here and type address]   [Put Phone, Fax and Email here]

Max Benson

Objective   [Click here and type objective]

Experience   1990–1994   Arbor Shoe   South Ridge, SC
National Sales Manager
- Increased sales from $50 million to $100 million.
- Doubled sales per representative from $5 million to $10 million.
- Suggested new products that increased earnings by 23%.

1985–1990   Ferguson and Bardwell   South Ridge, SC
District Sales Manager
- Increased regional sales from $25 million to $350 million.
- Managed 250 sales representatives in 10 Western states.
- Implemented training course for new recruits — speeding profitability.

1980–1984   Duffy Vineyards   South Ridge, SC
Senior Sales Representative
- Expanded sales team from 50 to 100 representatives.
- Tripled division revenues for each sales associate.
- Expanded sales to include mass-market accounts.

1975–1980   Lit Ware, Inc.   South Ridge, SC
Sales Representative
- Expanded territorial sales by 400%.
- Received company's highest sales award four years in a row.
- Developed Excellence in Sales training course.

Education   1971–1975   South Ridge State University   South Ridge, SC
- B.A., Business Administration and Computer Science.
- Graduated *summa cum laude*.

Interests   SR Board of Directors, running, gardening, carpentry, computers.

Tips   Select the text you would like to replace, and type your information.

Figure 3-19:
The
Professional
Resume.dot
template.

Publications

The Publications tab of the Templates dialog box contains four templates designed to create common types of business documents. The Brochure.dot template, shown in Figure 3-20, helps you create a simple three-fold brochure to advertise your business. The Directory.dot template, shown in Figure 3-21, creates a simple directory of services that you can adapt for your organization's needs. The Manual.dot template, shown in Figure 3-22, gets you started creating a manual, complete with title pages, a table of contents, and multiple chapters. Finally, the Thesis.dot template, shown in Figure 3-23, is the one to use if you're writing an educational paper.

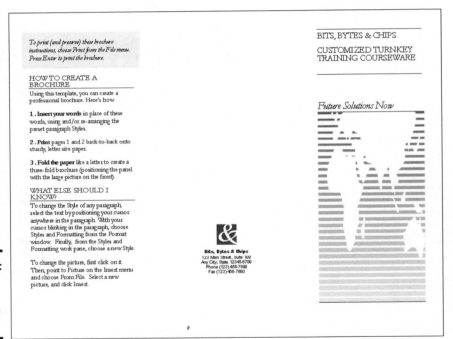

Figure 3-20a: The Brochure. dot template (first page).

HOW TO CUSTOMIZE THIS BROCHURE

You'll probably want to customize all your templates when you discover how editing and re-saving your templates would make creating future documents easier.

1. In this document, insert your company information in place of the sample text.

2. Choose Save As from the File menu. Choose Document Template in the Save as Type: box (the filename extensions should change from *.doc* to *.dot*) and save the updated template.

3. To create a document with your new template, on the File menu, click New. In the New Document task pane, under Templates, click On my computer. In the Templates dialog, your updated template will appear on the General tab.

ABOUT THE "PICTURES"

The "pictures" in this brochure are Wingdings typeface symbols. To insert a new symbol, highlight the symbol character and choose Symbol from the Insert menu—select a new symbol from the map, click Insert, and Close.

HOW TO WORK WITH BREAKS

Breaks in a Word document appear as labeled dotted lines on the screen. Using the Break command, you can insert manual page breaks, column breaks, and section breaks.

To insert a break, choose Break from the Insert menu. Select one option. Click on OK to accept your choice.

HOW TO WORK WITH SPACING

To reduce the spacing between, for example, body text paragraphs, click your cursor in *this* paragraph, and choose Paragraph from the Format menu. Reduce the Spacing After to 6 points, making additional adjustments as needed.

To save your Style changes, (assuming your cursor is blinking in the changed paragraph), click on the down arrow for the Style in the Styles and Formatting work pane. Select Update to match selection to save the changes, and update all similar Styles.

To adjust character spacing, select the text to be modified, and choose Font from the Format menu. Click Character Spacing and enter a new value.

OTHER BROCHURE TIPS

To change a font size, choose Font from the Format menu. Adjust the size as needed, and click OK or Cancel to exit.

To change the shading of shaded paragraphs, choose Borders and Shading from the Format menu. Select a new shade or pattern, and choose OK. Experiment to achieve the best shade for your printer.

To remove a character style, select the text and press Ctrl-Spacebar. You can also choose Default Paragraph Font from the Styles and Formatting work pane (accessible from the Format menu).

BROCHURE IDEAS

"Picture" fonts, like Wingdings, are gaining popularity. Consider using other symbol fonts to create highly customized "Icons."

Consider printing your brochure on colorful, preprinted brochure papers—available from many paper suppliers.

AT FEES YOU CAN AFFORD

We can often save you more than the cost of our service alone. So why not subscribe today?

Call 655-0000

Figure 3-20b:
The Brochure.
dot template
(second page).

Figure 3-21a:
The
Directory.dot
template
(first page).

SUMMER 1998 · DIRECTORY OF COMMUNITY SERVICES

Community Service Organizations

About the Symbol Pictures

The "pictures" are Wingdings typeface symbols. To insert a new picture, highlight the character and choose Symbol from the Insert menu—select a new symbol, choose Insert, and Close. To create new "icons," format a one-character paragraph as *Picture Style* (for the cover), or use *Icon 1 and 2* to create smaller icon styles.

HEADING 2 STYLE

Name Style   **123-4567**
List Style (with emphasis)   **123-4567**
List Style (without using the tab)
List Last Style (has extra space below)

How To Use Styles   **123-4567**
You can change the Style of any paragraph using Word's preset Styles. Open the Styles and Formatting workpane from the Format menu. Click your cursor in any paragraph. Read the Style name from the workpane.

ON CHANGING STYLES

Click on any paragraph   **123-4567**
Select a Style from the Styles and Formatting workpane (from Format menu). Choose a new Style from the list. Experiment (and use the Undo button).

TWO STYLE TYPES

Paragraph and Character   **123-4566**
In the Style list, a *f* icon next to a name indicates a paragraph Style, and the *a* icon indicates a character Style. Character Styles format **Words**.

Name Style   **123-4567**
List Style (using the tab)   123-4567
List Style (without using the tab)

List Last Style (has extra space below)

HOW TO CUSTOMIZE

Type Over Sample Text   **123-4567**
Select File New to re-open this template as a document. Choose File Save As. Choose Document Template in Save Save File as Type: box. See below.

ON SAVING FILES

Protecting Templates   **123-4567**
Templates that you save appear on the General tab of the Templates dialog box.

DIRECTORIES

Types of Directories   **123-4567**
Use the Name Style and/or List Style to create line-after-line directories. Use headings to create directories like this.

SECTION TITLE ABOVE

The Square "A" Above   **123-4566**
The Section Title Style creates a "letter icon." To create new "icons," format a one-character paragraph as the Section Title Style.
To Change the Shading   **123-4567**
Click on the gray-shaded (white) text. Choose Borders and Shading from the Format menu. Select a new shade.

ABOUT THE ICON 2 STYLE

The Big Arrow Below   **123-4567**
Highlight the arrow below and choose Symbol from the Insert menu. Select a new symbol, choose Insert, and Close.

Other Picture Symbols   **123-4567**
"Picture" fonts, like Wingdings, are gaining popularity. Consider using other symbol fonts to create highly customized company "icons."

WORKING WITH BREAKS

Breaks in Word Documents appear as "labeled," dotted lines on the screen. Using the Break command, you can insert a page, column, or section break.

TO INSERT A BREAK

Choose Break   **123-4566**
Choose Break from the Insert menu. Select one option.
Click OK to accept your choice.

Figure 3-21b:
The Directory.dot template (second page).

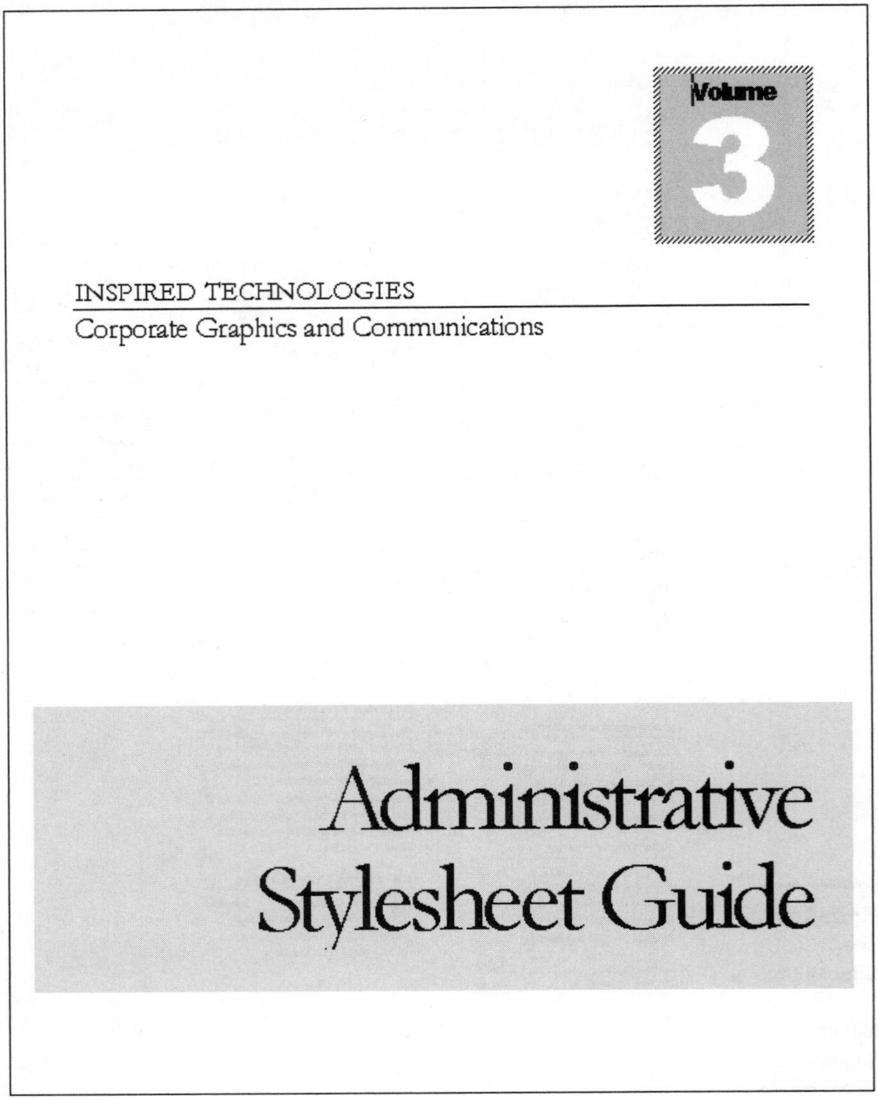

Volume

3

INSPIRED TECHNOLOGIES
Corporate Graphics and Communications

Administrative
Stylesheet Guide

Figure 3-22a:
The Manual.
dot template
(title page).

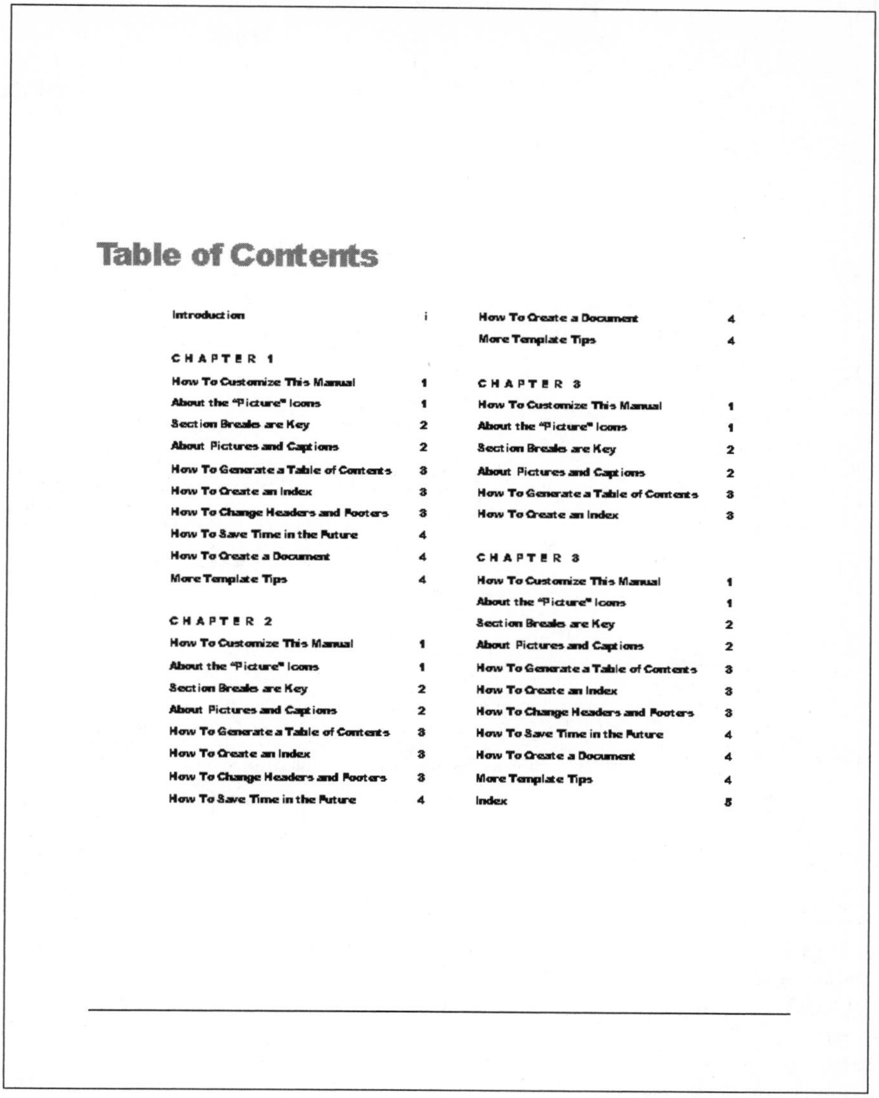

Table of Contents

Figure 3-22b:
The Manual.
dot template
(table of
contents).

DESIGN CUSTOMIZATION

Chapter

1

Seven Keys to Creating a Professional Manual

Like the Chapter Title Style above, and the Chapter Subtitle you're reading, Word's preset Styles are just a few clicks away.

To save time in the future, print a copy of this document. Choose Print from the File menu, and press Enter to receive all 9 pages of examples and instructions. With the printed document in hand, position yourself in Normal View to see the Style names next to each paragraph. Scroll through the document and write the Style names next to the paragraphs (press Ctrl-Home to reposition yourself at the beginning of the document).

ICON KEY
🗁 Valuable information
✏ Test your knowledge
⌨ Keyboard exercise
📖 Workbook review

To create a drop cap for the lead paragraph, like the example above, select and highlight the letter T, and type a new letter.

How to Customize This Manual

The "icon key" at left was produced using the Heading 8 Style for the words "icon key," and the List Bullet 5 Style for the text below—which uses a Wingdings symbol for the bullet character. To change the bullet symbol, double-click the bullet. Select a new symbol or create a custom bullet.

About the "Picture" Icons
The "picture" icons are Wingdings typeface symbols formatted in white with a shaded background. To insert a new symbol, highlight the character and choose Symbol from the Insert menu—select a new symbol, choose Insert, and Close. To create new "icons," format a one-character paragraph as the Icon 1 Style.

To change the shading of the Icon 1 Style, choose Borders and Shading from the Format menu. Select a new shade or color, and choose OK to accept your choice.

1

Figure 3-22c:
The Manual. dot template (chapter page).

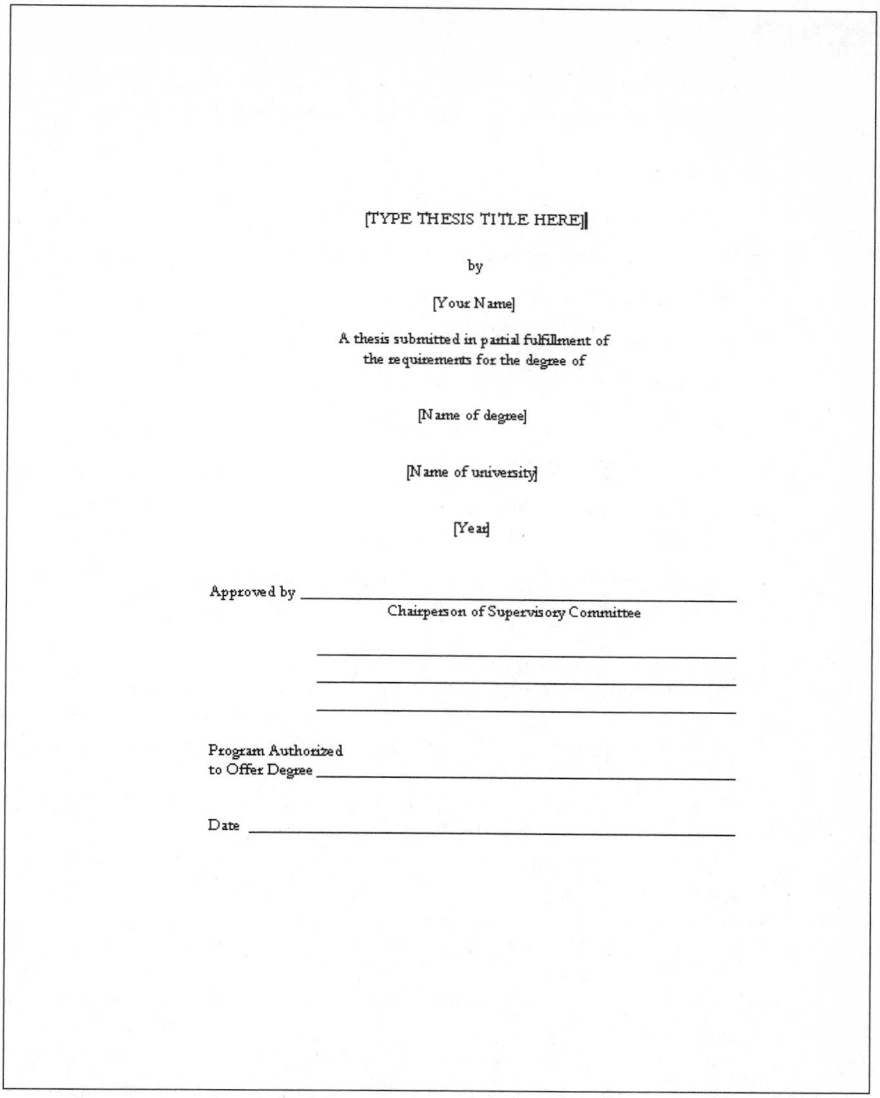

[TYPE THESIS TITLE HERE]

by

[Your Name]

A thesis submitted in partial fulfillment of
the requirements for the degree of

[Name of degree]

[Name of university]

[Year]

Approved by _____
Chairperson of Supervisory Committee

_____

_____

_____

Program Authorized
to Offer Degree _____

Date _____

Figure 3-23:
The Thesis.
dot template
(title page).

Using Wizards

Word comes with a collection of wizards designed to simplify the creation of routine documents. Word's wizards include the following:

- ✦ **Envelope:** Addresses envelopes.

- ✦ **Fax:** Creates faxes in various styles.

- ✦ **Letter:** Creates letters in various styles.

- ✦ **Mailing Label:** Creates mailing labels.

- ✦ **Memo:** Creates memos with attractive headers and body text.

- ✦ **Newsletter:** Sets up a newsletter with columns and other elements.

- ✦ **Pleading:** Creates legal documents.

- ✦ **Agenda:** Creates meeting agendas.

- ✦ **Calendar:** Creates Lemon Meringue pies. (Actually, it creates calendars, but pies would be more useful.)

- ✦ **Resume:** Creates resumes with pertinent sections, such as Education, References, and so on.

A wizard is nothing more than a special type of template given the extension WIZ instead of DOC. Each wizard contains specialized macros that run automatically to prompt you for the information it needs to create the document. After you answer the questions, the wizard creates the document for you.

To run a wizard, choose File⇨New and click the <u>On My Computer</u> link in the Templates section of the New Document task pane. Then, select a wizard instead of a template for the new document. Word loads the wizard and automatically runs it.

To illustrate how wizards work, I step you through one of the more popular wizards these days, the Resume Wizard. To create a resume using this wizard, start by summoning the Templates dialog box by choosing File⇨New and clicking the <u>On My Computer</u> link in the New Documents task pane. Click the Other Documents tab and double-click the Resume Wizard.wiz icon. (If the dialog box displays large icons, you may have to scroll the list to find the Resume Wizard.) Be patient while the Resume Wizard chugs and churns. Eventually, the Resume Wizard comes to life and displays the dialog box shown in Figure 3-24.

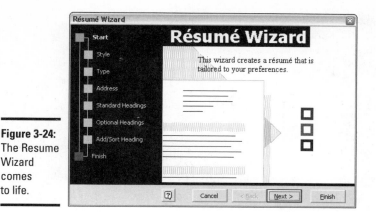

Figure 3-24:
The Resume
Wizard
comes
to life.

This dialog box shows the basic framework for all wizard dialog boxes. At the left of the dialog box is a flowchart that shows all of the steps in the wizard, with the current step highlighted in a different color from the other steps. The right side of the wizard dialog box contains various fields and option buttons you use to answer the wizard's questions. As you work your way through the wizard, these controls change depending on the information the wizard is seeking.

At the bottom of the dialog box are four buttons that you use to control the wizard:

✦ The Cancel button bails out of the wizard without creating a document.

✦ The Back button, which is grayed out in Figure 3-24, lets you work your way backwards through the wizard to change your answers to prior questions.

✦ The Next button tells the wizard to continue with the next question.

✦ The Finish button tells the wizard to stop the interview and create the document now, using whatever information it's gathered so far.

To proceed with the wizard, click the Next button, which displays the dialog box shown in Figure 3-25. Select from among the three different resume styles — Professional, Contemporary, or Elegant. These styles affect the appearance, not the content, of your resume.

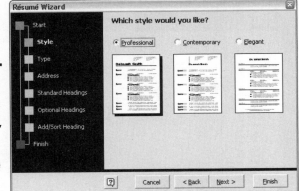

Figure 3-25:
You can create a Professional, Contemporary, or Elegant style resume.

Figure 3-26 shows the next dialog box displayed by the wizard, which allows you to select one of four basic resume types: Entry Level, Chronological, Functional, or Professional.

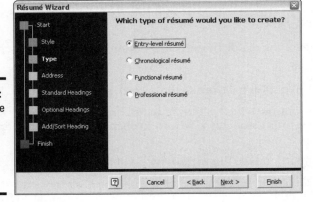

Figure 3-26:
The Resume Wizard lets you create one of four types of resumes.

Figure 3-27 shows the dialog box displayed next. Here, you type your name, address, and phone number. The Resume Wizard includes this information in the resume automatically.

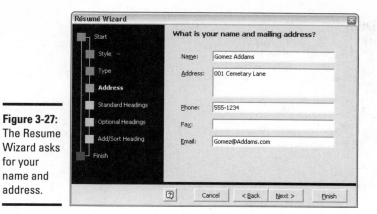

Figure 3-27:
The Resume
Wizard asks
for your
name and
address.

Figure 3-28 shows the next dialog box displayed by the Resume Wizard. Here, you are asked to select which commonly used headings to include in the resume. Note that the precise mix of sections that appear varies depending on which resume style you selected in the previous dialog box.

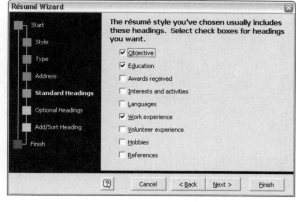

Figure 3-28:
The Resume
Wizard
offers to
include
these
standard
headings in
the resume.

Next, the Resume Wizard displays a list of optional sections you can include in your resume if you want, as shown in Figure 3-29. Again, these sections vary depending on which resume type you selected at the beginning.

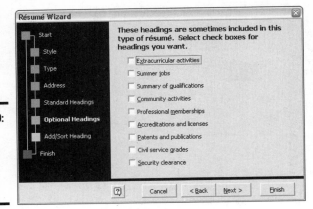

Figure 3-29:
Other
headings
you can
add to the
resume.

The Resume Wizard next displays the dialog box shown in Figure 3-30, which allows you to add your own headings to the resume or change the order in which the headings appear. To add a heading, type the title as you want it to appear in the resume in the text field and click the Add button. To move a heading, select it in the list box and click the Move Up or Move Down button.

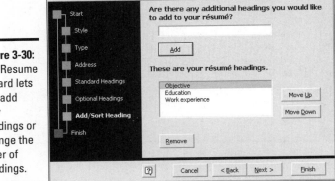

Figure 3-30:
The Resume
Wizard lets
you add
new
headings or
change the
order of
headings.

Finally, after you answer all the questions, you reach the final dialog box, shown in Figure 3-31. Click Finish to create the resume.

Book I
Chapter 3

Working with
Templates

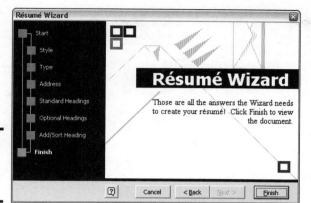

Figure 3-31:
You're
almost
finished!

When you click the Finish button, the wizard works for a few moments and then creates the resume as a new document, as shown in Figure 3-32. You can now edit the document however you want, filling in the blanks left by the wizard.

Note: The Office Assistant appears, offering to lend aid with the resume. You can opt to create a cover letter, change the visual style, shrink the resume to make it fit on fewer pages, send the resume to someone via fax or e-mail, or get help with something else. If all you want to do is edit the resume, click Cancel to dismiss the Assistant, and then get to work.

All the other wizards that come with Word work much the same as the Resume Wizard. Each displays a series of questions using the same dialog box format and the same Cancel, Back, Next, and Finish controls. Of course, the questions vary from wizard to wizard, and the document generated by the wizard is different. But the basic framework of the wizards is the same.

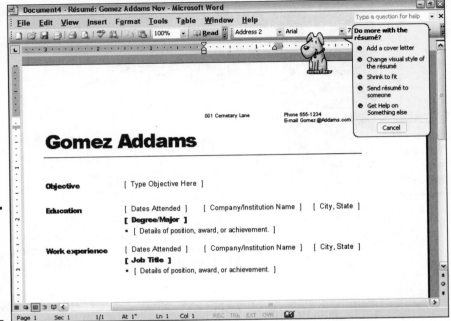

Figure 3-32:
A resume
created by
the Resume
Wizard,
ready for
editing.

Chapter 4: Printing Your Documents

In This Chapter

- ✓ Printing a document
- ✓ Playing with print options
- ✓ Previewing your output
- ✓ Cursing at your printer when it doesn't work

The Print command. The Printmeister. Big document comin' up. Printin' some pages. The Printorama. The Mentor of de Printor. Captain Toner of the Good Ship Laseroo.

Don't worry — when you print a Word document, no one's waiting to ambush you with annoying one-liners like that guy who used to be on *Saturday Night Live*. Just a handful of boring dialog boxes with boring check boxes. Point-point, click-click, print-print.

Printing the Quick Way

The fastest way to print your document is to click the Print button on the Standard toolbar. It's the one with the little picture of a printer on it. Clicking this button prints your document without further ado, using the current settings for the Print dialog box, which I explain in the remaining sections of this chapter. Usually, this action results in printing a single copy of all the pages in your document. But if you alter the Print dialog box settings, clicking the Print button uses the altered settings automatically.

Using the Print Dialog Box

For precise control over how you want your document to print, you must conjure up the Print dialog box shown in Figure 4-1. To summon this dialog box, choose File⇨Print or press Ctrl+P.

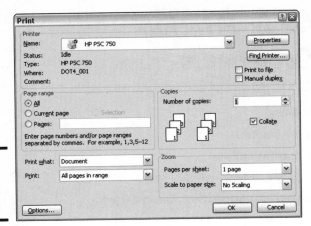

Figure 4-1:
Behold
the Print
dialog box.

After you call up the Print dialog box, click OK or press Enter to print a single copy of your entire document. Fiddle around with the settings to print just certain pages, to print more than one copy, or to change other aspects of how your document prints. This section shows you the treasures that lie hidden in this dialog box.

Printing can be es-el-oh-double-ewe, so don't panic if your document doesn't start printing right away. Word printouts tend to demand a great deal from the printer, so sometimes the printer has to work for a while before it can produce a finished page. Be patient. The Print dialog box has every intention of granting your request.

Changing printers

If you're lucky enough to have two or more printers at your disposal, you can use the Name field to pick which printer you want to use. You must first successfully install each printer in Windows — a topic beyond the reach of this humble book, but that you find plenty of information about in the appropriate version of Andy Rathbone's *Windows For Dummies* (published by Wiley).

Printing part of a document

When you first use the Print command, the All option is checked so that your entire document prints. The other options in the Print Range portion of the Print dialog box enable you to tell Word to print distinct portions of your document:

✦ **Current page:** Prints just the current page. Before you invoke the Print command, move to the page you want to print. Then check this option in the Print dialog box and click OK. This option is handy when you make a change to one page and don't want to reprint the entire document.

◆ **Selection:** Prints just the portion of the document you selected before invoking the Print command. First, select the pages you want to print. Then call up the Print command, select the Selection radio button, and click OK. (This option is grayed out in Figure 4-1.)

◆ **Pages:** Lets you select specific pages for printing. You can print a range of pages by typing the beginning and ending page numbers, separated by a hyphen, as in *5-8* to print pages 5, 6, 7, and 8. Or you can list individual pages, separated by commas, as in *4,8,11* to print pages 4, 8, and 11. And you can combine ranges and individual pages, as in *4,9-11,13* to print pages 4, 9, 10, 11, and 13.

Printing more than one copy

The Number of Copies field in the Print dialog box lets you print more than one copy of your document. You can click one of the arrows next to this field to increase or decrease the number of copies, or you can type directly in the field to set the number of copies.

Below the Number of Copies field is a Collate check box. If this box is checked, Word prints each copy of your document one at a time. In other words, if your document consists of ten pages and you select three copies and check the Collate box, Word first prints all ten pages of the first copy of the document, and then all ten pages of the second copy, and then all ten pages of the third copy. If you don't check the Collate box, Word prints three copies of the first page, followed by three copies of the second page, followed by three copies of the third page, and so on.

The Collate option saves you from the chore of manually sorting your copies. If your document takes forever to print because it's loaded down with heavy-duty graphics, however, you can probably save time in the long run by unchecking the Collate box. Why? Because many printers are fast when printing a second or third copy of a page. The printer may spend ten minutes figuring out how to print a particularly complicated page, but after it figures it out, the printer can print additional copies in ten seconds each. If you print collated copies, the printer must labor over each page separately for each copy of the document that it prints.

Choosing what to print

The Print What field in the Print dialog box enables you to select which type of output that you want to print. The following choices are available:

◆ **Document:** Prints your document. (Duh.)

◆ **Document Properties:** Prints information about your document.

◆ **Document Showing Markup:** If you enable the Track Changes feature, this option prints your document along with any revision marks.

- ✦ **List of Markup:** Prints a list of revisions made to the document.
- ✦ **Styles:** Prints the styles in the document.
- ✦ **AutoText entries:** Prints any AutoText entries in the document.
- ✦ **Key Assignments:** Prints any shortcut keys that are assigned.

Select the type of output you want to print and then click OK or press Enter. Off you go!

Zooming

The Print command has two Zoom options that let you print the text smaller or larger than actual size:

- ✦ **Pages per Sheet:** This option lets you print more than one page on each sheet of paper. This option is especially useful for creating quick proof pages to make sure your document is laid out properly. It is also useful if your document consists mostly of large text that is still readable when reduced 50 percent or more.
- ✦ **Scale to Fit Paper:** Adjusts the size of the printed output to fit the paper in the printer. You should usually leave this option unchecked.

Playing with Print Options

If you click the Options button at the bottom left of the Print dialog box, the Print Options dialog box appears, as shown in Figure 4-2. You can use this dialog box to control various aspects of how your document prints.

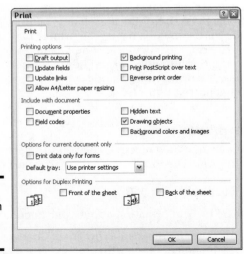

Figure 4-2:
Playing with the Print options.

The first group of options is the Print Options:

✦ **Draft Output:** Prints the document in draft format, with very little formatting. This option usually results in faster printing.

✦ **Update Fields:** Updates all of the document's fields before printing the document. You usually leave this option turned on.

✦ **Update Links:** Updates any linked information in the document before printing it. You usually leave this option turned on.

✦ **Allow A4/Letter Paper Resizing:** Automatically adjusts your document to fit the paper size.

✦ **Background Printing:** Prints documents in the background, so you can continue working while the document prints.

✦ **Print PostScript Over Text:** This option is important only if you're converting documents from Macintosh Word format.

✦ **Reverse Print Order:** Prints the document backwards, starting with the last page in your document.

The second group of options is titled Include with Document:

✦ **Document Properties:** Prints document properties on a separate page following the document.

✦ **Field Codes:** Prints field codes rather than field results. Use this option only if your document is filled with fields and you're trying to figure out why they aren't working right.

✦ **Hidden Text:** Prints any hidden text.

✦ **Drawing Objects:** Prints drawing objects.

✦ **Background Colors and Images:** Prints background colors and images.

The third group of options is titled Options for Current Document Only:

✦ **Print Data Only for Forms:** Prints the data entered into a form but doesn't print the form itself.

✦ **Default Tray:** Tells the printer to use its default tray.

The final group of options is titled Options for Duplex Printing. These options are useful when you want to print on both sides of the paper but your printer doesn't have a duplexing feature.

✦ **Front of the Sheet:** Sets the order of pages on the front of each sheet. Normally, the odd numbered pages are printed in order on the top of each page. Check this option to reverse the print order of the odd numbered pages.

✦ **Back of the Sheet:** Normally, even numbered pages are printed in order on the back of each page. Check this option to reverse the print order of the even numbered pages.

Using the Print Preview Command

The Print Preview feature lets you see how your pages will appear before committing them to paper (or transparencies). To use the Print Preview feature, choose File⇨Print Preview or click the Print Preview button. Or, you can choose File⇨Print to bring up the Print dialog box, and then click the Preview button. Either way, a preview of the printed page appears, as shown in Figure 4-3.

From the Print Preview screen, you can zoom in to examine the preview more closely by clicking anywhere in the preview area. Or, you can scroll through the pages using the scroll bar, the Page Up and Page Down keys, or the Prev Page and Next Page buttons located at the top-left corner of the screen.

After you're satisfied the printout will be to your expectations, click the Print button to print the document. If you discover a mistake in the preview, click Close to return to Word so that you can correct the mistake before printing your pages.

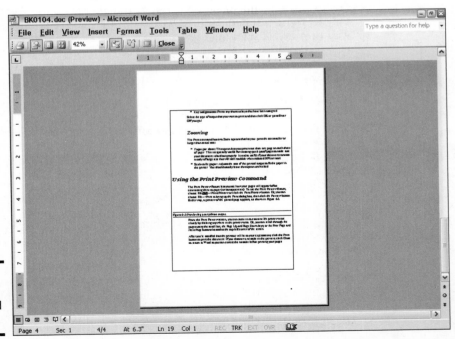

Figure 4-3: Previewing your printed output.

Chapter 5: Help!

*T*he ideal way to use Word is to have a Word expert sitting patiently at your side, answering your every question with a straightforward answer, gently correcting you when you make silly mistakes, and otherwise minding his or her own business. All you'd have to do is occasionally toss the expert a Twinkie and let him or her outside once a day.

The good news is that Word has just such an expert built-in. This expert is referred to as the Office Assistant, and he works not just with Word, but also with other Microsoft Office programs, including Excel, PowerPoint, and Outlook. You don't even have to feed the Office Assistant, unlike a real guru.

Meeting the Assistant

Alexander Graham Bell had Watson, Batman had Robin, and Dr. Frankenstein had Igor. Everybody needs an assistant, and Office users are no exception. That's why Microsoft decided to bless Office with the Office Assistant, a handy fellow who offers helpful assistance as you work with Office programs, including Word.

The Office Assistant is an animated persona who suddenly morphs onto your desktop with sage advice and suggestions. If the Office Assistant thinks you're struggling with something, he magically appears to offer help. Or, you can summon the Office Assistant to ask a question when you're not sure what to do.

The Office Assistant is actually one of several little cartoon characters. Figure 5-1 shows the one I like best. His name is Rocky. See the section "Changing Assistants" later in this chapter for instructions on how to switch to a different Assistant.

Figure 5-1:
Meet Rocky,
an Office
Assistant.

The fun thing about the Assistant is that he is animated. Watch the Assistant on-screen as you work. Every once in a while he blinks, and on occasion, he dances or makes a face. The Assistant often responds to commands that you choose in Word. For example, if you call up the Find command (Edit⇨Find or Ctrl+F), the Assistant makes a gesture as if he is searching for something. When you print your document, the Assistant does some cute little printer schtick. Microsoft went to a lot of trouble to make sure that the Assistant is entertaining, and the results are sometimes amusing. When you ask the Assistant for help, he sits down, plops his feet up on a desk, and takes copious notes — don't you wish real people cared so much!

Notice that the Assistant has a special type of dialog box called a *balloon,* which includes an area for you to type a question and several buttons you can click. The balloon functions like any other dialog box, but it has a special appearance that's unique to the Assistant.

When you first install Word, the Assistant is disabled. You can summon him by choosing Help⇨Show the Office Assistant. Then, right-click the Assistant, choose Options from the pop-up menu, and then check the Use the Office Assistant option and click OK.

Summoning the Assistant

You can summon the Assistant in several ways when you need help. In many cases, the Assistant shows up all by himself, so all you need to do to get his attention is click the Assistant. The balloon dialog box pops up and you can ask a question. If the Assistant isn't visible on-screen, you can summon him quickly by choosing Help⇨Show the Office Assistant, by pressing F1, or by clicking the Help button on the Standard toolbar (it's the button with the big question mark in it).

Sometimes the Assistant figures out that you're struggling with something and offers some helpful assistance all on his own. For example, if you try to select the bullet that appears next to a bulleted paragraph, the Assistant displays a light bulb to indicate that it has an idea. If you click the light bulb, the Assistant explains that you can't select the bullet as shown in Figure 5-2.

You're clicking on text you cannot select. Press BACKSPACE to delete the text, or press TAB to indent the paragraph.

OK

Figure 5-2:
The Assist-
ant offers
friendly
advice.

Asking a Question

If none of the Help topics offered by the Assistant seem to be what you're looking for, you can type a question right in the Assistant's balloon dialog box to look for help on a specific topic. For example, if you want to know how to create a bullet list, type **How do I create a bullet list?** in the text box and then click the Search button or press Enter. The Assistant searches Microsoft's extensive Help library, and then displays the results in the Search task pane, as shown in Figure 5-3.

If one of the topics looks promising, click it. Or click Can't Find It to see options for finding additional information.

If none of the topics seem related to the question you asked, try rephrasing the question and click Search again.

You don't actually have to phrase your question as a question. You can eliminate words such as *How do I,* and you can also usually eliminate "noise words" such as *a, an, the, of, in,* and so on. Thus, the brief question "change background color paragraph" yields exactly the same result as the more verbose "How do I change the background color of a paragraph?"

When you click one of the suggested topics, a separate Help window appears as shown in Figure 5-4.

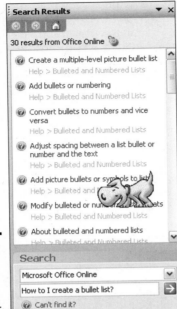

Figure 5-3:
The
Assistant
searches
for answers.

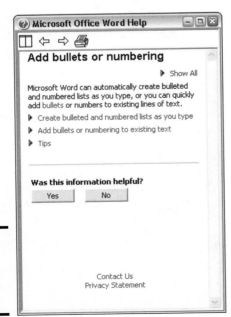

Figure 5-4:
Help
appears in
a separate
window.

When you get yourself this deep into Help, you need to heed the following advice to find your way around and get out when you find out what you want to know:

✦ **Print helpful information:** If you find a Help topic that you consider uncommonly useful, click the Print button and print the darn thing.

✦ **Navigate from page to page:** If you see an underlined word or phrase, you can click it to zip to a Help page that describes that word or phrase. By following these underlined words, you can bounce your way around from Help page to Help page until you eventually find the help that you need.

✦ **Get step-by-step instructions:** Sometimes, Help offers several choices under a heading such as "What do you want to do?" Each choice is preceded by a little button: Click the button to display step-by-step help for that choice.

✦ **Retrace your steps:** You can retrace your steps by clicking the Help window's Back button. You can use the Back button over and over again, retracing all your steps if necessary.

✦ **Work in Word and get help at the same time:** Help operates as a separate program, so you can work within Word while the Help window remains on-screen. When you display a help topic, a separate Help window appears, which you can resize, minimize, or drag as you wish.

✦ **Close Help:** When you have enough of Help, you can dismiss it by pressing Esc or clicking the close button in the upper-right corner of the Help window.

Changing Assistants

Rocky, the friendly and loyal cyberpup Assistant, is but one of seven Assistants from which you can choose. The others are a paperclip named ClipIt, a happy face named The Dot, a robot named F1, a puzzle piece named Office Logo, a globe named Mother Nature, and a cat named Links.

To select a different Assistant, summon the Assistant by choosing Help➪Show Office Assistant. Then click the Options button to display the Office Assistant dialog box. Click the Gallery tab located at the top of this dialog box. The Assistant Gallery displays, as shown in Figure 5-5.

To change to a different Assistant, click the Next button. Keep clicking the Next button to work your way through all the Assistants. When you find the one you want to use, click OK.

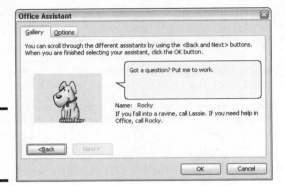

Figure 5-5:
The Office
Assistant
Gallery.

The Assistants differ only in appearance — not in their ability to offer assistance with using Word features. If I worked for Microsoft, I would have given the Assistants personalities. For example, Rocky would be eager to help. But every once in awhile, he'd lick the screen and the text under the spot would be out of focus. On the other hand, you'd have to press F1 five or six times before Links (the cat) would even appear on-screen.

You can also click the Options tab on the Office Assistant dialog box to set various options that affect how the Assistant works. In fact, you can use this dialog box to turn the Assistant off altogether if he annoys you.

Help the Old-Fashioned Way

The Assistant isn't the only way to get help in Word. You can still get help the old-fashioned Windows way through the traditional Help interface.

To summon old-fashioned Help, first turn off the Assistant by summoning the Office Assistant dialog box and unchecking the Use the Office Assistant check box. Then press F1 or choose Help⇨Microsoft Office Word Help, which summons the Help task pane. Next, click the <u>Table of Contents</u> link to summon the Help Table of Contents shown in Figure 5-6.

The topics with book icons next to them represent sections that have additional subtopics. You can click one of these sections to reveal the list of subtopics. Each of the actual Help topic pages has an icon that looks like a page with a question mark in it. You can click one of these topics to display the Help page.

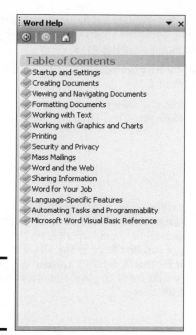

Figure 5-6:
Good old-
fashioned
help.

Searching for Lost Help Topics

If you can't find help for a nasty problem by browsing through the Help Contents, you can search for Help topics. On the main Help page in the task pane, just type the words that you want to search for in the text box and click Search. With luck, you can quickly find the help you need.

Getting Help on the Internet

In addition to the help that's built into Word, you can also get Word help from the Internet. All you need is an Internet connection. To seek help on the Internet, click one of the options in the Office on Microsoft.com section of the Help task pane. These options include the following:

✦ **Assistance:** This link connects you to the Microsoft Office Assistance home page at Microsoft.com. Here, you can find all kinds of useful information about Word and other Office programs.

✦ **Training:** This link takes you to the Training home page at Microsoft.com. Here you can find online training tutorials that teach you how to use specific aspects of Word or other Office programs.

✦ **Communities:** This link takes you to a Web page that has links to online forums where you can ask questions.

✦ **Downloads:** This link takes you to the Office Update home page on Microsoft.com, where you can download the latest updates to Office programs.

Repairing a Broken Office

If Word doesn't seem to be working right — for example, if it locks up your computer when you use certain commands or if features seem to be missing — you can use the built-in Office repair tool to detect and correct problems. To use the repair tool, first locate your Word or Office Setup CD. Then, choose Help⇨Detect and Repair. Follow the instructions that appear on-screen. If the repair tool needs to retrieve any files from the installation CD, it asks you to insert the CD in your computer's CD drive.

Book II

Formatting Text

The 5th Wave   By Rich Tennant

"The memo says that Chiller font is going to be the new company standard."

Contents at a Glance

Chapter 1: Basic Text Formatting

In This Chapter

- ✔ **Understanding formatting in Word**
- ✔ **Formatting characters**
- ✔ **Formatting paragraphs**
- ✔ **Understanding text flow**
- ✔ **Becoming familiar with tabs**
- ✔ **The ten commandments of formatting**

*H*ow I loved my first computer. It had one of those daisy-wheel printers that created pages that looked like they had been typed on an actual typewriter. And my word processing software was so advanced that I could actually underline individual words and even set tab stops. And it could print out an entire page of letter-quality text faster than Congress can give itself a pay raise!

Those were the good old days. Back then, you didn't worry too much about what your text looked like because you didn't really have that much control over appearances. So instead, you had to focus on — brace yourself — your actual words. Your document's words were actually more important than your document's appearance.

Nowadays, it seems as if appearance is everything. Who cares what your document says, as long as it looks great. The most brilliantly conceived proposal can go unread unless it looks like it was produced by a Madison Avenue ad agency. Sigh.

If you need a refresher in the basics of formatting text with Word, you landed in the right chapter. The formatting stuff in this chapter is pretty basic, so much of it may be review if you've been using Word for a while. But heck, a little review never hurt, and you may find a few juicy formatting tidbits in here that you didn't know you didn't know.

I hate this stuff as much as you do. Because I'm a writer, I like to concentrate on what my words *say* rather than how they look. If you agree, I highly recommend that you get to Chapter 3 of this minibook as soon as possible, where you are thrust into the world of *styles*. Styles are the secret to freedom from the bondage of all the formatting nonsense presented in this chapter.

Understanding Formatting in Word

Before getting into the details of applying specific formats to your document, review the *gestalt* of how Word formats your text. Word has three basic types of formats:

+ **Characters:** Characters are the smallest element that you can format in Word. You can make characters bold, italic, or underlined, change their font size, and more. If you're deranged enough, you can format every character of your document differently. Doing so gives your documents a ransom-note appearance, which is something you probably want to avoid.

+ **Paragraphs:** The next biggest element you can format in Word is a paragraph. You can format each paragraph so that it has its own tab stops, line spacing, extra space before or after the paragraph, indentation, alignment (left, right, centered, or justified), and more. Paragraphs also have default character formats. So the only time you need to apply a character format is when you want your characters to vary from the paragraph's default character format, such as when you want to italicize or bold a word.

+ **Sections:** Word also enables you to control the layout of pages. You can format each page by setting the top, bottom, left, and right margins, setting the number of columns and the size of each column, setting the paper size, controlling the placement of headers and footers, and more. You can format your document so that all pages have the same layout, or you can divide your document into *sections,* each with a different page layout. That's why Word refers to these formats as *section formats.*

Paragraph formatting information is contained within the paragraph mark at the end of the paragraph. This mark looks kind of like a backwards letter P. If you can't see any paragraph marks on your screen, choose Tools⇨Options and click the View tab. Then check the Paragraph Marks option.

Here are some additional things you need to know about how formatting works:

+ If you delete that paragraph mark, the paragraph merges with the following paragraph. Any formatting applied to the paragraph mark you deleted is lost — the text assumes the formatting of the following paragraph.

+ If you use more than one page layout in a document, the document is divided into two or more sections. Each section except the last one ends with a *section break,* which displays as a double line that spans the entire width of the page. Section marks work much like paragraph marks: If you delete one, the text before the section mark assumes the page layout of the section following the mark.

✦ Every document has at least one section, but you see section marks only if you divide the document into two or more sections. Where's the section mark for the last section of a document? There is none. The formatting information for the last section of a document is stored in the last paragraph mark in the document.

Formatting Characters

The sections that follow show you how to apply various formats to characters. Like most things in Word, you can apply these formats in more than one way. The easiest way is to use keyboard shortcuts (if you can remember them) or the various buttons and gizmos on the Formatting toolbar. Otherwise, you can use the Format➪Font command if you like to play with dialog boxes.

Fun with fonts

Ever notice the little icons that appear next to font names in Word's font lists? These icons identify the various types of fonts you can use with Word.

✔ **Printer fonts:** These fonts are designed for specific printers. For some reason known only by Windows moguls, they may not appear on-screen exactly as they appear on the printed page.

✔ **TrueType fonts:** These fonts are Windows fonts. The font displays on-screen exactly as it does on the printed page. Any printer that works with Windows can print TrueType fonts. Stick to TrueType for best results.

✔ **PostScript fonts:** These fonts are designed to work with PostScript-compatible laser printers, which are more expensive, but are the first choice of desktop publishing fanatics. Use these only if you have a PostScript laser printer.

If you make the wise decision to stick to TrueType fonts, follow this simple procedure to remove the non-TrueType font clutter from Word's font lists (and the font lists for all other Windows programs, for that matter):

1. **Click the Start button in the Windows task bar.**

2. **Click Control Panel.**

   The Control Panel appears. (If you're using an older version of Windows, you can get to the Control Panel by choosing Settings➪ Control Panel from the Start menu.)

3. **Double-click the Fonts icon.**

   A window listing all of the fonts installed on your computer appears.

4. **Choose Tools➪Options.**

   The Options dialog box appears.

5. **Click the TrueType tab at the top of the Options dialog box.**

6. **Check the Show Only TrueType Fonts in the Programs on My Computer check box.**

7. **Click OK and then click the Close button in the Fonts window.**

Now you don't have to worry about non-TrueType fonts; only TrueType fonts show up in Word.

Applying character formats the easy way

You can apply character formats before or after you type the text you want to format. To apply a character format to text as you type it, follow these steps:

1. **Type text up to the point where you want to apply a format.**

2. **Turn on the special character formatting by using one of the keyboard shortcuts or toolbar buttons listed in Table 1-1.**

Nothing happens at first, but wait. . . .

3. **Type away.**

Anything you type now assumes the format you applied in Step 2.

4. **Turn off the special character formatting by using the keyboard short-cut again.**

Or, if you clicked one of the buttons on the Formatting toolbar, click it again. Either way, Word discontinues the special formatting. Any text you subsequently type formats as usual.

Table 1-1	Character Formatting the Easy Way	
Toolbar Button	*Keyboard Shortcut*	*What It Does*
B	Ctrl+B	Bold
I	Ctrl+I	Italic
<u>U</u>	Ctrl+U	Underline (continuous)
	Ctrl+Shift+W	Word underline
	Ctrl+Shift+D	Double underline
	Ctrl+Shift+A	All caps
	Ctrl+Shift+K	Small caps
	Shift+F3	Change case
	Ctrl+=	Subscript
	Ctrl+Shift+=	Superscript
Arial	Ctrl+Shift+F	Change font
9.5	Ctrl+Shift+P	Change point size
	Ctrl+]	Increase size one point

Toolbar Button	Keyboard Shortcut	What It Does
	Ctrl+[	Decrease size one point
	Ctrl+Shift+>	Increase size to next available size
	Ctrl+Shift+<	Decrease size to previous available size
	Ctrl+Shift+Q	Switch to Symbol font ΓρεεκΤραγεδψ
	Ctrl+Shift+Z	Remove character formatting
	Ctrl+spacebar	Remove character formatting

To apply a character format to text you already typed, follow these steps:

1. **Highlight the text you want to format.**

To highlight a single word, double-click anywhere in the word. To highlight an entire paragraph, triple-click anywhere in the paragraph. Otherwise, highlight the text that you want to format by dragging the mouse over it while holding down the left mouse button or by using the arrow keys to move the cursor while holding down the Shift key.

If you enabled Word's Automatic Word Selection option, you don't have to double-click to select an entire word; Word automatically selects the entire word if the insertion point is anywhere in the word. To activate this option (or to deactivate it if it is already activated), choose Tools⇨ Options, click the Edit tab, and then click the Automatic Word Selection button. Click OK or press Enter to close the Options dialog box.

2. **Apply the format using one of the keyboard shortcuts or toolbar buttons listed in Table 1-1.**

The effects of your formatting are immediately apparent.

3. **Move on.**

Disperse. There's nothing more to see here. Return to your homes.

Some other tidbits on character formatting:

✦ You can gang tackle text with formats, if you want. For example, you can format text as ***bold italic double-underlined*** if you're really desperate for attention.

✦ To remove *all* character formatting, highlight the text that you want to return to normal; then press Ctrl+spacebar or Ctrl+Shift+Z.

✦ To remove a specific character format, such as bold or italic, but leave other character formats intact, highlight the text and press the keyboard shortcut or click the toolbar button for the format you want to remove.

✦ To paraphrase Chuck Yeager, there are old Word users, and there are bold Word users, but there are no old bold Word users.

Using the Format⇨Font command

The character formatting options you're likely to use most — bold, italics, underlining, font, and point size — are all readily accessible from the Formatting toolbar or easy-to-remember keyboard shortcuts. Most other character formatting options don't dare show their faces on the Formatting toolbar, and you probably won't use them enough to remember their keyboard shortcuts.

If you find yourself in the unenviable position of needing to apply a character format not on the toolbar and you can't remember the shortcut, you have three alternatives. First, you can try to talk yourself out of it. Who needs double underlining, anyway? If that doesn't work, you can flip open this book, turn to Table 1-1, and look up the keyboard shortcut.

As a last resort, you can use the Format⇨Font command. Yes, I know it pops up a dialog box that looks designed by Bill Z. Bub himself, but it does give you one-stop shopping for all of Word's character formatting options.

The Format⇨Font command is the only way to apply the following formats to characters:

◆ Underline styles

◆ Strikethrough

◆ Double strikethrough

◆ Shadow

◆ Outline

◆ Emboss

◆ Engrave

◆ Character spacing

These formats do not appear on any of the standard toolbars, and they have no keyboard shortcuts. So if you want to apply them, you have to use the Format⇨Font command. Here's the procedure for applying mystifying, strange formatting:

1. **Highlight the text you want to mangle with oddball formatting.**

2. **Conjure up Format⇨Font.**

Or, use the convenient and easy-to-remember mnemonic keyboard shortcut, Ctrl+D. (Just remember that the *D* stands for *those demonic character formats.* Works for me.)

3. Tremble before the Font dialog box.

After all, it was designed by Bill Z. Bub himself. Figure 1-1 shows its ghastly appearance.

4. Play with the controls.

Fiddle with the various controls to set the Font, the Font Style (bold, italic, and so on), and the Size. Click the Effects you want (strikethrough, superscript, and so on). Use the drop-down list boxes to set the underline and color. Have a ball.

5. Click OK when you have enough.

The dialog box vanishes, and your text magically transforms with the formats you selected.

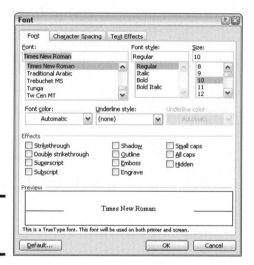

Figure 1-1:
The Font
dialog box.

Some notes about using the Font dialog box:

✦ If you haven't yet typed the text you want to mangle, use Format⇨Font, choose the formats you want, click OK, and then start typing. When you're done, press Ctrl+spacebar or Ctrl+Shift+Z to resume normal type.

✦ To remove oddball formats that you applied with the Format⇨Font command, select the text and press Ctrl+spacebar or Ctrl+Shift+Z. Or conjure up Format⇨Font once again and uncheck the formats you want to get rid of.

✦ Notice the tabs across the top of the Font dialog box? They enable you to switch between basic font formatting, character spacing, and special text animation effects. If you click the Character Spacing tab, you see options to control the spacing between characters, raise or lower characters from the baseline, and apply a spiffy desktop publishing feature called *kerning*. These options are in the realm of desktop publishing, so ignore them for now. If you can't wait, skip ahead to Book IV, Chapter 6 for information about using these options. I cover animation settings a bit later in this chapter, in the section "Animating your text."

✦ If you find yourself frequently using a formatting option that doesn't have a keyboard shortcut already assigned, you can create your own keyboard shortcut, which I describe in Book VIII, Chapter 2.

Spacing out your text

If you click the Character Spacing tab of the Font dialog box, the Character Spacing options appear, as shown in Figure 1-2.

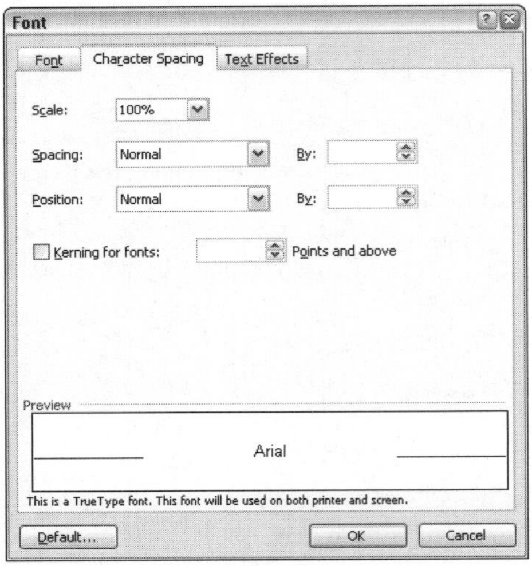

Figure 1-2: Character Spacing options.

The following paragraphs describe the options you can set via the Character Spacing tab:

✦ **Scale:** Lets you increase or decrease the size of the text.

✦ **Spacing:** Normal, Expanded, or Condensed. If you select Expanded or Condensed, you must then set the By field to indicate how many points the space between individual characters increase or decrease. You can experiment with different settings for these fields to create letters that appear scrunched together or spaced out.

Figure 1-3 shows how character spacing affects the appearance of your text. Here, I formatted the same paragraph three ways: first using 12-point Times New Roman with normal spacing, then with 12-point Times New Roman and character spacing expanded 0.5 points, and finally with 12-point Times New Roman and character spacing condensed 0.5 points.

Note: This option is not where you set the spacing between lines. That's done via Format➪Paragraph, which I describe in the "Formatting Paragraphs" section, later in this chapter.

✦ **Position:** Normal, Raised, or Lowered. If you select Raised or Lowered, you then indicate how many points above or below the baseline you want the text to move in the By field.

✦ **Kerning for Fonts:** Kerning means to adjust the amount of space between certain combinations of letters that otherwise appear to have too much space between them. If you check this field, you can also set the minimum character size for which kerning is used. This option is handy because kerning problems are more noticeable at larger type sizes.

Figure 1-4 shows two samples of type. The first is not kerned. As you can see, the amount of white space in the letter combinations *Yo, Ve,* and *Wo* appears excessive. The second sample shows the same text set in the same typeface but with Word's kerning feature activated. You can see that Word closed up the space for these letter combinations, giving the entire line a more balanced appearance.

Figure 1-3:
How
spacing
affects the
appearance
of your text.

12-Point Times New Roman, normal character spacing

The Old Grey Donkey, Eeyore, stood by himself in a thistly corner of the forest, his front feet well apart, his head on one side, and thought about things. Sometimes he thought sadly to himself, "Why?" and sometimes he thought, "Wherefore?" and sometimes he thought, "Inasmuch as which?"

12-Point Times New Roman, expanded 0.5 points

The Old Grey Donkey, Eeyore, stood by himself in a thistly corner of the forest, his front feet well apart, his head on one side, and thought about things. Sometimes he thought sadly to himself, "Why?" and sometimes he thought, "Wherefore?" and sometimes he thought, "Inasmuch as which?"

12-Point Times New Roman, condensed 0.5 points

The Old Grey Donkey, Eeyore, stood by himself in a thistly corner of the forest, his front feet well apart, his head on one side, and thought about things. Sometimes he thought sadly to himself, "Why?" and sometimes he thought, "Wherefore?" and sometimes he thought, "Inasmuch as which?"

Figure 1-4:
How
kerning
affects the
appearance
of your text.

Your Very Words

Your Very Words

Animating your text

Word has the ability to add simple animation effects to your text. These animation effects won't make your document look like Disney animators produced
it, but animation can draw attention to text you want highlighted. Of course,
animations are visible only when you view the document on your computer
using Word. Microsoft hasn't figured out a way to make the animations appear
on plain paper yet. (When they do, you'll wish you had bought stock.)

Word offers the following text animation effects:

✦ **Blinking Background:** The background flashes.

✦ **Las Vegas Lights:** Dots that flash on and off in changing colors surround
the text.

✦ **Marching Black Ants:** A series of black dashes appear to march around
the text.

✦ **Marching Red Ants:** Same as Marching Black Ants, only the "ants" are
red. (Watch out — Red Ants bite.)

✦ **Shimmer:** The text flashes with a fuzzy effect that makes you wonder if
you had too much beer last night.

✦ **Sparkle Text:** Little dots of color flash on and off in and about the text
giving it a festive party look.

To animate your text, follow these steps:

1. **Highlight the text you want to animate.**

2. **Choose Format⇨Font.**

   The Font dialog box appears.

3. **Click the Text Effects tab.**

   The Animation controls appear, as shown in Figure 1-5.

4. **Select the type of animation you want from the Animations list box.**

   Word displays a preview of the animation effect in the Preview area.

5. **Click OK.**

6. **Say "Ooh" and "Aah" when you see the animation in action.**

To remove an animation effect (which you'll probably end up doing after you realize that the whole idea is kind of silly), repeat the preceding steps but select None in Step 4.

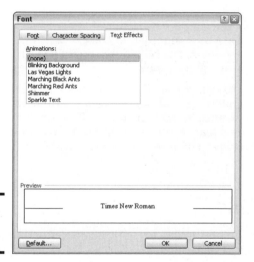

Figure 1-5:
Animating
your text.

Inserting Special Characters

You probably already know about the Insert⇨Symbol command. Did you know that several of the special symbols accessible from this command are assigned keyboard shortcuts? Table 1-2 lists the more useful of these symbols and their shortcuts.

Table 1-2		Keyboard Shortcuts for Special Symbols
Symbol	*Name*	*Keyboard Shortcut*
©	Copyright	Alt+Ctrl+C
®	Registered mark	Alt+Ctrl+R
™	Trademark	Alt+Ctrl+T
—	Em dash	Alt+Ctrl+— (minus sign on the numeric keypad)
–	En dash	Ctrl+— (minus sign on the numeric keypad)
. . .	Ellipsis	Alt+Ctrl+. (period)

The following things can aid you in your quest for special characters:

✦ If you can't remember the keyboard shortcuts for these symbols, choose Insert⇨Symbol and click the Special Characters tab in the dialog box that appears. A list of these characters appears, along with their keyboard shortcuts. The list also includes a few characters for which no keyboard shortcuts exist.

✦ You can add a keyboard shortcut to any special character by choosing Insert⇨Symbol, clicking the Symbols tab or the Special Characters tab in the Symbol dialog box that appears, and choosing the Shortcut Key button.

✦ An em dash is a dash the width of the letter M. An en dash is as wide as a letter N. If using a dash as a punctuation mark — like this — use an em dash instead of two hyphens. The old double-hyphen treatment is a carryover from the days of manual typewriters.

✦ The minus sign required for the em dash and en dash shortcuts is the minus sign on the numeric keypad, way off to the far-right side of the keyboard. (This key would probably be Rush Limbaugh's favorite key if he used a PC, but he's a Mac fanatic.) The shortcut won't work if you use the hyphen that's between the zero (0) and the equal sign (=) at the top of the keyboard.

Using the Format Painter

You can use the Format Painter to quickly copy character and paragraph formatting from one bit of text to another. The Format Painter works only if you already have some text formatted the way you like. Follow these steps to use the Format Painter:

1. **Highlight the text that has the format you want to copy.**

2. **Click the Format Painter button on the Standard toolbar.**

   It's the button that looks like a paintbrush.

3. **Point to the text you want to copy the format to, and then press and hold the mouse button and drag the pointer over the text.**

   Word automatically formats the new text to look just like the previously formatted text.

If you want to use the Format Painter to format two or more sections of text, highlight the text you want to use as your template, and then double-click the Format Painter button. The Format Painter then continuously formats text that you highlight until you either press a keyboard key, double-click the mouse again, or click the Format Painter button again.

If you really like keyboard shortcuts, you can copy a format by moving the insertion point to the text that has the format you want to copy and pressing Ctrl+Shift+C. Then, highlight the text you want to apply the format to and press Ctrl+Shift+V.

Formatting Paragraphs

The following sections show you how to apply various formats to a paragraph. Once again, you can apply these formats in more than one way. The easy way is to use keyboard shortcuts or toolbar buttons, but if you must, you can resort to the Format➪Paragraph, Format➪Tabs, or Format➪Borders and Shading commands.

Applying paragraph formats the easy way

To apply a paragraph format, follow this painless procedure:

1. **Click anywhere in the paragraph that you want to format.**

Where in the paragraph doesn't matter, as long as the cursor is some-where in the paragraph.

2. **Use one of the keyboard shortcuts or toolbar buttons listed in Table 1-3.**

The effect of your formatting is immediately obvious.

3. **There is no third step. You're done.**

Made you look!

Table 1-3	Paragraph Formatting the Easy Way	
Toolbar Button	*Keyboard Shortcut*	*What It Does*
▤	Ctrl+L	Left-aligns a paragraph
▤	Ctrl+R	Right-aligns a paragraph
▤	Ctrl+J	Justifies a paragraph
▤	Ctrl+E	Centers a paragraph

(continued)

Table 1-3 *(continued)*

Toolbar Button	Keyboard Shortcut	What It Does
![increase indent]	Ctrl+M	Increases left indent
![decrease indent]	Ctrl+Shift+M	Reduces left indent
	Ctrl+T	Creates hanging indent
	Ctrl+Shift+T	Reduces hanging indent
	Ctrl+1	Single-spaces paragraph
	Ctrl+2	Double-spaces paragraph
	Ctrl+5	Sets line space to 1.5
	Ctrl+0 (zero)	Removes space before or sets space before to 1 line
	Ctrl+Q	Removes paragraph formatting

Keep these notes in mind when formatting your paragraphs:

✦ As with character formats, you can heap paragraph formats atop one another. Just keep typing keyboard shortcuts or clicking toolbar buttons until you format the paragraph just right.

✦ To remove paragraph formatting, use the easy-to-remember Ctrl+Q keyboard shortcut (the Q stands for *quit using those diabolical paragraph formats*).

✦ Paragraph formats are stored in the paragraph marker at the end of the paragraph. Don't make the mistake of spending hours polishing a paragraph's appearance and then deleting the paragraph marker to merge the text into the following paragraph. If you do, you lose all the formatting you so carefully applied. (If that happens, quickly press Ctrl+Z to undo the deletion.)

Using the Format ⇨ Paragraph command

If you find yourself in the unenviable pickle of needing to use a formatting option that's not on the Formatting toolbar and you can't remember its keyboard shortcut, you can always conjure up the Format⇨Paragraph command and pick and choose your paragraph formats from a palette of delightful formatting treasures.

Here's the procedure for using the Format➪Paragraph command:

1. **Click anywhere in the paragraph that you want to format.**

Where in the paragraph doesn't matter, just so the cursor is somewhere in the paragraph.

2. **Choose Format➪Paragraph.**

Or press Alt+O and then P. The Paragraph dialog box appears, shown in Figure 1-6.

Figure 1-6:
The
Paragraph
dialog box.

3. **Play with the controls.**

You can set the paragraph alignment (Left, Right, Centered, or Justified) from the Alignment drop-down list. You can increase the Left or Right indentation, or you can choose a First Line or Hanging indent from the Special drop-down list box. You can also increase or decrease the amount of spacing Before and After the paragraph and set the Line Spacing.

As you play with the controls, keep an eye on the Preview box to see the effect of your changes.

4. **Click OK when you're done.**

Presto change-o! You're done.

You can set left and right indentation as well as first line and hanging indents by playing with the ruler. See the section "Setting tabs with the ruler" later in this chapter for details.

Measuring up

The way Word measures things, such as line spacing and indentations, is confusing if you don't understand the terminology. Here are the units of measure Word accepts:

in	Inches	You know what these are.
Cm	Centimeters	You should know by now, but in case you're not sure, 2.54 centimeters are in an inch.
Pt	Points	A term used by typographers to measure type. 72 points are in an inch and 12 points are in a pica.
pi	Pica	Another wacky term used by typographers. Roughly 6 picas are in an inch and 12 points are in a pica.
Li	Line	The same as a pica.
cb	Cubit, 17.5 inches	105 picas are in a cubit, and 1,260 points are in a cubit. (Just kidding. Word doesn't really accept cubits as a valid measurement unless the filename extension for the document you're working on is ARC.)

Here's some additional info on using paragraph formatting options:

✦ You can change the unit of measure used for setting indentation by choosing Tools⇨Options, clicking the General tab, and setting the Measurement Units field to the unit of measure you want to use. See the sidebar "Measuring up" for more information about units of measure.

✦ In the Line Spacing drop-down list, you can select several options for the paragraph's line spacing. The ones you use most are Single, 1.5 Lines, and Double. You can use Multiple to set some other line spacing, such as 3 lines. At Least lets you specify a minimum measurement for the line spacing, such as "At Least 14 Points." You can also use Exactly to set an exact measurement, but I recommend avoiding it. You can get into trouble if you use 12 point type in a paragraph, but set the line spacing to "Exactly 10 Points."

✦ Notice the Line and Page Breaks tab at the top of the Paragraph dialog box. Click it and you see options for controlling how paragraphs are positioned on the page. More information on these options is in the section "Line and page breaks," coming up in a jiffy.

✦ Oh, and the Paragraph dialog box has a Tabs button that zaps you over to the Tabs dialog box so that you can set tab stops. I cover tabs later, in the section "All about Tabs."

Line and page breaks

When you conjure up the Format⇨Paragraph command, you can click the Line and Page Breaks tab to awaken a different set of paragraph formatting options. Figure 1-7 shows the Line and Page Breaks tab of the Paragraph dialog box.

Figure 1-7: Setting the Line and Page Break options.

Here's what each of these options does:

+ **Widow/Orphan Control:** If a paragraph falls at the bottom of the page, Widow/Orphan Control prevents Word from splitting the paragraph to avoid stranding one line at the bottom of one page or the top of the next page. Instead, the entire paragraph is bumped to the next page. Widow/Orphan Control is on by default; I recommend leaving it on.

+ **Keep Lines Together:** Sometimes you have a paragraph that you don't want split up across pages. For example, suppose you want to quote a work of fine literature, such as a classic poem from Winnie-the-Pooh:

> Cottleston, Cottleston, Cottleston Pie,
> A fly can't bird, but a bird can fly.
> Ask me a riddle and I reply:
> *"Cottleston, Cottleston, Cottleston Pie."*

Obviously, you lose the stunning emotional impact of this powerful poem if you allowed Word to split it across two pages. Give it the Keep Lines Together option so that Word moves the whole thing to the next page if it doesn't fit in its entirety on the current page.

✦ **Keep with Next:** This option prevents Word from inserting a page break between a paragraph and the one that follows it. You use it mostly for headings, to prevent a heading from being stranded at the bottom of a page.

✦ **Page Break Before:** This option forces Word to place the paragraph at the top of the next page. Use it for chapter or section headings when you want each chapter or section to start on a new page.

✦ **Suppress Line Numbers:** If you use Word's line numbering feature, this option tells Word to skip the paragraph when numbering lines.

✦ **Don't Hyphenate:** If you use Word's hyphenation feature, this option tells Word to not hyphenate any words in the paragraph.

All about Tabs

You can set tab stops in one of two ways: by dropping them directly on the ruler or by ditzing around with the Format⇨Tabs command. Dropping tabs directly on the ruler is far and away the easier method of the two. Get involved with the Format⇨Tabs command only when you want to use *leaders* (little rows of dots that run across the page).

Setting tabs with the ruler

Here's the procedure for setting tabs with the ruler:

1. **If the ruler isn't visible, use View⇨Ruler to make it visible.**

2. **Type some text that you want to line up with tab stops.**

   Type several paragraphs if you want. Hit the Tab key once and only once between each column of information that you want lined up. Don't worry if everything doesn't line up at first. You can fix it later.

3. **Select the paragraph or paragraphs whose tabs you want to set.**

   If you're setting tabs for just one paragraph, click the mouse anywhere in the paragraph. If you're setting tabs for more than one paragraph, drag the mouse to select at least some text in each paragraph.

4. **Click the mouse on the ruler at each spot where you want a new tab stop.**

   Watch as the text you selected in Step 2 lines up under the tabs you create. Add one tab stop to the ruler for each column of information you want to align.

5. Adjust.

Nothing works quite right the first time. If you dropped a tab at 1½ inches and want to move it to 1¾ inches, just click and drag the tab marker with the mouse and slide it to the new location. When you release the mouse button, text in the currently selected paragraphs adjusts in the new tab position.

Here's more fascinating information about tabs:

✦ Default tab stops are placed every half an inch. However, each time you create a new tab stop, any default tab stops to the left of the new tab stops are deleted. In other words, default tab stops exist only to the right of tab stops you create.

✦ Word enables you to create seven types of tab stops: left, center, right, decimal, bar, first line indent, and hanging indent. To change the type of tab that's created when you click the ruler, click the Tab Alignment button at the far left edge of the ruler. Each time you click the button, the picture on the button changes to indicate the tab type, as shown in Table 1-4.

Book II
Chapter 1

Basic Text
Formatting

Table 1-4		Tab Types
Tab Alignment Button	*Tab Type*	*Explanation*
⌞	Left	Text left aligns at the tab stop. This is the default tab style.
⊥	Center	Text centers over the tab stop.
⌟	Right	Text right aligns at the tab stop.
⊥•	Decimal	Numbers align at the decimal point over the tab stop.
⏐	Bar	A vertical bar appears at the tab location.
▽	First Line Indent	Sets the indentation for the first line of the paragraph.
⊔	Hanging Indent	Creates a hanging indent.

Here are some miscellaneous thoughts to ponder concerning tab stops:

+ In spite of the recent political shifts in Washington, *left* tabs are still the most popular type of tab.

+ You can quickly summon the Tabs dialog box by double-clicking the lower half of the ruler. Watch where you double-click, though, because the first click adds a tab stop.

+ If you want to add a tab leader (a row of dots, dashes, or a solid line that precedes the tab, as is often found in a restaurant menu), first create the tab stop by dropping it on the ruler. Then conjure up Format➪Tabs, select the tab stop you want the leader added to, and select a leader type (dots, dashes, or solid line). Then click OK and check the results.

+ To remove a tab stop from the ruler, click the tab stop you want to remove and drag it straight down, off the ruler. When you release the mouse, the tab stop is deleted.

+ To quickly remove all tab stops, issue Format➪Tabs or double-click the bottom half of the ruler to summon the Tabs dialog box. Click the Clear All button to remove the tabs and then click OK to return to the document.

Using the Format➪Tabs command

If you have an unexplainable aversion to the ruler, you can set tab stops using the Format➪Tabs command instead. Just follow these steps:

1. **Choose Format➪Tabs.**

The Tabs dialog box appears, as shown in Figure 1-8.

2. **Type the position you want the new tab stop to appear in the Tab Stop Position field.**

3. **Select the Alignment option you want for the new tab stop (Left, Center, Right, Decimal, or Bar).**

For more information about bar tabs, see the upcoming section "Running a bar tab."

4. **Select the tab leader type for the tab stop. If you don't want leaders, select 1 None.**

I explain leaders later, in the section "Using tab leaders."

5. **Click Set.**

6. **Repeat Steps 2 through 5 for any other tab stops you want to create.**

7. **Click OK to dismiss the Tabs dialog box.**

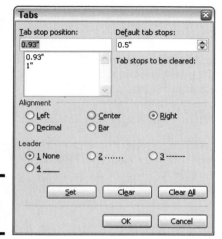

Figure 1-8:
The Tabs
dialog box.

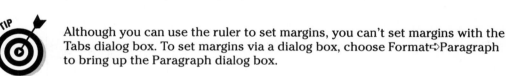

Although you can use the ruler to set margins, you can't set margins with the Tabs dialog box. To set margins via a dialog box, choose Format⇨Paragraph to bring up the Paragraph dialog box.

Removing all tabs

To remove all tab stops, highlight the paragraphs you want to remove the tab stops from. Then choose Format⇨Tabs or double-click the bottom half of the ruler to summon the Tabs dialog box. Then, click the Clear All button to remove the tabs and click OK to return to the document.

Using tab leaders

Price lists, tables of contents, or other lists commonly use tab leaders to help draw the eye from one item to its counterpart across the page. You can also use tab leaders to create fill-in-the-blanks forms. Just look at the table of contents for this book for an excellent example of tab leaders.

Word lets you create three types of leaders: dots, dashes, and solid line. Dots and dashes are the leader type you use for lists; solid lines are what you use for forms.

If you want the tab leader to end at a certain location, create a left-aligned tab at that location using the leader type of your choice. This technique is commonly used to create fill-in-the-blank forms. For example, the following line uses two left-aligned tab stops with solid-line leaders, one at 2.5", the other at 5":

Name: _____Rank: _____

Notice that no space is whatsoever between the end of the first solid-line leader and the word "Rank." To insert a small amount of space, you can type a few spaces, or you can create another tab, say at 2.625":

Name: _____ Rank: _____

If you are going to use dot or dash leaders to connect items in a list, you usually use right- or decimal-aligned tabs. For example, I formatted the following list with a single right-aligned dot-leader tab stop at 4.5":

Roland RS-50 ....*$799.99*

Novation KS-4..*$999.99*

Roland RD-700 ....*$1,799.99*

Yamaha S90..*Call!*

Running a bar tab

You must be 21 to use this feature in most states.

One of the more unusual things you can do with tabs is create vertical bars between columns of information, like this:

Hawkeye	James T. Kirk	Gilligan
B.J.	Mr. Spock	The Skipper
Charles	Dr. McCoy	The Professor
Hot Lips	Mr. Chekov	Mary Ann
Radar	Mr. Sulu	Ginger
Col. Potter	Lt. Uhura	Mr. Howell
Father Mulcahy	Nurse Chapel	Mrs. Howell

Here, the vertical bars between the columns are actually special deviant versions of tab stops. Bar tabs aren't like regular tab stops in that the Tab key doesn't stop at them. As a result, you use only one tab character between each column. To set bar tabs, first create a left tab for each column. Then, click the tab type button at the left of the ruler until the bar tab button appears. Then, add a bar tab a little to the left of each of the left tabs you created.

If the bar tab extends above or below the line, the paragraph format calls for extra space above or below the paragraph. Use Format⇨Paragraph to remove the Above or Below space. (If you need the extra space, add it to the adjoining paragraphs instead.)

Bar tabs is a crude way of making tables. A far better way to create tables with ruled line is to use Word's Table feature, which I cover in Chapter 6 of this minibook.

AutoFormat (Or, Make It Stop!)

Word's AutoFormat watches everything you type and steps in when it thinks you are trying to format something but you aren't doing it right. Here are just some of the changes AutoFormat may make to your document as you type along:

+ If you type a quotation mark, AutoFormat changes it to a left (") or right (") quotation mark depending on whether you use it before or after a word.

+ If you type (c) — that is, the letter "c" in parentheses — AutoFormat converts it to a copyright symbol: ©.

+ If you type an asterisk followed by a tab and some text, AutoFormat removes the asterisk and converts the paragraph to a bullet list.

+ If you type a number followed by a period and a space, AutoFormat removes the number and converts the paragraph to a numbered list.

The list goes on and on. Some of the changes are helpful, but some can be annoying. Fortunately, you can selectively disable most of the AutoFormat feature by following these steps:

1. **Choose Tools⇨AutoCorrect Options.**

The AutoCorrect dialog box appears.

2. **Click the AutoFormat As You Type tab.**

The AutoFormat As You Type options appear, as shown in Figure 1-9.

3. **Uncheck the AutoFormat options that annoy you.**

4. **Click OK.**

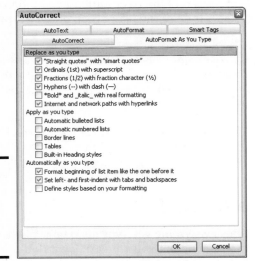

Figure 1-9:
Changing
the Auto-
Format As
You Type
options.

The Ten Commandments of Formatting

When Bill Gates came down from the mountain, he originally had 15 formatting commandments. But he dropped one of the three tablets, shattering it to pieces, so now we have but ten.

1. Thou shalt remember thy keyboard shortcuts to speed thy way

Don't bother memorizing the keyboard shortcuts for formats you rarely or never use. But do memorize the shortcuts for the formats you use frequently. Pressing Ctrl+B is much faster than clicking the mouse button or contending with menus and dialog boxes. Make a short list of the shortcuts you want to memorize and tape it to your computer or somewhere within eyesight.

II. Thou shalt not press Enter at the end of each line

You defeat the whole purpose of word processing if you press the Enter key at the end of each line you type. Let Word figure out where to break each line.

III. Thou shalt not create empty paragraphs

Don't press the Enter key twice to leave extra space between paragraphs. Instead, format the paragraph with 1½ or 2 blank lines before the first line.

IV. Thou shalt not use extraneous spaces

On a typewriter, you're supposed to hit the spacebar twice between sentences. With proportional fonts, use only one space following the period at the end of a sentence. Also, don't use spaces to align text in columns. Use tabs instead.

V. Thou shalt not use extraneous tabs

Don't hit the Tab key two or three times to move text across the page. Instead, press the Tab key once and then set a tab stop where you want to align the text.

VI. Thou shalt not underline when italics will do

Underlining is for typewriters. Italics is for computers. You paid lots of hard-earned money for your computer, so you may as well get your money's worth.

VII. Thou shalt not use more than three fonts on a page

Avoid the ransom note look at all costs. Use one font for your text, a second font for headings, and maybe a third font for emphasis. But no more than three fonts altogether, please.

VIII. Thou shalt not use Exact Line Spacing

The Exact Line Spacing option (found with Format⇨Paragraph) is a source of much trouble. Use Single, 1.5 lines, or Double instead.

IX. Thou shalt use the AutoCorrect feature

The AutoCorrect feature can correct typos on the fly, as well as help with simple formatting chores such as making sure sentences start with capital letters and using "curly quotes" properly.

To activate this feature, use Tools⇨AutoCorrect. When the AutoCorrect dialog box appears, check the things you want Word to automatically correct; then click OK.

X. Thou shalt use styles

The best way to deal with all this formatting nonsense is to put all the formatting you ever need into styles. Then you don't have to worry about line spacing, hanging indents, fonts and font sizes, or anything else. Just apply the correct style and everything is taken care of. (I discuss styles in detail in Chapter 3 of this minibook. Aren't you lucky?)

Chapter 2: The Border Patrol and Other Shady Characters

In This Chapter

- ✔ Drawing boxes around your paragraphs
- ✔ Wrapping a border around the whole page
- ✔ Shading the background behind your text

This short little chapter deals primarily with the features available from one formatting command: Format⇨Borders and Shading. With this command, you can draw borders around individual paragraphs or groups of paragraphs. Or, you can put a border around the entire page. And, you can add shading to your text.

You can also use borders and shading in conjunction with tables. For more information, refer to Chapter 6 of this minibook.

Creating Borders in Your Text

The following sections show you how to draw simple or elaborate borders around individual words, groups of words, single paragraphs, or groups of paragraphs.

Drawing a box around your text

If all you want to do is draw a simple box around some text, just follow these simple steps:

1. **Select the text you want to draw a border around.**

   You can select individual characters, a single word or group of words, or a single paragraph or even a group of paragraphs.

   If you don't select text at all, Word draws a border around the entire paragraph the cursor happens to be sitting in. As a result, if you want to draw a box around an entire paragraph, just click the mouse anywhere in the paragraph and proceed to the next step.

2. **Choose Format⇨Borders and Shading.**

   The Borders and Shading dialog box appears, as shown in Figure 2-1.

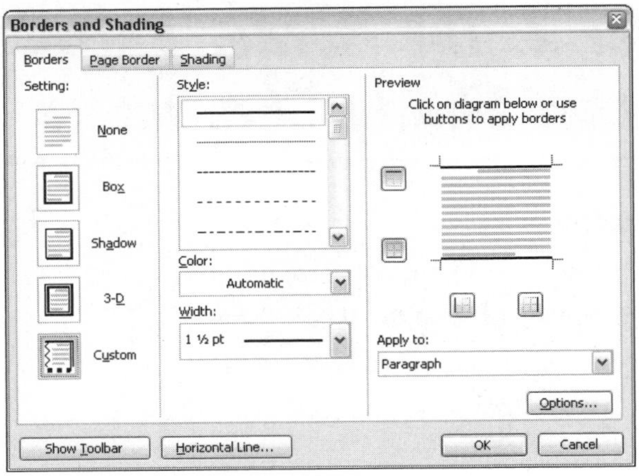

Figure 2-1:
The Borders
and Shading
dialog box
(Borders
tab).

3. **Click Box in the list of border types that appears at the left of the Borders and Shading dialog box.**

   The Borders and Shading dialog box has plenty of options that let you create fancier borders. For now, just click Box.

4. **Click OK.**

   The Borders and Shading dialog box vanishes, and your text now has a box around it.

The following paragraphs describe some of the additional tricks you can perform with the Borders and Shading dialog box:

✦ In addition to the Box border style, the Borders and Shading dialog box offers two other preset border styles: Shadow and 3-D. You can experiment with these settings to see what effect they have.

✦ You can also build a custom border one line at a time by clicking the buttons around the various edges of the paragraphs represented in the Preview area to indicate which edges you want a border to appear. These buttons control whether a border appears above, below, to the left, or to the right of the selection. If you select more than one paragraph, you also see a button that lets you add or remove lines between the paragraphs.

✦ The Style drop-down list lets you choose a fancy style for each line of the border. Various styles, such as double lines and dashed lines, are available. Note that you can change line styles as you apply individual borders, so that a paragraph can have a thin border at the top and a thick border at the bottom.

✦ The Color drop-down list lets you set the color for your border. You can select a standard color that appears in the list, or you can click More Line Colors at the bottom of the list of colors to bring up a dialog box that lets you choose any color you want.

✦ The Width drop-down lets you choose a width for each segment of the border.

By default, the borders are placed one point from the text they surround. If that placement is too right for you, you can adjust it by clicking the Options button in the Borders and Shading dialog box. The Borders and Shading Options dialog box comes up, shown in Figure 2-2.

Figure 2-2:
The Borders and Shading Options dialog box.

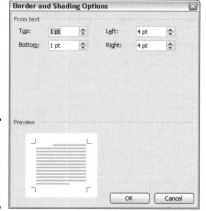

Putting borders around adjacent paragraphs

If you select more than one adjacent paragraph of text and format them using one of the preset border styles, all the paragraphs are contained within a single box, as shown in Figure 2-3.

If you want to box each paragraph separately, you can place an unboxed paragraph mark between each boxed paragraph, as shown in Figure 2-4. These "spacer" paragraphs need not contain any text, and you may want to vary their Before or After spacing so that the boxed paragraphs are spaced the way you want.

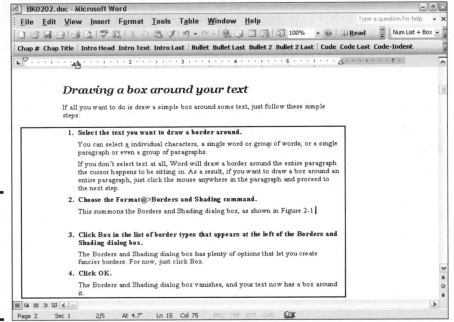

Figure 2-3:
Borders on adjacent paragraphs are merged to create a single border.

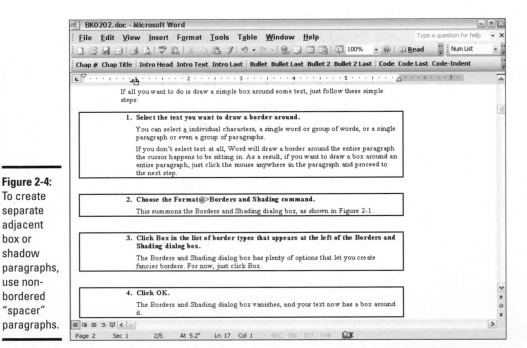

Figure 2-4:
To create separate adjacent box or shadow paragraphs, use non-bordered "spacer" paragraphs.

Using the Border button

The Formatting toolbar has a handy Border button you can use to apply basic borders with a single keystroke. You can click the button to apply the current border type to whatever text you select, or you can click the arrow next to the button to reveal a palette of border types, as shown in Figure 2-5.

Figure 2-5:
Using the
Border
button.

Keep these things in mind when playing around with borders:

✦ The Border button applies borders to one or more edges of the selected text or paragraph. The Borders and Shading dialog box controls the style, color, and width of those borders. You have to use Format➪Borders and Shading if you want to change those settings.

✦ Click the Border button once to apply a border. To remove a border, click the Border button again.

Shading Your Text

The Shading tab of the Borders and Shading dialog box lets you apply shading to a paragraph or a selection of text. Shading is a great way to draw attention to key parts of your document. For example, Figure 2-6 shows a document with a block of shaded text.

To apply shading to your text, follow these steps:

1. **Select the text you want to shade.**

You can select individual characters, a single word or group of words, or a single paragraph or even a group of paragraphs.

2. **Choose Format➪Borders and Shading.**

The Borders and Shading dialog box appears.

3. **Click the Shading tab.**

The Shading options appear, as shown in Figure 2-7.

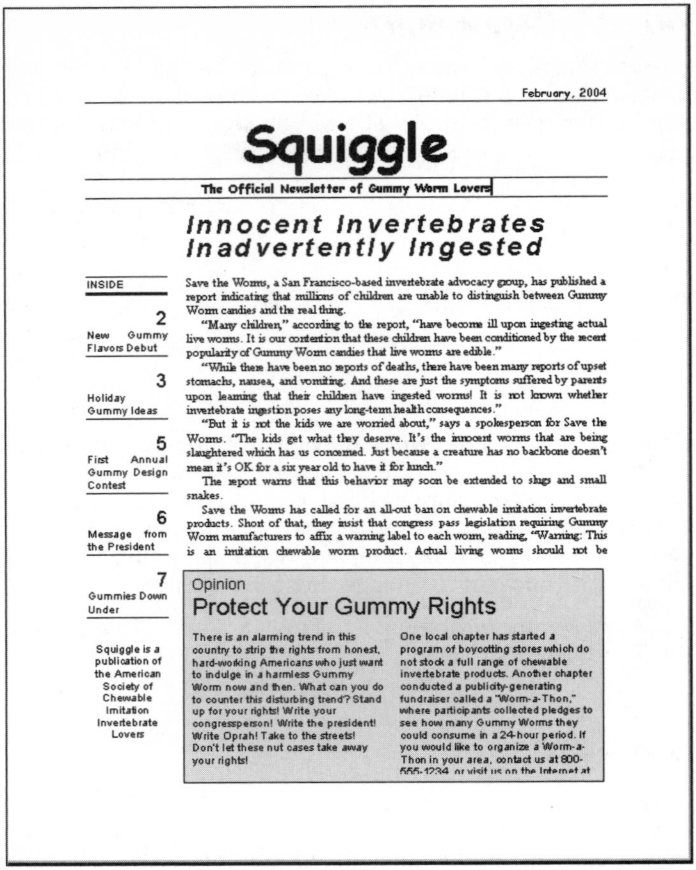

February, 2004

Squiggle

The Official Newsletter of Gummy Worm Lovers

Innocent Invertebrates Inadvertently Ingested

INSIDE

2 New Gummy Flavors Debut

3 Holiday Gummy Ideas

5 First Annual Gummy Design Contest

6 Message from the President

7 Gummies Down Under

Squiggle is a publication of the American Society of Chewable Imitation Invertebrate Lovers

Save the Worms, a San Francisco-based invertebrate advocacy group, has published a report indicating that millions of children are unable to distinguish between Gummy Worm candies and the real thing.

"Many children," according to the report, "have become ill upon ingesting actual live worms. It is our contention that these children have been conditioned by the recent popularity of Gummy Worm candies that live worms are edible."

"While there have been no reports of deaths, there have been many reports of upset stomachs, nausea, and vomiting. And these are just the symptoms suffered by parents upon learning that their children have ingested worms! It is not known whether invertebrate ingestion poses any long-term health consequences."

"But it is not the kids we are worried about," says a spokesperson for Save the Worms. "The kids get what they deserve. It's the innocent worms that are being slaughtered which has us concerned. Just because a creature has no backbone doesn't mean it's OK for a six year old to have it for lunch."

The report warns that this behavior may soon be extended to slugs and small snakes.

Save the Worms has called for an all-out ban on chewable imitation invertebrate products. Short of that, they insist that congress pass legislation requiring Gummy Worm manufacturers to affix a warning label to each worm, reading, "Warning: This is an imitation chewable worm product. Actual living worms should not be

Opinion

Protect Your Gummy Rights

There is an alarming trend in this country to strip the rights from honest, hard-working Americans who just want to indulge in a harmless Gummy Worm now and then. What can you do to counter this disturbing trend? Stand up for your rights! Write your congressperson! Write the president! Write Oprah! Take to the streets! Don't let these nut cases take away your rights!

One local chapter has started a program of boycotting stores which do not stock a full range of chewable invertebrate products. Another chapter conducted a publicity-generating fundraiser called a "Worm-a-Thon," where participants collected pledges to see how many Gummy Worms they could consume in a 24-hour period. If you would like to organize a Worm-a-Thon in your area, contact us at 800-555-1234 or visit us on the Internet at

Figure 2-6: Shading a region of text can make it stand out from the rest of the document.

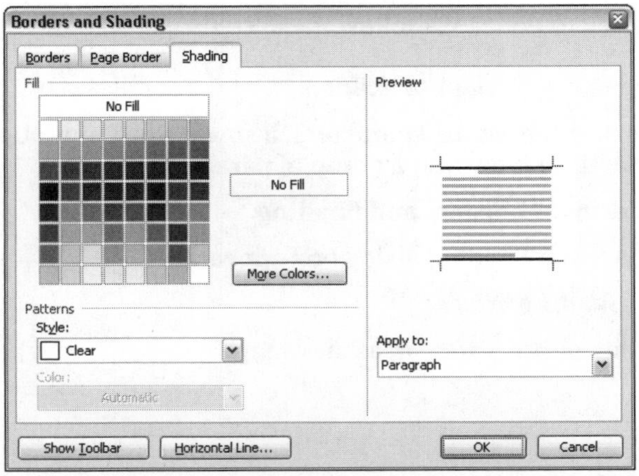

Figure 2-7: The Borders and Shading dialog box (Shading tab).

4. **Select the color you want to shade the text with.**

   The Borders and Shading dialog box lists a bunch of colors. However, if you're picky and don't find the color you like, you can click the More Colors button to bring up a dialog box that lists even more colors.

   Notice that the first three rows of colors in the Borders and Shading dialog box list various shades of gray. The remaining rows list basic colors.

5. **Click OK.**

   The Borders and Shading dialog box vanishes, and your text now has a box around it.

Here are a few points to keep in mind when shading your text:

✦ Make sure that you can still read the shaded text. With darker shades, you may need to change the font color to keep the text readable. For more information about changing font colors, see Chapter 1 of this minibook.

✦ A common text effect is to create white text on a black background. To do that, first use Format⇨Borders and Shading to set the background to black. Then, use Format⇨Font to set the font color to white.

✦ Don't forget that you have to have a color printer to print colors other than black or gray.

Bordering an Entire Page

Another feature of the Borders and Shading dialog box is that it lets you draw a border around an entire page. Perfect for such things as Perfect Attendance Certificates or other hokey documents.

Here's the procedure:

1. **Choose Format⇨Borders and Shading.**

   The familiar Borders and Shading dialog box appears.

2. **Click the Page Border tab.**

   The Page Border controls appear, as shown in Figure 2-8.

3. **Apply the border you want.**

   The technique for applying a border to the page is the same as for applying borders to selected text or paragraphs.

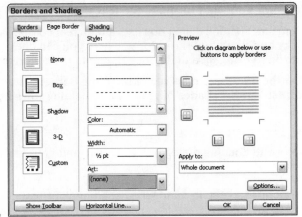

Figure 2-8:
The Borders and Shading dialog box (Page Borders tab).

If you want to create a really hokey border, use the Art drop-down list to choose a picture to use for the border. Word then creates the border from the picture you choose instead of using a boring old line. You can choose from all kinds of pictures, including hearts, butterflies, and pumpkins.

4. **Click OK.**

   The border is applied to the page.

Adding a Horizontal Line

Yet another feature of the Borders and Shading dialog box is its ability to insert artistic horizontal lines into your document. For example, Figure 2-9 shows some examples of the lines you can create using this feature. Pretty cool, huh?

To insert a horizontal line, follow these steps:

1. **Move the insertion point to the spot where you want to insert the horizontal line.**

2. **Choose Format⇨Borders and Shading.**

   The Borders and Shading dialog box appears.

3. **Click the Horizontal Line button.**

   The Horizontal Line dialog box appears, as shown in Figure 2-10.

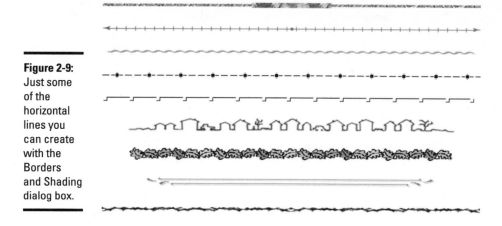

Figure 2-9:
Just some of the horizontal lines you can create with the Borders and Shading dialog box.

Figure 2-10:
The Horizontal Line dialog box.

4. **Choose the type of line you want to insert.**

   You can choose from several dozen styles.

5. **Click OK.**

   Both the Horizontal Line and the Borders and Shading dialog boxes are dismissed and the line you selected is inserted into the document.

Chapter 3: Working with Styles

In This Chapter

- ✔ Understanding styles
- ✔ Creating a new style
- ✔ Applying a style
- ✔ Changing a style
- ✔ Assigning a shortcut key to a style
- ✔ Basing one style on another
- ✔ Setting the style for the next paragraph automatically
- ✔ Using character styles
- ✔ Storing styles in a template
- ✔ Some tips for using styles

Styles are what Tiggers like best. They are the secret to freeing yourself from the tyranny of Word's Format menu. With styles, you toil at a paragraph's formatting until you get the paragraph just right; then you provide a name by which Word remembers all of the formatting you applied to the paragraph. From then on, you can apply the same formatting to other paragraphs simply by calling up the style. No more hunting and pecking your way through the Format menu commands, trying to recall how you got the paragraph to look so good.

If you're not yet using styles, I suggest you find out how to use them right away. Although the concept of styles may be confusing at first, they aren't really that hard to learn. An hour or so invested in becoming familiar with how styles work pays off in many saved hours of unnecessary formatting time later.

Understanding Styles

The basic idea behind styles is to store all the formatting information for a paragraph under a single name. That way, you can quickly apply the saved formats to other paragraphs simply by referring to the style's name. For example, suppose you want to format headings using 16-point Arial Bold, with 18 points of space above the heading and 6 points below, and with a line drawn beneath the paragraph. You have to bounce the mouse all over the place to format this heading manually. But if you store the formats in a style, you can apply all the formats with a single mouse click or a keyboard shortcut.

Styles contain all the formatting information specified with the following Word commands:

✦ **Format⇨Font:** Includes the font name, style (regular, bold, italic, or bold italic), and special character attributes such as small caps or superscripts, the font color, and character spacing and kerning.

✦ **Format⇨Paragraph:** Includes left and right indentation, first line indentation and hanging indents, line spacing, before and after spacing, and text flow (widow/orphan control, keep with next, and so on).

✦ **Format⇨Bullets and Numbering:** Enables you to set up numbered or bulleted lists. (See Chapter 7 of this minibook for more information about bullets and numbers.)

✦ **Format⇨Borders and Shading:** Includes borders and line styles as well as fill shades.

✦ **Format⇨Tabs:** Includes tab stop positions, tab types, leader tabs, and bar tabs.

✦ **Tools⇨Language:** Enables you to use an alternate dictionary for spelling and hyphenation or to tell Word to skip a paragraph specified with this style when the document is spell checked.

With all these formats stored together under one name, you can imagine how much time styles can save you.

Styles are an integral part of the way Word works. Even if you think you don't use styles, you do: Word documents start off with several predefined styles, including the ubiquitous Normal style. The Normal style governs the default appearance of paragraphs in your document.

Here are some other benefits of using styles:

✦ Suppose you don't know how to drop a line three points beneath the paragraph, and you don't want to learn how. No problemo. Just bribe your friendly Word guru into creating the style for you. After the style is created, you don't have to know how to use the formatting instructions contained in the style. All you have to know is how to apply the style, and that's as easy as clicking the mouse.

✦ The real beauty of styles comes when you decide that all the headings in your 200 page report are too small. Without styles, you have to adjust the size of each heading separately. With styles, you simply change the style and — voilà! — all the paragraphs assigned to that style automatically adjust.

✦ Styles are stored along with your text in the document file. Thus, each document can have its own collection of styles, and styles with the same name can have different formatting characteristics in different documents. For example, a style named Bullet List may have ordinary round bullets in one document but check marks or pointy index fingers in another.

✦ When you create a new document, the new document inherits its styles from the template you base the document on. For more information about templates, refer to Book I, Chapter 3.

✦ Another benefit of using styles is that some Word features, most notably Table of Contents and Outline view, work best when you use styles for your headings and body text. Don't even attempt to use these features if you don't use styles.

For more information about Tables of Contents, see Book VI, Chapter 6. To find out more about Outline view, see Book VI, Chapter 2.

Using the Style Drop-Down List

Sitting near the left edge of the Formatting toolbar is a helpful drop-down list called Styles. This drop-down list is the easiest way to work with styles.

Applying a style

To apply a style to a paragraph, follow these steps:

1. **Click anywhere in the paragraph you want to format.**

You don't have to select the entire paragraph; just move the insertion point anywhere in it.

2. **Choose the style you want from the Style list box.**

Click the down arrow next to the Style list box to reveal a list of styles, as shown in Figure 3-1. Then, scroll through the list of styles until you find the one you want and click it. The formatting contained in the style applies to the paragraph.

You can use the preceding steps to change the style assigned to a paragraph. When you do that, the formatting from the new style replaces all the formatting from the original style.

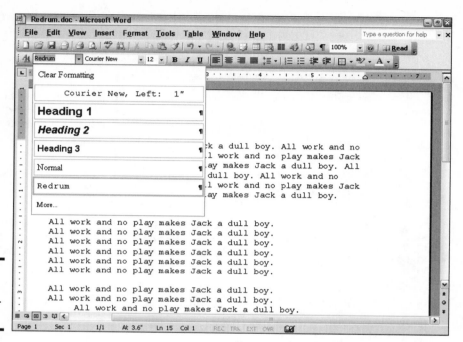

Figure 3-1:
Using the
Styles drop-
down list.

To apply a style to two or more adjacent paragraphs, simply select a range of text that includes all the paragraphs you want formatted. Then choose the style. When you press the Enter key to create a new paragraph, the new paragraph normally assumes the same style as the preceding paragraph. See the section "Setting the style of the next paragraph" later in this chapter for an important — and useful — exception.

Every paragraph in a document is assigned to a style. The default style for the first paragraph in a new document is called Normal.

You can tell which style is assigned to a paragraph by clicking anywhere in the paragraph and looking at the Style list box. It shows the name of the style assigned to the paragraph.

Here are some helpful hints to using styles effectively:

✦ The name of each style in the style list is formatted according to the style. This name gives you a hint of how your text will look before you apply the style.

✦ If a style that you are looking for doesn't appear in the style list, click More Styles at the bottom of the list.

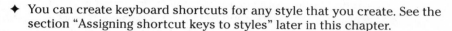

- ✦ To quickly return a paragraph to Normal style, press Ctrl+Shift+N.

- ✦ To assign the built-in Heading 1, Heading 2, or Heading 3 styles, press Ctrl+Alt+1, Ctrl+Alt+2, or Ctrl+Alt+3.

- ✦ You can create keyboard shortcuts for any style that you create. See the section "Assigning shortcut keys to styles" later in this chapter.

Creating a new style the easy way

To create a new style, follow these steps:

1. **Tweak a paragraph until it is formatted just the way you want it.**

Select the entire paragraph and set the font. Then use Format⇨Paragraph to set the line spacing, before and after spacing, and indentation for the paragraph. If you use tabs for the paragraph, set them using the ruler or with Format⇨Tabs. Add any other formatting you need, such as bullets, numbering, shading, borders, and so on.

2. **Click the Style list box on the Formatting toolbar.**

Don't click the arrow that's at the right side of the Style list box; that drops down the list to show all of the available styles. Instead, click in the text portion of the list box.

3. **Type a name for the style.**

Be descriptive. You can use more than one word, but avoid typing a name so long it doesn't fit in the Style list box.

4. **Press Enter.**

The style is added to Word's list of styles for the document so that you can reuse it.

Keep these points in mind when creating styles:

- ✦ When thinking up a name, try to come up with a name that describes the function of the paragraph in the document (for example, *Salutation* or *Vogon Poetry*) or that describes the type of formatting the style contains (like *Dbl Indent* or *Bullet List*).

- ✦ You can access the style you create only in the current document. To make the style accessible in other documents, you need to put it in a template. I cover templates in Book I, Chapter 3.

- ✦ If you really like styles, you'll want to use the Styles and Formatting task pane, which I describe later in this chapter in the brilliantly and aptly named section, "Using the Styles and Formatting Task Pane."

**Book II
Chapter 3**

Working with Styles

Overriding Style Formatting

Ordinarily, all the formatting you need for a paragraph comes from the paragraph's style. However, on some occasions, you may want to add additional formatting to a paragraph or change some aspect of a paragraph's formatting. The most common example of this instance is applying character formats, such as bold or italics, to individual characters or words within the paragraph. You can also apply paragraph formats to a paragraph formatted with a style. Any formats you apply simply augment or replace formats specified in the style.

Here are some guidelines:

✦ Formats that you apply to a paragraph directly rather than via a style are called, naturally enough, *direct formats*.

✦ Any direct paragraph formatting you apply is lost if you later decide to apply a different style to the paragraph. For example, if you apply the Normal style to a paragraph and then add 12 points of space above the paragraph, you lose the extra 12 points of space above if you apply a different style to the paragraph.

✦ Character formats are a little different. In most cases, Word preserves character formatting you applied directly even when you change the paragraph's style. For example, if you create a paragraph formatted with the Normal style, italicize a few words in the paragraph, and then apply another style to the paragraph, the italic words remain italicized.

✦ Sometimes, however, Word negates direct character formatting you applied, such as when you select a block of text in the paragraph and change the style. Word examines the text you selected, and if more than half the text has direct formatting applied, all the direct formatting in the paragraph is removed. This strange rule makes no sense to me, so I just ignore it. (This strategy works for many of life's little problems, doesn't it?)

Using the Styles and Formatting Task Pane

Although the Styles drop-down list on the Formatting toolbar lets you quickly assign styles and create new ones based on existing formatting, Word's more powerful style features are locked away in the Styles and Formatting task pane. You can summon it in one of the following ways:

✦ Click the AA button located on the Formatting toolbar, to the left of the Styles drop-down list.

+ Choose Format⊅Styles and Formatting.

+ Choose View⊅Task Pane, and then choose Styles and Formatting from the menu that appears at the top of the task pane.

Whichever method you choose, the Styles and Formatting task pane lists your styles as shown in Figure 3-2.

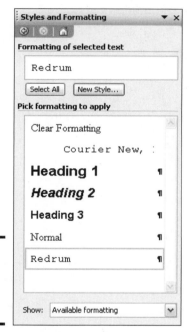

Figure 3-2:
The Styles and Formatting task pane.

When you point your mouse at a style in the task pane, two interesting things happen to the style:

+ The style is selected and a drop-down arrow appears. You can click this arrow to bring up a menu of commands for working with the style.

+ If you leave the mouse still for a moment, a box that describes the formatting applied by the style appears.

To apply a style using the task pane, select the text you want to apply the style to, and then click the style in the task pane.

Creating a new style the hard way

To create a new style using the task pane, follow these steps:

1. Choose Format⇨Styles and Formatting.

The Styles and Formatting task pane comes up; refer to Figure 3-2.

2. Click the New Style button.

The New Style dialog box appears, as shown in Figure 3-3.

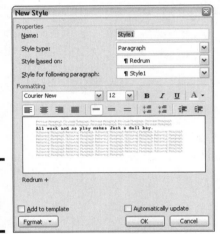

Figure 3-3:
The New Style dialog box.

3. Type a new name for the style in the Name text box.

The default value is something like Style1, which isn't very descriptive.

4. Set the formatting for the style.

You can use the controls that appear on the New Style dialog box to set common formats such as the text font and size, the paragraph alignment, paragraph spacing, and indentation.

For more control over style formatting, click the Format button to bring up a menu that reveals the following commands:

Font

Paragraph

Tabs

Border

Language

Frame

Numbering

Shortcut key

You can use these commands to bring up dialog boxes that let you apply advanced formatting. For example, if you click the Format button and choose Font, Word's standard Font dialog box appears. You can then apply any font formatting you want.

5. **Click OK.**

The style is created.

Modifying an existing style

The magic of styles is that when you make a change to a style, all paragraphs that use the style automatically update to reflect the style's new formatting. Here's the procedure for modifying a style:

1. **Choose Format⇨Styles and Formatting.**

The Styles and Formatting task pane comes up (refer to Figure 3-2).

2. **Point the mouse at the style you want to modify.**

Don't click the style; just point the mouse at it.

3. **Click the down-arrow that appears next to the style, and then choose Modify from the menu that appears.**

The Modify Style dialog box appears. It looks remarkably like the New Style dialog box (refer to Figure 3-3).

4. **Change the style.**

Change is good. You can change any feature of the style you want.

5. **Click OK.**

You're done! Any paragraphs the style is applied to updates to reflect the changed style.

Deleting a style

Styles can be very useful, so useful in fact that you may soon start creating them at the drop of a hat. Pretty soon, your documents are filled with styles you no longer use. When that happens, prune your style garden back, deleting styles you no longer use.

Fortunately, deleting styles is easy. Just follow these simple steps:

1. Conjure up Format⇨Styles and Formatting.

The familiar Styles and Formatting task pane appears.

2. Point the mouse at the style you want to delete.

Don't click the style; just point the mouse at it.

3. Click the down-arrow that appears next to the style, and then choose Delete from the menu that appears.

A dialog box appears asking if you've lost your mind, or do you really want to kill off that precious style you labored over so hard.

4. If you're from Caleefornia, say "Hasta la vista, Baby."

5. Click Yes.

When you delete a style, any paragraphs formatted with the style return to Normal style.

Do not attempt to delete the Normal style or any of the Heading styles. If you do, Jay Leno will make jokes about you for two weeks in his opening monolog. (As it turns out, Word won't let you delete these essential styles anyway. The Delete option is simply not available for these styles.)

Styles go in and out of fashion all the time, so don't feel bad about deleting them.

Neat Things to Do with Styles

You can do much more with styles than creating and applying them. The sections that follow chronicle some of the more interesting things you can do with styles.

Assigning shortcut keys to styles

Word enables you to assign keyboard shortcuts to your favorite styles. Then you can apply those styles by simply pressing the keyboard shortcut. You can assign keyboard shortcuts in two ways. Because I'm in a talkative mood, I show you both.

One way is to use the Styles and Formatting task pane. Follow these steps:

1. Choose Format⇨Styles and Formatting.

The Styles and Formatting task pane appears (refer to Figure 3-2).

2. **Point the mouse at the style you want to modify.**

   Don't click the style; just point the mouse at it.

3. **Click the down-arrow that appears next to the style, and then choose Modify from the menu that appears.**

   The Modify Style dialog box appears. It looks remarkably like the New Style dialog box (refer to Figure 3-3).

4. **Click the Modify button, and then choose Shortcut Key.**

   The Customize Keyboard dialog box appears, ready for you to assign a keyboard shortcut for the style. (See Figure 3-4.)

Figure 3-4: Assigning a keyboard shortcut to a style.

5. **Type the keyboard shortcut you want to assign to the style in the Press New Shortcut Key text box.**

   For example, Ctrl+Shift+R.

6. **Click Assign to assign the keyboard shortcut.**

7. **Click Close; then click OK and then Close again to get all the way out of there.**

You can assign a keyboard shortcut without bothering with the Styles and Formatting task pane. It involves an offbeat keyboard shortcut that turns the mouse pointer into a weird-looking pretzel. Try this method sometime when you really want to impress your friends:

1. **Press Ctrl+Alt+numeric plus.**

   That's the plus sign key on the numeric keypad, way over at the far right side of the keyboard.

2. **Check out the mouse pointer that looks like a pretzel.**

   Avoid the temptation to douse it with mustard.

3. **Choose the style from the Style list box on the Formatting toolbar.**

   Click the down arrow next to the Style list box; then click the style you want to assign a shortcut to. Word displays the Customize Keyboard dialog box, ready for you to type a shortcut. (Refer to Figure 3-4.)

4. **Type the keyboard shortcut that you want to use in the Press New Shortcut Key text box.**

   Like Ctrl+Alt+R.

5. **Click Assign to assign the shortcut to the style.**

6. **Click Close.**

   You're done.

Keep these tidbits in mind when using keyboard shortcuts for styles:

✦ When you type a keyboard shortcut in the Customize Keyboard dialog box, Word displays the current command assigned to the keyboard shortcut you press. Take note of this assignment to make sure that you aren't stepping on some other useful function's toes. However, if the keyboard shortcut is preassigned to a Word function you hardly ever use, don't hesitate to use the shortcut for your style.

✦ To remove a keyboard assignment you previously assigned, select it in the Current Keys list in the Customize Keyboard dialog box; then click the Remove button.

✦ The predefined heading styles already have keyboard shortcuts associated with them:

Ctrl+Alt+1	Heading 1
Ctrl+Alt+2	Heading 2
Ctrl+Alt+3	Heading 3

✦ You can create keyboard shortcuts using virtually any combination of keys on the keyboard. The shortcuts can utilize the Shift, Ctrl, and Alt keys, either alone or in combination. For example, you could assign Ctrl+K, Alt+K, Ctrl+Shift+K, Ctrl+Alt+K, or even Ctrl+Alt+Shift+K.

✦ You also can create complex keyboard shortcuts, such as Ctrl+Shift+I, 1. To activate this shortcut, you must press Ctrl+Shift+I; then release those keys and press the 1 key.

Basing one style on another

Suppose you create 20 different styles for various types of paragraphs in a complicated document, only to discover that your boss wants the entire document to use Palatino rather than Times New Roman as the base font. Do you have to change all 20 styles to reflect the new font? Not if you set up your styles using *base styles*.

A base style is a style that provides formatting information for other styles. For example, suppose you have a style named Bullet List, and you want to create a similar style named Bullet List Last that you use for the last paragraph of a series of bulleted paragraphs. The only difference between Bullet List and Bullet List Last is that Bullet List Last has additional space after the paragraph. Otherwise, the styles are identical. Base styles enable you to do this. In this case, Bullet List Last consists of all the formatting from its base style, Bullet List, plus 6 points of space after.

A style *inherits* all the formats specified in its base style. If the base style changes, the changes are inherited, too. However, a style can override the formats that it inherits from the base style. For example, if a style does not specify a point size, any paragraphs formatted with the style inherits the point size from the base style. However, if a style specifies a point size, then the point size of the base style is ignored.

Book II
Chapter 3

Working with Styles

Here's the procedure for creating a style that's based on another style:

1. **Choose the paragraph you want to format.**

2. **Apply the style that you want to use as the base style to the paragraph you selected.**

3. **Change the formatting of the paragraph.**

Add whatever extra formats you want applied to the new style. These formats are added to the base style's formats.

4. **Create the new style.**

See the earlier section "Creating a new style the easy way" for help with this step. The new style is based on the style originally applied to the paragraph.

You can also set the base style by using the New Style or Modify Style dialog box, which you access from the Styles and Formatting task pane.

Any styles based on the style you change automatically reflect any changes you make to a style. Thus, if all 20 of your paragraph styles are based on the Normal style, you can change the font for all 20 styles simply by changing the font for the Normal style. (Except for any styles based on Normal, but specify their own font to override the font picked up from the Normal style. In that case, those styles retain their own fonts.)

A style that serves as a base style may itself have a base style. For example, Bullet List Last may be based on Bullet List, which in turn may be based on Normal. In that case, the formats from Normal, Bullet List, and Bullet List Last are merged together whenever you apply the style.

Setting the style of the next paragraph

When you press the Enter key to create a new paragraph, the new paragraph normally assumes the same style as the previous paragraph. In some cases, you want to do exactly that. However, for some styles, the style of the following paragraph is almost always a different style. For example, a paragraph formatted with the Heading 1 style is rarely followed by another Heading 1 paragraph. Instead, a Heading 1 paragraph is usually followed by a Normal paragraph.

Instead of always changing the style assigned to a new paragraph in these situations, you can specify the style you want assigned to the next paragraph with Format⇨Style. Then, when you press the Enter key, the new paragraph is assigned the style you specified. This little trick can almost completely automate the chore of formatting your documents.

You can set the style for the following paragraph from the New Style or Modify Style dialog boxes, which you access via the Styles and Formatting task pane.

+ Examine the Style for Following Paragraph setting for each of your styles to see whether you can save yourself some work. Heading styles should specify Normal for the following paragraph, as should any other type of paragraph that usually occurs in singles. You may find other styles that should have this field set, too. For example, I have a Chapter Number style that specifies Chapter Title as Style for Following Paragraph.

+ This shortcut is such a great time-saver that I wish I had about eight more things to add to this short bullet list to make it look more important. But the only thing of note to say here is — just do it!

Viewing style assignments by enabling the style area

If you want to have a bird's eye view of the styles applied to each paragraph, open up the style area — a narrow band on the left edge of the document window. Figure 3-5 shows what Word looks like with the style area activated.

Follow these simple steps to enable the style area:

1. **Choose Tools⇨Options.**

The Options dialog box appears.

2. **Find the View tab and click it.**

The Options dialog box has 12 tabs, so you may have to hunt for a moment to find the View tab.

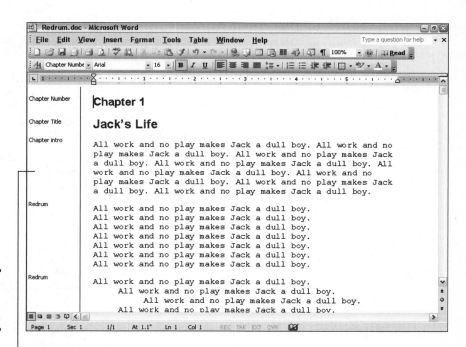

Figure 3-5: Viewing the style area.

The Style area

3. **Set the Style Area Width text box to at least 0.6 inch.**

   Locate the Style Area Width text box at the bottom left of the dialog box. You can set it to any width you want, but 0.6 inch is just about wide enough to accommodate most style names.

4. **Click OK.**

   The style area appears in your document.

Here are some helpful hints:

✦ You can adjust the width of the style area by dragging the line that separates it from the rest of the document window. Just position the mouse over the line and press the mouse button when the pointer changes shape. Drag the line to increase or decrease the width of the style area.

✦ To remove the style area altogether, drag the line all the way to the left of the window or invoke Tools⇨Options and set the Style Area Width text box to 0.

✦ You can select an entire paragraph by clicking the paragraph's style name in the style area.

✦ The problem with the style area is that it restricts the width of the document window. If you can't see the entire width of your text with the style area enabled, you may want to leave it off. Or, beg your boss for a brand new 19-inch monitor so that you have plenty of room on-screen for the Word document with the style area enabled.

✦ The style area is visible only in Normal and Outline views. If Word is in Print Layout view when you call up Tools⇨Options, you won't see the Style Area Width field. Use View⇨Normal or View⇨Outline to switch to Normal or Outline view.

Creating and using character styles

The vast majority of Word styles are *paragraph styles,* which affect formatting for an entire paragraph. Word has a little known and seldom-used feature called *character styles,* which enables you to create styles applied to specified characters rather than entire paragraphs.

Here's the blow-by-blow account of how you create a character style:

1. **Choose Format⇨Styles and Formatting.**

   The Styles and Formatting task pane comes up; refer to Figure 3-2.

2. **Click the New Style button.**

   The New Style dialog box appears. (Refer to Figure 3-3.)

3. **Type a new name for the style in the Name text box.**

   The default value is something like Style1, which isn't very descriptive.

4. **Change the Style Type text box to Character.**

   When you do so, the formatting options that relate to paragraphs (such as alignment and indentation) grow dim.

5. **Set the formatting for the style.**

   You can use the controls that appear on the New Style dialog box to set the text font and size. Or, for more control over the formatting, click the Format button and use the menu that appears.

6. **Click OK.**

   The style is created.

To apply a character style, select the range of characters you want to apply the style to and then apply the style using the Style list box on the Formatting toolbar or by pressing the style's keyboard shortcut.

Searching for and replacing style formatting

Want to quickly find every paragraph formatted with the Heading 1 style? You can activate the style area and scroll through the document, watching the style area to see whether the Heading 1 style comes up. But you can accomplish the same thing an easier way, courtesy of Edit⇨Find.

Here's the procedure for finding paragraphs tagged with a particular style:

1. **Invoke Edit⇨Find.**

   The keyboard shortcut is Ctrl+F. Either way, the Find dialog box appears.

2. **Click the More button.**

   Additional controls appear in the Find dialog box.

3. **Click the Format button and then choose the Style command from the pop-up menu.**

   The Find Style dialog box appears, as shown in Figure 3-6.

4. **Scroll through the list of styles until you locate the one you're looking for, select it, and then click OK.**

   Make sure that the Find What text box in the Find dialog box is blank; otherwise, the Find command searches for specific text formatted with the style you specify.

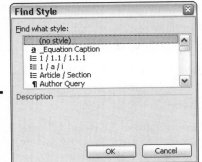

Figure 3-6:
The Find
Style dialog
box.

5. **Click the Find Next button to find the next occurrence of the style.**

    Click the Find Next button again to find the next occurrence. It's like déjà vu all over again.

6. **Press Esc when you're done.**

To replace paragraph styles, follow a similar procedure with Edit⇨Replace:

1. **Invoke Edit⇨Replace.**

    Or press Ctrl+H. The Replace dialog box appears.

2. **Click the More button to reveal the additional Replace controls.**

3. **Click in the Find What text box; then use the Format button to choose the style you want to find and replace.**

4. **Click in the Replace With text box; then use the Format button to choose the style you want to replace the Find What style with.**

5. **Click the Find Next button.**

    Word finds the first paragraph formatted with the style you specified and asks whether you want to replace its style.

6. **Click Replace if you want to replace the style.**

    Word replaces the style; then it finds the next paragraph formatted with the style and asks again. If you don't want to replace it, click Find Next. Either way, Word finds the next paragraph and asks again. Keep it up until all paragraphs are found.

When replacing one style with another, you can click the Replace All button to have Word replace all occurrences of the style without asking your permission. I suggest you start by clicking Find Next just to make sure Word is finding and replacing styles the way you intended. After you're sure, click the Replace All button to finish the laborious Find and Replace operation without your intervention.

Make sure that you leave both the Find What and Replace With fields blank. You're looking for all paragraphs formatted with a particular style; what text is in the paragraphs doesn't matter. If you accidentally leave text in the Replace With text box, Word replaces the entire paragraph with the Replace With text. If that happens, press Ctrl+Z and go fishing.

If all you want to do is quickly select all of the paragraphs in a document that use a given style, you can do so via the Styles and Formatting task pane. Point to the style you want to select, click the down-arrow to reveal the menu, and then choose the Select All *x* Instances command. (The *x* indicates how many times you used the style.)

Storing styles in a template

You can store styles directly in a document file or in a *template* file. When you apply a template to a document, you can copy all the styles in the template into the document, replacing any existing styles with the same name. You can change the entire look of a document simply by applying a different template.

Keep these hints in mind when using templates:

✦ To store a style in the current template rather than the current document, check the Add to Template box in the New Style dialog box when you use Format⇨Style to create the style.

✦ To copy styles from the document to the template, use Format⇨Style and then click the Organizer button.

✦ To apply a different template to the document, use Tools⇨Templates and Add-ins.

✦ For much more information about using templates, refer to Book I, Chapter 3.

Better Living through Styles

Styles are one of the keys to using Word effectively. I'd like to end this chapter by offering a list of my favorite tips for simplifying your life by using styles right:

✦ **Always use styles:** This advice is kind of redundant, because with Word, you *have* to use styles. Whether you realize it or not, all paragraphs in Word are based on a style. If you don't use styles, the paragraphs are based on the utilitarian Normal style.

My point here is that for all but the simplest of documents, create and apply styles instead of applying direct formatting to your paragraphs. In the long run, using styles rather than direct formatting saves you a great deal of time and grief. You may curse the computer while you climb the steep-at-times learning curve that comes along with using styles, but when you get to the top, you'll say to yourself, "That wasn't so hard."

✦ **Avoid the Style and Formatting task pane:** I hate the Styles and Formatting task pane. It takes up way too much space on-screen. Creating styles by example is much easier: Format a paragraph, click in the Style list box on the Formatting toolbar, and type a new style name. To apply a style, use a keyboard shortcut or choose the style name from the Style list box.

The Styles and Formatting task pane is useful in the following circumstances:

- You want to modify or delete a style.

- You want to assign a keyboard shortcut to a style, or you can't remember that Ctrl+Alt+numeric plus is the shortcut.

- You want to specify a style for the following paragraph.

- You want to use a different base style.

✦ **Check out the templates that come with Word:** Microsoft has already done a great deal of the hard work creating styles for you. Check out the various templates that come with Word to see whether any of them are suitable. If not, pick one that's close and modify it to suit your needs. For a bunch of information on using templates, check out Book I, Chapter 3.

✦ **Use the Style for Following Paragraph field to automate your formatting:** The fastest way to assign styles is to have Word do it automatically. Set the Style for Following Paragraph field in the Modify Style or New Style dialog box. Then, when you press the Enter key to create a new paragraph, Word automatically assigns the style.

✦ **Use keyboard shortcuts to assign styles quickly:** The second fastest way to assign styles is to use keyboard shortcuts. Assign a keyboard shortcut to each style that you use frequently. Don't bother with the ones you use infrequently, though. Remembering the keyboard shortcuts you use frequently is hard enough.

✦ **Use the built-in Heading 1, Heading 2, and Heading 3 styles for your headings:** Word has three predefined heading styles. If you don't like the way they look, redefine them. By using Heading 1, Heading 2, and Heading 3, you can work with your headings in Outline view (see Book VI, Chapter 2) or use them to create a Table of Contents (see Book VI, Chapter 6).

✦ **Base all text variants on the Normal style:** Most documents have several different types of paragraphs that are minor variations on normal text. For example, the bullet-list paragraphs in this book are variations of the book's normal-text paragraphs: They have the same typeface, point size, and line spacing, but the margins are different and they have bullets. Paragraphs such as bulleted lists should be formatted with styles that are based on the Normal style. That way, if you decide to make a sweeping change, such as moving from 10 to 11 point type or switching from Times New Roman to Palatino, you can change the Normal style rather than changing each style individually.

✦ **Use Space Before or Space After, but not both:** When you create your paragraph styles, decide in advance whether you prefer to add extra space before or after the paragraphs. As much as possible, stick to your decision. If you have two adjacent paragraphs, the first with extra space after and the second with space before, you may end up with more space than you intend between the paragraphs.

Chapter 4: Page Setup and Section Formatting

In This Chapter

✔ Understanding the relationship between sections and page layout

✔ Creating section breaks

✔ Setting margins, page size, orientation, and other basic page formats

✔ Adding page numbers to the bottom or top of your document pages

✔ Creating headers and footers

Sections are the third piece of the Word formatting puzzle, after characters and paragraph formats. In this chapter, you find out all about setting up basic page formats using sections. That includes such important tasks as setting up page margins, flipping pages from portrait to landscape orientation, and creating headers or footers at the top or bottom of each page.

Understanding Sections

Sections are the basis of Word's page layout formatting. Most documents consist of only a single section, so all the pages in the document receive the same formatting. If some pages require different formatting, you can break up the document into two or more sections, each with its own page format.

Sections control the following formatting information:

✦ The size of the paper.

✦ The left, right, top, and bottom margins.

✦ The orientation of the paper: whether the document is printed *portrait* (the height is bigger than the width) or *landscape* (the width is the larger measurement).

✦ The number and spacing of columns.

✦ Header and footer information, including the positioning of the header or footer as well as its appearance.

✦ Footnotes and endnotes, again including the positioning and appearance of the footnotes and endnotes.

✦ Page numbering.

✦ Line numbering.

One of the most confusing aspects of working with sections is that a single page can contain more than one section. For example, a page may start off with a single-column layout, then switch to two columns, and then switch back to a single column. Such a page would comprise three sections.

Unfortunately, Word does not include one convenient "Format⇨Section" command that allows you to set all these formats from one convenient location. In fact, you don't even set most of the section formats from the Format menu at all. Instead, section formatting is scattered about the Word menus:

✦ **File⇨Page Setup:** This command lets you set basic page formatting information such as margins, the position of headers and footers, and paper size and orientation.

✦ **View⇨Header and Footer:** This command displays the header and footer area so you can customize the headers and footers.

✦ **Insert⇨Break:** This command lets you create a new section that has the same format as the previous section.

✦ **Insert⇨Page Numbers:** This command adds a page number to the header or footer, lets you vary the page numbering style, and allows you to set the starting page number for the section.

✦ **Insert⇨Reference:** This command lets you create footnotes or endnotes and control their appearance and position. (I cover this topic in Chapter 8 of this minibook.)

✦ **Format⇨Columns:** This command lets you set the number of columns and the size and spacing for each column. (For more information about columns, refer to Chapter 5 of this minibook.)

All documents contain at least one section. In documents with only one section, the section formatting information is stored in the last paragraph mark of the document, along with the last paragraph's paragraph formats. If a document contains two or more sections, the end of each section except the last is indicated by a section break, which looks like this:

================================Section Break (Continuous)================================

The section break contains the section formatting information just as a paragraph mark contains paragraph formatting. As a result, if you delete a section break, the sections before and after the break combine and use the formatting information from the section that followed the break.

Creating Section Breaks

You can create a new section in several ways. One is to use Insert⇨Break. This method allows you to create a new section that inherits the formatting of the previous section. You can then make whatever formatting changes you want to the new section. To create a new section in this manner, follow these steps:

1. **Position the insertion point at the spot where you want the new section to begin.**

2. **Choose Insert⇨Break.**

The Break dialog box appears, as shown in Figure 4-1.

Figure 4-1:
Use the
Break dialog
box to
create a
section
break.

3. **Choose one of the four section break types:**

• **Next Page:** Creates a new section that begins at the top of the following page.

• **Continuous:** Creates a new section that begins on the next line of the same page. This type of section break is commonly used when changing the number of columns on a page.

• **Even Page:** Creates a new section that begins on the next even numbered page.

• **Odd Page:** Creates a new section that begins on the next odd numbered page.

4. **Click OK.**

You can also use Insert⇨Break to create a page break or a column break. A page break simply skips the text to the top of the next page without starting a new section. A column break skips to the top of the next column. For more information about column breaks, see Chapter 5 of this minibook.

Several of the commands that apply formatting to sections also let you create new sections. These commands include an Apply To field that lets you choose from among these options:

✦ **This Point Forward:** Select this option if you want to create a new section. Word inserts a section break and applies whatever formatting you select to the following section.

✦ **Whole Document:** Pick this option to apply a layout format to all the sections in the document.

✦ **This Section:** Use this option to apply formatting just to the current section. This option does not appear in the Apply To drop-down box if the document consists of only one section.

Using the File⇨Page Setup Command

The File⇨Page Setup command controls many page layout formats. When you call up this command, it displays the Page Setup dialog box, which sports three separate tabbed sections. The following sections describe each of the three tabs.

Margins

Figure 4-2 shows the Margins tab of the Page Setup dialog box.

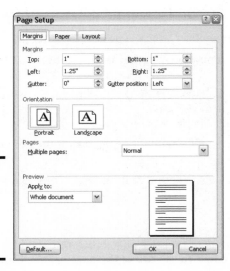

Figure 4-2:
The Page Setup dialog box (Margins tab).

Normally, this dialog box contains the following options:

✦ **Top:** Sets the distance from the top of the page to the first line of text. The default is 1".

✦ **Bottom:** Sets the distance from the bottom of the page to the last line of text. The default is 1".

✦ **Left:** Sets the distance from the left edge of the page to the start of the text. The default is 1.25".

✦ **Right:** Sets the distance from the right edge of the page to the end of the text. The default is 1.25".

✦ **Gutter:** Sets an additional amount of margin space for pages that are to be bound. The space is added to the left or top margin, depending on the setting of the Gutter Position option, unless you choose Mirror Margins, Two Pages Per Sheet, or Book Fold for the Multiple Pages option.

✦ **Portrait:** Orients the paper in an upright position, where the height is greater than the width.

✦ **Landscape:** Orients the paper sideways, such that the width is greater than the height. When you switch from Portrait to Landscape (and vice versa), the Height and Width values automatically swap.

✦ **Multiple Pages:** This option controls how pages are actually laid out on the sheets of paper that spit out of the printer. The options are Normal (one page per sheet), Mirror Margins (the left and right margins switch places every other page), 2 Pages Per Sheet (just what it says), and Book Fold (which lets you print booklets — for more information, see the side-bar "Printing booklets").

✦ **Apply To:** Whole Document, This Section, or This Point Forward.

**Book II
Chapter 4**

Page Setup and
Section Formatting

If you select the Mirror Margins from the Multiple Pages drop-down list, the Margins dialog box changes, as shown in Figure 4-3. The Left and Right options change to Inside and Outside and the Gutter Position option becomes unavailable. This setting allows the margins for each page to alternate: On odd-numbered pages, the inside margin is on the left; on even-numbered pages, the inside margin is on the right. Any additional space provided for by the Gutter field is added to the inside margin.

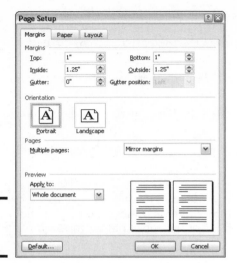

Figure 4-3:
Mirrored
Margins.

Printing booklets

The Book Fold option of the Multiple Pages drop-down list on the Margins tab of the Page Setup dialog box (wow, that's a mouthful) lets you create booklets from pages you fold in half and staple in the middle. If you've ever assembled a booklet like that, you know that you can't just print the pages in order. Instead, the first sheet of paper must have the first and last page on one side and the second and next-to-last page on the other. Each additional sheet has to have pages that alternate from the front of the booklet to the back of the booklet. The only sheet that has two consecutive pages side-by-side is the sheet that goes in the middle.

If you choose the Book Fold option, Word automatically shuffles the pages correctly when you print your document so that they come out ready to fold in half and staple together. This option is an enormous timesaver if you want to create religious tracts, company songbooks, or any other kind of booklet.

If you don't have a fancy printer that can automatically print on both sides of the page, choose the Manual Duplex option in the Print dialog box when you print your booklet. Then, Word prints the front side of each page of the booklet, and then tells you to take the pages out and put them back into the printer's paper tray to print the backsides.

Paper

The Paper tab of the Page Setup dialog box is shown in Figure 4-4.

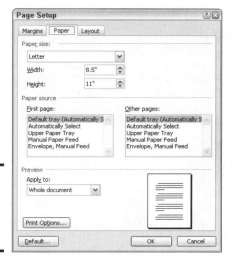

Figure 4-4:
The Page
Setup
dialog box
(Paper tab).

The Paper tab includes the following options:

✦ **Paper Size:** Sets the paper size. The drop-down list allows you to pick from a variety of paper sizes, including Letter, Legal, and various other envelope sizes.

✦ **Width:** Sets the width of the paper. This field is automatically set when you choose a Paper Size. If you change the value of this field, the Paper Size field changes to Custom Size.

✦ **Height:** Sets the height of the paper. This field is also set automatically according to the Paper Size you select, and changing the height automatically changes Paper Size to Custom Size.

✦ **Apply To:** Whole Document, This Section, or This Point Forward.

✦ **Paper Source — First Page:** Specifies which paper tray the printer uses for the first page of your document.

✦ **Paper Source — Other Pages:** Specifies which paper tray the printer uses for the second and subsequent pages of your document.

In most cases, you use the same source for both First Page and the Other Pages. However, using a different paper for the first page of business letters is common.

The Paper tab also includes a Print Options button that brings up a dialog box filled with printer options. It's the same as the Print tab of the Tools⇨ Options command.

Layout

The Layout tab, shown in Figure 4-5, sounds more exciting than it really is. "Layout" conjures up hopes of an all-encompassing dialog box wherein you can control at least the major aspects of your document's layout. Alas, the lowly Layout tab should have been named "Leftovers" because it contains nothing but a few obscure layout options that apparently didn't seem to fit anywhere else.

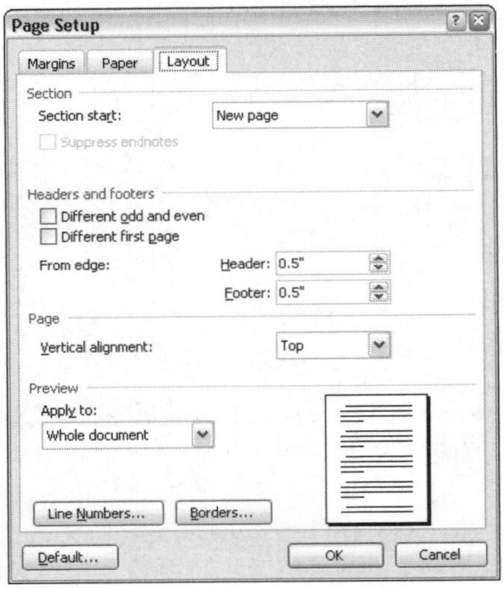

Figure 4-5: The Layout Options That Didn't Fit Anywhere Else But We Couldn't Bring Ourselves To Leave Them Out tab.

Here's the lowdown on the Layout options:

✦ **Section Start:** This drop-down box offers essentially the same options available with Insert⇨Break. It lets you change the section break type for the current section. For example, if you created the section originally specifying "Odd Page" and you want to change it to "New Page," you make the change with this option. (This dialog box is a pretty lame place to put this option, if you ask me. You initially set this option with Insert⇨ Break. Why should you have to come to the File⇨Page Setup command's Layout tab to change it? What Word desperately needs is a Format⇨Section command.)

✦ **Different Odd and Even** and **Different First Page:** These two options let you set up different headers and footers for even and odd pages or for the first page in a section. This option is useful if you are printing on both sides of the page or if you don't want the header to appear on the first page.

✦ **Header:** Sets the distance from the top of the page to the header area. The default is 0.5".

✦ **Footer:** Sets the distance from the bottom of the page to the footer area. The default is 0.5".

✦ **Vertical Alignment:** Top, Center, Justified, or Bottom. Top is the norm. Use Center if you want to center a title in the middle of the page and don't want to press the Enter key 10 or 12 times to center it. (I've never found a use for Justified or Bottom. If you do, write a letter to Bill Gates thanking him for these very useful features. In the PS, demand that the next version of Word have a Format⇨Section command.)

✦ **Apply To:** This drop-down list lets you choose whether you want the layout you specify in this dialog box to apply to the entire document or a portion of the document:

  • *This Point Forward*: Word creates a new section and applies the layout to the new section.

  • *Entire Document*: Word applies the layout to the entire document.

  • *This Section*: If the document already has two or more sections, this third option is available in the drop-down. The This Section option lets you apply the layout to just the current selection.

✦ **Borders:** Brings up the Page Border tab of the Borders and Shading dialog box where you can add a border to each page of the document.

✦ **Line Numbers:** Calls up the dialog box shown in Figure 4-6, which lets you print line numbers. You can select any starting line number, the increment to count lines by (5 or 10 is usually specified here), and whether line numbering restarts for each page or section or is continuous for the entire document.

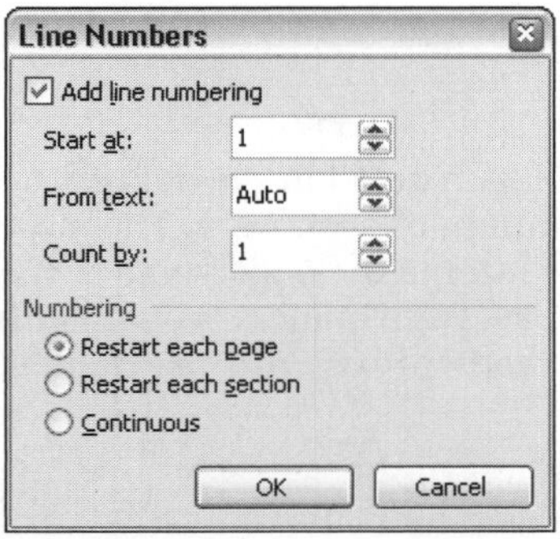

**Book II
Chapter 4**

**Page Setup and
Section Formatting**

Figure 4-6:
Setting
up line
numbers.

This feature is loved by lawyers and Shakespeare scholars alike. Figure 4-7 shows an example of a document formatted with line numbers. Notice that the title line at the top of the page is not figured into the line numbers. You can achieve this numbering in two ways:

- You can call up Format⇨Paragraph, click the Lines and Page Breaks tab, and select the Suppress Line Numbers option for the heading paragraph.

- You can create a continuous section break immediately after the title and turn off line numbering for the section that contains the title.

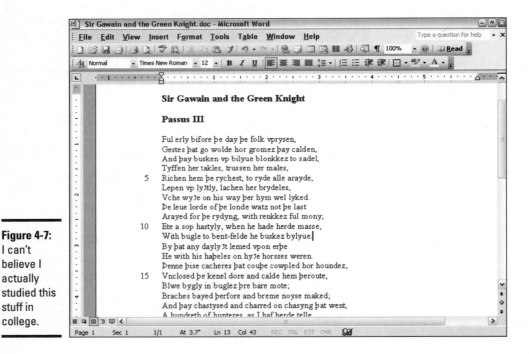

Figure 4-7: I can't believe I actually studied this stuff in college.

Inserting Page Numbers

Headers and footers, which I describe in detail in the next section, are for putting information at the top or bottom of each page. The most common type of information in a header or footer is the page number. If all you want to appear in your header or footer is a page number, you don't have to mess with headers and footers at all. Instead, just use the Insert⇨Page Numbers command, following these steps:

1. Choose Insert⇨Page Numbers.

The Page Numbers dialog box comes up, shown in Figure 4-8.

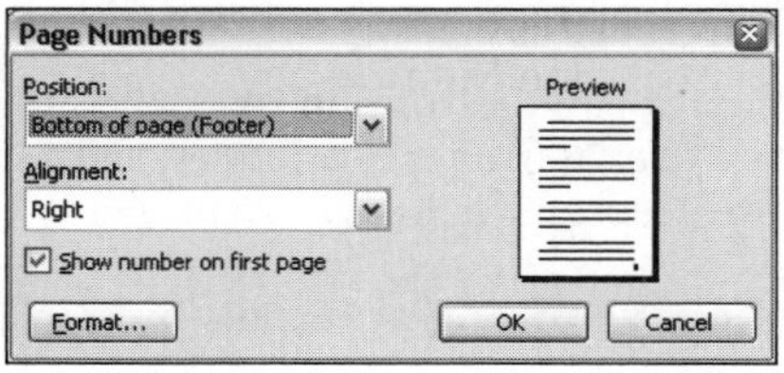

Figure 4-8:
The Page
Numbers
dialog box.

2. Choose the position of the page numbers using the Position drop-down list.

The choices are Bottom of Page or Top of Page.

3. Choose the alignment of the page numbers using the Alignment drop-down list.

The choices are Left, Center, Right, Inside, and Outside. (Inside and Outside apply only if you're using mirrored margins for two-sided printing.)

Note: As you set the page number position and alignment, the preview box updates so that you can see the positioning of the number.

4. If you want the page number printed on the first page, select the Show Number on First Page check box.

5. Click OK.

If you are not content with the page numbers Word shows when you use the Insert⇨Page Numbers command, click the Format button when the Page Numbers dialog box appears. The Page Number Format dialog box appears, as shown in Figure 4-9.

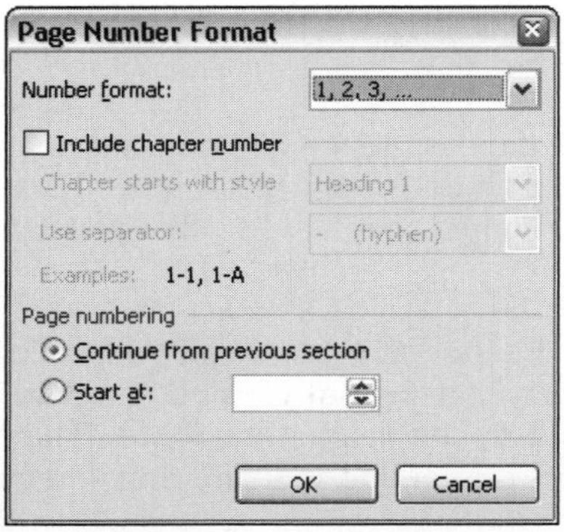

Figure 4-9:
The Page
Number
Format
dialog box.

This dialog box lets you control several aspects of page numbering. For starters, you can change the page number format by selecting an option from the Number Format drop-down list. You can choose normal Arabic numbering (1, 2, 3. . .), uppercase or lowercase letters (A, B, C. . . or a, b, c. . .), or uppercase or lowercase Roman numbering (I, II, III. . . or i, ii, iii. . .).

You can select the Include Chapter Number option to create compound page numbers that include a number drawn from a heading paragraph, such as 1-1, 1-2, and so on. Follow these steps:

1. **Format the chapter headings using one of Word's built-in heading styles.**

   In most cases, you should use the Heading 1 style.

2. **Choose Format⇨Heading Numbering and automatically number the headings, specify the numbering type, and then click OK.**

3. **Choose Insert⇨Page Numbers, and then click the Format button to summon the Page Number Format dialog box.**

4. **Check the Include Chapter Number check box, and then indicate which style to use for the chapter titles and what character you want to use as a separator between the chapter number and the page number.**

   You can use a hyphen, period, colon, or dash as the separator.

5. **Click OK to return to the Page Numbers dialog box, and then click OK to insert the page numbers into the document.**

The Page Number Format command also lets you set a starting page number for the document or section. Usually, you use Continue from Previous Section so that page numbers are continuous throughout the document. However, if you created a separate section for front matter such as a title page, Table of Contents, and so on, restarting the page numbers for the first chapter of the document at page 1 is customary.

Headers and Footers

The Insert⇨Page Numbers command is great if all you want to appear at the top or bottom of a page is a plain, unadorned page number. Fortunately, Word provides the View⇨Header and Footer command so that you can create fancier headers and footers.

To add a header or footer, use the View⇨Headers and Footers command. This command switches you into Page Layout view and activates the header and footer area so that you can edit the header and footer. The body of your document remains visible, but is dimmed to indicate that you cannot edit it. See Figure 4-10.

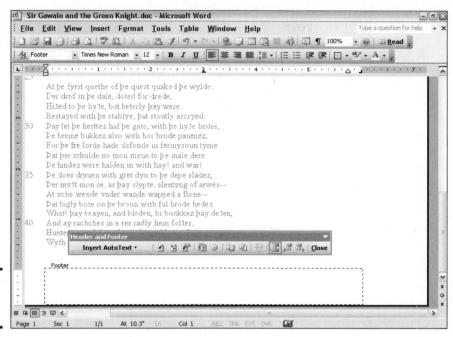

Figure 4-10:
Creating a
footer.

After activating the View⇨Headers and Footers command, you can use the
Header and Footer toolbar to work with headers and footers. Table 4-1
describes the function of each button on this toolbar.

Table 4-1	The Headers and Footers Toolbar Buttons
Button	*What It Does*
Insert AutoText ▾	Lets you insert a variety of pre-defined header or footer blocks.
	Switches from the header to the footer area. To switch back to the header, click the button again.
	Inserts the page number.
	Inserts the number of pages in the document.
	Calls up the Page Number Format dialog box. (Refer to Figure 4-9.)

(continued)

Table 4-1 *(continued)*

Button	What It Does
	Inserts the date.
	Inserts the time.
	Calls up the Layout tab of the Page Setup dialog box. (Refer to Figure 4-5.)
	Alternately hides and shows the document's text.
	Makes this header or footer identical to the one in the preceding section.
	Switches the display between the current page's header and footer.
	If the document has more than one section, moves to the header for the previous section.
	If the document has more than one section, moves to the header for the next section.
Close	Returns to Normal view.

You can type anything you want in the header or footer areas, and you can apply any type of formatting you wish. By default, Word creates a center-aligned tab stop dead set in the middle of the page and a right-aligned tab stop at the right margin. As a result, you can use the Tab key to create a header that has some text flush against the left margin, some more text centered on the page, and still more text flush against the right margin.

You can often spruce up the appearance of the page by adding a borderline beneath the header or above the footer. Just use Format➪Borders and Shading, or call up the Borders toolbar and click away.

Building a toolbar button to show headers

If you create a lot of documents that have headers and footers, you may want a more convenient way to access them than working your way through the View menu. Unfortunately, Word's standard toolbars do not have a Header and Footer button, but you can create one yourself easily enough. Just follow these steps:

1. **Call up Tools⇨Customize and click the Commands tab.**

   The Customize dialog box displays.

2. **In the Categories list, select View.**

3. **In the Commands list, select Header and Footer.**

You have to scroll most of the way down this list to find the Header and Footer command.

4. **Click and drag the Header and Footer command from the Commands list all the way to the toolbar where you want the button to appear.**

   When you release the mouse button, the Header and Footer button is added to the toolbar you select.

5. **Click Close to dismiss the Customize dialog box.**

Using a command that's placed on the View menu to "create" a header or footer may seem weird. The command makes sense, though, when you realize that *all* Word documents have headers and footers. As a result, you don't use the command to "create" a header or footer. All the View⇨Headers and Footers command does is allow you to view the header and footer area so that you can edit them, adding your own text and formatting.

Creating Sections with Different Page Numbers

Many documents require sections that have different page number formats. For example, many documents require that the first page or two — a cover page and perhaps an inside title page — have no page numbers at all. Then, a section of front matter begins, including a Table of Contents, an acknowledgments page, and perhaps a preface, forward, or introduction, which can be numbered with roman numerals (i, ii, and so on). Then, the body of the document begins, numbered with Arabic numerals starting with 1.

To create a document of this sort, you must use sections to format groups of pages with different numbering schemes. You don't have to perform a special action for the first group of pages — the ones with no page numbers.

Book II
Chapter 4

Page Setup and
Section Formatting

To create the proper page numbering for the front matter, follow these steps in Normal or Print Layout view:

1. **Place the insertion point at the beginning of the front matter.**

   If you already inserted a page break so that the first page of the front matter begins at the top of a new page, delete the page break. In the next step, you insert a section break that causes the front matter to start atop a new page.

2. **Choose Insert⇨Break.**

3. **Choose Next Page.**

4. **Click OK to insert the break.**

5. **Choose View⇨Header and Footer.**

6. **Click the Switch Between Header and Footer button to switch to the footer.**

   Skip this step if you positioned the page numbers at the top of the page.

7. **Click the Link to Previous button to detach the footer from the previous section's footer.**

8. **Click the Insert Page Number button.**

   A page number is inserted in the footer.

9. **Click the Format Page Number button.**

   The Page Number Format dialog box appears. (Refer to Figure 4-9.)

10. **For the front matter, choose the Roman numeral number format (i, ii, iii. . .) in the Number Format list box.**

11. **Select Start At 1.**

12. **Click OK.**

    The Page Number Format dialog box disappears

13. **Click Close to dismiss the Header and Footer toolbar.**

You can follow a similar procedure to begin a new section of page numbering for the body of the document, using Arabic numerals rather than Roman numerals.

Chapter 5: Column Formatting

In This Chapter

- ✔ Creating columns
- ✔ Adjusting column width
- ✔ Forcing a column break
- ✔ Hyphenating your text

If you use Word to create newsletters, brochures, and other stuff for which you really should be using a desktop publishing program like Adobe PageMaker, you'll be happy to know that Word enables you to create beautiful two- or three-column layouts. (Actually, you can create as many as 12 columns on a page, but unless you're using *really* wide paper, that's not such a good idea.)

 Word refers to two- and three-column layouts as *newspaper-style columns,* but that's just a bit misleading. To implement a true newspaper style column feature, Word would have to edit your prose automatically as you type it so that it focused on bad news and added a distinct left-wing slant to your text.

This chapter jumps head first into setting up newspaper-style columns in Word and tackles a related feature: hyphenation. Hyphenation isn't such a big deal in single-column layouts, but after you add two or three columns to a page, hyphenation is the key to making the columns look good. Plus, hyphenation didn't really fit anywhere else and this chapter was kind of short without it.

Creating Columns

When you create multiple columns, the column layout applies to the entire section. If the entire document consists of but one section, the column layout applies to the entire document. If you want part of the document to have one column and another part to have two or three columns, you have to create two or more sections to accommodate the different column layouts.

Creating columns the easy way

Here is the easiest way to create multiple columns in your document:

1. **Click the Columns button on the Standard toolbar.**

The drop-down menu shown in Figure 5-1 appears.

Figure 5-1:
The
Columns
button.

2 Columns

2. **Click and drag the mouse to pick the number of columns you want.**

3. **Let go.**

Voilà! The document is formatted with the number of columns you chose.

Some notes on using multiple columns:

✦ When you create a multi-column layout, Word switches you to Print Layout view so that the columns are visible side by side on the screen. If you switch back to Normal view (View⇨Normal), the text is formatted according to the width of the column, but the columns do not display side by side on-screen.

✦ For a quick glimpse of how the columns appear when printed, use File⇨ Print Preview. When you see enough, click the Close button to return to your document.

✦ Did you choke when you saw what your document looked like in columns? You can revert to single-column mode by pressing Ctrl+Z (the magic Undo command) or by using the Columns button to set the layout to one column.

✦ The Columns button enables you to set the number of columns, but it doesn't enable you to control the size of each column or the amount of space between columns. To do these latter actions, you need to use the Format⇨Columns command, described next.

Creating columns the hard way

For more control over the appearance of columns, use the Format⇨Columns command. Grab a cup of coffee and follow these steps:

1. **Move the cursor to the point in the document where you want the columns to begin.**

If you want to apply columns to the entire document, where you put the cursor doesn't matter.

2. **Hail Format⇨Columns.**

You are greeted with the Columns dialog box, shown in Figure 5-2.

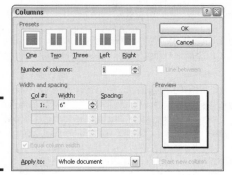

Figure 5-2:
The
Columns
dialog box.

3. **Click one of the five preset column layouts.**

   If you want more than three columns, drop everything. Take a nice long walk to clear your head of such nonsense. If you still want four or more columns when you return, use the Number of Columns control to set the number of columns you want.

4. **Change the Width or Spacing fields if you must.**

   If you want to change the width of the columns, change the Width field. To change the amount of space between columns, change the Spacing field.

5. **Click the Line Between button if you want a line between the columns.**

   This is the line between the stuff you read, not the stuff you read between the lines.

6. **Here's the tricky part: If you want the new column layout to begin at the cursor position, choose This Point Forward from the Apply To list box.**

   If you choose This Point Forward, Word adds a section break at the cursor position and applies the column layout to the new section. Thus, text that follows the cursor is formatted in columns, but text that comes before it is not.

   If you choose Whole Document, the column layout applies to the entire document.

7. **Periodically peer at the preview box to see whether you like the column layout.**

8. **Click OK.**

   Excellent!

Here are some things to remember as you twiddle with the Columns dialog box:

✦ If you check the Equal Column Width check box, Word balances the columns evenly. If you uncheck this check box, you can create columns of uneven width.

✦ Using the Apply To: This Point Forward option is the way to create a headline or title that spans the width of two or three columns. Start by creating the headline, using a large font and centering it. Position the insertion point at the end of the heading, and then use Format⇨Columns to create a two- or three-column layout. Set the Select Apply To field to This Point Forward to throw the columns into a new section so that the headline remains in a single column.

Adjusting the Column Width

If you don't like the width of columns you create, you can change them at any time. You have two ways to change column width:

✦ Call up Format⇨Columns and play with the Width and Spacing fields.

✦ Click and drag the *column marker,* the box-like separator between columns in the ruler. If you check the Equal Column Width check box in the Columns dialog box, all the column markers move in concert to preserve the equal column widths. Otherwise, you can adjust the column markers individually.

Some things to remember when you adjust column width:

✦ Even if you use unequal column widths, try to keep the gap between the columns the same widths. Otherwise, you create an unbalanced look.

✦ When adjusting column width by dragging the column marker, hold down the Alt key before clicking the mouse. Doing so causes Word to display measurements that show the width of each column and the size of the space between columns.

✦ *Remember:* Any formatting applied to paragraphs in columns is still in effect. If you gave a paragraph a left indent of ½ inch, the paragraph is indented ½ inch from the left column margin. This indentation reduces the column width.

Forcing a Column Break

Left to its own devices, Word decides when to jump text from the bottom of one column up to the top of the next column. Sometimes, however, you want to intervene and insert a column break of your own.

Follow these steps to force a column break:

1. **Place the cursor where you want the new column to begin.**

2. **Press Ctrl+Shift+Enter.**

   Or use Insert⇨Break, check the Column Break feature, and click OK.

In Normal view, a column break is indicated in the text by a solid line running all the way across the screen. In Page Layout view, the column break is obvious when you see the text jump to the next column.

Don't try to create two or three columns of equal length by inserting column breaks where you think the bottom of each column should fall. Instead, insert a continuous section break at the end of the last column. A continuous section break balances all the columns in the section so that they're of equal length and then starts a new section without forcing a page break. To insert a continuous section break, choose Insert⇨Break, select Continuous, and click OK.

**Book II
Chapter 5**

Column Formatting

Using Linked Text Boxes to Create Columns

Word offers an alternative to the Format⇨Columns command for creating complex multi-column layouts: linked text boxes. A linked text box is a drawing object that contains text. You can link a series of text boxes together so that if the first text box is not large enough to contain all of the text, the text spills over to the second text box. If the second text box isn't large enough to show all the text, a third text box is added to the link. Turn to Book IV, Chapter 4 if you want to know more about using text boxes.

Hyphenating Your Text

Word has the capability of automatically hyphenating words. You can set it up so that words are hyphenated as you type them, or you can wait until after you typed your text and then automatically hyphenate the document. Hyphenating as you type can slow Word down, especially if you don't have a blazingly fast computer. Thus, I suggest you type your document first and then hyphenate it.

Here's how:

1. **Type your text.**

   Don't worry about hyphens during this step.

2. **Activate Tools➪Language➪Hyphenation.**

   The Hyphenation dialog box, shown in Figure 5-3, appears.

Hyphenation

☐ Automatically hyphenate document
☐ Hyphenate words in CAPS

Hyphenation zone: 0.25"
Limit consecutive hyphens to: No limit

[Manual...]   [OK]   [Cancel]

3. **Check the Automatically Hyphenate Document check box.**

4. **Check the Hyphenate Words in CAPS check box if you want words made entirely of capital letters to be hyphenated.**

   Uncheck this option if your writing includes specialized jargon that appears in all capitals and should not be hyphenated. For example, if you use terms like TECHNOBABBLE VOCABULATOR, which must not under any circumstances be hyphenated, you'll love this option.

5. **Adjust the Hyphenation Zone if you're picky.**

   This zone is the area within which Word tries to end each line. If necessary, Word hyphenates words that cross into this zone. If you make this zone larger, Word hyphenates more words, but sometimes that results in lines that look too spaced out (for justified text) or right margins that are too ragged (for left-justified text).

6. **Set the Limit Consecutive Hyphens To list box to 3 or 4.**

   Having two hyphens in a row isn't wrong, and three is okay once in a while. But Word's default setting for this field places no limit to the number of consecutive lines that Word can hyphenate. You don't want to see a column of 20 hyphenated lines, do you?

7. **Click OK.**

   Word hyphenates the document.

8. **Check the results.**

   You may not be happy with Word's hyphenations. Always check the results and make any necessary corrections.

Here are some hyphenation pointers to keep in mind:

✦ Word uses its dictionary to determine where to hyphenate words. It probably spells better than you do. (I know it spells better than *I* do!)

✦ If you want to cause Word to hyphenate a word at a particular spot, place the cursor where you want the word hyphenated and press Ctrl+–. Pressing this shortcut creates an *optional hyphen,* which displays only when the word falls at the end of a line.

✦ Do *not* hyphenate words simply by typing a hyphen. It may work for the time being, but if you later edit the text so that the hyphenated word no longer falls at the end of a line, the hyphen still appears, now in the middle of the line where it does not belong. Use Ctrl+– instead.

✦ Sometimes you want to use a hyphen in a compound word, but you don't want the word to be split up at the end of the line because it may look funny — for example, *G-Men.* In that case, use Ctrl+Shift+– to create the hyphen rather than the hyphen key alone. Word displays the hyphen, but does not break the word at the hyphen.

✦ If you click the Manual button in the Hyphenation dialog box, Word leads you through the entire document, asking you about each word it wants to hyphenate, which is tiresome beyond belief. Better to just hyphenate the document and then review it and remove any hyphens you don't like.

**Book II
Chapter 5**

Column Formatting

Chapter 6: Using Tables

In This Chapter

- ✔ Setting up and using Word tables
- ✔ Formatting table cells using the Table AutoFormat command
- ✔ Editing a table by inserting and deleting cells, columns, and rows
- ✔ Formatting table cells yourself
- ✔ Using advanced table features

1 couldn't figure out what to call this chapter: Setting the Table? Turning the Tables? Sliding Under the Table? Dancing On the Table? Tabling the Motion? The Periodic Table? Table for Two? So I gave up and decided to call it just *Using Tables*.

This chapter describes the ins and outs of formatting text and graphics into tables. Word's table feature is remarkably versatile, so figuring out how it works really pays off.

If you're going to sit at my table, you have to remember the same two rules of table manners I've been trying to teach my kids for years: No talking with your mouth open and no eating with your mouth full.

Understanding Tables

You can think of a *table* as a mini-spreadsheet within your Word document. It consists of *rows* and *columns,* with *cells* at the intersections of each row and column. Each cell can contain text or graphics, and you can format the table in any way you wish. Figure 6-1 shows a simple Word table.

Survey Results

Figure 6-1:
A simple
table.

Word Feature	Like It	Hate It	What is It?
Mail Merge	20%	50%	30%
Styles	25%	20%	55%
Templates	10%	5%	85%
Columns	35%	30%	35%
Tables	20%	70%	10%

Each cell can contain one or more paragraphs of text, and text automatically wraps within its cell. Whenever text wraps to a new line, Word automatically increases the height of the row, if necessary, to accommodate the new line of text. This situation is where the versatility of tables becomes apparent. I could create the table in Figure 6-1 using tabs rather than the Table feature; in fact, creating the table using tabs is probably easier. Consider the table in Figure 6-2, however. To create a table such as this one using tabs, you have to manually break the lines for each column, using the tab key to separate columns from one another.

Figure 6-2:
A more
complex
table.

Feature	Advantages	Disadvantages
Tabs	Easy to set up for simple tables.	Difficult to use if the text must span several lines within a column.
Tables	Can apply any type of formatting within each cell. Text automatically wraps within cells.	More difficult to set up than simple tabs.

Figure 6-3 shows how this table appears in Word when it is being edited. Notice in the ruler how each table column has its own margins and indentation settings. (The ruler's indentation doohickeys are visible only for the column the insertion point is in; in this example, the second column is active.) Notice also that dotted gridlines appear around the table cells. These gridlines help you see the layout of the table as you are editing the table. They do not appear when you print the table.

If you do not see gridlines when you work with tables, choose Table⇨Gridlines.

Notice also that each cell has a little box in it, called the *end-of-cell marker.* You can think of these markers as the paragraph marks for cells. In fact, end-of-cell markers do not display unless you display paragraph marks also. If you don't see paragraph marks or end-of-cell markers in your documents, choose Tools⇨Options, click the View tab, and select the Paragraph Marks check box. Or, click the Show/Hide button on the Standard toolbar.

A Word table can contain as many as 31 columns. The number of rows is unlimited. When you create a table, Word adjusts the size of each column so that the table fits between the left and right margins. Each column is initially set to the same size, but you can adjust the size of individual columns later, and you can adjust the width of the entire table.

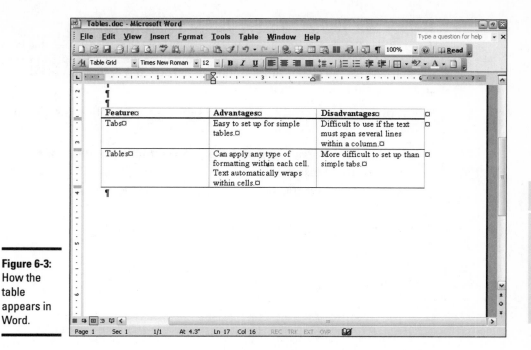

Figure 6-3:
How the
table
appears in
Word.

Creating Tables

The following sections describe several methods for creating tables.

Creating a table using the Insert Table button

The Insert Table button, which resides on the Standard toolbar, is the fastest way to create a simple table. When you click this button, a drop-down grid appears, as shown in Figure 6-4. Drag the mouse down and across the grid until the correct number of columns and rows are selected and release the button to create the table at the insertion point. (Naturally, place your insertion point where you want the table inserted first.)

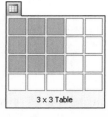

Figure 6-4:
Using the
Insert Table
button.

Using the Table➪Insert Table command

If you prefer the dialog-box approach to creating a table, use Table➪Insert Table. The advantages of using this command over the Insert Table button are that you can pick an arbitrary number of rows and columns and you can access the Table AutoFormat features.

Follow these steps to create a formatted table using the Table➪Insert Table command:

1. **Position the insertion point where you want to insert the new table.**

2. **Choose Table➪Insert Table.**

The Insert Table dialog box appears, as shown in Figure 6-5.

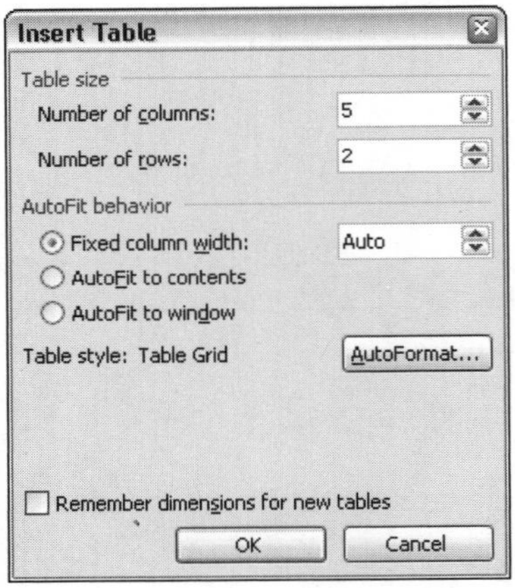

Insert Table

Table size
Number of columns: 5
Number of rows: 2

AutoFit behavior
⊙ Fixed column width: Auto
○ AutoFit to contents
○ AutoFit to window

Table style: Table Grid   [AutoFormat...]

☐ Remember dimensions for new tables

[OK]   [Cancel]

Figure 6-5:
The Insert Table dialog box.

3. **Adjust the number of rows and columns you want to create in the Number of Columns and Number of Rows fields.**

4. **If you want to apply an AutoFormat to the table, click the AutoFormat button.**

The Table AutoFormat dialog box comes up, which lets you choose from more than a few predefined table formats. Pick the format you want to apply and click OK to return to the Insert Table dialog box. For a more complete description of the Table AutoFormat dialog box, see the section "AutoFormatting a table" later in this chapter.

5. **Click OK to insert the table.**

Drawing a table

The Draw Table command lets you draw complicated tables on-screen using a simple set of drawing tools. This command is ideal for creating tables that are not a simple grid of rows and columns, but rather a complex conglomeration in which some cells span more than one row and others span more than one column.

Here's the procedure for creating a table using the Draw Table tool:

1. **Choose Table⇨Draw Table or click the Tables and Borders button on the Standard toolbar.**

Word goes into Print Layout View (if you aren't already there) and brings up the Tables and Borders toolbar, as shown in Figure 6-6.

2. **Draw the overall shape of the table by dragging the mouse to create a rectangular boundary for the table.**

When you release the mouse button, a table with a single cell is created, as shown in Figure 6-7.

3. **Carve the table up into smaller cells.**

For example, to split the table into two rows, point the mouse somewhere along the left edge of the table, and then press the mouse button and drag a line across the table to the right edge. When you release the mouse, the table splits into two rows.

You can continue to carve up the table into smaller and smaller cells. For each slice, point the mouse at one edge of where you want the new cell to begin and drag the mouse to the other edge.

**Book II
Chapter 6**

Using Tables

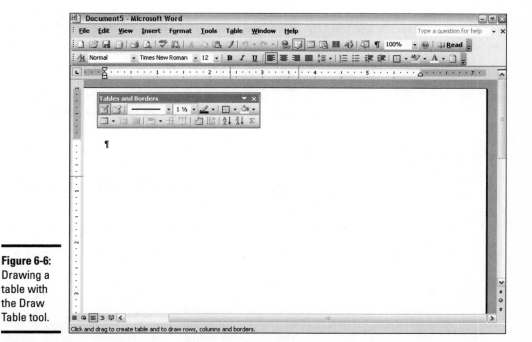

Figure 6-6:
Drawing a table with the Draw Table tool.

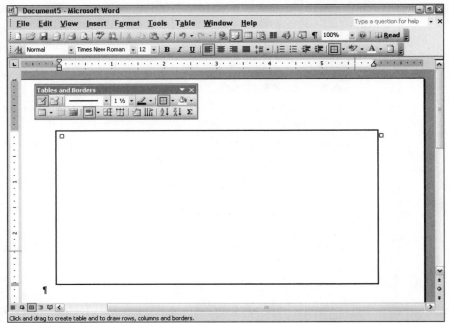

Figure 6-7:
First draw a
rectangle as
the outline
for the table.

4. **If you want to change the line size or style drawn for a particular segment, use the Line Style and Line Weight drop-down controls on the Tables and Borders toolbar.**

You can change the style of a line you've already drawn by tracing over the line with a new style.

5. **If you make a mistake while drawing the table cells, click the Erase (the one that looks like an eraser) button and erase the mistaken line segment.**

Click the Draw Table button if you want to draw additional segments after using the Erase tool.

6. **When you're done, click the Tables and Borders button again to dismiss the Tables and Borders toolbar.**

Figure 6-8 shows a table carved up into several cells, with various types of line style and line weights.

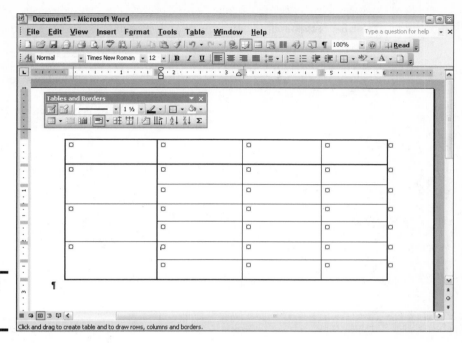

Figure 6-8:
A finished
table.

The Tables and Borders toolbar contains an assortment of tools that you can use not only to draw new tables, but also to work with existing tables. I describe many of these tools in detail in later sections of this chapter. Table 6-1 summarizes the function of each tool on this toolbar.

Table 6-1	The Tables and Borders Toolbar	
Button	**Name**	**What It Does**
	Draw Table	Draws the outline of the table, and then draws line segments to create new cells within a table.
	Erase	Erases line segments to remove cells from a table.
	Line Style	Sets the line style for line segments drawn with the Draw Table tool.
1 ½	Line Weight	Sets the width of line segments drawn using the Draw Table tool.

(continued)

Table 6-1 *(continued)*

Button	Name	What It Does
	Border Color	Sets the color of line segments drawn using the Draw Table tool.
	Outside Border	Shows or hides borders for selected cells.
	Shading Color	Sets the background color for the selected cells.
	Insert Table	Calls up the Insert Table dialog box.
	Merge Cells	Merges adjacent cells to create one large cell.
	Split Cells	Splits a merged cell into separate cells.
	Align	Sets the alignment of the selected cells. Click the down-arrow to reveal alignment types.
	Distribute Rows	Adjusts the height of the selected rows to distribute the rows evenly.
	Distribute Columns	Adjusts the width of the selected columns to distribute the columns evenly.
	Table AutoFormat	Summons the Table AutoFormat dialog box.
	Text Direction	Changes the direction of text in a cell.
	Sort Ascending	Sorts the selected cells in ascending order.
	Sort Descending	Sorts the selected cells in descending order.
	AutoSum	Creates an AutoSum field.

Editing Tables

The following sections describe the procedures for basic table-editing tasks: selecting cells, adding and deleting rows and columns, and changing column width.

Right-clicking table cells

Just about everything you can do to a table cell is accessible on the shortcut menu that appears when you right-click the cell. Different combinations of commands appear depending on whether you select a single cell, a range of cells including an entire column or row, or an entire table.

Moving and selecting in tables

You can move from cell to cell in a table using any of the keyboard shortcuts I list in Table 6-2.

Book II
Chapter 6

Using Tables

Table 6-2	Keyboard Shortcuts for Moving Around in a Table
To Move to This Cell	*Use This Keyboard Shortcut*
Next cell in a row	Tab
Previous cell in a row	Shift+Tab
First cell in a row	Alt+Home
First cell in a column	Alt+Page Up
Last cell in a row	Alt+End
Last cell in a column	Alt+Page Down
Previous row	Up Arrow
Next row	Down Arrow

You can combine the keyboard shortcuts listed in Table 6-2 with the Shift key to extend the selection over a range of cells. In addition, you can select the entire table by placing the insertion point anywhere in the table and pressing Alt+Numeric 5 (the 5 on the numeric keypad).

You can also select various portions of a table using the mouse actions listed in Table 6-3.

Table 6-3	Mouse Actions for Selecting Cells in a Table
To Select This	*Use This Mouse Action*
A single cell	Move the mouse over the left edge of the cell until the mouse pointer becomes a right-pointing arrow, and then click.

(continued)

Table 6-3 *(continued)*

To Select This	Use This Mouse Action
An entire row	Move the mouse just past the left edge of the leftmost cell in the row until the mouse pointer changes to a right-pointing arrow, and then click.
An entire column	Move the mouse just above the topmost cell in the row until the mouse pointer changes to a down-pointing arrow, and then click.
A range of cells	Drag the mouse across the rectangular area of cells you want to select.

Adding rows and columns

To add a new row or column to a table, you use the Table⇨Insert command. Depending on whether you select an individual cell or a range of cells, one or more complete rows, or one or more complete columns, this command appears on the Table menu as Table⇨Insert Cells, Table⇨Insert Rows, or Table⇨Insert Columns.

To add new rows to a table, follow one of these procedures:

✦ To insert a new row within the body of a table, select the row where you want to insert the new row and choose Table⇨Insert Row. The new row inserts above the selected row.

✦ To insert multiple rows, select the number of rows you want to insert and then choose Table⇨Insert⇨Rows Above. The new rows are inserted above the selected rows. For example, Figure 6-9 shows two rows inserted into a table.

Select two rows...

Word Feature	Like It	Hate It	What is It?
Mail Merge	20%	50%	30%
Styles	25%	20%	55%
Templates	10%	5%	85%
Columns	35%	30%	35%
Tables	20%	70%	10%

Then choose Table→Insert→Rows Above.

Figure 6-9: Inserting multiple rows in a table.

Word Feature	Like It	Hate It	What is It?
Mail Merge	20%	50%	30%
Styles	25%	20%	55%
Templates	10%	5%	85%
Columns	35%	30%	35%
Tables	20%	70%	10%

✦ To insert a new row at the bottom of the table, move the insertion point to the last cell in the last row of the table and press the Tab key.

To add new columns to a table, follow one of these procedures:

✦ To insert a new column within the body of the table, select the column where you want to insert the new column and choose Table⇨Insert Column. The new column inserts to the left of the selected column.

✦ To insert several columns, select the number of columns you want to insert and choose Table⇨Insert Column. The new columns insert to the left of the selected columns.

✦ To insert a new column at the right of the table, select the last column in the table. Then, choose Table⇨Insert⇨Columns to the Right.

Inserting cells

Word also allows you to insert individual cells within a table. Start by highlighting the cell or cells where you want to insert the new cells. Then choose Table⇨Insert Cells. The Insert Cells dialog box appears, as shown in Figure 6-10.

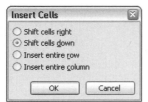

Figure 6-10:
The Insert
Cells dialog
box.

If you want to add new cells above the selected cells and shift the unselected cells in the same rows down, choose the Shift Cells Down option. If you want to insert the new cells to the left of the selected cells, with extra cells being added to the affected rows, choose the Shift Cells Right option. Then click OK.

The magic Insert Cells button

The Insert Table button has a peculiar feature: It changes to different table-related buttons when you select parts of the table. To be specific:

✦ If you select a single cell or a range of cells, the Insert Table button becomes an Insert Cells button. Click it to bring up the Insert Cells dialog box (refer to Figure 6-10).

✦ If you select an entire row of cells or no cells at all, the Insert Table button becomes an Insert Rows button.

✦ If you select an entire column, the Insert Table button becomes an Insert Columns button.

Deleting cells

If you want to delete the contents of one or more cells, select the cells and press the Delete key. The contents of the cells delete, but the cells themselves remain in place.

To completely remove one or more rows or columns from the table, select the rows or columns you want to delete and choose Table⇨Delete. (It appears in the Table menu as either Table⇨Delete Rows or Table⇨Delete Columns.)

To completely remove a range of cells in the table, select the cells you want to remove and choose Table⇨Delete Cells. The Delete Cells dialog box appears, as shown in Figure 6-11.

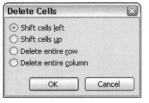

Figure 6-11: The Delete Cells dialog box.

Select whether you want to shift the surrounding cells up or left to fill the void left by the deleted cells or to just delete entire rows or columns, and then click OK.

Adjusting column width

When Word creates a table, it initially makes each column the same width. Having equal columns isn't appropriate for many tables, however, because the data in each column is rarely uniform in size. For example, the first column of a table may contain the names of famous composers, and the second column may list their birthdates. Obviously, the first column is wider than the second.

Fortunately, Word doesn't impose uniform column widths. You can manually adjust the width of each column individually, or you can let Word automatically adjust the width of each column based on the contents of the column.

To adjust the width of an individual column manually, drag the gridline to the right of the column to increase or decrease the column width. Grabbing the gridline so that you can move it is a little tricky, but if you hold the mouse still right on top of it, the mouse pointer changes into a double-beam thingy that indicates you got the gridline.

Alternatively, you can drag the column marker that appears in the ruler. Either way, the width of the columns to the right of the one you adjust automatically adjust so that the width of the entire table remains the same.

If you hold down the Alt key while adjusting column width, the width of each column displays in the ruler.

Another way to change column width is to choose Table⇨Properties and click the Column tab. The dialog box shown in Figure 6-12 then displays.

Figure 6-12:
Manually
setting
column
widths.

From this dialog box, you can set the width of each column to a precise measurement. The Table Properties dialog box shows the column width for one column at a time. Use the Previous Column and Next Column buttons to move from column to column.

Using the AutoFit command

The Table⇨AutoFit command automatically adjusts the size of a table's columns and rows so that you don't have to mess with each column and row separately. The Table⇨AutoFit command has five variations:

✦ **AutoFit to Contents:** Adjusts the size of the cells based on their contents.

✦ **AutoFit to Window:** Used for Web pages to resize the table so that it fits in the browser window.

✦ **Fixed Column Width:** Prevents the table from resizing itself as you type text in the cells.

✦ **Distribute Rows Evenly:** Vertically resizes the rows of the table so that they're all the same height.

✦ **Distribute Columns Evenly:** Adjusts the column widths so that the columns are all the same size.

Formatting Tables

You can format the contents of table cells just as you format any other document text in Word. You can change the font, font size, add bold, italics, and underlines. You can even add borders and shading to individual cells. Most of this formatting is pretty straightforward. The following sections describe the more tricky aspects of formatting tables.

Using tabs in a table

You can set tab stops for individual cells or a range of table cells. Tabs in tables work pretty much the way they do outside of tables, with two important exceptions:

✦ To insert a tab character into a cell, you must press Ctrl+Tab. Simply pressing the Tab key moves you to the next cell without inserting a tab.

✦ If you add a decimal tab to a table cell, the text in the cell automatically aligns over the decimal tab. You do not have to press Ctrl+Tab to move the data to the tab stop.

AutoFormatting a table

The Table⇨Table AutoFormat command spares you the hassle of formatting your tables cell by cell. Although it can't always give you the exact look for your table, it can often bring you close. You can then go back and tweak individual cell formats until your table is perfectly formatted.

To AutoFormat a table, follow these steps:

1. **Create a table using the Insert Table button on the Standard toolbar or Table⇨Insert Table.**

Create the table with the correct number of rows and columns and type in your data. If appropriate, use the first row and column as headings.

2. **Click the mouse anywhere in the table.**

3. **Choose Table⇨Table AutoFormat.**

   The Table AutoFormat dialog box appears, as shown in Figure 6-13.

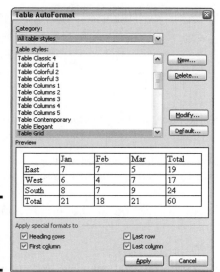

Figure 6-13:
The Table
AutoFormat
dialog box.

4. **Select the table format you like from the Table Styles list.**

   As you scroll through the list of available formats, the Preview box shows how a sample table appears with the format applied.

5. **Select which formatting elements you want applied to the table by checking or unchecking the appropriate boxes.**

   For example, if you don't have headings in the first row (or if you don't want the headings formatted in a special way), uncheck the Heading Rows box.

6. **Click OK.**

You can change the AutoFormat applied to a table at any time. Just click anywhere in the table and choose Table⇨Table AutoFormat again. Or, right-click in the table and choose the Table AutoFormat command.

Merging cells to create headings

If your table requires a heading that spans more than one column, you can use the Table⇨Merge Cells command. For example, Figure 6-14 shows a table in which the cell that contains the heading "Survey Results" is merged so that it spans three columns.

Figure 6-14:
A table
with a
multicolumn
heading.

Word Feature	Survey Results		
	Like It	Hate It	What is It?
Mail Merge	20%	50%	30%
Styles	25%	20%	55%
Templates	10%	5%	85%
Columns	35%	30%	35%
Tables	20%	70%	10%

To create a multicolumn heading, such as the one shown in Figure 6-14, follow these steps:

1. **Create the table as usual. For the heading that will span several columns, type the text into the cell over the first column you want the heading to span.**

2. **Highlight the cells in the row where you want to create a multicolumn heading.**

3. **Choose Table⇨Merge Cells.**

   The cells merge into one gigantic cell that spans several columns.

4. **If you want the heading centered over the cells, click the Center button on the Formatting toolbar or press Ctrl+E.**

If you want to separate cells you merged, select the merged cell and choose Table⇨Split Cells. When Word asks you how many columns to split the cell into, specify the number of columns the merged cell spans.

Designating heading rows

If you have an unusually long table that spans more than one page, you can designate the top row or rows of the table to serve as heading, which duplicate automatically at the top of each page. Select the row or rows you want to use for headings (include the top row of the table in the selection), choose Table⇨Properties, and click the Row tab. See Figure 6-15. Then, select the Repeat as Header Row at the Top of Each Page option. Word duplicates the selected rows at the top of each page where the table appears.

Figure 6-15:
The Table
Properties
dialog box
(Row tab).

Splitting a table

Suppose you create a large table and decide that you want to drop a paragraph or normal text right in the middle of the table, between two of its rows. In other words, you want to divide the table into two smaller tables. To do that, just select the row where you want to divide the table and choose Table⇨Split Table. Word divides the table into two and inserts a blank paragraph between the two tables.

What about splitting a table vertically, creating two side-by-side tables? Unfortunately, you can't split a table vertically in Word. However, you can simulate two side-by-side tables by using an empty table column to create empty space between two separately bordered areas of the table, as shown in Figure 6-16. Here, what appears to be two tables is actually a single table: The space between them is an unused column with no borders or shading.

Figure 6-16:
Creating the
appearance
of two side-
by-side
tables.

RED TEAM
Gilligan
Skipper
Professor
Ginger
Mary Ann
Mr. Howell
Mrs. Howell

BLUE TEAM
Hawkeye
B.J.
Col. Potter
Charles Emerson Winchester III
Radar
Klinger
Margaret

Sorting a Table

You can sort the rows of a table using the Table⇨Sort command. Here is the procedure:

1. **Select the rows you want to sort.**

For the best results, select entire rows, and leave out any heading rows you don't want sorted. Usually, you want to sort the entire table except for headings.

2. **Choose Table⇨Sort.**

The Sort dialog box comes up, as shown in Figure 6-17.

Figure 6-17:
The Sort
dialog box.

3. **Set the column you want to sort the table by and the type of sort you want.**

By default, the Sort dialog box sorts data into ascending sequence based on the first selected column. But you can pick a different column to sort by, or you can choose to sort in descending sequence, and you can tell Word whether the column contains text, numbers, or dates. You can also sort on up to three columns. (This setting tells Word which columns to use to determine the sorted order. Keep in mind that Word keeps rows together when it sorts them.)

4. **If your selection includes a heading row that you do not want sorted, check the Header Row option.**

5. **Click OK.**

Using Table Formulas

If you can't afford a real spreadsheet program, you can use Word tables as sort of a poor-man's spreadsheet. Like a spreadsheet, Word tables let you enter data into rows, columns, and cells. It even lets you perform simple calculations on cells using formulas similar to spreadsheet formulas.

The most common use for formulas in a Word table is to add up a row or column of cells. Here is the procedure:

1. **Select the cell where you want the total to appear.**

2. **Choose Table⇨Formula.**

**Book II
Chapter 6**

The Formula dialog box displays, shown in Figure 6-18.

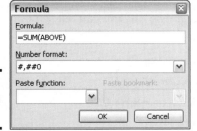

Figure 6-18:
The Formula
dialog box.

Using Tables

3. **Double-check the formula proposed by Word.**

Word takes its best guess at the cells you want to add. If you insert a formula to the right of a row of numbers, Word assumes you want to add up the numbers to the left. If you place it beneath a column of numbers, Word assumes you want to add up the cells above.

4. **Click OK.**

5. **Double-check the results to make sure the numbers add correctly.**

Yes, your computer does know how to add and subtract, but the formula may be set up to calculate the total differently than you expect.

Besides adding up the sum of a range of numbers, Word can perform a whole list of other functions. Table 6-4 summarizes the most common of these functions. In the Formula dialog box, you can use the Paste Function list box to select functions other than Sum.

Table 6-4	Formulas Most Commonly Used in Tables
Formula	*Explanation*
AVERAGE( )	The average of a list of cells.
COUNT( )	The number of items in a list of cells.
MAX( )	The largest value in a list of cells.
MIN( )	The smallest value in a list of cells.
PRODUCT( )	The product of a list of cells (that is, all of the cell values multiplied together).
SUM( )	The sum of a list of cells.

Word formulas use a reference system to refer to individual table cells just like a spreadsheet program. Each column is identified by a letter, starting with A for the first column, B for the second column, and so on. After the letter comes the row number. Thus, the first cell in the first row is A1, the third cell in the fourth row is C4, and so on. You can construct cell references in formulas as follows:

✦ A single cell reference, such as **B3** or **F7.**

✦ A range of cells, such as **A2:A7** or **B3:B13.**

✦ A series of individual cells, such as **A3,B4,C5.**

✦ **ABOVE** or **BELOW** referring to all the cells in the column above or below the current cell.

✦ **LEFT** or **RIGHT**, referring to all the cells in the row to the left or to the right of the current cell.

You can also construct simple math expressions, like **C3+C5*100**. You can use any of the standard mathematical operators:

+	Addition
-	Subtraction
*	Multiplication
/	Division
%	Percent

You can also control the format of numbers that appear in formulas by editing the Number Format field in the Formula dialog box. The Number Format drop-down list includes several predefined formats. If you want, you can create your own number formats using the characters listed in Table 6-5.

Table 6-5	Characters Used to Build Your Own Number Formats
Character	*Explanation*
0 (zero)	Displays a single digit of the result. If the result digit is zero, "0" displays. Use this setting to insure that a minimum number of digits displays. For example, 00.00 displays the value 1.01 as 01.01.
#	Displays a single significant digit of the result, but does not display leading zeros.
x	Used as the right-most digit on the right of the decimal point to round the result value at this digit. Use this setting in the right-most decimal position to display a rounded result.
. (decimal point)	The decimal point.
, (digit grouping symbol)	Separates series of three digits. For example, ##,##0.00.
- (minus sign)	Adds a minus sign to a negative result, or adds a space if the result is positive or 0 (zero).
+ (plus sign)	Adds a plus sign to a positive result, a minus sign to a negative result, or a space if the result is 0 (zero).
%, $, *, and so on	Displays the specified character.
'text'	Adds text to the result. Encloses text in single quotation marks.

You can provide separate number formats for positive, negative, and zero values by separating the number formats with semicolons. For example, **##,##0.00;(##,##0.00)** encloses negative numbers in parentheses. **##,##0.00; (##,##0.00);n/a** displays negative numbers in parentheses and zero values as "n/a."

Converting Text to a Table (And Vice-Versa)

If you have tabular information that you didn't originally enter as a table, you can use the Table⇨Convert Text to Table command to convert the text to a table. Word automatically creates a table for you, making its best guess at how many rows and columns the table contains based on the format of the data you highlighted. This guess is especially useful if the information was originally created outside of Word, for example as a simple text file that used tabs to align information into columns.

To convert text to a table, first highlight the text you want to convert, and then choose Table⇨Convert Text to Table. The dialog box shown in Figure 6-19 displays.

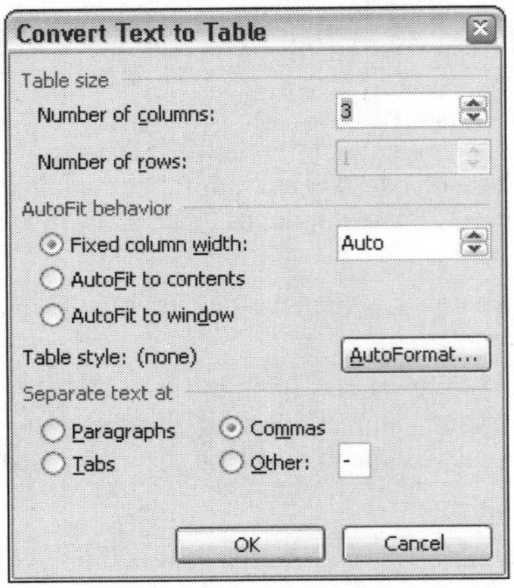

Figure 6-19: Converting text to a table.

The main thing to pay attention to here is the character Word uses to determine what text goes into each cell: tabs, paragraph marks, commas, or any arbitrary character you'd like to use. Word usually deduces the proper character based on the text you highlight, but double-checking it is worth your time.

You can also convert an existing table to text. Select the table you want to convert, and then choose Table⇨Convert Table to Text to summon the dialog box shown in Figure 6-20.

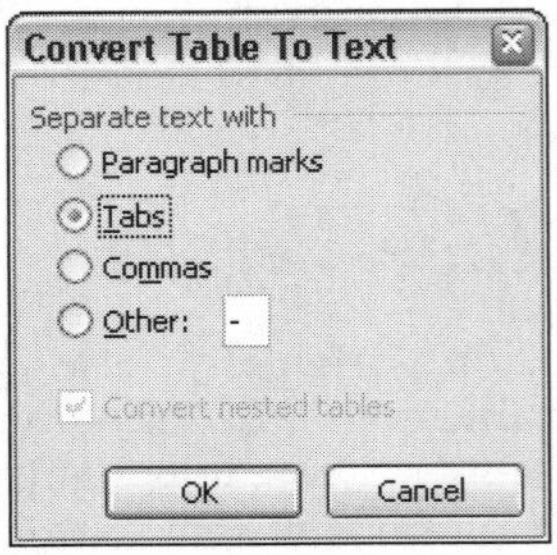

Figure 6-20: Converting a table to text.

Choose whether you want to use paragraph marks, tabs, commas, or some other character to separate the text for each table cell, and then click OK to convert the table to text.

Chapter 7: Creating Lists

In This Chapter

- Creating bulleted lists or numbered lists the easy way
- Allowing Word to automatically format bulleted and numbered lists
- Using deviant bullets
- Using crazy numbering schemes
- Creating an outline list

*B*ullets and numbered lists are great ways to add emphasis to a series of important points or to add a sense of order to items that fall into a natural sequence. Glance through this book and you see what I mean. It's loaded with bulleted and numbered lists.

In Word, you can add a bullet or a line number to each paragraph. The bullet or number is a part of the paragraph format, and Word adds the bullet character or the number so that you don't have to. Word even keeps the numbers in a numbered list in sequence, so if you add or delete a paragraph or rearrange paragraphs in the list, the numbers reorder automatically.

Creating a Bulleted or Numbered List the Easy Way

Nothing is easier than clicking a toolbar button, and that's about all you have to do to create a simple bulleted or numbered list. With the click of a button, you can create a bulleted list like this one:

- Cheery disposition
- Rosy cheeks
- No warts
- Plays games, all sorts

Click another button, and you transform the whole thing into a numbered list:

1. Cheery disposition
2. Rosy cheeks
3. No warts
4. Plays games, all sorts

Do *not* type bullet characters (either asterisks or special Wingdings characters) or numbers yourself. Instead, use the following procedures to create bulleted or numbered lists.

Creating a bulleted list the easy way

To create a bulleted list, follow this procedure:

1. **Type the first item of your list.**

   Don't press the Enter key yet.

2. **Click the Bullet button on the Formatting toolbar.**

   A bullet is added to the paragraph.

3. **Press the Enter key to begin the next item.**

   A new paragraph with a bullet is created.

4. **Type the rest of the list.**

   Press the Enter key between each item of the list. Word automatically adds bullets to each new paragraph.

5. **When you're done, press the Enter key twice in a row.**

   Pressing the Enter key the second time removes the bullet for the last item of the list.

When you create a bulleted list this way, Word uses a default bullet character (normally a small dot) and creates a ¼ inch hanging indent. (If the paragraphs already have hanging indents, the original indentation settings are preserved.) To discover how to use oddball bullets, find the section "Using Deviant Bullets" later in this chapter.

Here are a few additional tricks for bulleting your lists:

✦ To add additional items to the bulleted list, position the cursor at the end of one of the bulleted paragraphs and press Enter. Because the bullet is part of the paragraph format, it is carried over to the new paragraph.

✦ You can also add bullets to existing text. Just select the paragraph or paragraphs you want to riddle with bullets, and then click the Bullet button.

✦ You can remove bullets as easily as you add them. The Bullet button works like a toggle: Press it once to add bullets; press it again to remove them. To remove bullets from an entire list, select all the paragraphs in the list and click the Bullet button.

✦ Ever notice how the good guys never run out of bullets in the movies? Bad idea. The old notion of the six-shooter is a pretty good one. Placing more than six bullets in a row pushes the limits of just about any reader's patience. (Of course, I routinely disregard that advice throughout this book, but what are you going to do, shoot me?)

✦ Oh, and by the way, you probably shouldn't leave one bullet standing by itself. Bullets are used to mark items in a list, and you need more than one item to make a list. ("Army of One" may be a good slogan for the military, but "List of One" is a lousy slogan for this chapter.)

✦ Without doubt, the best way to work with bullets is to create a bullet style. This way, you can customize the bullet style all you want. With a bit of work, you can even mimic the bullets in this book or create your own custom bullet design. Assign a keyboard shortcut such as Ctrl+Shift+B to your custom bullet style, and you're on your way.

Creating a numbered list the easy way

To create a numbered list, follow this procedure:

1. **Type the first item of your list.**

   Don't press the Enter key yet.

2. **Click the Numbering button on the Formatting toolbar.**

   A number is added to the paragraph.

3. **Press the Enter key to begin the next item.**

   A new paragraph with the next number in sequence is created.

4. **Type the rest of the list.**

   Press the Enter key between each item of the list. Word automatically adds numbers to each new paragraph.

5. **When you're done, press the Enter key twice in a row.**

   Pressing the Enter key the second time removes the number for the last item of the list.

When you use the Numbering button to create a numbered list, Word uses a default numbering format and establishes a ¼ inch hanging indent for each paragraph. (If the paragraphs are already formatted with hanging indents, the original indentation settings are kept.) You can use all sorts of crazy numbering schemes if you want; to find out how, skip ahead to the section "Using Crazy Numbering Schemes."

Word is really cool about keeping the list in order. If you add or delete a paragraph in the middle of the list, Word renumbers the paragraphs to preserve the order. If you add a paragraph to the end of the list, Word assigns the next number in sequence to the new paragraph.

You can also apply numbering to existing text. Just select the paragraph or paragraphs you want to number, and then click the Numbering button.

The Numbering button works like a toggle: Click it once to add numbers to paragraphs; click it again to remove them. To remove numbering from a numbered paragraph, select the paragraph and click the Numbering button. To remove numbering from an entire list, select all the paragraphs in the list and click the Numbering button.

Automatic Bullets and Numbers

Word's AutoFormat feature can create bulleted and numbered lists automatically whenever Word determines you are trying to create a bullet or numbered list. Specifically:

✦ Word automatically formats text as a bulleted list whenever you begin a paragraph with an asterisk, period, or hyphen followed by a space or tab.

✦ Word automatically formats text as a numbered list whenever you type a number followed by a period, hyphen, right parenthesis, or greater-than sign (>) and a space or tab.

If you do not want this automatic formatting to occur, call up Tools⇨ AutoCorrect, click the AutoFormat as You Type tab, and uncheck the Automatic Bulleted Lists and Automatic Numbered Lists options.

Using Deviant Bullets

If you don't like the default bullet format you get when you click the Bullet button, change it! Here's how:

1. **Invoke Format⇨Bullets and Numbering.**

   The Bullets and Numbering dialog box appears, as shown in Figure 7-1. This dialog box has four tabs. If the bullet options don't appear, click the Bulleted tab to bring them forth. The Bulleted tab presents seven possible bullet formats.

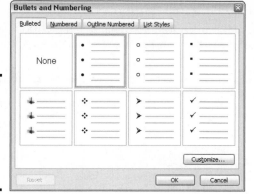

Book II
Chapter 7

Creating Lists

Figure 7-1:
The Bullets and Numbering dialog box (Bulleted tab).

2. **If one of the seven bullet formats shown in the dialog box suits your fancy, click it and then click OK.**

   You're done.

3. **Otherwise, click one of the bullet formats, and then click the Customize button.**

   The Customize Bulleted List dialog box appears, as shown in Figure 7-2.

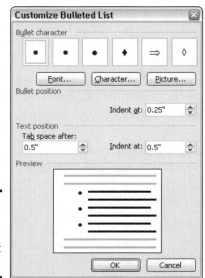

Figure 7-2:
The Customize Bulleted List dialog box.

4. **Modify the bullet format as you see fit.**

Play with the bullet character, font settings, bullet position, and text position. As you play, the preview box shows you how your bulleted list appears.

5. **If you don't like any of the bullet characters shown in the Customize Bulleted List dialog box, click the Character button.**

The Symbol dialog box, shown in Figure 7-3, appears.

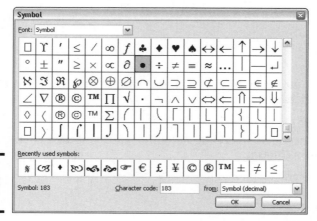

Figure 7-3: The Symbol dialog box.

6. **Pick the bullet character you want; then click OK.**

You can change the fonts displayed by choosing a different font from the Symbols From list box. You find the best bullet characters in the Wingdings font. Click the character you want to use and then click OK.

You can also change the font by clicking the Font button back in the Customize Bulleted List dialog box.

7. **If you'd rather use a picture for a bullet, click the Picture button, choose the bullet image you want to use, and then click OK.**

Figure 7-4 shows the Picture Bullet dialog box, which helps you choose a nice picture to use for your bullets.

8. **OK your way back to the document.**

Keep clicking OK until you get back to your document so that you can see the results of your bullet formatting efforts.

Creating custom bullets is a lot of work, isn't it? Better do it once and then save your bullet in a style. I tell you all about styles in Chapter 3 of this minibook.

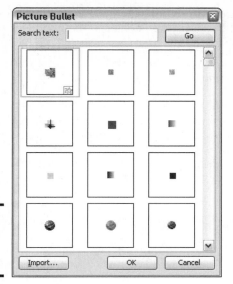

Figure 7-4:
The Picture
Bullet
dialog box.

Keep these points in mind when changing your bullets:

✦ If the characters in the Symbol dialog box seem too small to read, fear not. When you click one of them, Word blows it up about four times normal size so that you can see it.

✦ The Wingdings font (which comes with Windows) is filled with great bullet characters: pointing fingers, smiley faces, grumpy faces, thumbs up, thumbs down, peace signs for folks who were at Woodstock, time bombs, and a skull and crossbones. (Yo ho, yo ho, a pirate's life for me! I love that song more than Johnny Depp does!)

✦ You can apply any font formatting options you want to the bullet character by clicking the Font button, which brings up the normal Font dialog box.

Breaking and Continuing a Numbered List

The Numbered tab of the Bullets and Numbering dialog box includes two options useful in two situations: (1) When you are working with two or more numbered lists that are adjacent to one another; and (2) When you want to insert a non-numbered paragraph in the middle of a numbered list, but you want the list numbering to continue in sequence across the unnumbered paragraph. These options are:

✦ **Restart Numbering:** Use this option when you want to begin a new numbered list, even if the paragraph comes in the middle of an existing numbered list.

✦ **Continue with Previous List:** Use this option when you want a paragraph to continue the numbering from a previous list.

If you are trying to create a new numbered list, but the number for the first paragraph in the list refuses to start at 1, call up Format⇨Bullets and Numbering and select the Restart Numbering option.

On the other hand, if a paragraph in the middle of a list insists on starting with the number 1, try selecting the Continue with Previous List option.

Using Crazy Numbering Schemes

Most of us like to count 1, 2, 3, and so on. But some people count A, B, C, or maybe I, II, III, like a Roman. Not to fear. With Word, you can count just about any way you like.

Follow these prudent steps to create your own crazy numbering schemes:

1. **Invoke Format⇨Bullets and Numbering.**

   The Bullets and Numbering dialog box appears. Figure 7-5 shows the Bullets and Numbering dialog box with the Numbered tab up front. (If the Numbered tab isn't showing, click it.)

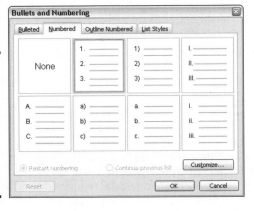

Figure 7-5: The Bullets and Numbering dialog box with the numbering options shown.

2. **If one of the seven numbering formats shown in the dialog box is acceptable, click it; then click OK.**

   You're home free.

3. **Otherwise, select one of the numbering formats and click the Customize button.**

   The Customize Numbered List dialog box appears, as shown in Figure 7-6.

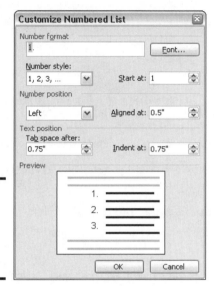

Figure 7-6:
The
Customize
Numbered
List dialog
box.

4. **Modify the numbering scheme to suit your fancy.**

   You can type text to include before and after the number, change the number format, and play with the indentation.

5. **Click OK.**

   Happy numbering!

I wouldn't want to create a number format more than once. Put it in a style so you can call up your hard-earned number format with the touch of a key. I tell you all about styles in Chapter 3 of this minibook.

Keep these points in mind when using numbered lists:

✦ Besides normal number formats like 1, 2, 3 . . . or A, B, C . . . or I, II, III . . .; you can specify One, Two, Three . . .; 1st, 2nd, 3rd; or even First, Second, Third as the number format. Believe it or not, these oddball formats work even with unreasonably long lists. Try it and see for yourself: Word knows how to spell one thousand one hundred eighty-seventh. It also knows that the Roman numeral equivalent is MCLXXXVII. Isn't that amazing?

✦ You can add text that appears before or after the number by typing the text into the Number Format text box. Note that the number itself is shown in the Number Format text box with a gray background.

✦ If you want to specify a different font for the numbers, click the Font button when the Customize Numbered List dialog box appears. The font applies not only to the number, but also to any text that appears before or after the number.

Creating an Outline List

You can create compulsive outline lists that can satisfy even the most rigid anthropology professor using Word's numbering feature. I wouldn't wish this task on anyone, but if you must create these types of lists, this feature is a godsend.

Here's an outline of the procedure for creating a multilevel list (I created my own outline list in the text for a visual example):

1. **Type the text that you want to make into an outline list.**

   • Type the top-level paragraphs as you normally do.

   • Don't worry about numbers yet.

2. **Adjust indentation using the Increase and Decrease buttons to reflect numbering levels.**

   • Use the Increase Indent button to create second- or third-level paragraphs.

   • Use the Decrease Indent button to promote a paragraph to a higher numbering level.

3. **Use Format⇨Bullets and Numbering, and then click the Outline Numbered tab to apply the outline list format.**

   • The Outline Numbered tab of the Bullets and Numbering dialog box appears, as shown in Figure 7-7.

   • Click the outline numbering format that you like.

   • Click OK.

4. **To create a custom outline numbering format, select one of the outline numbered formats, and then click the Customize button.**

   • The Customize Outline Numbered List dialog box appears, as shown in Figure 7-8.

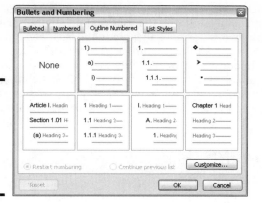

Figure 7-7:
The Outline
Numbered
tab of the
Bullets and
Numbering
dialog box.

Figure 7-8:
The
Customize
Outline
Numbered
List dialog
box.

- This dialog box enables you to customize each level of an outline list.
- The Level box indicates which level is shown. To change levels, move the scroll bar.
- You can format each level as a bullet or a number. Choose the bullet or number format from the Bullet or Number drop-down list box.
- When you have enough, click OK.

Here are some notes on outline lists:

✦ You can create styles for bulleted or numbered lists, but not for outline lists. Too bad.

✦ The outline list feature is good for small lists with two or three levels. But if what you really want to do is create an outline, use the Outline feature instead. See Book VI, Chapter 4 for details on how to create an outline.

✦ Did you notice in the Outline Numbered tab of the Bullets and Numbering dialog box (refer to Figure 7-7) that the four outline numbered formats listed in the second row of formats all include the text "Heading 1," "Heading 2," and "Heading 3" in the outline? These outline number formats work in conjunction with Word's built-in heading styles to format an outline list. Any paragraphs formatted with the built-in heading styles are numbered accordingly in the outline list. (In previous versions of Word, numbered lists based on heading styles was a separate feature.)

Numbering Your Headings

If you want to add numbers to a document's headings, you can do so by modifying the standard heading styles so they use outline numbering. Then, when you apply heading styles to your document's headings, the heading paragraphs number automatically according to the numbering scheme you pick.

Here is the procedure for adding numbering to your heading styles:

1. **Format your document's headings using Word's standard heading styles.**

   That is, Heading 1, Heading 2, and so on.

2. **Choose Format⇨Styles and Formatting.**

   The Styles and Formatting task pane appears.

3. **Point to the Heading 1 style and click the down-arrow to reveal the menu, and then choose Modify.**

   The Modify Style dialog box comes up.

4. **Click the Format button, and then choose Numbering from the menu that appears.**

   The Bullets and Numbering dialog box appears, with the Outline Numbering tab already selected.

5. **Apply the numbering style you want, and then click OK.**

   The Bullets and Numbering dialog box disappears.

6. **Click OK.**

   The Modify Style dialog box disappears.

7. **Repeat Steps 3 through 6 for the other heading styles you want numbered.**

Heading numbering always applies to all of the paragraphs in a document formatted with a given heading style. As a result, you cannot selectively apply it to some heading paragraphs but not to others.

Using Fields to Create Sequence Numbers

Word's numbered lists are great when you have a series of consecutive paragraphs that need sequence numbers. But many documents have lists spread out through the entire document. For example, every chapter in this book has figures numbered consecutively starting with 1. Word's numbered list feature can't help you with this type of list.

Fortunately, Word's field codes feature has a special field called seq that's designed just for this purpose. I refer you ahead to Book VI, Chapter 1, where you can find detailed information about this and other Word field codes.

**Book II
Chapter 7**

Creating Lists

Chapter 8: Working with Footnotes and Endnotes

In This Chapter

- ✔ Adding footnotes
- ✔ Changing the appearance of footnotes
- ✔ Changing the reference marks
- ✔ Changing the footnote separators
- ✔ Finding a footnote reference

*F*ootnotes. Back when I was in college, typing them was a major pain in the derriere[1]. You had to count out the lines just right to make sure you left enough room at the bottom of the page. I never did figure out how to deal with footnote references that fell right at the bottom of the page, too close to the margin to place the note on the same page.

Footnotes are one of the neatest features of word processors, at least while you're in college. After that, they're a pretty useless appendage, unless you happen to work at the college, in which case the footnote feature becomes a source of resentment — just one among many examples of how easy kids have it today. Hmph.

Adding a Footnote

Using footnotes is a snap, unless you want to get fancy with them. Here's the down-and-dirty procedure for adding plain-vanilla footnotes:

1. **Put the cursor where you want the little footnote reference number to appear in your text.**

2. **Call up Insert➪Reference➪Footnote.**

   The Footnote and Endnote dialog box appears, as shown in Figure 8-1. You can choose between footnotes and endnotes (footnotes appear at the bottom of the page on which the footnote reference appears; endnotes print together at the end of the document) and fiddle with numbering options, but usually you just give this dialog box a bothered glance before clicking OK.

[1]Hind part; rear appendage; stern.

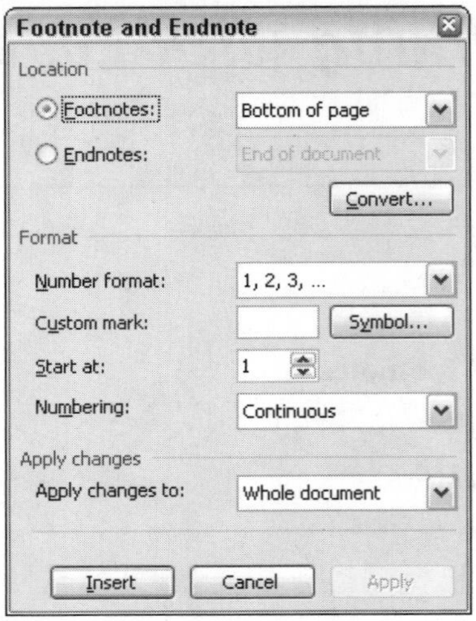

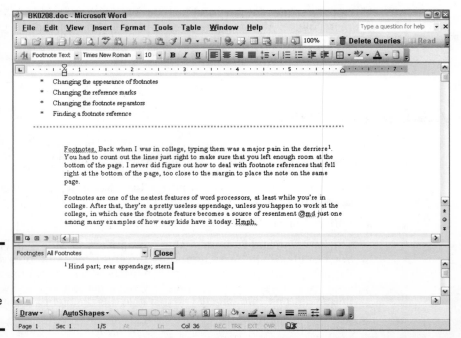

Figure 8-1:
The
Footnote
and Endnote
dialog box.

3. **Click Insert.**

A separate footnote window at the bottom of the screen opens, as shown in Figure 8-2.

Figure 8-2:
Typing a
footnote in
the footnote
window.

4. **Type your footnote in the space provided.**

5. **Click Close when you finish.**

Word automatically numbers footnotes for you. Heck, that's the point. When you insert a footnote, Word adds a little footnote reference number in the text and pairs it with a number in the footnote itself. If you go back later and insert a new footnote in front of an existing one, Word automatically juggles the footnote numbers to keep everything in sync.

Here are some more tips to remember when using footnotes:

✦ For an extra-quick way to create a footnote, use the keyboard shortcut Ctrl+Alt+F. This keyboard shortcut means "Go directly to the footnote window. Do not display the Footnote and Endnote dialog box; do not collect $200."

✦ To look at your footnotes, use View➪Footnotes.

✦ If you start off with endnotes but then decide that you want to convert your endnotes to footnotes (or vice versa), fear not! Just choose Insert➪Reference➪Footnote, click the Convert button in the Note Options dialog box, and click OK to convert your footnotes to endnotes. Click Close to dismiss the Footnote and Endnote dialog box.

✦ If you made a goof in the footnote, double-click the footnote reference in the text. The footnote window pops up and you can fix the note.

✦ To delete a footnote, select its footnote reference number in the text and press the Delete key.

Changing the Footnote Format

The formatting of footnotes is governed by the Footnote Text style. You can change the appearance of all the footnotes in your document by simply modifying the Footnote Text style.

Similarly, you can format footnote reference numbers using the Footnote Reference style. This style is a character style, so it doesn't affect formatting for the entire paragraph.

For details on how to change a style, see Chapter 3 of this minibook.

The initial setting for footnote text is Normal + 10 point. Therefore, footnotes are formatted using the same font as in your Normal paragraphs, except that they are 10 point regardless of the Normal text size. If you want your footnotes to appear in a different font from the rest of the document, change the font for the Footnote Text style.

The initial setting for footnote references is Default Character Format + Superscript. As a result, footnote reference numbers print using the same font as the rest of the text in the paragraph, except that the superscript attribute applies. If you want to see footnote references in a different font, all you have to do is change the Footnote Reference style.

Both footnote text and footnote references automatically apply when you create footnotes, so you shouldn't have any cause to apply these formats directly.

Changing the Reference Marks

Most footnotes are numbered 1, 2, 3, and so on, but Word enables you to change this standard numbering format to use letters, roman numerals, or the special reference symbols *, †, ‡, and §.

Follow these steps to change reference marks:

1. **Summon Insert⇨Reference⇨Footnote.**

The Footnote and Endnote dialog box appears; refer to Figure 8-1.

2. **Choose the Number Format you want.**

This list shows your choices:

> 1, 2, 3 . . .
>
> a, b, c . . .
>
> A, B, C . . .
>
> i, ii, iii . . .
>
> I, II, III . . .
>
> *, †, ‡, § . . .

3. **Click Apply.**

All the footnotes in a section must use the same numbering scheme. You can't mix and match.

If you choose the special symbols *, †, ‡, and § for your reference marks, Word doubles them if necessary to create unique reference marks. The first four footnotes use the symbols singly. The mark for the fifth through eighth notes are **, ††, ‡‡, and §§. After that, the symbols are tripled.

To keep this doubling and tripling of symbols in check, choose the Restart Each Page option in the Note Options dialog box. That way, the mark for the first note on each page is always an asterisk (*). Otherwise, you end up with reference marks like §§§§§§§§§§, which look really silly.

You can bypass Word's automatic footnote-numbering scheme at any time by entering any text you want to use for the mark in the Custom Mark text box in the Footnote and Endnote dialog box. For example, you can specify that an asterisk (*) mark all footnotes. If you want to enter a symbol that's not readily available from the keyboard, click the Symbol button and choose the symbol you want from the resulting Symbol dialog box.

Changing the Footnote Separators

Word automatically adds a short horizontal line called the *footnote separator* to separate footnotes from the text on a page. If the footnote is too long to fit at the bottom of the page, Word automatically continues the footnote to the next page and adds a *footnote continuation separator,* a longer horizontal line. You can customize the appearance of these separators by following this procedure:

1. **Create at least one footnote.**

Don't bother with customized separators for a document that doesn't yet have any footnotes. Word doesn't let you anyway.

2. **Summon View⇨Footnotes.**

The footnote window appears.

3. **In the list box at the top of the footnote window, choose the separator that you want to edit.**

You can choose the footnote separator, the footnote continuation separator, or the footnote continuation notice. (The continuation notice prints beneath a footnote that is being continued to the next page; the continuation separator prints atop the continued note on the next page.)

4. **Edit the separator.**

Delete the horizontal line if you want. Add text, such as "Footnotes," above or below it. Or change the amount of space before or after the separator. Whatever.

5. **Click Close.**

You're finished.

If you mess with a separator and then wish you hadn't, use View⇨Footnotes, choose the separator you messed up, and click the Reset button.

Finding a Footnote Reference

To quickly find the reference mark for a particular footnote or endnote, follow these steps:

1. **Call up Edit⇨Go To.**

Or press Ctrl+G. A dialog box that isn't worthy of a separate figure here displays.

2. **In the Go To What list box, choose Footnote or Endnote.**

3. **In the Enter Footnote Number text box, type the number of the footnote that you want to go to.**

If the notes are numbered with reference symbols (*, †, ‡, and §), type the corresponding number (1, 2, 3, and so on).

4. **Click OK.**

There it is.

Or, for an even easier method, click the Select Browse Object button located near the bottom of the scroll bar on the right edge of the document window. Then choose one of the following buttons from the pop-up menu that appears:

 Browse by endnote

 Browse by footnote

The double-headed up and down arrow buttons that appear above and below the Select Browse Object button change so that they go to the previous and next footnote or endnote, respectively.

Book III

Editing Techniques

The 5th Wave   By Rich Tennant

"It's a ten step word processing program. It comes with a spell-checker, grammar-checker, cliche-checker, whine-checker, passive/aggressive-checker, politically correct-checker, hissy-fit-checker, pretentious pontificating-checker, boring anecdote-checker, and a Freudian reference-checker."

Contents at a Glance

Chapter 1: Getting Around

In This Chapter

✓ Moving around in your document

✓ Figuring out helpful mouse tricks

✓ Playing with the browse control

✓ Working with bookmarks

✓ Charting your course with the document map

✓ Introducing thumbnails

*O*dds are you already know at least some of the basics of getting around a Word document, such as using the arrow keys to move up or down, working the scroll bar, and so on. However, Word offers a plethora of ways to move around your document. This chapter presents the basic document navigation techniques as well as some obscure ones that can come in handy on occasion.

Basic Movement

The most basic way to move around your document is to press the arrow keys to move the insertion pointer around. The four arrow keys move the insertion pointer around as follows:

Key	Where It Goes
←	Back one character
→	Forward one character
↑	Up one line
↓	Down one line

If moving one character or line is too slow for you, you can move the insertion pointer around faster by holding down the Ctrl key while you press the arrow keys. The arrow keys behave as detailed in the following table when you use them in combination with the Ctrl key:

Key	Where It Goes
Ctrl+←	To the previous word
Ctrl+→	To the next word
Ctrl+↑	To the start of the previous paragraph
Ctrl+↓	To the start of the next paragraph

Most computer keyboards actually have two sets of arrow keys. The ones you'll use most are in a little group all by themselves. The second set of arrow keys are on the numeric keypad part of the keyboard. To use those keys, make sure that the Num Lock light is turned off. This light is usually near the top right of the keyboard. If the Num Lock light is on, press the Num Lock key to turn it off.

In addition to the four arrow keys, your keyboard also sports four additional navigation keys located in a group along with the Insert and Delete keys immediately above the arrow keys. The following table describes the functions of these keys when used by themselves and in combination with other keys:

Key	Where It Goes
PageUp	To the previous screen
PageDown	To the next screen
Home	To the beginning of the current line
End	To the end of the current line
Ctrl+PageUp	To the previous browse object
Ctrl+PageDown	To the next browse object
Ctrl+Home	To the beginning of the document
Ctrl+End	To the end of the document

If you're confused by the function of the Ctrl+PageUp and Ctrl+PageDown shortcuts, join the club. These keys work differently depending on the browse object you've selected for use with Word's Go To feature. For more information, see the section "Going Places with Edit⇨Go To" later in this chapter.

Using the Scroll Bar

The scroll bar in Word works pretty much like the scroll bar in other Windows programs. Here are a few of the things you can do with the scroll bar:

✦ Click the arrow buttons at the top or bottom of the scroll bar to scroll the document up or down. The document continues scrolling as long as you hold down the button.

✦ Drag the scroll box (which is sometimes called the *thumb*) to scroll the document up or down. As you drag the scroll box, a balloon appears indicating the current page number to help you gauge your position in the document.

✦ Click the scroll bar above or below the scroll box to scroll up or down one screen at a time. Pressing PageUp or PageDown does the same thing.

✦ Just below the scroll bar is a doohickey called the *browse control,* which consists of a double-arrow pointing up, on top of a button that looks like a marble, on top of a double-arrow pointed down. The browse control is not a part of the scroll bar, but it is used for navigation. For more information, see the section "Just Browsing" later in this chapter.

Scrolling with the scroll bar does *not* move the insertion pointer. When you get to where you want to be, you must click the mouse somewhere on the page to actually move the insertion pointer to that page. If you start typing before you click the mouse, you are instantly transported back to the page where the insertion pointer is, which is where the text you type appears.

Besides the vertical scroll bar, Word also has a horizontal scroll bar that appears at the bottom of the screen. You probably won't ever use it, except maybe when you're working with Word's drawing features and you zoom way in to get a close look at your work. In normal usage, the entire width of your text fits on-screen, so you have no reason to scroll left or right.

Rolling Around with the Mouse Wheel

Newer mice, such as the Microsoft IntelliMouse, have a cool little wheel between the mouse buttons. You can roll the wheel forward or backward, or you can click it as if it were a third mouse button. Word supports the mouse wheel control in the following ways:

✦ You can scroll your document by rolling the wheel, which is equivalent to clicking the up or down arrow buttons in the scroll bar.

✦ You can *pan* the document by pressing and holding the wheel, and then dragging the mouse up or down. When you do so, the document scrolls in the direction you slide the mouse. The farther you drag the mouse, the faster the document scrolls.

✦ You can *autoscroll* the document by clicking the mouse wheel once. The document starts to slowly scroll down and continues to scroll down until you click any mouse button (including the wheel) or press any key. (As with panning, you can increase the speed of autoscrolling by dragging the mouse. The farther you drag the mouse, the faster the document scrolls. You can also reverse the autoscroll direction by dragging the mouse up.)

✦ You can zoom in or out by holding down the control key while rotating the mouse wheel. For fun, hold down the Ctrl key and roll the mouse wheel back and forth to watch your document zoom in and out.

Going Places with Edit⇨Go To

The Go To command is the Word equivalent of the Go Directly To Jail card in Monopoly. This command enables you to jet over to any of several specific locations in your document, without passing Go or collecting $200.

Like anything worth doing in Word, you can call up the Go To command in multiple ways. Here are some of my favorites:

✦ Choose Edit⇨Go To.

✦ Press F5.

✦ Press Ctrl+G.

✦ Double-click the page number in the status bar.

Whichever way you choose, the Go To dialog box appears, as shown in Figure 1-1.

Figure 1-1: The Go To dialog box.

The Go To dialog box is used most often to go to a specific page number. To do that, simply type the page number into the Enter Page Number field, click Go To (the Next button changes to a Go To button the moment you type a page number), and then click Close or press the Esc key to dismiss the Go To dialog box.

Besides going to a specific page, you can also go forward or backwards a certain number of pages. To go forward, type a plus sign followed by the number of pages you want to skip. For example, to go 3 pages forward, type **+3**. To go backward, type a minus sign instead of a plus sign. For example, type **-20** to go backward 20 pages.

In addition, besides going to a specific page, the Go To command enables you to go to a particular section or line, or any of several types of goodies that may reside in your document, such as bookmarks, annotations, footnotes, and so on. To go to something other than a page, just change the setting of the Go To What drop-down list box.

One of the most annoying bugs I found in Word is right here in the Go To dialog box. The problem is that the Go To dialog box stays on-screen after Word finds the page and takes you to it. If you Go To Page 11, you have to press the Esc key to dismiss the Go To dialog box before you can begin working on page 11. Microsoft would probably tell you that it designed the feature that way. I guess they figure that most users, after going to page 11, don't want to do anything to page 11 but want instead to go to page 23, and making them press F5 to call up the Go To dialog box again would be a nuisance. Humperdink! If I were king, the Go To dialog box would disappear after taking you to wherever you want to go instead of sticking around like an unwanted houseguest.

Just Browsing

Just below the vertical scroll bar is a fancy device called the *browse control*. The browse control consists of three buttons. The top and bottom buttons allow you to navigate forward and backwards through your document. Normally, these buttons move your document to the previous or next page. However, you can use the middle button to change the way these buttons work.

When you click the Select Browse Object button (sandwiched between the two double-arrow controls), a menu appears that lets you access several navigation features from one convenient location, as shown in Figure 1-2.

Figure 1-2:
The Select
Browse
Object
menu.

The first two buttons on the second row of this menu invoke the familiar Edit⇨Go To and Find commands. The ten remaining buttons change the unit by which the document is browsed when you click the double up or double down arrow controls immediately above and below the Select Browse Object button. Table 1-1 describes the function of each of the twelve buttons that appear on the Browse menu.

Table 1-1	Options on the Select Browse Object Menu
Button	*What It Does*
{a}	Browse by Word fields
[i]	Browse by endnote
[1]	Browse by footnote
▢	Browse by comments
▢	Browse by section
▢	Browse by page
→	Invokes Edit⇨Go To
🔍	Invokes Edit⇨Find
✎	Browse by edits (works in conjunction with revision tracking)
☰	Browse by headings as indicated by standard heading styles
🖼	Browse by graphic objects
▦	Browse by Word table objects

Yes, You Can Go Back

A funny thing about Word is that it has more than a few useful commands that aren't accessible from the menus or toolbars. One such command is the Go Back command. Most Word users don't know about the Go Back command because they can only access it via its keyboard shortcut, Shift+F5, and if they didn't read the manual, they'd probably never stumble across it on their own. Yet the Go Back command can be very useful. Word remembers the last five locations at which you edited your document, and each press of Shift+F5 returns you to one of those previous editing locations. So if you inadvertently use or misuse one of the navigation commands presented in this chapter and find yourself where you don't want to be, press Shift+F5 to go back to where you were.

I can't tell you how many times I've pressed Ctrl+Z (Undo) to try to undo the effect of an errant navigation command. For example, I accidentally hit Ctrl+End and find myself at the end of the document. Then, I press Ctrl+Z thinking that takes me back to where I was. Unfortunately, Undo doesn't apply to navigation commands. So what happens instead is that the last editing operation I did gets undone. If this misfortune happens to you, just press Ctrl+Y, the magic Redo command, which reinstates the editing undone by your inadvertent use of Ctrl+Z.

Working with Bookmarks

A *bookmark* is a name you assign to a location in a document or to a selection of text so that you can easily return to that location at a later time. Using a bookmark is a safer and more effective method than attempting to fold down the corner of your monitor to mark a page.

To create a bookmark, position the insertion point where you want to place the bookmark and press Ctrl+Shift+F5. If you can't remember Ctrl+Shift+F5, use Insert⇨Bookmark instead. Either way, the Bookmark dialog box appears, as shown in Figure 1-3. Type the name of the bookmark and click the Add button.

Book III
Chapter 1

Getting Around

Bookmark

Bookmark name:

Appendix

Figures
Sources
Tables

Sort by: ● Name ○ Location

☐ Hidden bookmarks

Add | Delete | Go To

Close

Figure 1-3:
Adding a
bookmark.

The bookmark name can include letters and numbers, but no spaces, punctuation, or special symbols except the underscore character (_). The bookmark name must begin with a letter. Notice that the Add button doesn't become active until you start typing a valid bookmark name, and if you type an incorrect bookmark name (for example, if you include a space or any special character except the underscore), the Add button deactivates.

You can create a bookmark for a selection of text rather than for a specific insertion point location, but you usually have little reason to bother selecting the text. If the only reason you are creating the bookmark is to go to it later, don't bother selecting a range of text; just place the insertion point at the location you want to return to and create a bookmark.

After you create a bookmark, you can go to it at any time by pressing Ctrl+ Shift+F5 to call up the Bookmark dialog box, clicking the bookmark you want to go to, and then clicking the Go To button.

You can also go to a bookmark by calling up Edit⇨Go To, selecting Bookmark in the Go To What list, selecting the bookmark in the Enter Bookmark Name drop-down list, and then clicking the Go To button. Going to the bookmark using Ctrl+Shift+F5 is a lot easier, though.

Actually, you don't have to select Bookmark in the Go To What list if you remember the bookmark name. Simply type the bookmark name in the Enter Page Number field and press the Enter key. Word is smart enough to figure out that what you entered was a bookmark, not a page number.

To delete a bookmark, press Ctrl+Shift+F5 to call up the Bookmark dialog box, select the bookmark you want to delete, and then click the Delete button.

Using the Document Map

When you're working with a document that has lots of headings, Word's *document map* feature is especially useful. It displays a list of the document's headings in a separate pane that appears to the left of the document's text, as shown in Figure 1-4. You can instantly navigate to any heading in your document by clicking the heading in the document map.

Because most of the documents I work with have lots of headings (like this chapter, for example), I use the document map a lot. To display the document map, choose View⇨Document Map or click the Document Map button on the Standard toolbar (it's the one that looks like a page with a magnifying class, not to be confused with the Print Preview button, which also happens to look like a page with a magnifying glass).

If you grow weary of the document map, choose View⇨Document Map or click the Document Map button again.

The Document Map button

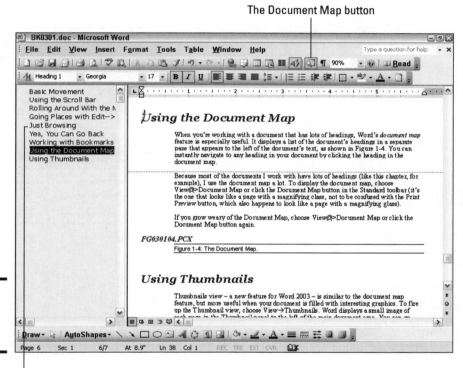

Figure 1-4:
The
document
map.

The Document map

Using Thumbnails

Thumbnails view — a new feature for Word 2003 — is similar to the document map feature, but more useful when your document is filled with interesting graphics. To fire up the Thumbnail view, choose View⇨Thumbnails. Word displays a small image of each page in the Thumbnail panel to the left of the main document area, as shown in Figure 1-5. You can go directly to any page in your document by clicking the page in the Thumbnail panel.

To get rid of the thumbnails, choose View⇨Thumbnails again.

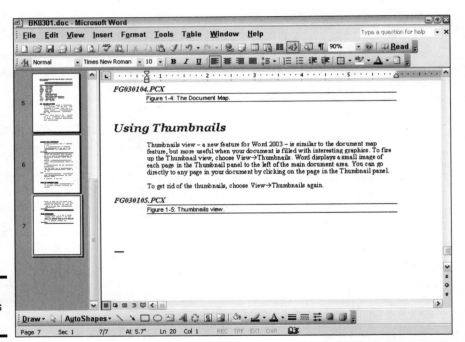

Figure 1-5:
Thumbnails
view.

Chapter 2: Basic Document Editing Techniques

In This Chapter

✔ Watching out for Overtype mode

✔ Selecting text

✔ Deleting text

✔ Copying, cutting, and pasting in many ways

✔ Using the Undo command

✔ Counting your words

✔ Changing text case

If you're like Mary Poppins ("Practically Perfect in Every Way"), you can skip this chapter. Perfect people never make mistakes, so everything they type in Word comes out right the first time. They never have to press Backspace to erase something they typed incorrectly, go back and insert a word they left out, or shuffle their sentences because they didn't write them in the correct order to begin with.

If you're more like Jane ("Rather Inclined to Giggle; Doesn't Put Things Away"), Michael ("Extremely Stubborn and Suspicious"), or me ("Not Sure Why He's Here"), you probably make mistakes along the way. This chapter shows you how to go back and correct those mistakes.

Reviewing your work and correcting it if necessary is called *editing*. Editing is not a fun job, but it has to be done. A spoonful of sugar usually helps.

Avoiding the Evil Overtype Mode

Word has an evil editing feature called *Overtype mode*. When you're in Overtype mode, any text you type obliterates text on-screen. For example, move the insertion pointer to the beginning of this paragraph, switch to Overtype mode, and type the letter G to change "Word" to "Gord." In Overtype mode, typing a character replaces the character at the insertion pointer with the character you type.

I have no idea why you would ever want to do that. As far as I can tell, Overtype mode has no logical reason to even exist, except perhaps as a cruel joke. The only reason I even bring it up here is that you may fall into Overtype mode by accident. If that happens, don't panic. I've heard of people who sold their computers because they fell into Overtype mode by accident and couldn't get out.

Most likely, the way you got into Overtype mode was by pressing the Insert key, thinking it may do something useful like insert something. Fortunately, you can get back to normal mode (which, by the way, is technically called *Insert mode*) by pressing the Insert key again.

When you're in Overtype mode, the letters OVR appear in boldface in the status bar. If you like secret double-click tricks, here's a good one: You can double-click directly on the letters OVR to switch between Overtype and Insert mode.

Selecting Text with the Mouse and Keyboard

One of the most basic editing skills is selecting text. After you select some text, you can delete it, copy it, move it, apply formatting to it, change its capitalization, and do all sorts of other neat stuff to it.

The easiest way to select text is by dragging the mouse over the text you want to select. You can also use the following mouse actions to select text:

✦ Another way to select a block of text with the mouse is to click at the start of the block, hold down Shift, and click at the end of the block. This action selects all text in-between the clicks.

✦ To select a single word, double-click the mouse anywhere on the word. Click, click.

✦ To select an entire paragraph, triple-click the mouse anywhere on the paragraph. Click, click, click.

✦ To select an entire sentence, hold down Ctrl and click the mouse anywhere in the sentence.

✦ To select a column of text, hold down Alt, press and hold the left mouse button, and drag. Drag the mouse left or right to increase or decrease the width of the column selected, and drag the mouse up or down to extend the column up or down. (This technique is especially useful if you arrange text into columns by using tabs and you want to rearrange the columns.)

Using the invisible selection bar

Way off to the left of your text is an invisible, secret region of the Word screen that is officially called the *selection bar.* To find it, slide the mouse over towards the left edge of the screen until the mouse pointer turns into a right-pointing arrow. When the mouse pointer changes, say "Gotcha!" quickly so Word knows you're up to its game.

Here are a few selection tricks that use the selection bar:

✦ Click the selection bar once to select an entire line of text. Click.

✦ Double-click the selection bar to select an entire paragraph. Click, click.

✦ Triple-click the selection bar to select the entire document. Click, click, click.

✦ To select several paragraphs, double-click the selection bar to select the first paragraph, hold the mouse button down after the second click, and drag the mouse up or down the selection bar to select additional paragraphs.

Selecting with the keyboard

If you are allergic to the mouse, you can use the keyboard shortcuts summarized in Table 2-1 to select text.

**Book III
Chapter 2**

Table 2-1	Keyboard Shortcuts for Selecting Text
Keyboard Shortcut	*What It Does*
Ctrl+A	Select entire document.
Ctrl+NumPad5	Select entire document.
Alt+NumPad5	Select entire table. (NumLock must be off for this shortcut to work.)
Shift key	If you hold down the Shift key, the selection extends as you move the insertion pointer by using the arrow keys.
F8	Places Word in Extend mode, which lets you extend the selection by using the arrow keys without holding down the Shift key.
Ctrl+Shift+F8	Extends a column selection, similar to using the Alt key with the mouse.

After you press F8 to enter Extend mode, you can press it again to select the current word (like double-clicking). Press it a third time to select a sentence. Press it a fourth time to select the entire paragraph, and a fifth time to select the entire document.

To turn off Extend mode, press the Escape key.

Selecting cells in a table

If you create a table, you can use the following tricks to select individual cells, columns, or rows:

✦ To select a cell, click the mouse in the cell. To select several cells, hold down the left mouse button and drag the mouse across the cells you want to select.

✦ To select an entire column, click the top gridline of the column. The mouse pointer changes to a down arrow when it's in the right position to select the column. You can select several columns by dragging the mouse in this position.

✦ To select an entire row, click the selection bar to the left of the row. To select several rows, drag the mouse in the selection bar.

Deleting Text

Deleting text is one of the basics of good editing. Some people think they're such good writers that they shouldn't have to delete anything. Not me. I delete about half of what I write. And that's probably not enough.

Word has many ways to delete text. The most basic deletion technique is to delete characters one at a time using one of these two keys:

✦ **Backspace:** Deletes the character to the left of the insertion pointer.

✦ **Delete:** Deletes the character to the right of the insertion pointer.

If you immediately catch a typing mistake, use the Backspace key to obliterate it, and then type the correct text. The Delete key is more appropriate when you discover your mistake a few moments after the fact. Then, you can move the insertion pointer to the text in error, use the Delete key to erase the mistake, and then type the correct text.

You can also use the Backspace and Delete keys in combination with the Ctrl key to delete whole words. The same distinction between Backspace and Delete applies when you use the Ctrl key: Ctrl+Backspace deletes the previous word; Ctrl+Delete deletes the next word.

Note: Ctrl+Backspace and Ctrl+Delete work best when the insertion pointer is positioned between words. If the insertion pointer is in the middle of a word, Ctrl+Backspace and Ctrl+Delete delete only part of the word. Ctrl+Backspace deletes everything from the insertion pointer to the beginning of the word and Ctrl+Delete deletes everything from the insertion pointer to the end of the word.

If you select text before you use the Backspace or Delete key, the forward and backward distinction between these two keys fades into the distance. With text selected, both the Backspace and the Delete key simply delete the selected text. You can use this ability to delete large amounts of text with one blow. For example:

✦ To delete a sentence, hold down the Ctrl key and click the mouse in the sentence to select it, and then press Delete or Backspace.

✦ To delete a paragraph, triple-click the paragraph to select it, and then press Delete or Backspace.

✦ To delete the entire document (an act of extreme desperation, I would think), press Ctrl+A to select the entire document and then press Delete or Backspace.

If you become overzealous with the Delete or Backspace key, you can restore your smitten text by pressing Ctrl+Z to summon the Undo command. For more information, see the section "The Magic of Undo and Repeat" later in this chapter.

Copy, Cut, and Paste

Copying, cutting, and pasting are the basic editing operations not only in Word, but in all Windows applications. These operations rely on a special storage area called the *Clipboard,* which Windows uses to temporarily stash information you copy or cut so that you can paste that information to another location.

You can access the Copy, Cut, and Paste commands from the Edit menu, or from the Standard toolbar. However, these commands are important enough that you should endeavor to commit their keyboard shortcuts to memory. Table 2-2 lists the keyboard shortcuts for the Copy, Cut, and Paste commands.

Table 2-2	The Three Most Important Word Keyboard Shortcuts
Keyboard Shortcut	*What It Does*
Ctrl+C	Copies the selected text to the Clipboard.
Ctrl+X	Cuts the selected text to the Clipboard. The original text is removed from the document.
Ctrl+V	Pastes the contents of the Clipboard at the insertion point.

Memorizing these keyboard shortcuts will prove worth the effort. Not only do they save you time when working in Word, you'll soon discover that just about all Windows programs — including Windows itself — honor these three keyboard shortcuts.

If you have trouble remembering these shortcuts, consider first that they are positioned adjacent to one another on the bottom row of the keyboard. Then consider the following memory aids:

* **Ctrl+X:** The X is reminiscent of the X drawn to cross out something you want removed.

* **Ctrl+C:** The C is short for Copy.

* **Ctrl+V:** The V is reminiscent of a proofreading mark (a caret, ^) that indicates where something should be inserted.

If the preceding memory aids don't help, have these shortcuts tattooed on the back of your hand. That way, you can see them as you type.

Using the Clipboard Task Pane

The Clipboard task pane is a nifty feature that lets you gather up to 24 different items of text or graphics from Word or any other Office application (such as Excel or PowerPoint), and then selectively paste them into your document. Figure 2-1 shows the Clipboard task pane in action.

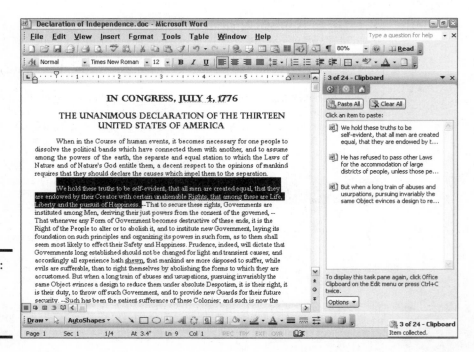

Figure 2-1:
The Clipboard task pane in action.

You can summon the Clipboard task pane in several ways so that you can work with the items you add to the Clipboard:

✦ Choose Edit⇨Office Clipboard

✦ Press Ctrl+C twice

✦ Copy or cut two items consecutively, without doing anything else in between

To paste an item from the Clipboard task pane, first click to mark the location in the document where you want to insert the item, and then click the item in the Clipboard that you want to insert.

If you like everything you copied to the Clipboard, you can paste it all into your document in one swell foop by clicking the Paste All button. You find this button lurking near the top of the Clipboard task pane.

To remove an item from the Office Clipboard, right-click the item and choose Delete from the menu that appears. To clear out everything from the Clipboard, click the Clear All button that appears near the top of the Clipboard task pane.

Dragging and Dropping

Drag-and-drop editing (or *dragon dropping*) helps you to move text from one location in a document to another by using only the mouse, without using the Clipboard. You simply highlight the text you want to move and use the mouse to drag the text to a new location. When you release the mouse button, the text is cut from its original location and pasted to the new location.

If you hold down the Ctrl key while dragging text, you can copy the text, instead of moving it, to the new location. In other words, the text is not deleted from its original location.

You can drag and drop text between two open documents, which is easier if both documents are visible on-screen. To ensure that both documents are visible, use Window⇨Arrange All. To drag text from one open document to another without rearranging your windows, try this technique:

1. **Select the text you want to drag to another document.**

2. **Press and hold the mouse button.**

3. **While still holding down the mouse button, press Alt+Tab to switch to the document you want to drop the text into.**

Note: You may have to press Alt+Tab more than once to switch to the right document.

4. **While still holding down the mouse button, drag the text to the location where you want to drop it.**

5. **Release the mouse button to drop the text.**

By my reckoning, this way is more trouble than it is worth. I'd put my money on simple copy and paste (Ctrl+C and Ctrl+V) any day.

Before you step in the dragon dropping, consider the following:

✦ If you don't like this feature — and you may well find that you don't — you can disable it via Tools➪Options. Select the Edit tab and then uncheck the Drag-and-Drop Text Editing check box.

✦ On the other hand, if you can't get the dragon drop technique to work, check the Tools➪Options command Edit tab to make sure that the Drag-and-Drop Text Editing check box is checked.

The Magic of Undo and Repeat

The Undo command is one of the best ways to become a Word guru. Without the Undo command, you would be afraid of experimenting with Word for fear of losing your document. But with this command at hand, you can try anything you want, knowing that the worst that can happen is that you may have to use the Undo command to undo your mistake.

You can access the Undo command from the Edit menu (Edit➪Undo), but Undo is used frequently enough that you should simply memorize its keyboard shortcut: Ctrl+Z. While you're at it, go ahead and memorize Ctrl+Y, the keyboard shortcut for an almost equally useful command: Repeat. Table 2-3 summarizes these shortcuts.

Table 2-3	Two More Keyboard Shortcuts You Should Memorize
Keyboard Shortcut	*What It Does*
Ctrl+Z	Undoes the previous action.
Ctrl+Y	Repeats the previous action. If the previous action was Undo, Ctrl+Y redoes the undone action.

The Repeat command, as its name implies, repeats the last action. If you just used Format➪Font to make a bevy of formatting changes all at once, select some other text that you want similarly formatted and then press Ctrl+Y. By using this Repeat command, you can apply the same formats to the other text.

The Repeat command repeats just about any action you can do in Word. But when the most recent command is Undo, the Repeat command becomes the Redo command: It redoes the action undone by the Undo command. Undo and Redo are a perfect combination for people who can't decide whether they like something or not.

Word keeps track of more than one recent action. In fact, you can undo hundreds of recent actions. I don't think undoing more than one or two at a time is a good idea, but who am I to second-guess what you do with Word. To undo more than one action at a time, click the down-arrow of the Standard toolbar's Undo button to reveal a list of all the undoable actions. Drag the mouse to select the actions you want to undo, as shown in Figure 2-2. Then, release the mouse to undo them all.

Figure 2-2:
Undoing
more than
one
command.

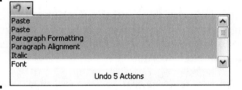

Paste
Paste
Paragraph Formatting
Paragraph Alignment
Italic
Font

Undo 5 Actions

The Redo button on the Standard toolbar has a similar capability to redo recently undone actions.

Word and Character Counts

An important part of editing is knowing how long your document is. Trust me, I know. When a magazine editor says she needs a 1,750-word article on the mating habits of Australian slugs, she means 1,750 words. Don't try to cheat by delivering an article of only 1,749 words. You won't get paid.

To find out whether you've written enough or too much, all you have to do is pop up Tools⇨Word Count. The Word Count dialog box displays, shown in Figure 2-3, loaded with all the information you need.

Word Count

Statistics:

Pages	8
Words	2,876
Characters (no spaces)	13,435
Characters (with spaces)	16,226
Paragraphs	128
Lines	263

☐ Include footnotes and endnotes

[Show Toolbar] [Close]

Figure 2-3:
Oops, this
document
is way too
long.

Note: A check box allows you to include footnotes and endnotes in the count.

Changing Case

The Format➪Change Case command is useful when you want to change the case of a sentence, paragraph, or other arbitrary selection of text. For example, you can use it to capitalize an entire selection, just the first letter of the selection, or the first letter of each word.

Personally, I think Microsoft made a mistake placing the Change Case command on the Format menu. I would have placed it on the Edit menu instead. All the other commands on the Format menu change the appearance of your text. But the Change Case command actually changes your text by selectively changing lowercase letters to uppercase, and vice versa.

To use the Format➪Change Case command, follow these steps:

1. **Select the text whose case you want to change.**

2. **Choose Format➪Change Case.**

The Change Case dialog box, shown in Figure 2-4, appears.

3. **Pick the capitalization option you want to apply to the selection.**

The options in this dialog box are pretty self-explanatory, except the toggle case option. It changes all uppercase letters to lowercase, and vice versa. For example, if you select the text "Click OK" and apply toggle case to it, the text transforms to "cLICK ok."

4. **Click OK.**

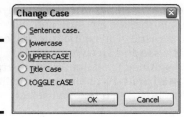

Figure 2-4:
The Change
Case dialog
box.

An easier way to change case is to use the keyboard shortcut Shift+F3. Each time you press Shift+F3, Word "cycles" through a different case option. As a result, you can just keep pressing Shift+F3 until the text is capitalized the way you want.

The programmers at Microsoft decided that they could try to anticipate the type of case change you want to make based on how much text you select. If you select less than a complete sentence, the Shift+F3 shortcut alternates among the following options:

> all lowercase
>
> ALL UPPERCASE
>
> Initial Capital Letters (Title Case)

If you select more than one full sentence, Shift+F3 alternates among a *different* set of options:

> all lowercase
>
> ALL UPPERCASE
>
> First capital letter (Sentence case)

This shortcut might seem to make sense at first, but unfortunately it doesn't deal well with headings, which are typically one sentence or less. For headings, Shift+F3 would be better if it alternated among the following options:

> ALL UPPERCASE
>
> First capital letter (Sentence case)
>
> Initial Capital Letters (Title Case)

Unfortunately, Word insists on throwing headings into the one-sentence-or-less category because headings do not include a period and therefore are never longer than one sentence. As a result, you cannot quickly convert a heading from Sentence Case to Title Case and vice versa. Frankly, Shift+F3 would be much more useful if Microsoft had tried not to anticipate what type of case you wanted and simply allowed Shift+F3 to always cycle through all of the case options without regard to how much text you select.

Chapter 3: Finding and Replacing

In this chapter, I show you how to use two of Word's most useful commands: Find and Replace. The Find command enables you to locate specific text in your document. For example, you may remember that somewhere in your 200-page report you discussed the famous Bandersnatch, but you can't recall exactly where. So you fire up the Find command and ask it to find the first mention of Bandersnatch in your document.

You may then decide that whenever you mention the Bandersnatch, you should add the word *Frumious*. So you then summon the Replace command to replace all occurrences of "Bandersnatch" with "Frumious Bandersnatch." See? I told you these commands are useful.

Using the Find Command

The Edit⇨Find command enables you to search for text anywhere in your document. The command also lets you search for specific formats, such as a particular font or style, and for special symbols, such as paragraph marks or annotations.

You summon the Find command by choosing Edit⇨Find from the menu or by pressing Ctrl+F. Unfortunately, the Find command has no toolbar button, but you can add one if you're willing to customize your toolbars. Word even supplies a predefined toolbar button image that looks like a set of binoculars. For information about customizing the toolbars, see Book VIII, Chapter 2.

However you invoke it, the Find command displays the Find dialog box, as shown in Figure 3-1. The following sections explain how to use this dialog box for various and sundry searches.

Find and Replace

Find | Replace | Go To

Find what: | Bandersnatch

☐ Highlight all items found in:

Main Document

More ≭ | Find Next | Cancel

Finding missing text

You can use the Edit⇨Find command to find text anywhere in a document. Just follow these steps:

1. **Choose Edit⇨Find or press Ctrl+F to summon the Find dialog box.**

   Refer to Figure 3-1 for a glimpse of this dialog box.

2. **Type the text you want to find in the Find What field.**

   For example, **Bandersnatch**.

3. **Click the Find Next button.**

4. **Wait a second while Word searches your document.**

   When Word finds the text, it highlights that text on-screen. The Find dialog box remains on-screen so that you can click Find Next to find yet another occurrence of the text.

5. **Stop when you see the message indicating that no more occurrences of the text are found.**

Here are a few pointers to using the Find command more efficiently:

✦ Word starts searching from the current position of the insertion pointer. If it reaches the end of the document without finding your search text, a dialog box appears asking whether you want to continue searching from the start of the document. Click Yes to continue your search.

✦ You can click the Find Next button to repeat the search to find additional occurrences of your search text.

✦ If Word doesn't find the search text, check your spelling. You may have spelled it wrong in the Find dialog box.

✦ You can bail out of the Find dialog box at any time by clicking Cancel or pressing the Esc key.

✦ Ctrl+F is the shortcut key for the Find command.

Advanced Searches

To gain additional control over the Find operation, click the More button. The dialog box expands to the larger form shown in Figure 3-2. The following sections explain the advanced search options available when you click the More button.

You can shrink the expanded Find dialog box down to size by clicking the Less button.

Figure 3-2:
Clicking the More button shows additional search options.

Changing the search direction

You can change the direction of Word's search by changing the setting in the Search drop-down box. Three choices are available:

✦ **All:** Searches the entire document without regard to the position of the insertion point.

✦ **Down:** Starts the search at the position of the insertion point and searches forward toward the end of the document.

✦ **Up:** Searches backward from the insertion point, toward the beginning of the document.

Both the Down and Up options search until they reach the bottom or top of the document; then they ask whether you want to continue searching the rest of the document.

Refining your findings

The check boxes at the bottom of the expanded Find dialog box let you refine your searches in sometimes helpful ways, as described in the following sections.

Matching case

Check the Match Case check box before beginning the search if it matters whether the text appears in uppercase or lowercase letters. This option is handy when you have, for example, a document about Mr. Smith the blacksmith.

Finding whole words

Speaking of Mr. Smith the blacksmith, use the Find Whole Words Only check box to find your text only when it appears as a whole word. If you want to find the text where you talk about Mr. Smith the blacksmith's mit, for example, type **mit** in the Find What text box and check the Find Whole Words Only check box. That way, the Find command looks for *mit* as a separate word and doesn't show you all the *mit*s in *Smith* and *blacksmith*.

Using wildcards

Check the Use Wildcards check box if you want to include wildcard characters or other search operators in the Find What field. Table 3-1 summarizes the search operators you can use if you select this option.

Table 3-1	Advanced Search Operators for the Find Command
Operator	*What It Does*
?	Finds a single occurrence of any character. For example, f?t finds fat or fit.
*	Finds any combination of characters. For example, b*t finds any combination of characters that begins with b and ends with t, such as bat, bait, ballast, or bacteriologist.
#	Any numerical digit.
[abc]	Finds any one of the characters enclosed in the brackets. For example, b[ai]t finds bat or bit, but not bet or but.
[a-c]	Finds any character in the range of characters enclosed in the brackets. For example, b[a-e]t finds bat or bet, but not bit or but.
[!abc]	Finds any character except the ones enclosed in the brackets. For example, b[!ai]t finds bet or but, but not bat or bit.
@	Finds one or more occurrences of the preceding character. For example, 10@ finds 10, 100, or 1000.

Operator	What It Does
{n}	Specifies the preceding character must be repeated exactly n times. For example, 10{2} finds 100, but not 10 or 1000.
{n,}	Specifies the preceding character must be repeated at least n times. For example, 10{2,} finds 100 or 1000, but not 10.
{n,m}	Specifies the preceding character must be repeated from n to m times. For example, 10{2,3} finds 100 or 1000, but not 10 or 10000.
<	Finds the following text only if it appears at the beginning of a word. For example, <pre finds predestined and prefabricated, but not appreciate or apprehend.
>	Finds the preceding text only if it appears at the end of a word. For example, ing> finds interesting and domineering, but not ingenious or ingest.

First word, short, sounds like . . .

Check the Sounds Like check box if you're not sure exactly how to spell the text for which you're searching. Word can search for words that are pronounced the same as the word you're searching for. For example, if you search for **your** with the Sounds Like option on, Word stops when it finds *you're*. Don't expect too much from this option, however. For example, if you typed **low** in the Find What field, you'd expect the option to find *Lowe* (well, *I* would anyway). But it doesn't.

Finding all word forms

If you select the Find All Word Forms check box, Word looks for alternate forms of most verbs. For example, if you search for **run**, Word finds *runs, running,* and *ran.* And the program is smart enough to know about certain oddball words such as go: If you search for **go**, Word finds not only *goes, going,* and *gone,* but also *went.* Searching for **be** finds *is, was, am, were, being,* and *been.*

Don't expect miracles, however. Find All Word Forms doesn't pick up every imaginable word form, especially where nouns are concerned. For example, a search for **introduction** doesn't pick up *introductory,* and **religion** doesn't catch *religious.* Find All Word Forms is more adept at finding alternate word forms for verbs than for nouns.

Finding formats

To find specific types of formatting, choose the Edit➪Find command or press Ctrl+F, and then click the More button to display the advanced search options; refer to Figure 3-2. Click the Format button and choose the type of format you want to search for from the pop-up menu. The following options are available:

**Book III
Chapter 3**

**Finding and
Replacing**

+ **Font:** Enables you to search for specific font formatting. You can search for specific fonts or for font formatting, such as bold, italics, font size, and so on.

+ **Paragraph:** Enables you to search for specific paragraph formatting, such as indentation and alignment.

+ **Tabs:** Enables you to search for paragraphs with specific tab settings.

+ **Language:** Enables you to search for paragraphs formatted for a particular language.

+ **Frame:** Enables you to search for specific frame formatting.

+ **Style:** Enables you to search for paragraphs formatted with a particular style.

+ **Highlight:** Enables you to search for highlighted text.

Make sure that the Find What field itself is blank; otherwise, the Find command searches for specific text formatted with the style you specify.

Finding special characters

You can also use the Find command to search for special characters such as em dashes or annotation marks. Call up the Find command (Edit⇨Find or Ctrl+F), click the More button to reveal the advanced Find options, and then click the Special button to reveal a list of special characters that you can search for, as shown in Figure 3-3. Select the character you want to search for and click Find Next to begin the search.

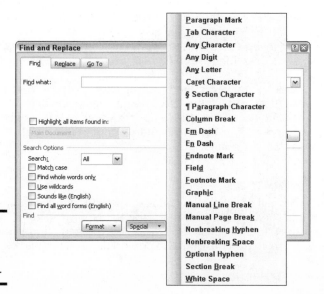

Figure 3-3:
Searching for special characters.

When you select a special character, Word inserts a code into the Find What text box. If you know the code, you can bypass the Special button and its huge menu by typing the code directly into the Find What field. Table 3-2 summarizes the codes.

Table 3-2	Search Codes for Special Characters
Character	*Code*
Paragraph mark	^p
Tab character	^t
Comment mark	^a
Any character	^?
Any digit	^#
Any letter	^$
Section character	^%
Paragraph character	^v
Caret character	^^
Column break	^n
Em dash	^+
En dash	^=
Endnote mark	^e
Field	^d
Footnote mark	^f
Graphic	^g
Manual line break	^l
Manual page break	^m
Nonbreaking hyphen	^~
Nonbreaking space	^s
Optional hyphen	^-
Section break	^b
White space	^w

Replacing Text

You can use the Edit⇨Replace command to replace all occurrences of one bit of text with other text. The following steps show you the procedure:

1. **Choose Edit⇨Replace or press Ctrl+H.**

The Replace dialog box appears, as shown in Figure 3-4.

Find and Replace

| Find | Replace | Go To |

Find what: Bandersnatch

Replace with: Frumious Bandersnatch

More ▼   Replace   Replace All   Find Next   Cancel

Figure 3-4:
The Replace
dialog box.

2. **Type the text you want to find in the Find What text box.**

   For example, **Bandersnatch**.

3. **Type the text you want to substitute for the Find What text in the Replace With text box.**

   For example, **Frumious Bandersnatch**.

4. **Click the Find Next button.**

   When Word finds the text, it highlights that text on-screen.

5. **Click the Replace button to replace the text.**

6. **Repeat the Find Next and Replace sequence until you finish.**

If you're absolutely positive that you want to replace all occurrences of your Find What text with the Replace With text, click the Replace All button. Taking this step automatically replaces all remaining occurrences of the text.

Replace All can be dangerous. You're bound to encounter at least one spot where you don't want the replacement to occur. Replacing the word **mitt** with **glove**, for example, changes *committee* to *comgloveee* (imagine the confusion *that* could cause).

As for the Find command, you can click the More button to expand the dialog box so that additional options are visible, as shown in Figure 3-5. You can then use the Match Case, Find Whole Words Only, Use Wildcards, Sounds Like, and Find All Word Forms options. The last option is even smart enough to properly replace alternate word forms with the correct version of the replacement text. For example, if you replace **run** with **walk**, Word replaces *running* with *walking* and *ran* with *walked*.

Because Word is not 100-percent confident in its capability to properly replace all alternate word forms, you get a warning message if you select the Find All Word Forms option and click Replace All. Find All Word Forms is tricky enough that you should verify each replacement.

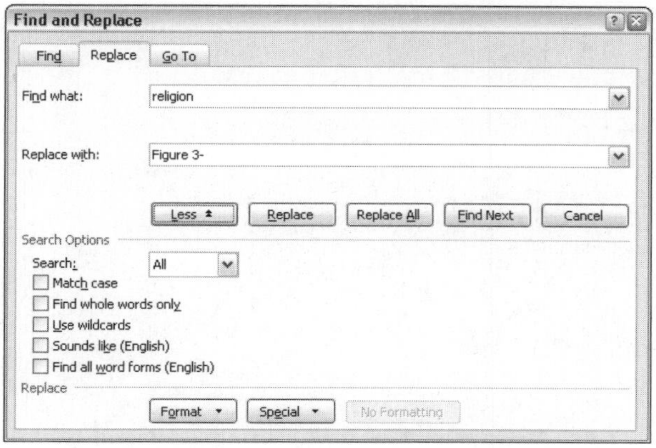

Figure 3-5:
Advanced
options for
the Replace
command.

Chapter 4: All About AutoCorrect and Its Siblings

In This Chapter

- ✔ Utilizing AutoCorrect
- ✔ Formatting with AutoFormat
- ✔ AutoFormatting as you type
- ✔ Inserting AutoText
- ✔ Creating smart tags

T his chapter covers several advanced editing features of Word that are available from Tools⇨AutoCorrect. These features include AutoCorrect itself as well as several similar features: AutoFormat, AutoFormat As You Type, AutoText, and Smart Tags. Depending on the type of documents you create, these features may or may not prove invaluable.

Using AutoCorrect

AutoCorrect is a Word feature that monitors your typing, carefully watching for common typing mistakes and fixing them quicker than you can say "Bob's Your Uncle." For example, type **adn** and AutoCorrect changes it to *and.* Typing **teh** becomes *the; ***recieve*** becomes *receive.* You get the idea. AutoCorrect has other features as well: It corrects capitalization including accidental use of the Caps Lock key, and it lets you insert special symbols.

If you don't like a change made by AutoCorrect, press Ctrl+Z, choose Edit⇨ Undo, or click the Undo button to undo the change. Alternatively, you can play with the AutoCorrect Options button, as I describe in the following steps:

1. **When Word automatically makes a correction to your text, move the insertion pointer mouse pointer to the changed word.**

Point with the mouse or use the arrow keys. When you get to the changed word, a little blue line appears beneath the modified text, as shown in the margin.

2. **Point right at the blue underline until the insertion pointer changes to an arrow pointer.**

The AutoCorrect Options button magically appears in place of the blue underline, as shown in the margin.

3. **Click the mouse to reveal a menu.**

   The menu includes the following commands:

   - **Undo Automatic Corrections:** This option is the same as pressing Ctrl+Z, choosing Edit⇨Undo, or clicking the Undo button. Because any of these three alternatives are easier than hunting for the AutoCorrect Options menu, I doubt you'll use this command often.

   - **Stop Doing That:** Well, this menu command won't actually say "Stop Doing That." Instead, it offers to stop making whatever type of AutoCorrect change was just made. For example, if AutoCorrect automatically capitalizes the first letter of a sentence, this command is called "Stop automatically capitalizing the first letter of a sentence." You can choose this command to disable the particular AutoCorrect action that led you to find the AutoCorrect Options menu.

   - **Control AutoCorrect Options:** Brings up the AutoCorrect Options dialog box so you can further customize your AutoCorrect options.

4. **Choose the command you want to apply and be done with it.**

If you find the AutoCorrect Options button to be more of an annoyance than a help, you can turn it off as I describe in the next section.

Setting AutoCorrect options

AutoCorrect is controlled from the AutoCorrect tab of the AutoCorrect Options dialog box, shown in Figure 4-1. To summon this dialog box, choose Tools⇨AutoCorrect and click the AutoCorrect tab if it isn't already selected. This dialog box lets you activate specific AutoCorrect features; in Figure 4-1, I enabled all the AutoCorrect features, but you may find that one feature or another doesn't suit your fancy. If that's the case, use Tools⇨AutoCorrect to disable the feature you don't like.

AutoCorrect settings, including specific AutoCorrect entries that replace typing, are treated as a Word option rather than as a template or document option. Thus, any changes you make to the AutoCorrect settings are available no matter with what document or template you are working.

The following sections describe each of the AutoCorrect options in detail.

Show AutoCorrect options buttons

If you select this option, Word displays the AutoCorrect Options button whenever AutoCorrect changes your text and you point at the changed word. You can uncheck this option to disable the button.

Figure 4-1:
The
AutoCorrect
dialog box.

Correct TWo INitial CApitals

If you're an average typist, you probably have the bad habit of occasionally leaving the Shift key down a bit too long when typing the initial capital letter of a sentence or a proper noun. The result is that two letters of the word wind up being capitalized rather than just one. If you enable this option, AutoCorrect watches for this mistake and changes the second capital letter to lowercase.

This feature is very useful, unless of course you *want* to type the first two letters of a word in capitals. As an example, I had a devil of a time typing the heading for this section. AutoCorrect kept correcting my capitalization. When I typed *INitial,* Word changed it to *Initial.* One way around this problem is to type *INitial,* let Word change it to *Initial,* and then go back and change the lowercase *n* to a capital letter. Another option is to press Ctrl+Z, the magic Undo keyboard shortcut.

Unfortunately, both of these two techniques lead you into a potential problem: The next time you accidentally type *INitial,* Word doesn't correct your mistake. Why? Because AutoCorrect's default behavior is to watch for any capitalization it corrects that you immediately change back. It remembers those words and doesn't correct them in the future.

You can click the Exceptions button to call up the AutoCorrect Exceptions dialog box, as shown in Figure 4-2. This dialog box contains three *exception lists* (that is, specific words that you do not want Word to correct): one for First Letter capitalizations, one for INitial CAps corrections, and one for other corrections. As you can see, the exception list includes the three words in the heading for this section. Word automatically added these words because the Automatically Add Words to List check box is checked. To disable Word's capability of remembering which words you do not want it to correct, uncheck this box. (I have it unchecked on my system because I find that Word is all too likely to add words that don't belong in the exception list.)

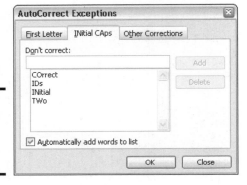

Figure 4-2:
The INitial
CAps
exception
list.

You can remove a word from the exception list by clicking the word to select it and clicking the Delete button. To add a word of your own, type the word with the first two letters capitalized in the Don't Correct field and click Add.

Capitalize first letter of sentences

If you choose the Capitalize First Letter of Sentences option, Word automatically ensures that the first letter of each sentence is capitalized. The poet e.e. cummings should have used this feature.

The Capitalize First Letter of Sentences option works by looking for periods or other sentence-ending punctuation. A problem arises when you want to use an abbreviation that ends with a period: Word is liable to capitalize the word following the abbreviation, thinking that the previous sentence ended. Fortunately, Word provides an extensive exception list that includes many common abbreviations. To access it, click the Exceptions button and click the First Letter tab. See Figure 4-3.

If you select the Automatically Add Words to List option, Word watches for any words it automatically capitalizes that you then immediately uncapitalize. Word assumes that the preceding word is an abbreviation and adds it to the list. Because Word is likely to add a word that doesn't belong on the exception list, you may want to disable this option.

To remove a word from the exception list, select the word and click Delete. To add a word, type the word in the Don't Capitalize After field and click Add.

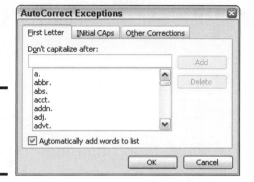

Figure 4-3:
The First
Letter
exception
list.

Capitalize first letter of table cells

This option automatically capitalizes the first letter of any text in a table cell. Because that's usually what you want, I suggest you leave this option checked and use Ctrl+Z to undo the autocorrection for those occasional table cells that you want to begin with a lowercase letter.

Capitalize names of days

If you enable this option, Word always capitalizes the first letter of the names of days: Monday, Tuesday, Wednesday, and the like. Thus, if you type **thursday**, Word automatically changes it to *Thursday*.

Correct accidental usage of cAPS lOCK key

This AutoCorrect feature can figure out if you accidentally press the Caps Lock key, and automatically turns it off for you. If you're like me, you frequently press the Caps Lock key by mistake when reaching for the Shift key. With this option enabled, Word watches for the telltale pattern of inverted capitalization: a word that begins with a lowercase letter, and then continues with uppercase letters. When it detects the pattern, it corrects the incorrectly capitalized letters and disables the Caps Lock key.

Replace text as you type

This option is the heart of AutoCorrect; the other options are merely gravy. At its core, AutoCorrect is a list of replacements that are made whenever you type certain words. For example, whenever you type **adn**, Word automatically substitutes *and*. Word only make these substitutions if you select the Replace Text as You Type check box.

Word comes with an extensive list of built-in AutoCorrect entries. Some of these entries correct commonly misspelled words, such as *adn* for *and* and *teh* for *the*. Others provide a convenient way to insert special symbols quickly. Table 4-1 summarizes these AutoCorrect entries.

Table 4-1	Built-In AutoCorrect Entries for Creating Symbols
Type This	*To Create This*
(c)	Copyright symbol: ©
(r)	Registered symbol: ®
(tm)	Trademark symbol: ™
...	Ellipsis: ...
-->	Small right arrow: →
<--	Small left arrow: ←
==>	Big right arrow: →
<==	Big left arrow: ←
<=>	Double arrow: ⇔
:)	Happy face: ☺
:(	Sad face: ☹
:|	Neutral face: ☺

You can use the Undo command to undo a change made by AutoCorrect. For example, if you type --> and do not want it converted to an arrow, press Ctrl+Z immediately after Word changes it to the arrow. The text is restored to -->.

Creating your own AutoCorrect entries

To add your own AutoCorrect entries, type the text you want replaced in the Replace field, followed by the text you want to replace it with in the With field. For example, if you want to set up an AutoCorrect entry so that every time you type **february**, Word replaces it with *February,* type **february** in the Replace field, type **February** in the With field, and click Add.

If you want Word to preserve the formatting for an AutoCorrect entry, first type the replacement text in your document and format it however you want. Then, select the text and call up Tools⇨AutoCorrect. The replacement text is placed in the With field. All you have to do is type the Replace field and click Add.

That's how you can add additional symbols to the AutoCorrect list. For example, suppose you routinely use the open book symbol in the WingDings font. Follow these steps to add it as an AutoCorrect entry so that whenever you type <b>, the open book symbol is inserted:

1. **Choose Insert⇨Symbol.**

   The Symbol dialog box appears.

2. **Select the Wingdings font and click the open book symbol, as shown in Figure 4-4.**

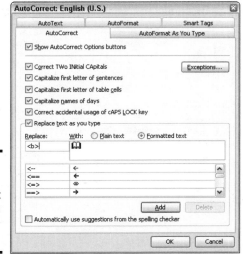

Figure 4-4:
Inserting the
open book
symbol into
a document.

3. **Click the Insert button to insert the symbol into the document and then click Close to close the Symbol dialog box.**

4. **Use the mouse to highlight the symbol you just inserted.**

5. **Choose Tools⇨AutoCorrect.**

   The AutoCorrect dialog box appears with the book symbol already placed in the With field, as shown in Figure 4-5.

Figure 4-5:
Creating an
AutoCorrect
entry for the
open book
symbol.

6. **Type <b> in the Replace field.**

7. **Click Add and click Cancel to dismiss the AutoCorrect dialog box.**

Now, whenever you type <b>, Word automatically substitutes the open book symbol formatted in the WingDings font.

Using AutoFormat

Word's AutoFormat feature cleans up your document and fixes common formatting problems. AutoFormat tries to deduce such things as which paragraphs in your document should be formatted as headings, which paragraphs should be bulleted or numbered lists, and so on. It doesn't always get it right, so you need to carefully review the changes that it makes.

Using AutoFormat

Here's the procedure for using AutoFormat:

1. **Save your document.**

   AutoFormat performs drastic surgery on your document, so you best save it first. That way, if you don't like what AutoFormat does, you have a saved copy to fall back on.

2. **Choose Format⇨AutoFormat.**

   The AutoFormat dialog box comes up, as shown in Figure 4-6.

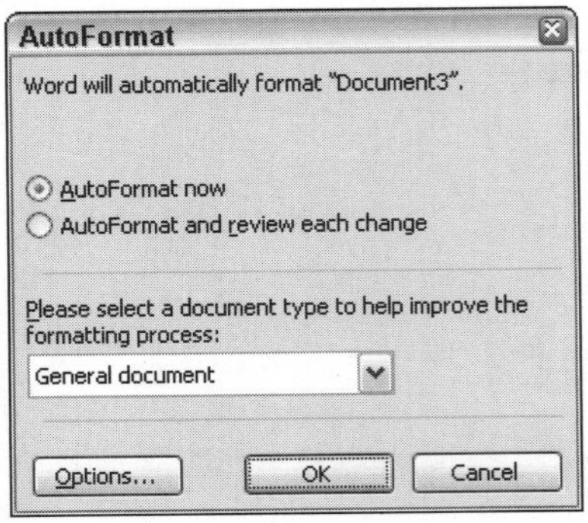

Figure 4-6:
The
AutoFormat
dialog box.

3. **Click OK.**

   AutoFormat reviews your entire document and makes whatever changes it deems necessary to spiff it up.

4. **Review the changes.**

Look over your document carefully to make sure you like the way it looks.

If AutoFormat makes a complete mess of your document, use the Undo command (Edit⇨Undo or Ctrl+Z) to restore your document to its previous condition.

If you don't trust AutoFormat, select the AutoFormat and Review Each Change option. Then, AutoFormat gives you an opportunity to review each change.

Setting AutoFormat options

You can control the changes made by AutoFormat by calling up the Auto-Format Options dialog box, shown in Figure 4-7. To display this dialog box, choose Tools⇨AutoCorrect, and then click the AutoFormat tab. (Alternatively, you can choose Format⇨AutoFormat, and then click the Options button.)

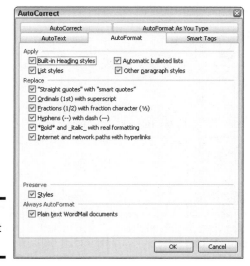

Figure 4-7:
AutoFormat
options.

You can also find most of these options on the AutoFormat As You Type tab of this dialog box, which I describe in the next section. Because AutoFormat As You Type is a more interesting and useful feature, I describe these options in the next section rather than here.

Using AutoFormat As You Type

The Word AutoFormat As You Type feature automatically improves the formatting of documents written with little concern for appearance. This feature applies document formatting as you type, so it's closely related to the AutoCorrect feature. In fact, you find the options for controlling AutoFormat As You Type right next to the options for controlling AutoCorrect. Call up Tools⇨AutoCorrect Options, and then click the AutoFormat As You Type tab to display the options shown in Figure 4-8.

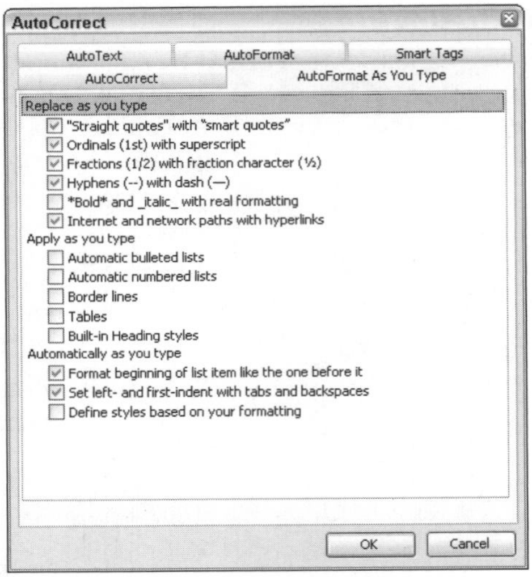

Figure 4-8:
The
AutoFormat
As You Type
options.

Replace as you type

The first section of AutoFormat As You Type options are for items that are automatically replaced as you type them. These items work essentially the same as AutoCorrect items: When you type a particular bit of text, Word steps in and replaces the text with other, more appropriate text.

The following sections summarize the Replace As You Type options.

"Straight quotes" with "smart quotes"

This option tells Word to replace ordinary apostrophes and quotation marks automatically with curly quotes and apostrophes. The trick of quotes is figuring out whether to use the left or right variety of curly quote or apostrophe. The left variety appears to the left of quoted material; the right quote or apostrophe appears on the right. Word does its best to figure it out, and usually gets it right. If a character immediately follows the apostrophe or quote, Word replaces it with a left quote or apostrophe. If a non-blank character is immediately before the quote or apostrophe, Word replaces it with a right quote or apostrophe. Verdict: Thumbs up, with the following caveats:

The Smart Quotes feature works most of the time, but it bombs when you want to use a simple curly apostrophe. For example, try typing **Stop 'n Go**. You can't do it: Word insists on turning the apostrophe the other way 'round. (See, I did it again: Bet you can't!)

Okay, here's the secret to getting these apostrophes right: Simply type *two* apostrophes in a row. Word curls them both, the first one left, the second one right: ''. Now go back and delete the first one.

Another way to do it is to hold down the Ctrl key and press the apostrophe key twice. This trick emits a right apostrophe.

Smart Quotes is such a useful feature that you have little reason to turn it off. If you need to type an ordinary, non-curled apostrophe or quote once in awhile, just type the apostrophe or quote and press Ctrl+Z (Undo).

Ordinals (1st) with superscript

This option replaces ordinal numbers, such as 1st, 2nd, 3rd with properly formatted superscripts: 1st, 2nd, and 3rd. AutoCorrect can also accomplish ordinals, but the AutoFormat option is convenient. For most people, ordinals are one of the main reasons to use superscripts (the other being footnotes), so automatically converting them in this way is a real convenience.

Replace fractions (1/2) with fraction characters (½)

The standard Windows character set, which most fonts adhere to, includes three fraction characters: ½, ¼, and ¾. Prior to Word, the most convenient way to access these characters was via Insert⇨Symbol. When you enable this option, however, Word automatically converts 1/2, 1/4, and 3/4 to their fraction equivalents.

Too bad the Windows character set doesn't include a few other fractions, at least 1/3 and 2/3. Sigh.

Two hyphens (--) with dash (—)

This option does two things:

✦ It replaces two hyphens with a typographical dash called an em dash, so called because it is about as wide as a capital letter M. For example, — is an em dash.

✦ It replaces two hyphens preceded and followed by a space with an en dash, so called because it is about the width of a capital letter N. For example, June – July, Aug – Sep, and so on.

Internet and network paths with hyperlinks

This option watches for text that looks like an Internet address, such as www.wiley.com or Gomez@Addams.com, or network paths, such as \\SERVER01\ADMIN. It then formats these items as hyperlinks so that you can double-click them in Word to open the Web page or network location they point to in a browser window.

Apply as you type

The Apply As You Type section of the AutoFormat As You Type tab lets you select various formatting options that apply to text as you type. The following sections describe each of these options.

Automatic bulleted lists

If you start a paragraph with a character that resembles a bullet, such as an asterisk, hyphen, "o," or >, followed by a space or tab, Word removes the bullet character and the space or tab and instead formats the paragraph as a bullet list. Automatic bullets are pretty convenient for users who haven't yet learned how to use the Bullets button on the Formatting toolbar, but I don't particularly care for it.

Automatic numbered lists

If you start a paragraph with a number followed by a period, space, or tab; Word removes the number and instead formats the paragraph as a numbered list. This option is okay for users who haven't yet learned how to use the Numbering button on the Formatting toolbar, but it drives me batty. Usually, if I start a paragraph with a number followed by a tab, I'm creating a numbered list in a format that is too complicated for the Numbering button to handle, and I don't want to take the time to mess with Word's multilevel numbered list feature. For simple numbered lists, I always just click the Numbering button anyway.

Border lines

If you type three or more hyphens, underscores, or equal signs in a row and press the Enter key with this option selected, Word deletes the characters and instead applies a border to the bottom of the paragraph. You get a thin line for dashes, a thick line for underscores, or a double line for equal signs. This feature is pretty neat.

Tables

This feature is the strangest of all the AutoFormat As You Type features. It automatically creates a table whenever you type a plus sign followed by one or more hyphens, another plus sign, and optionally another set of hyphens and plus signs. For example, to create a table with four columns, you could type this:

```
+----+----+----+----+
```

The number of hyphens you type between the plus signs determines the width of each column.

If you ask me, using the Insert Table command is just easier.

Built-in heading styles

Whenever you type a line that starts with a capital letter, has no ending punctuation, and is at least 20 percent shorter than the maximum line length, Word makes the paragraph a heading if you select this option. Frankly, the rules for AutoFormatting headings as you type are too restrictive. What if the heading needs to be more than one line long? (Some do.) What if the heading ends with a question mark? What if you need to use two or more levels of headings? Memorizing the keyboard shortcuts for applying Word's built-in heading styles is much easier: Ctrl+Alt+1 for a Heading 1, Ctrl+Alt+2 for a Heading 2, and so on.

Automatically as you type

The last group of AutoFormat As You Type options applies the formatting described in the following sections.

Format beginning of list item like the one before it

This feature attempts to apply consistent formatting to the first portion of each item in a list. For example, if the first list item begins with boldface text and switches to normal after a colon, Word automatically applies that formatting to subsequent list items.

Set left- and first-indent with tabs and backspaces

When you select this feature, the Tab key sets the indentation for paragraphs. For example, if you press the Tab key at the beginning of a new paragraph, Word automatically increases the paragraph's indentation by half an inch. Press the Backspace key to decrease the indentation by half an inch. If you press the Tab key at the beginning of an existing paragraph, Word increases the first line indent by half an inch.

Personally, I'd rather use styles to set indentation so that it's consistent throughout the document.

Define styles based on your formatting

This option automatically creates styles based on AutoFormat formatting. Normally, this option is turned off, and I recommend you leave it off. Styles are the best way to apply formatting consistently throughout your document, but you have much more control if you create and apply styles yourself rather than let Word automatically create them.

Using AutoText

The AutoText feature lets you store words, phrases, or longer portions of text and graphics under a user-defined name. Then, to recall the stored text, you simply type the AutoText name and press F3, the AutoText key. For example, you might store your address in an AutoText entry named *addr.* Then, to include your address in a document, you just type **addr** and press F3.

An AutoText entry can contain more than text; it can also contain complete formatting information as well as graphics. In essence, an AutoText entry can contain any part of a Word document that you can select.

Judicious use of AutoText can often help speed up your typing. I generally use AutoText on a project-by-project basis. For example, while writing this book, I found that I frequently need to refer to specific Word commands, for example, Tools⇨Options or File⇨Print. Rather than retype these commands over and over again, I created AutoText entries for most of them. The Auto-Text name for each is the two-letter hotkey sequence for the command. For example, Tools⇨Options is *to* and File⇨Print is *fp.* Typing **fp** and pressing F3 is a lot easier than typing **File⇨Print**.

Another way to insert AutoText entries is to use the AutoText toolbar, which I describe a bit later in this section.

Creating an AutoText entry

To create an AutoText entry, follow these simple steps:

1. **Type and format the text exactly as you want to store it.**

2. **Select the text and choose Tools⇨AutoCorrect Options, and then click the AutoText tab.**

   The AutoText options appear, as shown in Figure 4-9.

3. **Type a name for the AutoText entry.**

Comparing AutoCorrect and AutoText

The Word AutoCorrect and AutoText features are similar enough that you can easily become confused about which is which, and which feature you use in a given situation. The following table should help clarify the difference between AutoCorrect and AutoText:

AutoCorrect	*AutoText*
Associates a name with stored text, formatting, and graphics.	Associates a name with stored text, formatting, and graphics.
Entries are automatically recalled when you type the entry name followed by a space or punctuation.	Entries are manually recalled when you type the entry name and press the AutoText key (F3).
AutoCorrect is intended for correcting simple spelling errors or typing special symbols.	AutoText is intended for storing commonly used text for quick recall.
AutoCorrect entries are stored with Word options and are always available.	AutoText entries are stored in templates and are only available when the template is open.
AutoCorrect provides other typing-related features, such as Smart Quotes, capitalization correction, and so on.	AutoText is just AutoText.

Word suggests the text itself as the AutoText Name, but you want to change it to something more succinct. For example, I typed **ta** for the Name in Figure 4-9.

4. **Click Add to create the AutoText entry.**

Figure 4-9:
Creating an
AutoText
entry.

If you want the AutoText entry to retain its paragraph formatting, you must select the paragraph mark along with the rest of the text before you create the AutoText entry. If you don't include the paragraph mark in the AutoText entry, the text picks up its paragraph formats from the paragraph where you insert the AutoText entry.

Another way to create AutoText entries is to use the AutoText toolbar, which I describe later in this section.

Editing an AutoText entry

You cannot directly edit an AutoText entry. You have to follow a roundabout procedure such as the following:

1. **Switch to a new document.**

2. **Insert the AutoText entry by typing its name and pressing F3.**

3. **Edit the entry however you want.**

4. **Select the entire entry.**

5. **Choose Edit⇨AutoText and save the entry using the same name you previously saved it under.**

Using the AutoText toolbar

If you work with AutoText a lot, you may want to activate the AutoText toolbar, shown in Figure 4-10. To call up this toolbar, just choose View⇨ Toolbars⇨AutoText. This toolbar sports three buttons:

✦ **AutoText:** This button simply calls up the AutoText tab of the AutoCorrect Options dialog box so that you can play with your AutoText settings.

✦ **Entries:** This button displays a menu of all your AutoText entries. You can use this menu to insert an AutoText entry if you can't remember the entry's name.

✦ **New:** This button is available only if you first select some text. It lets you quickly create an AutoText entry from the selected text. A small dialog box appears asking for a name for the new AutoText entry.

Figure 4-10:
The
AutoText
toolbar.

Using Smart Tags

Smart Tags is a feature that identifies certain text and marks it as special. For example, if Word recognizes a company's financial symbol (like IBM or MSFT), it underlines the text with little purple dots as shown in the margin.

If you see text underlined with little purple dots, you can point the mouse at the text to summon the Smart Tags icon. You can then click this icon to reveal a menu of things you can do with Smart Tags. For example, the Smart Tags menu for a financial symbol includes commands that let you get a stock quote, a market report, or news about the company.

You can play with the options for Smart Tags by choosing Tools➪AutoCorrect Options and clicking the Smart Tags tab. These options are shown in Figure 4-11. You can use this dialog box to disable Smart Tags altogether, or you can enable or disable specific types of Smart Tags such as financial symbols, phone numbers, address book contacts, and so on.

Figure 4-11:
Setting
options for
Smart Tags.

Chapter 5: Proofing and Research Tools

In This Chapter

- ✓ Spell checking your document with the spell checker
- ✓ Correcting your grammar with the grammar checker
- ✓ Utilizing the thesaurus
- ✓ Employing the dictionary
- ✓ Translating your document

This chapter shows you how to tap into several Word features designed to help you improve your writing. The spell checker automatically detects and offers to correct spelling mistakes. The grammar checker can help you avoid embarrassing gaffs like using it's instead of its or your instead of you're. The thesaurus can help you find just the right word — that is, the correct, true, accurate, and precise word. And Word's research feature can help you look up words or topics in online dictionaries and encyclopedias.

Using the Spell Checker

I was voted "Worst Speler" in the sixth grade. Not that being "Worst Speler" qualifies me to run for president or anything, but it shows how much I appreciate computer spell checkers. Spelling makes no sense to me. Many years ago, I saw a program on public television called *The Story of English*. It made me feel better. Now at least I know whom to blame for all the peculiarities of English spelling: the Anglos, the Norms (including the guy from *Cheers*), and the Saxophones.

Fortunately, Word has a pretty decent spell checker. In fact, the spell checker in Word is so smart that it knows that you made a spelling mistake almost before you make it. The spell checker watches over your shoulder as you type and helps you to correct your spelling errors as you work.

You can use the spell checker in two basic ways. The first is to let it do its work as you type your document, pointing out and correcting mistakes as you make them. The second is to wait until you finish typing your document, and then check it for spelling mistakes all at once. You can use whichever of these two techniques best fits your style. If you're an especially bad speller, you may want to use them both for good measure.

Checking Spelling as You Go

Word's on-the-fly spell checker watches over your shoulder as you type, politely pointing out spelling mistakes as you make them. The spell checker actually looks up every word you type in its dictionary to make sure you spelled it right. If you type something it can't find in its dictionary, the spell checker underlines the mistake with a wavy red line, as shown in Figure 5-1. (The misspelled word is also shown in the margin.)

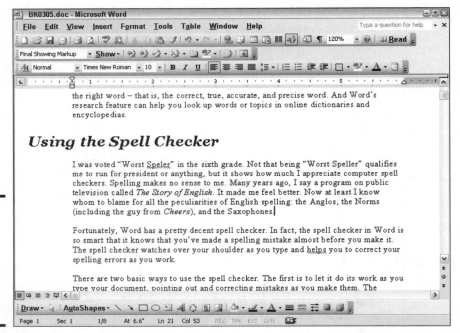

Figure 5-1:
Word
usually
knows
before you
do that you
misspell a
word.

I tried to convince the good people at John Wiley & Sons to pop for an expensive four-color printing process for this book so you could actually see the red line in Figure 5-1. They informed me that they would be happy to oblige, but the added cost would be deducted from my royalty check. That's when I realized that you could probably just pretend that the wavy black line in Figure 5-1 is really a wavy red line.

Word doesn't beep, chime, or yell at you when you misspell a word. As a result, unless you watch the screen as you type, you may not immediately notice a spelling error. Periodically checking the screen is a good idea, even if you are a 90-word-per-minute touch typist who never looks up.

In Figure 5-1, the word *Speler* is marked as misspelled. When you see the tell-tale wavy red line, you have some options:

✦ **Make the correction:** You can use the Backspace key to delete the word, and then retype the word using the correct spelling. After you do that, Word removes the wavy red underline.

✦ **Let Word help:** You can click the word with the right mouse button to call up a menu that lists suggested spellings for the word. In most cases, Word can figure out what you meant to type and suggests the correct spelling. For example, when you right click *Speler,* the following suggestions appear:

> Speller
>
> Spellers
>
> Speer
>
> Spiller

To replace the misspelled word with the correct spelling, just choose the correctly spelled word from the menu.

The quick menu that appears when you right-click a misspelled word also shows the following commands:

✦ **Ignore All:** Sometimes, you want to misspell a word on purpose. For example, you may just happen to be writing a chapter about how to use the spell checker, and you want to misspell the word Speler on purpose. In that case, you want to just ignore the misspelling. To do that, right click the word and choose Ignore All. Then, the word is ignored throughout the document.

✦ **Add to Dictionary:** In some cases, the underlined word is spelled correctly after all; it just happens Word's dictionary doesn't include it. Right click the word and choose Add to Dictionary to add the word to Word's spelling dictionary. That way, Word won't flag the word as misspelled in the future.

✦ **AutoCorrect:** This command reveals a menu that lists the correct spelling suggestions for the misspelled word. When you select one of the suggestions, Word creates an AutoCorrect entry that automatically corrects this spelling error from now on. Choose this option only for words that you frequently misspell that aren't already in the AutoCorrect list. (For more information about AutoCorrect, see Chapter 4 of this minibook.)

If you accidentally use this feature, and then you want to remove the AutoCorrect entry it creates, don't rely on the Undo command. The Undo command undoes the correction, but it won't remove the AutoCorrect entry. To remove the AutoCorrect entry, choose Tools➪AutoCorrect, select the entry you want to remove from the list, and click Delete.

✦ **Language:** This command lets you access the Language dialog box, shown in Figure 5-2. You can use this dialog box to specify the language dictionary that is used to check your spelling. You can also use it to suspend spell checking for the entire paragraph. For more information, see the section "Excluding text from spell checking" later in this chapter.

Figure 5-2:
The
Language
dialog box.

The spell checker can't tell you when you use the wrong word but spell it correctly. For example, you may type *dime navels* when you mean *dime novels*. Cheap literature may be a bad thing, but cheap citrus certainly is not.

Using the Spelling Icon

When you enable automatic spell checking, you find a spelling icon in the form of an open book at the bottom of the Word window, near the right edge of the status bar. This icon indicates the status of your document's spelling:

	Word is spell checking the document. The pencil animates to give the feeling of motion. When you enable the Automatic Spell Check option, the pencil moves whenever you are typing.
	The document contains one or more spelling errors. You can go directly to the next spelling error by double-clicking the Spelling icon.
	The document does not contain any spelling errors.

You can double-click the spelling icon to display the shortcut menu that lists the suggested corrections for the next misspelled word.

Spell Checking After the Fact

If you prefer to ignore the constant nagging by Word about your spelling, you can always check your spelling the old-fashioned way: by running the spell checker after you finish your document. The spell checker works its way through your entire document, looking up every word in its massive list of correctly spelled words and bringing any misspelled words to your attention. It performs this task without giggling or snickering. As an added bonus, the spell checker even gives you the opportunity to tell it that you're right and it's wrong and that it should discern how to spell words the way you do.

The following steps show you how to check the spelling for an entire document:

1. **If the document you want to spell check is not already open, open it.**

2. **Fire up the spell checker.**

   Click the Spelling button on the Standard toolbar, press F7, or choose Tools⇨Spelling.

3. **Tap your fingers on your desk.**

   Word is searching your presentation for embarrassing spelling errors. Be patient.

4. **Don't be startled if Word finds a spelling error.**

   If Word finds a spelling error, it displays the misspelled word along with a suggested correction, as shown in Figure 5-3.

Book III
Chapter 5

Proofing and
Research Tools

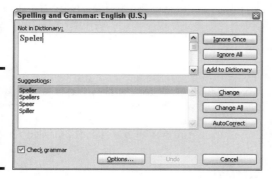

Figure 5-3: The Word spell checker points out a boo-boo.

5. **Choose the correct spelling or laugh in Word's face.**

   If you agree that the word is misspelled, scan the list of corrections that Word offers and select the one that you like. Then click the Change button.

If you like the way that you spelled the word in the first place (maybe it's an unusual word that isn't in the Word spelling dictionary, or maybe you like to spell like Chaucer did), click the Ignore Once button. Watch as Word turns red in the face.

If you want Word to ignore all occurrences of a particular misspelling, click the Ignore All button. Likewise, if you want Word to correct all occurrences of a particular misspelling, click the Change All button.

If you want Word to automatically correct this particular spelling error without asking, click AutoCorrect. The correction is added as an AutoCorrect entry.

6. **Repeat Steps 4 and 5 until Word gives up.**

   When you see the following message:

   ```
   The spelling check is complete
   ```

   you're finished.

If Word detects a repeated word (that is, the same word occurring twice in a row), it displays a variation of the Spelling dialog box that gives you two choices: Ignore or Delete. If you want to repeat the word, click Ignore. To delete the second occurrence of the repeated word, click Delete.

If Word can't come up with a suggestion or if none of its suggestions are correct, you can type your own correction and click the Change button. If the word that you type isn't in the dictionary, Word asks whether you're sure that you know what you're doing. Double-check and click OK if you really mean it.

If you get tired of Word always complaining about a word that's not in its standard dictionary, click Add to Dictionary to add the word to the custom dictionary. If you can't sleep at night until you know more about the custom dictionary, see the next section.

The speller can't tell the difference between *your* and *you're, ours* and *hours, angel* and *angle,* and so on. In other words, if the word is in the dictionary, Word passes it by regardless of whether you used the word correctly. The Word spell checker, however, is no substitute for good, old-fashioned proofreading. Print your document, sit down with a cup of tea, and *read* it.

Custom dictionaries

Word comes with a large dictionary of spellings, called the *main dictionary,* which contains billions and billions of words that were checked for correctness by Noah Webster himself. As exhaustive as the main dictionary is, it isn't comprehensive. Many technical fields have their own specialized jargon, and new words are being invented every day (especially in Washington).

That's where custom dictionaries come in. A *custom dictionary* is a list of words (spelled correctly, of course) that supplements the main dictionary. Words are added to a custom dictionary when you click the Add to Dictionary button, or when you select the Add command from the pop-up menu that appears when you right-click a misspelled word.

By default, Word sets up and maintains a single custom dictionary, named CUSTOM.DIC. Microsoft stores the custom dictionary in the Application Data\Microsoft\Proof folder, which is located in your My Documents folder.

If all your writing needs are similar, a single custom dictionary is adequate. However, some people need more than one custom dictionary. For example, if you're an attorney by day and a Chaucer scholar by night, you probably don't want to store all of Chaucer's weird spellings in your default CUSTOM.DIC dictionary. After all, a contract or a will with spellings such as *commissioun* (*commission*), *symple* (*simple*), or *statut* (*statute*) probably wouldn't hold up in court.

For this purpose, Word lets you set up and maintain more than one custom dictionary, and you can have more than one dictionary active at once. You can create alternate custom dictionaries in the same folder as the default CUSTOM.DOC, and they must use the extension .DIC.

To manage custom dictionaries, choose Tools⇨Options, click the Spelling & Grammar tab, and then click the Custom Dictionaries button to summon the Custom Dictionaries dialog box shown in Figure 5-4.

**Book III
Chapter 5**

**Proofing and
Research Tools**

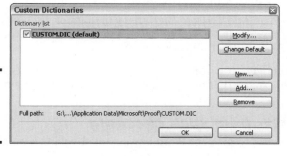

Figure 5-4:
The Custom
Dictionaries
dialog box.

All the available custom dictionaries appear in the Dictionary list. To enable a custom dictionary, click it to select its check box. To temporarily disable a custom dictionary, uncheck its check box.

Five buttons are provided for managing custom dictionaries:

✦ **Modify:** Brings up the dialog box shown in Figure 5-5 so that you can edit the custom dictionary. You can use this dialog box to add or remove words from the custom dictionary.

Figure 5-5:
Editing a
custom
dictionary.

The dialog box shown contains:

CUSTOM.DIC

Word:

Dictionary:

Binford Razzle-Dazzle
LoweWriter.com
Marcellus
Mazzei
Razzle
rebuckles
Ronko Slide-O-Matic
Saviour
stateful
subnetting

Add   Delete

Language

All languages

OK   Cancel

✦ **Change Default:** Makes the selected dictionary the default custom dictionary.

✦ **New:** Click this button to create a new custom dictionary. Word prompts you for a name for the new dictionary.

✦ **Add:** Displays an Add Custom Dictionary dialog box that is similar to the Open dialog box. It allows you to browse your hard disk for dictionary files to be added to the Dictionary list.

✦ **Remove:** Removes a custom dictionary from the Dictionary list. The file is not actually deleted; it merely deletes Word's knowledge of the file.

Excluding text from spell checking

Sometimes, you want to prevent Word from spell checking a range of text, either a text selection or an entire paragraph. For example, you may quote a passage from Chaucer or Shakespeare, and you don't want Word to flag its misspelled words every time you spell check the document.

To prevent Word from spell checking text, follow these steps:

1. **Select the text in question.**

2. **Choose Tools⇨Language⇨Set Language.**

The Language dialog box appears. Refer to Figure 5-2.

3. **Check the Do Not Check Spelling or Grammar option.**

4. **Click OK.**

Word skips over the text formatted with (no proofing) whenever it does a spell check.

 If you frequently write entire paragraphs of text that you don't want spell checked, I suggest you create a style for this purpose. You can access the Language dialog box from the Modify Style dialog box by choosing Format⇨Language.

Spelling options

You can set options for Word's spell checker by choosing Tools⇨Options and clicking the Spelling & Grammar tab, or by clicking the Options button from the Spelling dialog box. Either way, the spelling and grammar options display in the Options dialog box, shown in Figure 5-6.

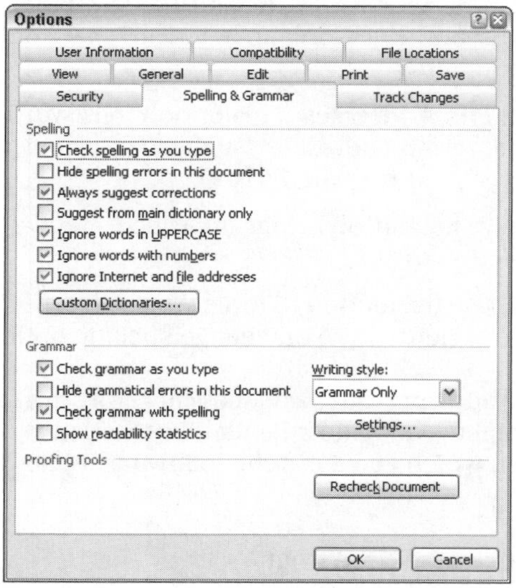

Figure 5-6:
Spelling
options.

The following paragraphs describe the proper use of each of the spelling options:

✦ **Check Spelling as You Type:** Use this option if you want Word to automatically check your spelling as you type.

✦ **Hide Spelling Errors in This Document:** Hides the red wavy underline that marks misspelled words.

✦ **Always Suggest Corrections:** If your computer is fast enough that searching the dictionary for correct spellings doesn't slow down your spell check too much, leave this option selected. However, if you find that Word spends an inordinate amount of time whenever you advance to the next misspelling, turn off this option.

✦ **Suggest from Main Dictionary Only:** Select this option if you do not want Word to consult your custom dictionaries when suggesting words.

✦ **Ignore Words in UPPERCASE:** Tells Word not to look up words that are in all uppercase. Many common acronyms and business names, including FEMA (Federal Emergency Management Agency) and IBM are not in the dictionary. With this option selected, Word won't even bother to spell check them if you type them in all uppercase.

✦ **Ignore Words with Numbers:** Technical documents are often filled with words that intermix text and numbers and shouldn't be spell checked. For example, product part numbers or government form numbers often mix letters and numbers, such as BX-104 and 1040-A. With this option enabled, Word doesn't bother to look up any word that contains a mixture of letters and numbers.

✦ **Ignore Internet and File Addresses:** This option tells Word to ignore words that look like Internet addresses (such as `www.dummies.com`) or file addresses (such as `C:\Program Files`).

✦ **Custom Dictionaries:** This button brings up a separate dialog box for managing custom dictionaries.

✦ **Recheck Document:** Use this button to force Word to recheck the spelling and grammar of a document after you change spelling options.

The Check Grammar as You Type, Hide Grammatical Errors in This Document, Check Grammar with Spelling, and Show Readability Statistics options are for the grammar checker, which I cover in the following section.

Using the Grammar Checker, or Not

I think Word's much-touted grammar checker is a letdown. Not because anything is wrong with it. Actually, as grammar checkers go, it's pretty good. In my opinion, though, grammar checkers are a waste of time. They aren't really intelligent enough to distinguish between genuine grammatical errors and stylistic license, so if you're a halfway decent writer already, the majority of the messages generated by the grammar checker are most likely incorrect. And if you aren't, you can't distinguish between the good suggestions and the bogus ones.

For example, consider Figure 5-7. Here, I used the grammar checker to check the sentence *Only one of the runner's finished under 26 minutes.* This sentence contains a simple grammatical error: *runner's* should be *runners*. The grammar checker caught the error, but suggested *runners's* as an alternative.

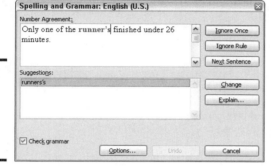

Figure 5-7:
The grammar checker seems confused.

Aside from its occasional grammatical mistakes, the grammar checker has a nasty habit of imposing its idea of good writing on your prose. Try running Abraham Lincoln's Gettysburg Address through the grammar checker to see if it makes any good suggestions that would improve Lincoln's masterpiece. All it does is call for the elimination of passive voice and suggest that Lincoln use *however* or *nevertheless* instead of *but*.

I've run the grammar checker on many other specimens of outstanding writing, with similar results. Ernest Hemingway's *The Old Man and the Sea* is sexist. Winston Churchill mixes up his prepositions. Thomas Jefferson should have used more periods. And on and on.

One line of reasoning in favor of using the grammar checker is that it can help a poor writer become more proficient. Becoming a better writer would be possible, were it not for the fact that the grammar checker is just as apt to offer bad advice as good; how is a poor writer supposed to know the former from the latter?

If you must use the grammar checker, feel free to ignore its advice. And by all means choose Tools➪Options, click the Spelling & Grammar tab, click Settings, and review the rules used by the grammar checker. Disable any rules you don't agree with or find the grammar checker cannot reliably detect. The section, "Customizing the grammar checker," explains how.

**Book III
Chapter 5**

**Proofing and
Research Tools**

Checking for grammar errors

By default, Word checks for grammatical errors as you type. When it spots what it thinks is an error, it underlines the suspected text with a wavy green underline. You can right-click the underlined text to display a menu of suggested changes. If you choose Grammar from the menu that appears when you right-click the underlined text, the Spelling and Grammar dialog box appears (refer to Figure 5-7).

You can also do your grammar check after the fact, by choosing Tools⟳ Spelling and Grammar or by pressing F7. Word checks grammar and spelling at the same time, so it points out spelling and grammatical errors in the order in which it finds them.

When the Spelling and Grammar dialog box displays a grammatical error, it offers the following buttons:

✦ **Ignore Once:** Tells the grammar checker to ignore the alleged error. You click this button nine times out of ten (with the possible exception of Cancel).

✦ **Ignore Rule:** The grammar checker ignores the rule that caused it to flag the text. After Word incorrectly accuses you of using sentence fragments ten or twelve times in a row, you may want to click this button to make it stop.

✦ **Next Sentence:** Many times, the grammar checker reports multiple errors for a single sentence. You can often tell when the grammar checker isn't making heads or tails out of a sentence. For example, the grammar checker usually has trouble with headings, captions, and other bits of text that aren't complete sentences. Rather than wade through message after message for these non-sentences, you can click Next Sentence to direct the grammar checker to skip ahead to the next sentence.

✦ **Change:** This button allows you to edit the sentence directly in the Grammar dialog box, and then record your change in the document.

✦ **Explain:** Displays a description of the rule that caused the sentence to be flagged as a possible error. Some of the explanations are brief; others are elaborate grammar lessons. For example, Figure 5-8 shows an explanation triggered by Abraham Lincoln's use of the word "which" in the following sentence from the Gettysburg Address:

*It is for us the living, rather, to be dedicated here to the unfinished work **which** they who fought here have thus far so nobly advanced.*

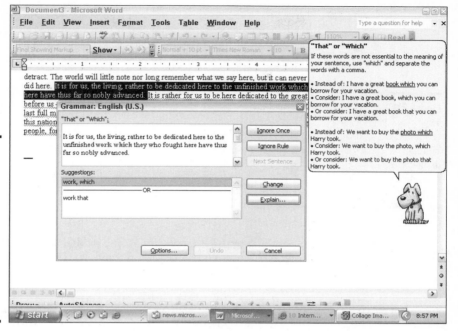

Figure 5-8:
The grammar checker's explanation of why Lincoln should have considered "that" instead of "which."

✦ **Options:** Calls up the Options dialog box so that you can change the behavior of the grammar checker. I describe these options in the section "Customizing the grammar checker" later in this chapter.

✦ **Undo:** Undoes the last grammar checker action.

✦ **Cancel:** My favorite button in the Grammar dialog box.

Readability statistics

After the grammar checker finishes its futile effort at tearing apart your prose, it does an often useful analysis of your document's readability, using several well-known methods for determining the "grade level" of your document. Figure 5-9 shows these readability statistics; in this case, calculated for the very chapter you are reading now.

Readability Statistics	☒
Counts	
Words	2711
Characters	12265
Paragraphs	109
Sentences	119
Averages	
Sentences per Paragraph	2.9
Words per Sentence	19.5
Characters per Word	4.3
Readability	
Passive Sentences	8%
Flesch Reading Ease	63.9
Flesch-Kincaid Grade Level	9.1
OK	

Figure 5-9:
The grammar checker displays readability statistics.

The first two sections of the Readability Statistics dialog box show various counts and averages compiled from your document. Then, the following readability statistics are shown:

✦ **Passive Sentences:** This score reports the percentages of sentences in the text that use passive voice. Most experts agree that passive voice is harder to read than active voice; the lower this score, the more readable your prose is.

✦ **Flesch Reading Ease:** This score computes document readability based on the average number of syllables per word and the average number of words per sentence. Scores range from 0 (zero) to 100. Most good writing falls in the range of 60 to 70. The higher the number, the more readable the text.

✦ **Flesch-Kincaid Grade Level:** Computes document readability based on the average number of syllables per word and the average number of words per sentence, similar to the Flesch Reading Ease measurement. However, the resulting score is stated as a grade-school level. For example, a score of 8.0 means an eighth grader can read and understand the document. Most writers shoot for seventh- to ninth-grade level on this scale.

Don't put too much stock in these readability statistics. They are helpful as a general guide, but don't take them too seriously.

Customizing the grammar checker

You can use Tools⇨Options to customize the grammar checker so that it checks only for specific types of grammatical errors. Choose Tools⇨Options and click the Spelling & Grammar tab to see the spelling and grammar options. That dialog box is shown in Figure 5-6, so I won't repeat it here.

The following options in the Spelling & Grammar tab of the Options dialog box relate to the grammar checker:

✦ **Check Grammar as You Type:** This option enables the on-the-fly grammar checker, which I describe earlier in this chapter, in the "Checking for grammar errors" section.

✦ **Hide Grammatical Errors in This Document:** This option hides grammar errors.

✦ **Check Grammar with Spelling:** This option causes Word to check grammar whenever you do an after-the-fact spell check.

✦ **Show Readability Statistics:** If you enable this option, statistics that indicate how readable your document is display when you do a grammar check.

✦ **Writing Style:** This option lets you specify whether you want to check for simple grammar mistakes or for stylistic blunders as well as grammatical errors.

You can change the specific rules that are checked by the grammar checker by clicking the Settings button. The Grammar Settings dialog box appears, shown in Figure 5-10. Here, you can choose which specific rules to check for.

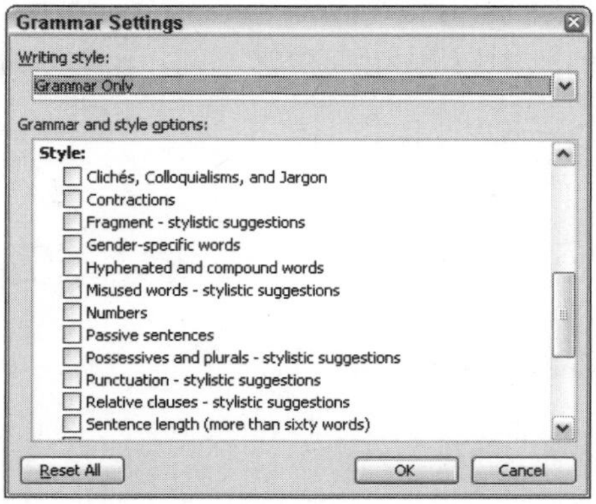

Figure 5-10:
The Grammar Settings dialog box.

Using the Thesaurus

One of the nifty Word features is a built-in thesaurus that can quickly show you synonyms for a word that you type. Using it is easy:

1. **Right-click a word that you typed and choose Synonyms from the menu that appears.**

   A menu listing synonyms for the word appears. (Sometimes Word throws an antonym into the list just to be contrary.)

2. **Click the word that you want to replace your word.**

   Word replaces the original word with your selection.

If you choose Thesaurus from the Synonyms menu, the Thesaurus section of the Research task pane appears with the synonyms listed, as shown in Figure 5-11. You can also summon this task pane by pressing Shift+F7. The Thesaurus task pane lets you look up words to find even more synonyms. For example, if you select *occasionally* from the list of synonyms, you get another set of words. You can keep clicking words to find other synonyms as long as you like, until you're ready to get back to real work.

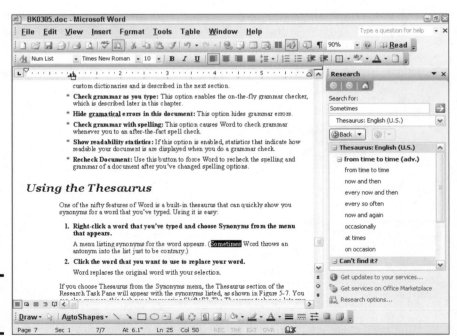

Figure 5-11:
The
Thesaurus.

Using the Dictionary

If you have an Internet connection, you can look up a definition of any word in your document by right-clicking the word you want to look up, and then choosing Look Up from the shortcut menu that appears. The Research task pane comes up, shown in Figure 5-12, displaying the definition of the word you selected. In this example, the word Thesaurus is defined.

If the definition doesn't appear, make sure that the drop-down list beneath the Search For text box specifies the dictionary. You can use this drop-down list to select other research tools, such as an online encyclopedia or an Internet search service.

You can also look up words by opening the Research task pane (choose View⇨Task Pane, and then click Research), typing the word you want to look up in the Search For text box, and then clicking the Start Searching button (the green button with the big arrow).

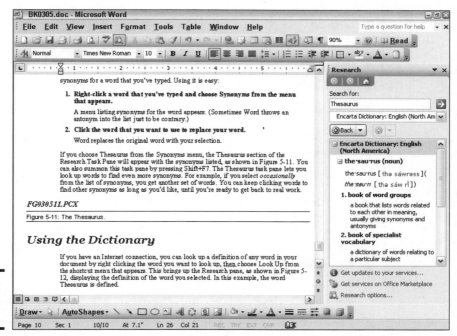

Figure 5-12:
Looking up
a word.

Losing Something in the Translation

Remember the Universal Translator, that cool device they had on Star Trek that could translate into any language spoken anywhere in the galaxy? They didn't need it much because most of the alien civilizations they encountered spoke English anyway. But for those species that communicated with high-pitched squeals and shrieks, the Universal Translator came in handy.

Fortunately, Word has the equivalent of a Universal Translator built right into the Research task pane. You can use it to translate to and from the following languages:

+ Chinese (PRC or Taiwan)
+ Chinese
+ Dutch
+ English (U.S. only — sorry, not British translation)
+ French
+ German
+ Greek
+ Italian
+ Japanese
+ Korean
+ Portuguese
+ Russian
+ Spanish

To translate some text, follow these steps:

1. **Type the text you want to translate in your document, and then highlight the text.**

2. **Right-click the text and choose Translate.**

   The Research task pane appears with Translation selected as the option for the drop-down list below the Search For text box.

3. **Choose the languages you want to translate from and to in the From and To drop-down lists.**

4. **Click the green arrow button to translate your text.**

5. **Scroll down in the Research task pane to see the result.**

You have to scroll down a bit to see the translation.

So how good is the translation? About as good as you can expect for a computer-based translation. I wouldn't use it to negotiate an arms treaty, but it may work for casual correspondence.

However, be aware that most computer-based translations are way too literal. And sometimes, that leads to strange results. For example, I used Word's translation feature to translate the sentence, "By the way, I love football" into Italian. The result was "A proposito, Amo il gioco del calcio." Because I don't speak Italian, I have absolutely no idea if this translation is good. But for fun, I then used the translation feature to translate this translation back into English. The result was "On purpose, I love the game of soccer."

Huh? Obviously, the "By the way" didn't get translated right. And the American game of football became soccer. But that's okay; I like soccer, too.

Chapter 6: Track Changes and Other Collaboration Features

Rumor has it that Benjamin Franklin was first given the opportunity to write the Declaration of Independence but declined because he refused to write a document that others would edit.

Ha!

Old Ben would have hated this chapter. The very thought that Word had features that enabled other people to edit his documents would have sent him out into the storm to fly another kite.

This chapter covers several Word features designed for group work. I discuss how to track the changes you and others make to a document by using revision marks, how to add comments to a document, how to save different versions of a document in a single file, and a few other goodies.

Using Reading Layout

The first topic for this chapter is a new feature of Word 2003 called *Reading Layout.* Reading Layout is a special document view designed for easy on-screen reading. As shown in Figure 6-1, it shows two pages side by side, just like a real book. Note that these pages don't correspond to printed pages. In Reading Layout, each page holds much less text than a full size printed page.

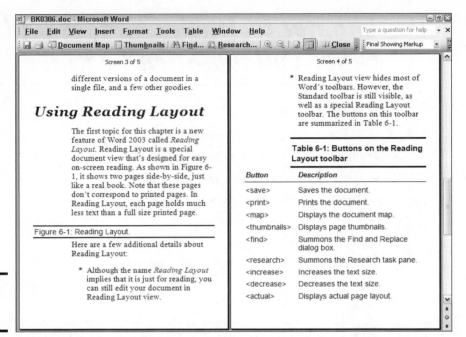

Figure 6-1:
Reading
Layout.

Here are a few additional details about Reading Layout:

✦ Although the name *Reading Layout* implies that it is just for reading, you can still edit your document in Reading Layout view.

✦ Reading Layout view hides most of Word's toolbars, as well as the ruler and the status bar, to maximize the amount of screen space available for reading your document. However, the Standard toolbar is still visible, as well as a special Reading Layout toolbar. I summarize the buttons on this toolbar in Table 6-1.

✦ To leave Reading Layout view, click the Close button that appears on the toolbar. Or just switch to another view.

Table 6-1	Buttons on the Reading Layout Toolbar	
Button	*Name*	*What It Does*
💾	Save	Saves the document.
🖨	Print	Prints the document.

Button	Name	What It Does
Document Map	Document Map	Displays the document map.
Thumbnails	Thumbnails	Displays page thumbnails.
Find...	Find	Summons the Find and Replace dialog box.
Research...	Research	Summons the Research task pane.
	Increase Text Size	Increases the text size.
	Decrease Text Size	Decreases the text size.
	Actual Page	Displays actual page layout.
	Allow Multiple Pages	Allows two pages to be displayed side by side.
Close	Close	Closes Reading Layout view.

All Hail the Honorable Reviewing Toolbar

Many of Word's group editing features are handled by a dedicated Reviewing toolbar, which is shown in Figure 6-2. The Reviewing toolbar contains all the buttons you need to track changes to your documents and to add comments that other reviewers can read. I give you the details of how to use these features later in this chapter. For now, Table 6-2 summarizes the function of each button on the Reviewing toolbar.

Figure 6-2:
The Reviewing toolbar.

Table 6-2		Buttons on the Reviewing Toolbar
Button	*Name*	*What It Does*
Final Showing Markup ▼	Display for Review	Selects which version of the document to display: Final, Final Showing Markup, Original, or Original Showing Markup.
Show ▼	Show	Opens a menu that lets you select various options for viewing changes made by other users.
	Previous	Goes to the previous change or comment.
	Next	Goes to the next change or comment.
	Accept Change	Accepts the current change, making it a permanent part of the document.
	Reject Change/ Delete Comment	If the insertion pointer is positioned at a change, rejects the change and restores the original version. If the insertion pointer is positioned at a comment, deletes the comment.
	Insert Comment	Inserts a comment into a document.
	Highlight	Activates the highlighter tool.
	Track Changes	Turns change tracking on or off.
	Reviewing Pane	Opens or closes the Reviewing task pane.

Using the Highlighter

The highlighter tool allows you to draw attention to a portion of a document by shading it with a background color that is similar to a highlighter pen. It is intended to be used in workgroup settings. For example, you may use it to highlight a portion of a colleague's document that you think needs to be reworked. When you send the document back to your colleague, he or she can easily find the highlighted section of text.

To highlight text, click the Highlight button on the Reviewing toolbar, and then paint the text you want highlighted by dragging the special highlight pointer over the text you want highlighted. Alternatively, you can double-click a word to highlight the entire word, or you can triple-click a paragraph to highlight the entire paragraph. When you finish highlighting, click the Highlight button again. (***Note:*** The highlighter also appears on the Formatting toolbar, so you can use the highlighter even if the Reviewing toolbar isn't visible.)

Another way to use the highlighter tool is to first select the text you want to highlight, and then click the Highlight button. The selected text is immediately highlighted, and the mouse pointer does not change to the highlighter tool.

The highlighter tool doesn't have a keyboard shortcut, but you can easily assign one using Tools⇨Customize. Look for the Highlight command in the Format category. (For more information about using Tools⇨Customize, see Book VIII, Chapter 2.)

The default color for the highlighter is yellow, but you can change colors by clicking the arrow next to the Highlight button. A menu drops down offering 15 different highlighter colors, plus None. If you choose None, the highlighter becomes a highlight eraser that you can use to remove highlighting.

To remove highlighting, simply paint the area you want to remove highlighting from again. Or, select None as the highlight color and highlight away. Highlighting is removed from everything you paint, plus you don't have to worry about accidentally highlighting areas that aren't already highlighted.

To remove all highlighting in your document, press Ctrl+A to select the entire document, and then click the down-arrow next to the Highlight button and choose None.

Keeping Your Comments to Yourself (Not!)

A comment is a way of adding a note to part of a document without modifying the document. When you insert a comment, Word adds a hidden comment mark to the text at the location of the comment. Word then adds your comments to a separate Comment pane, which is keyed to the comment marks so that you can come back later and view each of the comments.

In previous versions of Word, comments were known as *annotations*.

To insert a comment, follow these steps:

1. **Summon the Reviewing toolbar by choosing View⇨Toolbars⇨ Reviewing.**

   The Reviewing toolbar appears.

2. Select the text you want to comment on.

If the text is really long, just move the cursor to the end of the text. If you select the text before creating the comment, Word highlights the text later when you display the comment.

3. Click the Insert Comment button.

Or, if you prefer, use Insert⇨Comment. Either way, a comment mark is inserted as hidden text following the text you selected. Then the screen is split in two, revealing the comments in the bottom portion of the screen. Word refers to the screen's bottom portion as the Reviewing pane, and Word's right — it is a pain. Figure 6-3 shows a Word document with comments.

Note: If you're working in Page Layout view, comments display with special comment bubbles that appear at the location of the comment. You can still use the Reviewing pane, but the comment bubbles are easier to work with.

4. Type your comments.

Word adds your comments to the Comment pane at the correct position.

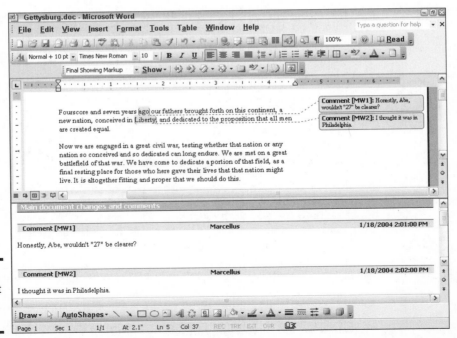

Figure 6-3: A document with comments.

5. **Click the Close button to dismiss the Comment Pane and return to the document.**

Here are some things to keep in mind when you insert comments:

✦ Notice how the comment marks in the document are keyed to comments in the Comment pane. Word uses your initials (it gets them from the User Info options), followed by a sequence number. For example, the first comment in Figure 6-3 is identified as MW1; the second is MW2; and so on. With the user identification feature, several people can add comments to a document, and you can easily determine which comment came from each person.

✦ If you're going to insert a bunch of comments, you can leave the Comment pane open. After typing a comment, just click the mouse anywhere in the document. Both the Document pane and the Comment pane remain visible. Find the next bit of text you want to comment on, select it, and click the Insert Comment button to insert another comment.

✦ If you have a sound card, a microphone, and more disk space than you know what to do with, you can add a voice comment by clicking the cassette-tape button in the Comment pane.

✦ If you can't say something nice, don't say nothin' at all.

Viewing comments

The easiest way to view comments is to switch to Page Layout view. Then, any comments in the document display in special comment bubbles.

If you want to work with comments in the Reviewing pane, click the Reviewing Pane button on the Reviewing toolbar. You can then scroll through the Document pane or the Comment pane to look at comments along with the corresponding document text. Notice that as you scroll through either pane, the other pane scrolls in sync. When you select a comment by clicking it in the Comment pane, Word scrolls the Document pane to the text that the comment refers to, and highlights the referenced text.

If the document contains comments created by more than one user, you can restrict the Reviewing pane so that it shows just that user's comments by choosing that user from Show➪Reviewers (the Show button is on the Reviewing toolbar). To display all comments regardless of who inserted them, select All Reviewers.

If you want to copy a comment directly into the document, select the comment text you want to copy. Press Ctrl+C, click in the document at the location where you want the text inserted, and then press Ctrl+V.

**Book III
Chapter 6**

**Track Changes and
Other Collaboration
Features**

If the Comment pane is too big or too small, you can change its size. Hold the mouse steady over the top edge of the Comment pane for a moment, and the mouse cursor changes to a double-headed arrow. Hold down the left mouse button and drag the Comment pane up or down to increase or decrease its size.

You can quickly scroll to the next or previous comment in the document by clicking the Next Comment or Previous Comment buttons on the Reviewing toolbar.

Another way to navigate through your comments is to click the Select Browse Object button (the ball that's located between the double-up and double-down arrow buttons beneath the vertical scroll bar) and choose Browse By Comment. You can then use the double-up and double-down buttons beneath the scrollbar to go to the next or previous comment.

You can print comments by choosing File➪Print and choosing Document Showing Markup from the Print What drop-down list.

You can view a comment without calling up the Reviewing pane simply by hovering the mouse over text that is highlighted as a comment. After a moment, the comment appears in a box just above the text. When you move the mouse, the comment disappears.

Removing comments

To delete a comment, highlight the hidden comment mark in the document text, and press the Reject Change/Delete Comment button.

To remove all of the comments in a document, click the arrow next to the Reject Change/Delete Comment button, and then choose Delete All Comments in Document.

Tracking Changes

Wouldn't it be great if you could quickly see what changes have been made to a document? Such a feature would be great for anyone in charge of maintaining corporate bylaws, legal documents, records about investments in failed savings and loans, congressional testimony, and so on.

With Word's Track Changes feature, you can. Track Changes lets you indicate what changes have been made to a document. Any deleted text is shown with a line running through it (strikethrough). Inserted text is underlined. Any line that contains a change is marked with a vertical line in the margin, so you can quickly scan through a document to find changes. Figure 6-4 shows an example of a document with revision marks. To create revision marks like these, read on.

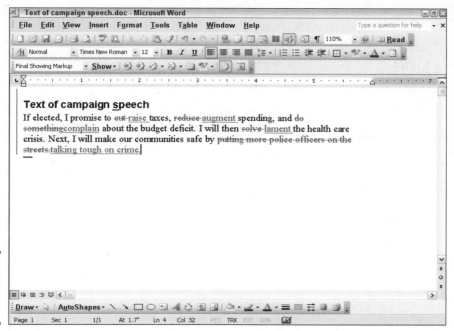

Figure 6-4:
A document with revisions.

To track changes to a document while editing the document, turn on the Track Changes feature before you begin editing your document. Then Word keeps track of revisions as you make them. You can then print the document with or without the changes, and you can later accept or reject the changes.

Follow these steps to track changes:

1. **Choose Tools⇨Track Changes.**

The Reviewing toolbar appears and Word begins tracking your changes.

2. **If you do not want the change marks to appear on-screen while you edit the document, choose Final in the Display for Review drop-down list.**

Normally change marks appear on-screen as you type, which can be annoying, so you may want to switch to Final display. As long as Track Changes is still turned on, Word continues tracking your changes even though it doesn't display the revision marks.

3. **Proceed!**

Now you can feel free to edit the document to pieces.

To disable revision marking, click the Track Changes button on the Reviewing toolbar. I sometimes do turn off Track Changes to correct a simple and obvious typographical error that doesn't need to be highlighted by a revision mark. Then I turn revision marking back on again.

TIP

You can quickly activate Track Changes by double-clicking the letters TRK in the status bar.

You can change the way to display changes by choosing Tools⇨Options and clicking the Track Changes tab. As Figure 6-5 shows, a page of options let you set the color to display insertions, deletions, formatting changes, and the vertical bar displayed next to changed lines. You can also control whether or not balloons highlight comments and editing.

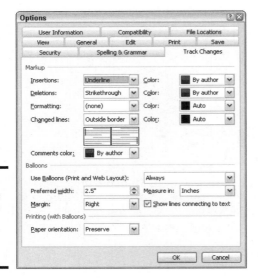

Figure 6-5: Setting the options for the Track Changes feature.

Comparing documents

Word tracks changes only when you activate change tracking as I describe in the section, "Tracking Changes." If you forget to activate Track Changes, you can still re-create change marks by comparing a document with an earlier version of the same document. Word does its best to mark text that has been inserted or deleted from the older version of the document.

For example, suppose you e-mail a buddy a copy of a document. Your buddy then makes some changes to the document and e-mails it back to you. You now have two versions of the document: the original (a copy of which you sent your buddy) and the version edited by your buddy. If you want to find out exactly what changes your so-called friend made to the document, you can use the Compare Documents feature to find out.

Follow these steps to compare documents:

1. **Open the newer version of the two documents you want to compare.**

2. **Choose Tools⇨Compare and Merge Documents.**

    The Compare and Merge Documents dialog box appears, which is almost identical to a normal File Open dialog box.

3. **Choose the file to which you want to compare the current file.**

    In other words, choose the older version of the file you opened in Step 1.

4. **Click OK.**

Word compares the files and automatically inserts change marks in the newer document.

Don't expect Word to insert change marks perfectly when it compares documents. Word is good at marking minor revisions, but some changes may confuse Word and cause it to insert wacky change marks. You are better off marking revisions as you make them, if possible.

Accepting or rejecting changes

When you have accumulated a bunch of change marks, sooner or later you want to accept or reject the revisions. If you accept the changes, the revisions are permanently incorporated into the document, and the change marks are removed. If you reject the changes, the document reverts to its previous state and the revisions are deleted along with the change marks.

To accept or reject all of the changes to a document in one swift stroke, follow these steps:

1. **Summon the Reviewing toolbar.**

    Choose View⇨Toolbars⇨Reviewing to display this toolbar.

2. **Click the arrow next to the Accept Change button, and then choose Accept All Changes in Document.**

    The changes are accepted.

Skim through your document to confirm that changes have indeed been accepted or rejected as you intended. It should be obvious.

If you have second thoughts, press Ctrl+Z. The revision marks are restored.

If you prefer to work your way through the changes one at a time, accepting or rejecting each one on its own merits, use the Next Change or Previous Change buttons on the Reviewing toolbar to move to the next or previous change, and then click the Accept Change or Reject Change button, depending on what you think of the change.

Change marks accumulate in a document until you either accept or reject them. You can collect a set of revision marks over a period of days or weeks and then deal with them all by accepting or rejecting them.

Sending a Document to Reviewers

Word includes a File⇨Send To command, which lets you send a copy of the current document to one or more e-mail recipients. Then, the recipients can review the document, make changes, add comments, and send the marked-up document back to you.

When you're ready to put a document out for review, follow these steps:

1. **Open the document you want to send out for review.**

If the document is already open, use File⇨Save to save any changes you made since you opened it.

2. **Choose File⇨Send To⇨Mail Recipient (for Review).**

Word summons Outlook and creates a new message, as shown in Figure 6-6. As you can see, the message already has the Subject line filled in ("Please review. . . "), the document is attached to the message, and the message text reads "Please review the attached document."

Send	Cut	Copy	Paste	Undo	Check	Spelling	Attach	Priority	Sign		

File   Edit   View   Insert   Format   Tools   Message   Help

From:	doug@lowewriter.com (Doug@LoweWriter)	▼
To:		
Cc:		
Bcc:		
Subject:	Please review 'BK0306'	
Attach:	BK0306.doc (75.0 KB)	

Please review the attached document.

Figure 6-6:
Sending a
document
for review.

3. **In the To field, add an e-mail address for each person you want to send a review copy to.**

   You can type the e-mail addresses directly into the To field, or you can click the To button to call up the Address Book. You can then use the Address Book to select your reviewers.

   If you want to send the document to more than one person, separate the e-mail addresses with semicolons.

4. **If you want, change the Subject field or message body.**

   You probably want to say something a little more cordial than the bland "Please review. . . " messages created automatically by Word.

5. **Set any other Outlook options you want for the message.**

   You can set a whole bevy of options for Outlook messages, such as high or low importance, signatures, stationery, plain or HTML formatting, and more. But this book isn't about Outlook, so I don't go into them here.

6. **Click the Send button.**

   Your message is whisked away, to be delivered as soon as possible.

Another way to send a document out for review is to use File➪Send To➪ Routing Recipient. This command enables you to send a single copy of a document to a list of recipients. Each recipient in the list can review the document, make changes and add comments, and then forward the document to the next recipient on the list. When the last recipient finishes his or her review, the document is sent back to you. You can then see the changes and comments made by all your reviewers at once.

**Book III
Chapter 6**

Track Changes and
Other Collaboration
Features

Using SharePoint Team Services

SharePoint Team Services, also known as STS, is a nifty feature that lets you set up a Web site where users can collaborate on documents. An STS site enables you do to the following:

✦ Save documents in shared libraries so that everyone in your group can access the documents.

✦ Have online discussions in which you comment on each other's work, argue about politics, and otherwise confer, consult, and cajole.

✦ Track the progress of your project, post announcements, assign tasks, and even schedule meetings.

✦ Take surveys to gauge the opinions of your team members.

✦ Control who can access the site.

Setting up an STS Web site is a job for someone who's a bit of a computer guru and is well beyond the scope of this book. Whoever sets up your STS Web site can give you the information you need to access it. Specifically, you need to know three bits of information:

✦ The Internet address (URL) of the STS site, such as `rivercity.sts.conman.com`. I just made this name up as an example, so don't bother trying to go there.

✦ A user ID, such as `RCITY/Harold`.

✦ A password.

To facilitate use of your STS site, open a My Network Places folder and create a new network place for the STS site. To do so, click Add a Network Place in the task pane of the My Network Places folder, and then answer the questions asked by the Add Network Place Wizard.

Using a document library

One of the basic features of an STS site is the document libraries, which allow you to store documents that can be worked on by members of your group. You can choose File⇨Save As and File⇨Open to save or retrieve documents in one of these libraries. Click the My Network Places icon in the Open or Save As dialog box, and then double-click the icon for the STS site. Then, double-click the library that you want to access. Figure 6-7 shows a shared document library in an Open dialog box.

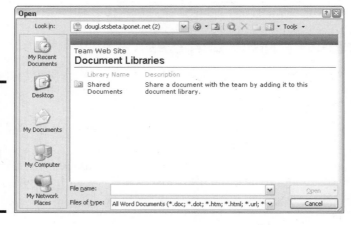

Figure 6-7: Opening a document from a SharePoint Team Services site.

Checking out

Like any good library, SharePoint document libraries let you check out a document so that others know you're using them. After you finish working with the document, you can check it back in. (Fortunately, the Check Out feature doesn't charge a fine for overdue items.)

To check out a document, open the document as usual. Then, choose File➪ Check Out. While you have the document checked out, other users can access a read-only copy of the document. They can't save changes to the document or see any changes that you make until you check the document back in.

To check in a document, choose File➪Check In. A dialog box appears in which you can type comments about the changes you made to the document. Then, Word saves the document. The document remains open in Word, but because it is no longer checked out, other users can open the document and make changes to it.

Using the Shared Workspace task pane

The Shared Workspace task pane gives you direct access to many of the features of a SharePoint Team Services site. The Shared Workspace task pane automatically displays whenever you open a document from an STS site. You can also display it by choosing Tools➪Shared Workspace.

The Shared Workspace task pane has six tabbed areas:

 ✦ **Status:** This tab displays information about the shared documents on which you're currently working.

 ✦ **Members:** This tab displays information about other members of the STS site. You can use this tab to find out who else is currently logged in to the site to send e-mail, schedule meetings, and perform other related tasks.

 ✦ **Tasks:** This tab is a handy to-do list. You can create new tasks for yourself or other members of your team, track pending tasks, and even send annoying e-mail reminders about uncompleted tasks.

 ✦ **Documents:** This tab provides quick access to the site's document folders.

✦ **Links:** This tab provides an area where you can create a list of useful links. For example, you can create links to Web sites that have information about topics that interest you.

 ✦ **Information:** This tab displays information about the document you're working on, such as who created it and when it was created.

Visiting a SharePoint Team Services site

SharePoint Team Services sites have many features, such as discussion forums and announcements, that aren't available from within Word. To use these features, you can visit the SharePoint Team Services site from a Web browser, such as Internet Explorer. Just type the address of the team site in the browser's address bar and type your user ID and password when prompted. Figure 6-8 shows a typical SharePoint Team Services site.

One of the best features of SharePoint is that it lets you customize the STS site in many ways. For starters, you can add your own announcements, add links to your important Web sites in the Links section, and create additional document libraries. You can also click the <u>Modify This Page</u> link to access a menu that lets you add or remove optional elements and change the appearance of the pages. And if you're gutsy, you can use the Microsoft Web page editor, FrontPage, to customize many other aspects of an STS site.

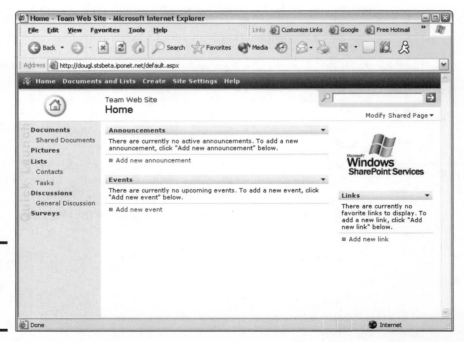

Figure 6-8:
A Share-Point Team Services site.

Book IV

Getting Graphic

The 5th Wave   By Rich Tennant

©RICHTENNANT

"Eddy, I said, 'Make a Word chart,' not 'Make a WORM chart.'"

Contents at a Glance

Chapter 1: Inserting Pictures and Clip Art

In This Chapter

✔ Using free pictures

✔ Finding a picture you like

✔ Moving, sizing, cropping, and stretching pictures

✔ Adjusting the appearance of an image

✔ Adding a border to a picture

✔ Wrapping text around your pictures.

*F*ace it: Most of us are not born with even an ounce of artistic ability. Some day (soon, I hope), those genetic researchers combing through the billions and billions of genes strung out on those twisty DNA helixes will discover The Artist Gene. Then, in spite of protests from the DaVincis and Monets among us (who fear that their NEA grants will be threatened), doctors will splice the little bugger into our own DNA strands so that we can all be artists. Of course, this procedure won't be without its side effects: Some will develop an insatiable craving for croissants, and others will inexplicably develop French accents and whack off their ears. But artists we shall be.

Until then, you have to rely on clip art, pictures you find on the Internet, or pictures that you scan into the computer using a scanner or take with a digital camera.

Exploring the Many Types of Pictures

The world is awash with many different formats in which you can store pictures on your computer. Fortunately, Word works with almost all these formats. The following sections describe the two basic types of pictures that you can work with in Word: bitmap pictures and vector drawings.

Bitmap pictures

A *bitmap picture* is a collection of small dots that comprise an image. Bitmap pictures are most often used for photographs and for icons and other buttons used on Web pages. You can create your own bitmap pictures with a scanner, a digital camera, or a picture drawing program, such as Adobe Photoshop or Corel PHOTO-PAINT. You can even create crude bitmap pictures with Microsoft Paint, which is the free painting program that comes with Windows.

The dots that comprise a bitmap picture are called *pixels*. The number of pixels in a given picture depends on two factors: the picture's resolution and its size. *Resolution* refers to the number of pixels per inch. Most computer monitors (and projectors) display 72 pixels per inch. At this resolution, a 1-inch square picture requires 5,184 pixels (72×72). Photographs printed on an inkjet or laser printer usually have a much higher resolution, often 300 pixels per inch or more. At 300 pixels per inch, a 4" x 6" photograph requires more than 2 million pixels.

The amount of color information stored for the picture — also referred to as the picture's *color depth* — affects how many bytes of computer memory the picture requires. The color depth determines how many different colors the picture can contain. Most pictures have one of two color depths: 256 colors or 16.7 million colors. Most simple charts, diagrams, cartoons, and other types of clip art look fine at 256 colors. Photographs usually use 16.7 million colors.

16.7 million color pictures are also known as *TrueColor* pictures or *24-bit color* pictures.

A 4" x 6" photograph, which has more than two million pixels, requires about 2MB to store with 256 colors. With TrueColor, the picture size jumps to a whopping 6.4MB. Fortunately, you can compress bitmap pictures to reduce their size without noticeably distorting the image. Depending on the actual contents of the picture, a 6MB picture may reduce to 250KB or less.

Bitmap picture files usually have filename extensions such as `.bmp`, `.gif`, `.jpg`, `.png`, or `.pcx`. Table 1-1 lists the bitmap file formats that Word supports.

Table 1-1	Word's Bitmap Picture File Formats
Format	*What It Is*
BMP	Garden variety Windows bitmap file, used by Microsoft Paint and many other programs
GIF	Graphics Interchange Format, a format commonly used for small Internet pictures
JPG	JPEG, a common format for photographs (JPEG stands for Joint Photographic Experts Group, but that won't be on the test)

Format	What It Is
PCD	Kodak Photo CD format
PCT	Macintosh PICT files
PCX	A variant type of bitmap file, also used by Microsoft Paint
PNG	Portable Network Graphics file, an image format designed for Internet graphics
TGA	Targa files
TIF	Tagged Image Format file, another bitmap program most often used for high-quality photographs

Victor, give me a vector

Besides bitmap pictures, the other category of picture files that you can use with Word are vector drawings. A *vector drawing* — sometimes called a *line drawing* — is a picture file that contains detailed instructions for how to draw the basic shapes, such as lines, curves, rectangles, and so on, that comprise drawn pictures. You usually create vector drawings with high-powered drawing programs, such as CorelDRAW or Adobe Illustrator.

Word supports all the most popular vector drawing formats, as I describe in Table 1-2.

Table 1-2	Word's Vector File Formats
Format	What It Is
CDR	CorelDRAW, a popular, upper-crust drawing program
CGM	Computer Graphics Metafile
DRW	Micrografx Designer or Micrografx Draw, two popular ooh-aah drawing programs
DXF	AutoCAD, a popular drafting program
EMF	An Enhanced Windows MetaFile picture
EPS	Encapsulated PostScript, a format used by some high-end drawing programs
WMF	Windows MetaFile, a format that many programs recognize
WPG	A WordPerfect drawing

Book IV
Chapter 1

Inserting Pictures and Clip Art

Where to Get Pictures

Whether you buy Word by itself or get it as part of Microsoft Office, you also get a collection of thousands of pictures, sound, and motion clips that you can pop directly into your documents.

A program called the Clip Organizer manages the Word clip art pictures. This nifty little program keeps track of images, sounds, and movies spread out all over your hard drive and spares you the unpleasant chore of rummaging through your directories to look for that picture of Elvis that you know you have somewhere. Clip Organizer also takes the guesswork out of using clip art: Rather than choosing a filename like `elvisfat.jpg` and hoping that it's the one you are looking for, you can see the clip art before you add it to your document.

Clip Organizer lets you search for clip art pictures using keywords. Keywords make searching for the perfect clip art pictures for your pages easy.

The first time you access the clip art, Word launches the Clip Organizer, which offers to search your entire hard drive and create a catalog of all the pictures that it contains. I suggest you accept this offer so that you can use the Clip Organizer to access your own picture files in addition to the clip art files that come with Word. However, be prepared to spend a few minutes waiting for this initial search to finish. This would be a good time to take a walk.

If you don't like the pictures that come with Word, you can scour the Internet for pictures to use. Beware, though, that copyright restrictions usually apply to pictures you find on the Internet. You can't legally point your browser to an Internet site, download any old picture, and use it in your documents without permission of the picture's owner. For more information about finding clip art pictures on the Internet, see the section "Getting clip art from the Internet" later in this chapter.

If you have a scanner connected to your computer, you can scan photographs and images directly into Word. And if you have a digital camera, you can connect it to your computer and copy its pictures into Word. For more information, see the section "Inserting a picture directly from a scanner or digital camera."

Inserting Pictures into Your Documents

The following sections describe various ways to insert pictures into your documents: inserting clip art, downloading a clip art picture from the Internet, inserting a picture from a file, and inserting an image directly from a scanner or digital camera.

Inserting clip art

The following steps explain how to drop clip art into your document:

1. **Move the insertion point to the location where you want to insert the clip art.**

2. **Choose Insert⇨Picture⇨Clip Art.**

   Sorry, Word offers no shortcut key for this command. If you like the mouse, though, you can click the Insert Clip Art button instead. It's the one with the picture of the little cartoon person located near the middle of the Drawing toolbar at the bottom of the screen.

3. **Behold the Clip Art task pane in all its splendor.**

   After a brief moment's hesitation, the Clip Art task pane pops up, as shown in Figure 1-1.

4. **Type a keyword in the Search For text box, and then click the Go button.**

   For example, to search for pictures of trombones, type **Trombone** in the Search For text box, and then click Go.

   Word searches through the Clip Organizer to locate the clip art you're looking for, and then displays thumbnails of the pictures it finds in the Clip Art task pane.

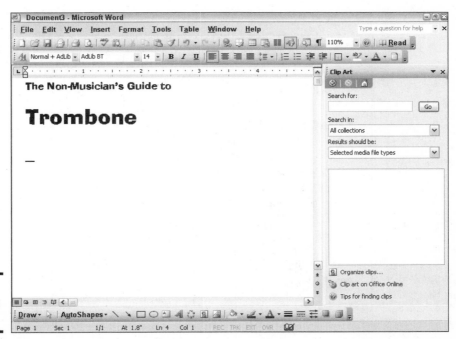

Figure 1-1:
The Clip Art task pane.

**Book IV
Chapter 1**

Inserting Pictures and Clip Art

5. **Click the picture that you want to use.**

   The picture is inserted, as shown in Figure 1-2.

6. **When you finish inserting pictures, click the Clip Art task pane's Close button (the X in the upper-right corner of the task pane).**

   The task pane vanishes.

You probably want to move the picture and change its size. To find out how, see the section "Sizing and stretching a picture" later in this chapter.

If you find a clip art picture you like, you can find other pictures that are drawn in a similar style by right-clicking the picture in the Clip Art task pane (or by clicking the down-arrow on the right side of the picture) and then choosing Find Similar Style.

The Clip Art task pane also has a Search In drop-down list that lets you choose which clip art collections to search. In addition, the Results Should Be drop-down list lets you limit your search to clip art, pictures, sounds, or videos.

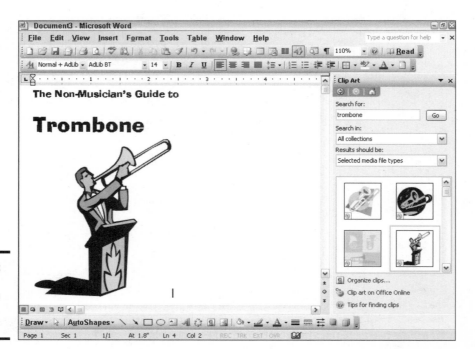

Figure 1-2: Word inserts the picture on the page.

Inserting clip art from the Internet

As if the vast collection of clip art that comes with Office and Word isn't enough, Microsoft also maintains a clip library on the Internet that you can use. If you have access to the Internet, you can access this additional clip art library by clicking the Clip Art on Office Online link at the bottom of the Clip Art task pane. A separate Internet Explorer window opens, as shown in Figure 1-3.

To search for clip art images, change the media type drop-down list near the top right of the page from All Media Types to Clip Art, type one or more search words, and then click the Search button (the green button with the arrow). If you find a clip art image you want, you can mark it for later download. Then, after you find all the images you want to download, you can choose an option that allows you to download the images directly into the Clip Organizer. You can then call up the images using the Clip Art task pane, which I describe earlier in this chapter.

Figure 1-3: The Microsoft Office Online site, where you can find loads of free clip art.

Inserting a picture from a file

If you happen to already have an image file on your computer that you want to insert into a document, Word lets you insert the file by choosing Insert➪ Picture➪From File. With this command, you bypass the Clip Art task pane altogether. These steps show you how:

1. **Move to the location where you want to splash a picture.**

2. **Choose Insert➪Picture➪From File.**

If you prefer, click the Insert Picture button (the icon that looks like a pretty mountain sunset) on the Picture toolbar. Either way, you are rewarded with the Insert Picture dialog box, shown in Figure 1-4.

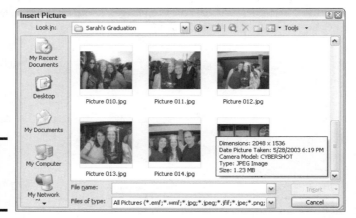

Figure 1-4:
The Insert Picture dialog box.

3. **Dig through the bottom of your hard drive until you find the file that you want.**

The picture you want may be anywhere. Fortunately, the Insert Picture dialog box has all the controls you need to search high and low until you find the file. Just click the icons at the left side of the box or click in the Look In drop-down list, and you are halfway there.

4. **Click the file and then click Insert.**

You're done!

You also can paste a picture directly into Word by way of the Clipboard. Anything that you can copy to the Clipboard you can paste into Word. For example, you can doodle a sketch in Paint, copy it, and then zap over to Word and paste it. Voilà — instant picture! Or, if you find a picture you like on the Internet — and the picture isn't protected by copyright — you can right-click the picture and choose Copy, and then scoot over to Word and paste the picture in.

Inserting a picture directly from a scanner or digital camera

If you have a scanner connected to your computer and properly configured, you can insert pictures from it directly into Word. First, put the picture you want to scan into your scanner. Then, choose Insert➪Picture➪From Scanner or Camera. The dialog box shown in Figure 1-5 appears. If you have more than one imaging device connected to your computer, choose the device that you want to use from the drop-down list. Then, click the Insert button and wait a minute or so for the scanner to scan the picture and insert it into your document. You probably need to crop and resize the picture to get it just right. (You find out how to do that later in this chapter.)

Figure 1-5:
The Insert Picture from Scanner or Camera dialog box.

Insert Picture from Scanner or Camera

Device

Hewlett-Packard PSC 750 Scanner

Resolution: ⦿ Web Quality   ◯ Print Quality

☑ Add Pictures to Clip Organizer

[Insert]   [Custom Insert]   [Cancel]

If you prefer to crop the picture before you scan it or set other scanning options, click the Custom Insert button instead. A dialog box comes up that lets you set various options for the scanner. You can choose whether to scan the image in color, grayscale, or black and white. You can also preview the image, and crop it before scanning it. Figure 1-6 shows the custom scan in action.

Don't ask who the kid in the picture is. Cute, though, huh?

You can also use the Custom Insert button to retrieve pictures directly from a digital camera. First, connect the camera to the computer via its USB cable. Then, choose Insert➪Picture➪From Scanner or Camera, select the camera from the list, and click the Custom Insert command. A dialog box comes up that lets you select the picture that you want to insert.

**Book IV
Chapter 1**

**Inserting Pictures
and Clip Art**

Rather than insert a picture directly from a camera into Word, you may prefer to first copy all of the pictures from the camera to your My Pictures folder. To do that, simply plug the camera into the computer via the USB cable. Then, when the Scanner and Camera Wizard appears, follow its instructions to copy the pictures to the My Pictures folder. After you copy the pictures, follow the steps in the section "Inserting a picture from a file."

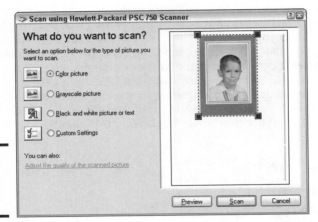

Figure 1-6: Using a custom scan.

Playing with Your Pictures

After you get a picture into Word, you'll have an irresistible urge to play with it. You'll want to make it bigger, make it smaller, make it taller, make it skinnier, move it here, move it there, make it brighter, make it darker, and so on. With luck, you are able to play with the picture the entire afternoon, and everyone will think you are working really hard.

Welcoming the Picture toolbar

Whenever you select a picture, a handy Picture toolbar appears, floating conveniently near the picture. This toolbar contains a dozen or so useful buttons that enable you to manipulate the picture. I describe the functions of many of these buttons in the sections that follow. For now, I summarize them in Table 1-3.

Table 1-3		Picture Toolbar Buttons
Button	*Name*	*What It Does*
	Insert Picture	Calls up the Insert Picture dialog box so you can insert another picture.

Button	Name	What It Does
	Color	Lets you choose whether the picture is color, grayscale, black and white, or washout.
	More Contrast	Increases the contrast.
	Less Contrast	Decreases the contrast.
	More Brightness	Increases the brightness.
	Less Brightness	Decreases the brightness.
	Crop	Crops the picture.
	Rotate	Rotates the picture.
	Line Style	Creates a border around the picture.
	Compress Pictures	Compresses the pictures in a document to save space.
	Text Wrapping	Lets you specify how text wraps around the picture.
	Format	Calls up the Format Picture dialog box.
	Set Transparent Color	Lets you create a transparent background for the picture.
	Reset Picture	Restores the picture to its original appearance.

The Picture toolbar disappears automatically whenever you select something other than a picture. Don't worry; it returns again all by itself when you select a picture again. As a result, you never have to summon the Picture toolbar manually — that is, by choosing View⇨Toolbars⇨Picture.

Book IV
Chapter 1

Inserting Pictures and Clip Art

Sizing and stretching a picture

In most cases, you need to resize your picture after you insert it. To do so, click the picture to select it. Notice the eight handles that appear around the picture. You can drag any or all of these handles to resize the picture. When you click one of the corner handles, the proportion of the picture stays the same as you change its size. When you drag one of the edge handles (top, bottom, left, or right) to change the size of the picture in just one dimension, you distort the picture's outlook as you go.

Stretching a picture by dragging one of the edge handles can dramatically change the picture's appearance. For example, you can stretch an object vertically to make it look tall and thin or horizontally to make it look short and fat. I usually like to stretch pictures of me vertically.

Cropping a picture

Sometimes, you want to cut off the edges of a picture so that you can include just part of the picture in your document. For example, you may have a picture of two people, only one of whom you like. You can use Word's cropping feature to cut off the other person.

To crop a picture, select the picture and click the Crop button located in the middle of the Picture toolbar. The selection handles change to special crop marks. You can then drag the crop marks around to cut off part of the picture. When you're satisfied, just click outside of the picture.

After you crop a picture, click anywhere outside the picture to turn off the cropping tool.

If you decide later that you don't like the cropping, you can click the Reset button on the Picture toolbar.

Adjusting the color and such

After you size and crop your picture, you may want to play with its color. You can do that in several ways:

✦ Use the Color button to select whether the picture displays in color (Automatic), black and white, or grayscale. Clicking the Color button reveals a menu that offers these choices as well as Washout, which adjusts the picture's brightness and contrast to create a washed-out appearance.

✦ Use the More Contrast and Less Contrast buttons to change the picture's contrast.

✦ Use the More Brightness and Less Brightness buttons to change the picture's brightness.

You can also adjust these settings by clicking the Format Picture button to bring up the Format Picture dialog box, shown in Figure 1-7. Then, use the controls in the Image Control section on the Picture tab to adjust the color type, brightness, and contrast.

Format Picture

| Colors and Lines | Size | Layout | Picture | Text Box | Web |

Crop from

Left: 0"   Top: 0"

Right: 0"   Bottom: 0"

Image control

Color: ▼

Brightness: ◄ ░░░ ► 86 %

Contrast: ◄ ░ ► 11 %

Compress...   Reset

OK   Cancel

Figure 1-7:
The Format
Picture
dialog box.

Rotating a picture

If your picture is upside down or sideways, you can use the Rotate button on the Picture toolbar to flip it around. Each time you click the Rotate button, the picture rotates counter-clockwise 90 degrees. So you may have to click the Rotate button two or three times to orient the picture the way you want.

If you want to rotate a picture to some arbitrary angle, you can do so by selecting the picture, and then dragging the picture's rotation handle. The rotation handle is the little green dot that appears above the picture when you select it. You can use the rotation handle to drag the picture to any angle you wish.

Yet another way to rotate a picture is to select the picture, and then click the Format Picture button on the Picture toolbar to bring up the Format Picture dialog box. Click the Size tab, and then adjust the Rotation spin control to the exact rotation you want.

Drawing boxes around your pictures

The Line Style button on the Picture toolbar lets you add a border around your picture. For example, Figure 1-8 shows three copies of a picture — one without lines, the other two with different line styles. This figure also shows the menu of line styles that's revealed when you click the Line Style button. To apply a border, simply select the picture, click the Line Style button, and then choose one of the line styles that appears in the menu.

**Book IV
Chapter 1**

**Inserting Pictures
and Clip Art**

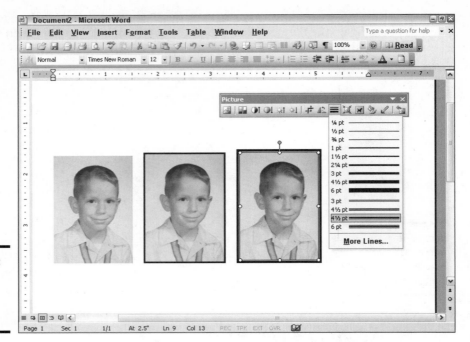

Figure 1-8:
Putting
boxes
around a
picture.

If you don't like any of the line styles predefined in the Line Styles menu, you can choose More Lines. The Format Picture dialog box, shown in Figure 1-9, comes up with the Colors and Lines tab showing. You can use this dialog box to specify a custom width for a line, to create dashed lines, or to change the color for the line.

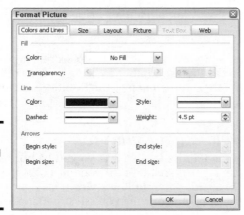

Figure 1-9:
Customizing
the lines
around a
picture.

Wrapping text around your picture

When you first insert a picture, the picture is inserted inline with the text. Any text that appears before or after the picture is lined up with the bottom of the picture; no text appears alongside the picture. For example, have a look at the text in the top half of Figure 1-10. Here, I inserted the picture of a cute little kid right before the first word of the paragraph.

In many cases, you want the text to wrap around the picture. The text in the bottom half of Figure 1-10 shows one way to do this. *Tight wrapping* causes the text to hug as close to the picture as possible. To switch to tight wrapping, select the picture, click the Text Wrapping button on the Picture toolbar, and choose Tight from the menu that appears.

The Text Wrapping button includes several other options:

✦ **In Line with Text:** The default wrapping option, and the one you're least likely to use. It places the picture inline with your text. The height of the line on which the picture appears is adjusted to match the height of the picture. In most cases, this wrapping doesn't look right.

✦ **Square:** Wraps the text squarely around the picture.

✦ **Tight:** Word figures out where the actual edges of the picture are and snuggles the text up as closely as possible.

✦ **Behind Text:** This option allows the text to spill right over the top of the picture, as if the picture weren't even there. The picture appears behind the text.

✦ **In Front of Text:** This option places the picture on top of the text. The picture may obscure some of the text, so use this option only if that's what you want.

✦ **Top and Bottom:** This option places text above and below the picture but doesn't allow any text to appear beside the picture.

✦ **Through:** This option is kind of like the Tight option, but results in an even tighter fit. If Word finds any blank spaces within the picture, it fills the space with text.

✦ **Edit Wrap Points:** This option lets you design your own wrapping shape around your picture by dragging little handles on a wrapping outline.

When you choose tight wrapping (or any other type of wrapping besides In Line with Text), the picture becomes a free-floating object and is no longer tied to a specific position within the text. You can drag the picture around to any location you want. You can even put it right in the middle of a paragraph, and Word wraps the text around both sides. See Figure 1-11 for an example. Here, I set the wrapping style to Tight, and then I dragged the picture to the middle of the paragraph.

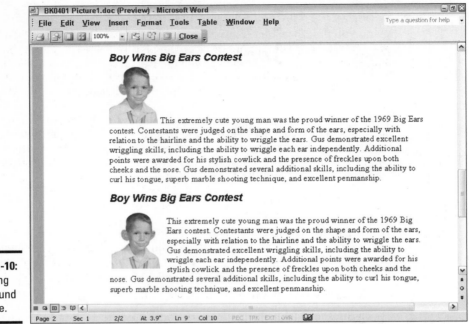

Figure 1-10:
Wrapping
text around
a picture.

Figure 1-11:
Plopping
a picture
into the
middle of a
paragraph.

Boy Wins Big Ears Contest

This extremely cute young man was the   proud winner of the 1969 Big Ears
contest. Contestants were judged on the   shape and form of the ears,
especially with relation to the hairline   and the ability to wriggle the ears.
Gus demonstrated excellent wriggling   skills, including the ability to
wriggle each ear independently.   Additional points were awarded for
his stylish cowlick and the presence   of freckles upon both cheeks and
the nose. Gus demonstrated several   additional skills, including the
ability to curl his tongue, superb marble shooting technique, and excellent penmanship.

Chapter 2: Drawing on Your Documents

In This Chapter

✔ Using the Word drawing tools

✔ Drawing lines, rectangles, and circles

✔ Using predefined AutoShapes

✔ Drawing polygons or curved lines

✔ Changing colors and line types

✔ Flipping and rotating objects

✔ Understanding layers and groups

✔ Lining things up and spacing them out

Chim-chiminey, chim-chiminey, chim-chim cheroo, I draws what I likes and I likes what I drew. . . .

Art time! Everybody get your crayons and glue and don an old paint shirt. You're going to cut out some simple shapes and paste them on your Word documents so that people either think that you are a wonderful artist or scoff at you for not using clip art.

This chapter covers the drawing features of Word 2003. One of the best things about Word is the cool drawing tools. Once upon a time, Word had but rudimentary drawing tools — the equivalent of a box of crayons — but Word now has powerful drawing tools that are sufficient for all but the most sophisticated aspiring artists among us.

Some General Drawing Tips

Before getting into the specifics of using each Word drawing tool, this section describes a handful of general tips for drawing pictures.

Activating the Drawing toolbar

You can find most of Word's drawing goodies on a special Drawing toolbar that appears at the bottom of the Word window. If you're missing the Drawing toolbar, call it forth by choosing View⇨Toolbars⇨Drawing. For more information, see the section "Working with the Drawing Toolbar."

Zooming in

When you work with the Word drawing tools, you may want to increase the zoom factor so that you can draw more accurately. I often work at 200, 300, or even 400 percent when I'm drawing. To change the zoom factor, click the down arrow next to the Zoom Control button (near the right side of the Standard toolbar) and choose a zoom factor from the list. Or you can click the zoom factor, type a new zoom percentage, and press Enter.

Yet another way to zoom in is to hold down the Ctrl key and spin the wheel that's between the buttons on your mouse.

Also, get rid of the task pane when you're drawing in order to make more room on-screen for the document. And to create even more room, close the document map or Thumbnail pane if either are open.

Saving frequently

Drawing is tedious work. You don't want to spend two hours working on a particularly important drawing only to lose it all just because a comet strikes your building or an errant Scud lands in your backyard. You can prevent catastrophic loss from incidents such as these by frequently pressing Ctrl+S or clicking the Save button with your mouse as you work. And always wear protective eyewear.

Don't forget Ctrl+Z

In my opinion, Ctrl+Z (the ubiquitous Undo command) is the most important key in any Windows program, and Word is no exception. Always remember that you're never more than one keystroke away from erasing a boo-boo. If you do something silly — like forgetting to group a complex picture before trying to move it — you can always press Ctrl+Z to undo your last action. Ctrl+Z is my favorite and most frequently used Word key combination. (For left-handed mouse users, Alt+Backspace does the same thing.) And for those who climb shrieking on a chair at the first sign of a mouse, try the handy Undo button on the Formatting toolbar or choose Edit⇨Undo.

Working with the Drawing Toolbar

Word provides a whole row of drawing tools, located on the Drawing toolbar. If the Drawing toolbar has disappeared, you can make it appear again by choosing View⇨Toolbars⇨Drawing.

Table 2-1 shows you what each drawing tool does.

Table 2-1	Buttons on the Drawing Toolbar	
Drawing Tool	*What It's Called*	*What It Does*
Draw ▾	Draw	Displays a menu of drawing commands.
	Select Objects	Not really a drawing tool, but rather the generic mouse pointer used to choose objects.
AutoShapes ▾	AutoShapes	Pops up the AutoShapes menu, which contains a bevy of shapes that you can draw, including fancy lines, arrows, crosses, flowchart symbols, stars, and more!
	Line	Draws a line.
	Arrow	Draws an arrow.
	Rectangle	Draws a rectangle. To make a perfect square, hold down the Shift key while you draw.
	Oval	Draws circles and ovals. To create a perfect circle, hold down the Shift key while you draw.
	Text Box	Adds a text object.
	Insert WordArt	Summons forth WordArt, which lets you create all sorts of fancy text effects.
	Insert Diagram or Organization Chart	Inserts a diagram or organization chart.

**Book IV
Chapter 2**

Drawing on Your Documents

(continued)

Table 2-1 *(continued)*

Drawing Tool	What It's Called	What It Does
	Insert Clip Art	Summons the Clip Art task pane.
	Insert Picture	Inserts a picture.
	Fill Color	Sets the color used to fill solid objects, such as circles and ellipses, as well as AutoShapes.
	Line Color	Sets the color used to draw lines, including lines around rectangles, ellipses, and AutoShapes.
	Font Color	Sets the color used for text.
	Line Style	Sets the style used for lines.
	Dash Style	Creates dashed lines.
	Arrow Style	Creates lines with arrowheads.
	Shadow Style	Creates shadows.
	3-D Style	Creates 3-D effects.

The good folks at Microsoft couldn't decide whether the Drawing toolbar should contain buttons or menus, so they threw in some of both. The Draw and AutoShapes buttons are actually menus that behave just like menus on a normal menu bar: Click them to reveal a menu of choices or use the Alt key shortcuts to activate them. (Alt+R activates the Draw menu, and Alt+U activates the AutoShapes menu.)

Canvassing the Situation

Every artist needs a canvas on which to work. So whenever you add one of the drawing objects that I describe in this chapter to a document, Word creates a gizmo called a *canvas* and places the object in it. For example, Figure 2-1 shows a drawing in a canvas. (The canvas is the big rectangle around the face.)

The purpose of the canvas is to group together multiple objects that make up a single drawing. That way, you can easily resize the drawing, change the way text flows around it, or move the drawing to another location in your document.

The canvas has its own toolbar that lets you play tricks on the canvas. The Canvas toolbar doesn't appear automatically, but you can summon it by right-clicking on the canvas and choosing Show Canvas Toolbar. Table 2-2 describes the buttons on the Canvas toolbar.

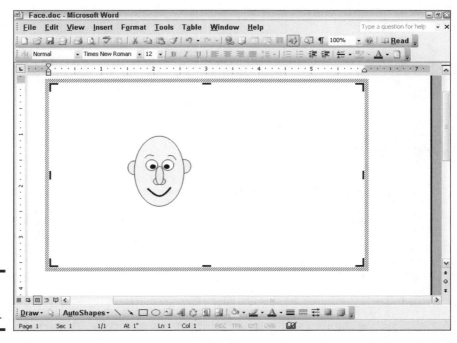

Figure 2-1: A drawing in a canvas.

Book IV Chapter 2

Drawing on Your Documents

Table 2-2	Buttons on the Canvas Toolbar	
Drawing Tool	*What It's Called*	*What It Does*
Fit	Fit Drawing to Canvas	Resizes all of the objects in the drawing to make it fit the canvas.
Expand	Expand Canvas	Makes the canvas a tad bit bigger. Each time you click it, the canvas grows a little, kind of like what happens to me each time I eat an Oreo.
Scale Drawing	Scale Drawing	Lets you adjust the size of the drawing while keeping the drawing objects in proportion. Click Scale Drawing, and then drag one of the corners of the canvas to resize the drawing.
	Text Wrapping	Displays a menu of text wrapping options for the drawing.

If you don't want to use a drawing canvas when you create a drawing object, press the Esc key after you select one of the drawing buttons on the toolbar but before you draw the object. For example, to create a rectangle without a canvas, click the Rectangle button on the Drawing toolbar, press Esc to banish the canvas, and then draw your rectangle.

Drawing Simple Objects

To draw an object on a document, click the Drawing toolbar button that represents the object you want to draw and then use the mouse to draw the object on the document. Well, drawing is not always as simple as that. You find detailed instructions for drawing with the more important tools in the following sections. Before I get to that, though, I want to give you some pointers to keep in mind:

✦ **Choosing a location:** Before you draw an object, move the insertion point to the location where you want the object to appear. You can always move the object later, but starting it in the right position is best.

✦ **Adding text to an object:** Word has two types of objects: shapes (such as circles, rectangles, and crosses) and lines/arcs. Word enables you to add text to any shape object, but you can't add text to a line or arc object.

✦ **Using or loosing the canvas:** When you first click an object to begin a drawing, Word inserts a canvas for the drawing. If you don't want to draw on a canvas, press Esc to get rid of it.

✦ **Fixing a mistake:** You can delete the object that you just drew by pressing the Delete key; then try drawing the object again. Or you can change its size or stretch it by clicking it and dragging its love handles.

Table 2-3 summarizes some handy shortcuts that you can use while drawing.

Table 2-3	Drawing Shortcuts
Shortcut	*What It Does*
Shift	Force lines to be horizontal or vertical, arcs and ellipses to be true circles, rectangles to be squares; and draw other regular shapes.
Ctrl	Draw objects from the center rather than from end to end.
Ctrl+Shift	Draw from the center and enforce squareness or circleness.
Double-click any button on the Drawing toolbar	Draw several objects of the same type.

The last shortcut in Table 2-3 needs a bit of explanation. If you click a drawing tool button once (such as the rectangle or ellipse button), the mouse cursor reverts to an arrow after you draw an object. To draw another object, you must click a drawing tool button again. If you know in advance that you want to draw more than one object of the same type, double-click the drawing tool button. Then you can keep drawing objects of the selected type. To stop drawing, click the Selection tool button (the arrow at the left end of the Drawing toolbar).

Drawing straight lines

You use the Line button to draw straight lines on your documents. Here are the steps:

1. **Click the Line button.**

2. **Point to where you want the line to start.**

3. **Click and drag the mouse cursor to where you want the line to end.**

4. **Release the mouse button when you reach your destination.**

You can choose Format➪Colors and Lines to change the line color and other features (thickness, dashes, and arrowheads) for a line or arc object. Or you can click the Line Style button or Line Color button on the Drawing toolbar (refer to Table 2-1) to change these attributes.

After you draw a line, you can adjust it by clicking it and then dragging the handles that appear on each end of the line.

Remember: You can force a line to be perfectly horizontal or vertical by holding down the Shift key while you draw. And if you hold the Shift key and drag diagonally while you draw the line, the line is constrained to perfect 45-degree angles.

Drawing rectangles, squares, ovals, and circles

To draw a rectangle, follow these steps:

1. **Click the Rectangle button.**

2. **Point to where you want to position one corner of the rectangle.**

3. **Click the mouse button and drag to where you want to position the opposite corner of the rectangle.**

4. **Release the mouse button.**

The steps for drawing an oval are the same as the steps for drawing a rectangle except that you click the Oval button rather than the Rectangle button.

You can choose Format⇨Colors and Lines to change the fill color or the line style for a rectangle or oval object. You also can use the Line Style button or the Fill Color button on the Drawing toolbar.

To apply a shadow, click the Shadow button. See Chapter 3 of this minibook for more information.

To draw a square or perfectly round circle, select the Oval button or the Rectangle button, but hold down the Shift key while you draw. And you can adjust the size or shape of a rectangle or circle by clicking it and dragging any of its love handles.

Using AutoShapes

Rectangles and circles aren't the only two shapes that Word can draw automatically. When you click the AutoShapes button on the Drawing toolbar, a whole menu of AutoShapes appears. These AutoShapes make drawing common shapes, such as pentagons, stars, and flowchart symbols, easy.

The AutoShapes menu organizes AutoShapes into the following categories:

✦ **Lines:** Straight lines, curved lines, lines with arrowheads, scribbly lines, and freeform shapes that can become polygons if you want. The freeform AutoShape is useful enough to merit its own section, "Drawing a Polygon or Freeform Shape," which immediately follows this section.

 ✦ **Connectors:** Lines with various shapes and arrowheads with connecting dots on the ends.

 ✦ **Basic Shapes:** Squares, rectangles, triangles, crosses, happy faces, lightning bolts, and more.

 ✦ **Block Arrows:** Fat arrows pointing in various directions.

 ✦ **Flowchart:** Various flowcharting symbols.

 ✦ **Stars and Banners:** Shapes that add sparkle to your presentations.

 ✦ **Callouts:** Text boxes and speech bubbles like those used in comic strips.

 ✦ **More AutoShapes:** In fact, 73 more.

The following steps explain how to draw an AutoShape:

1. **Click the AutoShapes button on the Drawing toolbar.**

The AutoShapes menu appears.

2. **Choose the AutoShape category that you want.**

A toolbar of AutoShapes appears. Figure 2-2 shows all the toolbars that you can access from the AutoShapes menu. Look this figure over to see what kind of AutoShapes are available. (Of course, when you actually use Word, only one of these toolbars is visible at a time.)

3. **Click the AutoShape that you want to draw.**

4. **Click in the document where you want the shape to appear and then drag the shape to the desired size.**

Hold down the Shift key while drawing the AutoShape to create an undistorted shape.

When you release the mouse button, the AutoShape object takes on the current fill color and line style.

5. **Start typing if you want the shape to contain text.**

After you type your text, you can use Word's formatting features to change its typeface, size, color, and so on. For more information, refer to Chapter 4 of this minibook.

**Book IV
Chapter 2**

**Drawing on Your
Documents**

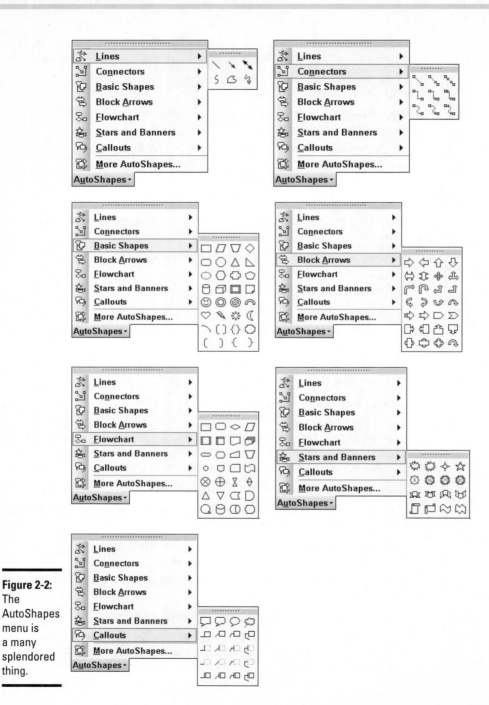

Figure 2-2:
The
AutoShapes
menu is
a many
splendored
thing.

You can change an AutoShape object to a different type of AutoShape object by selecting the object and then choosing Draw⇨Change AutoShape.

Many AutoShape buttons have an extra handle shaped like a yellow diamond that enables you to adjust some aspect of the object's shape. For example, the block arrows have a handle that enables you to increase or decrease the size of the arrowhead. The location of these handles varies depending on the shape you're working with. Figure 2-3 shows how you can use these extra handles to vary the shapes produced by six different AutoShapes. For each of the six shapes, the first object shows how the AutoShape is initially drawn; the other two objects drawn with each AutoShape show how you can change the shape by dragging the extra handle.

Figure 2-3: You can create interesting variations by grabbing the extra handles on these Auto-Shapes.

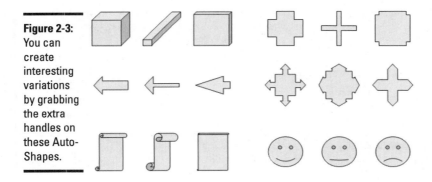

Drawing a Polygon or Freeform Shape

Mr. Arnold, my seventh-grade math teacher, taught me that a *polygon* is a shape that has many sides and has nothing to do with having more than one spouse (one is certainly enough for most of us). Triangles, squares, and rectangles are polygons, but so are hexagons and pentagons, as are any unusual shapes whose sides all consist of straight lines. Politicians are continually inventing new polygons when they revise the boundaries of congressional districts.

One of the most useful AutoShapes is the Freeform tool. It creates polygons, with a twist: Not all the sides have to be straight lines. The Freeform AutoShape tool lets you build a shape whose sides are a mixture of straight lines and freeform curves. Figure 2-4 shows three examples of shapes that I created with the Freeform AutoShape tool.

Flowcharting 1970s style

I remember when I took my first computer programming class. The year was 1976. I had to buy a plastic template with flowcharting symbols cut into it so that I could learn how to draw proper flowcharts for my COBOL programs.

The 2003 edition of Microsoft Word has flowcharting symbols on the AutoShapes menu — a very good thing. Now I can throw away that old plastic template. You never know when you may need one of these symbols, just for old time's sake:

	Card	Most computer users have never even seen one of these. They were considered old-fashioned 25 years ago.
	Punched Tape	I used a computer that worked with punched tape once. The paper tape always broke, but you could easily mend it with Scotch tape.
	Tape	Few PCs have reel-to-reel tape drives. But if you want to see one, tune into the SciFi channel late at night.
	Delay	Back in the 1970s, computers were so fast that sometimes you had to program in a delay so that the users wouldn't get spoiled.
	Summing Junction	This popular TV series was a spin-off from *Petticoat Junction*.

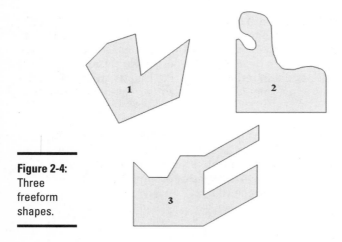

Figure 2-4:
Three
freeform
shapes.

Follow these steps to create a polygon or freeform shape:

1. **Click the AutoShapes button and then choose Lines.**

   The Lines toolbar appears.

2. **Click the Freeform button.**
3. **Click where you want to position the first corner of the object.**
4. **Click where you want to position the second corner of the object.**
5. **Keep clicking wherever you want to position a corner.**
6. **To draw a freeform side on the shape, hold down the mouse button when you click a corner and then draw the freeform shape with the mouse. When you get to the end of the freeform side, release the mouse button.**

   You can then click again to add more corners. Shape 2 in Figure 2-4 has one freeform side.

7. **To finish the shape, click near the first corner — the one that you created in Step 3.**

   You don't have to be exact: If you click anywhere near the first corner that you put down, Word assumes that the shape is finished.

You're finished! The object assumes the line and fill color from the document's color scheme.

You can reshape a polygon or freeform shape by double-clicking it and then dragging any of the love handles that appear on the corners.

If you hold down the Shift key while you draw a polygon, the sides are constrained to 45-degree angles. I drew shape 3 in Figure 2-4 in this manner. How about a constitutional amendment requiring Congress to use the Shift key when it redraws congressional boundaries?

You also can use the Freeform AutoShape tool to draw a multi-segmented line, called an *open shape*. To draw an open shape, you can follow the preceding steps, except that you skip Step 7. Instead, double-click or press the Esc key when the line is done.

Drawing a Curved Line or Shape

Another useful AutoShape tool is the Curve button, which lets you draw curved lines or shapes. Figure 2-5 shows several examples of curved lines and shapes drawn with the Curve AutoShape tool.

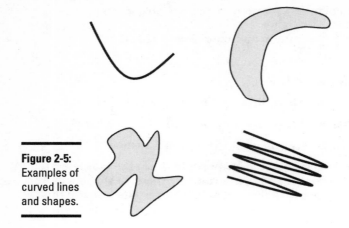

Figure 2-5:
Examples of
curved lines
and shapes.

Here are the steps for drawing a curved line or shape:

1. **Click the AutoShapes button and then choose Lines.**

The Lines toolbar appears.

2. **Click the Curve button.**

3. **Click where you want the curved line or shape to begin.**

4. **Click where you want the first turn in the curve to appear.**

The straight line turns to a curved line, bent around the point where you clicked. As you move the mouse, the bend of the curve changes.

5. **Click to add additional turns to the curve.**

Each time you click, a new bend is added to the line. Keep clicking until the line is as twisty as you want.

6. **To finish a line, double-click where you want the end of the curved line to appear. To create a closed shape, double-click over the starting point, which is where you clicked in Step 3.**

Setting the Fill, Line, and Font Color

The three color controls that appear on the Drawing toolbar let you set various colors for drawing objects:

 ✦ **Fill Color:** This color fills a solid object.

 ✦ **Line Color:** The color used for an object's lines.

 ✦ **Font Color:** This color fills an object's text.

These buttons behave a little strangely, so they merit a bit of explanation. *Note:* The current color for each button displays in a little horizontal stripe beneath the button's icon.

Each of the color buttons actually consists of two parts: a button and an arrow. Click the button to assign the current fill, line, or text color to the selected object. Click the arrow to apply any color that you want to the selected object.

When you click the arrow, a menu appears. For example, Figure 2-6 shows the Fill Color menu that appears when you click the arrow attached to the Fill Color button. As you can see, this menu includes a palette of colors that you can select.

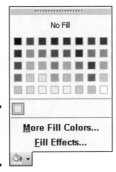

Figure 2-6:
The Fill
Color menu.

If you set the Fill Color, Line Color, or Font Color to Automatic, the fill color changes whenever you change the presentation's color scheme.

If you want to use a color that isn't visible on the menu, click More Fill Colors; clicking this option displays the Colors dialog box shown in Figure 2-7, which resembles a tie-dyed version of Chinese checkers. You can choose any color you want from this dialog box.

**Book IV
Chapter 2**

**Drawing on Your
Documents**

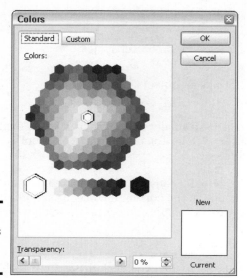

Figure 2-7:
More colors
to choose
from.

The Standard tab of the Colors dialog box shown in Figure 2-7 shows 127 popular colors, plus white, black, and shades of gray. If you want to use a color that doesn't appear in the dialog box, click the Custom tab. This step summons the custom color controls, shown in Figure 2-8. Here, you can construct any of the 16 million colors theoretically possible with Word. You need a Ph.D. in physics to figure out how to adjust the Red, Green, and Blue controls, though. Play here if you want, but be careful. You can create some really ugly colors if you aren't careful.

You can also apply a fill effect — such as a gradient fill, pattern, texture, or picture — to an object by choosing the Fill Effects command from the Fill Color menu. The Fill Effects dialog box pops up, which I describe in Chapter 3 of this minibook to a tee.

The Line Color and Font Color menus have similar commands. In addition, the Line Color menu includes a Patterned Lines command that lets you pick a pattern to apply to lines. For more about lines, see the next section, "Setting the Line Style."

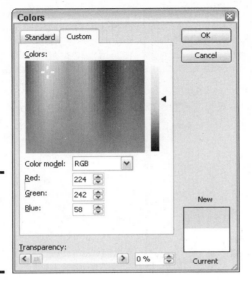

Figure 2-8:
Billions and
billions of
colors to
choose
from.

Setting the Line Style

Three buttons on the Drawing toolbar let you change the style of line
objects:

✦ **Line Style:** The thickness of the lines that outline the object.

✦ **Dash Style:** The dashing pattern used for the lines that outline the
object. The default uses a solid line, but different patterns are available
to create dashed lines.

✦ **Arrow Style:** Lines can have an arrowhead at either or both ends.
Arrowheads are used mostly on line and arc objects.

To change any of these object attributes, simply select the object or objects
that you want to change and then click the appropriate button to change the
style. A menu of style options appears.

The Line Style menu includes a More Lines command that summons the Format AutoShape dialog box shown in Figure 2-9. From this dialog box, you can control all aspects of a line's style: its color, width, dash pattern, and end style (you can apply various arrowheads). The Arrow Style command includes a More Arrows command that summons the same dialog box.

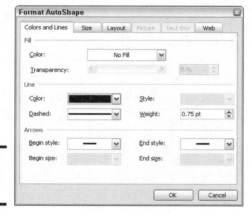

Figure 2-9: Setting the line style.

Flipping and Rotating Objects

To *flip* an object means to create a mirror image of it. To *rotate* an object means to turn it about its center. Word lets you flip objects horizontally or vertically, rotate objects in 90-degree increments, or freely rotate an object to any angle.

Rotation works for text boxes and AutoShape text. Thus, you can use rotation to create vertical text or text skewed to any angle you want. However, flipping an object doesn't affect the object's text.

Flipping an object

Word enables you to flip an object vertically or horizontally to create a mirror image of the object. To flip an object, follow these steps:

1. **Choose the object that you want to flip.**

2. **Click the Draw button to reveal the Draw menu, choose Rotate or Flip, and then choose Flip Horizontal or Flip Vertical.**

Rotating an object 90 degrees

You can rotate an object in 90-degree increments by following these steps:

1. **Choose the object that you want to rotate.**

2. **Click the Draw button to reveal the Draw menu, choose Rotate or Flip, and then choose Rotate Left or Rotate Right.**

3. **To rotate the object 180 degrees, click the appropriate Rotate button again.**

Using the rotate handle

Remember how all the bad guys' hideouts were slanted in the old *Batman* TV show? The rotate handle lets you give your drawings that same kind of slant. With the rotate handle, you can rotate an object to any arbitrary angle just by dragging it with the mouse.

The rotate handle is the green handle that appears above the object, connected to the object by a line, as shown in Figure 2-10. You can rotate an object to any angle simply by dragging the rotate handle.

Figure 2-10:
Rotate handles enable you to rotate an object to any arbitrary angle.

Rotate handles

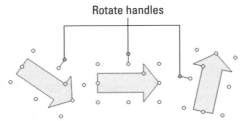

The following steps show you how to use the rotate handle:

1. **Click the object that you want to rotate.**

2. **Drag the rotate handle in the direction that you want to rotate the object.**

   As you drag, an outline of the object rotates around. When you get the object's outline to the angle you want, release the mouse button, and the object is redrawn at the new angle.

Another way to rotate an object is to select the object, click the Draw button, click Rotate or Flip, and then choose Free Rotate. Rotation handles then appear at all four corners of the object. You can rotate the object by dragging any of the four handles.

To restrict the rotation angle to 15-degree increments, hold the Shift key while dragging around the rotation handle.

When you hold down the Ctrl key while dragging a corner handle, the object rotates about the opposite corner handle rather than the center. This feature is very strange, but it's occasionally useful.

Drawing a Complicated Picture

When you add more than one object to a document, you may run into several problems. What happens when the objects overlap? How do you line up objects so that they don't look like they were thrown at the document from a moving car? And how do you keep together objects that belong together?

This section shows you how to use Word features to handle overlapped objects, and how to align and group objects. If you're interested in a description of how to use these features together to draw a picture, check out the sidebar titled "Don't let me tell you how I drew that funny face!" at the end of this chapter.

Changing layers

Whenever you have more than one object on a document, the potential exists for objects to overlap one another. Like most drawing programs, Word handles this problem by layering objects like a stack of plates. The first object that you draw is at the bottom of the stack; the second object is on top of the first; the third is atop the second object; and so on. If two objects overlap, the one that's at the highest layer wins; objects below it are partially covered. (*Note:* Word's layers aren't nearly as powerful as layers in programs, such as Adobe Illustrator or CorelDRAW. All layers really do in Word is set the stacking order when you place objects on top of one another.)

So far, so good — but what if you don't remember to draw the objects in the correct order? What if you draw a shape that you want to tuck behind a shape you've already drawn, or what if you want to bring an existing shape to the top of the pecking order? No problem. Word enables you to change the stacking order by moving objects toward the front or back so that they overlap just the way you want.

The Draw menu on the Drawing toolbar provides four commands for changing the stacking order, all grouped under the Order command:

✦ **Draw➪Order➪Bring to Front:** Brings the chosen object to the top of the stack.

✦ **Draw➪Order➪Send to Back:** Sends the chosen object to the back of the stack.

✦ **Draw➪Order➪Bring Forward:** Brings the chosen object one step closer to the front of the stack.

✦ **Draw➪Order➪Send Backward:** Sends the object one rung down the ladder.

Layering problems are most obvious when objects have a fill color. If an object has no fill color, objects behind it show through. In this case, the layering doesn't matter much.

If you have two objects that overlap and you don't want the one behind to show through, fill the one on top with a color.

To bring an object to the top of another, you may have to use the Bring Forward command several times. The reason is that even though the two objects appear to be adjacent, other objects may occupy the layers between them.

Line 'em up

Nothing looks more amateurish than objects dropped randomly on a document with no apparent concern for how they line up with each other. The Draw menu on the Drawing toolbar provides several alignment commands. To use them, first select the objects that you want to align. Then click the Draw button, click Align or Distribute, and then choose one of the following commands from the menu that appears:

	Align Left
	Align Center
	Align Right
	Align Top
	Align Middle
	Align Bottom

The first three commands align items horizontally; the last three align items vertically.

You can also distribute several items so that they are spaced evenly. Select the items that you want to distribute, click the Draw button, choose Align or Distribute, and then choose Distribute Horizontally or Distribute Vertically.

If you want objects to automatically adhere to an invisible grid when you draw them or move them about, click the Draw button, click Snap, and then choose To Grid. To turn the snap-to-grid feature off, choose Draw⇨Snap⇨To Grid again.

Using the grid

To help you create well-ordered documents, Word lets you display a grid of evenly spaced lines over the drawing canvas. These lines aren't actually a part of the drawing, so they won't appear when you print the document. They exist simply to make the task of lining things up a bit easier. Figure 2-11 shows an example of a drawing canvas with the grid turned on.

To display the grid, choose Draw⇨Grid. This command summons the Drawing Grid dialog box, shown in Figure 2-12. (You can also summon this dialog box by pressing Ctrl+G.)

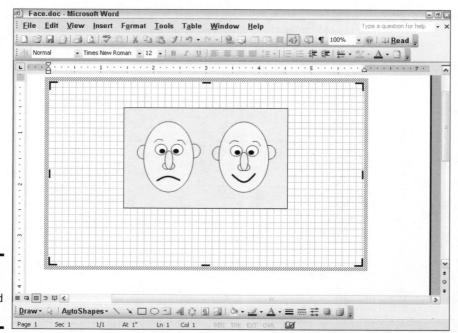

Figure 2-11: A drawing with the grid turned on.

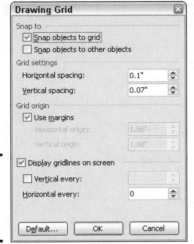

Figure 2-12:
The
Drawing
Grid dialog
box.

To activate the grid, select the Snap Objects to Grid check box, and then adjust the horizontal and vertical spacing to whatever settings you want. If you want to actually see the grid on-screen, select the Display Gridlines on Screen check box.

Note: You can check the Display Gridlines on Screen check box without checking Snap Objects to Grid. In that case, the gridlines appear, but objects don't automatically snap themselves to the grid.

Group therapy

A *group* is a collection of objects that Word treats as though it were one object. Using groups properly is one key to putting simple shapes together to make complex pictures without becoming so frustrated that you have to join a therapy group. ("Hello, my name is Doug, and Word drives me crazy.")

To create a group, follow these steps:

1. **Choose all objects that you want to include in the group.**

   Hold down the Shift key and click each of the items or hold down the mouse button and drag the resulting rectangle around all the items.

2. **Click Draw on the Drawing toolbar and then select the Group command.**

To take apart a group so that Word treats the objects as individuals again, follow these steps:

1. **Select the object group that you want to break up.**

2. **Choose Draw⇨Ungroup.**

Don't let me tell you how I drew that funny face!

In case you're interested, you can follow the bouncing ball to see how I created the goofy face that appears in a few figures in this chapter. By studying this creature, you can get an idea of how you use layers, groups, and alignment to create complicated pictures, as shown in these steps:

1. Draw the face shape using the Oval tool.

I filled the face with pale yellow.

2. Draw the eyes using the Oval tool.

To draw the eyes, I started by using the Oval button to draw an oval for the left eye, which I filled with white. Next, I pressed Ctrl+D to make a duplicate of the oval. Then I dragged the duplicate eye to the right side of the face. Next, I used the oval again to draw a little pupil inside the left eye, which I filled with black. I then duplicated the pupil and dragged the duplicate over to the right eye. Finally, I used the Curve AutoShape to draw the eyebrows.

3. Draw the ears using the Oval tool.

The only trick with the ears is using the Send to Back command to send the ears behind the face where they belong.

4. Draw the nose using the Oval tool.

The nose is actually three ovals. The first is the center part of the nose: It's a tall but narrow oval. The other two ovals are the nostrils, which are almost round. I used the Send Backward command on the nostrils to place them behind the first oval.

5. Draw the mouth using the Curve AutoShape.

6. Draw the body using the Freeform AutoShape.

When the body is drawn, I used Send to Back to send it behind the face. Then, I used a pattern as the fill for the body to create a lovely striped shirt.

Oh, I almost forgot. The last step is to choose all the objects that make up the face (by dragging and clicking a dotted-line square around the entire picture) and group them using Draw⇨Group. That way, I don't have to worry about accidentally dismembering my little friend.

If you create a group and then ungroup it so that you can work on its elements individually, you can easily regroup the objects. These steps show you how:

1. **Select at least one object that was in the original group.**

2. **Choose Draw⇨Regroup.**

    Word remembers which objects were in the group and automatically includes them.

Word enables you to create groups of groups. This capability is useful for complex pictures because it enables you to work on one part of the picture, group it, and then work on the next part of the picture without worrying about accidentally disturbing the part that you already grouped. After you have several such groups, select them and group them. You can create groups of groups of groups and so on, ad nauseam.

Chapter 3: Fill Effects, Ghosts, Shadows, and Other Effects

In This Chapter

✔ **Creating gradients**

✔ **Adding textures**

✔ **Playing with patterns**

✔ **Inserting pictures**

✔ **Turning on transparent fills**

✔ **Discovering shadows**

✔ **Checking out 3-D objects**

*T*his chapter builds on the basic drawing techniques that I describe in Chapter 2 of this minibook. In this chapter, you discover how to apply advanced fill effects, how to create shadows, and how to create 3-D effects. Have fun!

Working with Fill Effects

In Chapter 2 of this minibook, I show you how to use the Fill Color button on the Drawing toolbar to fill an object with a solid color. But the Fill Color button is not limited to just solid colors. If you choose the Fill Effects command from the menu that appears when you click the Fill Color button, you can apply four different types of fill effects to your drawing objects.

Figure 3-1 shows some drawing objects filled with each of the four types of effects that I describe in the following sections.

Making the gradient

A *gradient fill* is a fill effect that smoothly blends two or more colors. Gradient effects can be subtle or bold, depending on how similar the blended colors are. For example, if you blend a bright shade of yellow into a not-so-bright shade of yellow, the effect is subtle. But if you blend a bright shade of yellow into a bright shade of red, the effect is bold.

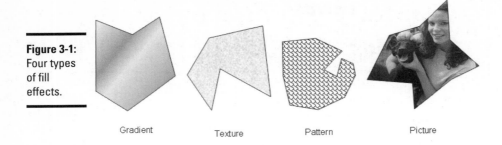

Figure 3-1:
Four types
of fill
effects.

Gradient   Texture   Pattern   Picture

To apply a gradient fill, click the Fill Color button, choose the Fill Effects command, and click the Gradient tab if it isn't already selected. The Gradient fill options display, as shown in Figure 3-2.

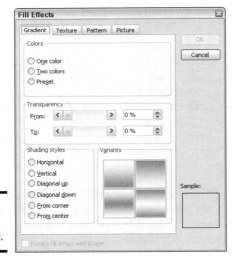

Figure 3-2:
Creating a
gradient fill.

Start by selecting a one-color shade, in which a single color fades to white or black, or a two-color shade, in which one color fades into another. Then select the Shade Style — Horizontal, Vertical, Diagonal Up, and so on. Finally, select one of the variants in the Variants area of the dialog box.

Alternatively, you can select one of several preset shadings by picking the Preset option. The preset shading options include Early Sunset, Nightfall, Rainbow, and several other interesting effects.

Applying a texture

A *texture* is a photo-quality bitmap image designed so that it can be repeated throughout without any noticeable tiling. Textures let you create objects that look like they're made of wood, stone, parchment, and so on.

To apply a texture, click the Fill Color button, choose the Fill Effects command, and click the Texture tab. The Texture options display, as shown in Figure 3-3. Here you can choose one of several textures to give your illustration a polished Formica look.

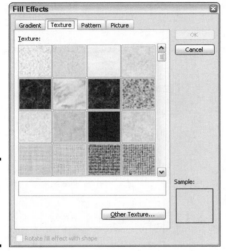

Figure 3-3:
The Formica dialog box (just kidding).

Using a pattern

If you select the Pattern tab in the Fill Effects dialog box, as shown in Figure 3-4, you can choose from any of 48 different patterns using your choice of foreground and background colors.

My personal favorites are the patterns that resemble bricks and cobblestones.

Note: You can change the background and foreground colors used to draw the pattern. You can create a nice brick pattern by setting the foreground color to a light gray and the background color to a deep red.

The problem with patterns

My only beef with Word's pattern fill feature is that you can't control the scale of the pattern. No matter how large or small the object being filled, the pattern always remains the same size. And, in general, the patterns are too small. In fact, the brick pattern is so small that when you print it, you almost have to use a magnifying glass to see the individual bricks.

What's even weirder is that the patterns all display the same size on-screen regardless of the zoom factor. For example, if you draw a 1-inch rectangle and fill it with bricks, each row of bricks has about 12 bricks in it. If you zoom in to 200%, the bricks don't get bigger. Instead, each row now has 24 bricks. Likewise, if you zoom down to 50%, each row now has 6 bricks. When I print the rectangle on my HP psc750 printer, each row has 18 bricks!

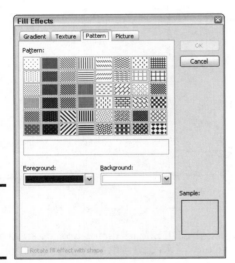

Figure 3-4:
Filling an
object with
a pattern.

Filling an object with a picture

If you click the Picture tab in the Fill Effects dialog box, the dialog box shown in Figure 3-5 appears. This dialog box allows you to select a picture to be used as a drawing object's fill. Just click the Select Picture button to bring up a dialog box that lets you rummage through your computer's hard disk to find a suitable picture.

Figure 3-5:
Filling an
object with
a picture.

Creating Transparent Fills

If you like scary movies, you can create a ghostly semitransparent fill for an object. This fill allows objects behind the semitransparent object to show through. To apply this effect, select the object that you want to turn into a ghost, and then choose the command that appears at the bottom of the Format menu. The exact name of this command varies depending on the type of object you select. For example, if you select a text box, choose Format⇨Text Box. However, if you select an AutoShape object, such as a circle or a rectangle, the command is Format⇨AutoShape.

Either way, the dialog box shown in Figure 3-6 appears. You can then slide the Transparency slider to set the amount of transparency for the object. If you move the Transparency slider all the way to the left (0%), the object is a solid color. Increasing the Transparency value from 0% lets more and more of whatever lies behind the object show through. If you move the slider all the way to the right (100%), the object is completely transparent, so the object's fill color doesn't show at all. In the figure, I set the transparency to 75%.

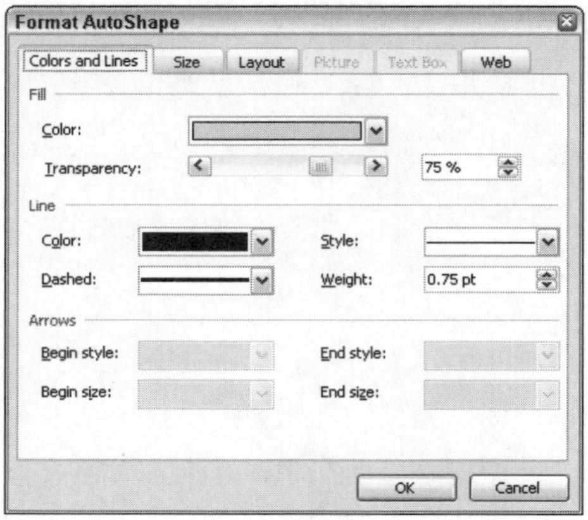

Format AutoShape

| Colors and Lines | Size | Layout | Picture | Text Box | Web |

Fill

Color: [   ] ▼

Transparency: ◄ [ⅢⅢ] ► [75 %] ⬍

Line

Color: [   ] ▼   Style: [   ] ▼

Dashed: [   ] ▼   Weight: [0.75 pt] ⬍

Arrows

Begin style: [   ] ▼   End style: [   ] ▼

Begin size: [   ] ▼   End size: [   ] ▼

[OK] [Cancel]

Figure 3-6:
Making a
ghost.

Applying a Shadow

To apply a shadow effect to an object, select the object and click the Shadow button. The Shadow menu shown in Figure 3-7 appears, offering several shadow styles. Click the shadow style that you want the object to assume.

If you select the Shadow Settings command from the Shadow menu, the Shadow Settings toolbar appears. The buttons on this toolbar allow you to nudge the shadow into exactly the right position and change the shadow color to create a custom shadow effect. Table 3-1 describes these buttons.

Table 3-1	Buttons on the Shadow Settings Toolbar	
Drawing Tool	*What It's Called*	*What It Does*
	Shadow On/Off	Turns the object's shadow on or off.
	Nudge Shadow Up	Moves the shadow up a bit.
	Nudge Shadow Down	Moves the shadow down a bit.
	Nudge Shadow Left	Moves the shadow left a bit.

Drawing Tool	What It's Called	What It Does
	Nudge Shadow Right	Moves the shadow right a bit.
	Shadow Color	Sets the shadow color.

Figure 3-7:
The Shadow menu.

Adding 3-D Effects

The 3-D button is one of the coolest buttons on the Drawing toolbar. This button lets you transform a dull and lifeless flat object into an exciting, breath-taking three-dimensional object. Figure 3-8 shows how you can use the 3-D button to transform several shapes into 3-D objects. In each case, the object on the left is a simple AutoShape, and the three objects to the right of the simple AutoShape are three-dimensional versions of the same shape.

To apply a 3-D effect to a shape, select the shape and click the 3-D button. The 3-D menu shown in Figure 3-9 appears. Click the effect that you want to apply. Or click No 3-D if you want to remove 3-D effects.

If you select 3-D Settings from the 3-D menu, the 3-D toolbar appears. You can use the controls on this toolbar to tweak the 3-D settings of the object to obtain just the right effect. You can tilt the object in any direction, set its depth, and change the lighting and surface textures. I describe the buttons on this toolbar in Table 3-2.

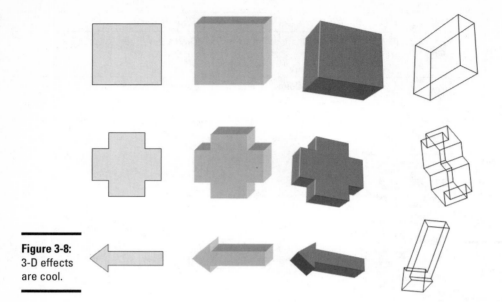

Figure 3-8:
3-D effects
are cool.

Figure 3-9:
The 3-D
menu.

Table 3-2	**Buttons on the 3-D Toolbar**	
Drawing Tool	*What It's Called*	*What It Does*
	3-D On/Off	Turns the 3-D feature on or off.
	Tilt Down	Rotates the object down.

Drawing Tool	What It's Called	What It Does
	Tilt Up	Rotates the object up.
	Tilt Left	Rotates the object left.
	Tilt Right	Rotates the object right.
	Depth	Sets the depth of the object.
	Direction	Sets the direction from which the 3-D object is viewed.
	Lighting	Sets the position and intensity of the lighting that illuminates the 3-D surfaces.
	Surface	Sets one of four styles for the 3-D surfaces: Wire Frame, Matte, Plastic, or Metal.
	3-D Color	Sets the color used for the 3-D surfaces.

Chapter 4: Working Graphically with Text

In This Chapter

- ✔ Creating text boxes
- ✔ Framing frames
- ✔ Using captions
- ✔ Inserting WordArt
- ✔ Employing callouts

*B*et you thought that text was text and graphics were graphics. Wrong! This chapter describes several Word features that let you incorporate text into your drawings. For example, you can add captions to pictures. You can also add text to most AutoShape objects. And you can use a special type of drawing object called *WordArt* to create fancy logos.

Have fun!

Using Text Boxes

A text box is a special type of shape designed to place text on your document without regard to the normal margins of the page. The most common use of text boxes is to add little bits of text to drawings. However, as I discuss in Chapter 5 of this minibook, text boxes are also sometimes used to create interesting desktop publishing effects, such as pull quotes or sidebars. For example, Figure 4-1 shows a document with a pull quote — a floating text box that highlights a quote from the document.

The following sections describe the ins and outs of working with text boxes.

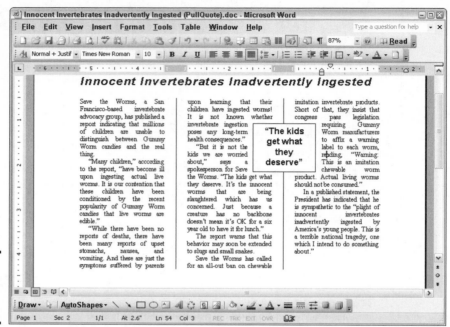

Figure 4-1:
A document with a text box.

Creating a text box

To create a text box, follow these steps:

1. **Click the Text Box button on the Drawing toolbar.**

2. **If you don't want to create a drawing canvas, press Esc.**

Keep the drawing canvas if the text box is part of a larger drawing. If the text box stands all by itself, you don't need the canvas.

3. **Click where you want one corner of the text box to appear and drag to where you want the opposite corner.**

Drawing a text box is similar to drawing a rectangle.

4. **Release the mouse button, and then type your text.**

The insertion pointer is automatically positioned in the text box, so you can immediately start typing text after you draw the text box.

Note: The default wrapping style for a text box is In Front of Text. With this setting, the text box obscures any normal document text that happens to fall behind the text box. In most cases, you want to change this setting to something more appropriate, such as Tight or Square. To do that, right-click the text box, choose the Format Text Box command, click the Layout tab, and change the Wrapping style. (For more information about what the different wrapping styles do, see Chapter 1 of this minibook.)

Most AutoShapes also function as text boxes. If you want to add text to an AutoShape, just click the shape and start typing. The text appears centered over the shape. (The only AutoShapes that do not accept text are lines and connectors.)

Formatting a text box

After your text box is in place, you want to apply some formatting. To start, you can format the text you type in the text box by highlighting the text and using the text formatting controls on the Formatting toolbar. For more information about formatting text, refer to Book II, Chapter 1.

You can format the text box itself by using the Fill Color, Line Color, and Line Style buttons, which I describe in the next section. By default, text boxes fill with white and have a thin black line. If you don't want a line around the text box, click the Line Color button and choose No Line.

By default, the text in a text box is indented a tenth of an inch from the left and right of the text box and five hundredths of an inch from the top and bottom. If you want to change this indentation (I often set it to zero), right-click the text box, choose Format Text Box, and click the Text Box tab, as shown in Figure 4-2. Here, you can set the top, left, right, and bottom margins. In addition, you can set the following two options:

✦ **Word Wrap Text in AutoShape:** You almost always want to leave this option turned on. If you turn it off and the text box isn't wide enough, the text may get cut off.

✦ **Resize AutoShape to Fit Text:** This option automatically adjusts the size of the text box to fit the text you type in it. You usually leave this option turned off. You can always adjust the size of the text box manually by dragging any of the text box's corner handles.

Changing text direction

One of the most disappointing limitations of text boxes is that you can't freely rotate their text. When you select a text box, no rotation handle appears and the options on the Draw⇨Rotate and Flip command are disabled. Text boxes with rotation handles would be great so that you could spin the text to any angle, but Word is a word processing program, not a desktop publishing program. I guess the programmers at Microsoft figure that if you want to rotate text, you should buy Publisher instead.

Figure 4-2:
The Text
Box tab of
the Format
Text Box
dialog box.

But wait! You can rotate other types of shapes, can't you? And didn't I say a
few pages back that you can add text to any AutoShape? Yes I did. But unfortunately, when you add text to an AutoShape, and then rotate the AutoShape,
the text doesn't rotate with the shape. Sigh.

You have hope, however. Word provides a somewhat helpful Format⇨Text
Direction command that can rotate the text in a text box left or right 90
degrees. It doesn't let you rotate text to any arbitrary angle, but 90 degrees
is better than nothing.

To use the Text Direction command, simply select a text box and choose
Format⇨Text Direction. The dialog box shown in Figure 4-3 appears. Choose
the text orientation you want to use and click OK. That's all you have to do!

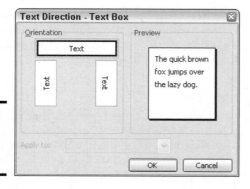

Figure 4-3:
The Text
Direction
dialog box.

You can still edit text after you rotate it. However, seeing letters crawl up or down the screen as you type them is a little disconcerting, unless you turn your head sideways. To save your neck, I suggest you enter the text for a text box *before* you rotate the text.

Using linked text boxes

If a text box isn't big enough to display all of its text, Word lets you continue the text into another text box. For example, you might use text boxes to create a sidebar that has text related to the main topic of your document. If the sidebar is particularly long, you can continue it in another text box.

Just follow these steps to create a set of nicely linked text boxes:

1. **Type the text you want to place in a series of text boxes.**

   Linked text boxes work best if you first create the text they contain. You can even type the text in a separate document if you want.

2. **Create two or more text boxes to hold the text.**

   Position the text boxes where you want them to appear in your document. They don't have to be on the same page.

3. **Select the text you typed in Step 1 and press Ctrl+C.**

   The text copies to the Clipboard.

4. **Select the first text box and press Ctrl+V.**

   The text from the Clipboard pastes into the first text box. The text box displays as much of the text as it can; the rest is hidden.

5. **Right-click the text box and choose Create Text Box Link.**

   The mouse pointer changes to a weird looking coffee cup.

6. **Click the second text box.**

   This action spills the coffee into the second text box. In other words, the text from the first text box continues into the second.

7. **If you want to spill text into additional text boxes, repeat Steps 5 and 6.**

   You can link as many text boxes together as you want.

Word has a handy Text Box toolbar that sometimes appears when you select a text box. If this toolbar is missing, you can summon it by selecting a text box and choosing View⇨Toolbars⇨Text Box. Table 4-1 lists the functions of the buttons that appear on this toolbar.

**Book IV
Chapter 4**

**Working
Graphically
with Text**

Table 4-1	Buttons on the Text Box Toolbar	
Drawing Tool	*What It's Called*	*What It Does*
	Create Text Box Link	Lets you create a link to another text box. Clicking this button is the same as right-clicking the text box and choosing Create Text Box Link.
	Break Forward Link	Breaks the link to the next text box.
	Previous Text Box	Goes to the previous linked text box.
	Next Text Box	Goes to the next linked text box.
	Change Text Direction	Changes the text from horizontal to vertical orientation.

To remove a text box from a chain of linked text boxes, right-click the text box and choose Break Forward Link. Alternatively, you can select the text box and click the Break Forward Link button on the Text Box toolbar.

I've Been Framed!

Frames are an archaic but sometimes useful Word feature. At one time, frames were the only way to insert pictures into a Word document. And before the days of text boxes, you had to use frames if you wanted to put text in arbitrary locations on the page. But then along came text boxes, and frames are now hardly used at all.

Text boxes can do almost everything that frames can, and more. However, frames can do a few tricks that text boxes can't. In particular, frames can contain certain text elements that text boxes can't:

✦ Footnotes and endnotes.

✦ Comments.

✦ Certain field codes — mostly those that number items in your document or build lists, such as AUTONUM, TOC, and TOA.

Another major benefit of frames is that you can incorporate them into a style. In other words, you can create a style that places the paragraph it's applied to in a frame. In Chapter 6 of this minibook, I show you how to create a frame style for side heads that appear in the margin.

Creating a frame

Interestingly, Word doesn't provide a direct way to create a frame. Instead, you must first create a text box, and then convert it to a frame. Here are the steps:

1. **Create a text box.**

2. **Right-click the text box and choose Format Text Box and click the Text Box tab.**

   Figure 4-2 shows this dialog box, so I won't repeat it here.

3. **Click the Convert to Frame button.**

   A dialog box with the following warning message appears:

   ```
   When you convert this drawing object to a frame, some of the drawing
   object's formatting may be lost. Do you want to continue?
   ```

4. **Throw caution to the wind and click OK.**

   The text box converts to a frame, which looks exactly like a text box.

5. **Congratulate yourself.**

   You're done. You can now include footnotes, comments, or weird field codes in the frame's text.

Formatting a frame

You can set some formatting options for a frame by right-clicking the frame and choosing the Format Frame command from the shortcut menu. The Frame dialog box comes up, shown in Figure 4-4.

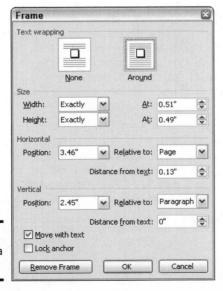

Figure 4-4: Formatting a frame.

Here's the lowdown on the various options in the Frame dialog box:

Text Wrapping: Read this carefully: It's text *wrapping,* not text *warping.* To warp your text, you must dig deeply into your own deviant sense of humor. To wrap your text around a frame, click Around. To interrupt your text when the frame appears and resume it after the frame, click None.

Note: Frames have much more limited wrapping options than text boxes. That's one of the reasons to use text boxes instead of frames whenever you can.

Size: Controls the Width and Height of the frame. You can leave both fields set to Auto to make Word figure out how big the frame needs to be. Or you can change either field to Exactly and then type a number in the corresponding At field to set the width or height precisely.

Horizontal: Controls the horizontal left-to-right position of the frame. In the Position field, you can type a measurement or you can choose Left, Right, Center, Inside, or Outside and allow Word to do the measuring for you. (Use Inside and Outside when even- and odd-numbered pages have different margins. Inside means left on a right-hand page and right on a left-hand page; outside means left on a left-hand page and right on a right-hand page.)

Stop me, Smee, before I drop the anchor!

Every frame is *anchored* to a particular paragraph. When you move a frame around on the page, Word automatically picks up the frame's anchor and drops it on the nearest paragraph. This paragraph is referred to when you set the Frame dialog box's Vertical Relative To field to Paragraph. When you switch to Normal view, the frame displays immediately before the paragraph it is anchored to.

If you don't want Word to change the paragraph that a frame is anchored to when you move the frame, check the Lock Anchor option in the Frame dialog box. Then the frame anchor remains in the same paragraph even if you move the frame around the page.

You can actually see the anchors in Page Layout view if you click the Show/Hide button on the Standard toolbar. When you select a frame, the paragraph it is anchored to has a little anchor next to it. You can change the anchor paragraph by dragging the anchor from paragraph to paragraph, and you can pop up the Frame dialog box by double-clicking the anchor. Shiver me timbers!

(Truth be told, text boxes and other drawing objects have anchors too. Anchors are a behind-the-scenes thing for those types of objects. You have to worry about anchors only when you work with frames, and even then only if you want to mess with the Lock Anchor option.)

In the Relative To field, you can choose Page, Margin, or Column. This option tells Word where to measure from when applying the Position setting. For example, to place the frame flush left against the margin, set Position to Left and Relative To to Margin. To line it up against the right edge of the column, set Position to Right and Relative To to Column.

In the Distance from Text field, you tell Word how much empty space to leave between the right and left edges of the frame and any text that wraps around the frame. Increase this option if the text seems too crowded.

Vertical: Sets the vertical, up-and-down position of the frame. You can type a number in the Position field or set it to Top, Bottom, or Center and let Word figure it out.

Set the Relative To field to Page, Margin, or Paragraph to control placement of the frame. For example, to set the frame down on the bottom margin, set Position to Bottom and Relative To to Margin. To place a frame one inch below a particular paragraph, set Position to 1" and Relative To to Paragraph.

Move with Text/Lock Anchor: Select the Move with Text check box if you want the frame to travel along with the paragraph it's anchored to. If extensive editing causes the anchor paragraph to move to the next page, the frame moves to the next page too. If you want to force the frame to stay on the same page even if the anchor paragraph jumps pages, deselect the Move with Text check box. See the sidebar, "Stop me, Smee, before I drop the anchor!" if you're not sure what I mean by *the anchor paragraph.*

Adding Captions to Your Pictures

A *caption* is a bit of text that identifies a figure, table, chart, or other visual element you include in a document. Captions usually include a reference number, for example, Figure 58 or Table 293. Figure 4-5 shows a document with a captioned illustration.

If you want, you can create captions simply by creating a text box to hold the caption. (I cover text boxes earlier in this chapter.) But Word includes a Caption feature that automatically numbers your captions when you insert them, keeps the numbers in order, and lets you create a table of figures, tables, charts, or whatever when you're all done. You paid for this program, so you may as well know how to use as much of it as possible.

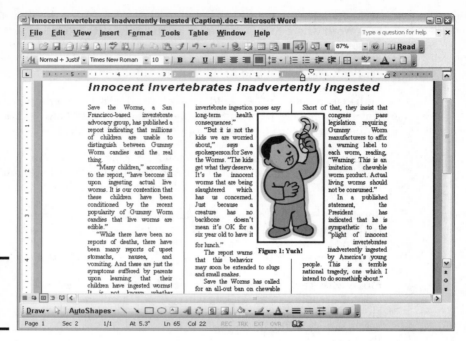

Figure 4-5:
A picture
with a
caption.

To add a caption to a picture, table, chart, or other graphic goodie, follow these steps:

1. **If you haven't done so already, choose Insert⇨Picture to insert a picture into your document.**

2. **Select the picture that you want the caption attached to.**

3. **Choose Insert⇨Reference⇨Caption.**

   You see the dialog box shown in Figure 4-6.

Figure 4-6:
The Caption
dialog box.

4. Type the caption.

Word starts the caption for you by providing the reference number. Type whatever text you want to describe the figure, table, chart, or whatever.

5. Change the Label field if it is incorrect.

Word keeps track of caption numbers for figures, tables, and equations separately. When you insert a caption, make sure the Label field is set to the type of caption you want to create.

6. Change the Position field if you want to change the positioning.

The two options are Above or Below the selected item.

7. Click OK.

Word inserts the caption.

Here are a few rapid-fire thoughts designed to inspire your use of captions:

✦ If you want to create captions for something other than figures, tables, and equations, click the New Label button and type a label for whatever you want to create captions for; say, for example, a limerick. Click OK, and from then on, Limerick appears as one of the Label types.

✦ When you create a caption, Word automatically applies the Caption style to the caption paragraph. You can control the format of all captions in a document by modifying the Caption style.

✦ You can create a table of figures, tables, equations, or limericks by using Insert➪Index and Tables. Pick the Table of Figures tab and then choose the type of caption you want to create a table for from the Caption Label field. Click OK and treat yourself to a Snickers bar. (For more detailed information about this feature, see Book VI, Chapter 6.)

✦ At various and sundry times, caption numbers get out of sequence. Fear not! Word can put the caption numbers back into sequence when you print the document. If you're tired of looking at out-of-sequence numbers, choose Edit➪Select All to select the entire document and then press F9 to recompute the caption numbers.

✦ If you want Word to always create a caption whenever you insert a particular type of object into your document, click the AutoCaption button in the Caption dialog box. A dialog box lists all the various types of objects you can insert into a Word document. Check the ones you want to automatically create captions for and then click OK.

Creating Fancy Text with WordArt

WordArt is a nifty little feature that takes a snippet of ordinary text and transforms it into something that looks like you paid an ad agency an arm and a leg to design. Figure 4-7 is an example of what you can do with WordArt in about three minutes.

Figure 4-7:
You, too, can create fancy text effects like these by using WordArt.

Follow these steps to transform mundane text into something worth looking at:

1. **Click the WordArt button on the Drawing toolbar.**

Or, if you prefer, choose Insert⇨Picture⇨WordArt. Either way, the WordArt Gallery appears, as shown in Figure 4-8.

Figure 4-8:
The WordArt Gallery offers a choice of WordArt styles.

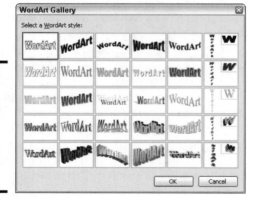

2. **Click the WordArt style that most closely resembles the WordArt that you want to create and then click OK.**

   The Edit WordArt Text dialog box appears, as shown in Figure 4-9.

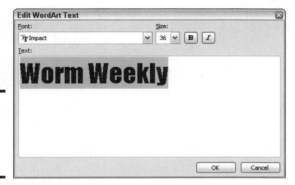

Figure 4-9:
The Edit
WordArt
Text dialog
box.

3. **Type the text that you want to use for your WordArt in the Text field and then click OK.**

   The WordArt object appears along with the WordArt toolbar.

4. **Fool around with other WordArt controls.**

   I identify the various controls available on the WordArt toolbar in Table 4-2. Experiment as much as you want until you get the text to look just right.

Table 4-2	Buttons on the WordArt Toolbar	
Drawing Tool	*What It's Called*	*What It Does*
	Insert WordArt	Creates another WordArt object.
Edit Text...	Edit Text	Brings up the Edit WordArt Text dialog box.
	WordArt Gallery	Brings up the WordArt Gallery dialog box.
	Format WordArt	Brings up a dialog box that lets you control the layout and other formatting options for the WordArt object.

(continued)

Table 4-2 *(continued)*

Drawing Tool	What It's Called	What It Does
	WordArt Shape	Lets you choose one of several 40 different shapes for the WordArt text.
	WordArt Text Wrapping	Lets you choose the text wrapping style for the WordArt object.
	WordArt Same Letter Heights	Makes each letter in the WordArt object the same height.
	Vertical Text	Switches the text to a vertical format.
	WordArt Alignment	Changes the alignment of the text.
	WordArt Character Spacing	Changes the spacing between each character in the WordArt object.

The WordArt Shape button is the key to creating fancy logos, such as text that wraps around circles. Figure 4-10 shows the menu that appears when you click this button. You need to experiment a bit with these shapes to see how they work. Note that some of them have two or three sections. For those shapes, enter the text you want to appear in each section of the shape on a separate line in the Edit WordArt Text dialog box.

Figure 4-10:
The
WordArt
Shapes
menu.

Don't forget that, in the eyes of Word, a WordArt object is not text. Unlike a text box or frame, you can't edit it just by clicking it and typing. Instead, you have to edit the text from the Edit WordArt Text dialog box.

Drawing a Callout

A *callout* is a special type of AutoShape object that is like a text box but has a line or a series of bubbles connecting the callout to some other object, as shown in Figure 4-11. In the figure, I use callouts to illustrate the thoughts of the donkey.

Figure 4-11:
The proper use of callouts.

Follow these steps to create callouts to contain your own thoughts:

1. **Click the AutoShapes button, and then choose Callouts.**

A toolbar showing 20 different callout styles appears.

2. **Choose the callout type you want to use.**

3. **Click where you want the upper-left corner of the callout to appear, and then drag out the shape of the callout.**

After you release the mouse, a big one-inch-square callout box appears.

4. **Drag the little yellow dot that appears at the end of the connecting line (or bubbles, if you choose the *thought bubble* type of callout used in Figure 4-11) to the point where you want the callout to indicate.**

As you drag the little yellow dot around, the shape of the callout changes.

5. Click in the callout, and then type some callout text.

Word inserts the text into the callout.

Presto! You're finished.

Keep the following points in mind when you work with callouts:

✦ Notice that if you drag a callout around the screen, the callout remains attached to the same point in your document. Cool!

✦ If the text doesn't fit inside the callout, try dragging the callout by one of its love handles to increase the size. Or select the callout, and then choose Format⇨AutoShape. Click the Text Box tab and reduce the margins for the callout. Margins allow the text to creep closer to the inside boundaries of the callout.

Chapter 5: Charts and Diagrams

*T*his chapter shows you how to insert charts and diagrams into your document. Charts are really the strength of Excel because Excel is great at crunching the numbers that lead to a good chart. However, you can also create a simple chart directly in Word. Word diagrams are things such as organization charts, Venn diagrams, Pyramid diagrams, and so on.

Creating a Chart

One of the best ways to prove a point is with numbers, and one of the best ways to present numbers is in a chart. With Word, adding a chart to your document is easy. And getting the chart to look the way you want is usually easy, too. It takes a little bit of pointing and clicking, but it works.

Understanding charts

If you've never attempted to create a chart, the process can be a little confusing. A chart is simply a series of numbers rendered graphically. You can supply the numbers yourself, or you can copy them from a separate file, such as an Excel spreadsheet. You can create all kinds of different charts, ranging from simple bar and pie charts to exotic doughnut and radar charts. Very cool, but a little confusing to the uninitiated.

The following list details some of the jargon that you have to contend with when you're working with charts:

✦ **Graph or chart:** Same thing. These terms are used interchangeably. A graph or chart is nothing more than a bunch of numbers turned into a picture. After all, a picture is worth a thousand numbers.

✦ **Microsoft Graph:** Charts (or graphs, if you prefer) are actually created by a separate program called Microsoft Graph. However, Microsoft Graph is so well integrated with Word that if I hadn't just told you, you probably wouldn't realize that it's a separate program from Word.

✦ **Chart type:** Microsoft Graph supports several chart types: bar, column, pie, line, scatter, area, radar, Krispy Kreme Donut, and others. Different types of charts are better suited to displaying different types of data.

✦ **3-D chart:** Some chart types have a 3-D effect that gives them a jazzier look. Nothing special here — the effect is mostly cosmetic.

✦ **Datasheet:** Supplies the underlying data for a chart. A chart is nothing more than a bunch of numbers made into a picture. The numbers come from the datasheet, which works like a simple spreadsheet program. If you know how to use Excel, finding out how to use the datasheet takes you about 30 seconds. If you don't know Excel, allow five minutes. The datasheet is part of the Graph object, but it doesn't appear on the page. Instead, the datasheet appears only when you edit the Graph object.

✦ **Series:** A collection of related numbers. For example, a chart of quarterly sales by region may have a series for each region. Each series has four sales totals, one for each quarter. Each series is usually represented by a row on the datasheet, but you can change the datasheet so that each column represents a series. Most chart types can plot more than one series. The notable exception is the common pie chart, which can chart only one series at a time.

✦ **Axes:** The lines on the edges of a chart. The *X-axis* is the line along the bottom of the chart; the *Y-axis* is the line along the left edge of the chart. The X-axis usually indicates categories. Actual data values plot along the Y-axis. Microsoft Graph automatically provides labels for the X- and Y-axes, but you can change them.

✦ **Legend:** A box used to identify the various series plotted on the chart. Microsoft Graph can create a legend automatically if you want one.

Microsoft Graph that comes with Word is also used for charting functions in Excel. So if you know how to use Excel to create charts, you can pretty much skip the rest of this section: You already know everything you need to know.

When you create or edit a chart, Microsoft Graph comes to life. Rather than popping up in its own window, though, Microsoft Graph sort of takes over the Word window and replaces the Word menus and toolbars with its own. So don't panic if the room seems to spin and your toolbar changes. You're not having a seizure; this change is normal.

Microsoft Graph has its own Help system. To see Help information for Microsoft Graph, first call up Microsoft Graph by inserting a chart object or by double-clicking an existing chart object. Then press F1, click the Help button, or use the Help menu to access Graph Help directly.

Inserting a chart

The following steps show you how to insert a new page that contains a chart:

1. **Click at the position where you want to insert a chart.**

2. **Choose Insert⇨Picture⇨Chart.**

   Microsoft Graph comes to life, inserting a chart into your document as shown in Figure 5-1. Notice that the Word toolbars and menus give way to a new set of toolbars and menus designed specifically to work with charts.

3. **Change the sample data to something more realistic.**

   The *datasheet,* visible in Figure 5-1, supplies the data on which the chart is based. The datasheet is in a separate window and is not a part of the page. The datasheet works just like a spreadsheet program. For more information about using it, see the section "Working with the datasheet" later in this chapter.

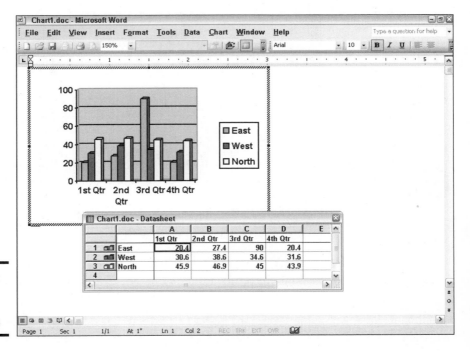

Figure 5-1: Microsoft Graph takes over.

4. **Fiddle with the chart until it's just right.**

   To accomplish this feat, use the editing and formatting techniques that I describe throughout this chapter.

5. **When the chart is just right, click outside it to return to the rest of the page.**

   Word regains control of your screen so that you can continue editing the rest of your document. You can then see the chart with the new numbers and formatting, as shown in Figure 5-2.

   You can always return to Microsoft Graph to make further adjustments to the chart by double-clicking the chart.

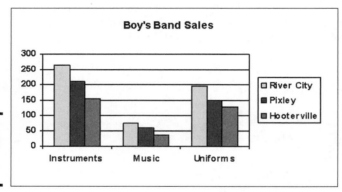

Figure 5-2:
A page with
a finished
chart.

Another way to create a chart is to first create a Word table that holds the data you want charted. Arrange the table so that the first row and the first column contain labels, and the rest of the table contains the values to plot. Select the entire table (click anywhere in the table, choose Table⇨Select⇨ Table), and then choose Insert⇨Picture⇨Chart. Word creates a chart based on the data in the table.

Working with the datasheet

The datasheet contains the numbers that are plotted in your Microsoft Graph chart. The datasheet works like a simple spreadsheet program with values stored in cells arranged in rows and columns. Like in a spreadsheet, each column is assigned a letter, and each row is assigned a number. You can identify each cell in the datasheet, therefore, by combining the column letter and row number, as in A1 or B17. (Bingo!)

Finding the lost Insert Chart button

If you work with charts a lot, you may want to place an Insert Chart button on the Standard toolbar. Fortunately, you can add this button by following these steps:

1. **Choose Tools➪Customize.**

2. **Click the Commands tab.**

3. **Select Insert from the Categories list.**

4. **Drag the Chart button from the Commands list to the Standard toolbar and release it at the location where you want it to appear.**

5. **Click Close to dismiss the Customize dialog box.**

Ordinarily, each series of numbers is represented by a row in the spreadsheet. You can change this orientation so that each series is represented by a column; to do so, click the By Column button on the Microsoft Graph toolbar or choose Data➪Series in Columns. The Data menu is a function of Microsoft Graph and, like the toolbar, it vanishes when your datasheet is complete.

The first row and column in the datasheet are used for headings and are not assigned a letter or number.

If you want to chart a large number of data values, you may want to increase the size of the datasheet window. Unfortunately, someone forgot to put the Maximize button on the datasheet window, but you can still increase the size of the datasheet window by dragging any of its corners.

You can choose an entire column by clicking its column letter, or you can choose an entire row by clicking its row number. You also can choose the entire datasheet by clicking the blank box in the upper-left corner of the datasheet.

You can change the font used in the datasheet by choosing Format➪Font. You also can change the numeric format by choosing Format➪Number. Changing the font and number format for the datasheet affects not only the way the datasheet displays, but also the format of data value labels included in the chart.

Although the datasheet resembles a spreadsheet, you can't use formulas or functions in a datasheet. If you want to use formulas or functions to calculate the values to plot, use a spreadsheet program — preferably Excel — to create the spreadsheet and then import it into Microsoft Graph. (Or create

**Book IV
Chapter 5**

Charts and
Diagrams

the chart in Excel rather than in Word. Then import the Excel chart into the Word document by choosing Insert⇨Object or copy the chart into Word by way of the Clipboard.)

To get rid of the datasheet, click the datasheet's Close button. This action doesn't delete the datasheet; it just hides the datasheet. You can call it up again later by choosing View⇨DataSheet.

Changing the chart type

Microsoft Graph enables you to create 14 basic types of charts. Each type conveys information with a different emphasis. Sales data plotted in a column chart may emphasize the relative performance of different regions, for example, and the same data plotted as a line chart may emphasize an increase or decrease in sales over time. The best type of chart for your data depends on the nature of the data and which aspects of it that you want to emphasize.

Fortunately, Word doesn't force you to decide the final chart type up front. You can easily change the chart type at any time without changing the chart data. These steps show you how:

1. **Double-click the chart to activate Microsoft Graph.**

2. **Choose Chart⇨Chart Type.**

   Microsoft Graph displays the Chart Type dialog box, shown in Figure 5-3. From this dialog box, you can choose the chart type that you want to use. The chart types are arranged in two groups: standard on the Standard Types tab and custom on the Custom Types tab. (To show the custom types, click the Custom Types tab at the top of the dialog box.)

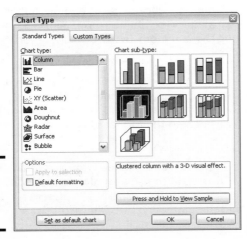

Figure 5-3:
The Chart
Type dialog
box.

3. **Click the chart type that you want.**

4. **To use a variant of the chart type, click the chart subtype that you want to use.**

   For example, the column chart type has seven subtypes that enable you to use flat columns or three-dimensional columns and to change how the columns are positioned relative to each other.

5. **Click OK and you're done.**

Another way to summon the Chart Type dialog box is to double-click the chart object and then right-click the chart. When the quick menu appears, choose Chart Type. Make sure your arrow is on a series value when you double-click (one of those bars in the graph), or it won't work. The chart area is very sensitive to random clicking, so be careful and proceed with patience.

You can change the chart type another way by using the Chart Type button on the Microsoft Graph Standard toolbar. When you click the down arrow next to the button, a palette of chart types appears. The Chart Type button provides an assortment of 18 popular types of charts. If you want to use a chart type that isn't listed under the button, choose Chart⇨Chart Type.

The Microsoft Graph Standard toolbar has more than 30 buttons. Unfortunately, Word displays only a dozen or so of them by default. To see the additional buttons, click the down-arrow that appears at the right edge of the toolbar, and then choose Show Buttons on Two Rows.

If you choose one of the 3-D chart types, you can adjust the angle from which you view the chart by choosing Chart⇨3-D View. Experiment with this one; it's kind of fun.

Embellishing a chart

Microsoft Graph enables you to embellish a chart in many ways: You can add titles, labels, legends, and who knows what else. You add these embellishments by choosing Chart⇨Chart Options, which summons a Chart Options dialog box that has several tabs from which you can control the appearance of the chart.

To add a chart embellishment, choose Chart⇨Chart Options, click the tab that relates to the embellishment that you want to add, fiddle with the settings, and click OK. The following paragraphs describe each of the Chart Options tabs in turn.

**Book IV
Chapter 5**

**Charts and
Diagrams**

✦ **Titles:** Figure 5-4 shows the Titles tab of the Chart Options dialog box. You can add two types of titles to your chart: a *chart title,* which describes the chart's contents, and *axis titles,* which explain the meaning of each chart axis. Most charts use two axes: the *value axis* and the *category axis.* Some 3-D chart types use a third axis called the *series axis.*

In most cases, the page title serves as a chart title for a chart included on a Word page. If that's the case, you don't need to use a chart title.

Figure 5-4:
Adding titles
to your
chart.

✦ **Axes:** Sometimes an axe is what you'd like to use to fix your computer. But in the case of the Axes tab shown in Figure 5-5, *axes* refer to the X- and Y-axis on which chart data is plotted. The *X-axis* is the horizontal axis of the chart, and the *Y-axis* is the vertical axis. For 3-D charts, a third axis — *Z* — is also used. The Axes tab of the Chart Options dialog box lets you show or hide the labels used for each chart axis.

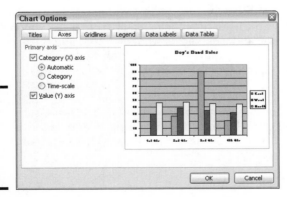

Figure 5-5:
The Axes
tab of the
Chart
Options
dialog box.

✦ **Gridlines:** *Gridlines* are light lines drawn behind a chart to make judging the position of each dot, bar, or line plotted by the chart easier. You can turn gridlines on or off via the Gridlines tab, shown in Figure 5-6.

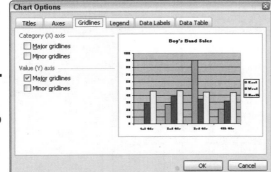

Figure 5-6:
The Gridlines tab of the Chart Options dialog box.

✦ **Legend:** A *legend* explains the color scheme used in the chart. If you want a legend to appear in your chart, click the Legend tab of the Chart Options dialog box (shown in Figure 5-7), indicate where you want to place the legend (Bottom, Corner, Top, Right, or Left), and then click OK.

Microsoft Graph enables you to create a legend, but you're on your own if you need a myth or a fable.

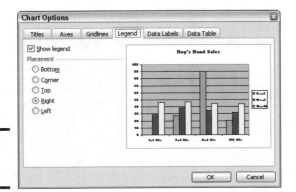

Figure 5-7:
Creating a legend.

✦ **Data Labels:** A *data label* is the text attached to each data point plotted on the chart. You can tell Microsoft Graph to use the actual data value for the label, or you can use the category heading for the label. The Data

Labels tab, shown in Figure 5-8, controls this setting. For most page types, data labels add unnecessary clutter without adding much useful information. Use labels only if you think that you must back up your chart with exact numbers.

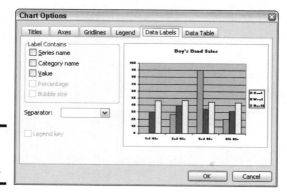

Figure 5-8:
Creating
data labels.

+ **Data Table:** The *data table* is a table that shows the data used to create a chart. The Data Table tab, shown in Figure 5-9, holds the controls that let you add a data table to your chart.

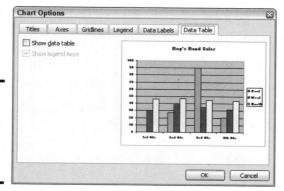

Figure 5-9:
The Data
Table tab of
the Chart
Options
dialog box.

Creating and Inserting a Diagram

Word includes a nifty little feature called the Diagram Gallery, which lets you add several different types of useful diagrams to your documents. With the Diagram Gallery, you can create organization charts, and Cycle, Radial, Pyramid, Venn, and Target diagrams.

Of the six types of diagrams that you can create with the Diagram Gallery, all of them, except the organization chart, are variations on the same theme: They show simple relationships among the elements in a diagram. In fact, after you create a diagram, you can easily change the diagram to a different type. Thus, if you start with a Radial diagram but decide that a Pyramid diagram better makes your point, you can change the diagram to a Pyramid diagram. Organization charts, however, show more complex relationships. So you can't change an Organization chart to one of the other diagram types.

To create a diagram, follow these steps:

1. Click the Insert Diagram or Organization Chart button.

You find this button on the Drawing toolbar. Clicking it brings up the Diagram Gallery dialog box, shown in Figure 5-10.

Figure 5-10:
The Diagram Gallery dialog box comes to life.

2. Select the type of diagram you want to create.

The Diagram Gallery lets you create six different types of diagrams:

- **Organization Chart:** Shows hierarchical relationships among elements.

- **Cycle Diagram:** Shows a process that repeats a continuous cycle.

- **Radial Diagram:** Shows how elements relate to a central element.

- **Pyramid Diagram:** Shows how elements build upon one another to form a foundation.

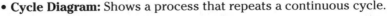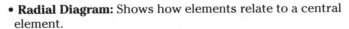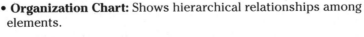

- **Venn Diagram:** Shows how different elements overlap one another.

- **Target Diagram:** Shows elements that progress towards a goal.

3. Click OK.

The chart or diagram is created. Figure 5-11 shows how an Organization chart appears when you first create it. The other diagram types have a similar appearance.

4. Modify the diagram however you see fit.

For more information on modifying diagrams, see the following sections, "Working with Organization Charts" and "Working with Other Diagrams."

5. You're done!

Well, you're never really done. You can keep tweaking your diagram until the end of time to get it perfect. But at some point, you have to say, "Enough is enough" and call it finished.

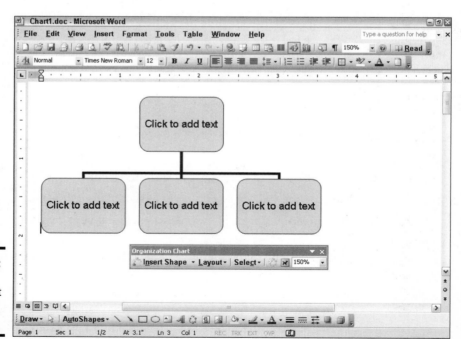

Figure 5-11:
An organization chart ready to be organized.

Working with Organization Charts

Organization charts — you know, those box-and-line charts that show who reports to whom, where the buck stops, and who got the lateral arabesque — are an essential part of many documents. You can draw organization charts by using regular rectangles and lines, but that process is tedious at best. If Jones gets booted over to advertising, the task of redrawing the chart can take hours.

Mercifully, the Diagram Gallery feature is adept at drawing organization charts. You can create diagrams that show bosses, subordinates, coworkers, and assistants. You can easily rearrange the chain of command and add new boxes or delete boxes. Figure 5-12 shows a finished organization chart.

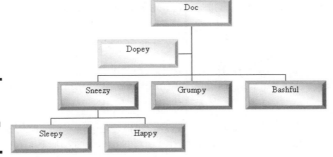

Figure 5-12:
A finished organization chart.

Keep in mind that organization charts are useful for more than showing employee relationships. You also can use them to show any kind of hierarchical structure. For example, back when I wrote computer programs for a living, I used organization charts to plan the structure of my computer programs. They're also great for recording family genealogies, although they don't have any way to indicate that Aunt Milly hasn't spoken to Aunt Beatrice in 30 years.

Previous versions of Word used a clumsy program called Microsoft Organization Chart to handle organization charts. The new Diagram Gallery Organization Chart feature is easier to use, though it isn't as adept at creating complicated charts as the old program was.

**Book IV
Chapter 5**

Charts and Diagrams

Organization chart terms you can skip

Organization charts thrust a bunch of specialized terminology in your face. This list explains some of the more important terms:

🗸 **Manager:** A box that has subordinate boxes reporting to it.

🗸 **Subordinate:** A box beneath a manager box that reports to that manager in a line relationship.

🗸 **Coworker:** Two or more boxes that report to the same manager.

🗸 **Assistant:** A box that has a staff relationship to another box rather than a line relationship. Assistant boxes are drawn differently to indicate their different relationship to the chart.

🗸 **Level:** All the boxes on the same level in a chart.

🗸 **Branch:** A box and all the boxes that report directly and indirectly to it.

Adding text to boxes

To add text to an organization chart box, click the box and start typing. If necessary, Word adjusts the size of the box to accommodate the text you type.

You can use any of the Word text formatting features to format text in your organization chart boxes. To keep the boxes small, avoid typing long names or job titles. To create two or more lines of text in a box, just press Enter whenever you want to start a new line.

Adding boxes to a chart

To add a new box to an organization chart, follow these steps:

1. **Click the box you want the new box to be below or next to.**

2. **Click the arrow next to the Insert Shape button on the Organization Chart toolbar, and then click one of the following buttons:**

- **Subordinate:** Inserts a new box beneath the selected box.

- **Coworker:** Inserts a new box at the same level as the selected box.

- **Assistant:** Inserts a new box beneath the selected box, but connected with a special elbow connector to indicate that the box is an assistant, and not a subordinate.

3. **Click in the new box, and type whatever text you want to appear in the box.**

4. **If necessary, drag the box to adjust its location.**

Deleting chart boxes

To delete a box from an organization chart, click the box to select it and press Delete. Word automatically adjusts the chart to compensate for the lost box.

When you delete a box from an organization chart, you should observe a moment of somber silence — or throw a party. It all depends on whose name was on the box, I suppose.

Moving a box

To move a box to a different position on the chart, drag the box with the mouse until it lands right on top of the box that you want it to be subordinate to. Word automatically rearranges the chart to accommodate the new arrangement. Dragging boxes can be a handy way to reorganize a chart that has gotten a little out of hand.

Word won't let you move a box that has subordinates unless you select all the subordinate boxes. You can do that easily by selecting the box you want to move, clicking the Select button on the Organization Chart toolbar, and clicking the Branch button. You can then move the entire branch.

Changing the chart layout

Word lets you choose from one of four methods of arranging subordinates in an organization chart branch:

✦ **Standard:** Subordinate shapes are placed at the same level beneath the superior shape.

✦ **Both Hanging:** Subordinates are placed two per level beneath the superior with the connecting line between them.

✦ **Left Hanging:** Subordinates are stacked vertically beneath the superior, to the left of the connecting line.

✦ **Right Hanging:** Subordinates are stacked vertically beneath the superior, to the right of the connecting line.

Figure 5-13 shows an organization chart that uses all four of these layouts. The first layer of shapes beneath the top level uses the Standard layout. Beneath the first shape on this layer are two shapes with the Both Hanging layout. The other two shapes each have three subordinate shapes with the Left Hanging and Right Hanging layout.

To change the layout of a branch of your chart, first click the shape at the top of the branch. Then, click the Layout button on the Organization Chart toolbar and choose the layout type you want to use from the menu that appears.

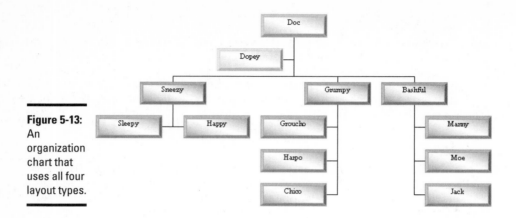

Figure 5-13:
An
organization
chart that
uses all four
layout types.

Changing the chart style

You can fiddle for hours with the formatting for the boxes, lines, and text of an organization chart. But if you want to quickly apply a good-looking format to your chart, click the AutoFormat button on the Organization Chart tool-bar. The Organization Chart Style Gallery appears, as shown in Figure 5-14. Select the style that you want to apply to your chart, and then click OK.

Figure 5-14:
The
Organization
Chart Style
Gallery lets
you create
a good-
looking
chart
without
much fuss.

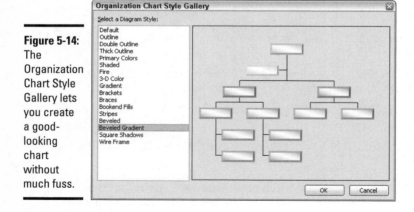

Working with Other Diagrams

Cycle, Radial, Pyramid, Venn, and Target diagrams are all useful in various situations to illustrate how different items relate to one another. For example, a Target diagram can help readers see how working through a series of steps or achieving a series of goals helps advance you toward your ultimate goal. A Pyramid diagram helps show how one task or idea provides a foundation for other tasks or ideas.

You use similar toolbar controls and menus to create and format all five of these chart types. In fact, you can even switch a chart from one type to another. So if you decide that a Venn diagram is better than a Pyramid diagram, you can simply switch types.

If you don't believe me, look at the two diagrams in Figure 5-15. Both present the same information, one as a Pyramid diagram, the other as a Target diagram. To create these diagrams, I first created the Pyramid diagram. Then, I chose Edit➪Duplicate to duplicate the chart, and then changed the chart type to Target diagram.

Figure 5-15:
Two diagrams that present the same information in different ways.

The following list describes the basics of working with these types of diagrams:

✦ **Change the diagram type:** To change the diagram type, click the Change To button on the Diagram toolbar and choose the type of diagram you want to change to.

✦ **Format the diagram:** Any formatting changes you make to the chart, such as changing the colors of individual shapes or changing text fonts or size, is lost if you change the diagram type. As a result, settle on a diagram type before you make extensive modifications to the diagram's formatting.

✦ **Add text to a shape:** To add text to a shape, click the shape and type. You can use the Word text formatting features to change the font, size, color, and style of your text.

✦ **Add a shape to the diagram:** To add a shape to the diagram, click the Insert Shape button. Word adds a shape that is appropriate for your diagram type and automatically resizes and repositions the other shapes in the diagram to accommodate the new shape.

Book IV
Chapter 5

Charts and Diagrams

✦ **Delete a shape:** To delete a shape, click the shape to select it and press Delete.

 ✦ **Reverse the order of shapes:** You can reverse the order of shapes in the diagram by clicking the Reverse Diagram button.

 ✦ **Change the order of shapes:** To change the order of shapes in the diagram, click the shape that you want to move, and then click the Move Shape Forward or Move Shape Backward button. (Each diagram type uses a different icon for these buttons, but they are always located next to the Reverse Diagram button.)

 ✦ **Apply a built-in format to the diagram:** To apply a built-in format to the diagram, click the AutoFormat button. The Diagram Style Gallery dialog box comes up. Select the diagram style you want, and then click OK.

✦ **Change the color or style of a shape:** To change the color or style of an individual shape, click the shape to change it, and then use buttons on the Drawing toolbar to change the shape's fill or line color, line style, shadow style, or 3-D style. (If you apply an AutoFormat to the diagram, you must first right-click the diagram and uncheck the Use AutoFormat command.)

Chapter 6: A Pocket Full of Desktop Publishing Tricks

In This Chapter

- ✔ **Inserting sidebars**
- ✔ **Employing pull quotes**
- ✔ **Raising eyebrows**
- ✔ **Discovering icons**
- ✔ **Using side heads**

This chapter is a compendium of ideas on how to incorporate common graphic design elements into a Word document to make it look like you used a more expensive desktop publishing program, such as Adobe PageMaker.

This chapter is written along the lines of "Here's how to use styles, borders, drawing objects, and other stuff you know about to create some really cool effects that only graphic artists used to be able to do." You may come across a feature or two that you're not sure how to use. That's okay; no reason to feel bad. Just hop back to the relevant chapter for a quick refresher and all is well.

On with the show.

Sidebars

A *sidebar* is a short portion of text — usually a paragraph or two — that is incidental to the main flow of text in your document and is given special graphical treatment. This book is filled with sidebars: They're those gray boxes of text.

Sidebars are frequently used in newsletters. If your newsletter has a two- or three-column layout, a sidebar can help you break up the monotony created by column after column of pure text. Sidebars are also often used for elements such as a table of contents. For example, Figure 6-1 shows a newsletter page with two sidebars. The one on the left lists the articles that appear in this issue of the newsletter. The one at the bottom of the page spans two columns, breaking up an otherwise long and boring article.

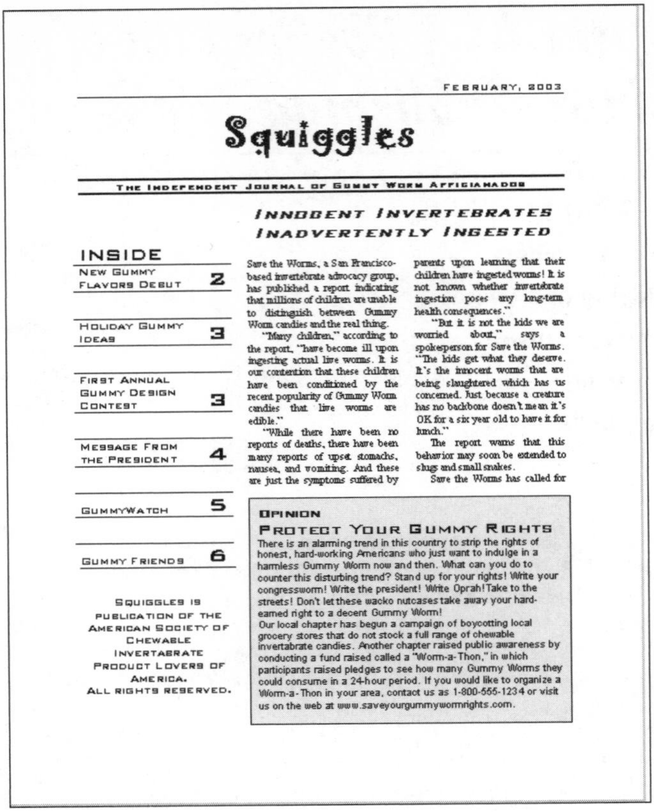
FEBRUARY, 2003

Squiggles

THE INDEPENDENT JOURNAL OF GUMMY WORM AFFICIANADOS

INSIDE

New Gummy Flavors Debut	2
Holiday Gummy Ideas	3
First Annual Gummy Design Contest	3
Message From the President	4
GummyWatch	5
Gummy Friends	6

Squiggles is publication of the American Society of Chewable Invertabrate Product Lovers of America. All rights reserved.

INNOCENT INVERTEBRATES INADVERTENTLY INGESTED

Save the Worms, a San Francisco-based invertebrate advocacy group, has published a report indicating that millions of children are unable to distinguish between Gummy Worm candies and the real thing.

"Many children," according to the report, "have become ill upon ingesting actual live worms. It is our contention that these children have been conditioned by the recent popularity of Gummy Worm candies that live worms are edible."

"While there have been no reports of deaths, there have been many reports of upset stomachs, nausea, and vomiting. And these are just the symptoms suffered by parents upon learning that their children have ingested worms! It is not known whether invertebrate ingestion poses any long-term health consequences."

"But it is not the kids we are worried about," says a spokesperson for Save the Worms. "The kids get what they deserve. It's the innocent worms that are being slaughtered which has us concerned. Just because a creature has no backbone doesn't mean it's OK for a six year old to have it for lunch."

The report warns that this behavior may soon be extended to slugs and small snakes.

Save the Worms has called for

OPINION

PROTECT YOUR GUMMY RIGHTS

There is an alarming trend in this country to strip the rights of honest, hard-working Americans who just want to indulge in a harmless Gummy Worm now and then. What can you do to counter this disturbing trend? Stand up for your rights! Write your congressworm! Write the president! Write Oprah! Take to the streets! Don't let these wacko nutcases take away your hard-earned right to a decent Gummy Worm!

Our local chapter has begun a campaign of boycotting local grocery stores that do not stock a full range of chewable invertabrate candies. Another chapter raised public awareness by conducting a fund raised called a "Worm-a-Thon," in which participants raised pledges to see how many Gummy Worms they could consume in a 24-hour period. If you would like to organize a Worm-a-Thon in your area, contact us as 1-800-555-1234 or visit us on the web at www.saveyourgummywormrights.com.

Figure 6-1: A sidebar can spice up an otherwise dull page.

To create sidebars like the ones in Figure 6-1, follow these steps:

1. **Click the Text Box button on the Drawing toolbar, and then draw a text box where you want the sidebar to appear.**
2. **Click in the text box and type the text for the sidebar.**
3. **Apply whatever formatting you want to the sidebar text.**

   The easiest way to format sidebars is to create styles for the sidebar heading and body. Then you simply apply the styles to format the sidebar properly.
4. **Use the Fill Color and Line Style controls to add shading and an outline to the sidebar.**
5. **You're done.**

   Wasn't that easy?

Here are some random thoughts about creating sidebars:

✦ Pick a contrasting font for the sidebar. In Figure 6-1, I used sans-serif fonts (BankGothic and Arial) for the sidebar's heading and text.

✦ Unfortunately, Word doesn't let you set up a two-column text box. If you absolutely must have two-column sidebars, you need to switch to Adobe PageMaker.

✦ To keep the sidebar from moving around the page after you find a good spot for it, call up Format⇨Text Box, click the Layout tab, and then click the Advanced button. Uncheck the Move with Text option.

✦ Tables are sometimes a handy way to format elements within a sidebar. For example, the table of contents sidebar in Figure 6-1 uses a table to format the article names and page numbers.

✦ Don't overuse sidebars. Sidebars lose their impact if they take up more space than the main text.

Pull Quotes

A *pull quote* (also referred to as a *lift-out quote*) is a short quotation pulled out of the article and given special treatment. Its purpose is to pique the reader's interest so that he or she is drawn to read the article.

Pull quotes are usually set in a larger type and are often sandwiched between columns in a two- or three-column layout, as shown in Figure 6-2. To achieve this effect, you create the pull quote in a text box.

Follow these steps to create a pull quote like the one in Figure 6-2:

1. **Draw a text box to hold the pull quote.**

To draw the text box, select the Text Box tool on the Drawing toolbar, position the mouse pointer where you want one of the pull quote's corners to appear, and then drag out the text box to the size you want.

2. **Click in the text box and type the text that you want to appear in the pull quote.**

3. **Format the pull quote however you want.**

In Figure 6-2, I use a larger italic version of the body text typeface and center the paragraph.

4. **Right-click the text box border and choose Format Text Box from the pop-up menu.**

The Format Text Box dialog box appears. (If it doesn't, you probably didn't click right on the text box border. Try again.)

5. **Click the Layout tab and choose Square for the wrapping style.**

6. **Click the Text Box tabs and set all margins to zero.**

7. **Click the Colors and Lines tab and set the Line Color to No Line.**

8. **Click OK to dismiss the Format Text Box dialog box.**

9. **Use Format➪Borders and Shading to add a border to the pull quote.**

   In Figure 6-2, I use a thin border for the left, right, and bottom edge of the paragraph and provide a thicker border at the top. Other border designs are just as effective.

10. **Adjust the text box position if necessary.**

    Place the pull quote text box in a location that is not too close to the spot where the quote appears in the article. And make sure that you place the text box in the middle of paragraphs, not between them. If you place the pull quote between paragraphs, the reader may think the pull quote is a heading.

 You probably have to make several small adjustments to the pull quote to position it just right. Each time you nudge the pull quote, Word reflows the text around it. Sometimes you end up with unsightly gaps in the text as Word tries to make it fit. Nudging the pull quote up or down a bit often closes these gaps.

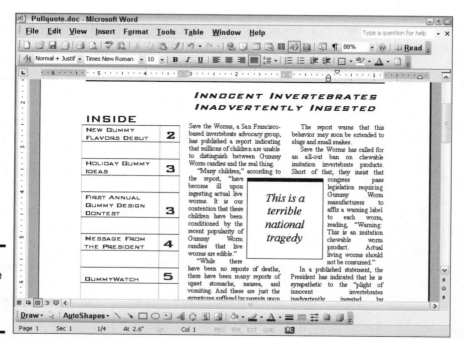

Figure 6-2:
A pull quote draws the reader into the text.

Keep these thoughts in mind when you create pull quotes:

✦ The purpose of the pull quote is to draw the reader into your text. Pick the most interesting or provocative quotes from the article.

✦ Pull quotes are typically enclosed in a box border, but sometimes a simple rule above and below does the job of highlighting the quote without imprisoning it.

✦ Experiment with different column positions for your pull quotes. In Figure 6-2, I sandwich the pull quote between the columns. You can also set a pull quote within a column, or you can create pull quotes that are a full two-columns wide.

Eyebrows

Eyebrows are the short department descriptions that appear over article titles in magazines and newsletters. Eyebrows are a good place to have some typographical fun (if that's possible). Because they're so short (a word or two does the job), you don't have to worry much about readability.

You can create some eyebrows using Word's basic formatting options. For example, you can format your eyebrows with 10-point bold Century Gothic with the letter spacing expanded 6 points, centered over the article title:

E D I T O R I A L

Or use the same typeface, but condense the letter spacing to 1 point:

EDITORIAL

Or add a special symbol from the Wingdings font to characterize the eyebrow and left-align it:

■EDITORIAL

You can use borders and shading to create interesting effects:

`EDITORIAL`

In that last example, I used two paragraphs for the eyebrow. For the first paragraph, I typed the word EDITORIAL, formatted it with the right font, switched to white characters on a black background, and then played with the paragraph indents until the black shading extended just a bit past each side of the word. For the next paragraph, I added a line border above, with zero space between the line and the text. Oh, and I made sure the space after for the first paragraph and the space before for the second paragraph were both zero.

Some thoughts to think about as you ponder the meaning of eyebrows and other great issues of life:

✦ Format your eyebrows consistently. Consistent eyebrows give your publication a more unified look.

✦ Put the eyebrow formatting information in a style. That's the best way to format them consistently.

✦ For a really dramatic look, try letting your eyebrows run together like Nikita Khrushchev or shaving them off.

Icons

Ever wonder how to insert icons similar to the ones found throughout the margins in this and other *For Dummies* books using Word? Actually, it's pretty easy. You just insert a picture to use for an icon and line it up where you want it. Figure 6-3 shows an example.

To add icons to a document, follow these steps:

1. **Come up with a really good icon.**

   Use one of the Word clip art files or create your own using Word's drawing tools.

2. **Put the cursor in the paragraph you want the icon attached to.**

3. **Choose Insert⇨Picture⇨Clip Art to insert the icon graphic.**

4. **Right-click the picture and choose Format Picture.**

   The Format Picture dialog box appears.

5. **Click the Layout tab.**

6. **Select In Front of Text for the wrapping style, and then click OK.**

7. **Resize the picture.**

   The picture is probably way too big when you insert it. Cut it down to size.

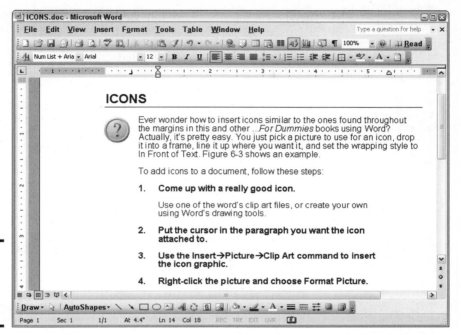

Figure 6-3:
Inserting
an icon
in a Word
document.

8. **Drag the picture to the margin.**

9. **There is no Step 9. You're done.**

    Made you look.

As you lie awake nights thinking about icons, keep these points in mind:

✦ The beauty of icons set up as described here is that they follow the text they are attached to. For example, if you add a paragraph above the paragraph the icon is attached to, the icon moves down so it stays next to the original paragraph. Unfortunately, Word doesn't always immediately move the icon as you edit. If an icon fails to move when it should, just nudge the scroll bars a little to force Word to redraw the page. The icon snaps right into place.

✦ Icons work best if you lay out your document so that a wide margin is at the left side of the page. A wide margin allows room for you to insert the icon without disrupting the text.

✦ The purpose of icons is to call attention to text that may be of particular interest. Study the way icons are used in this book and other *For Dummies* books for the ultimate example of the proper use of icons (but don't share any of this knowledge with other publishers).

Book IV
Chapter 6

A Pocket Full
of Desktop
Publishing Tricks

✦ Icons work especially well in procedure manuals. For example, you may design a File Cabinet icon to use whenever you tell the reader to file something away. Or you may create a Computer icon to use whenever the reader is told to do something on a computer.

✦ The Wingdings font that comes with Windows includes quite a collection of little pictures that may be suitable for icons. To insert a Wingdings character, first create a text box. Then, use Insert⇨Symbol to insert a Wingding symbol into the text box. You also need to set the text box's Line Color to No Line and its left, right, top, and bottom indentations to zero. And you need to adjust the size of the symbol until it is as large as you want.

Side Headings

A *side heading* is a heading that appears in a separate column next to the text it relates to, as shown in Figure 6-4. You may think that side headings are easy to do: Just give all your body text paragraphs a generous left indent, and format the heading paragraph with a hanging indent. But this method works only when the heading consists of only one line. To create multi-line side headings, such as the one in Figure 6-4, you have to use a text box.

To create a side head, do the following:

1. **Use File⇨Page Setup to lay out your page with a generous left margin.**

In Figure 6-4, I set the left margin to 3.25 inches.

2. **Type the heading text where you want the heading to appear in your document.**

3. **Assign the appropriate Heading style to the paragraph.**

For top-level headings, assign Heading 1 to the paragraph. Use Heading 2 or Heading 3 for lower-level headings.

4. **Format the characters however you want.**

In Figure 6-4, the text is 12-point BankGothic.

5. **Select the entire heading and choose Insert⇨Text Box to place the heading in a text box.**

Word converts the heading to a text box. It probably doesn't look the way you want just yet, but in a few more steps it will.

6. **Choose Format⇨Text Box or right-click the text box and choose Format Text Box from the pop-up menu.**

The Format Text Box dialog box appears.

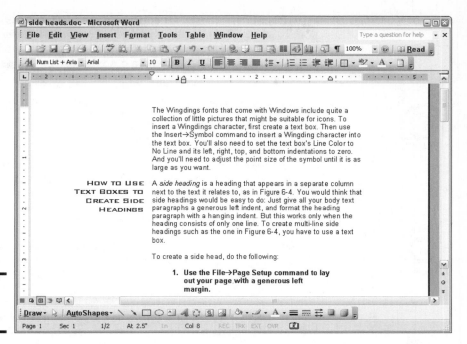

The Wingdings fonts that come with Windows include quite a collection of little pictures that might be suitable for icons. To insert a Wingdings character, first create a text box. Then use the Insert→Symbol command to insert a Wingding character into the text box. You'll also need to set the text box's Line Color to No Line and its left, right, top, and bottom indentations to zero. And you'll need to adjust the point size of the symbol until it is as large as you want.

HOW TO USE TEXT BOXES TO CREATE SIDE HEADINGS

A *side heading* is a heading that appears in a separate column next to the text it relates to, as in Figure 6-4. You would think that side headings would be easy to do: Just give all your body text paragraphs a generous left indent, and format the heading paragraph with a hanging indent. But this works only when the heading consists of only one line. To create multi-line side headings such as the one in Figure 6-4, you have to use a text box.

To create a side head, do the following:

1. Use the File→Page Setup command to lay out your page with a generous left margin.

Figure 6-4:
A side
heading.

7. **Adjust the Format Text Box settings.**

    You must adjust settings on several tabs in this dialog box:

    -   **Colors and Lines:** Set the Line Color to No Color to remove the border around the text box.

    -   **Size:** On the Size tab, set the Width setting to match the heading area. For Figure 6-4, I set the Width to 1.75 inches.

    -   **Layout:** On the Layout tab, click the Advanced button, and then set an absolute horizontal position. For Figure 6-4, I set the horizontal position to 1.25 inches to the right of the page. Added to the width (1.75 inches), that puts the right edge of the frame at 3 inches, leaving a 0.25 inch empty space between the side head and the left margin of the text (which I set to 3.25 inches in Step 1).

    Make sure you leave the Move with Text option checked so that the heading travels with the text.

8. **Click OK to dismiss the Format Text Box dialog box.**

    Sometimes, Word stubbornly refuses to adjust the width of the text box. If that happens, manually adjust the size until it's pretty close to what you want. Then call up the Format Text Box dialog box again and set the width to the exact size.

**Book IV
Chapter 6**

**A Pocket Full
of Desktop
Publishing Tricks**

The hardest part about side headings is planning the layout. The best way to plan the layout is with a blank piece of paper and a ruler. Mark the location of the heading text box and the text column. Set the page margins to accommodate the text column. Set the heading text box's horizontal position and width accordingly.

If you're not sure that a heading text box is anchored to the text that follows it, select the text box and look for the little anchor. If you can't see the anchor, click the Show/Hide button.

Note: Word may not instantly move the heading when you edit your text. If a heading doesn't seem to move when it should, give the scroll bars a nudge. The heading immediately snaps into place.

If you want to create a style that can format a side heading, one step remains: You must convert the text box to a frame. Frames are an older method of creating text that you can position precisely on a page. Microsoft has all but dropped frames in favor of text boxes, but frames still have a few advantages over text boxes; the most important being that you can incorporate a frame into a style.

To convert a text box to a frame, first follow the preceding steps in this section to format the heading as a text box. Then choose Format⇨Text Box; on the Text Box tab, click the Convert to Frame button. Word converts the text box into a frame.

After you convert the text box to a frame, select the entire heading and type an appropriate style name (such as Side Heading) in the Style box on the Formatting toolbar. The new style picks up the formatting you apply, including the frame.

For more information about frames, see Chapter 4 of this minibook.

Chapter 7: Move Over, Einstein (Creating Equations)

In This Chapter

⊭ Creating an equation

⊭ Editing an equation

⊭ Adding text to an equation

Steven Hawking wrote in the preface to his book, *A Brief History of Time,* that his editor warned him that every mathematical equation he included in the book would cut the book's sales in half. So he included just one: the classic $e=mc^2$. See how easy that equation was to type? The only trick was remembering how to format the little two as a superscript.

My editor promised me that every equation I included in this book would double its sales, but I didn't believe her; not even for a nanosecond. Just in case, Figure 7-1 shows some examples of the equations you can create by using Word's handy-dandy Equation Editor program. You wouldn't even consider trying to create these equations by using ordinary text, but they took me only a few minutes to create by using Equation Editor. Aren't they cool? Tell all your friends about the cool equations you saw in this book so that they'll all rush out and buy copies for themselves. Or better yet, read this chapter to find out how to create your own knock-'em-dead equations, and then try to convince your friends that you understand what they mean.

$$\mu_{YX} = \overline{Y}_X \pm t_a s_{Y.X} \sqrt{\frac{1}{n} + \frac{(X-\overline{X})^2}{\sum X^2 - n\overline{X}^2}}$$

$$I = \frac{\sum \left(\frac{P_1}{P_0} \times 100\right) v}{\sum v}$$

Figure 7-1:
Eight
equations
that
probably
won't affect
the sales of
this book
one way or
the other.

$$t = \frac{\overline{X}_A - \overline{X}_B}{\sqrt{\frac{(n_A-1)s_A^2 + ((n_B-1)s_B^2}{n_A + n_B - 2}} \sqrt{\frac{1}{n_A} + \frac{1}{n_B}}}$$

$$f(x) = y = \sqrt[3]{\frac{x-1}{x^2+1}}$$

$$\sigma_p = \sqrt{\frac{\pi(1-n)}{n}} \sqrt{\frac{N-n}{N-1}}$$

$$\sqrt{(x-h-c)^2 + (y-k)^2} = \left|h + \frac{c}{e^2} - x\right|e$$

$$t = \frac{b}{\frac{s_{Y.X}}{\sqrt{\sum X^2 - n\overline{X}^2}}}$$

$$d_1^* = -z_{a/2} \sqrt{P_c(1-P_c)\left(\frac{1}{n_A} + \frac{1}{n_B}\right)}$$

Introducing Equation Editor

Equation Editor is a special version of a gee-whiz math program called MathType, from Design Science. You don't have to know anything about math to use Equation Editor. I don't have a clue what any of the equations in Figure 7-1 do, other than increase my royalties. But they sure look great, don't they?

Don't forget to tell your friends how great the equations in Figure 7-1 are. They alone are worth the price of the book.

Equation Editor has its own, complete help system. After you're in Equation Editor, press F1 or use the Help command to call up complete information about using it.

Creating an Equation

To add an equation to a document, follow these steps:

1. **Choose Insert⇨Object.**

The Object dialog box appears, as shown in Figure 7-2.

2. **Choose Microsoft Equation 3 from the Object Type list and then click OK.**

This step summons Equation Editor, which argues with Word for a few moments about who's really in charge. Then it replaces Word's menus with its own and pops up a floating toolbar that's chock-full of mathematical doohickies (see Figure 7-3).

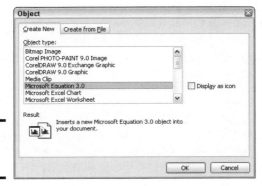

Figure 7-2:
The Object
dialog box.

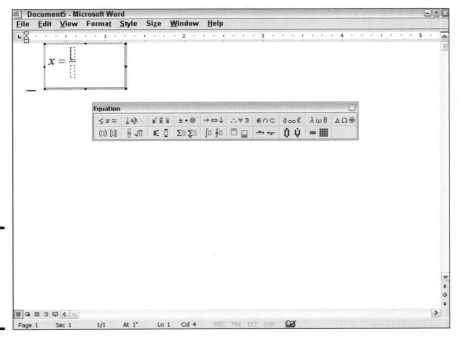

Figure 7-3:
Creating an
equation
with
Equation
Editor.

3. **Start typing your equation.**

   The variables and basic operators, such as plus and minus signs, are easy enough: Just type them with the keyboard. But how do you get those fancy symbols, such as square root and summation? The answer lies in the floating Equation toolbar.

4. **To add a symbol that's not on the keyboard, use one of the buttons in the top row of the Equation toolbar.**

   Each button yields a menu of symbols, most of which only Robert Oppenheimer could understand. There's nothing special about the tools in the top row of the Equation toolbar; they simply insert special characters into your equation. I summarize these symbol buttons in Table 7-1.

   The magic of Equation Editor lies in the bottom row in the toolbar, which I summarize in Table 7-2. These buttons let you build the parts of the equation that have elements stacked on top of one another or inside of one another, such as fractions, superscripts, and roots.

5. **To add a stacked symbol, use one of the buttons in the bottom row of the Equation toolbar.**

   Each button in the bottom row of the toolbar is attached to a menu of templates, which you use to create stacked symbols (not to be confused with document templates, which are altogether different). Most templates include a symbol and one or more slots, in which you type text or insert other symbols. Back in Figure 7-3, for example, I used a template to create a fraction. You can see that the fraction template consists of a horizontal stroke with a slot for the numerator above and the denominator below.

   To complete this fraction, you can type a number in each slot. Or — and here's the whole trick of it — you can add another symbol or template to make the equation more interesting. Most equations consist of templates nestled within the slots of other templates. The beauty of it is that Equation Editor adjusts the equation on the fly as you add text or other templates to fill a slot. If you type something like ax^2+bx+c in the top slot, for example, Equation Editor stretches the fraction bar accordingly.

   To move from one template slot to the next, press the Tab key.

6. **When you finish, click anywhere outside the equation.**

   Equation Editor bows out, enabling Word to restore its menus and toolbars. You can now drag the equation object to change its size or location.

Confused? I don't blame you. After you latch on to the idea behind templates and slots, you can slap together even the most complex equations in no time. But the learning curve here is steep. Stick with it.

✦ The *denominator* is the bottom part of a fraction, not an Arnold Schwarzenegger movie.

✦ Sometimes Equation Editor leaves droppings behind and obscures the clean appearance of the equation. When that happens, use View⇨ Redraw to clean up the equation.

✦ Spend some time exploring the symbols and templates available on the toolbar. Enough stuff is here to write an entire book about building your own atomic bomb.

Note: None of the equations in Figure 7-1 has anything to do with atomic bombs. Honest. I stole them all from a statistics book.

Table 7-1	Buttons in the Top Row of the Equation Editor Toolbar	
Button	*What It's Called*	*What It Does*
≤ ≠ ≈	Relational Symbols	Greater-than-or-equal-to and other similar symbols.
⅄ a͟b ∵	Spaces and Ellipses	Spacing symbols and various types of ellipses.
x́ ā̄ ä	Embellishments	Primes, hats, bars, dots, and other goodies. (These items are often called *diacriticals* or *accents*.)
± • ⊗	Operator Symbols	Standard math operators that aren't found on the keyboard.
→ ⇔ ↓	Arrow Symbols	Various and sundry arrows.
∴ ∀ ∃	Logical Symbols	Illogical logic symbols, such as a backwards E and an upside-down A.
∉ ∩ ⊂	Set Theory Symbols	Unions and such.
∂ ∞ ℓ	Miscellaneous Symbols	Odds and ends.
λ ω θ	Greek Characters (Lowercase)	Alpha, beta, gamma, and so on.
Λ Ω ⊕	Greek Characters (Uppercase)	Uppercase greeks.

Table 7-2	Buttons in the Bottom Row of the Equation Editor Toolbar	
Button	*What It's Called*	*What It Does*
(⣿) [⣿]	Fence Templates	Big parentheses, brackets, braces, and their ilk.
▦ √⣿	Fraction and Radical Templates	Templates for creating fractions and roots.
▦⣿ ⣿	Subscript and Superscript Templates	Templates with little boxes above or below for subscripts and super-scripts.
Σ⣿ Σ⣿	Summation Templates	Summation templates for using that big Greek Fraternity Sigma thing.
∫⣿ ∮⣿	Integral Templates	I knew I should have paid more attention in Mr. Yerxa's Calculus class.
⎺⣿ ⣿	Underbar and Overbar Templates	Templates with bars above or below.
→⣿ ←⣿	Labeled Arrow Templates	Arrows with templates above or below for text.
Π̬ U̬	Products and Set Theory Templates	Templates for working with sets.
□□□ ▦	Matrix Templates	Matrices of templates.

Editing an Equation

To edit an equation, follow these steps:

1. **Double-click the equation.**

This step summons Equation Editor. If double-clicking doesn't work, select the equation and choose Edit⇨Equation Object⇨Edit.

2. **Make your changes.**

Add stuff, delete stuff, move stuff around. Indulge yourself.

3. **Click outside the equation when you finish.**

All the standard Windows editing tricks work in Equation Editor, including the Ctrl+X, Ctrl+C, and Ctrl+V shortcuts for cutting, copying, and pasting text.

Adding Text to an Equation

Equation Editor watches any text you type in an equation and does its level best to figure out how to format the text. If you type the letter x, for example, Equation Editor assumes that you intend for the x to be a variable, so the x displays in italics. If you type **cos**, Equation Editor assumes that you mean the Cosine function, so the text is not italicized.

You can assign several different text styles to text in an equation:

✦ **Math:** The normal equation style. When you use the Math style, Equation Editor examines text as you type it and formats it accordingly by using the remaining style types.

✦ **Text:** Text that is not a mathematical symbol, function, variable, or number.

✦ **Function:** A mathematical function, such as sin, cos, or log.

✦ **Variable:** Letter that represents an equation variable, such as a, b, or x. Normally formatted as italic.

✦ **Greek:** Letters from the Greek alphabet that use the Symbol font.

✦ **Symbol:** Mathematical symbols such as +, =, summation, integral, and so on. Based on the Symbol font.

✦ **Matrix-Vector:** Characters used in matrices or vectors.

You can change the text style by using the Style commands, but you normally leave it set to Math. That way, Equation Editor can decide how to format each element of your equation.

On occasion, Equation Editor's automatic formatting doesn't work. Type the word **cosmic**, for example, and Equation Editor assumes that you want to calculate the cosine of the product of the variables m, i, and c. When that happens, highlight the incorrectly formatted text and use Style⇨Text.

Don't use the spacebar to separate elements in an equation — let Equation Editor worry about how much space to leave between the variables and the plus signs. The only time you use the spacebar is when you're typing two or more words of text formatted with the Text style.

The Enter key has an interesting behavior in Equation Editor: It adds a new equation slot, immediately beneath the current slot. This key is sometimes a good way to create stacked items, but using an appropriate template instead is a better way.

Keyboard Shortcuts for Equation Editor

Just like Word itself, Equation Editor is loaded with helpful keyboard shortcuts. You have my deepest sympathies if you are forced to use Equation Editor often enough to commit these keyboard shortcuts to memory, but just in case, I list them in Table 7-3.

Table 7-3	Keyboard Shortcuts for Equation Editor
Keyboard Shortcut	*What It Does*
Navigating and Editing Keys	
Tab	Moves to the end of the current slot; if the insertion point is already at the end of the slot, moves to the beginning of the next slot
Shift+Tab	Moves to the end of the preceding slot
Ctrl+Tab	Inserts a tab character
Ctrl+D	Redraws the equation
Ctrl+Y	Shows the entire equation
Ctrl+Shift+L	Left-align
Ctrl+Shift+C	Center
Ctrl+Shift+R	Right-align
Ctrl+1	Zooms to 100%
Ctrl+2	Zooms to 200%
Ctrl+4	Zooms to 400%
Ctrl+↑	Nudges selected item up one pixel
Ctrl+↓	Nudges selected item down one pixel
Ctrl+←	Nudges selected item left one pixel
Ctrl+→	Nudges selected item right one pixel
Applying Styles	
Ctrl+Shift+=	Applies Math style
Ctrl+Shift+E	Applies Text style
Ctrl+Shift+F	Applies Function style
Ctrl+Shift+I	Applies Variable style
Ctrl+Shift+G	Applies Greek style
Ctrl+Shift+B	Applies Matrix-Vector style

Keyboard Shortcut	What It Does
Inserting Symbols	
Ctrl+K, I	Infinity (∞)
Ctrl+K, A	Arrow ($\rightarrow$)
Ctrl+K, D	Derivative (∂)
Ctrl+K, <	Less than or equal to ($\leq$)
Ctrl+K, >	Greater than or equal to ($\geq$)
Ctrl+K, T	Times ($\times$)
Ctrl+K, E	Element of ($\in$)
Ctrl+K, Shift+E	Not an element of ($\notin$)
Ctrl+K, C	Contained in ($\subset$)
Ctrl+K, Shift+C	Not contained in ($\subseteq$)
Inserting Templates	
Ctrl+9 or Ctrl+0	Parentheses
Ctrl+[or Ctrl+]	Brackets
Ctrl+{ or Ctrl+}	Braces
Ctrl+F	Fraction
Ctrl+/	Slash fraction
Ctrl+H	Superscript (High)
Ctrl+L	Subscript (Low)
Ctrl+J	Joint superscript/subscript
Ctrl+I	Integral
Ctrl+T, |	Absolute value
Ctrl+R	Root
Ctrl+T,N	Nth Root
Ctrl+T, S	Summation
Ctrl+T, P	Product
Ctrl+T, M	Matrix
Ctrl+T, U	Underscript (limit)

**Book IV
Chapter 7**

**Move Over, Einstein
(Creating Equations)**

Book V

Web Publishing

The 5th Wave   By Rich Tennant

"Face it, Vinnie — you're gonna have a hard time getting people to subscribe online with a credit card to a newsletter called 'Felons Interactive!'"

Contents at a Glance

Chapter 1: Going Online with Word

In This Chapter

- ✔ Saving and retrieving documents on a Web server
- ✔ Creating a Network Places icon for a Web server
- ✔ Accessing FTP sites from Word
- ✔ Using the Web toolbar

*I*n the early, Bronze Age era of computing, the only way to the Internet was through special Internet programs, such as e-mail programs and Web browsers. Now, however, you can access the Internet directly from the comfort of your favorite application programs, including Word. If you have access to a Web server, Word lets you save a document directly to the server. And you can open a document directly from the Internet without leaving Word. Pretty cool, eh?

This entire chapter assumes that you have access to the Internet. If you don't have Internet access, you should first pick up a copy of my book, *Internet Explorer 6 For Dummies* (published by Wiley), which shows you how to get connected to the Internet, and as a bonus, shows you how to use Internet Explorer 6 to access the Internet.

Saving a Document on a Web Server

Suppose that you create a Word document and decide to make it available to the general public via the Internet. You can do that by saving the document as an HTML file so that anyone with a Web browser can access the document. You find out how to do that in the next chapter. A simpler method is to save the .dpc file to a Web server. This way, anyone who has Word can open the document directly from the Web server and view the file from within Word.

Before you can save a Word document to a Web server, you need to obtain access to a Web server. You can do that by purchasing space on a Web server from a Web hosting company or by setting up your own Web server. The details for doing that are a little beyond the scope of this book, but you can find out more in my book, *Internet Explorer 6 For Dummies*.

After you gain access to a Web server, you need the address of the Web server. In addition, you need a user ID and password that grants you access to the server. You need to get those details from the person responsible for setting up the server.

After your Web server is set up, the next step is to set up a network place in your My Network Places folder. You can easily access the Web server from the folder when you want to save or retrieve documents. Complete instructions for this task are in the next section, "Creating a Network Place."

When you add a network place for your Web site, you can save a document to the site by opening the document and choosing File➪Save As. In the Save As dialog box, click the My Network Places icon, double-click the icon for your Web server, and then click Save. The document saves to your Web server.

Creating a Network Place

Creating a network place simplifies the task of saving or retrieving documents on a Web server. To create a network place, follow these steps:

1. **Choose My Network Places from the Start menu.**

The Network Places folder opens up.

2. **Click the <u>Add Network Place</u> link that appears in the task pane.**

The Add Network Place Wizard launches, as shown in Figure 1-1.

Figure 1-1:
The opening
window of
the Add
Network
Place
Wizard.

3. **Click Next.**

   The Add Network Place Wizard asks if you want to create a network place for an MSN Communities page or some other network location.

4. **Select Choose Another Network Location, and then click Next.**

   The Add Network Place Wizard asks for the address of the Web site you want to create a network place for, as shown in Figure 1-2.

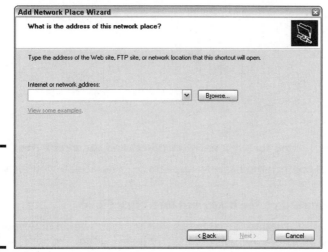

Figure 1-2: Enter the address of your network place here.

5. **Type the Web site address in the text box.**

   For example, `http://www.mywebsite.com`.

   Note: You must include `http://` before the actual Web site address. If you omit this key bit, the Add Network Place Wizard gets confused and passes out.

6. **Click Next.**

   You're prompted to enter a username and password.

7. **Enter your username and password, and then click Next.**

   The Add Network Place Wizard asks for a name for your network place, as shown in Figure 1-3. This name displays in the Network Places folder, so pick a meaningful name that helps you identify the Web site.

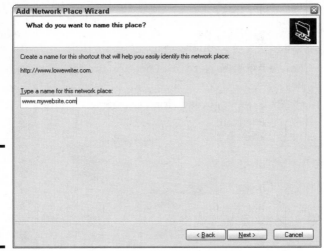

Figure 1-3:
Enter a
name for
your
network
place here.

8. **Enter a name for your network place, and then click Next.**

   A final confirmation screen appears to congratulate you for your ingenuity.

9. **Pat yourself on the back, and then click Finish.**

   You're returned to the Network Places folder, which now sports a shiny new icon for the network place you just created.

Opening a Document from a Web Server

You can use Word's File⇨Open command to open a Word document that resides on a Web server. Note that although any users can open a document you saved to a Web server, they must have a user ID and password for the server in order to save any changes they make to the document back to the server.

To open a document located on a Web server, you must know the complete address (called a *URL*) of the document that you want to open. This address usually consists of three parts: a server address, one or more directory names, and a filename for the document. The address must always begin with `http://` so that Word can distinguish the address from a normal filename. The other parts of the URL are separated by slashes.

For example, consider this address:

`http://www.LoweWriter.com/squiggle.doc`

Here, the host name is `www.LoweWriter.com` and the filename is `squiggle.doc`.

When you know the URL, all you have to do to open a document in Word is type its URL in the File Name field on the standard Open dialog box. Here's the complete procedure for opening a document at a Web site:

1. **Find out the complete URL of the document that you want to open.**

2. **Choose File⇨Open.**

Alternatively, click the Open button or use the keyboard shortcut Ctrl+O. One way or the other, the Open dialog box appears.

3. **In the File Name field, type the URL of the document that you want to open.**

For example, type **http://www.LoweWriter.com/squiggle.doc.**

4. **Click Open.**

If you're not already connected to the Internet and you use a dialup connection, a Connect To dialog box appears so that you can make a connection.

5. **If prompted, enter the username and password for the site where the document resides.**

Depending on how the Web site is set up, it may allow you to access the document without entering a username and password. If a username and password is required, you have to get the required information from the person who administers the site.

6. **Play a quick game of Solitaire.**

Copying the file over the Internet to your computer takes a bit of time — perhaps even several minutes if the document is large and your connection is slow. When the transfer finishes, the document displays as normal.

If you display the Web toolbar, you can enter the address in the Address box, press Enter, and voilà! The document displays. You can find more about the Web toolbar by reading the section "Using the Web Toolbar" later in this chapter.

Word doesn't care if the file identified by the URL is on a computer halfway around the globe, on a computer two floors up from you, or on your own computer. So long as the URL is valid, Word retrieves the document and displays it.

Opening a Document in Internet Explorer

You can also open a Word document directly from Internet Explorer. Just type the complete address of the document (such as `http://www.lowewriter.com/squiggle.doc`) in Internet Explorer's address bar. The dialog box shown in Figure 1-4 appears to warn you that downloading files can be dangerous. Do not proceed unless you know that the file is actually what it purports to be.

Figure 1-4: Word cautiously cautions you to be cautious.

Depending on the speed of your Internet connection and the size of the document, opening the document may take a few seconds or minutes. When the document does open, you're greeted by an interesting amalgam of Internet Explorer and Word, as shown in Figure 1-5.

Some strange things lurk just beneath the surface of this unusual relationship:

✦ Judging from the title bar in Figure 1-5, this window is an Internet Explorer window. Notice that the big fat Internet Explorer toolbar appears just beneath the menu bar.

✦ But wait! The menu bar belongs to Word. All the familiar menu commands, including Format, Tools, and Table, are there.

✦ But wait some more! A few extra menu commands are around: Go To and Favorites. These belong to Internet Explorer, not Word.

✦ Word's Reviewing toolbar is hanging around.

✦ You can edit the document directly in the Internet Explorer window. If you try to save the document back to the Web server, you may be prompted for a username and password. But you can choose File⇨Save As to save the document to your own hard disk without a username or password.

Internet Explorer's toolbar

Word's menu

Word's Reviewing toolbar

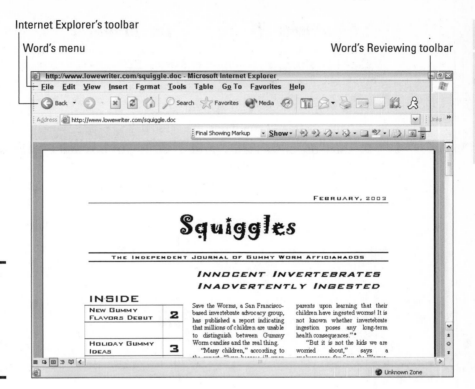

Figure 1-5:
Word and
Internet
Explorer
appear to
be cohab-
itating.

Using an FTP Site

FTP, which stands for *File Transfer Protocol,* is one of the oldest parts of the
Internet. FTP is designed to create Internet libraries in which files are stored
and retrieved by other Internet users. Although FTP is old, it is still one of
the most common ways of saving and retrieving files on the Internet.

FTP uses a directory structure that works much like Windows folders. The
main directory of an FTP site is called the *root.* Within the root are other
directories, which may contain files, additional directories, or both. For
example, a typical FTP server for a business may have directories such as
Products (for storing files that contain product information), Company (for
company information), Software (for software files that can be downloaded),
and Docs (for documentation about the company's products).

The following section ("Adding an FTP site to your computer") explains how
to set up an FTP site so that you can access it from within Word. The section
after that ("Opening a document from an FTP site") shows how to actually
access an FTP site from Word.

Adding an FTP site to your computer

Before you can access files on an FTP site, you must add the address (URL) of the FTP site to your computer's list of FTP sites. To do that, follow these steps:

1. **In Word, choose File⇨Open.**

This command summons the Open dialog box.

2. **Click the down arrow for the Look In list box and then scroll down to select Add/Modify FTP Locations.**

The dialog box shown in Figure 1-6 appears.

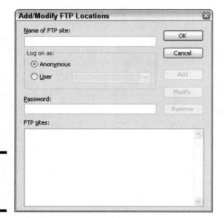

Figure 1-6:
Adding an
FTP site.

3. **Type the URL of the FTP site in the Name of FTP Site field.**

Be sure to include `ftp://` at the start of the URL. (You don't usually have to type `http://` to access Web sites, but you do have to type `ftp://` to access an FTP site.)

4. **If this FTP site requires you to enter a username and password to gain access, select the User option and then type your username and password.**

You have to get the name and password to use from the administrator of the FTP site you are accessing. (At many FTP sites, the username of "Anonymous" works, and the password is your e-mail address.)

5. **Click Add.**

The new FTP site is added.

6. Click OK.

The Add/Modify FTP Locations dialog box vanishes, returning you to the Open dialog box.

7. Click Cancel to return to Word.

The FTP site is now added to the list of FTP sites that are available from within Word. To open a document from this site or another site you have previously added, follow the steps I detail in the next section.

Opening a document from an FTP site

To open a document from an FTP site, follow these steps:

1. Choose File⇨Open.

The Open dialog box opens.

2. Click the down arrow of the Look In list box and then scroll down to find and select the FTP site containing the document that you want to open.

Your computer hesitates for a moment as it connects with the FTP site. Then the Open dialog box displays, listing the directories that appear at the FTP site's root.

3. Select the file that you want to open.

To open a directory, double-click the directory's icon. Click the icon of the file that you want to select.

4. Click Open.

Depending on the size of your document, you may have to wait for a few minutes for Word to download the document.

You're done!

Saving a document to an FTP site

If you have access to an FTP site that lets you store your file (that is, if you have *write privileges* for the FTP site), you can also save a document directly to the FTP site from Word by choosing File⇨Save As. Here are the steps:

1. Choose File⇨Save As.

The familiar Save As dialog box appears.

2. Click the down arrow for the Look In list box and then scroll down to find and select the FTP site on which you want to save the document.

Your computer connects to the FTP site (which may take a moment) and then displays the FTP site's root directory in the Save As dialog box.

3. **Navigate to the directory where you want to save the file.**

4. **Type a name for the file.**

5. **Click Save.**

   The file copies to the FTP server. Depending on the size of the file, the copying may take a while. If the file has dozens of pages, each with large graphics, you may have enough time to catch a quick lunch while the file copies to the FTP server.

Using the Web Toolbar

Word sports a toolbar called the Web toolbar. The Web toolbar allows you to view documents that contain hyperlinks or that you retrieved from the World Wide Web easier. Table 1-1 lists the function of each button and control on the Web toolbar.

To summon the Web toolbar, choose View⇨Toolbars⇨Web or click the Web button on the Standard toolbar.

Table 1-1	Buttons on the Web Toolbar	
Button	*Name*	*What It Does*
	Back	Goes to the previously displayed page.
	Forward	Returns to the page you went back from.
	Stop	Stops downloading the current page.
	Refresh	Reloads the current page.
	Start Page	Displays your designated start page. (Internet Explorer uses the term *home page* for the start page.)
	Search the Web	Displays your designated search page.
Favorites ▾	Favorites	Displays your favorites list, similar to clicking the Look In Favorites button in an Open or Save As dialog box.

Button	*Name*	*What It Does*
Go ▾	Go	Displays a menu that includes the Back, Forward, Start, and Search commands that correspond to the Back, Forward, Start, and Search buttons. Also includes an Open Hyperlink command and commands to designate the current page as your start page or search page.
	Show Only Web Toolbar	Temporarily hides everything on-screen except the page area and the Web toolbar. Click this button again to get the screen back to normal.

If you find that you don't have all the buttons you want on your Web toolbar, remember the down arrow that leads you to the Add or Remove Buttons button. If you whisper "Button, button, who's got the button?" while performing this task, it works a lot better.

Chapter 2: Creating Web Pages with Word

In This Chapter

✔ Finding out about Web pages in Word

✔ Discovering how to host a Web site

✔ Setting Word's Web options

✔ Creating and saving pages in Web format

Do you want to make yourself known on the World Wide Web with your own Web page, but are afraid that you're not enough of a geek for the complex task of HTML programming? Fear not! Word has the ability to save your documents in HTML format so that you can publish them to the Web. All you have to add is a Web site to save your pages to.

This chapter covers the basics of creating Web pages with Word. You find additional information and more advanced techniques in the chapters that follow. But the information in this chapter gets you started.

Before you get started, you should realize that Word isn't really the ideal program for maintaining Web sites that consist of more than a few pages. For more complicated Web sites, you need to use a Web publishing program, such as Microsoft FrontPage that comes with some editions of Office.

Understanding Web Page Basics

Before you start creating Web pages with Word, you need to know a few basics about Web pages. So bear with me while I trudge through some.

Clarifying some basic terminology

Before getting too far into this chapter, I want to clarify some basic terminology you're probably familiar with already. A *Web page* is a single page that you can view with a Web browser, such as Internet Explorer. A *Web site* is a collection of one or more pages linked together so that you can move from one page to another. A *home page* is the top-level page in a Web site — the page most users view first when they visit the site.

Many people — myself included — tend to use these three terms interchangeably. For example, if I tell you that I just set up a home page for my company, what I probably really mean is that I set up a company Web site with a home page and several other Web pages.

HTML, which stands for *HyperText Markup Language,* is the language used to compose individual Web pages. HTML consists of a bunch of pre-defined *tags* that mark various elements of a Web page to indicate how to format them. A Web page is sometimes called an *HTML document.*

Recounting the differences between Web pages and printed pages

Word is designed primarily as a word processor for creating printed pages. Web pages are fundamentally different from printed pages. In particular:

+ Printed pages are designed to print on paper. Web pages are designed to be viewed on the computer screen in a Web browser — most likely, Microsoft Internet Explorer.

+ Printed pages are usually 8½" x 11". Web browser windows are smaller. Typically, a browser window can display about half the amount of information as can be shown on a printed page.

+ The appearance of a printed page is fixed. Web users can resize their browser windows, so you can't predict the size at which a Web page displays. As a result, Web pages are designed to be formatted according to the size of the window they're displayed in.

+ All pages that make up a printed Word document are stored on a disk as a single .doc file. In contrast, each page in a Web site is stored as a separate file. In addition, the various elements that make up each page — such as graphic images — are also stored as separate files. A Web site with a few dozen pages may require a hundred or more files, depending on the complexity of each page.

+ Word documents have many more formatting options than Web pages. Web pages are limited to the type of formats that can be created with HTML, the language used to format Web pages. Some HTML formatting features (such as tables, bulleted lists, and heading styles) are similar to Word's, but aren't as flexible.

+ By the same token, Web pages have features that printed documents don't. For example, most Web pages include hyperlinks that a user can click to go to a different Web page. In addition, Web pages can have animations and scripts.

Setting Up a Web Site

To publish your Web pages on the Internet so that other people can see them, you must have access to a Web server. A *Web server* is a special computer that's connected to the Internet and runs special Web server software, which enables the computer to store Web page files other Internet users can view on their computers. A Web server is also known as a *Web host.*

The following sections give you some ideas for where to find Web server space to host your Web site.

Internet service providers

If you access the Internet through an Internet service provider (ISP), you probably already have space set aside to set up a small Web site. Most ISPs give each of their users a small amount of disk space for Web pages included in their monthly service fee. The space may be limited to a few megabytes, but that is enough to set up a modest Web site with several pages. You can probably get additional disk space, if you need it, for a small monthly fee. Some service providers also limit the amount of traffic your Web site receives. In other words, you can't host a wildly popular site that receives millions of visits per day on your ISP account.

Your ISP can give you step-by-step instructions for copying your Web pages to the ISP's Web server. Visit the help section of your ISP's home page for more information.

Web hosting services

A *Web hosting service* is a company that specializes in hosting Web sites on its own server computers. Unlike ISPs, which include limited Web hosting features as a part of their normal fee for Internet access, a Web hosting service charges you for hosting your Web site.

Web hosting services offer much more than an ISP: your own domain name for your Web site, more disk space for your Web site and a larger traffic allowance, technical support for your Web server, help designing and creating your Web site, and support for advanced Web server features.

Of course, you have to pay for all this, and the cost varies from one service to the next. A typical Web hosting package includes

✦ Your own domain name so that you can pick the Web address users use to access your site. The Web hosting service may register this name for you, or you can register it yourself. For more information, see the nearby sidebar, "Obtaining a domain name."

If you let the hosting service register the domain name for you, make sure that you're listed as the owner of the name so that you can take the name with you to another Web hosting service if you decide to switch later. The best way to make sure that you own the domain name is to register it yourself.

✦ A limited amount of disk storage on one of the hosting company's Web server computers — typically from 100MB to 200MB for a basic package, with more space available at additional charge.

✦ A high-speed connection to the Internet for your Web site, with a relatively high limit on the amount of traffic, such as 5GB or 6GB per month. If your Web site becomes very popular, you may have to pay extra for the increased traffic. On the other hand, some Web host services provide unlimited traffic even with basic packages.

A claim of unlimited traffic can be misleading — the Web host service may not have the equipment necessary to allow an unlimited amount of traffic for all its customers with acceptable speed. To find out, try accessing a few Web sites hosted by the Web host service you're considering to see how long accessing the Web pages takes.

✦ One or more e-mail accounts using your domain name.

Getting a free site

If you can't find a home for your Web site at your Internet service provider and you don't want to pay for a Web hosting service, you can opt for one of the many free Web servers to host your Web site. You can't create a huge site on a free server, but most give you several megabytes of Web server space free of charge — enough to set up a few pages at least.

What's the catch? Advertising. Users who visit your Web site have to put up with advertisements that pop up in their own windows or appear as banners on your pages. If you don't mind the advertisements, a free Web server can be an easy way to get started creating Web pages.

If you don't want to mess with HTML, most free Web servers include simple fill-in-the-blank tools that make creating basic Web pages easy. For example, you can create a basic home page by selecting one of several templates, typing the page title and information you want on the page — such as your name and a description of your family, hobbies, or interests — and uploading pictures you want to appear on the page.

Obtaining a domain name

The best part about using a Web hosting service is that you get to register your own domain name. With an ISP-hosted Web page, your Web page address is based on a combination of your user ID and your ISP's domain name. For example, if your username is wilbur and your ISP's Web domain name is `www.mydity provider.com`, your Web page has an address, such as `www.mydityprovider.com/~wilbur`. But if you host your page with a Web hosting service, you can register your Web site with a name of your choosing, such as `www.myveryowncompany.com`.

Registering a domain name is inexpensive — about $25 per year. You can easily register a name yourself by going to the Network Solutions Web site at `www.networksolutions.com`. From there, you can search for a domain name that hasn't been taken yet. When you find a name that isn't already in use, you can sign up over the Web by providing the contact information for the domain name and a credit card number for payment.

Setting Word's Web Options

Before you save a Word document as a Web page, spend a few moments with the Web Options dialog box, shown in Figure 2-1. This dialog box lets you set various options that affect how Word creates the Web pages for a presentation. To summon the Web Options dialog box, choose Tools➪Options. In the Options dialog box, click the General tab, and then click the Web Options button.

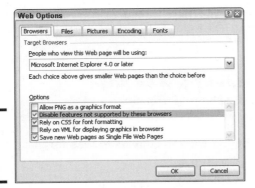

Figure 2-1:
The Web
Options
dialog box.

The Web Options dialog box has five tabs:

+ **Browsers:** This tab lets you set the browsers that you want the document to be compatible with. For example, you can require that users must have Internet Explorer version 6, version 5 or later, or version 4 or later, and you can allow Netscape browsers. The higher browser versions enable more advanced features but limit the number of people who can view the page. Unless you are certain that everyone has a certain browser version, your best bet is to stick with the default choice, Internet Explorer 4 or later. You can choose from a drop-down list of browsers, or you can pick the specific browser capabilities that you want the document to support.

+ **Files:** This tab lets you control how Word organizes the various files that are generated for a Web page. The most important option on this tab is Organize Supporting Files in a Folder. Select this option if you want Word to create a folder to hold the files. If you already created a folder structure for the files, uncheck this option.

+ **Pictures:** This tab lets you select the screen resolution you want to target your pages for. The default — 800 x 600, 96 pixels per inch — is appropriate for most pages.

+ **Encoding:** This tab lets you choose alternate language schemes for your pages. Best steer clear of this one.

+ **Fonts:** This tab lets you choose the default fonts to use for your pages. These fonts display text when the font isn't specified.

Creating Web Page Documents

You have two basic ways of creating Web pages in Word. You can save an existing Word document in Web page format, or you can create a new document in Web page format. The following sections describe both of these techniques.

Saving a document as a Web page

You can convert an existing Word document to a Web page document by following these steps:

1. **Open the document you want to convert to Web format.**

2. **Choose File⇨Save as Web Page.**

   The Save As dialog box appears, as shown in Figure 2-2. As you can see, the Save as Type drop-down list is preset to Single File Web Page (*.mht, *.mhtml).

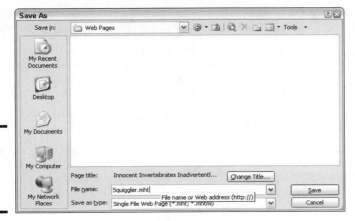

Figure 2-2:
Saving a
document
as a Web
page.

3. **Type a name for the Web page in the File Name text box.**

4. **Click the Change Title button.**

   The Set Page Title dialog box comes up, shown in Figure 2-3. This dialog box lets you set the title that displays in the Web browser's title bar when a user views the page.

Figure 2-3:
Setting the
page title for
a Web page.

5. **Change the title if you want, and then click OK.**

   You're returned to the Save As dialog box.

6. **Set the Save as Type drop-down list to the Web page format you want to use.**

   Three formats are for saving Web pages:

   - **Single File Web Page:** This format saves the entire page in one file. Images and other attachments embed in the file in a special format. Pages saved in this format are viewed only with Internet Explorer version 5.0 or later.

- **Web Page:** Saves the document as an HTML file. This format includes special tags that enable you to edit the page later in Word.

- **Web Page, Filtered:** Saves the document as an HTML file and removes the special tags that allow you to edit the document with Word. With this format, the file is smaller than the normal Web page format. However, after you save the document in this format, you can't open it in Word.

7. Click Save.

If Word encounters any formatting in the document that isn't rendered correctly in the Web page, a dialog box similar to the one shown in Figure 2-4 displays.

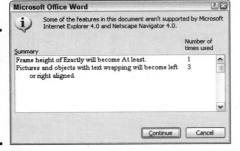

Figure 2-4:
Word warns you about possible Web formatting problems.

8. Click Continue.

The document saves as a Web page. You're done!

Creating a new Web page

You can create a Web page from scratch by choosing File⇨New to summon the New task pane, and then clicking the Web page icon. Word automatically switches to Web Layout view, which lets you edit the Web page as you see fit. When you're done, use File⇨Save to save the Web page.

Editing and Formatting Web Pages

In general, you can edit and format text in a Web page the same as you format it in a normal Word document. The toolbar buttons and keyboard shortcuts for such common formatting as bold and italic work the same. Even features such as bulleted lists, numbered lists, and even tables work pretty much the same.

You can also use any of the Word drawing features I cover in Book IV on a Web page. AutoShapes, diagrams, charts, WordArt objects, and even text boxes convert to image files, so they can efficiently display with any Web browser.

Previewing Web Pages

As you work with Web page documents, you frequently need to preview the page to see how it appears when viewed in a Web browser. To do that, choose File➪Web Page Preview. A separate browser window displays the page, as shown in Figure 2-5.

When you're done previewing the document, you can return to Word by pressing Alt+Tab, or you can close the browser window.

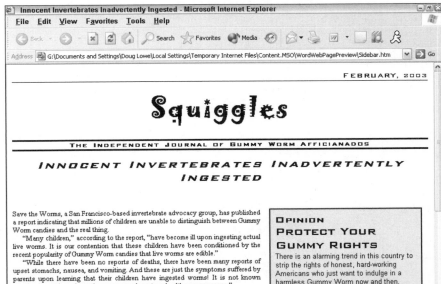

Figure 2-5:
Previewing a Web page in a browser window.

Chapter 3: Basic Web Formatting Features

In This Chapter

✔ Adding hyperlinks to create links to other pages

✔ Inserting images into your Web pages

✔ Adding multimedia features, such as sound and video

✔ Looking at the HTML for a Web page

*I*n this chapter, I show you some of the basic editing and formatting features of Word that are unique to Web pages, such as creating hyperlinks, working with Web graphics, and editing HTML. If you've worked with HTML before, most of this information is old hat. But if you're new to HTML, or if you just want to find out how standard HTML features translate into Word, this chapter is for you.

Creating Hyperlinks

A *hyperlink* is simply a bit of text or a graphic image that you can click when viewing a Web page to summon a different page. The other page can be another page within the same Web site or a page in another Web site. Or, the hyperlink can point to some other type of document, such as an Excel spreadsheet or a PowerPoint presentation.

Hyperlinks are commonly used to allow users to navigate through the pages of your Web site. For example, you may include a hyperlink to the major pages of your Web site on every page in the site. That way, users can easily find those pages no matter what page they're currently viewing.

Here are a few additional thoughts to ponder concerning hyperlinks:

✦ A hyperlink consists of two parts: an *anchor* and a *target*. The anchor is the part of the hyperlink that appears in the Web page. The target is the Internet address of the page the hyperlink refers to.

✦ A hyperlink can also have a *screen tip,* which displays in a small box when the user hovers the mouse over the anchor.

✦ The anchor can either be text or a graphic image.

✦ You can also create an *e-mail hyperlink* that specifies an e-mail address as its target. Then, when the user clicks the e-mail hyperlink, an e-mail window opens that allows the user to compose and send a message to the user indicated in the hyperlink's target.

✦ Word's AutoCorrect feature automatically creates hyperlinks from Web addresses and e-mail addresses you type. For example, if you type a sentence such as "Send e-mail to George@Jetson.com," Word automatically turns George@Jetson.com into a hyperlink.

Linking to an existing Web page

Adding a hyperlink to an existing Web page is easy. Just follow these steps:

1. **Move the insertion pointer to the spot where you want to insert the link.**

2. **Choose Insert⊃Hyperlink.**

Alternatively, click the Insert Hyperlink button on the Standard toolbar or use the keyboard shortcut Ctrl+K. One way or the other, the Insert Hyperlink dialog box, shown in Figure 3-1, is summoned.

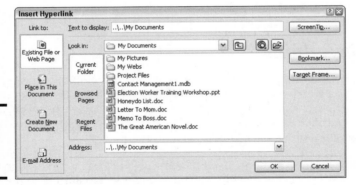

Figure 3-1:
The Insert
Hyperlink
dialog box.

3. **Select the Existing File or Web Page icon in the Link To list.**

The Link To list is the stack of four icons that appears on the left edge of the Insert Hyperlink dialog box. The four icons are:

• **Existing File or Web Page:** You can link to another page you already created or to a Web page on the Internet.

• **Place in This Document:** You can link to one part of the current Web page. For long pages, providing links to the page's major sections at the top of the page is common.

- **Create New Document:** This option does just what it says. You can, however, choose now or another time to edit the new document by clicking the appropriate button.

- **E-mail Address:** Link to an e-mail address. This feature is useful in an intranet or Internet setting because this link allows the reader to write e-mail to the e-mail address that you link to.

4. **Select the page you want to link to.**

   You can indicate the page you want to link to in several ways:

   - To link to a Web page on your own computer, select the Current Folder icon, and then navigate to the page you want to link to.

   - If you recently edited the page you want to link to, you can click the Recent Files icon and select the page.

   - To link to a page on another Web site, type the complete address of the page in the Address box.

   - If you don't know the address of the page but recently viewed it in your Web browser, click the Browsed Pages icon and select the page.

5. **Type the text you want to display as the anchor for the hyperlink in the Text to Display box.**

   The text you type here inserts into your document at the insertion point.

6. **Click the Screen Tip button.**

   The Set Hyperlink ScreenTip dialog box opens, as shown in Figure 3-2.

Figure 3-2:
Setting a
hyperlink
screen tip.

7. **Type the text you want to appear in the screen tip.**

   This text appears in a box when the user hovers the mouse over the hyperlink.

8. **Click OK.**

   You return to the Insert Hyperlink dialog box.

***9.* Click OK again.**

This time, you return to your document and the hyperlink is created.

Here are a few additional thoughts regarding hyperlinks:

✦ If you prefer, you can type the text to use as the hyperlink anchor before you insert the hyperlink. Select the text, and then choose Insert⇨ Hyperlink. The text you selected automatically appears in the Text to Display box.

✦ To create a graphic anchor, first add the graphic element you want to use as the anchor. Then, select it and choose Insert⇨Hyperlink. The Text to Display box is disabled.

✦ To edit a hyperlink after you create it, right-click the hyperlink's anchor in the Web page and choose Edit Hyperlink from the shortcut menu that appears.

✦ To remove a hyperlink without removing the anchor text or graphic, right-click the anchor and choose Remove Hyperlink from the shortcut menu that appears.

Linking to a location in the current page

Besides creating links to other Web pages, you can also create hyperlinks that go to other locations in the current page. Links are most useful for large pages to save the user the hassle of scrolling down the page to find the information he or she is looking for.

To create a hyperlink to a location in the current page, follow the steps I describe in the preceding section. In Step 3, choose the Place in This Document icon instead of the Existing File or Web Page icon. Then, you can select the location in the current document, as shown in Figure 3-3.

Figure 3-3: Linking to a location in the current page.

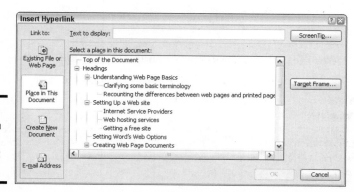

You can create a link to any heading in your document by selecting the heading from the Insert Hyperlink dialog box. If you want to link to a location other than a heading, create a bookmark for the location before calling up the Insert Hyperlink dialog box. Then, you can select the bookmark as the target for the hyperlink. (For more information about creating bookmarks, refer to Book III, Chapter 1.)

Linking to a new document

If the document you want to link to doesn't yet exist, you can create it at the same time you create the hyperlink. Follow the steps I outline in the section "Linking to an existing Web page," earlier in this chapter. But in Step 3, choose the Create New Document icon instead of the Existing File or Web Page icon. The dialog box shown in Figure 3-4 appears. Here, you can specify the name and path for the new file. In addition, you can choose whether you want to open the document for editing right now or later. If you select the Edit the New Document Later option, don't forget to open the new document later to edit it. Otherwise, the hyperlink leads to an empty page.

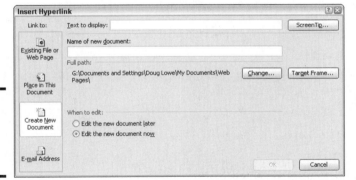

Figure 3-4:
Creating
a new
document
to link to.

Creating an e-mail link

You can create a hyperlink that sends an e-mail message by following the steps I describe in the section "Linking to an existing Web page," earlier in this chapter, but choosing the E-mail Address icon rather than the Existing File or Web Page icon in Step 3. The dialog box shown in Figure 3-5 appears.

You can then type the e-mail address you want the message delivered to and the subject for the e-mail message. When the user clicks the hyperlink, a New Message window appears with the To and Subject fields already filled in. The user can then type the body of the message and click Send to send the message on its way.

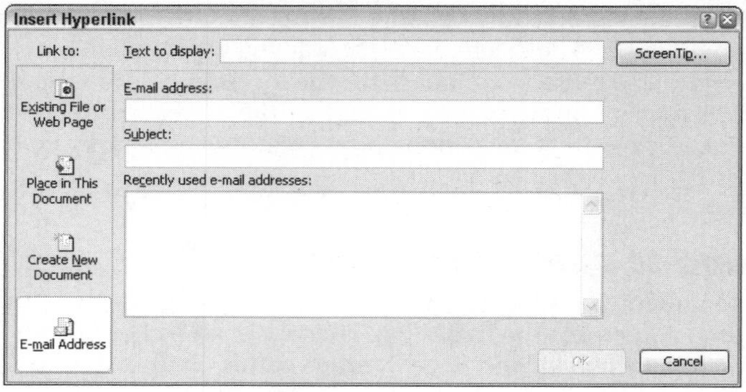

Insert Hyperlink

| Link to: | Text to display: | | ScreenTip... |

Existing File or Web Page

E-mail address:

Place in This Document

Subject:

Create New Document

Recently used e-mail addresses:

E-mail Address

OK   Cancel

Figure 3-5:
Creating an
e-mail link.

Working with Images

One of the coolest features of Word Web pages is that Word automatically converts graphic elements to GIF image files when you save the document. As a result, you can use any of the graphics features I describe in Book IV in a Word Web page. In particular, Word Web pages can include

✦ Images inserted from files via Insert⇨Picture⇨From File

✦ Clip art images inserted via Insert⇨Picture⇨Clip Art

✦ Scanned images or digital photographs inserted via Insert⇨Picture⇨ From Scanner or Camera

✦ AutoShapes

✦ Text boxes

✦ WordArt

✦ Diagrams inserted via Insert⇨Diagram

✦ Charts created with Microsoft Graph

In addition, you can apply any of the Word graphic effects to these objects, such as line and fill effects, shadows, or 3-D effects. Word includes these effects when it converts your graphic to an image file.

Whenever you insert a graphic object in a Word Web page, you need to specify *alternate text* for the object. Alternate text displays in browsers that are not configured to display pictures. Users with slow Internet connections sometimes disable pictures to increase download speeds.

To provide alternate text, right-click the graphic item and choose the Format command from the shortcut menu. Then click the Web tab, shown in Figure 3-6. Enter the alternate text in the text box, and then click OK.

Figure 3-6:
Creating
alternate
text.

The following sections describe several additional ways to work with images in a Word Web page.

Adding a background image

Many Web pages use a background image to create an interesting appearance for the page. You can use Format➪Background➪Fill Effects to set the background for a Web page. The Fill Effects dialog box appears — the same one you use to apply a fill effect to a graphic object. You can then select a gradient fill, texture, image, or pattern to use for the page background. I describe this dialog box in detail in Book IV, Chapter 3, so I won't repeat all of its options here.

Inserting a horizontal line

One of the commonly used formatting features in Web pages is the horizontal line, which is drawn across the page to visually separate groups of information. To insert a horizontal line, follow these steps:

1. **Position the insertion point where you want to insert the horizontal line.**

2. **Choose Format➪Borders and Shading.**

   The Borders and Shading dialog box appears.

3. **Click the Horizontal Line button.**

   You find this button at the bottom of the Borders tab. When you click it, the dialog box shown in Figure 3-7 appears.

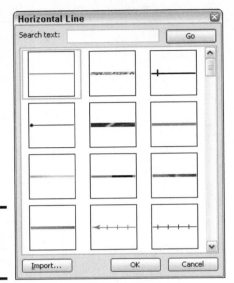

Figure 3-7:
Inserting a
horizontal
line.

4. **Select the horizontal line you want to use.**

   Word offers quite a selection of lines to choose from.

5. **Click OK.**

   The line inserts into the page.

6. **Right-click the line and choose Format Horizontal Line from the short-cut menu.**

   The Format Horizontal Line dialog box appears, as shown in Figure 3-8.

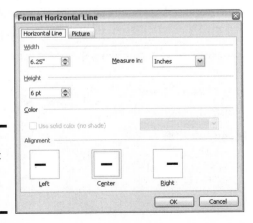

Figure 3-8:
The Format
Horizontal
Line dialog
box.

7. Adjust the width, height, and alignment if desired.

8. Click OK.

You're done!

To remove a line later on, select it by clicking anywhere on the line and then press the Delete key.

Inserting picture bullets

Web pages frequently have bulleted lists. Although you can use the normal small black dots for your bullets, Word lets you jazz up your bulleted lists by using a picture for the bullet. To use picture bullets, follow these steps:

1. Create a normal bulleted list.

Use the Bullets button the way you normally do to format the list.

2. Select the entire list.

3. Choose Format⇨Bullets and Numbers.

The Bullets and Numbers dialog box appears.

4. Click the Customize button.

The Customize Bulleted List dialog box appears, as shown in Figure 3-9.

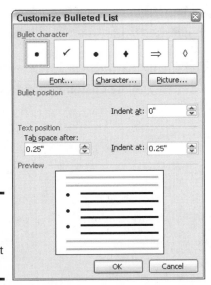

Figure 3-9:
The
Customize
Bulleted List
dialog box.

5. Click the Picture button.

The Picture Bullet dialog box shown in Figure 3-10 appears.

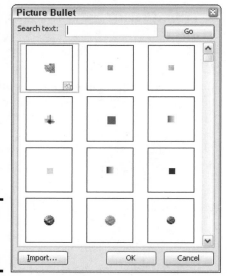

Figure 3-10:
Choosing
a picture
bullet.

6. Choose the picture bullet you want to use, and then click OK.

Word offers many picture bullets to choose from.

The bullets with a little star in the bottom-right corner are animated picture bullets; they move when you display them in a Web browser.

When you click OK, you're returned to the Customize Bulleted List dialog box.

7. Click OK again.

You return to the Bullets and Numbers dialog box.

8. Click OK again.

I'm OK, you're OK.

Book II, Chapter 7 has a lot more information about bulleted lists.

Inserting Multimedia with the Web Tools Toolbar

Word has a special Web Tools toolbar that displays several buttons that add features to your Web pages. Three of the buttons on this toolbar let you insert multimedia items on your Web pages:

 ✦ **Movie:** Inserts a video into your Web page.

 ✦ **Sound:** Inserts a background sound that plays whenever the page is viewed.

 ✦ **Scrolling text:** Inserts text that automatically scrolls across the page.

Before you can insert any of these items, you must display the Web Tools toolbar by choosing View⇨Toolbars⇨Web Tools.

 The Web Tools toolbar also includes a Design Mode button that switches between design and preview mode. When the page is in preview mode, movies, sounds, and scrolling text display as they appear when the page is viewed in a browser. To edit or remove a movie, sound, or scrolling text, click the Design Mode button to place the page in design mode. You can then select and edit the movie, sound, or scrolling text.

Inserting a movie

 You can insert a movie clip directly on a Web page by clicking the Movie button on the Web Tools toolbar. The Movie Clip dialog box comes up, as shown in Figure 3-11. You can type the path and filename of the movie clip directly in the Movie text box, or you can click the Browse button to locate the file. You can also provide an image file and text to display for browsers that don't support movies.

In addition, you can specify one of three options for starting the movie:

✦ **Open:** Plays the movie automatically whenever the page is viewed.

✦ **Mouse Over:** Plays the movie whenever the user moves the mouse over it.

✦ **Both:** Plays the movie once when the page loads, and then again when the user moves the mouse over it.

You can also use this dialog box to play the movie over and over again in a loop.

Figure 3-11:
The Movie
Clip dialog
box.

Inserting a background sound

Before you read this section, I want to point out that most Internet users (myself included) find background sounds very annoying. They're cute the first time you visit a page, but after that they get old. I'd skip this section if I were you.

If you want to ignore my warning, you can insert a background sound by clicking the Sound button on the Web Tools toolbar. The dialog box shown in Figure 3-12 opens, which lets you specify the file that contains the sound to play and whether or not you want to loop the sound.

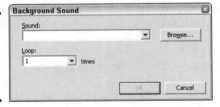

Figure 3-12:
The
Background
Sound
dialog box.

Inserting scrolling text

Scrolling text — sometimes called a *marquee* — is a bit of text that travels across the screen from one side to the other. To create scrolling text in your Web page, click the Scrolling Text button on the Web Tools toolbar. The dialog box shown in Figure 3-13 appears. You can type the text you want to scroll into the text box, and you can play with the other settings to control the direction and speed with which you want the text to scroll and whether you want the text to scroll just once or to repeat in a loop.

Scrolling Text

Behavior: Scroll | Background color: ☐ Auto

Direction: Left | Loop: Infinite

Speed

Slow ————————————|———————— Fast

Type the scrolling text here:

Singin' in the Rain

Preview

Singin' in the Rain

OK | Cancel

Figure 3-13:
Creating a
scrolling
marquee.

Editing HTML

Normally, Word displays your Web pages pretty much as they appear when
displayed by a Web browser. However, on some occasions, you may want to
view the actual HTML codes that comprise your Web page. To do that, just
choose View⇨HTML Source, and Microsoft Script Editor opens. Microsoft
Script Editor is a special window that's designed to let you work with HTML
code, scripts, and macros as shown in Figure 3-14.

If you want to, you can actually edit the HTML in this window. Just click anywhere and start typing. Or, if you have better judgment, just look at the HTML
for a moment, gasp in amazement that some people are actually interested in
such arcane subjects, and choose File⇨Exit to close the script editor and
return to your document.

If you do decide to play with the HTML that appears in the script editor
window, be sure to use the Save button in the script editor to save your
changes. If you return to the document without saving any changes, you see
a toolbar called the Refresh toolbar. This toolbar has two buttons: Refresh
and Do Not Refresh. Click the Refresh button to update the document to
reflect any changes you made.

Note: If you save changes in the script editor, the document window refreshes
automatically, so the Refresh toolbar doesn't appear.

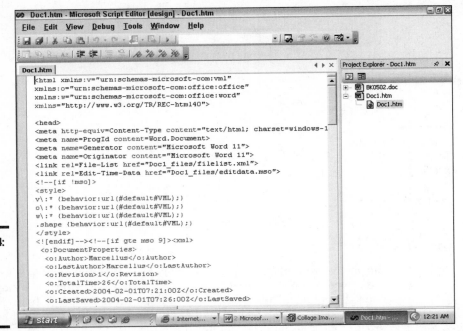

Figure 3-14:
Viewing
HTML in
Microsoft
Script
Editor.

Chapter 4: Using Themes and Cascading Style Sheets

In This Chapter

✔ Using themes to format a Web page

✔ Formatting a page with cascading style sheets

This chapter presents two specific features you can use for formatting Web pages: themes and cascading style sheets.

Themes allow you to quickly make drastic formatting changes to a Web page by applying a preset collection of formatting elements. The themes that come with Word have been put together by professional designers, so they look pretty good — better than what most of us can come up with on our own.

Cascading style sheets are a fairly advanced Web design feature that removes the details of how a Web page is formatted from the page itself, and puts those details in a separate style sheet file. Word doesn't let you create the style sheets, but it does let you assign an existing style sheet to a Web page. So if you or someone else has developed a style sheet for your Web site, you can incorporate it into the pages you create with Word.

Using Themes

A *theme* is a collection of design elements and a color scheme that can give your page a professionally designed appearance. Word comes with a collection of themes you can choose from to apply to your Web pages.

Themes are sort of like templates, in that they define fonts, styles, and other formatting elements for your documents. However, the two are significantly different:

✦ Unlike templates, themes do not automatically include macros, AutoText, or customized settings.

✦ Themes include elements that aren't found in templates, such as a set of graphic elements, which can be background images, picture bullets, and horizontal lines designed to look good together.

Although you can use themes for printed pages, themes are designed for Web pages. If you use a theme with a printed page, you may want to remove the background graphic or color before you print the document.

Applying a theme to a document

To apply a theme to a document, follow these steps:

***1.* With the document open, select Format⇨Theme.**

The Theme dialog box opens, as shown in Figure 4-1. Whether you already worked on the document or whether you're just starting doesn't matter. Just make sure that you can see an active cursor within the document screen and that no text is highlighted.

Figure 4-1:
The Theme
dialog box.

***2.* Choose the theme you want to apply.**

The Theme dialog box shows you a list of available themes in the Choose a Theme list on the left; the window on the right displays a sample of the currently selected theme. Scroll through the list and look at the samples until you find one you like.

***3.* If you want the theme to use brighter colors, check the Vivid Colors check box.**

Checking this box switches the theme to brighter versions of the theme's basic colors. The new colors immediately appear in the preview box when you select this check box, so you can see how the change affects the appearance of your page.

4. **If you want the theme to use animated graphics, check the Active Graphics check box.**

   Animated graphics are cute but annoying, so I suggest you leave this option unchecked unless you want your Web page to be cute and annoying.

5. **If you want to leave the background blank, uncheck the Background Image check box.**

   This option omits the theme's background image, which can sometimes make the page look cluttered and difficult to read.

6. **Click OK.**

Depending on the options you selected when you installed Word, some of the themes may not be installed on your computer. If you select a theme that hasn't been installed, an Install button appears instead of the preview box when you select the theme. You can click this button to install the theme. You are then asked to insert the Word or Office installation CD so that the installation program can copy the theme onto your hard drive.

At the bottom of the Theme dialog box is the Style Gallery button. If you click this button, the Style Gallery dialog box opens. From this dialog box, you can choose different styles and see what your document looks like using that style with the theme you've chosen. Nifty, eh?

Changing the default theme

Word has a default theme that it applies to all documents when you first open them. You can change this default so that a new theme always appears whenever you open a new Word document. To do this:

1. **Choose Format⇨Theme to open the Theme dialog box.**

2. **Select the theme that you want to use as the default theme.**

3. **Click the Set Default button.**

   A dialog box appears asking whether you want to set a new default theme for new documents.

4. **If you really want to do this, click Yes.**

5. **Click OK to dismiss the Theme dialog box.**

   From now on, every new Word document you create has that theme applied to it, until you decide to change it.

Using External Cascading Style Sheets

Cascading style sheets are to Web pages what Word's templates are to normal Word documents. Style sheets allow you to keep the formatting specifications for a Web page in a separate file called an *external style sheet*. Then, to apply a consistent look to all of the pages in your Web site, you can attach (the proper HTML term is *link*) a style sheet to each page. If you decide later to change the appearance of your Web site, you can often make most of the changes via the style sheet file rather than to each individual Web page.

For example, with a style sheet, you can create a Web page in which all the first level headings are centered on a page, appear in 26-point Arial Bold, and are colored teal. If you later decide that you want the headings to be blue, you can change the color specified in the style sheet rather than in every heading that appears in your entire Web site.

Unfortunately, creating cascading style sheet files is not one of Word's strengths. Your best bet is to use another program, such as FrontPage, to actually create your style sheets. You can even use the free text editor Notepad to create style sheets if you like coding HTML yourself.

Although Word doesn't let you create cascading style sheets, you can attach an existing style sheet to any Web page by following these steps:

1. **Open the page you want to apply the style sheet to.**

2. **Choose Tools⇨Templates and Add-Ins.**

   The Templates and Add-Ins dialog box appears.

3. **Click the Linked CSS tab.**

   The Linked Style Sheets options appear, as shown in Figure 4-2.

4. **Click Add.**

   The Add CSS Link dialog box appears. This dialog box is almost identical to a standard Open dialog box.

5. **Locate and select the style sheet file you want to attach.**

6. **Click OK to return to the Templates and Add-Ins dialog box, and then click OK again.**

   The dialog box shown in Figure 4-3 appears. This dialog box informs you that you have to save and reload your document to use the styles.

This dialog box is kind of annoying because using the styles is probably what you had in mind when you attached the style sheet, so why would you *not* want to save and reload the document? If I were King of Microsoft, Word would just do this automatically without asking.

Figure 4-2:
Attaching
cascading
style sheets.

Figure 4-3:
Word asks
one of its
annoying
questions.

7. **Click Yes.**

   You return to your document. The styles in the style sheet are now available via the Style drop-down list on the Formatting toolbar.

   You can attach more than one style sheet to a document. When you do, Word uses the style in the higher-ranking sheet if two or more style sheets have styles with the same name. The order the style sheets appear in the Templates and Add-Ins dialog box determines their ranking. (The style sheet at the top of the list has the highest priority.) You can use the Move Up and Move Down buttons to shuffle the rankings if you want.

Chapter 5: Working with Frames

In This Chapter

✓ Understanding how frames work

✓ Creating a page with frame layouts

✓ Working with hyperlinks that use frames

✓ Creating a table of contents frame

✓ Previewing a frames page

This chapter shows you how to work with *frames,* one of the keys to designing Web pages. Frames allow you to slice up a Web page into multiple regions, each of which displays the contents of a separate Web document. Frames are commonly used to add design elements, such as banners and navigation menus that should appear on each page of your Web site.

Before you dig too deep into frames, I want to remind you that Word is not designed primarily as a Web site designer. If you're creating Web pages complicated enough to require frames, you really need to consider using a more advanced Web page designer, such as Microsoft FrontPage. That being said, Word's frames are useful for small Web sites. And, as you see in this chapter, the Table of Contents in a Frame feature is very useful.

Understanding Frames

Frames enable you to divide a Web page into separate areas that each display the contents of a separate Web document. The advantage of using frames is that the user can interact with each frame independently. For example, a frame that contains a long text document can have its own scroll bars so that the user can scroll through the document while other elements of the page, such as a title banner and navigation bar, remain on-screen.

Figure 5-1 shows how I might use frames to create a Web site to promote my books and brag about my hobbies and other activities. This page uses three frames:

✦ The first frame displays the top banner and the site menu, which provides links to the major areas on the Web site: Books, Halloween, and so on.

✦ The second frame displays a sidebar menu that changes when the user selects one of the major site areas. In this case, the user clicked Books in the main site menu, so the sidebar menu displays a page that contains links to information about some of my books.

✦ The third frame is the main display area of the page. It displays a different page depending on which item the user clicks in the sidebar menu. In this case, the user clicked the <u>Networking All-In-One Desk Reference For Dummies</u> link, so this frame displays a page about that book.

The Web page shown in Figure 5-1 is actually four distinct HTML documents displayed together. The main HTML document is called the *frames page*. The frames page itself doesn't contain any content. Instead, it defines the frames layout of the page. Each of the frames defined in the frames page displays the contents of a different HTML document. Because the frames page in Figure 5-1 has three frames, a total of four different HTML documents display: one for each frame, plus the frames page itself.

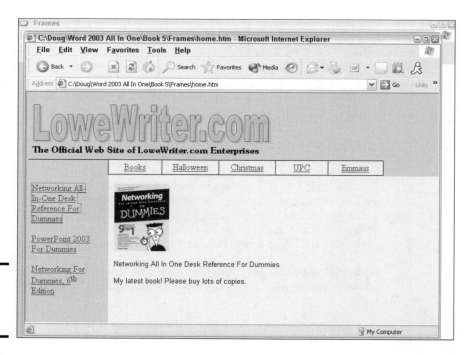

Figure 5-1:
A page with three frames.

The menus that appear in the top and left frames of Figure 5-1 are simply hyperlinks that link to the page that displays when the user clicks the link. In a frames page, a hyperlink can specify not only a document to link to, but also a *target frame* in which to display the document. As a result, the hyperlinks in the top frame refer to pages that contain the Web sites area menus and specify the left frame as the target frame. For example, when the user clicks Books, the Books.html document displays in the left frame.

The Books.html document, in turn, contains hyperlinks for each of the content pages in the Books area of the Web site and specifies the center frame as the target frame. So, for example, when the user clicks the <u>Networking All-In-One Desk Reference For Dummies</u> link, the naio.html page displays in the center frame.

I hope that makes sense. If not, read on. Things should clear up when you see how you actually stitch a page like this together.

In the following sections, you discover how to set up Web pages that use frames in this way.

Creating a Frames Page

To create a new frames page, follow these steps:

1. **Create a new Web document by choosing File⇨New to open the New Document task pane, and then clicking Web Page in the task pane.**

    This step creates a blank Web document that serves as the source for the first frame you create when you complete the next step.

2. **Use File⇨Save to save the document.**

    Remember: This document is not the frames page, but rather the content page for the first frame in the frames page.

3. **Choose Format⇨Frames⇨New Frames Page.**

    This step creates a new frames page with a single frame. The document that was open is placed in this frame. Also, the Frames toolbar shown in Figure 5-2 appears.

Figure 5-2:
The Frames
toolbar.

4. **Choose File⇨Save to save the frames page.**

The name you specify for this page is the name a Web user uses to retrieve the frames page.

5. **Click one of the New Frame buttons on the Frames toolbar to create a frame.**

The Frames toolbar sports four buttons that let you create a new frame:

New Frame Left

New Frame Left: Creates a new frame to the left of the current frame.

New Frame Right

New Frame Right: Creates a new frame to the right of the current frame.

New Frame Above

New Frame Above: Creates a new frame above the current frame.

New Frame Below

New Frame Below: Creates a new frame below the current frame.

When you click one of the New Frame buttons, a new frame is added to the page.

6. **Drag the frame border to change the size of the frame.**

7. **Choose File⇨Save to save the page displayed by the new frame.**

When the Save As dialog box appears, specify the name you want to save this page under. *Remember:* You're saving the Web document that appears in the current frame here, not the frame page itself.

The name of the Web document displayed in the current frame displays in the Address box on the Web toolbar.

8. **To create additional frames, click in one of the existing frames, and then click one of the New Frame buttons and resize the frame.**

The new frame divides the current frame horizontally or vertically, depending on whether you click New Frame Left or Right (divides the frame vertically) or New Frame Above or Below (divides the frame horizontally). Use the File⇨Save command to save the page displayed by the new frame.

9. **Repeat Step 8 until you're happy.**

Most pages require just three or four frames, but some complicated pages need more. Figure 5-3 shows a frames page after three frames are created: one above, one on the left.

10. **You're done, for now.**

After you create the frames, the next step is to format them and assign Web pages to them, as I describe in the next section.

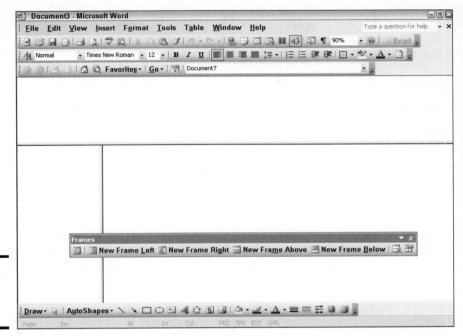

Figure 5-3:
A page
with three
frames.

Here are some additional ideas regarding frames:

✦ Getting the overall frame layout of your page set before you start working on the content of any of the frames is best.

✦ If you want to create a banner frame at the top or bottom of the page, create those frames first.

✦ To delete a frame, click anywhere in the frame, and then click the Delete Frame button on the Frames toolbar.

Formatting Your Frames

After you create and size the frames for your page, you can set the formatting options for each frame to make the frame look just the way you want. Here are the steps:

1. **Click in the frame you want to format.**

2. **Click the Frame Properties button on the Frames toolbar or choose Format⇨Frames⇨Frame Properties.**

The Frames Properties dialog box appears, as shown in Figure 5-4.

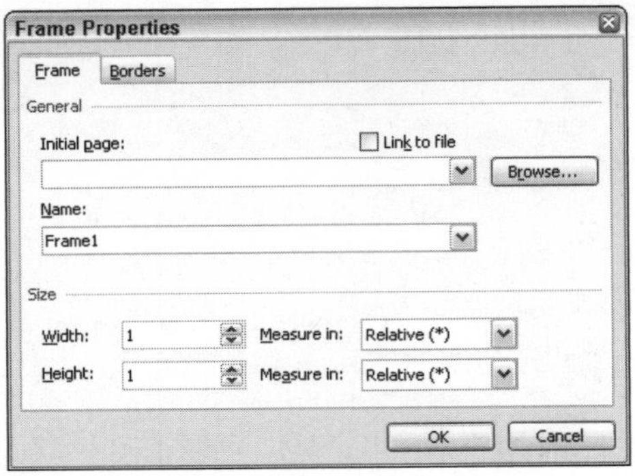

Figure 5-4:
Setting
frame
properties.

3. **Select the page you want to initially display in the frame.**

   The Initial Page drop-down list includes every Web document that's currently open in Word. So if the page you want to place in the frame is already open in another Word window, you can just select it from the list. Otherwise, click Browse and select the page from the Open dialog box that appears.

4. **Type a meaningful name for the frame.**

   The frame name initially defaults to something like Frame1 or Frame2. You can choose one of the more sensible names that appears in the Name drop-down list, or you can type a name of your own choosing.

5. **Tweak the size if you want.**

   You can specify an exact size for the frame by using the Size options that appear in the bottom half of the Frame Properties dialog box.

6. **Click the Borders tab.**

   Another set of frame properties appears, as shown in Figure 5-5.

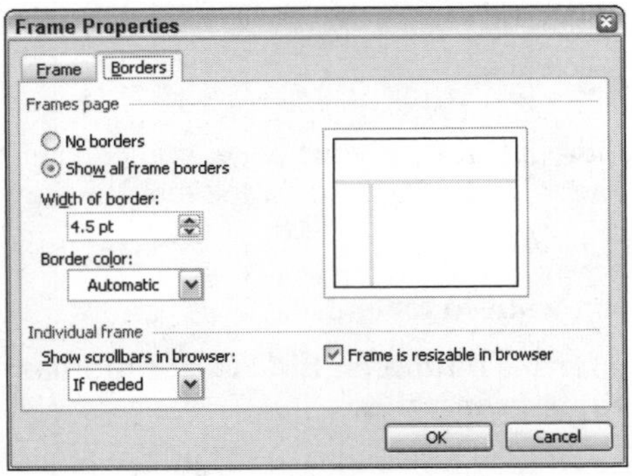

Figure 5-5:
Setting
frame
border
properties.

7. Set the border style for the frames page.

Note: The Frames Page border options in the top portion of this dialog box apply to the entire frames page, not just the current frame. You can choose no border, or you can select a border with a specified width and color.

8. Use the Show Scrollbars in Browser drop-down list to set the scroll bar option you want to use for this frame's border.

You have three choices:

- **If Needed:** Scroll bars appear only if the frame is not large enough to display the entire contents of the HTML page.

- **Never:** Scroll bars never display. If the page is too large to fit in the frame, the portion of the page that doesn't fit isn't visible.

- **Always:** Scroll bars always display, whether the page fits in the frame or not.

9. If you want to allow the user to resize the frame, choose the Frame Is Resizable in Browser option.

Leave this option unchecked if you want the frame to be a fixed size.

10. Click OK to dismiss the Frame Properties dialog box.

If you remove the frame borders, you may have trouble keeping track of where each frame is when you work with the document in Word. I suggest you leave the borders on until you have the whole frame page working pretty much the way you want. Then, remove the borders and make any necessary last-minute adjustments to the frame sizes to make everything line up the way you want.

Editing Pages in Frames

When you work with a frames page, you can edit the document currently displayed in any of the frames on the page by clicking in the frame and editing away. Any editing or formatting features that work in a normal Web page work in a frame. Be sure to periodically save your changes.

When you use File⇨Save while working in a frames page, all of the pages visible in frames are saved.

You can also save the contents of a single frame in a separate file. To do so, right-click anywhere in the frame and choose Save Current Frame As from the shortcut menu. Then supply a name for the file and click Save.

Working with Hyperlinks and Frames

Hyperlinks are one of the keys to building frames pages. When you create a hyperlink, you can specify a *target frame* in which the linked document displays when the user clicks the link. This feature allows you to build a menu in one frame that controls the contents displayed in another frame.

To set the target frame for a hyperlink, first make sure you assign a meaningful name to the target frame. Then, when you create the hyperlink with the Insert Hyperlink command, click the Target Frame button. The Set Target Frame dialog box appears, shown in Figure 5-6.

Figure 5-6:
Setting the target frame for a hyperlink.

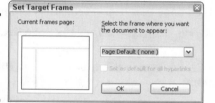

The Set Target Frame dialog box contains a thumbnail view of the frames on the page. To set the target frame, click the frame in this thumbnail or select it from the drop-down list. Then click OK.

If you select the Set as Default for All Hyperlinks check box, the frame you select automatically is used as the target frame for any hyperlinks you create from now on, until you click the Target Frame button again and change the setting. This option can save you some time if you're inserting a series of hyperlinks to create a menu.

Inserting a Table of Contents in a Frame

One of the more useful of Word's Web features is its ability to automatically create a Table of Contents in a frame that lets you browse directly to all of the headings in a document. This feature is especially useful for longer documents. For example, Figure 5-7 shows a Web page set up this way. The Table of Contents frame on the left lets you quickly go to any heading in the document.

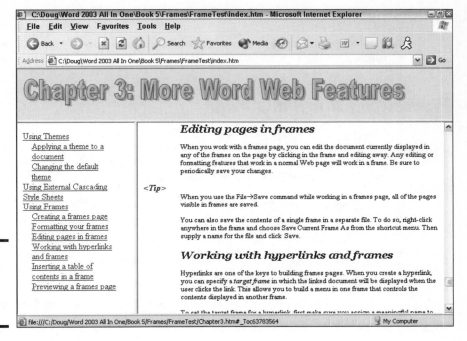

Figure 5-7:
A frames
page with
a table of
contents.

To use this feature, follow these steps:

1. Set up a frames page with the frames you want, except for the frame in which you want to include the Table of Contents.

For example, if you want a banner frame at the top, add a top frame. But don't add a frame to hold the Table of Contents. That frame is created automatically in Step 3.

2. Open the Frame Properties dialog box for the main frame and set the document you want to browse as the initial page for the document. Then close the Frame Properties dialog box.

The document appears in the frame.

3. Click the Table of Contents In Frame button on the Frames toolbar.

Word automatically adds a new frame to the left of the current frame, and then inserts a Table of Contents in which each heading in the document is formatted as a hyperlink.

4. **Save the document.**

For more information about creating and formatting a Table of Contents, refer to Book VI, Chapter 6.

Previewing a Frames Page

As you work with frames pages, you'll want to frequently check their appearance in a Web browser window. Unfortunately, File⇨Web Page Preview doesn't work very well for frames pages. I suggest you preview the Web page in a separate browser window. Follow these steps:

1. **Open a separate Internet Explorer browser window.**

   To do so, click the Internet Explorer icon on your desktop or choose Start⇨Internet.

2. **Choose File⇨Open, and then click Browse.**

   The standard Open dialog box comes up.

3. **Locate your frames page, select it, click Open, and then click OK.**

   The frames page displays in the browser window.

As you work with the frames page in Word, you can easily switch over to the browser window to see the effect of your changes. To do so, save the document in Word, press Alt+Tab to switch to the browser window, and then click the Refresh button to retrieve a fresh copy of the page.

Chapter 6: Word and XML

In This Chapter

✔ Understanding XML

✔ Saving a Word document in XML format

✔ Editing XML data directly in Word

*O*ne of the more obscure new features of Word is its ability to work with XML documents. You can save your Word documents in XML format, which allow other programs designed to read Word's special XML document format to read them. Or, you can open other people's XML documents in Word and work with them there.

According to Microsoft, XML compatibility is the most important feature added to Word since the invention of the Save command.

In reality, 99 percent of Word users have no idea what XML is. Another .9 percent of Word users know what XML is but have no reason to use it with Word. So, if you're one of the lucky one-in-a-thousand Word users who not only know what XML is but who would also like to use it with Word, this chapter is for you.

What Exactly Is XML, Anyway?

XML is the latest fad in computing. *XML* stands for *eXtensible Markup Language*. It's a way to create text files that have special tags (that's the markup) that identify the meaning of each element of data in the file. XML is called extensible because you can use it for an almost limitless variety of data applications. (Normal human beings would have called it *EML,* but the computer nerds who came up with the name thought it would be cool to capitalize the X instead.)

Most computer industry pundits agree that XML is going to completely change the way you work with computers. Here are just some of the ways XML will revolutionize the world of computers:

✦ XML will unlock all of the data that's locked up in the vaults of corporate mainframe computers.

✦ XML will enable every electronic device on the planet from the most complex supercomputers to desktop computers to cell phones to wrist watches to communicate with one another.

✦ XML will allow every computer program ever written to exchange data with every other computer program ever written.

✦ XML will probably cure cancer and solve the budget deficit, too.

Yawn.

So what is XML, really? Simply put, XML is a way to store and exchange information in a standardized way that's easy to create, easy to retrieve, and easy to exchange between different types of computer systems or programs.

When XML is stored in a file, the file is usually given the extension .xml. Word 2003 has the ability to open and save XML files.

Tags

Like HTML, XML uses tags to mark the data. For example, here's a bit of XML that describes a book:

```
<Book>
  <Title>Word 2003 All-In-One Desk Reference For Dummies</Title>
  <Author>Lowe</Author>
</Book>
```

This chunk of XML defines an *element* called Book, which contains information for a single book. The Book element, in turn, contains two subordinate elements: Title and Author.

Notice how each element begins with a tag that lists the element's name. This tag is called the *start tag*. The element ends with an element that repeats the element name, preceded by a slash (an *end* tag).

Everything that appears between the start tag and the end tag is the element's *content*. An element's content can consist of text data, or it can consist of one or more additional elements.

The highest level element in an XML document is called the *root element*. Strictly speaking, a properly formed XML document consists of a single root element, which can contain elements nested within it. For example, suppose you want to create an XML document with information about two books. The XML document looks something like this:

```
<Books>
  <Book>
    <Title>Word 2003 All-In-One Desk Reference For Dummies</Title>
    <Author>Lowe</Author>
  </Book>
```

```
<Book>
  <Title>Networking All-In-One Desk Reference For Dummies</Title>
  <Author>Lowe</Author>
</Book>
</Books>
```

Here, the root element named `Books` contains two `Book` elements, each of which contains a `Title` and an `Author` element.

Although XML superficially resembles HTML, you find two key differences between XML and HTML:

✦ The tags used in HTML indicate the format of data that displays. In contrast, tags in an XML document indicate the meaning of the data. For example, HTML has tags such as `<B>` and `<I>` that indicate data is bold or italic. In contrast, an XML document that holds information about books may have tags such as `<Title>` and `<Author>` that provide the title and author of the book.

✦ The tags used in an HTML document are set in stone. In contrast, you can make up any tags you want to use in an XML document. If you're creating an XML document about cars, you may use tags such as `<Make>`, `<Model>`, and `<Year>`. But if you're creating an XML document about classes taught at a university, you may use tags such as `<Course>`, `<Title>`, `<Instructor>`, `<Room>`, and `<Schedule>`.

Schemas

An XML document can have a *schema,* which spells out exactly what tags are used within the document. The schema also spells out how the tags are used. For example, a schema for an XML document about books may specify that each book can have only one title but can have multiple authors. It may also specify that the title and at least one author are required, but a subtitle is optional.

The main purpose of the schema is to spell out the structure of an XML document so that users of the document know how to interpret it. But another equally important use of the schema is to *validate* the document to make sure it doesn't have any structural errors. For example, if you create a books XML document that has two titles for a book, you can use the schema to detect the error.

You can store the schema for an XML document in the same file as the XML data, but more often you store the schema in a separate file. That way, you can use a schema to govern the format of several XML documents of the same type.

Creating a schema is complicated work, requiring an in-depth understanding of XML Schema Definition (XSD) language. If you need to use a schema, try to cajole one of your computer-nerd friends into creating one for you. With luck, your company's Information Technology department can send out one of its resident nerds to do this unpleasant task for you.

If you just want a simple schema to experiment with, type in the schema shown in Listing 6-1 and save it with the name `books.xsd`. (If you prefer, you can download this schema file from my Web site, `www.LoweWriter.com`.)

Listing 6-1:   A Simple Schema File (books.xsd)

```
<xs:schema xmlns:xs="http://www.w3.org/2001/XMLSchema">
  <xs:annotation>
    <xs:documentation xml:lang="en">
      Books schema for Word 2003 All-In-One Desk Reference For Dummies.
    </xs:documentation>
  </xs:annotation>

  <xs:element name="Books" type="BooksType"/>

  <xs:complexType name="BooksType">
    <xs:sequence>
      <xs:element name="Book" type="BookType" minOccurs="0"
          maxOccurs="unbounded"/>
    </xs:sequence>
  </xs:complexType>

  <xs:complexType name="BookType">
    <xs:sequence>
      <xs:element name="Title" type="xs:string"/>
      <xs:element name="Author" type="xs:string"/>
    </xs:sequence>
  </xs:complexType>

</xs:schema>
```

Working with XML Documents in Word

Word 2003 has several features that work with XML documents. I describe these features in the following sections.

Saving a Word document as XML

You can convert any Word document to XML format by choosing File⇨Save As, and then selecting XML Document (*.xml) in the Save as Type drop-down list. The document saves using Microsoft's default schema for Word documents, which uses XML tags to identify each element of the document.

Frankly, you have little reason to ever do this. You should save a Word document in XML format only if you need to use the file as input to some other program or system that expects the document in XML format, and knows how to deal with the Word schema. In fact, the main reason I even mention it here is so you understand that when you see XML Document as one of the choices listed in the Save as Type drop-down list, you know to steer clear.

Creating an XML document

The features I describe in this section (and in the rest of this chapter) work only if you're using Microsoft Office 2003 Professional Edition. If you have the Standard Edition or the Student and Teacher edition, you can read on to find out what you're missing.

To create a new XML document in Word, follow these helpful steps:

1. **Choose File⇨New, and then click XML Document in the New Document task pane.**

A new XML document is created, and the XML Structure task pane appears, as shown in Figure 6-1.

Frankly, a new XML document isn't much to look at. You can't really do anything with it until you attach a schema.

2. **Choose Tools⇨Templates and Add-Ins, and then click the XML Schema tab.**

The dialog box shown in Figure 6-2 appears.

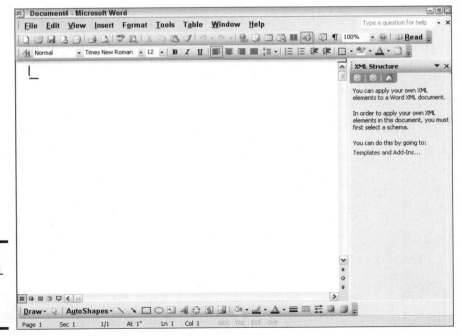

Figure 6-1:
A new XML document springs to life.

3. **If the schema you want to use appears in the list of schemas, select it. Otherwise, click the Add Schema button, locate the schema file you want to attach, click Save, and then select the schema in the schema list.**

4. **Click OK.**

   The schema applies to the document, and the XML Structure task pane becomes more interesting, as shown in Figure 6-3. In particular, the bottom part of the task pane lists the XML tags you can insert at the current position in the document according to the schema.

5. **To insert an XML element, select the element that you want to insert from the list at the bottom of the XML Structure task pane.**

   When you select the element in the task pane, Word inserts a start and end tag for the element in the document, along with space between the tags where you can type the content for the element.

   The elements listed here vary as you work with the document depending on the position of the insertion pointer. For example, assuming that you use the books.xsd schema, only one element (Books) is listed in the XML Structure task pane because a Books element is the only element you can insert at the root level of the document.

   If you insert a Books element, position the insertion pointer in the document between the start and end tags for the Books element; this list shows that you can now insert a Books element. If you do so, then position the insertion pointer between the Books start and end tags; the list shows that you can now insert a Title or an Author element.

   If an element calls for text content (such as the Title or Author elements), click in the document between the start and end tags and type whatever text you want.

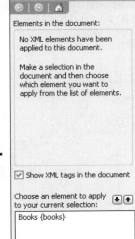

Figure 6-3:
The XML Structure task pane after applying a schema to a document.

6. **Repeat Step 5 for each element you want to create.**

   Figure 6-4 shows a document after several elements have been added.

7. **When you're done, choose File⇨Save to save your document.**

   When the Save As dialog box appears, provide a name for your document, and then click Save.

Here are a few other interesting tidbits to remember when you work with XML documents:

✦ You can edit an existing XML document by opening the document using File⇨Open. Choose XML Files (*.xml) in the Files of Type drop-down list to display XML documents in the Open dialog box, locate the file you want to edit, and then click Open.

✦ Word has a bunch of XML options you can set if you want to tweak the way XML documents are used. Funny thing, though: You can't find these options with Tools⇨Options (where they belong). To find the XML options, choose Tools⇨Templates and Add-Ins, and click the XML Options button on the XML Schema tab. A bevy of XML options appear, as shown in Figure 6-5.

One XML option you probably need to check is the Save Data Only option. If you leave this option unchecked, Word saves a bunch of extraneous Word XML tags along with the document, which makes the document readable only to programs that know about Word's schema. In most cases, you want to check this option to omit the extra Word tags.

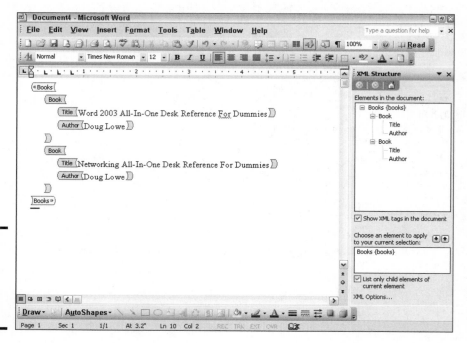

Figure 6-4:
An XML
document
with
elements
added.

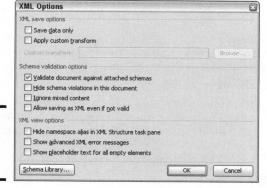

Figure 6-5:
The hidden
XML
options.

Book VI

Advanced Document Features

The 5th Wave   By Rich Tennant

"I'm using the 'Cab Driver's' edition of NaturallySpeaking, so it understands words like '⊙✦✦✳' and '✓⊠⊙✦!'"

Contents at a Glance

Chapter 1: Working with Fields

A field is a special placeholder code that tells Word to insert something (usually text of some sort) into the document. A date field, for example, tells Word to insert the current date into the document. No matter when you edit or print the document, the date field causes the document to contain the current date.

Fields are everywhere in Word. Many of the commands you have come to know and love rely on fields to do their business. Fields let you put the page number in a header or footer, create a Table of Contents or an index, and print mail-merged letters. These fields are often inserted into your document without your knowledge, as a result of you using some other command, such as Insert⇨Page Numbers or Tools⇨Letters and Mailings⇨ Mail Merge.

This chapter shows you what you need to know to insert fields directly, by using Insert⇨Field. Word provides many different types of fields (more than 60). At the end of this chapter is a table that lists them all.

Understanding Fields

A *field* is a code that Word translates into some result, usually text, which then inserts into the document. When you insert a date field, for example, you're really saying to Word, "Insert the current date right here, and make sure that you get the date right. When I print this document, I want to see today's date. If I print it tomorrow, I want to see tomorrow's date. Next week, I want to see next week's date. A year from now. . . ." You get the idea. A date field is like a placeholder for an actual date, which Word inserts automatically.

Other fields work in the same way. The text Word inserts in place of the field code is called the *result.* For a date field, the result is the current date. For a page-number field, the result is the current page number. Other field types produce more complicated results, such as a Table of Contents or an index. For some fields, the result isn't text at all, but a picture or a chart.

When you print a document, you can't distinguish between text you typed directly into the document and text that is a field result. Consider, for example, the following text you may use in a letter:

As of today, Saturday, August 21, 2004, you have been banished from Remulak and sentenced to live out the remainder of your existence among the Blunt Skulls of Earth.

You can't tell that *Saturday, August 21,2004* is a field result.

When you edit a document in Word, you must have some way to distinguish between regular text and field results. Word normally displays field results so that the document appears on-screen just as it does when you print it. If the result isn't quite what you expect, however, or if you want to make sure that you used the correct field to produce a result, you can switch the display to show field codes.

Word also has an option that displays field results but shades them so that you can distinguish field results from ordinary text. Call up Tools⇔Options and click the View tab. Then, select one of the following three values for the Field Shading drop-down list box:

✦ **Never:** Field results display as normal, with no shading.

✦ **Always:** Field results are shaded with a gray background.

✦ **When Selected:** Field results are shown with a gray background when selected.

Then, click OK to put the option you selected into effect.

The preceding letter fragment with field codes displayed looks like this:

As of today, { TIME \@ "dddd, MMMM dd, yyyy" }, you have been banished from Remulak and sentenced to live out the remainder of your existence among the Blunt Skulls of Earth.

The field is the stuff marked by the curly braces ({ }), which are called *field characters*. Their whole purpose in life is to tell Word that a field lives there. They look just like the curly braces you can type with the keyboard, but they're not. The only way you can create these field characters is by using Insert⇔Field or some other Word command that inserts a field.

Sandwiched between the field characters is the field itself. Each field begins with a *field type* that tells you what type of field you have there. In the preceding example, you're looking at a TIME field, which provides the current date or time in many different formats.

Following the field type are *instructions,* which tell the field what to do. The TIME field in the preceding example contains an instruction that tells Word how to format the time: *ddd, MMMM dd, yyyy.*

Inserting a Field

Many Word commands, such as Insert⇨Date and Time and Insert⇨ Reference⇨Index and Tables, quietly insert fields into your document without boasting. But Word provides many other fields you can insert only by using Insert⇨Field.

Follow these steps to insert a field in your document:

1. **Move the insertion point to the spot where you want to insert the field.**

2. **Call up Insert⇨Field.**

The Field dialog box appears, as shown in Figure 1-1.

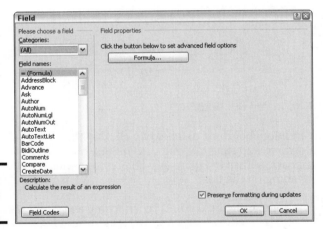

Figure 1-1:
The Field dialog box.

3. **Choose the field type you want to insert.**

Because so many field types exist, Word breaks them down into categories so that you can find them easier. First, pick the category that contains the field you want to use. Then, pick the field from the Field Names list. If the field you want doesn't appear, try a different category. If you're not sure which category contains the field you want to insert, choose All as the category. This action lists all of Word's field types in the Field Names list.

4. **Use the other controls in the Field dialog box to add additional instructions required by the field.**

I'd like to be more specific here, but I can't. The appearance of the Field dialog box changes when you select a field because each type of field accepts a different combination of options. For example, Figure 1-2 shows how the Field dialog box appears if you select an Info field. The Field dialog box for an Info field includes a New Value text box, an Info Categories drop-down list, and a Format drop-down list.

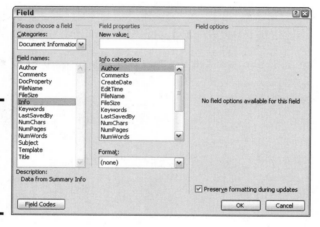

Figure 1-2: The Field dialog box changes when you select a field type.

5. **Click OK to insert the field.**

You can add additional options to a field by clicking the Field Codes button in the Field dialog box, and then clicking the Options button. The Field Options dialog box appears, shown in Figure 1-3. The options presented in the dialog box vary depending on the field.

You can add options to the field codes by choosing an option you want to add in the list and then clicking the Add to Field button. Every time you click the Add to Field button, the selected option is added to the Field Codes box. Also, a terse description of each field option appears at the bottom of the Field Options dialog box.

When you insert a field, either the field code or the result displays, depending on whether the Fields Codes view option is set. You can switch between field codes and field results by pressing Alt+F9, or you can right-click the field and select the Toggle Field Codes command.

Figure 1-3:
The Field
Options
dialog box.

If you see something like Error! Unknown switch argument rather than
the field result you expect, you made a mistake when you composed the
field instructions. You have to edit the field directly by pressing Alt+F9 to
reveal the field codes and then clicking in the field and typing your correction. (Or, once again, right-click the field and choose the Toggle Field Codes
command.)

Keyboard Shortcuts for Working with Fields

A whole bevy of specialized keyboard shortcuts are available for working
with fields. Table 1-1 summarizes them for your convenience.

Table 1-1	Keyboard Shortcuts for Fields
Keyboard Shortcut	*What It Does*
F9	Updates the selected field or fields.
Shift+F9	Switches the display between field codes and field results for the selected field or fields. You must place the insertion point in a field to use this command.
Alt+F9	Switches the display between field codes and field results for all fields in the document. You do not have to select a field before using this command.
Ctrl+F9	Inserts a blank field into a document.
Ctrl+Shift+F9	Converts a field to text (unlinks the field).
F11	Finds the next field in the document.
Shift+F11	Finds the previous field in the document.
Ctrl+F11	Locks a field so that it cannot be updated.
Ctrl+Shift+F11	Unlocks a field.

Another Way to Insert Fields

If you are good at typing commands, you can insert a field by typing it directly in your document. Just follow these steps:

1. **Position the cursor where you want to insert the field.**

2. **Type the field name and instructions for the field you want to insert.**

Don't worry about the curly braces for now. Just type the field and its instructions.

3. **Select the text you typed in Step 2.**

4. **Press Ctrl+F9.**

Ctrl+F9 converts the selected text to a field by enclosing it in field codes: those curly little braces that look just like the curly braces you can type with the keyboard but aren't the same thing at all. If you prefer, you can reverse these steps: Position the cursor where you want to place the field and press Ctrl+F9 and an empty field appears, which you can select. Then you can type the field name and instructions within the braces.

Formatting Field Results with Switches

Word provides several switches you can use on almost any field to control the formatting applied to the field result. You don't have to use any of these switches if you don't want to. If you omit them, Word makes an educated guess about the format of the field result.

You can use three switches to format a field's result:

✦ The Format switch (*) tells Word whether to capitalize the field results and, for fields that produce numeric results, which type of numbers to create (Arabic or Roman numerals, for example).

✦ The Numeric Picture switch (\#) controls the format of numbers.

✦ The Date-Time Picture switch (\@) sets the format of dates and times.

Each of these switches has numerous options you can mix and match to format the field in just about any way you want. I explain the various uses of these three switches in the following sections.

Preserving formatting when you update fields: The * mergeformat switch

When you update a field, Word usually removes any formatting, such as bold or italics, you applied to a field result. If you want Word to keep this type of formatting, include the * mergeformat switch in the field. Preserving formatting is usually a good idea, so I recommend you use this switch most of the time.

You can tell Word to automatically add a * mergeformat switch to a field by checking the Preserve Formatting During Updates check box in the Field dialog box.

Capitalizing field results

Use the Format switch (*) options I list in Table 1-2 to control capitalization in a field result. The following field, for example, inserts the name of the current file in lowercase letters:

{ filename * lower * mergeformat }

Table 1-2	Capitalizing Field Results
Switch	*What It Means*
* caps	The First Letter Of Each Word Is Capitalized.
* firstcap	The first letter of the first word is capitalized.
* lower	all the letters are lowercase.
* upper	ALL THE LETTERS ARE UPPERCASE.

Setting the number format

Numbers usually display with Arabic numerals. You can change the format of numbers in field results, however, by using the switches listed in Table 1-3. Consider this text, for example:

This is the { page * OrdText * mergeformat } page.

This line produces a result like this:

This is the thirty-third page.

In this case, the * OrdText switch spells out the page number.

Note: The capitalization used in the table doesn't matter except for the Alphabetic and Roman formats. In that case, the capitalization determines whether upper or lowercase letters display for the field value.

Table 1-3	Setting the Number Format
Switch	*What It Means*
* alphabetic	Converts numbers to lowercase letters (*1* becomes *a, 2* becomes *b,* and so on).
* ALPHABETIC	Converts numbers to uppercase letters (*1* becomes *A, 2* becomes *B,* and so on).
* Arabic	The usual number format (nothing special here).
* CardText	Spells out the number (for example, *1994* becomes *one thousand nine-hundred ninety-four*).
* DollarText	Spells out a dollar amount the way you write it on a check (*289.95* becomes *two hundred eighty-nine and 95/100*).
* Hex	A favorite of computer nerds, converts numbers from the normal earth dweller base 10 numbering system to base 16 (for example, *492* becomes *1EC*).
* Ordinal	Adds *st, nd, rd,* or whatever is appropriate to the end of the number (for example, *307* becomes *307th*).
* OrdText	Spells out the number and adds *st, nd, rd,* or whatever is appropriate to the end (for example, *307* becomes *three hundred seventh*).
* roman	Converts the number to lowercase roman numerals. Film directors use this format to mark copyright dates (for example, *1953* becomes *mcmliii*).
* ROMAN	Converts the number to uppercase roman numerals.

Creating custom number formats

If you don't like the way Word displays numbers, you can create your own custom number formats by using the Numeric Picture switch (\#). Numeric pictures are created by stringing together a bunch of pound signs, zeros, commas, decimal points, plus or minus signs, dollar signs, and other characters to show how you want numbers to appear. Table 1-4 lists the numeric picture switches you're most likely to use.

You can automatically add the numeric pictures listed in Table 1-4 to formulas if you use Table⇨Formula rather than Insert⇨Field to create the formula. Table⇨Formula provides a drop-down list box that lists these pictures. You just choose the number format you want, and Word inserts the appropriate switch into the field.

Table 1-4	Sample Numeric Picture Switches
Picture Switch	*Description*
\# #,##0	Prints whole numbers with commas to separate groups of thousands (for example, 1,024 and 1,244,212).
\# #,##0.00	Prints numbers with commas to separate groups of thousands and two decimal positions. Both decimal positions print even if one or both of them is zero (for example, 1,024.00 and 8.47).
\# $#,##0.00;($#,##0.00)	Prints numbers as money: commas to separate groups of thousands, two decimal positions, and a leading dollar sign; negative numbers are enclosed in parentheses: for example, $1,024.00 and ($97.38).
\# 0	Prints whole numbers without commas (for example, 38 and 124873345).
\# 0%	Prints whole numbers without commas, followed by a percent sign (for example, 98%).
\# 0.00	Prints numbers without commas but with two decimal positions (for example, 1024.00 or 3.14).
\# 0.00%	Prints numbers without commas, with two decimal positions, and followed by a percent sign (for example, 97.99%).

Creating custom date and time formats

When you use Insert⇨Field to insert a date field, you can click the Options button and choose from one of 17 different formats. If you don't like any of the 17 formats, you can compose your own custom date format by using the Date-Time Picture switch (\@). You just string together the various components of the date or time by using combinations of characters, such as MMM to stand for the three-letter month abbreviation, and dddd to stand for the day of the week, spelled out.

You'd think with 17 date formats to choose from, you can always find the one you need. That's not always the case, though. For example, if you want the current year (as in 1995), you have to create a custom date format using the switch **\@ "yyyy"**. Word doesn't provide this seemingly basic date format among its 17 formats.

Updating a Field

When you first insert a field, Word calculates the field's result. Thereafter, the field result may become out of date. To recalculate a field result to make sure that it is up to date, follow one of these procedures:

- ✦ Call up Tools➪Options and choose the Print tab. Check the Update Fields check box and then click OK. Word automatically updates all the fields every time you print the document.

- ✦ To update a specific field, select the field and press F9. If you select several fields, pressing F9 updates all of them. You can quickly update all the fields in a document by pressing Ctrl+A to select the entire document and then pressing F9 to update the fields.

- ✦ If you point to a field and click the right mouse button, a shortcut menu appears. Choose the Update Field command from this menu to update the field.

Preventing a Field from Being Updated

If you do *not* want to update a field, you can either lock the field or unlink the field. If you lock the field, Word prevents it from updating until you *unlock* the field. If you *unlink* the field, Word deletes the field code and replaces it with the result text. Locking a field temporarily prevents it from being updated; unlinking the field is permanent.

How I learned to love the SEQ field

Seq is one of my favorite fields because it lets me create a type of numbered list that I use all the time and that can't be done by using Format➪Bullet and Numbering. When I plan the Table of Contents for a book, I have to create a list that looks something like this:

Part I: Basic PowerPoint 2003 Stuff
Chapter 1: Opening Ceremonies
Chapter 2: Editing Slides
Chapter 3: Outlining Your Presentation

Part II: Making Your Presentations Look Mahvelous
Chapter 4: Fabulous Text Formats
Chapter 5: Working with Pictures and Clip Art
Chapter 6: A Slide of a Different Color

Do you see in this example how the chapters are numbered sequentially (1 through 6) and the parts also are numbered sequentially (I, II, and so on)? You can't create this type of list by using Format➪Bullet and Numbering. But you can do it if you use a Seq field. For the part numbers, use the Seq field like this:

{ seq part * ROMAN *mergeformat }

For the chapter numbers, use the Seq field like this:

{ seq chapter * mergeformat }

The *part* and *chapter* in the fields let Word keep track of two separate lists at the same time.

To lock, unlock, or unlink a field, first select it. Then use the keyboard shortcuts I list in Table 1-5.

Table 1-5	Keyboard Shortcuts for Locking, Unlocking, or Unlinking a Field
Keyboard Shortcut	**What It Does**
Ctrl+F11	Locks the field
Ctrl+Shift+F11	Unlocks the field
Ctrl+Shift+F9	Converts the field to results text (unlinks the field)

Field Code Reference

Table 1-6 lists all of the field codes available in Word 2003, along with a brief description of what each code does. For more detailed information about each field code, check the information available via the Insert Field Code dialog box.

Table 1-6	Word Field Codes
Field Code	**Description**
AddressBlock	Inserts a mail-merge address block.
Advance	Moves the text that follows the Advance field to the right or left, up or down, or to a specific position. In most cases, adjusting the positioning with Format⇨Font, Format⇨Paragraph, or Format⇨Tabs or by framing the text is better.
Ask	Prompts for information from the user and stores the result in a bookmark. A separate dialog box displays to ask the question.
Author	Obtains the Author name from the document properties, or sets the Author property to a new value.
AutoNum	Automatically numbers the paragraph. This field has been made obsolete by Format⇨Bullets and Numbering. AutoNum has no options.
AutoNumLgl	Automatically numbers heading paragraphs using legal or technical format (for example, 1.1, 1.2, and so on). Place an AutoNumLgl field at the beginning of each paragraph that you want numbered. This field has been rendered obsolete by Format⇨Bullets and Numbering.
AutoNumOut	Automatically numbers heading paragraphs using outline form. Place an AutoNumOut field at the beginning of each paragraph that you want numbered. This field has been rendered obsolete by Format⇨Bullets and Numbering.
AutoText	Inserts an AutoText entry.

(continued)

Table 1-6 *(continued)*

Field Code	Description
AutoTextList	Creates a shortcut menu in the document that allows the user to select AutoText entries.
BarCode	Inserts a postal bar code based on an address. You can do this more easily by using Tools⇨Envelopes and Labels.
BidiOutline	This field code wins the prize for Word's most obscure. It reverses the direction of outline numbering for languages that support right-to-left text.
Comments	Shows the contents of the comments field from the document's properties, and allows you to change the comments.
Compare	Compares two expressions and returns a value of 1 if the comparison is true and 0 if false. It is similar to the If field code.
CreateDate	Inserts the document's creation date.
Database	Inserts the result of a database query into the document as a table.
Date	Inserts the current date into the document. (Word gets the date from Windows. If the date appears wrong, double-click the date that appears at the right side of the Windows task bar to reset the date.)
DocProperty	Retrieves a specified document property. Many of these document properties are also available via their own field codes, such as Author, TotalEditingTime, and so on. Some are also available via the Info field.
DocVariable	Inserts the value of a document variable into your text.
EditTime	Inserts the total editing time in minutes since the document was created. Don't be fooled into thinking that this number somehow reflects a meaningful measure of how long you spent working on the document because the clock continues to run while a document is open whether you're working on it or not. If you get paid based on this field, I recommend you leave your documents open overnight.
Eq	Before Microsoft added the Equation Editor to Word, the Eq field was the only way to create equations. The Equation Editor is much easier to use and has many more options, so don't bother with this field. If you need to create equations, install the Equation Editor and be done with it.
FileName	Inserts the filename of the current document, with or without the complete path.
FileSize	Inserts the size of the document file in bytes, kilobytes, or megabytes.
Fillin	The Fillin field prompts the user for text, and then inserts the text into the document as the field result. It is similar to the Ask field, except that Ask places the user's input in a bookmark rather than in the document.
GoToButton	Creates a button that moves the insertion point to a specified location when clicked.
GreetingLine	Inserts the greeting line for a mail merge.
HyperLink	Inserts a hyperlink.

Field Code	Description
If	Compares the results of two expressions and supplies one of two result values depending on the outcome of the comparison.
IncludePicture	Inserts a picture into the document. Inserting a picture is much easier with Insert⇨Picture, so this field is pretty much obsolete.
IncludeText	Inserts another document into the current document.
Index	Inserts an index. You must first mark entries to be included in the index with XE fields. Note that creating an index is much easier by using Insert⇨Reference⇨Index and Tables.
Info	Retrieves the specified document information. Many of these document properties are also available via their own field codes, such as Author, TotalEditingTime, and so on. Most are also available via the DocProperty field. The Info field also lets you set a new value for several of the properties.
Keywords	Displays the keywords from the document properties.
LastSavedBy	Displays the name of the user who last saved the document.
Link	Inserts a file or portion of a file created by another application using an OLE link. This result is similar to using Insert⇨Object and selecting the Link to File option to insert an object into a file.
MacroButton	Inserts a button that, when clicked, runs a macro.
MergeField	Sets up a merge field that is replaced by data from the data source when the mail merge is processed.
MergeRec	Sets up a merge field that displays the number of the data record being processed during a mail merge.
MergeSeq	Displays a count of the number of records that are merged so far.
Next	Skips to the next record in the data source without starting a new merge document. Use this field if you want each merge document to include data from two or more records.
NextIf	Skips to the next merge record if the specified condition is true. Mail Merge Helper (Tools⇨Mail Merge) handles conditional merging better.
NoteRef	Allows you to refer to a footnote or endnote that is already marked so that if the footnote or endnote changes, the reference changes along with it.
NumChars	Inserts the number of characters in the document.
NumPages	Inserts the number of pages in the document.
NumWords	Inserts the number of words in the document.
Page	Inserts the current page number. This field is inserted into the header or footer when you click the Page Number button.
PageRef	Inserts the number of the page on which a specified bookmark appears.

Book VI
Chapter 1

Working with Fields

(continued)

Table 1-6 *(continued)*

Field Code	Description
Print	Sends printer codes directly to the printer when the document prints. To use this field properly, you need to be an expert in the printer codes used by your printer. It works best with HP LaserJet printers or PostScript printers.
PrintDate	Displays the date the document was last printed.
Private	Holds information stored when a document converts from one format to another. This field is intended for use only by the document converters.
Quote	Inserts text into a document.
RD	Allows you to create a Table of Contents or index for a multi-file project without dealing with Word's master document feature. Unfortunately, this method does not automatically number pages consecutively from one document to the next. Instead, you must manually set the page numbers and update any TOC, TOA, or Index fields in the separate documents.
Ref	Inserts the contents of the specified bookmark. This is the only field for which the field code itself is optional. As a result, you can just cite the name of the bookmark if you wish.
RevNum	Inserts the number of times the document is saved. Unfortunately, this result is probably not what you or I think of as a true revision number, as most users frequently save their work. Thus, if you save a document ten times in the course of an hour (not an unreasonable rate), you produce ten revisions.
SaveDate	Inserts the date the document was last saved.
Section	Inserts the current section number.
SectionPages	Inserts the total number of pages in the current section.
Seq	Creates sequence numbers, such as a numbered list, chapter or heading numbers, and so on. For simple lists, using Format⇨ Bullets and Numbering or Format⇨Heading Numbering is best. However, the Seq field is useful as a more general numbering tool.
Set	Allows you to create a bookmark for text that isn't visible in the document.
SkipIf	Conditionally skips the next merge record during a mail merge, based on the results of a comparison. Mail Merge Helper (Tools⇨Mail Merge) can handle conditional merging, so avoid using this field.
StyleRef	Inserts text that is formatted with a particular style. This field is most useful for creating dictionary-style headers or footers that cite the first or last heading on the page.
Subject	Inserts the document subject taken from the document's properties.
Symbol	Inserts a symbol into the document. This result is far easier to accomplish by using the Insert⇨Symbol command.

Field Code	Description
TA	Marks a citation to be included in a Table of Authorities. This field is inserted when you press Alt+Shift+I to mark a citation.
TC	Marks an entry to be included in a Table of Contents. You can more easily compile Tables of Contents based on heading styles, but if you must do it the hard way, use TC fields instead.
Template	Inserts the filename of the template attached to the document.
Time	Inserts the current time. (Word gets the time from Windows. If the time appears wrong, double-click the date that appears at the right side of the Windows task bar to reset the time.)
Title	Inserts the document title taken from the document's properties.
TOA	Compiles a Table of Authorities based on TA fields inserted into the document. This field is inserted when you use Insert⇨ Index and Tables.
TOC	Compiles a Table of Contents. This field is inserted when you use Insert⇨Index and Tables.
UserAddress	Inserts the user's address taken from Tools⇨Options (on the User Info tab).
UserInitials	Inserts the user's initials taken from Tools⇨Options (on the User Info tab).
UserName	Inserts the user's name taken from Tools⇨Options (on the User Info tab).
XE	Marks an entry for inclusion in an index. XE fields insert when you press Alt+Shift+X.
= (Formula)	Lets you insert formulas into your documents.

**Book VI
Chapter 1**

Working with Fields

Chapter 2: Form Follows Function (Setting Up and Using Forms)

In This Chapter

- ✔ Understanding forms
- ✔ Creating a form template
- ✔ Inserting a text field
- ✔ Creating a check box field
- ✔ Adding a drop-down field
- ✔ Filling in a form
- ✔ Using macros in a form
- ✔ A sample form that uses macros
- ✔ Adding help to a field

My guess is that Microsoft had a big contract with the government — probably the military — to sell a million copies of Word to the government if the program provided a feature for creating and filling in forms, preferably in triplicate. So here I am, ready to write another chapter for this book. I'd really rather call it a day and maybe catch a quick round of golf, but who knows — maybe the government will buy a truckload of copies of this book at $913 each if I throw in a chapter about creating and filling in forms. So what the heck.

You may not realize it, but creating a form that you or someone else can fill out later qualifies as a type of programming. As such, you must adopt a bit of a programmer's mentality, distasteful as that may seem. In this chapter, I use the word *user* to refer to the person — you or someone else — who fills out a form that you create, just to keep you alert.

Understanding Forms

A *form* is a special type of document in which parts of the document are protected from the user modifying it. The user is allowed to enter information only in predefined fill-in-the-blank portions of the document, which are called *form fields*.

Figure 2-1 shows an example of a form that I created with Word. Most of the text you see in the document is protected. The only parts of the document that the user can modify are the shaded parts: the name and address fields, the answers to the two questions, and the check boxes.

I provide the exact steps for creating and filling out a blank form later in this chapter, but the general idea goes something like this. First, you create a new template. Then you add any text that you want to appear in the form to the template and you add the form fields using buttons available on the Forms toolbar. When you finish the blank form, use Tools⇨Protect Document to prevent the user from modifying any part of the document other than the form fields, and finally, you save the template.

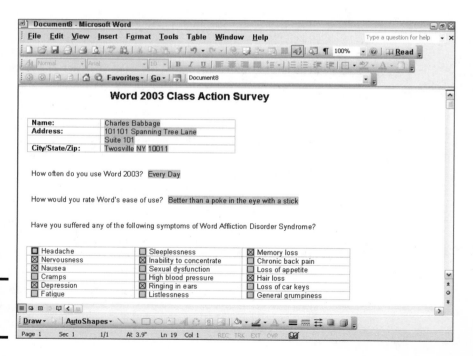

Figure 2-1:
A Word
form.

To fill in a form, you have to create a new document based on the form template. Then fill in the blanks. Word doesn't allow you to move the insertion point anywhere outside the form fields, so you don't have to worry about accidentally messing up the form.

◆ Think of the template as a pile of blank forms. To fill out a form, first you have to grab a form off the pile by opening the template. After you fill out the form (the template), you can save it as a normal document. The saved document contains the form itself that's copied from the template, plus whatever information you typed into the form fields.

◆ Although it's not apparent from Figure 2-1, the form fields for the first two questions are actually drop-down list boxes. Instead of typing in a response to the question, the user selects one of several permissible responses. If, for example, the user clicks the mouse in the form field for the first question ("How often do you use Word 2003?"), the drop-down list shown in Figure 2-2 appears.

◆ Microsoft offers several form templates for download at the Microsoft Office Online Web site. To see what you can do with forms, try downloading a few of these templates.

Book VI
Chapter 2

Form Follows
Function (Setting Up
and Using Forms)

Figure 2-2:
A drop-
down list.

Every Day ▲
Every Day
Once a Week
Once a Month
As Little as Possible

Creating a Form Template

Before you can fill out a form, you must create a template. The template contains any text and graphics that appear on the blank form as well as the form fields, into which the user enters information.

To create a form template, follow these steps:

1. **Click the New Blank Document button on the Standard toolbar.**

Or, if you prefer, choose File⇨New, and then click the <u>Blank Document</u> link in the New Document task pane.

If you prefer to base your new form on an existing template, choose File⇨New to bring up the New Document task pane, click the <u>On My Computer</u> link in the Templates section, and then select a template to base the new form on.

2. **Choose File⇨Save As.**

The Save As dialog box appears.

3. **Choose Document Template in the Save as Type drop-down list.**

4. **Type a name for your new form template and click Save.**

The initial copy of the template is saved.

5. **Choose View➪Toolbars➪Forms.**

The Forms toolbar appears, which you use to add elements to your form.

6. **Create your form.**

Type text where you want text to appear, insert graphics where you want graphics to appear, and insert form fields where you want form fields to appear.

You can insert three basic types of fields into a form: text fields, list box fields, and check box fields. To create any of these, use the appropriate buttons on the Forms toolbar. For more specific information on creating these fields, see the following three sections.

7. **Call up Tools➪Protect Document.**

The Protect Document task pane appears, as shown in Figure 2-3.

8. **Check the Allow Only This Type of Editing in the Document check box, and then choose Filling in Forms from the drop-down list.**

This action protects the document so that the user can enter data into the form fields only.

Figure 2-3:
The Protect
Document
task pane.

9. **Click the Yes, Start Enforcing Protection button in the Protect Document task pane.**

   The dialog box shown in Figure 2-4 appears.

Figure 2-4:
The Start
Enforcing
Protection
dialog box.

Start Enforcing Protection	☒
Enter new password (optional):	
Reenter password to confirm:	
OK	Cancel

10. **Type the password you want to use to protect the document in both text boxes, and then click OK.**

    Using a password helps insure that only you can unprotect the form to make changes to the form's layout. If you don't care about password protecting the form, just click OK without typing a password.

11. **Use File⇨Save to save the template.**

12. **That's all.**

    You're done.

Here are some suggestions for creating forms:

✦ If you're converting a paper form to Word, create the Word form so that it looks as much like the current paper form as possible. Work in Print Layout view so that you can see how things line up.

✦ If you want the form to be laid out on a grid with ruled lines and boxes, use tables, text boxes, borders, shading, and whatever other Word features you can muster.

✦ If you're creating a template for the first time, you may want to refer to Book I, Chapter 3 to make sure you know the ins and outs of working with templates.

✦ Creating a form is tedious work. You may not want to wait until the very end to save the template. In fact, you should probably press Ctrl+S to save your work every few minutes or activate the AutoSave feature so that the template automatically saves at regular intervals.

✦ If you protect the template by using Tools⇨Protect Document, you must unprotect the template if you need to change the layout of the form later. Call up Tools⇨Unprotect. If you used a password when you protected the document, you are asked to enter the password to unprotect the document. Don't forget to protect the form again when you finish!

Using the Forms Toolbar

Word provides a Forms toolbar, shown in Figure 2-5, that includes buttons you can use for developing forms. To summon this toolbar, choose View➪ Toolbars➪Forms.

Figure 2-5:
The Forms
toolbar.

Table 2-1 lists the buttons that appear on the Forms toolbar.

Table 2-1	Buttons on the Forms Toolbar
Button	*What It Does*
ab|	Inserts a text field
☑	Inserts a check box field
	Inserts a drop-down field
	Calls up the Form Field Options dialog box for a field
	Calls up the Tables and Borders toolbar so that you can draw a table
	Inserts a table
	Inserts a frame
a	Turns field shading on or off

Button	What It Does
	Sets form fields back to their default settings
	Protects or unprotects a form

Creating a Text Field

A *text field* is a form field that the user can type information into. You use text fields to provide a space on the form where the user can enter information, such as a name or address. The form shown in Figure 2-1 uses four text fields: one for the name and three for the address lines.

To create, or insert, a text field in a form, follow these steps:

1. **Position the insertion point on the template where you want the text field to appear.**

2. **Click the Text Form Field button on the Forms toolbar.**

A text box is inserted.

The text field is inserted in the template.

Typing some sort of text in the template next to the field to tell the user what to type into the field is a good idea. For example, in Figure 2-1, I typed **Name:** next to the text field that is supposed to contain the name.

If you want to provide a *default value* for the text field — that is, a value that the field assumes if the user doesn't type anything into the field — select the text field and then click the Form Field Options button on the Forms toolbar. Or, just double-click the text field. Either way, the Text Form Field Options dialog box appears, as shown in Figure 2-6. Type a default value for the field in the Default Text box and then click OK.

The Text Form Field Options dialog box also enables you to set the field type. Word lets you create six different types of text fields, as I summarize in Table 2-2.

Table 2-2	The Six Types of Text Fields
Text Field Type	*What It Does*
Regular Text	This field consists of ordinary text, like a name or address. The user can type anything into the field.
Number	The user must type a number into the field.
Date	The user must type a date into the field. The date must be in the usual date format (for example, 05/31/04 or 6-24-04) or may include the month spelled out (as in March 28, 2004).
Current Date	Word automatically inserts the current date into the field. The user can't type anything in the field.
Current Time	Word automatically inserts the current time into the field. The user can't type anything in the field.
Calculation	The field contains a formula field (=) to calculate a result value, usually based on the value of one or more number fields. The user also can't type anything into this field.

If you uncheck the Fill-in Enabled check box in the Text Form Field Options dialog box (see Figure 2-6), Word displays the text field, but the user can't modify it. Use this field only if you plan on doing some fancy macro programming, in which a macro enables or disables the field at will. This kind of macro programming requires programming knowledge that is way beyond the realm of reasonableness.

After you create a text field, you can call up the Text Form Field Options dialog box by double-clicking the field or right-clicking the field (that is, pointing to the field and clicking the right mouse button) and selecting the Properties command from the shortcut menu that appears.

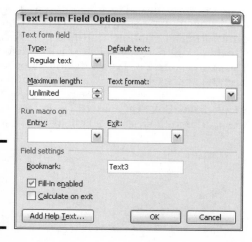

Figure 2-6: The Text Form Field Options dialog box.

Creating a Check Box Field

A *check box field* is a field that the user can check or uncheck to provide a yes or no answer. Check box fields work just like regular check boxes in dialog boxes: You click them with the mouse to check or uncheck them.

Follow these steps to create or insert a check box field:

1. **Position the insertion point in the template where you want the check box field to appear.**

2. **Click the Check Box button on the Forms toolbar.**

   A check box is inserted.

3. **If you want the check box to not be checked when the form first displays, you're done. Otherwise, click the Forms Field Options button on the Forms toolbar.**

   Or, double-click the check box you created in Step 2. Either way, the Check Box Form Field Options dialog box appears, as shown in Figure 2-7.

4. **Select the Checked option.**

   The check box will be checked when the form first displays.

5. **Click OK.**

The check box is now inserted in the document.

Figure 2-7:
The Check
Box Form
Field
Options
dialog box.

Check Box Form Field Options

Check box size

- ⦿ Auto
- ○ Exactly: 10 pt

Default value

- ⦿ Not checked
- ○ Checked

Run macro on

Entry: Exit:

Field settings

Bookmark: Check1

☑ Check box enabled
☐ Calculate on exit

Add Help Text...   OK   Cancel

Here are some pointers for creating a check box field:

+ Obviously, a check box by itself is of little worth. You want to place some text in the template right next to the check box so that the user knows what the check box field means.

+ Unless you're into writing macros, the only thing you can do with a check box is check it or uncheck it. If you want to roll up your sleeves and do some heavy-duty macro programming, you can come up with all sorts of exotic uses for check box fields.

+ If you want to change the default size of the check box field, select Exactly (at the top of the Check Box Form Field Options dialog box) and type the size of the check box in points.

+ If you uncheck the Check Box Enabled check box, Word displays the check box field, but the user can't modify it. Use this field only if you plan to do some fancy macro programming, in which a macro enables the field if the user enters a certain value into another field. To reenable the check box again, check the Check Box Enabled check box.

Sounds like a scene from *Airplane,* doesn't it?

Roger: Chuck, check the Check Box Enabled Check Box.

Chuck: Roger, Roger. Now checking the Check Box Enabled check box. Chuck out.

Roger: Check, Chuck.

+ You can call up the Check Box Form Field Options dialog box after you insert a check box field by double-clicking the field or right-clicking the field (that is, pointing to it and clicking the right mouse button) and selecting the Properties command from the shortcut menu that appears.

Creating a Drop-Down Field

A *drop-down field* is like a text field, except that the user isn't allowed to type text directly into the field. Instead, the user must select from a list of preset choices that are given in a list box. List boxes are great for fields such as marital status, shipping instructions, or gender. In other words, fields that have only a limited set of correct answers.

Follow these steps to create, or insert, a drop-down field:

1. **Position the insertion point where you want the text field to appear.**

 2. **Click the Drop Down Form Field button on the Forms toolbar.**

A default drop-down list is created.

3. Click the Form Field Options button on the Forms toolbar.

Or, double-click the drop-down form field. Either way, the Drop-Down Form Field Options dialog box appears, as shown in Figure 2-8.

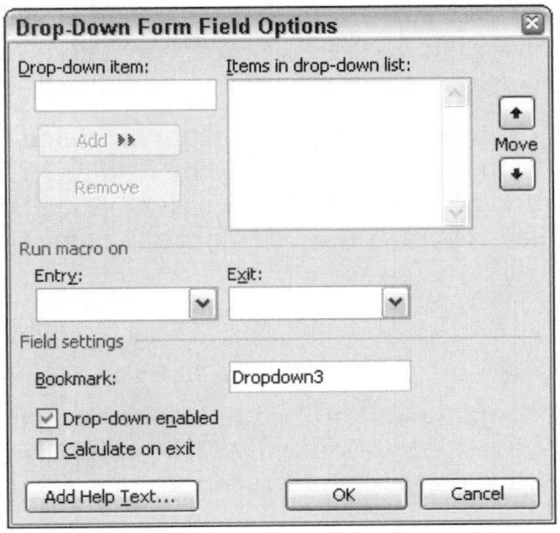

Figure 2-8:
The Drop-Down Form Field Options dialog box.

4. To add an item to the drop-down list, type some text in the Drop-Down Item box and then click the Add button.

The text is added to the Items in Drop-Down List field.

5. Repeat Step 4 for each item you want to include as a choice in the drop-down list.

6. When you add all the items you want in the list, click OK.

That's it!

If you're going to the trouble of creating drop-down list fields, keep the following hot tips in mind:

✦ The first item in the drop-down list is the default selection — that is, the item that is initially selected for the field.

✦ To rearrange items in the drop-down list, call up the Drop-Down Form Field Options dialog box, select the item that you want to move to another position in the list, and click the up or down Move buttons.

✦ To delete an item from the list, select the item and click the Remove button.

✦ To correct a mistake in a list item, delete the incorrect item. Word copies the deleted item to the Drop-Down Item box, where you can correct the mistake and click the Add button to reinsert the item.

✦ If you uncheck the Drop-Down Enabled check box, Word displays the drop-down list field, but the user can't modify it. Use this field only if you plan to do some fancy macro programming, in which a macro enables or disables the field on the fly. Better con a computer nerd friend into doing this macro for you.

✦ You can call up the Drop-Down Form Field Options dialog box after you insert a drop-down field by double-clicking the field or right-clicking (that is, pointing to the field and clicking the right mouse button) the field and selecting the Properties from the shortcut menu that appears.

Filling Out a Form

After you create a form template and protect it, it's time to put the form to good use collecting the vital information that you so carefully designed it to record. In other words, it's time to fill out the form.

To fill out a form using a form template that you or someone else created, follow these steps:

1. **Call up File⇨New, and then click the <u>On My Computer</u> link in the Templates section of the New Document task pane.**

   The New dialog box appears, listing all the available templates.

2. **Select the correct form template from the Template list.**

3. **Click OK.**

4. **Fill in the form fields.**

   When you fill in the form fields, you can use any of the keyboard actions I list in Table 2-3. For the most part, you use the Tab key to move from field to field.

5. **Print the document.**

   Use File⇨Print or click the Print button on the Standard toolbar.

6. **Save the file, if you want.**

   Use File⇨Save or click the Save button on the Standard toolbar. Word asks for a filename.

Table 2-3	Keys You Can Use When Filling Out a Form
Key	*What It Does*
Enter, Tab, or ↓	Moves the insertion point to the next field
Shift+Tab, or ↑	Moves the insertion point to the previous field
Alt+↓, or F4	Displays a drop-down list
↑ or ↓	Moves up or down in a drop-down list
Space or X	Checks or unchecks a check box field
F1	Displays the help text for a field
Ctrl+Tab	Inserts a tab character into a text field

Adding Help to a Form Field

Word lets you add your own help text to form fields. Then if you forget what a field is for when you're filling out a form, the help text reminds you.

You can create two types of help text for each field. The status bar help is a single line of text that appears on the status bar whenever the insertion point moves into the field. Word limits this help text to 138 characters so that it fits in the space provided on the status bar. If the status bar help isn't enough, you can supply help text, which the user can summon by pressing F1. You can provide up to 256 characters for help text. Figure 2-9 shows an example of help text.

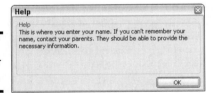

Figure 2-9:
Help text for
a form field.

To create help text for a field, follow these steps:

1. **Select the field you want to add help text to.**

Make sure the form is unprotected. You can't add help text to a field while the form is protected.

2. **Double-click the field to call up the Form Field Options dialog box.**

3. **Click the Add Help Text button.**

   The Form Field Help Text dialog box appears, as shown in Figure 2-10.

4. **Type the status bar help text on the Status Bar tab and the help text on the Help Key (F1) tab.**

5. **Click OK.**

   The help text is now attached to the field. The user can display it by pressing F1.

Figure 2-10:
Adding help
information
to a form
field.

Using Pre-Printed Forms

If you are creating an online form for a document for which you have pre-printed forms that you can use with your printer, format the form template so that its fields align exactly with the form fields on the pre-printed form. Then, when you want to print to the pre-printed form, first call up the Print options (choose Tools⇨Options, and then click the Print tab, or File⇨Print, and then click the Options button) and select the Print Data Only for Forms option. Word prints just the data you enter into the form fields, not the form template itself. If your pre-printed forms and your form template are lined up properly, the data fits snugly in the fields on the pre-printed form.

Exporting Form Data to a Text File

Word lets you save the data you enter into a form in a comma-delimited text file, which you can then input to another program, such as a database program. To use this feature, choose Tools⇨Options, click the Save tab, and then select the Save Data Only for Forms option. Then, when you save the file, it saves to a text file rather than to a document file.

A File Conversion dialog box similar to the one shown in Figure 2-11 appears before the file actually saves. You can play with the options that appear in this dialog box if you want to tweak the details of how the file is stored.

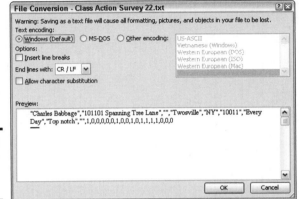

Figure 2-11: Saving only data for a form.

All the fields in the form write to the text file, whether the user enters data into the field or not. The fields are separated from one another with commas, and text values are enclosed in quotation marks. List fields are given the text value for the item selected for the field, and check boxes are written as 1 if they are selected, 0 if they are not.

You can display the saved file with a text editor, such as Notepad. For example, Figure 2-12 shows how a text file for a form based on the template used throughout this chapter may appear when displayed in Notepad.

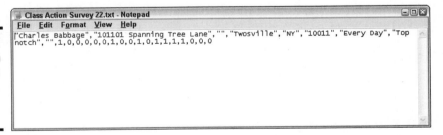

Figure 2-12: Displaying a text file that contains saved form data only.

Chapter 3: More about Outlining

In This Chapter

✔ Switching to Outline view

✔ Understanding Outline view

✔ Collapsing and expanding an outline

✔ Promoting and demoting paragraphs

✔ Editing in Outline view

✔ Printing an outline

✔ Working with the document map

Some writers have the outlining gene — others don't. Some writers manage to concoct at least a rudimentary outline only through an extraordinary act of self-will. Other writers spend days polishing the world's most perfect outline before they write a word. Their outlines are so good that they can write with their eyes closed after finishing the outline. Hmph. I fall somewhere in between. I spin a fairly decent outline up front, but I'm not compulsive about it. I rarely write with my eyes closed and usually revise the outline substantially as I go, sometimes beyond the point of recognition.

Word has a built-in outlining tool that's handy whether you like to create detailed outlines in advance, or you just want to check occasionally on the overall structure of your document to see how it is evolving. I use it all the time, even though I'm not an outline fanatic. If you use Word to create reports, proposals, or other types of documents that have some sense of structure to them, you owe it to yourself to find out the basics of working with outlines.

Switching to Outline View

Word usually runs in *Normal view,* which displays your document in a manner that's most convenient for on-screen editing. *Outline view* shows the contents of your document in the form of an outline. You can switch to Outline view in three ways:

◆ Using View⇨Outline

 ◆ Clicking the Outline View button (shown in the margin) next to the horizontal scroll bar, near the bottom-left corner of the document

◆ Pressing Ctrl+Alt+O

Figure 3-1 shows an example of a document in Outline view.

 To return to Normal view, use View⇨Normal, click the Normal View button (shown in the margin), or press the keyboard shortcut Ctrl+Alt+N.

 To switch to Print Layout view, use View⇨Print Layout, click the Print Layout View button (shown in the margin), or press the keyboard shortcut Ctrl+Alt+P.

You can also work with a document's outline by turning on the Document Map feature. For more information, see the section "Using the Document Map" at the end of this chapter.

Outlining toolbar

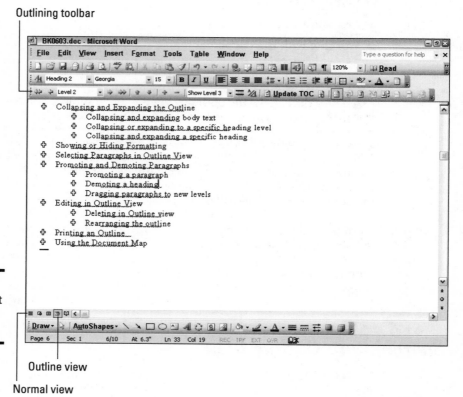

Figure 3-1:
A document in Outline view.

Outline view

Normal view

Understanding Outline View

The key to understanding Word's Outline view is realizing that an outline is just another way of looking at a document. The outline is not a separate entity from the document. Instead, when you switch to Outline view, Word takes the headings from your document and presents them in the form of an outline. Any changes you make to your document while in Outline view automatically reflect in the document when you return to Normal view, and any changes you make in Normal view automatically appear when you switch to Outline view. The reason is because Normal view and Outline view are merely two ways of displaying the contents of your document.

Note some important concepts about Outline view:

✦ The outline is made up of the headings and body text of the document. Any paragraph formatted with one of the built-in heading styles (Heading 1, Heading 2, Heading 3, and so on) is considered to be a heading; any other paragraph is considered body text.

✦ When you switch to Outline view, an extra toolbar appears on-screen, replacing the ruler (which isn't needed in Outline view). This toolbar, appropriately called the Outlining toolbar, contains buttons for performing routine outlining tasks. Refer to Figure 3-1 to see the Outlining toolbar; I list the toolbar buttons used for working with outlines in Table 3-1. (The Outlining toolbar contains additional buttons that are used for working with Tables of Contents and master documents. You find information about Tables of Contents in Chapter 6 of this minibook. And I cover the Master Documents feature in Chapter 4 of this minibook.)

✦ When you first switch to Outline view, your document may not appear dramatically different than it does in Normal view. In the following sections, you see how Outline view enables you to view your document quite differently from the way you view it in Normal view.

✦ While in Outline view, you can type new text or edit existing text just as you do in Normal view. You can also apply character formatting, such as bold or italic, and you can apply styles to paragraphs. However, you can't apply direct paragraph formats, such as indentation, tab stops, alignment, and so on. To apply these types of formats, you must return to Normal view.

✦ Outline view has its own set of keyboard shortcuts (which I summarize in Table 3-2) to help you move things along.

Table 3-1	Buttons on the Outlining Toolbar
Button	*What It Does*
	Promotes the selected text to Heading 1
	Promotes the selected text to the next higher heading level
Level 1	Sets the heading level of the selected text
	Demotes the selected text to the next lower level
	Demotes the selected text to body text
	Moves the selected text up in the outline
	Moves the selected text down in the outline
	Expands the selection
	Collapses the selection
Show Level 1	Selects the level to be shown
	Displays only the first line of each paragraph
	Shows or hides text formatting

Table 3-2	Keyboard Shortcuts for Outline View
Keyboard Shortcut	*What It Does*
Ctrl+Alt+O	Switches to Outline view
Ctrl+Alt+N	Switches back to Normal view
Alt+Shift+A	Collapses or expands all text
Alt+Shift+hyphen	Collapses the selection

Keyboard Shortcut	What It Does
Alt+Shift+plus	Expands the selection
Alt+Shift+1	Collapses/expands to Heading 1
Alt+Shift+*(number)*	Collapses/expands to specified heading level
/ (on numeric keypad)	Hides/shows formatting
Shift+Tab	Promotes the selection
Alt+Shift+←	Promotes the selection
Tab	Demotes the selection
Alt+Shift+→	Demotes the selection
Ctrl+Shift+N	Demotes selection to body text by applying Normal style
Alt+Shift+↑	Moves the selection up, similar to cutting and pasting it
Alt+Shift+↓	Moves the selection down, similar to cutting and pasting it

**Book VI
Chapter 3**

More about
Outlining

Showing or Hiding Formatting

Before you spend too much time working in Outline view, you may want to hide the formatting from the outline so that you can concentrate more closely on the document's structure. Hiding the formatting in Outline view doesn't actually remove the formatting from your text; it just temporarily hides it. The outline shown in Figure 3-1 has the formatting hidden.

To remove formatting from an outline, click the Show Formatting button or press the slash (/) key on the numeric keypad.

Keep these tips in mind when using the Show Formatting button:

✦ To restore formatting, click the Show Formatting button or press the slash (/) key again.

✦ You don't need the formatting to distinguish among heading levels because the headings are indented for you. So I usually work in Outline view with formatting off.

✦ When you hide formatting, you're doing just that: hiding it. You're not actually removing it. When you click the Show Formatting button again or return to Normal view, all the formatting that you so carefully applied to your document is restored.

Collapsing and Expanding the Outline

One of the main reasons for working in Outline view rather than in Normal view is so that you can get a handle on the overall structure of your document. The secret lies in collapsing the outline so that the portions of your document you're not interested in are hidden.

The Outlining toolbar includes a Show Level drop-down list that lets you collapse or expand the entire outline to a specific heading level. For example, if you want to see just the top level headings (paragraphs formatted with the Heading 1 style), select Show Level 1 in the Show Level drop-down list. Figure 3-2 shows what the document from Figure 3-1 looks like when Level 1 is selected.

Here are some important features to note about working with collapsed text in Outline view:

✦ Notice that some of the headings have fuzzy lines under them. These fuzzy lines represent collapsed body text.

✦ Notice also that each heading has a large plus sign or minus sign next to it. Headings with plus signs have other headings or body text subordinate to them. Headings with minus signs do not. Body text paragraphs always have a hollow square bullet next to them.

✦ If you're good with keyboard shortcuts, Alt+Shift+A quickly toggles between Show Level 9 and Show All Levels. This handy shortcut quickly shows or hides all of the body text in an outline.

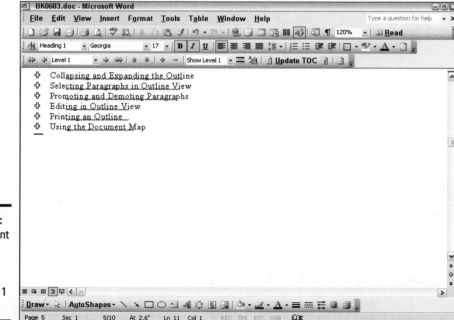

Figure 3-2:
A document in Outline View showing only Level 1 headings.

Collapsing and Expanding a Specific Heading

You can selectively collapse or expand specific headings in Outline view so that you can focus on specific portions of your document. For example, you can collapse the entire document to Heading 1 and then expand only the heading that you want to work on.

To collapse and subsequently expand a heading, follow these simple steps:

1. **Select the heading that you want to collapse.**

Click anywhere in the heading to select it.

2. **Click the Collapse button (shown in the margin).**

All the subordinate headings and body text paragraphs for the heading temporarily hide.

3. **To expand the heading again, click the Expand button (shown in the margin).**

The hidden paragraphs reappear.

Another way to collapse a heading is to double-click the big plus sign next to it. Double-click it again to expand the heading. You can also use the keyboard shortcuts:

✦ **Alt+Shift+- (hyphen):** Collapse the outline.

✦ **Alt+Shift++ (plus sign):** Expand the outline.

Selecting Paragraphs in Outline View

When you work in Outline view, you can easily become confused about how to select various portions of the document. This section is a quick summary of the techniques:

✦ Most of the techniques for selecting text that work in Normal view also work in Outline view. For example, you can select a block of text by dragging the mouse or holding down the Shift key while using the keyboard arrows.

✦ To select an entire heading or body text paragraph, point the mouse to the left of the paragraph in the invisible zone (actually, the left margin) called the *selection bar* and click. (The mouse arrow points northeast when it's in the selection bar.)

✦ To select a heading paragraph and all its subordinate paragraphs, click the big plus sign next to the paragraph or double-click to the left of the paragraph in the selection bar. This action selects subordinate heading paragraphs as well as body text paragraphs.

Selecting an entire paragraph to perform most outline operations isn't necessary. For example, you can select a paragraph for promotion or demotion just by clicking anywhere in the paragraph.

Promoting and Demoting Paragraphs

To *promote* a paragraph means to move it up one level in the outline. If you promote a Heading 2, it becomes a Heading 1. You can't promote a Heading 1 paragraph; it's already as high as it can get. If you promote a body text paragraph, it becomes a heading paragraph at the same level as the heading it is subordinate to. Thus, if you promote a body text paragraph that follows a Heading 2, the body text paragraph becomes a Heading 2.

To *demote* a paragraph is to move the paragraph down one level in the outline. If you demote a Heading 1, it becomes a Heading 2. Demote it again and it becomes a Heading 3. You cannot demote a body text paragraph, but you can demote any heading to a body text paragraph.

When you promote or demote headings, the body text paragraphs that fall under the heading always go along for the ride. You don't need to worry about losing a heading's body text. Whether or not subordinate headings get swept up in the move depends on how you handle the promotion or demotion.

Promoting a paragraph

To promote a paragraph, place the cursor anywhere in the paragraph and then perform any of the following techniques:

✦ Click the Promote button on the Outlining toolbar.

✦ Press Shift+Tab.

✦ Use the keyboard shortcut Alt+Shift+←.

The paragraph moves up one level in the outline pecking order.

You cannot promote a Heading 1; it is already at the highest level in the outline hierarchy.

If you want to promote a heading *and* all its subordinate headings, click the big plus sign next to the paragraph or double-click in the invisible selection bar to the left of the paragraph. Then promote it. If you promote a body text paragraph, it assumes the heading level of the heading paragraph it used to belong to.

You also can promote paragraphs by dragging them with the mouse. See the section, "Dragging paragraphs to new levels," later in this chapter.

 You can promote any paragraph directly to a Heading 1 paragraph by clicking the Promote to Heading 1 button.

Demoting a heading

To demote a heading, place the cursor anywhere in the heading and then do one of the following:

+ Click the Demote button (shown in the margin) on the Outlining toolbar.
+ Press Tab.
+ Use the keyboard shortcut Alt+Shift+→.

The heading moves down a level in the outline pecking order.

To demote a heading *and* any headings unfortunate enough to be subordinate to it, click the paragraph's big plus sign or double-click in the hidden selection bar just left of the paragraph. Then demote it.

Don't be insensitive when you demote a paragraph. It can be a traumatic experience.

You can also demote paragraphs by dragging them with the mouse. See the section, "Dragging paragraphs to new levels," later in this chapter.

You can't demote a body text paragraph. It's already at the bottom of the rung.

 You can quickly demote a heading paragraph to body text by clicking the Demote to Body Text button on the Outlining toolbar or by pressing the keyboard shortcut Ctrl+Shift+N. (Recognize this shortcut? Demoting a paragraph to body text is accomplished by assigning the Normal style to it.)

Dragging paragraphs to new levels

When you move the mouse pointer over the big plus or minus sign next to a heading or body text paragraph, the pointer changes from a single arrow to a four-cornered arrow. This arrow is your signal that you can click the mouse to select the entire paragraph (and any subordinate paragraphs) and then use the mouse to promote or demote a paragraph along with all its subordinates.

To promote or demote with the mouse, follow these steps:

1. **Point to the big plus or minus sign for the paragraph you want to demote or promote.**

   The mouse pointer changes to a four-cornered arrow, as shown in the margin.

2. **Click and hold the mouse button down.**

3. **Drag the mouse to the right or left.**

   The mouse pointer changes to a double-pointed arrow, as shown in the margin, and a vertical line appears that shows the indentation level of the selection. Release the button when the selection indents the way you want. The text automatically assigns the correct heading style.

If you mess up, press Ctrl+Z to undo the promotion or demotion. Then try again.

You can't demote a heading to body text using the preceding technique. You must either click the Demote to Body Text button or press Ctrl+Shift+N.

Editing in Outline View

Outline view is a great place to perform large-scale editing on your document, such as rearranging or deleting whole sections of text. If you edit a document while the body text is hidden, any edits you perform on headings automatically extend to the body text that belongs to them. Thus, if you delete a heading, all its body text deletes, too. If you move a heading to a new location in the document, the body text moves as well.

Deleting in Outline view

To delete large portions of your document quickly, switch to Outline view. Select the text that you want to delete; then press the Delete key and — Pow! — the text is gone.

Some helpful hints when using Outline view to delete text:

✦ Click the mouse in the magic invisible selection bar just to the left of a heading paragraph to select the entire paragraph. Then press the Delete key and kiss the paragraph good-bye.

✦ Click the big plus sign next to a heading paragraph to select it *and* all its subordinate headings and body text. Press the Delete key to send everything — headings and body text alike — into oblivion.

✦ Click and drag the mouse over a block of heading paragraphs to select them and then press the Delete key to delete everything that you selected.

✦ Obviously, using the Delete key in Outline view is risky business. Don't do it unless you're certain that the body text and subordinate paragraphs are preserved. When in doubt, switch to Normal view and delete text the old-fashioned way.

Rearranging the outline

To rearrange your document on a large scale, switch to Outline view and move entire headings up or down in the outline. ***Remember:*** Body text always travels with its headings. Whether subordinate headings travel as well depends on whether you select them before moving headings around.

To move just one paragraph, click anywhere in the paragraph. To move a paragraph along with its subordinates, click the big plus sign next to it. Then use one of the following techniques.

To move the selected paragraphs up, use one of these methods:

✦ Click the Up button (shown in the margin) on the Outlining toolbar.

✦ Press Alt+Shift+↑.

✦ Drag the text with the mouse.

To move the selected text down, use one of the following techniques:

✦ Click the Down button (shown in the margin) on the Outlining toolbar.

✦ Press Alt+Shift+↓.

✦ Drag the text with the mouse.

If you don't like the result of your move, you can always undo it by pressing Ctrl+Z.

Printing an Outline

You can quickly print an outline of your document by following these steps:

1. **Switch to Outline view.**

2. **Collapse or expand the outline to show just the portion of the outline you want to print.**

3. **Click the Show Formatting button if you don't want the outline to include heading formats.**

4. **Click the Print button on the Standard toolbar.**

   The outline prints.

A printed outline is no substitute for a Table of Contents. See Chapter 6 of this minibook for details on printing a Table of Contents — complete with page numbers.

Sorting a Document Alphabetically by Headings

If you are working on a document whose headings you want to appear in alphabetical order, Outline view can be a real timesaver. The following steps sort an entire document into alphabetical order based on the Heading 1 paragraphs. All body text and Heading 2 and lower headings travel along with their Heading 1 paragraph when sorted.

1. **Use View⇨Outline or click the Outline View button to switch to Outline view.**

2. **Choose Show Heading 1 from the Show Level drop-down list.**

   The entire outline collapses so that only Heading 1 paragraphs show.

3. **Press Ctrl+A to select the entire document.**

4. **Choose Table⇨Sort Text.**

   The Sort Text dialog box appears, as shown in Figure 3-3.

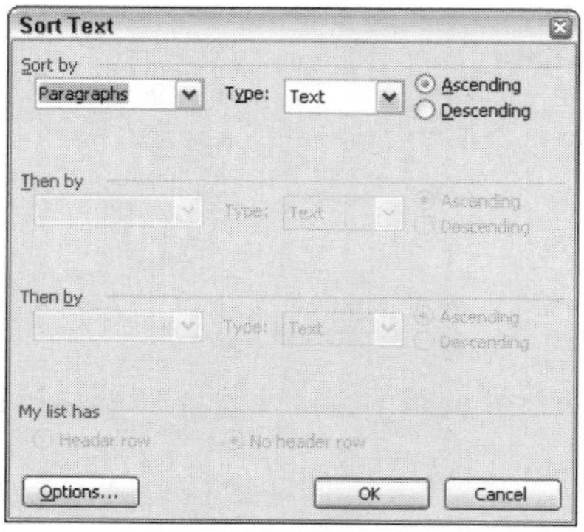

Figure 3-3:
The Sort Text dialog box.

5. **Click OK.**

   The headings are sorted.

6. **Click the Normal View button to return to Normal view.**

Using the Document Map

The *document map* is a handy way to view the headings that make up a document in a separate pane, as shown in Figure 3-4. When the document map is visible, you can scroll the text window to any location in the document by clicking a heading in the document map.

To display the document map, just click the Document Map button found on the Standard toolbar. To hide the document map, click the button again. You can also access the document map via View➪Document Map.

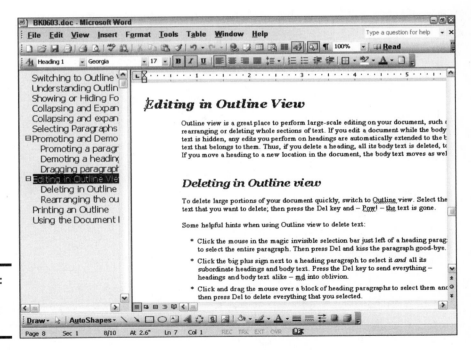

Figure 3-4:
Using the
document
map.

Chapter 4: Mystical Master Documents

In This Chapter

✔ Understanding master documents

✔ Creating a master document from scratch

✔ Inserting existing files into a master document

✔ Breaking down an existing document into smaller subdocuments

✔ Cool things to do after you make a master document

Suppose a great honor is bestowed upon you: serving as the moderator of this year's Neat Freaks Convention. As moderator, one of your jobs is assembling a little 1,200-page book titled *Neat Freaks '04: Proceedings of the Annual Neat Freaks Trade Show and Conference*. Notable Neat Freaks from all across the globe will present papers, and your job is to assemble all of these documents into one huge book. Fortunately for you, the International Neat Freak Association (INFA) has adopted Word 2003 as its standard word processor, so each neat freak of note will send you a document on disk. All you have to do is combine the files into a single document and print them.

This job is definitely for Word's Master Document feature. It lets you create long documents by piecing them together from small documents. Master documents are all very confusing and worth figuring out only if you have to do this sort of thing often. If you find yourself needing to read this chapter, I offer my sincerest condolences.

You probably shouldn't tackle master documents until you have a pretty good understanding of Word's Outline view because the Master Document feature is sort of an advanced form of outlining. If you haven't yet read Chapter 3 of this minibook, I'd go back and read it now if I were you.

What Is a Master Document?

A *master document* contains special links to other documents, which are called *subdocuments*. If you are putting together a book that consists of 30 chapters, for example, you probably don't want to put the entire book into one document. Instead you probably want to create a separate document for each chapter. That's all well and good, but what happens when you want to print the whole thing with page numbers that begin at page one and run through the end of the book rather than restart at page one at the beginning of each chapter? Or what if you want to print a Table of Contents for the book or create an index?

That's where master documents come in. With a master document, you create each chapter as a separate document. Then you create a master document for the entire book. In the master document, you create links to each of the chapters or subdocuments. Then you can print the entire book, and Word takes care of numbering the pages for you. You can also create a Table of Contents or index in the master document, and the page numbers automatically adjust.

Word has a whole separate view for working with master documents, called — drumroll, please — *Master Document view.* Master Document view is a variation of Outline view, except that little icons indicate the portions of the master documents that are subdocuments. You can double-click one of these icons to open a subdocument in a separate window to edit it.

For the most part, you use Master Document view to create a new master document, to change the order in which individual subdocuments appear in the master document, or to add or remove subdocuments. If all you want to do is edit one of the individual chapters in your book, you just open the chapter document as you normally do, without worrying about it being a subdocument in a master document.

If you open a master document and switch to Normal view or Page Layout view, Word treats the master document and all the subdocuments as though they are a part of one large document. You can scroll through the master document all the way to Chapter 12 and begin typing, for example, or you can use File⇨Print to print the entire book, or you can use Edit⇨Replace to replace all occurrences of *WordPerfect* with *Word* throughout the entire document.

You can assemble a master document in three ways:

✦ If you know that you need a master document beforehand, you can create the master document and all the subdocuments from scratch. This technique results in a master document and a collection of empty subdocuments, which you can then call up and edit as you see fit. See the section, "Whipping Up a Master Document," later in this chapter.

✦ If you get part of the way into a project and realize, "Hey! This document is way too long! I should have used a master document," it's not too late. You can bust a big document into several smaller subdocuments. See the section "Break It Up!" later in this chapter.

✦ If you already have a bunch of Word documents you want to assemble into a master document, you can create a master document by using the existing documents as the subdocuments. See the section "Putting an Existing File into a Master Document," later in this chapter.

All this stuff about master documents is confusing, I'm sure, but it makes more sense when you begin to use them. (I promise.) Just to muddy the waters a little more, the following list shows you some additional things you need to know about master documents before I jump into the steps for creating and using them:

✦ In the master document, each subdocument is contained within its own section. Each subdocument, therefore, can have its own page layout, column arrangement, and any of the other niceties that go along with being in your own section.

✦ When you work in Master Document view, the Outlining toolbar appears and displays additional buttons specially designed to work with master documents. Table 4-1 summarizes each Master Document toolbar button's function.

Table 4-1	Buttons on the Master Document Toolbar
Button	*What It Does*
	Switches to Master Document view
	Collapses or expands a subdocument
	Breaks the selected text into subdocuments and assigns a filename based on the first heading in the subdocument
	Deletes the selected subdocument
	Inserts an existing file as a subdocument
	Combines two subdocument files into one subdocument file
	Splits a subdocument into two subdocuments
	Locks or unlocks a subdocument

◆ Basing the master document and all the subdocuments on the same templates is best. Otherwise, trying to figure out which styles, macros, and other template goodies are available is a nightmare.

◆ Word uses hyperlinks to indicate subdocuments, as shown in Figure 4-1. The hyperlink is underlined and displayed in blue so that you can recognize it quickly, as shown in Figure 4-1. To open a subdocument, all you have to do is click the subdocument's hyperlink. (For more information about hyperlinks, refer to Book V, Chapter 3.)

You can switch between Outline view and Master Document view by clicking the Master Document View button on the Outlining toolbar.

You can open a subdocument in two ways. The first way is to open the master document. Word displays any subdocuments contained in the master document as hyperlinks. To open a subdocument, all you have to do is click the subdocument's hyperlink. Alternatively, you can ignore the master document and open the subdocument file the way you open any other Word document: by using File⇨Open or clicking the Open button on the Standard toolbar.

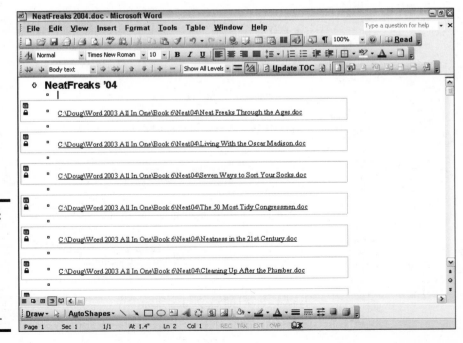

Figure 4-1:
A master document with subdocuments shown as hyperlinks.

If you have a network and more than one person is involved with the creation of your documents, Word keeps track of who owns which subdocument, based on the Author Name field of the subdocuments. Before you can edit a subdocument that someone else created, you must unlock it by clicking the Lock/Unlock button on the Master Document toolbar.

 You can spread the master document and its subdocuments across different folders and can even live on different computers if you have a network. Life is much easier, however, if you create a separate folder for just the master document and all its subdocuments. If more than one person is working on the project, place this folder on a shared network disk so that everyone involved in the project can access it.

Whipping Up a Master Document

If none of the documents you want to combine by using a master document is created yet, the best way to begin is to create the master document and all its subdocuments at the same time. Then you can call up each subdocument individually to fill in the missing chapters of your book.

These steps show you the procedure for creating a master document and its subdocuments from scratch:

1. Choose File⇨New or click the New button.

2. Use View⇨Outline View.

 Outline view displays. You can also get to Outline view by clicking the Outline View button at the bottom left of the Word window (shown in the margin).

3. Click the Master Document View button on the Outlining toolbar.

 The Master Document portion of the Outlining toolbar activates.

4. Create a Heading 1 paragraph for the title of the master document.

If you're creating a book, for example, type the book's title as a Heading 1 paragraph.

5. Create a Heading 2 paragraph for each subdocument you want to create.

If each subdocument represents a chapter, type the chapter titles as Heading 2 paragraphs.

Figure 4-2 shows an example of a master document with a Heading 1 paragraph for the master document title and a Heading 2 paragraph for each subdocument title.

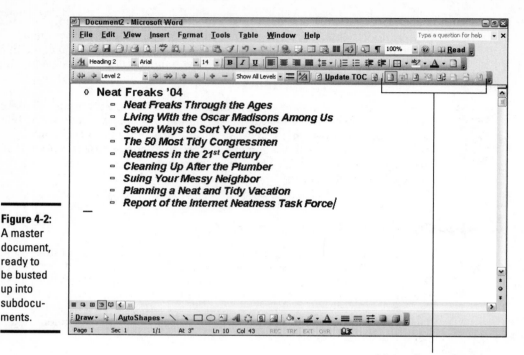

Figure 4-2:
A master
document,
ready to
be busted
up into
subdocu-
ments.

Master Document tools

6. Select the Heading 2 paragraphs.

Drag the mouse or hold down the Shift key while you move the cursor with the arrow keys. Each Heading 2 paragraph you select converts to a separate subdocument in the next step. (Make sure you don't select the Heading 1 paragraph at the beginning of the document.)

 7. Click the Create Subdocument button on the Master Document toolbar.

Clicking this button tells Word to bust up the selected heading paragraphs into smaller subdocuments, sort of like what the Justice Department would like to do to Microsoft.

8. Admire your handiwork.

Figure 4-3 shows a document that's been busted up. Notice how Word draws a box around each subdocument and adds a little subdocument icon in the top-left corner of the box.

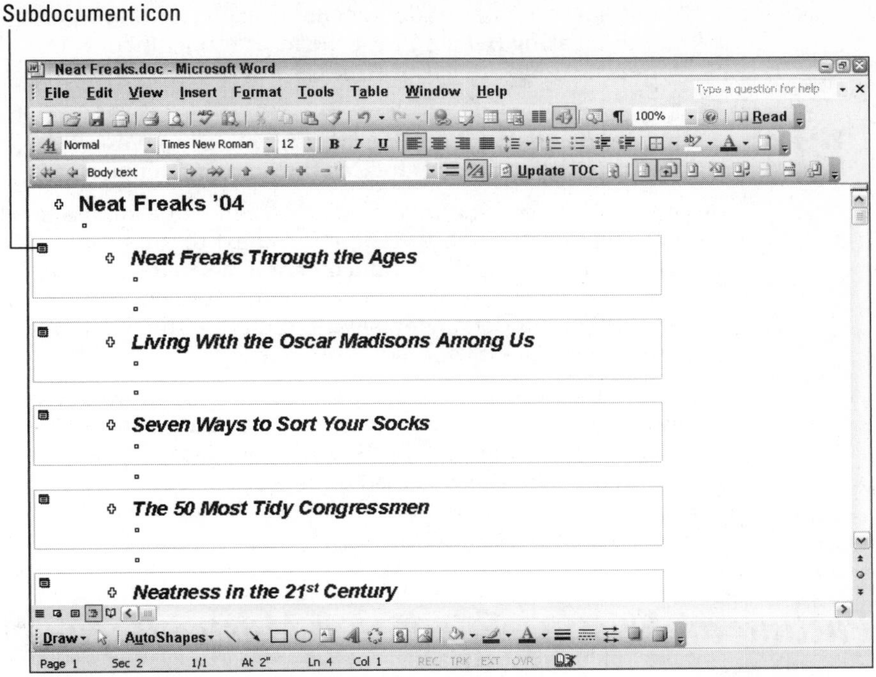

Subdocument icon

Figure 4-3:
You're
busted.

9. **Use File⇨Save to save the files.**

You have to provide the name and location of the master document. Word makes up names for all the subdocuments, using the first eight characters of the heading paragraph if possible.

10. **You're finished.**

Well, not quite. All you have is the outline of a book with a bunch of empty subdocuments. You still have to write the chapters!

Here are a few thoughts to keep in mind when you're creating a master document from scratch:

✦ You don't *have* to use the Heading 1 style for the master document title and Heading 2 for the subdocument titles. But doing so makes sense. Word examines the text you selected before you click the Create Subdocuments button to find the first Heading paragraph. Then it creates a separate subdocument for each paragraph in the selected text that's formatted with the same heading style as the first heading. If the first heading paragraph is formatted with the Heading 3 style, Word creates a separate subdocument for each Heading 3 paragraph. Most of the time, using Heading 1 for the master document title and Heading 2 for each subdocument title makes sense.

✦ The subdocuments aren't saved until you use File⇨Save to save the master document. Then Word automatically saves all the subdocuments in the same directory as the master document.

✦ After you create subdocuments, you can edit a subdocument by double-clicking the little subdocument icon next to the subdocument heading. This action opens the subdocument in a separate document window and leaves the master document open in its own window, too. After you finish editing the subdocument, save it and close the window to return to the master document window.

✦ Notice that the document shown in Figure 4-3 shows the contents of each subdocument in the master document window rather than just hyperlinks, as shown in Figure 4-1. When you close and reopen the document, the hyperlinks show instead of the actual subdocument text. Then, to edit a subdocument, press Ctrl while clicking the link to the subdocument you want to edit.

Putting an Existing File into a Master Document

If you (or your buddies) have already created a bunch of smaller files that you want to combine into one larger publication, you can plug each file into a master document as a subdocument. Then you can create a Table of Contents or an index for the whole publication or print the publication with uninterrupted page numbers.

Follow these steps to create a master document and insert existing documents into it as subdocuments:

1. **Using the My Computer window or Windows Explorer, copy the various files you need into a single folder.**

This step isn't strictly necessary, as creating a master document from subdocuments spread throughout your hard drive is acceptable. But life is simpler if the master document and all its subdocuments live together in a single folder.

2. **Click the New button.**

Or, if you're allergic to buttons, choose File⇨New, and then click the <u>Blank Document</u> link in the New Document task pane.

3. **Choose View⇨Outline (or click the Outline View button), and then click the Master Document View button.**

Word switches you into Master Document view.

4. **Click the Insert Subdocument button on the Master Document toolbar.**

   An Insert Subdocument dialog box appears. This dialog box is identical to the Open dialog box except for its name.

5. **Find the file you want to insert as a subdocument, choose it, and click Open.**

   The file is inserted into the master document as a subdocument. Word creates section breaks before and after it.

6. **Repeat Steps 4 and 5 for any other subdocuments you want to insert.**

7. **Use File⇨Save to save the master document.**

8. **You're finished.**

Here are a few points to ponder when you insert subdocuments into a master document:

+ Inserting a subdocument doesn't change the subdocument file's filename or folder location.

+ When you click the Insert Subdocument button, the subdocument is inserted at the position of the insertion point. Make sure that the insertion point is either at the beginning or end of the master document or between two previously inserted subdocuments. If the insertion point is within a subdocument when you click the Insert Subdocument button, the subdocument you select is inserted *within* the subdocument, not within the master document. If you're not careful, you can end up with subdocuments within subdocuments within subdocuments, kind of like those fancy Russian nesting dolls.

The contents of the subdocument file do not copy into the master document. Instead, a link to the subdocument file is created so that whenever you open the master document, you access the subdocument file also. You can still open the subdocument file separately, apart from the master document.

Break It Up!

Sometimes a project just gets out of hand. It starts out as a half-page memo about where to keep spare pencils and ends up being a 300-page office-procedures manual. You obviously wouldn't use a master document for the half-page memo (unless you're really bored), but somewhere around page 100 you may wish that you had. No problem! Just bust up the big document into two or more subdocuments.

Follow these steps to break a large document into smaller subdocuments:

1. **Open the document.**

2. **Choose View⇨Outline (or click the Outline View button), and then click the Master Document View button on the Outlining toolbar to switch to Master Document view.**

3. **Change the headings to make each section of text you want to become a subdocument begin with a Heading 2 style.**

The most logical thing is to format the document title as a Heading 1 and each subdocument as a Heading 2. You may have to use the Promote and Demote buttons to accomplish this task. Bother. (For more information about promoting and demoting, refer to Chapter 3 of this minibook.)

4. **Select the range of text you want to convert into subdocuments, beginning with the heading for the first subdocument and ending with the last paragraph of the last subdocument.**

5. **Click the Create Subdocument button.**

Word breaks up the document into smaller subdocuments based on the heading paragraphs and inserts section breaks before and after each subdocument.

6. **Call up File⇨Save to save your work.**

The master document saves, as does each of the subdocuments. Word retains the name of the original file for the master document and makes up names for the subdocuments, using the first eight characters of each subdocument's heading, if possible.

7. **You're finished!**

Celebrate by taking the rest of the day off.

You can promote or demote all the headings in a document by selecting the entire document (press Ctrl+A) and then by clicking the Promote or Demote buttons on the Outlining toolbar.

Numbering Subdocument Pages Consecutively

When you use a master document, you can number all the pages of your publication consecutively. In other words, the first page of a subdocument is one greater than the last page of the subdocument that precedes it.

These steps show you the procedure:

1. **Open the master document.**

You can work in Normal view or Master Document view, but you have to be working with the master document, not with an individual subdocument.

2. **Call up View⇨Header and Footer.**

Word temporarily throws you into Page Layout view, confines you to the header area of the page, and throws the Headers and Footers toolbar up on-screen.

 To add a footer rather than a header, click the Switch Between Header and Footer button.

3. **Format the header or footer to include a page number.**

 Type whatever text you want to include in the header or footer. To add a page number, click the Page Numbers button.

4. **Click the Close button when you're happy with the header or footer.**

Word returns you to Normal view or Master Document view.

5. **Print the master document and check the page numbers.**

Pretty cool, eh?

 If you want each subdocument to begin on a new page, add the Page Break Before option to the Heading 2 style's Paragraph format (or whatever style you use for the title of each subdocument). You can find the Page Break Before option on the Text Flow tab of the Format⇨Paragraph command.

Chapter 5: So You Want to Make an Index, Eh?

In This Chapter

- ✔ Marking index entries
- ✔ Creating an index
- ✔ Marking a range of pages
- ✔ Building an index from a list of words
- ✔ Creating subentries
- ✔ Creating cross-references
- ✔ Updating an index

*I*f all you ever use Word for is to create one- and two-page memos on mundane subjects, such as how to clean the coffee maker, you can skip this chapter. After all, you don't need an index for a two-page memo on coffee maker cleaning unless you work at the Pentagon. If, on the other hand, your memo turns into a 200-page policy manual on appliance maintenance, an index may well be in order.

As luck has it, Word just happens to have a most excellent indexing feature that can help you with the tedious task of indexing. It doesn't create the index for you automatically, but it does help you identify which words to include in the index, and Word compiles and formats the index from the words you mark without too much complaining.

Creating an index is a three-stage affair. First, you must mark all the words and phrases within your document that you want to appear in the index. Second, you call on the Insert⇨Reference⇨Index and Tables command to create the index. This command takes all the words and phrases you mark, sorts them in alphabetical order, and combines identical entries. Third, you carefully review the index, lament that Word didn't do a better job, and fix what you can.

I've indexed quite a few books in my day, and I have yet to find a word processor with an indexing feature that really does the trick. Word is no exception. It does a better job than any other word processors I've had the pleasure of working with, but you should still be prepared to do a ton of work yourself.

You can mark the words you want to include in an index in two ways: manually, marking each word one by one; or automatically, giving Word a list of words you want in the index and letting it mark the words in the document. First I show you the manual way and then, later in the chapter, I show you the automatic way (in the section, "Isn't There an Easier Way?").

Mark Those Index Entries

The first — and most important — task in creating an index is to mark the words or phrases you want to include in the index. The most common way to do that is to insert an index marker in the document at each occurrence of each item you want to appear in the index.

To mark index entries manually, follow these steps as long as you can stay awake:

1. **Choose File⇨Open to open the document you want to index.**

2. **Highlight the word or phrase you want in the index by using the mouse or the keyboard.**

Start at the beginning of the document and select those items you deem worthy of an entry in the index.

3. **Press the keyboard shortcut Alt+Shift+X.**

Alt+Shift+X is one of Word's more memorable keyboard shortcuts, to be sure. It pops up the Mark Index Entry dialog box, shown in Figure 5-1.

Figure 5-1:
The Mark
Index Entry
dialog box.

4. **Double-check the contents in the Main Entry field. If correct, click the Mark button. If not, correct it and then click Mark.**

The text does not have to appear in the index exactly as it appears in the document. You may highlight an abbreviation to include in the index, for example, but then edit the Main Entry field so that the full spelling of the word, rather than the abbreviation, appears in the index.

5. **To index an entry under a different word, type the alternative entry in the Main Entry field and click the Mark button again.**

   For example, you may want to create an entry for "mutt, mangy" in addition to "mangy mutt."

6. **Mark any additional index entries by highlighting them in the document and clicking the Mark button.**

   The Mark Index Entry dialog box works somewhat like the Spelling dialog box in the way it stays on-screen so that you can efficiently mark additional index entries. So, while the Mark Index Entry dialog box remains visible, you can select the text for another index entry, and then click Mark to mark it. You can keep indexing for as long as you have the energy.

7. **After you mark each of the index entries you want, click the Close button.**

The index entries are marked with special codes formatted as hidden text so that you can't normally see them and they don't print. They are there, however, waiting to be counted when you create the index.

Here are some timely tips for preparing your index entries:

+ The most efficient way to create an index is after you write and edit your document. Set aside some time to work through the document with the Mark Index Entry dialog box. Don't bother to create index entries as you write your document; it just slows you down and distracts you from your primary task: writing.

+ Another way to summon the Mark Index Entry dialog box is to call up Insert➪Reference➪Index and Tables, click the Index tab, and then click the Mark Entry button.

+ If you come across a word or phrase while marking index entries that you know occurs elsewhere in your document, click the Mark All button. By clicking the Mark All button, you create an index entry not only for the selected text, but also for any other occurrence of the selected text within the document.

+ Each time you mark an index entry, Word activates the All check box of the Tools➪Options command's View tab. The All check box then reveals not only the hidden text used to mark index entries, but also other characters normally hidden from view, such as field codes, tab characters, optional hyphens, and so on. This behavior is normal, so don't be surprised when it happens. To return your display to normal, just click the Show/Hide button on the Standard toolbar (shown in the margin).

✦ Index entries look something like this: { XE "mangy mutt" }, formatted as hidden text. You can edit the index entry text (the part between quotation marks) if you want to change an index entry after you create it.

Creating an Index

After you mark the index entries, the process of generating the index is relatively easy. Here are the steps:

1. **Move the insertion point to the place where you want the index to appear.**

The index generally begins on a new page near the end of the document. Press Ctrl+Enter to create a new page if necessary, and click the mouse to position the insertion pointer on the empty page. You may want to add a heading, such as Index, at the top of the page.

2. **Call up Insert⇨Reference⇨Index and Tables and click the Index tab.**

The Index and Tables dialog box appears, as shown in Figure 5-2.

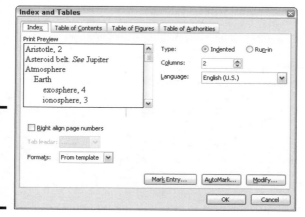

Figure 5-2:
The Index tab of the Index and Tables dialog box.

3. **Choose the index style that you want from the Formats list.**

As you click the various formats, the Preview window shows how the resulting index will appear.

4. **Play with the other controls in the Index tab to fine-tune the index.**

- **Type:** Lets you place index subentries on separate indented lines (Indented) or run together (Run-in).

- **Columns:** Sets the number of columns you want in the index. Two is the norm.

- **Language:** If you have multiple language options installed in Word, you can select the language to use in this drop-down list.

- **Right Align Page Numbers:** Check this box if you want the page numbers placed at the right edge of the index.

- **Tab Leader:** Changes or removes the dotted line that connects each index entry to its page number. You can only remove the dotted line when you select the Right Align Page Numbers option.

- **Formats:** Lets you choose one of several preset formats for the index. Or, you can specify From Template to use styles in the document's template to determine the formatting for the index.

5. Click OK.

The index is inserted into the document.

If the index looks like { INDEX \r \h "A" \c "2" }, call up Tools⇔Options, click the View tab, and uncheck the Field Codes check box. Click OK, and the index appears correctly.

To delete an index, select the entire index and then press the Delete key.

The entries in an index format with a set of standard styles named Index 1, Index 2, Index 3, and so on. If you don't like any of the predefined formats listed in the Formats list in the Index and Tables dialog box, choose From Template in the Formats list and then click the Modify button. A special version of the Style dialog box appears listing only the standard Index styles. You can then change the appearance of your index by modifying the various Index styles.

Updating an Index

Whenever you edit your document, you run the risk of messing up the index. Even a slight change can push text from the bottom of one page to the top of the next and possibly invalidate the index. Fortunately, this section gives you several ways to keep your index up to date.

In the Tools⇔Options dialog box, click the Print tab, check the Update Fields check box, and then click OK. Word automatically updates the index every time you print your document.

To update an index without printing the document, select the index and press F9. If you point to the index and click the right mouse button, the shortcut menu that appears includes an Update Field command. Using this command works the same as pressing F9.

Marking a Range of Pages

If a particular topic is discussed for several pages in your document, you may want to create an index entry that marks a range of pages (for example, 26-29) rather than each page individually (26, 27, 28, 29).

Unfortunately, the procedure for marking page ranges isn't as slick as it could be. You have to mess around with a Word doohickey called a bookmark. A *bookmark* is a name you can assign to a selection of text. You usually use bookmarks to mark locations in your document so that you can get back to them later, but they have all sorts of more interesting uses. Marking a range of pages for an index is just one.

To use a bookmark for range of pages, follow these steps (it gets tricky, so hang on to your hat):

1. **Highlight the entire range of text you want included in the index entry's page range.**

A long discussion of a single topic could go on for pages, so be prepared.

2. **Call up Insert⇨Bookmark.**

The Bookmark dialog box appears, as shown in Figure 5-3.

Figure 5-3:
The
Bookmark
dialog box.

3. **Type a bookmark name to identify the bookmark.**

Bookmark names can be as long as 40 characters and can be made up of any combination of letters and numbers. Spaces aren't allowed, but you can use an underscore to double as a space.

4. **Click Add to create the bookmark.**

5. **Position the cursor at the beginning of the bookmark and press Alt+Shift+X.**

    The Mark Index Entry dialog box appears.

6. **Type the text you want to appear in the index in the Main Entry field.**

7. **Select the Page Range option.**

8. **Choose the bookmark you just created from the list of bookmark names in the Bookmark drop-down list box.**

    All the bookmarks in the current document appear in this drop-down list.

9. **Click the Mark button to create the index entry.**

After you create the bookmark and an index entry naming the bookmark, the index includes the range of page numbers for the entry.

The location of various bookmarks in your document are indicated by large brackets in the text. These brackets appear only if you check the Bookmarks option with the Tools⇨Options command (View tab).

Make the bookmark name as close to identical to the index entry text as you can. Use underscore characters rather than spaces: master_document for master document, for example.

Creating Subentries

A *subentry* is used when a word is used for two different meanings or when a word serves as a category organizer for several related words. For example, you may want to create an index entry that looks like the following example:

> crew
>
> > Kirk, James T., 15
> >
> > McCoy, Leonard H., 16
> >
> > Scott, Montgomery, 16
> >
> > Spock, Mr., 17

Here, the index entries for Kirk, McCoy, Scott, and Spock are all subentries of the main entry: crew.

To create index subentries, you follow the normal procedure for marking index entries. You type text for both the main entry and the subentry, however, in the Mark Index Entry dialog box. Each of the preceding index entries, for example, has crew for the Main Entry field and the individual crew member's name as the subentry.

You can create a subentry directly in the Main Entry field by typing the main entry, a colon, and the subentry. For example, type **crew:Kirk, James T.** to create *Kirk, James T.* as a subentry of *crew*.

See Also . . .

A cross-reference is one of those annoying messages signaling that you're about to embark on a wild goose chase:

crew, see cast.

To create a cross-reference, begin by marking an index entry as you normally do. On the Mark Index Entry dialog box, check the Cross-reference option and then type some text in the accompanying text box. Word automatically merges the cross-reference with other index entries for the same text.

Isn't There an Easier Way?

Yet another way to create index entries is to use an *automark file,* which is simply a list of the words that you want Word to include in the index. Word then creates an index entry for each occurrence of each word in the list. Sounds like a great timesaver, eh? It is, sometimes.

Here are the steps:

1. **Create a new document for the word list.**

2. **Type the list of words you want to index, each on its own line.**

For example:

Kirk

Spock

McCoy

Scotty

3. **If you want the text in the index to be different from the text in the document, press the Tab key and then type the text exactly as you want it to appear in the index.**

For example:

Kirk   Kirk, James T.

Spock   Spock, Mr.

McCoy McCoy, Leonard H.

Scotty Scott, Montgomery

Note: You can have more than one line referring to the same index entry. For example:

McCoy   McCoy, Leonard H.

Bones   McCoy, Leonard H.

4. **Save the word list document by choosing File⇨Save.**

5. **Close the word list document by choosing File⇨Close.**

6. **Open the document you want to index with File⇨Open.**

7. **Call up Insert⇨Reference⇨Index and Tables and click the Index tab.**

    The Index and Tables dialog box pushes its way to the front. If the Index tab isn't on top, click it to bring the indexing options into view.

8. **Click the AutoMark button.**

    A dialog box similar to the File Open dialog box appears.

9. **Find the file you saved in Step 4, choose it, and click Open.**

10. **Hold your breath while Word adds the index entries.**

    If your word list or the document is long, adding the index may take a while. Be patient.

11. **Select the index and press F9 to update your index with the marks added in Step 10.**

    It's done.

**Book VI
Chapter 5**

So You Want to
Make an Index, Eh?

After the automatic index entries are created, you probably want to work your way through the document by creating additional index entries.

Unfortunately, the AutoMark option doesn't account for running discussions of a single topic that span several pages. It results in index entries such as *Vogons, 14, 15, 16, 17, 18* that should read *Vogons, 14-18*.

When you use tabs to separate the keywords used to locate the items to index and the actual text you want inserted in the index for those items, keep in mind that the tab-stop positions in the word list document don't matter.

If you want, you can use Word's Table feature to create the word list. Create a two-column table and use the first column for the text to find in the document and the second column for the text to include in the index.

Word sometimes refers to the word list as a *concordance.* Just thought you'd want to know.

Chapter 6: Creating a Table of Contents or Table of Figures

In This Chapter

✔ **Formatting your document to make a Table of Contents easy to create**

✔ **Creating a Table of Contents**

✔ **Using other styles to create a Table of Contents**

✔ **Creating a table of figures or other similar tables**

✔ **Updating a Table of Contents or tables of figures**

*I*n the old days, creating a Table of Contents for a book, manual, or other long document was a two-step affair. First you created the Table of Contents, leaving blanks or Xs where the page numbers eventually went. Then after the pages of the document were in their final form, you browsed through the entire document, made a list of the page numbers for each chapter, and went back to the Table of Contents and changed all the Xs to the actual correct page numbers.

Now, assuming that you format your document properly, creating a Table of Contents is a matter of clicking the mouse a few times. Word assembles the Table of Contents for you using the headings you cleverly placed throughout your document. And it takes care of the drudgery of counting pages and even adjusts the Table of Contents for you if you make changes to the document that affect page numbers in the table.

This chapter shows you all the ins and outs of making a Table of Contents. It also shows you how to create a table of figures or other types of similar tables.

The term Table of Contents is a little cumbersome to use over and over again throughout this chapter. Being a bit of a computer nerd myself, I kind of like using TLAs (three-letter acronyms). So I frequently use *TOC* to stand for Table of Contents in this chapter, if for no other reason than to save paper.

Understanding Tables of Contents

A Table of Contents is simply a list of the headings that appear in a document, typically with the page number for each heading as shown in Figure 6-1. Word can create a Table of Contents for you automatically based on the heading paragraphs in your document.

Table of Contents

Figure 6-1:
A simple
Table of
Contents.

The Table of Contents feature is one of several Word features that depend on the proper use of styles for trouble-free operation. When you create a table of contents, Word searches through your document and looks for heading paragraphs to include in the table. How on earth does Word know which paragraphs are supposed to be headings? By looking at the style you assign to each paragraph: You format the heading paragraphs with heading styles, such as Heading 1, Heading 2, and so on.

If you plan to create a Table of Contents, make sure that you use heading styles to format your document's headings, especially those headings that you want to appear in the TOC. You should do this anyway, of course: Styles help you format all your headings consistently, and let you take advantage of Word's Outline view (see Chapter 3 of this minibook for more on outlines).

Word provides three shortcut keys for applying heading styles:

Shortcut Key	*Description*
Ctrl+Alt+1	Heading 1
Ctrl+Alt+2	Heading 2
Ctrl+Alt+3	Heading 3

If you routinely use additional heading styles for additional heading levels, you can assign those styles to keyboard shortcuts, such as Ctrl+Alt+4, Ctrl+Alt+5, and so on, by using Tools⇨Customize (Book VIII, Chapter 2) or Format⇨Style (Book II, Chapter 3).

If you want, you can tell Word to use different styles to create a TOC. If you format your chapter titles with a Chapter Title style, for example, you can tell Word to include paragraphs formatted with the Chapter Title style in the TOC. For more information, see the section "Beyond Heading Styles" later in this chapter.

Word can also create a Table of Contents for a Web page. The Web TOC enables quick document navigation for pages that use frames. For more information, see Book V, Chapter 5.

Creating a Table of Contents

If you assign heading styles to your document's headings, creating a Table of Contents is easy. Just follow these simple steps:

1. **Move the insertion point to the place where you want the Table of Contents to appear.**

The TOC generally appears on its own page near the beginning of a document. Press Ctrl+Enter to create a new page if necessary, and click the mouse to position the insertion pointer in the empty page.

You may want to add a heading, such as Contents or Table of Contents, at the top of the page. Format this heading however you want, but don't use one of the heading styles unless you want the TOC to include the page number of the Table of Contents.

2. **Call up Insert⇨Reference⇨Index and Tables and click the Table of Contents tab.**

The dialog box appears, as shown in Figure 6-2.

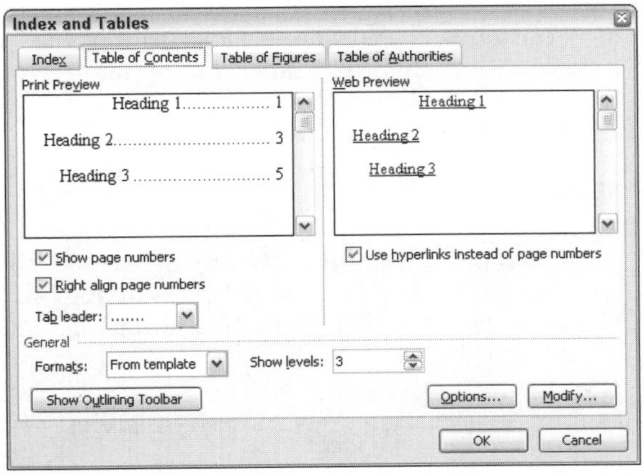

Figure 6-2:
The Table
of Contents
tab of the
Index and
Tables
dialog box.

3. **Choose the Table of Contents style you want from the Formats list.**

   As you click the various formats, the Preview window shows how the resulting TOC will appear.

4. **Play with the other controls to fine-tune the Table of Contents.**

   • **Show Page Numbers:** Uncheck this box if you want the TOC to show the document's outline but not page numbers.

   • **Right Align Page Numbers:** Uncheck this box if you want the page numbers placed right next to the corresponding text rather than at the right margin.

   • **Tab Leader:** Use this drop-down list to change or remove the dotted line that connects each TOC entry to its page number.

   • **Formats:** Use this drop-down list to choose one of several pre-defined formats for the Table of Contents.

   • **Show Levels:** Use this control to specify which heading levels to include in the table.

5. **Click OK.**

   The TOC is inserted into the document.

Here are some things to remember when you compile a TOC:

✦ If the Table of Contents looks like {TOC \o "1-3" \p " "}, call up Tools⇨Options, click the View tab, and uncheck the Field Codes check box. Click OK and the table appears correctly.

✦ You can make changes directly to a TOC by clicking in the table and typing, but that's a bad idea because any changes you make are lost the next time you regenerate the Table of Contents. See the section, "Updating Tables of Contents or Figures," for more information.

✦ Unfortunately, Word doesn't add Chapter 1 in front of the TOC entry for Chapter 1. If you want chapter numbers to appear in your TOC, you must include them in the paragraphs formatted with a style that is included in the TOC (such as Heading 1).

✦ To delete a TOC, select the entire table and then press the Delete key.

✦ Word formats entries in a TOC with a set of standard styles named TOC 1, TOC 2, TOC 3, and so on. If you don't like any of the predefined formats listed in the Formats list in the Index and Tables dialog box (refer to Figure 6-2), choose From Template from the Formats list and click the Modify button. A special version of the Style dialog box appears, which shows only the standard TOC styles. You can then change the appearance of your table by modifying the various TOC styles.

Beyond Heading Styles

Using the standard heading styles to create a Table of Contents is convenient but not always exactly what you want to do. What if you created a document that consists of several chapters and you marked the title of each chapter with a Chapter Title style ? Fortunately, Word lets you create a Table of Contents based on paragraphs formatted with any style you want, not just the standard heading styles.

Only a crazy person would use fields to create a Table of Contents

Because of styles, compiling a Table of Contents in Word is as easy as pie — as easy as popping a frozen pie in the oven, that is. The Table of Contents equivalent of baking a pie from scratch is using fields rather than styles to create the TOC. The only real reason to use fields is if you want the text that appears in the TOC to vary slightly from the document text on which you base the TOC. You may want to add "Chapter 1" in front of the title for Chapter 1, for example.

To create a TOC from fields rather than from styles, you first must insert special TC fields throughout your document wherever you want a TOC entry created. Here are the painful steps for inserting these fields:

1. **Place the insertion pointer where you want to insert the TC field.**

2. **Call up Insert⇨Field.**

   The Field dialog box appears.

3. **Choose Index and Tables from the Categories list.**

4. **Choose TC from the Field Names list.**

5. **In the Text Entry field, type the text that you want to include in the TOC in quotation marks immediately after the TC field code, as shown in this example:**

   ```
   Chapter 1: I Am Born
   ```

6. **Click OK or press Enter.**

The field is inserted in the document at the cursor location. It looks something like this:

```
{ TC "Chapter 1: I Am Born" }
```

Word formats it as hidden text, so you may not be able to see it. If you can't, call up Tools⇨Options, click the View tab, check the Hidden Text check box, and then click OK.

After you insert all the TC fields, you create the TOC by using Insert⇨Reference⇨Index and Tables, the same as when you base the TOC on styles. Click the Options button and then check the Table Entry Fields check box in the Table of Contents Options dialog box. Click OK to return to the Table of Contents dialog box, and then click OK again to compile the table.

To create a Table of Contents by using styles other than the standard heading styles, follow these steps:

1. **Call up Insert⇨Reference⇨Index and Tables and click the Table of Contents tab.**

   The Table of Contents dialog box appears.

2. **Click the Options button.**

   The Table of Contents Options dialog box appears, as shown in Figure 6-3. This dialog box lists all the styles available in the document and lets you assign a Table of Contents level to each style.

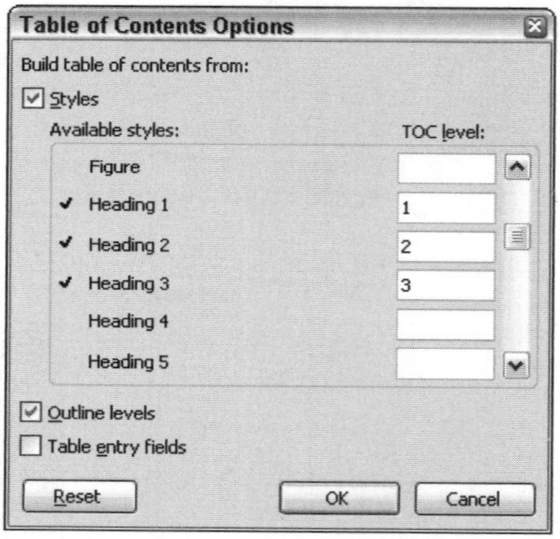

Figure 6-3: The Table of Contents Options dialog box.

3. **Adjust the TOC level fields to reflect the styles you want to include in your Table of Contents.**

   The TOC level fields initially are set to include standard heading styles, but that's easy to change. To exclude a style from the Table of Contents, select the style's TOC level field and delete the number in the field. To add a style to the Table of Contents, choose the style's TOC level field and type the outline level you want that style to represent.

4. **Click OK to return to the Table of Contents dialog box.**

5. **Click OK again to insert the Table of Contents.**

   Voilà! You're finished.

Keep in mind the following when using styles other than the standard style to create a Table of Contents:

✦ The initial settings for the TOC level fields reflect the Show Levels setting in the Table of Contents dialog box (refer to Figure 6-2). If you plan to exclude the standard heading levels from your Table of Contents, set the Show Levels drop-down list to 1 before calling up the Table of Contents Options dialog box. Then you have to clear only the TOC level field for the Heading 1 style.

✦ If you really mess up the Table of Contents options, you can click the Reset button to return everything to the default settings.

✦ No rule says that the styles you include in the Table of Contents all have to appear at different levels. Suppose that you want to include paragraphs formatted with the Chapter Title, Preface Title, Foreword Title, and Appendix Title styles in the Table of Contents at the top level. No problem. Just type 1 in the TOC level field for each of these styles in the Table of Contents Options dialog box.

Creating a Table of Figures or Other Similar Tables

Tables of Contents aren't the only kind of tables you can create with the Insert⇨Reference⇨Index and Tables command. You can also use this command to compile tables of figures, tables, equations, or other similar collectibles. Chapter 5 of this minibook shows how to use this command to create an index, and Chapter 7 of this minibook shows how to create a table of authorities for legal documents.

These steps show you how to create tables of figures or other similar tables:

1. **Choose Insert⇨Reference⇨Caption to create a caption for each item you want to include in the table.**

   Figure 6-4 shows the Caption dialog box. Choose the type of caption you want to create (Figure, Table, or Equation) in the Label field. Then type the caption in the Caption field. After you finish, click OK.

   Repeat this step for every caption you want to insert.

2. **Move the insertion pointer to where you want to insert the table.**

3. **Call up Insert⇨Reference⇨Index and Tables and click the Table of Figures tab.**

   Figure 6-5 shows the resulting dialog box.

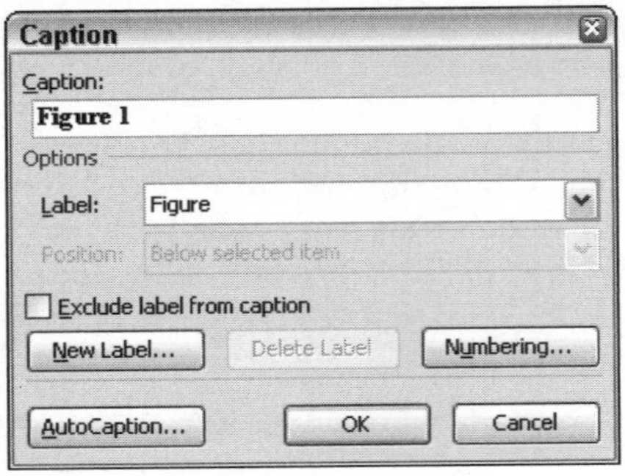

Figure 6-4:
The Caption dialog box.

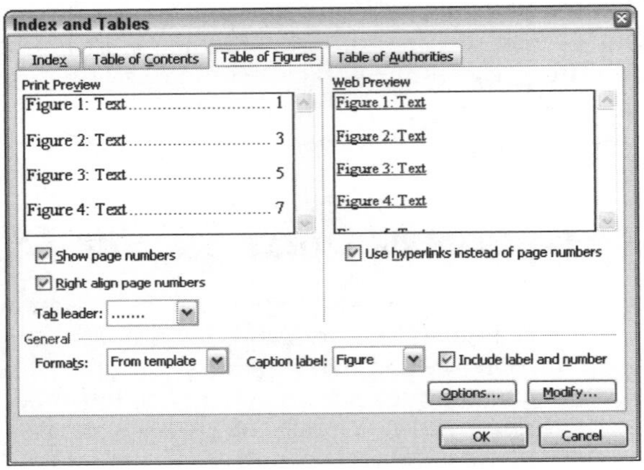

Figure 6-5:
The Table of Figures tab of the Index and Tables dialog box.

4. Choose the type of table you want to create from the Caption Label list.

The Caption Label setting corresponds to the Label setting in the Caption dialog box. To create a table of all figure captions, for example, choose Figure in the Caption Label field.

5. Choose the style you want from the Formats list.

As you click the various formats, the Preview window shows how the resulting table appears.

6. Fiddle with the other controls to fine-tune the table's appearance.

- **Show Page Numbers:** Uncheck this box if you want the table to list the captions but not page numbers.

- **Right Align Page Numbers:** Uncheck this box if you want the page numbers placed right next to the corresponding text rather than at the right margin.

- **Tab Leader:** Use this drop-down list to add or remove the dotted line that connects each table entry with its page number.

- **Formats:** Use this drop-down list to choose one of several pre-defined formats for the table of figures.

- **Caption Label:** Use this drop-down list to choose whether you want to build a table of figures, a table of equations, or a table of tables.

- **Include Label and Number:** Uncheck this box if you want the table to include the caption text (for example, "A Heffalump and a Woozle" or "Ratio of Red M&Ms") but not the number (for example, Figure 1 or Table 3).

7. Click OK.

The table is inserted into the document.

Book VI
Chapter 6

Creating a Table
of Contents or
Table of Figures

Here are some things to remember when you compile a table of figures or other similar tables:

✦ If the table looks like { TOC \c "Figure" }, call up Tools⇨Options, click the View button, and uncheck the Field Codes check box. Click OK and the table appears correctly.

✦ Word is set up to create captions and tables for equations, figures, and tables. If you want to create other types of captions and tables — for limericks or cartoons, for example — you can add items to the list of labels that appears in the Caption and Table of Figures dialog boxes. Call up Insert⇨Reference⇨Caption and click the New Label button. Then type a new label (such as Limerick or Cartoon) and click OK. Type the caption text and click OK to insert the first caption of the new type. Later, when you call up Insert⇨Reference⇨Index and Tables and click the Table of Figures tab, the label you created appears in the Caption Label list.

✦ For more information about captions, see Book IV, Chapter 4.

If you detest the Insert⇨Reference⇨Caption command, type your captions as separate paragraphs and create a style for them. Then call up Insert⇨Reference⇨Index and Tables, click the Table of Figures tab, and click the Options button. Check the Style check box, and choose the style you used to format the captions.

To delete a table of figures, select the entire table, and press the Delete key.

The entries in a table of figures are formatted with a standard Table of Figures style. If you don't like any of the predefined formats listed in the Formats list in the Index and Tables dialog box, choose From Template and click the Modify button. A special version of the Style dialog box appears, showing only the standard Table of Figures style. You can then change the appearance of your table by modifying the Table of Figures style.

Updating Tables of Contents or Figures

As you edit your document, the Table of Contents or table of figures you create will likely become out of date. The page numbers may change, you may delete headings or captions, or you may insert headings or captions.

When you print your document, you can make sure that your tables are up to date in several ways:

✦ Call up Tools➪Options, click the Print tab, check the Update Fields check box, and then click OK. Any tables and other fields in the document automatically update every time you print your document.

✦ To update a table without printing the document, select the table and press F9. A dialog box appears, asking whether you want to just refresh the table's page numbers or completely rebuild the table. Just refreshing the page numbers is faster, but it doesn't account for items you added or deleted since you created the table.

✦ If you point to a table and click the right mouse button, the shortcut menu that appears includes an Update Field command. Using this command works the same as pressing F9.

✦ To update all tables in your document, press Ctrl+A to select the entire document and then press F9.

Don't forget to save your file after you update the tables.

Chapter 7: Objection, Your Honor (Creating a Table of Authorities)

In This Chapter

✔ Marking citations

✔ Creating a table of authorities

✔ Adding your own categories

✔ Updating a table of authorities

✔ Disclaimer of warranties and limit of liability

*I*nasmuch as you, hereinafter referred to as the *reader,* have deemed it necessary, appropriate, and befitting to create, prepare, and otherwise compile a table, list, or enumeration of various and sundry citations, references, and quotations from legal authorities and other sources, including, but not limited to, cases, statutes, rules, treatises, regulations, constitutional provisions, and other authorities occurring within and among documents, files, and other materials prepared with the word-processing software known as Microsoft Word 2003, hereinafter referred to as *Word,* now therefore and thereupon I, hereinafter referred to as *I,* agree to provide within this chapter a thorough and comprehensive description, discussion, and presentation of the techniques, methods, and procedures required to prepare such aforementioned tables, lists, or enumerations. In consideration hitherto, so let it be written, so let it be done.

In other words, this chapter shows you how to use Word's Table of Authorities feature. If you're a lawyer or legal secretary, you already know what a table of authorities is. If you aren't, put this book down before it's too late.

Creating a table of authorities is much like creating an index. First you mark the citations where they appear within the document. Then you use Insert⇨ Reference⇨Index and Tables to compile the table of authorities based on the citations you marked. If necessary, you can then edit the table or adjust its formatting. You can also update the table to make sure that all the entries are up to date.

Marking Citations

The first step in creating a table of authorities is reviewing the entire document and marking any citations you want to include in the table. Follow these steps:

1. **Find a citation you want to mark.**

   Start at the beginning of the document and work through the whole thing, marking citations as you go. You can simply read through the document to find citations or you can let Word find the citations for you.

2. **When you find a citation you want to mark, highlight it with the mouse or keyboard and press Alt+Shift+I.**

   The Mark Citation dialog box appears, as shown in Figure 7-1.

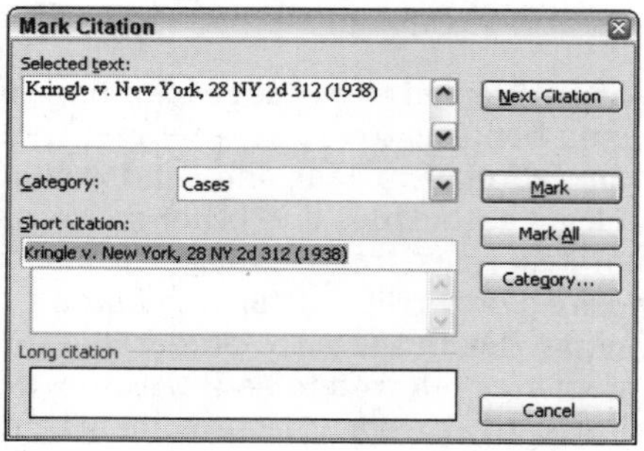

Figure 7-1:
The Mark
Citation
dialog box.

3. **Edit the Selected Text field so that it is exactly the way you want the citation to appear in the table of authorities.**

   The Selected text field initially contains the text that you selected when you pressed Alt+Shift+I. If the citation in the document isn't how you want it to appear in the table of authorities, click in the Selected Text field and type away. If you want to split the citation into two lines, just position the cursor where you want the line to split and press the Enter key.

4. **Edit the Short Citation field so that it exactly matches the way the short version of the citation is used in subsequent references throughout the document.**

   The first time you cite an authority, you must provide a complete citation (such as "Kringle v. New York, 28 NY 2d 312 (1938)"), but thereafter you use the short form ("Kringle v. New York"). Edit the Short Citation field to match the short form of the citation. That way, Word can automatically locate subsequent citations and mark them.

5. **Choose the type of authority being cited from the Category list box.**

   Word comes equipped with several common categories: Cases, Statutes, Other Authorities, Rules, Treatises, Regulations, and Constitutional Provisions. You can also create your own categories.

6. **Click the Mark button to mark the citation.**

   Word inserts a hidden field code to mark the citation.

7. **The Mark Citation dialog box stays on-screen so that you can mark additional citations. Click the Next Citation button to find the next citation.**

   The Next Citation button searches for the next citation in the document by looking for text that is commonly found in citations, such as v.

8. **Highlight the complete text of the citation found by the Next Citation button.**

   The Next Citation button doesn't highlight the complete citation — only the text it finds that convinces it to stop because a citation is probably nearby. Use the mouse to highlight the citation in the document. (The Mark Citation dialog box patiently stays on-screen while you mark the citation.)

9. **Repeat Steps 3 through 8 until you mark all the citations you can stand.**

10. **After you finish marking citations, click the Close button.**

Word marks citations with field codes formatted as hidden text so that they are normally invisible. They jump to life, however, when you compile a table of authorities. See the next section, "Creating a Table of Authorities," for the steps.

Another way to summon the Mark Citation dialog box is to call up Insert⇨ Reference⇨Index and Tables, click the Table of Authorities tab, and then click the Mark Citation button.

If the screen suddenly changes to Print Preview mode when you try to mark a citation, don't panic. You probably pressed Ctrl+Alt+I rather than Alt+Shift+I. Ctrl+Alt+I is the keyboard shortcut for toggling Print Preview on and off. These two keyboard shortcuts are perilously close to one another, but don't worry if you hit the wrong one. Just press Ctrl+Alt+I again to return to Normal view and then start over.

If you stumble onto a citation that you know occurs later in your document, click the Mark All button. The Mark All button creates a citation not only for the selected text, but also any subsequent occurrences of the citation.

Each time you mark a citation, Word activates the All check box of the Tools⇨Options command's View tab, which reveals not only the hidden text used to mark citations, but also perverts the screen with dots for spaces, paragraph and tab marks, and other obnoxious codes. To return your display to normal, click the Show/Hide button (shown in the margin) on the Standard toolbar.

The field codes for citations look like the following example:

```
{ TA \l "Kringle v. New York
28 NY 2d 312 (1938)" \s "Kringle v. New York" \c 1 }
```

The preceding codes are formatted as hidden text, so you don't normally see them. You can edit the long citation text (the part between quotes following \l) or the short citation text (the quoted text that follows \s) if you want to change a citation after you create it.

Creating a Table of Authorities

After you mark all the citations in your document, follow these steps to create the table of authorities:

1. **Move the insertion point to the place where you want the table of authorities to appear.**

You can place the table of authorities at the front or back of the document. If you want the table to appear on its own page, press Ctrl+Enter to create a page break. You may also want to type a heading, such as Table of Authorities.

2. **Call up Insert⇨Reference⇨Index and Tables and click the Table of Authorities tab.**

The Index and Tables dialog box appears with the Table of Authorities tab in plain view, as shown in Figure 7-2.

3. **Pick the style you want from the Formats list.**

As you click the various formats, the Preview area shows how the resulting table of authorities appears.

4. **Play with the other controls to fine-tune the table of authorities.**

• **Use Passim:** Check this box if you want Word to use the word passim when a citation occurs on five or more pages. (Passim is a Latin word that means either "scattered throughout," or "an ugly, overgrown, rat-like creature that hangs upside down by its tail.")

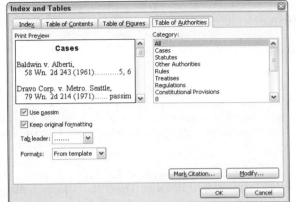

Book VI
Chapter 7

Objection, Your
Honor (Creating a
Table of Authorities)

Figure 7-2:
The Table of
Authorities
tab of the
Index and
Tables
dialog box.

- **Keep Original Formatting:** Check this box if you want the character formatting (such as underline and italics) that Word applies to the document's citation to carry over into the table of authorities.

- **Tab Leader:** Use this drop-down list to add or remove the dotted line that connects each table entry with its page number.

- **Formats:** Use this drop-down list to choose one of several pre-defined formats for the table of authorities.

- **Category:** Use this list box to choose the citation category you want compiled. Usually you leave the category set to the default, All. If you want to compile a table of one category, (cases, rules, regulations, and so on) choose the category from the drop-down list.

5. **Click OK.**

   The table of authorities is created.

Here are some things to remember when you compile a table of authorities:

✦ If the table of authorities looks like { TOA \h \c "1" \p }, call up Tools⇨Options, click the View button, and uncheck the Field Codes check box. Click OK and the table appears correctly.

✦ To delete a table of authorities, select the entire table and then press the Delete key.

✦ Word formats the entries in a table of authorities with a standard Table of Authorities style, and the category headings are formatted with a TOA Heading style. If none of the predefined formats listed in the Formats list tickles your fancy, choose From Template and click the Modify button. A special version of the Style dialog box appears showing only the standard table of authorities styles. You can customize the appearance of your table by modifying the Table of Authorities and TOA Heading styles.

Updating a Table of Authorities

If you edit a document after creating a table of authorities, the table may become out of date. To make sure that the table is up to date, use one of these techniques:

✦ In the Tools⇨Options command, click the Print tab, check the Update Fields check box, and then click OK. Then the table of authorities automatically updates every time you print your document.

✦ To update a table of authorities without printing the document, select the table and press F9.

✦ If you point to a table of authorities and click the right mouse button, the shortcut menu that appears includes an Update Field command. Using the Update Field command works the same as pressing F9.

Disclaimer of Warranties and Limit of Liability

The author, Doug Lowe, and the publisher, Wiley Publishing, Inc., make no representations or warranties with respect to the accuracy or completeness of the contents of this chapter and specifically disclaim any implied warranties or merchantability or fitness for any particular purpose and shall in no event be held liable for any loss of profit or any other commercial damage, including, but not limited to, such damages as losing a big case because of a key citation's being omitted from a pleading or a brief; tripping, falling, or stumbling over this book; or the cost of medical treatment and/or hospitalization, pain and suffering, lost wages, or emotional anguish due to stress inflicted or sustained while using or attempting to use the Table of Authorities feature in the Word 2003 software program. Et cetera, et cetera, et cetera.

Book VII

Letters, Envelopes, and Labels

The 5th Wave   **By Rich Tennant**

The new desktop publishing software not only lets Rags produce a professional looking greeting card quickly and inexpensively, but it also allows him to say it his way.

©RICHTENNANT

ARF!!
Whooof arf!

Arf, arf arf

Contents at a Glance

Chapter 1: Creating Letters and Envelopes

In This Chapter

✔ Using the Letter Wizard to whip out a letter

✔ Adding an envelope to a letter

✔ Printing return-address labels

✔ Creating a custom label for odd-sized labels

I read recently that Ronald Reagan was a prolific letter writer, with at least 6,500 of his letters on file in various libraries and private collections. I doubt that I've written 65 letters in my entire life. Apparently, Reagan wrote most of his letters out in longhand on a yellow legal pad, and then had them typed up by his secretary.

Think of how many more letters he could have written if Word 2003 had been available back then, with the special letter writing features that I describe in this chapter. Then he could have devoted more time to his favorite hobbies, like tearing down the Berlin Wall or building Star Wars missile defense systems.

Using the Letter Wizard

Word comes with a special letter-writing wizard that can practically write your letter for you. All you have to do is fill in the details. Here are the steps for writing a letter with the Letter Wizard:

1. **Choose File⇨New, and then click the <u>On My Computer</u> link in the Templates section of the New Document task pane.**

   The Templates dialog box comes up.

2. **Click the Letters & Faxes tab, and then double-click the Letter Wizard icon.**

   The dialog box shown in Figure 1-1 appears. (If you have the Office Assistant turned off, this message is displayed in a normal dialog box instead of in an Office Assistant bubble.)

Figure 1-1:
The Office Assistant asks if you want to create one letter or a bunch of letters.

3. **Click Send One Letter.**

   The Letter Wizard launches, which makes its initial appearance as shown in Figure 1-2.

   If you select Send Letters to a Mailing List, the Mail Merge Helper starts. For more information about how it works, refer to Chapter 3 of this minibook.

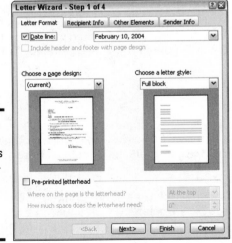

Figure 1-2:
The Letter Wizard asks for information about the format of your letter.

4. **Select the Letter Format options you want to use for your letter.**

   The first choice to make is whether to include the date at the top of the letter. If you check the Date Line option, you can select a date format from the drop-down list.

You can choose a page design and a letter style. The preview boxes beneath these drop-down lists give you a peek at what each of the choices for these options look like.

If you're using pre-printed letterhead, check the Pre-printed Letterhead option, and then tell the wizard how much room to leave at the top or bottom of the page for the letterhead.

5. **Click Next.**

   The second page of the Letter Wizard comes to life, as shown in Figure 1-3. (If you prefer, you can just click the Recipient Info tab rather than the Next button.)

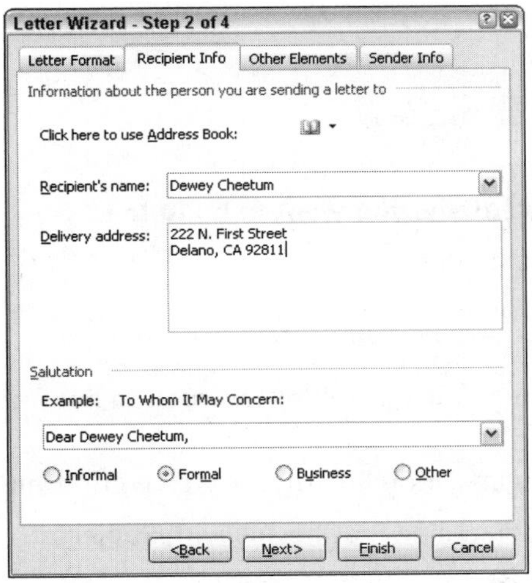

Figure 1-3:
The Letter Wizard asks for information about the recipient of your letter.

6. **Enter the recipient's name and address and choose the Salutation style.**

   If you have the recipient's name on file in your Outlook address book, click the Address Book icon, and then choose the recipient. Otherwise, type the information in manually.

   Notice the radio buttons that appear beneath the Salutation drop-down list: Informal, Formal, Business, and Other. When you choose one of these options, the salutations that appear in this drop-down list change.

7. **Click Next.**

   The third page of the Letter Wizard comes to life, as shown in Figure 1-4. (If you prefer, you can click the Other Elements tab rather than the Next button.)

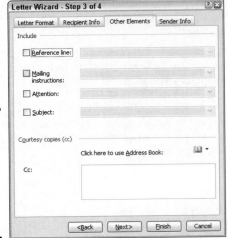

Figure 1-4:
The Letter
Wizard asks
if you want
to include
other items
in your
letter.

8. **Select any optional elements you want to include in your letter.**

The option elements include:

- **Reference Line:** Adds a reference line, such as RE:, In regards to:, and so on.

- **Mailing Instructions:** Adds a mailing instruction line, such as Special Delivery.

- **Attention:** Adds an attention line that begins with Attention: or Attn:.

- **Subject:** Adds a subject line that begins with Subject:.

To select one or more of the optional elements, check the check box for the element, choose the form you want to use from the drop-down list, and then type any additional information you want to include.

You can also add Courtesy Copy names to the letter by adding the names to the Cc: text box. If the names are in your address book, you can click the Address Book icon to select them.

9. **Click Next.**

The fourth and final page of the Letter Wizard comes to life, as shown in Figure 1-5. (If you prefer, you can click the Sender Info tab rather than the Next button.)

10. **Enter your name and address in the top portion of the wizard.**

You can type your name and address or select it from the address book by clicking the Address Book icon. If don't want to include your return address on the letter, check the Omit check box.

Figure 1-5:
The Letter
Wizard
asks for
information
about you.

11. **Choose the options you want to use for the closing.**

    You can choose one of several complimentary closings, such as Sincerely, Regards, Warmly, and so on. Then, you can add additional lines to the closing, such as your job title, company, the writer/typist initials, and an Enclosures line.

12. **Click Finish.**

    Presto! Word builds a letter using the elements you chose for the wizard. Figure 1-6 shows a typical letter created by the Letter Wizard.

13. **Replace the boilerplate letter body with your own text.**

    Unless, of course, you want to send your friend a letter that says "Type your letter here." — which would cause your friend to worry about you.

14. **Add an envelope if you want.**

    For details on how to add an envelope, see the section "Printing an Envelope" later in this chapter.

15. **Print the letter.**

    Click the Print button or choose File➪Print.

16. **Save the letter if you want to keep it.**

    Click the Save button or choose File➪Save.

17. **You're done!**

**Book VII
Chapter 1**

**Creating Letters and
Envelopes**

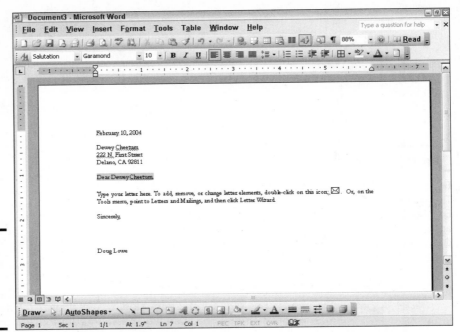

Figure 1-6:
The Letter
Wizard
creates
a letter
for you.

Now all you have to do is mail the letter.

Here are a few interesting things to note about the Letter Wizard:

✦ After you create a letter, you can bring up the Letter Wizard again by choosing Tools⇨Letters and Mailings⇨Letter Wizard. Any changes you make in the Letter Wizard are applied to your letter when you click OK.

✦ The Letter Wizard remembers your settings. Because the only information that usually changes from letter to letter is the recipient information and the optional elements, you can usually head straight to the Recipient Info tab, type the recipient's name and address, click the Other Elements tab to adjust those settings, and then click Finish to create a new letter.

Printing an Envelope

Word includes a special Envelopes and Labels command that can quickly create an envelope to stuff your letter into. To add an envelope to a letter you already created, open the letter (if it isn't already open) and follow these steps:

1. **Choose Tools⇨Letters and Mailings⇨Envelopes and Labels.**

The Envelopes and Labels dialog box appears, as shown in Figure 1-7.

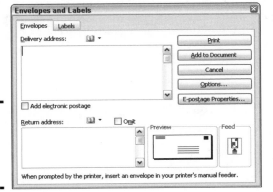

Figure 1-7:
The
Envelopes
and Labels
dialog box.

2. **If necessary, type the delivery address.**

Word can usually find the address, so this field is usually already filled in. But sometimes Word gets lost and can't find the address, so you have to type it in yourself.

If the Envelopes and Labels dialog box appears without the delivery address filled in, you can click Cancel to dismiss the dialog box. Then, use the mouse to select the recipient's address in the letter and choose Tools⇨Letters and Mailings⇨Envelopes and Labels again. This time, the address is filled in.

3. **If you want your return address to print on the label, type it in the Return Address text box.**

4. **Click the Add to Document button to add the envelope to the letter.**

The envelope is added to your document as a separate page that appears before the first page of your letter.

When you print the letter, the envelope prints first. So you have to be prepared to insert an envelope into the printer. The exact steps for inserting an envelope depend on your printer. But most printers prompt you to insert an envelope when it wants to print one. Be an obedient printer user and do as you're told.

If your envelope prints upside down, you may need to configure Word so that it knows how your printer handles envelopes. From the Envelopes and Labels dialog box, click the Options button. When the Envelope Options dialog box appears, click the Printing Options tab to reveal the printing options, as shown in Figure 1-8. Then, select the Feed Method options that correspond to the way your printer accepts envelopes. Then click OK to dismiss this dialog box. Word memorizes these options, so you only have to set them once.

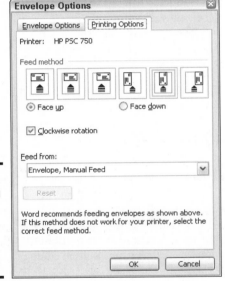

Figure 1-8:
The Printing Options tab of the Envelope Options dialog box.

Printing Labels

Word also lets you quickly print labels rather than envelopes. You can use labels in Word three ways:

✦ You can print just one label, which you usually don't want to do because it wastes an entire sheet of labels just to get one label.

✦ You can print an entire sheet of the same label. This option is useful for printing return address labels. I do this approximately once a year, when I send out a few hundred Christmas cards to my inner circle of close and dear friends.

✦ You can print labels from a database. This option is really a mail merge topic, so you have to skip ahead to Chapters 3 and 4 of this minibook to find out more about how to do it.

Because I don't recommend printing single labels 'cause it wastes paper, and I cover printing mail merge labels in Chapter 3 of this minibook, that leaves me with the steps for creating a whole sheet of return address labels. Follow these handy steps:

1. **Get some labels.**

   You find a huge assortment of labels at your handy office supply store. Pick whichever ones you like, but make sure you get labels that work with your printer.

   Note: Word works best with Avery labels, but you can buy a cheaper brand if you want. Most cheaper labels list the Avery equivalent on the package.

2. **In Word, choose Tools⇨Letters and Mailings⇨Envelopes and Labels, and then click the Labels tab.**

   The dialog box shown in Figure 1-9 appears.

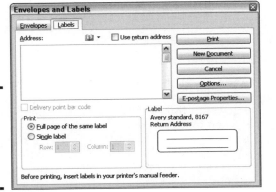

Book VII
Chapter 1

Creating Letters and Envelopes

Figure 1-9:
The Labels tab of the Envelopes and Labels dialog box.

3. **Type the address you want to print in the label in the Address text box.**

   Naturally, if you're printing labels for something other than addresses (for example, name tags or file folders), you don't actually type an address here. Instead, type whatever you want to appear on each label in this text box.

4. **Make sure the right labels are selected.**

   The label number appears in the lower-right corner of the dialog box. If this number doesn't match the number you're using, click the Options button and select the right label type from the Label Options dialog box, shown in Figure 1-10. Then click OK to return to the Envelopes and Labels dialog box.

Figure 1-10:
The Label
Options
dialog box.

A dialog box titled "Label Options" containing:

Printer information
- Dot matrix
- Laser and ink jet   Tray: Manual Paper Feed

Label information
Label products: Avery standard

Product number:
8162 - Address
8163 - Shipping
8164 - Shipping
8165 - Full Sheet
8166 - File Folder
8166-18CB - File Folder
8167 - Return Address

Label information
Type: Return Address
Height: 0.5"
Width: 1.75"
Page size: Letter (8 ½ x 11 in)

Details... | New Label... | Delete | OK | Cancel

5. **Click New Document.**

   A new document is created with an entire page of labels, all lined up in a nice table.

6. **If you want to format the labels differently, choose Edit⇨Select All, and then apply any formatting you want to use.**

   For example, you may want to change the font and size to make your text fit better in the space available in the label.

7. **Insert a sheet of labels in the printer.**

   Be sure to insert the labels with the correct orientation. If you're not sure, try this time-honored trick: Draw an arrow on a plain sheet of paper indicating the direction in which you feed the paper, and then test print the labels on that page. When the page comes out of the printer, make a note of whether labels print on the same side of the page as the arrow or on the opposite side. That helps you determine whether to insert the labels face up or face down. (Printing a test page on plain paper is a good idea before using a sheet of labels anyway.)

8. **Choose File⇨Print to print the labels.**

   That's it; you're done.

Creating Custom Labels

If your labels don't appear in the list of predefined labels, you have to create a custom label format. To do so, select a label type that's close in size to the labels you want to create and click the New Label button in the Label Options dialog box. Either the New Custom Laser dialog box shown in Figure 1-11 or the New Custom Dot Matrix dialog box appears, depending on what type of printer is selected. The two are identical except for the title.

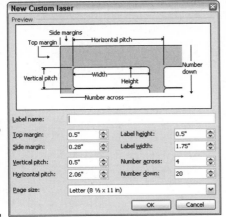

To set up your custom label, enter appropriate values for each of the fields in this dialog box:

+ **Label Name:** The name for your custom label type.

+ **Top Margin:** The distance between the top of the sheet and the top of the first label.

+ **Side Margin:** The distance between the left edge of the sheet and the left edge of the first margin.

+ **Vertical Pitch:** The distance between the top of one label and the top of the label beneath it.

+ **Horizontal Pitch:** The distance between the left edge of one label and the left edge of the label to its right.

+ **Label Height:** The height of each label.

+ **Label Width:** The width of each label.

+ **Number Across:** The number of labels in each row.

+ **Number Down:** The number of labels in each column.

+ **Page Size:** The size of each sheet of labels, usually 8½" x 11".

Notice that as you change these values, the diagram in the Preview window changes to reflect the settings you enter. When you're satisfied with the layout, click OK. Word asks if you're sure you want to change the label format; click Yes to proceed.

Chapter 2: Faxing and E-Mailing Documents

In This Chapter

✔ Faxing a document the old-fashioned way

✔ Faxing a document with a fax modem

✔ Faxing a document with an Internet fax service

✔ Sending a document via e-mail

✔ Sending a document as an e-mail attachment

This chapter covers two features in Word that let you send documents to other people. First, you find out how to send a Word document as a fax to anyone who has a fax machine. Then, you discover how to e-mail a Word document directly to anyone who has an e-mail address.

Given the choice, e-mailing a document is usually the better solution: The user who receives a document via fax gets a pile of paper, crudely printed on a low-resolution fax machine. But if you e-mail the document, the recipient gets an actual copy of your Word document file, which he or she can then save to disk, print, and perhaps even modify and send back. But the choice is yours.

Sending a Fax

Betcha didn't know that the first patent for a workable fax machine was issued in England in 1843, and that by the 1920s, AT&T offered a fax service that could send copies of photographs over telephone lines for use in newspapers.

Point being that faxing is a pretty old technology. And Word has supported document faxing almost from the very beginning. You can fax a Word document three basic ways:

✦ The easiest way is to print the document, and then use a separate fax machine to actually send the fax. I know it doesn't sound very elegant, but if you send only occasional faxes and you have a fax machine at your disposal, this technique saves you the hassle of figuring out how to deal with Word's built-in faxing features.

✦ If you have a fax modem installed in your computer and the modem is plugged into a telephone line, you can use File⇨Send To to send the document via your fax modem. I describe this technique in the upcoming section, "Using a fax modem."

✦ If you don't have a fax modem but do have a connection to the Internet, you can send a fax by using one of the many Internet-based faxing services. For more information, see the section "Using a fax service" later in this chapter.

Using a fax modem

To send a fax using a built-in fax modem, you must properly install the modem in your computer and plug it in to a phone line. In addition, your computer must have Windows Fax Services installed.

If the Fax Services aren't installed, you can install them by choosing Start⇨ Control Panel to open the Control Panel folder. Double-click the Add/Remove Programs icon, and then click Add/Remove Windows Components. When the Windows Components Wizard appears, select Fax Services, click Next, and follow any other instructions Windows throws in your face.

To send a document using your fax modem, follow these steps:

1. **Open the document you want to send.**

2. **Choose File⇨Send To⇨Recipient Using a Fax Modem.**

The Fax Wizard appears, as shown in Figure 2-1.

Figure 2-1:
The Fax Wizard leads the way into fax land.

3. **Complete the wizard.**

   The Fax Wizard consists of five pages that gather the information needed to send the fax. After completing the information for each page, click Next to advance to the next page.

   The Fax Wizard displays five pages:

   - **Document to Fax:** On this page, you can choose the document to fax. The default is the current document. You can also choose whether or not you want to include a cover sheet.

   - **Fax Software:** This page lets you choose which software to use to send your fax. Usually, you choose Microsoft Fax. If you purchased and installed some other faxing software, it's listed on this page. You can also elect to skip the faxing software and just print the page so that you can manually fax it later.

   - **Recipients:** On this page, you indicate to whom you want to send the fax. You can type names and fax numbers manually, or you can select names from your address book.

   - **Cover Sheet:** This page lets you choose the style for your cover sheet.

   - **Sender:** This page lets you fill in your name, address, phone number, and fax number.

4. **Click Send Fax Now to send the fax.**

   The fax is sent to the recipient.

5. **Click Finish to quit the Fax Wizard.**

   You're done.

Using a fax service

If you don't have a fax modem installed in your computer but do have an Internet connection, you can use an Internet faxing service to send a fax. Unfortunately, these services aren't free. Fees range from $5 to $20 or more per month, depending on the features you sign up for. In addition, you must have Outlook 2003 installed on your computer to use a fax service.

To send a document via a fax service, choose File⇨Send To⇨Recipient Using Fax Service. The first time you do this, a dialog box appears telling you that you have to first sign up for a faxing service. When you click OK, Word launches an Internet Explorer window that goes to a Microsoft Web page that lists Internet fax services. You can then follow the links to sign up for a service.

After you properly sign up, the File⇨Send To⇨Recipient Using Fax Service command adds a special header at the top of the document that lets you specify the subject and recipient information. Fill in this information, and then click Send to send your fax.

Sending a Document as an E-Mail Message

If your computer is connected to a network or to the Internet, you can send a copy of the document you're working on to a friend or co-worker via e-mail by using File⇨Send To. You find several variations of this command:

✦ **File⇨Send To⇨Mail Recipient:** Sends a copy of the document as an e-mail message. The text of your document is inserted directly into the body of the message.

✦ **File⇨Send To⇨Mail Recipient (As Attachment):** Sends a copy of the document as an attachment.

✦ **File⇨Send To⇨Mail Recipient (For Review):** Attaches a copy of the document file to the e-mail message and inserts the message "Please review the attached document" in the body of the message.

✦ **File⇨Send To⇨Routing Recipient:** Allows you to send the document to a list of users. The users in the list receive the document one at a time. When each user finishes reviewing the document, he or she can forward the document to the next user in the route list by choosing File⇨Send To⇨Next Routing Recipient.

The following sections present steps for sending documents using Outlook. If you're using a different e-mail program, the steps are similar, but you may encounter minor variations.

E-mailing a document

To send a document as an e-mail message, follow these steps:

1. **Open the document you want to send.**

2. **Choose File⇨Send To⇨Mail Recipient.**

A special e-mail pane is added to the top of the document, as shown in Figure 2-2.

3. **Type the e-mail address of the person you want to send the document to in the To text box.**

If you have the recipient's e-mail address on file in your address book, click the To button to summon the Address book. Then, select the correct recipient and click OK.

Figure 2-2:
Sending a
document
as an e-mail
message.

4. **Type a subject for your message in the Subject text box.**

5. **Click the Send a Copy button to send the message.**

   The document is sent. Now all you have to do is wait for a reply.

Sending a document as an attachment

If your document is large, you may want to send it as an attachment rather than as a regular e-mail message. That way, the entire document doesn't appear in the body of the message. To e-mail a document as an attachment e-mail message, follow these steps:

1. **Open the document you want to send as an attachment.**

2. **Choose File⇨Send To⇨Mail Recipient (as Attachment).**

   The New Message window opens, as shown in Figure 2-3.

3. **Type the e-mail address of the person you want to send the document to in the To text box.**

   If you have the recipient's e-mail address on file in your address book, click the To button to summon the Address book. Then, select the correct recipient and click OK to return to the New Message dialog box.

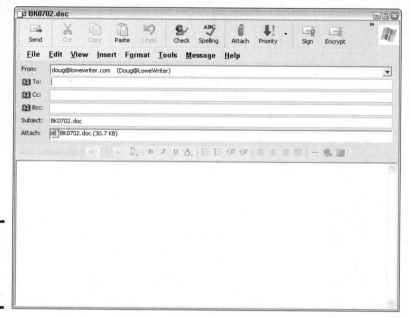

4. **Type a subject for your message in the Subject text box.**

5. **Type a message in the message body area of the New Message dialog box.**

6. **Click the Send button to send the message.**

   Your message is sent on its way. Hopefully it receives a warm welcome.

Chapter 3: Using the Mail Merge Wizard

In This Chapter

✔ Understanding how mail merge works

✔ Getting started with the Mail Merge Wizard

✔ Following the Mail Merge Wizard's instructions to complete a mail merge

✔ Working with the Mail Merge toolbar

Mail merge. Just the sound of those two words is enough to drive even veteran Word users into a state of utter and complete panic. Just when you think that you've figured out enough about mail merge to put out a simple form letter, along comes Word with a bunch of additional mail merge features. Arghhhh! What next?

This chapter shows you how to use Word's Mail Merge Wizard to perform basic mail merges. After you master the basics, you may want to also read the next chapter, which presents some more advanced mail merge features that come in handy from time to time.

Word has a Tools➪Compare and Merge Documents command that is not related at all to the Mail Merge feature. Instead, the Tools➪Compare and Merge Documents command is a part of the revision tracking feature, which I cover in Book III, Chapter 6. Don't get these two distinctly different features confused.

Understanding Mail Merge

Mail merge refers to the process of merging a file that contains a list of names and addresses with another file that contains a model letter to produce a bunch of personalized form letters. Suppose that you decided to do some volunteer work for the local public library, and the library decided to put you in charge of getting deadbeats to return long overdue books. A personalized letter is the ideal way to communicate your message to these good-for-nothings. And Word's mail merge feature is ideal for preparing such a personalized letter.

The beauty of the whole thing is that you can keep the names and addresses in a separate file and use them over and over again. After all, you know these same people are probably going to have overdue books again soon.

Mail merge involves three basic steps:

1. Create the *main document*. The main document contains the letter you want to send. It includes the text printed for each letter, plus special *merge fields* that indicate exactly where to place in each letter the information from your mailing list, such as the recipient's name and address.

2. Create the *data source,* the list of names and addresses that is used to create the form letters. The data source can be a Word document, in which case the information is stored in a table, with one row for each name and address. Individual fields, such as name, address, city, state, zip code, and so on, are stored in separate columns. Or, the data source can be a list of contacts maintained by Outlook, a database created by a program such as Access, or some other type of file.

3. *Merge* the main document with the data source. This step creates a form letter for each row in the data source table. You can create the form letters as a separate document, with one letter on each page, or you can send the merged letters directly to the printer. You can also send the merged letters to e-mail or to a fax machine.

You can use mail merge to produce more than form letters. You can also use it to print envelopes or mailing labels, or even documents that don't have anything to do with mailing, such as a directory or a catalog. In short, mail merge is useful for any application in which a list of repeating data must be converted into a document in which each record in the data source is formatted in a similar way.

Using the Mail Merge Wizard

To start the Mail Merge Wizard, first create a new blank document or open an existing letter. Then, choose Tools⇨Letters and Mailings⇨Mail Merge. The wizard appears in the task pane in the right side of the document window, as shown in Figure 3-1.

After you call up the wizard, you can follow the steps I outline in the following sections.

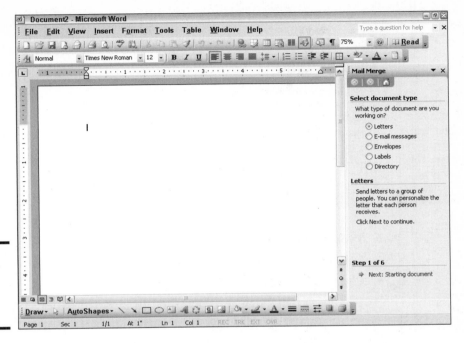

Figure 3-1:
The Mail
Merge
Wizard in
action.

Creating the main document

The first Mail Merge task the wizard helps you accomplish is setting up your main document. Here are the steps:

1. **Select the type of documents that you want to create for your mailing.**

    The choices are:

    - Letters
    - E-mail messages
    - Envelopes
    - Labels
    - Directory

    For normal, run-of-the-mill mass mailings, select Letters.

2. **Click Next at the bottom of the Mail Merge Wizard.**

    Step 2 of the Mail Merge Wizard appears, as shown in Figure 3-2.

3. **Click the Use the Current Document option if it is not already selected.**

    If you prefer to start a new document based on a template rather than using the current document, choose Start from a Template. Then, click the Select template link and choose the template you want to use.

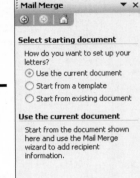

Figure 3-2:
Step 2, in
which you
select the
starting
document.

4. **Type the body of your letter.**

   Leave out the address block and greeting line. You add those later.

5. **Choose File⇨Save to save the file when you're done.**

   Your letter looks something like the one shown in Figure 3-3.

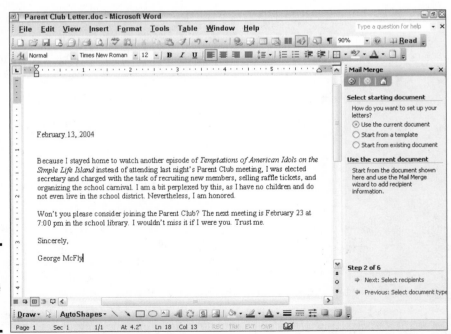

Figure 3-3:
A letter
ready to use
as a main
document.

Creating an address list

The next big step in Mail Merge is to select the recipients who will receive your letters. This step is usually the hardest part of the entire procedure, because it often involves creating an address list with the names and addresses of your recipients. Here are the bothersome steps:

1. **If you haven't already done so, click Next at the bottom of the wizard to proceed to the Select Recipients step.**

Step 3 of the wizard makes its appearance, as shown in Figure 3-4.

Figure 3-4: Step 3, in which you select the lucky recipients.

2. **Select the Type a New List radio button, and then click the <u>Create </u>link.**

The New Address List dialog box appears, shown in Figure 3-5.

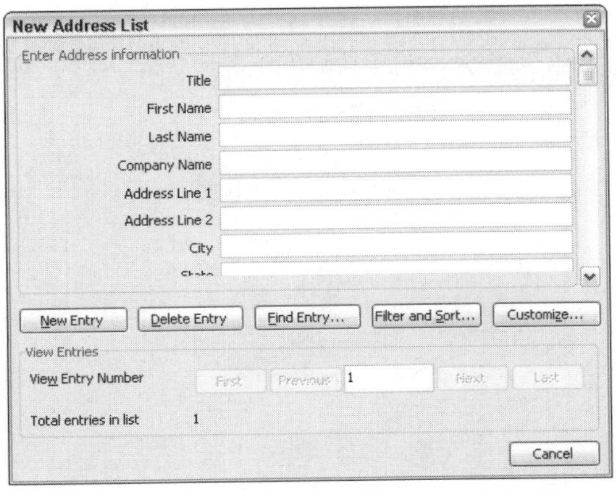

Figure 3-5: The New Address List dialog box.

If you already created the address list, you can call it up by choosing the Use an Existing List option. Then, click Browse. When the Select Data Source dialog box appears, locate the file you previously saved the address list as and click Open. Then, the Mail Merge Recipients dialog box appears, as shown in Figure 3-6, and you can skip ahead to Step 8.

3. **Type the information for a person that you want to add to the address list.**

   Press Tab to move from field to field or to skip over fields in which you don't want to enter any data. (You don't need to enter a value for every field.)

4. **After you type all the data for the person, click the New Entry button to add that person's data to the address list.**

5. **Repeat Steps 3 and 4 for each person that you want to add to the data source.**

   You can use the First, Previous, Next, and Last arrow buttons near the bottom of the New Address List dialog box to move forward or backward through the address list. You can use the Previous button to call up a record you already entered to correct a mistake if necessary.

   To delete a record, move to the record that you want to delete and then click the Delete Entry button.

6. **After you add all the names that you want to, click the Close button.**

   A Save Address List dialog box appears.

7. **Type a name for your address list, and then click Save.**

   The file is saved to your computer's hard drive. Then, the Mail Merge Recipients dialog box appears, as shown in Figure 3-6.

Figure 3-6: The Mail Merge Recipients list.

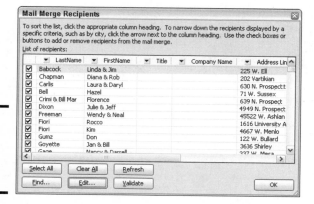

From the Mail Merge Recipients list, you can get back to the New Address List dialog box by clicking the Edit button.

8. **Click the column heading for the column that you want to sort the list by.**

   For example, if you want the letters to print in Zip Code sequence, click the heading for the Zip Code column (you have to scroll the list to the right to see the Zip Code column).

9. **Uncheck any records that you don't want to include in the mailing.**

   The mailing will be sent to every record that's checked, and the records are all initially checked. So you can manually remove people from the list by unchecking them.

   If the mailing will be sent to only a few people on the list, click the Clear All button to remove all the check marks. Then, go through the list and check the ones you want to send the mailing to.

10. **Click OK.**

The Address List feature is actually a built-in database program designed especially for Mail Merge. You can customize the fields that are used for each record in the address list by clicking the Customize button in the New Address List dialog box. The Customize Address List dialog box appears, shown in Figure 3-7, which lets you add fields, remove existing fields, or change the order in which the Address List fields appear.

Figure 3-7:
The Mail
Customize
Address List
dialog box.

Word offers ways other than the address list to store the names and addresses for your mailings. The two most popular choices are in an Access database or in your Outlook Address book. To use names and addresses from Outlook, choose the Select from Outlook Contacts option in Step 2. To use an Access database (or any other database), choose Use an Existing List in Step 2, and then locate the database in the dialog box that appears.

Inserting the address block and greeting line

After you add names and addresses to the data source, finish your letter by adding placeholders for the address block, greeting line, and any other information you want to insert from the address list. In Wordspeak, these placeholders are called *merge fields*.

If the main document isn't already displayed, select it from the Window menu. Then, follow these steps:

1. Click Next at the bottom of the wizard to bring up Step 4 of the wizard.

As Figure 3-8 shows, this step allows you to add the address block and other merge fields to your letter.

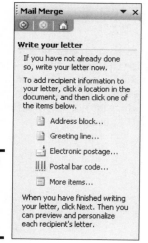

Figure 3-8:
Step 4, in which you complete the letter.

2. Position the insertion point where you want to insert the address block.

3. Click the <u>Address Block</u> link.

The Insert Address Block dialog box appears, as shown in Figure 3-9.

4. Choose the options that you want to use for the address block, and then click OK.

You can select the format to use for the recipient's name, whether to use the company name, and whether to use country and region information in the address.

When you click OK, the Insert Address Block dialog box is dismissed and the address block is inserted.

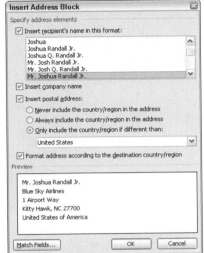

Figure 3-9:
The Insert
Address
Block dialog
box.

5. **Position the cursor where you want to insert the greeting line and click the <u>Greeting Line</u> link.**

   The Greeting Line dialog box appears, as shown in Figure 3-10.

Figure 3-10:
The
Greeting
Line dialog
box.

6. **Choose the options that you want to use for the greeting line, and then click OK.**

   The Greeting Line dialog box lets you choose several options for creating casual or formal greeting lines. When you click OK, the greeting line is inserted into the document.

7. **If you want to insert a field from the address list into the body of the letter, move the insertion point to where you want to insert the field and click the <u>More Items</u> link.**

   The Insert Merge Field dialog box comes up, as shown in Figure 3-11.

Figure 3-11:
The Insert
Merge Field
dialog box.

8. **Choose the field you want to insert and click Insert.**

   The field is inserted into the document. The Insert Merge Field dialog box remains on-screen so that you can insert other fields, if you're so inclined.

9. **Repeat Step 8 for any other fields you want to insert, and then click Close.**

   When you click Close, the Insert Merge Field dialog box is dismissed.

Figure 3-12 shows how a letter appears after you insert the Address Block, Greeting Line, and the First and Last Name fields in the body of the document. Notice that merge fields display within special chevron characters — for example: «AddressBlock» and «FirstName».

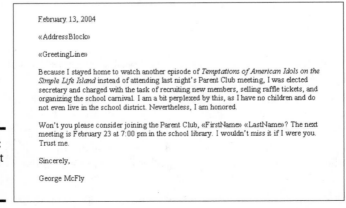

Figure 3-12:
A document
with fields
inserted.

Merging the documents

After you set up the main document and the address list, you're ready for the show. Follow these simple steps to merge the main document with the data source to produce form letters:

1. **Click Next for the next step of the wizard — Preview Your Letters.**

The first letter in your mail merge appears on-screen, as shown in Figure 3-13.

2. **Review each letter in the merge.**

You can click the >> or << button in the Mail Merge Wizard to move forward or backward through the letters. If you find a mistake in a name or address, correct the mistake directly on the letter.

If you find a letter that you don't want to include, click the Exclude This Recipient button.

If you review the first few letters and they look okay, you can skip ahead to the next step without reviewing them all.

**Book VII
Chapter 3**

**Using the Mail
Merge Wizard**

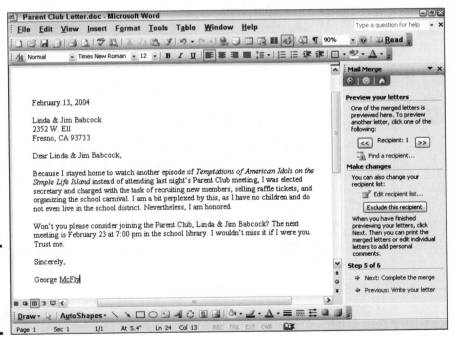

Figure 3-13: Step 5, in which you preview the mail merge.

3. **When you review the entire mailing, click Next at the bottom of the wizard.**

   The final step of the wizard appears, as shown in Figure 3-14.

4. **Click the <u>Print</u> link to print your letters.**

   The letters are printed.

   If you want to edit the letters individually and print them later, click the <u>Edit Individual Letters</u> link instead of the <u>Print</u> link. The merged letters move to a new document, which you can then edit and save.

Figure 3-14: Step 6, in which you print the mail merge.

Using the Mail Merge Toolbar

If you are an experienced Mail Merge user, you can save time by skipping the Mail Merge Wizard and jumping straight to the Mail Merge toolbar to complete your mail merge tasks. To call up the Mail Merge toolbar, choose Tools⇨Letters and Mailings⇨Show Mail Merge Toolbar or View⇨Toolbars⇨ Mail Merge.

The following table lists the buttons that appear on the Mail Merge toolbar. In general, you use these buttons in sequence from left to right to complete a mail merge.

Button	*What It Does*
	Lets you choose Letters, E-mail messages, Envelopes, or Labels for the main document type
	Opens the data source

Button	What It Does
	Lets you select which names to include in the mailing and lets you determine the sort order (for example, by last name or by zip code)
	Inserts an address block
	Inserts a greeting line
	Inserts a merge field, which lets you add additional information from the data source
Insert Word Field ▾	Inserts a Word field, which gives you more precise control over the contents of your merged letters
«»ABC	Displays the merged data
	Highlights merged fields
	Allows you to specify which fields in a database to use for certain mail merge functions
	Duplicates the contents of one label into all other labels on the page
◀	Goes to the first record in the data source
◀	Goes to the previous record in sequence in the data source
1	Goes to a specific record in the data source
▷	Goes to the next record in the data source
▷|	Goes to the last record in the data source
	Searches for records
	Checks for merge errors

(continued)

Book VII
Chapter 3

Using the Mail
Merge Wizard

(continued)

Button	What It Does
	Merges the main document and data source, placing the result in a new document
	Merges the main document and data source, and sends the result directly to the printer
	Merges the main document and data source, and e-mails the resulting letters
	Merges the main document and data source, and faxes the results

Chapter 4: More Mail Merge Tricks

In This Chapter

✔ **Doing an e-mail merge**

✔ **Printing envelopes or labels from an address list**

✔ **Creating a directory**

✔ **Sorting and filtering data**

✔ **An interesting computer science lesson based on chicken**

his chapter covers some of the more interesting things you can do with Word's mail merge feature, such as print mailing labels, choose only certain names to print letters for, use data from sources other than Word, and create an address directory.

This chapter assumes you already know the basics of performing a mail merge. If you're completely new to mail merge, stop where you are. Back up very slowly, make no sudden moves, and read the previous chapter. Only after that should you return to this chapter.

Other Types of Merges

Although creating form letters is the most popular use for mail merge, the Mail Merge Wizard can also send e-mail, create personalized envelopes, print address labels, and even create a directory. The following sections show you how.

Merging to e-mail

If you want to send your letters via e-mail rather than snail mail, you can use the Mail Merge Wizard to merge your letters, and then send them to e-mail addresses rather than print them. For this merge to work, your computer must have an e-mail program such as Microsoft Outlook installed. And your data source must have an e-mail address for each recipient.

Don't be a spammer! You should send e-mail merges only to people you know, or to customers you've done business with and who have agreed to let you send them e-mail.

All you have to do is choose E-mail Messages rather than Letters as the document type in the first step of the Mail Merge Wizard. Then, you follow the normal steps for using the Mail Merge Wizard as I describe in Chapter 3 of this minibook, until you get to the last step. Instead of the normal choices (Print and Edit Individual Letters), you have only one choice: Electronic Mail. Click this link to summon the Merge to E-Mail dialog box, as shown in Figure 4-1.

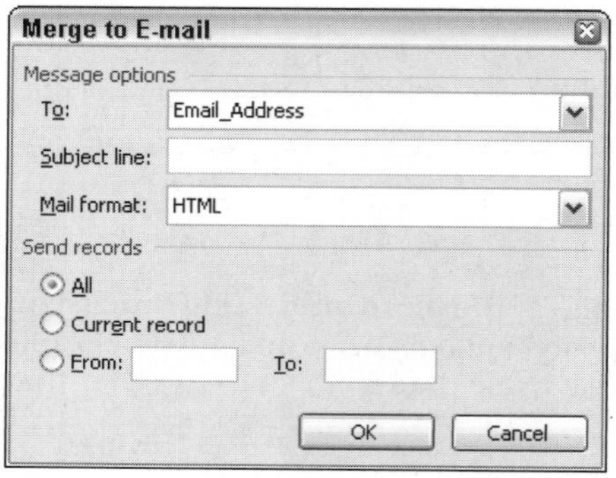

Figure 4-1:
The Merge
to E-Mail
dialog box.

Use this dialog box to specify the options you want to use for the e-mail merge. The options include:

+ **To:** Use this drop-down list to choose the field in the data source that contains the recipients' e-mail addresses.

+ **Subject Line:** Type the subject line you want to appear in the e-mail messages.

  Unfortunately, Word doesn't let you personalize the subject line for each recipient. Each recipient in your mailing gets exactly the same subject line.

+ **Mail Format:** This drop-down list lets you choose one of three ways to send the e-mail. You can format the messages as Plain Text, HTML, or Attachments. Choose HTML if you applied text formats or included images in the message. Otherwise, choose Plain Text.

+ **Send Records:** Use these radio buttons to choose whether to send messages to all of the recipients in the merge, just the current recipient, or a range of recipients.

Merging envelopes

Ever spend 30 minutes printing 50 personalized letters by using mail merge and then another 30 minutes hand-addressing envelopes? Never again! Word can easily transform a mail merge address list into a set of nicely printed envelopes.

For business mail, a good alternative to printing addresses on envelopes is to simply use window envelopes. That way, the inside address on the letters shows through the window. This feature has two advantages. First, you don't have to mess around with printing the envelopes. And second, you eliminate the risk of mixing up the letters and the envelopes and inadvertently sending Mr. Smith's overdue notice to Mr. Jones.

If you still insist on merging envelopes, follow the normal Mail Merge Wizard procedure, with these variations:

✦ In Step 1 of the Mail Merge Wizard, select the Envelopes option rather than Letters as the document type.

✦ In Step 2 of the Mail Merge Wizard, click Envelope Options to bring up the Envelope Options dialog box, shown in Figure 4-2. Use this dialog box to select the envelope size and to format the font used for the delivery and return addresses. You can also click the Printing Options tab to adjust Word's envelope layout to match the way envelopes feed into your particular printer. You may need to fiddle with these settings in case your envelopes print upside down or on the wrong side.

Figure 4-2:
The
Envelope
Options
dialog box.

✦ In Step 4 of the Mail Merge Wizard, click in the recipient address area in the center of the envelope, and then click the <u>Address Block</u> link to insert a standard address block. Then, click in the return address area in the upper left corner of the envelope and type your return address (unless you're using pre-printed envelopes). Figure 4-3 shows how the envelope appears when it's been set up properly.

You can also use this step of the Mail Merge Wizard to add a postal bar code to the envelope. And, if you subscribe to an electronic postage service, you can print e-postage right on the envelope so that you don't have to use stamps.

The postal bar code is not a secret password that gets you into pubs where mail carriers hang out — it's a bar code that speeds mail delivery. If you do bulk mailing and have the proper permits, using this bar code can earn postage discounts.

You can complete the rest of the Mail Merge Wizard steps as you do for a printed letter.

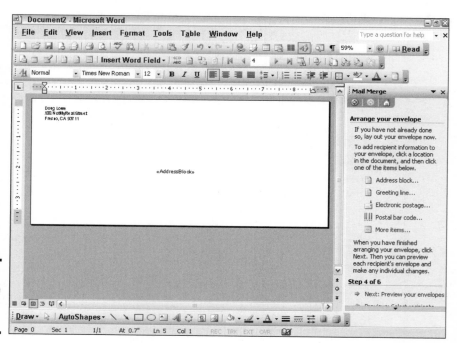

Figure 4-3:
An envelope all ready to be merged.

Merging to labels

If you want to create mailing labels instead of envelopes, choose Labels as the document type in the first step of the Mail Merge Wizard. Then, follow the normal Mail Merge Wizard steps, with these exceptions:

✦ In Step 2 of the wizard, click Label Options to bring up the Label Options dialog box, as shown in Figure 4-4. Use this dialog box to specify the type of labels you're using.

Figure 4-4:
The Label
Options
dialog box.

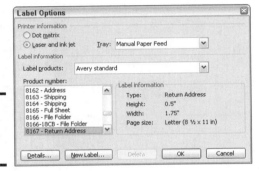

✦ In Step 4 of the wizard, you format the labels. To do that, click in the first label, and then click the <u>Address Block</u> link to insert an address block in the label. If you want, change the font or size of the address block. Then click the Update All Labels button at the bottom of the Mail Merge Wizard task pane. The contents of the first label copy to all the other labels on the page. It also adds a «Next Record» field to each label except the first to tell Word to skip to the next recipient. When you're done, your main document resembles Figure 4-5.

You can complete the rest of the Mail Merge Wizard the usual way.

If the addresses don't fit properly in the labels, first check to make sure that you selected the right type of label in the Label Options dialog box. If the labels are correct and the addresses still don't fit, return to Step 4 and try reducing the font size for the address block. You can do this by changing the size for the first label. Then, click the Update All Labels button to propagate the change to all the other labels.

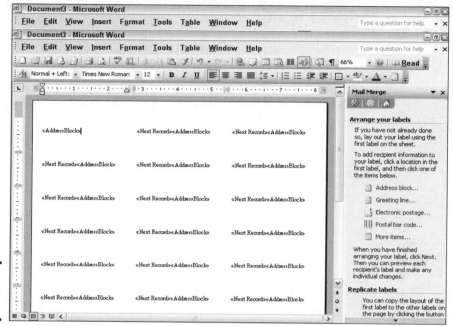

Creating a directory

You can use the Mail Merge Wizard to create a directory that lists all the addresses in a data source by choosing Directory as the document type in Step 1 of the wizard. Then, follow the wizard's normal steps with these variations:

✦ In Step 4, add the merge fields you want to appear for each item in the directory. For a simple address listing, you can just click the <u>Address Block</u> link. Or, you can create a more customized directory by clicking the <u>More Items</u> link to bring up the Insert Merge Field dialog box, as shown in Figure 4-6.

For example, here's one way to format an address listing that lists people in alphabetical order, with last name first:

```
«LastName», «FirstName»
    «Address_Line_1»
    «Address_Line_2»
    «City», «State» «ZIP_Code»
    «HomePhone»
```

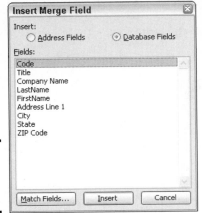

+ When the preview of the document appears in Step 5, only the first record is shown. Don't panic. All the records appear when you complete the merge.

+ In Step 6, click the <u>To New Document</u> link. A new document is created for your directory. Then, use File➪Save to save the directory to a file.

Fun Things to Do with the Data Source

Mail merge is useful enough if all you do with the data source is store your names and addresses. But Word's data sources have more tricks up their sleeves than meet the eye. With a little chutzpah and a bit of wrestling with the dialog boxes, you can do several cute and moderately useful tricks with the data source. The following sections explain these amazing feats.

Sorting records

Suppose that you enter all the names in whatever sequence they were sitting in the pile, but you want to print the letters in alphabetical order. No problem! Just sort the data source.

Sorting is controlled from the Sort Records tab of the Filter and Sort dialog box. To get to this dialog box and sort your merge records, follow these steps:

1. **Start a mail merge as usual. When you get to Step 3 of the Mail Merge Wizard, select the recipient list you want to use.**

The Mail Merge Recipients dialog box appears. (If you have already selected a recipient list, Step 3 includes an Edit Recipient List option you can click to bring up this dialog box.)

2. Click the Edit button.

A dialog box opens that lets you edit recipient addresses, as shown in Figure 4-7.

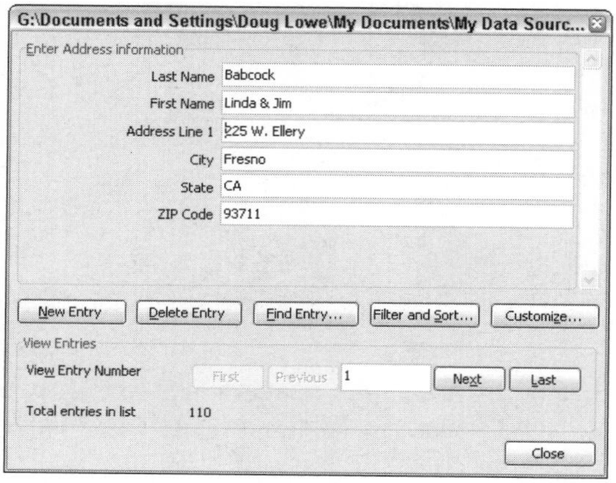

Figure 4-7:
Editing the recipient list.

3. Click the Filter and Sort button.

The Filter and Sort dialog box comes up.

4. Click the Sort Records tab.

The Sort Records tab is brought to the forefront, as shown in Figure 4-8.

Figure 4-8:
The Sort Records tab of the Filter and Sort dialog box.

5. In the Sort By list box, choose the merge field that you want to sort the data source by.

Click the down arrow next to the Sort By list box to reveal a list of all the merge fields in the data source and then choose the one you want to sort the data by. (In Figure 4-8, I already chose LastName for the first sort field.)

If you want to sort records in reverse order, click the appropriate Descending button. Records are then sorted on that field in reverse order, beginning with the *Z*s and working back up to the *A*s.

6. If you want a second or third sort field, set them in the two Then By fields.

The Then By field is used as a tiebreaker when two or more records have the same main Sort By field. For example, in Figure 4-8, I chose FirstName as the second sort field. Then, if the data source has more than one record with the same LastName, they sort into sequence by their first names, like this:

```
King    Larry
King    Martin Luther
King    Stephen
```

If you have a third field you can use as a tiebreaker, set it in the next Then By field.

7. Click OK.

You return to the Mail Merge Wizard.

8. Finish the merge.

Your letters (or envelopes, labels, or whatever) now print in the proper sequence.

Filtering records

Filtering lets you automatically select certain names from your database based on some arbitrary criteria. For example, you may want to send letters only to bald-headed starship captains of French descent. Sending letters to this group is possible if you have fields in your data source for Starfleet rank, degree of baldness, and country of origin.

Unlike the filters in your car, mail merge filters don't fill up with gunk, so you don't have to change them every 5,000 miles. You do have to be careful about how you set them up, though, to be sure that they choose just the records you want to include in your mail merge.

To mail letters to only those lucky few, follow these steps:

1. Start a mail merge as usual. When you get to Step 3 of the Mail Merge Wizard, choose a recipient list.

The Mail Merge Recipients dialog box appears. (If you already have chosen a recipient list, click Edit Recipient List to summon this dialog box.)

2. Click the Edit button.

The dialog box opens that lets you edit recipient addresses (refer to Figure 4-7).

3. **Click the Filter and Sort button and click the Filter Records tab.**

   The Filter Records tab comes to the front, as shown in Figure 4-9.

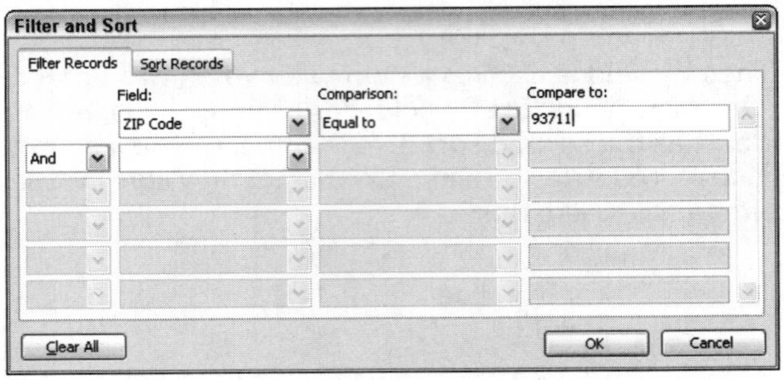

Figure 4-9:
The Filter
Records tab
of the Filter
and Sort
dialog box.

4. **Set the criteria for including records in the mail merge by specifying a Field, Comparison, and Compare To value for each criteria.**

   To create a letter only for people who live in the 93711 zip code, for example, set the first Field to ZIP Code, the first Comparison to Equal To, and the Compare To field to 93711. This filter means the mail merge includes only the records whose ZIP Code field is equal to 93711. (That's how the filter shown in Figure 4-9 is set up.)

   The following section contains an explanation of the options in the Comparison fields.

5. **Click OK, click Close, and then click OK.**

   All the dialog boxes hanging around are dismissed and you go back to your document.

6. **Finish the mail merge.**

   Now, only the records that match the filter criteria are included in the merge.

Understanding relationships

You can set up ten different kinds of tests in the Comparison fields:

✦ **Equal To:** Selects records if the field matches the Compare To value exactly.

✦ **Not Equal To:** Selects records if the field does not match the Compare To value exactly.

✦ **Less Than:** Selects records if the field is less than the Compare To value.

- ✦ **Greater Than:** Selects records if the field is greater than the Compare To value.

- ✦ **Less Than or Equal:** Selects records if the field is less than or equal to the Compare To value.

- ✦ **Greater Than or Equal:** Selects records if the field is greater than or equal to the Compare To value.

- ✦ **Is Blank:** Selects records in which the field is blank.

- ✦ **Is Not Blank:** Selects records in which the field is not blank.

- ✦ **Contains:** Selects records if the field contains the Compare To value.

- ✦ **Does Not Contain:** Selects records if the field does not contain the Compare To value.

Computerniks call these tests *relational tests* because they test the relationship between two things (in this case, a merge field and a specific value). You can use these relational tests to create different kinds of selection filters.

You can set up complicated queries that check the contents of several fields. You may want to mail letters only to people who live in a particular city and state, for example. You set up the query like this:

```
City Equal to Bakersfield
And State Equal to CA
```

In this query, the merge includes only records whose City field is equal to *Bakersfield* and whose State field is equal to *CA*.

You can also set up queries that test the same field twice. To mail to addresses with zip codes 93711 or 93722, for example, set up the query like this:

```
Zip Code Equal to 93711
Or Zip Code Equal to 93722
```

Notice that I change the And/Or field from And to Or. That way, a record is selected if its Zip Code field is 93711 or 93722. If you test the same field for two or more specific values, do not leave the And/Or field set to And. If I left the And/Or field set to And in the preceding example, a record is selected only if its Zip Code field is equal to 93711 and if it is also equal to 93722. Obviously, this situation isn't possible: The zip code may be 93711 or 93722, but it can't be both at the same time. Leaving the And/Or field set to And is natural because you want to "mail letters to everyone in the 93711 *and* 93722 zip codes." But when in this situation, you have to specify Or, not And.

On the other hand, suppose that you want to mail to anyone whose zip code is 93711, 93722, or any value in between. In that case, you use two condition tests linked by And, as shown in this example:

```
Zip Code Greater Than or Equal to 93711
And Zip Code Less Than or Equal to 93722
```

For an even more interesting twist concerning And/Or, see the sidebar "Unprecedented stuff about precedence."

Unprecedented stuff about precedence

Be careful when you set up a query that uses three or more field tests and mixes And and Or. You're confronted with the issue of precedence, which means, in layperson's terms, "The Chicken or the Egg?" You may suppose that Word tests the conditions you list in the Filter and Sort dialog box in the order in which you list them. Not necessarily. Word groups any condition tests linked by And, and then checks them out before combining the results with tests linked by Or.

Confused? So am I. The following example shows how it works. Suppose that you open the menu at a restaurant and see that the fried chicken dinner comes with a "leg or wing and thigh." Which of the following statements represents the two possible chicken dinner combinations you can order:

✔ You can order a meal with a leg and a thigh or you can order a meal with a wing and a thigh.

✔ You can order a meal with a leg or you can order a meal with a wing and thigh.

According to the way Word processes queries, the answer is the second one. Word lumps together as a group the two options linked by And.

If you want the first example to be the right answer, you have to state the menu choice as "leg and thigh or wing and thigh."

For a more realistic Word for Windows example, suppose that you want to mail to everyone who lives in Olympia, WA just across the way in Aberdeen, WA. You may be tempted to set the query up like this:

State Equal To WA
And City Equal To Olympia
Or City Equal To Aberdeen

Unfortunately, that doesn't work. You end up with everyone who lives in Olympia, WA, plus anyone who lives in any town named Aberdeen, regardless of the state (you can find an Aberdeen in Maryland and South Dakota).

You could just petition the federal government to make Aberdeen MD and Aberdeen SD change their names. But the better way is to set up the filter like this:

State Equal To WA
And City Equal To Olympia
Or State Equal To WA
And City Equal to Aberdeen

Book VIII

Customizing Word

The 5th Wave By Rich Tennant

@RICHTENNANT

I'M JUST HAVING TROUBLE DATING A GUY WHOSE NAME DEFAULTS TO "LOONY FRUITCAKE" ON MY SPELL CHECKER.

Contents at a Glance

Chapter 1: Opting for Options

In This Chapter

✔ What's with all these options?

✔ View options

✔ General options

✔ Edit options

✔ Print options

✔ Save options

✔ User information options

✔ Compatibility options

✔ File location options

✔ Security options

✔ Spelling and grammar options

✔ Track changes options

Sometimes I long for the old pre-Windows days, when my favorite word processor was WordPerfect 4.2 and the only real options I had to worry about were whether to change WordPerfect's screen colors or take the afternoon off and catch a quick round of golf. My golf game fell all to pieces after I began using Word. Now, I spend all my free time playing with the options on the Tools⇨Options command, so I don't have any time left over for such luxuries as golf.

You should read this chapter when you finally decide to give in to the Tools⇨ Options command and you want to know what all those options do. This chapter describes the most useful options but, more importantly, it tells you which options you can safely ignore so that you (unlike some people I know — me, for example) can catch up on your golf.

I am aware, of course, that for many people, golf is a more frustrating game than playing with Word. And for some, golf is more boring than reading Word's online help. If you're one of those poor, unenlightened souls, feel free to substitute your favorite non-golf pastime in the preceding paragraphs.

What's with All the Options?

When you choose Tools⇨Options, you are presented with one of the most heavily laden dialog boxes of all time. This dialog box has so many options that it earned Microsoft a Lifetime Achievement Award from the American Society of Windows Programmers.

Like many other dialog boxes in Word, the Options dialog box organizes its settings into tabs. Each tab has its own set of option controls. To switch from one tab to another, just click the tab label at the top of the dialog box.

Most Word dialog boxes that use tabs have two or three tab labels, but the Options dialog box has eleven — that's right, *eleven* — tabs:

+ **View:** Contains options that control the way your document displays on-screen.

+ **General:** Contains a hodgepodge of miscellaneous options that the Microsoft programmers couldn't fit on any of the other tabs.

+ **Edit:** Contains options that affect the way Word's basic text-editing features work.

+ **Print:** Contains options that affect the way the File⇨Print command works.

+ **Save:** Has important options that control the way Word saves your documents.

+ **User Information:** Stores your name and address and other personal information, such as your birth date, height, weight, credit card numbers, bank account balance, and other information Microsoft might be interested in when Bill Gates finally decides to take over the world. (Just kidding.)

+ **Compatibility:** Sets options that determine how Word works with documents created with older versions of Word.

+ **File Locations:** Tells Word where to look for files.

+ **Security:** Sets various security and privacy options, such as password protection for the current document.

+ **Spelling & Grammar:** Turns the spelling and grammar checkers on and off.

+ **Track Changes:** Contains options used in conjunction with the Tools⇨ Track Changes command, which you can find out about in Book III, Chapter 6.

To set options in Word, follow these steps:

1. **Call up Tools⇨Options.**

The Options dialog box appears.

2. **Click the tab that contains an option you want to change.**

If you're not sure which tab contains the option you're looking for, just cycle through the tabs until you find the option.

3. **Set the option however you want.**

Most of the options are simple check boxes that you click to check or uncheck. Some require that you select a choice from a drop-down list, and some have the audacity to require that you type a filename or otherwise demonstrate your keyboard proficiency.

4. **Repeat Steps 2 and 3 until you exhaust your options or until you're just plain exhausted.**

You can set more than one option with a single use of the Tools⇨ Options command.

5. **Click OK.**

You're done!

As you fritter away your day playing with these tabs, keep the following points in mind:

✦ Several of the Options tabs have more than one road that leads to them. You can reach the Print tab, for example, by choosing File⇨Print and then clicking the Options button.

✦ As big as the Options dialog box is, it still isn't big enough to hold all of Word's options. As a result, some of the Options tabs have buttons that bring up additional dialog boxes that have additional tabs. In fact, some of those additional options dialog boxes have more than one tab full of options. Sheesh!

✦ To move to a tab, just click the tab label. You can also move from tab to tab by using the keyboard's arrow keys. To move from the General tab to the Edit tab, for example, press the right arrow key.

Many settings that a normal person would consider *options* are located elsewhere in Word's sinuous menu structure. You use the View⇨Toolbars command, for example, to display or hide toolbars. And you access the AutoCorrect and AutoFormat As You Type features, which control many basic editing options, such as automatically capitalizing new sentences and using fancy curly quotes, from the Tools⇨AutoCorrect command.

Book VIII Chapter 1

Opting for Options

The ten best options

Direct from the Home Office in sunny Fresno, California, here are my top ten favorite options:

1. **Automatic Save (Save options):** This option can be a real lifesaver. Set it to save your work every ten minutes or so and you won't have to worry about losing an entire day's work because of a power failure.

2. **Use Smart Cut and Paste (Edit options):** No more worrying about whether the space is before or after the text cut to the Clipboard. This option handles that for you.

3. **Automatic Word Selection (Edit options):** Without this option, you have to select an entire word and then press Ctrl+B or Ctrl+I to make the word bold or italicized. With this option set, just put the cursor anywhere in the word and any formatting you apply is applied to the entire word.

4. **Recently Used File List (General options):** Saves you from navigating through the Open dialog box. Set it to as high a number as you can tolerate.

5. **Background Printing (Print options):** Why wait for the computer while it prints?

6. **Prompt for Document Properties (Save options):** Summary information is good only if you create it for every document. Turning on this option improves the odds that you remember to type a subject, keywords, and comments for each document you create.

7. **Documents (File Locations options):** You can set this option to direct Word to look in any folder you want.

8. **Style Area Width (View options):** If you use lots of styles, setting this option to 0.6 inches can help you keep track of which styles you use.

9. **Text Boundaries (View options):** When you're trying to line up columns and frames, this option is a must. It is available only in Page Layout view.

10. **Eighteen holes of golf:** Better than the other nine options put together.

Vivid View Options

The options on the View tab, shown in Figure 1-1, let you customize the appearance of Word's humble display. The View options are arranged in four groups: Show, Formatting Marks, Print and Web Layout, and Outline and Normal.

A few of the Show options are available only when you work in Print Layout view. As a result, you need to switch to Print Layout view before calling up Tools⇨Options to set those features.

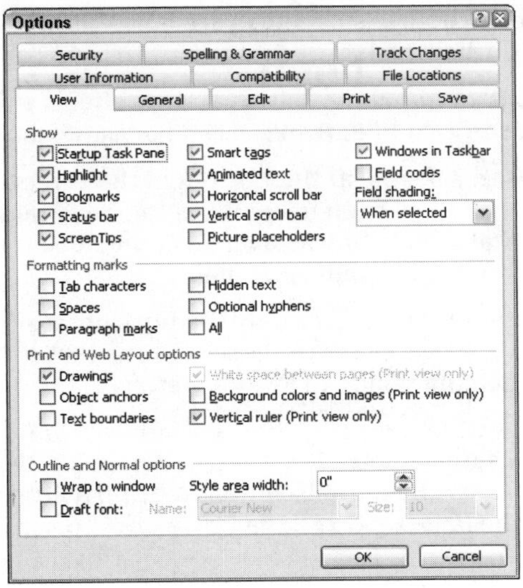

Figure 1-1:
The View
options.

The Show options

The View options grouped under the Show heading control the amount of detail displayed in the document window. The following list gives you the lowdown on each of the options you can set from this tab:

✦ **Startup Task Pane:** Indicates whether the task pane displays when Word starts.

✦ **Highlight:** Turns off the highlighting made by Word's Highlight feature.

✦ **Bookmarks**: Takes text referred to in a bookmark and sandwiches it between gray brackets.

✦ **Status Bar:** Word's dashboard. It tells you what page you're on, where you are on the page, whether you pressed the Insert key to switch to Overtype mode, and so on. If all this stuff just takes up space, you can remove it by unchecking the Status Bar option. This action leaves more room for your document.

✦ **ScreenTips:** Check this option to enable screen tips that appear when you hover the mouse over certain Word items, such as comments or hyperlinks.

This option does not control the screen tips that display when you hover the mouse over a toolbar button. That option is controlled via Tools➪Customize. For more information, see Chapter 2 of this minibook.

✦ **Smart Tags:** Controls whether smart tags are highlighted. For more information, see Book III, Chapter 4.

✦ **Animated Text:** Controls whether text animation effects show. (Text animations are set via the Text Effects tab of the Format⇨Font command.)

✦ **Horizontal Scroll Bar:** The one at the bottom of the screen. If you discover one day that you have been using Word for two years and didn't know that a horizontal scroll bar was available, uncheck this option to free up more space to display your document.

Unchecking this option removes not only the horizontal scroll bar, but also the view buttons next to it. With these buttons removed, you have to use the View menu commands to switch views.

✦ **Vertical Scroll Bar:** At the right edge of the window. If your text is just a wee bit wide for the screen, consider unchecking the Vertical Scroll Bar option to remove the scroll bar. This action frees up a little space, and you can still press the Page Up and Page Down keys to scroll through your document.

✦ **Picture Placeholders:** If you insert a picture into a document, you notice that Word hesitates a little when you scroll the picture into the document window. If you add 20 pictures to a document, the hesitations may come so often that you want to scream. Checking the Picture Placeholders option causes Word to display a simple rectangle where the picture goes. This step eliminates the hesitation, but of course hides the pictures so you can't see what they look like until you print the document.

✦ **Windows in Taskbar:** Displays each open document as an icon on the Windows task bar. If you uncheck this option, only one icon for Word appears on the task bar regardless of how many documents are open.

✦ **Field Codes:** Shows the codes inserted for each field rather than the results of the field. Use this option when you're struggling with a maniacal mail merge.

✦ **Field Shading:** Shades field results to draw attention to them. You can set this option to Never (which never shades field results), Always (which always shades field results), and When Selected (which shades field results only when some or all of the field is selected).

The Formatting Marks options

The View options grouped in the Formatting Marks section let you control which special characters display in the document window:

✦ **Tab Characters:** Displays tab characters as an arrow. I usually leave this option checked so that I can keep track of tabs.

✦ **Spaces:** Displays spaces as little dots. I usually leave this option unchecked. But some people like to see the little dots so they can tell where they type spaces.

✦ **Paragraph Marks:** Displays paragraph marks. I usually leave this option checked so that I can quickly find extraneous paragraphs.

✦ **Hidden Text:** Displays hidden text. Hidden text is text that is in your document, but isn't printed. It's marked as hidden via the Format⇨ Font command.

✦ **Optional Hyphens:** Displays optional hyphens, which are helpful when you want precise control over hyphenation.

✦ **All:** Displays all hidden characters. Choosing this option is the same as clicking the Show/Hide button on the Standard toolbar.

When the Show/Hide button on the Standard toolbar is depressed, all non-printing characters display. When the button is not depressed, only those nonprinting characters specified on the View tab display. Set the options on the View tab so that only those nonprinting characters you *always* want to display — such as tab characters and paragraph marks — are checked. You can display the other nonprinting characters at any time simply by clicking the Show/Hide button.

The Print and Web Layout options

The View options grouped under the Print and Web Layout Options heading let you tweak the appearance of Word documents when viewed in Print Layout or Web Layout view. This list shows the details:

✦ **Drawings:** Displays drawing objects. If you uncheck this option, Word displays a rectangle for each drawing object rather than the object itself.

✦ **Object Anchors:** Displays anchors for frames and drawing objects.

✦ **Text Boundaries:** Displays lines around columns and margins so that you can quickly see the page layout.

✦ **White Space Between Pages:** Displays extra space between each page.

✦ **Background Colors and Images:** Displays background colors and images for Web pages.

✦ **Vertical Ruler:** Places a ruler at the left edge of the window.

The Outline and Normal options

The options in the last section of the View tab apply only when you're work-ing in Normal view or Outline view. The options are

✦ **Wrap to Window:** Keeps text within the document window by breaking lines too wide to fit in the window. When you use this option, the line endings you see on-screen are different from the line endings that print.

✦ **Style Area Width:** If you want to see the names of styles you assign to your paragraphs all lined up in a neat row down the left side of the window, increase the setting of this option from 0 inches to about 0.6 inches. To remove the style area, return this setting to 0.

✦ **Draft Font:** This option displays all text in the same font regardless of what font the text is actually formatted with. The default is 10pt Courier New, but you can change the font if you want. If you're running Word on a computer that was manufactured in the 1940s, you may want to turn on this option. Otherwise, ignore it.

Gregarious General Options

Back in the days of Microsoft Word Version 1.0, the options on the General tab were lowly Private Options. But they re-upped for Version 2 and eventually decided to become career options. Now they've made it all the way to the rank of General. You'd better snap-to whenever you call up these options (see Figure 1-2).

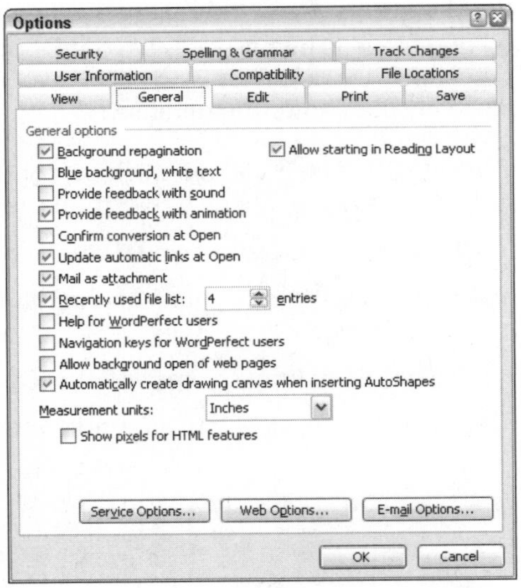

Figure 1-2:
The General
options.

This list gives you the lowdown on what the General options do:

✦ **Background Repagination:** Ever notice that when you take a breather from your sustained typing rate of 90 words per minute, Word sometimes causes page breaks to dance about? This dance is Word's

Background Repagination feature at work, constantly surveying the length of your document and inserting page breaks where they rightfully belong. If you uncheck this box, Word repaginates the document only when you print it; create a Table of Contents, index, or other table; or work in Page Layout or Print Preview view.

Turning Background Repagination off may make your computer run a little faster, but you'll always be wondering whether you're at the top or bottom of the page. I don't recommend it. (You can't turn off Background Repagination when you're in Page Layout view because Page Layout view requires that page breaks always be up to date.)

✦ **Allow Starting in Reading Layout:** Allows Word to start up in Reading Layout view.

✦ **Blue Background, White Text:** Once upon a time, there was a word processing program called WordPerfect. It displayed white text on a blue background. If you long for the old days, turn on this option. (Okay, I know WordPerfect is still around. It probably still has a white-on-blue option too.)

✦ **Provide Feedback with Sound:** Causes Word to beep, boop, and otherwise chortle whenever it needs to get your attention. Turn this option on if you want to constantly remind your neighbors that you haven't yet mastered Word.

✦ **Provide Feedback with Animation:** Lets Word show off by displaying clever animations when you perform certain actions, such as saving files or printing.

✦ **Confirm Conversion at Open:** This option is not some kind of religious awakening. Instead, it merely instructs Word to ask for your consent before opening a document that was created by some other program.

✦ **Update Automatic Links at Open:** Automatically updates any files that are linked to a document when you open the document. Leaving this option on is usually best.

✦ **Mail as Attachment:** When you send a document by e-mail, this option causes the document to be sent as an attachment rather than as the body of the message.

✦ **Recently Used File List:** Tells Word how many files to list at the bottom of the File menu. You can list as many as nine files.

✦ **Help for WordPerfect Users:** For those of you who are just now switching from WordPerfect to Word, this option can come in handy. If you momentarily forget that you're using Word and press a WordPerfect function key, such as Shift+F7, you receive a minor electric shock as a gentle reinforcement to use the correct Word command instead.

For maximum effectiveness, use this option in conjunction with the WordPerfect Help Assistance Coupler (WHAC), a device that plugs into your computer's USB port and attaches to your wrist. You need to also make sure you're properly grounded.

✦ **Navigation Keys for WordPerfect Users:** Yet another futile attempt to help WordPerfect users who have been forced at gunpoint to switch to Word, this time by making the Page Up, Page Down, Home, End, and Esc keys behave in the same brain-damaged manner as they do in WordPerfect.

✦ **Allow Background Open of Web Pages.** When you open HTML pages that take a long time to load, this option allows you to continue working on other documents while the Web page loads.

✦ **Automatically Create Drawing Canvas When Inserting AutoShapes:** If the drawing canvas really annoys you, you can turn it off by unchecking this option. If you find that you do need a drawing canvas for a particularly complex picture, you can always insert one manually by using Insert⇨Picture⇨New Drawing. For more information about drawing canvases, see Book IV, Chapter 2 for more information.

✦ **Measurement Units:** In case you don't like inches, you can change Word's measurements to centimeters, points, picas, fathoms, leagues, cubits, or parsecs.

✦ **Show Pixels for HTML Features:** Makes pixel the default choice for the measurement unit for Web documents.

At the bottom of the General tab, you find three buttons that bring up additional dialog boxes stuffed with options:

✦ **Service Options:** Brings up the dialog box shown in Figure 1-3. This dialog box lets you control several options that come into play when you connect to the Internet. For some reason, Microsoft decided not to provide tabs in this dialog box. Instead, you choose one of the categories in the Categories list to display the various options. The categories are:

   • **Customer Feedback Options:** Lets you grant Microsoft permission to snoop on you as you use Word. Microsoft promises that this snooping is anonymous, and that it only gathers information about how you use Microsoft products.

   • **Online Content:** This category has one particularly useful option — the Search Online Content When Connected option. If this option is selected, which it is by default, Word downloads help information from the Internet every time you use Help. If you use Help a lot (as I do, especially when I'm writing a book), that can grow annoying. On the other hand, if you don't use Help very often, this option ensures that when you do use Help, you get the most current Help information that's available.

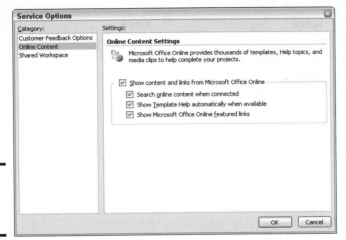

Figure 1-3:
Setting the
Service
options.

- ✦ **Shared Workspace:** If you use the Shared Workspace feature, you can use this category to set various options. For more information about this feature, see Book III, Chapter 6.

- ✦ **Web Options:** Brings up a separate dialog box that lets you set options for working with Web pages. I describe these options in Book V, Chapter 2.

- ✦ **E-mail Options:** This button brings up a dialog box that lets you set options for working with e-mail. For example, you can automatically add a signature to the end of every message you compose.

Extraordinary Edit Options

The Edit tab, shown in Figure 1-4 and in the following list, affects the way Word's basic editing operations work. The first group of options is bundled under the Editing Options heading:

- ✦ **Typing Replaces Selection:** If you highlight text by dragging the mouse over it or by holding down the Shift key while moving the cursor and then type something, the whatever-it-was-you-typed obliterates the whatever-it-was-you-highlighted. If this behavior drives you bonkers, you can turn it off by unchecking the Typing Replaces Selection check box.

- ✦ **Drag-and-Drop Text Editing:** More commonly known as dragon dropping, this option lets you move text by selecting it and then dragging it with the mouse. If it annoys you, turn it off by unchecking this field.

**Book VIII
Chapter 1**

Opting for Options

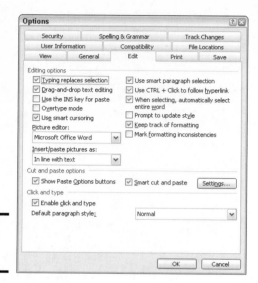

Figure 1-4:
The Edit
options.

✦ **Use the INS Key for Paste:** Way back in Book III, Chapter 2, I told you about Overtype mode, which is actually a cruel practical joke invented by a Word programmer who worked on Word version 1. If you want to make the Insert key do something more useful than throw you into Overtype mode, check this option. Then, the Insert key doubles as a shortcut for Edit⇨Paste.

✦ **Overtype Mode:** Speaking of Overtype mode, sneak into someone's office late at night, call up Tools⇨Options, and check this option. Then let out an evil laugh when they shout obscenities every time they start up Word and don't discover that it's in Overtype mode until it's too late.

I don't know what got into me. Don't under any circumstances do this. Please. Playing with other people's computers isn't nice.

✦ **Use Smart Cursoring:** This option automatically moves the insertion point as you scroll your document using the scrolling keys (such as Page Up or Page Down).

✦ **Picture Editor:** Lets you use a graphics program other than Word to edit imported graphics.

✦ **Insert/Paste Pictures As:** Lets you set the default text wrapping mode for inserted or pasted pictures. For more information, refer to Book IV, Chapter 1.

✦ **Use Smart Paragraph Selection:** Keeps paragraph formatting intact when you cut and paste paragraphs.

✦ **Use CTRL+Click to Follow Hyperlink:** If selected, this option allows you to follow a hyperlink by clicking it while holding down the Ctrl key.

✦ **When Selecting, Automatically Select Entire Word:** One of the niftiest features in Word. It causes Word to assume that you meant to select an entire word. For example, if you place the cursor in the middle of a word and press Ctrl+I, the entire word is italicized. It can be disconcerting at first, though. If it's against your religion, you can turn it off by unchecking the Automatic Word Selection check box.

✦ **Prompt to Update Style:** If this option is on, Word asks what you want to do if you modify the format of some text, and then reapply the previously applied style . The prompt asks if you want to revert to the formatting specified by the style or if you want to update the style to reflect the new formatting.

✦ **Keep Track of Formatting:** This option tells Word to automatically create a style every time you apply formatting. This feature is pretty cool because you can then modify the style to make consistent changes to your document. On the other hand, Word can go a little overboard creating styles. You may find that your style list fills up with dozens of styles that Word created as it tracked every little formatting change you made.

✦ **Mark Formatting Inconsistencies:** This nifty option causes Word to alert you when you apply formatting that is similar to, but not exactly the same as, other formatting in the document. A wavy blue underline indicates inconsistent formatting. You can right-click the underlined words to see one or more suggested changes to make the formatting more consistent.

The Cut and Paste Options section of the Edit tab contains the following options:

✦ **Show Paste Options Buttons:** This option displays a Paste Options button at the bottom corner of text you paste into your document. You can click this button to reveal a menu of options for formatting the pasted text.

✦ **Smart Cut and Paste:** Adjusts spaces before and after text you cut and paste so that you don't end up with two spaces between some words and no spaces between others. Leave this option checked; it's too good to turn off.

You can also click the Settings button, which brings up the Settings dialog box shown in Figure 1-5. This dialog box gives you more control over exactly how smart cut and paste works.

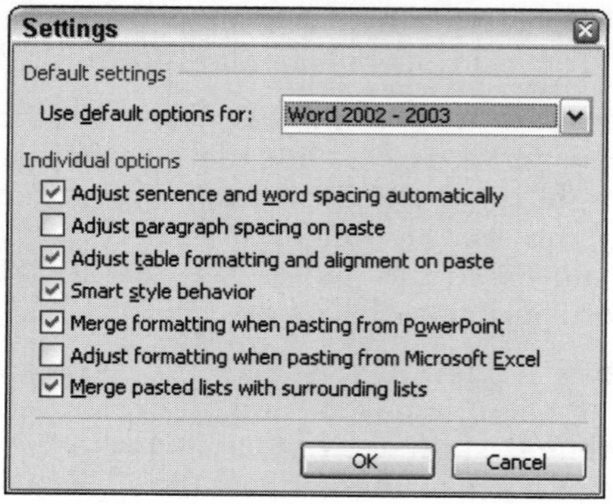

Settings

Default settings

Use default options for: Word 2002 - 2003

Individual options

- ☑ Adjust sentence and word spacing automatically
- ☐ Adjust paragraph spacing on paste
- ☑ Adjust table formatting and alignment on paste
- ☑ Smart style behavior
- ☑ Merge formatting when pasting from PowerPoint
- ☐ Adjust formatting when pasting from Microsoft Excel
- ☑ Merge pasted lists with surrounding lists

OK   Cancel

Figure 1-5:
Changing
the smart
cut and
paste
settings.

The Click and Type section contains two additional options:

✦ **Enable Click and Type:** This option enables the Click and Type feature, which lets you place text anywhere on a page by double-clicking where you want to place the text and typing. Word automatically adjusts the indentation or tabs necessary to get the text at the right place. This feature works only in Print Layout or Web Layout view.

✦ **Default Paragraph Style:** Lets you specify the style to apply to text created with the Click and Type feature.

Precocious Print Options

Figure 1-6 shows the options available from the Print tab. You can reach this tab by choosing Tools⇨Options, or you can access it from File⇨Print and clicking the Options button. I describe these options in detail in Book I, Chapter 4, so I won't repeat each of the options here. Instead, I just remind you about the most important ones:

✦ **Update Fields:** Updates the contents of fields before printing. I recommend turning on this option.

✦ **Background Printing:** Speeds printing and allows you to continue working while a long document is printing.

✦ **Document Properties:** If you want document properties to print as a separate page, select this option.

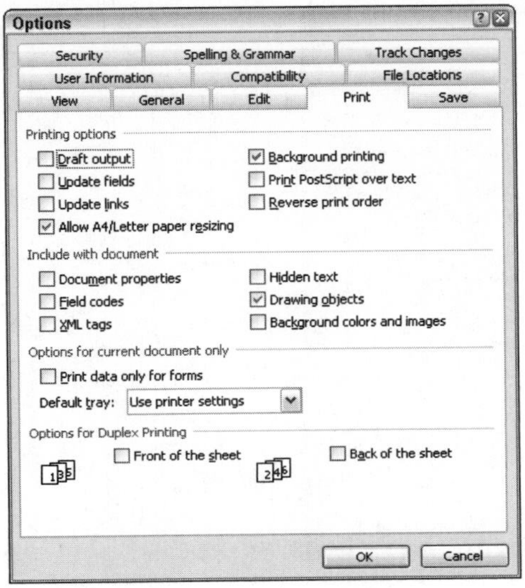

Figure 1-6:
The Print
options.

Savvy Save Options

The Save tab of the Tools⇨Options command contains several options that affect how Word saves document files. Figure 1-7 shows these options. Because I describe these options in detail in Book I, Chapter 2, I won't review them in detail here. Instead, I just review the most important Save options:

✦ **Always Create Backup Copy:** This option isn't nearly as useful as you may think at first, especially if you frequently save your documents, which you should. Still, it's a good safety net, so I recommend it.

✦ **Allow Fast Saves:** Use this option if you work on large documents that take a long time to save. Avoid it if your documents are small and save quickly.

✦ **Embed TrueType Fonts:** Use this option if you want to share the document with another user who doesn't have the same fonts that you do.

✦ **Save AutoRecovery Info Every *N* Minutes:** Automatically saves recovery information at regular intervals. The default setting is to save the recovery information every 10 minutes, but you can change the time interval if you want. I like to set it for 5 minutes.

Options

Security	Spelling & Grammar	Track Changes
User Information	Compatibility	File Locations
View	General	Edit	Print	Save

Save options

☐ Always create backup copy
☐ Allow fast saves
☑ Allow background saves
☐ Embed TrueType fonts
    ☐ Embed characters in use only
    ☐ Do not embed common system fonts
☐ Make local copy of files stored on network or removable drives
☑ Save AutoRecover info every: 5 ⏶ minutes
☑ Embed smart tags
☐ Save smart tags as XML properties in Web pages

☐ Prompt for document properties
☐ Prompt to save Normal template
☐ Save data only for forms
☑ Embed linguistic data

Default format

Save Word files as: Word Document (*.doc) ▼
☐ Disable features introduced after: Microsoft Word 97 ▼

[OK]   [Cancel]

Figure 1-7:
The Save
options.

Unbelievable User Information Options

The User Information tab, shown in Figure 1-8, lets you provide your own name, initials, and address. This information is used in several ways:

✦ In the document properties when you save a document

✦ In comments and in revision marks when you track changes

✦ In envelopes, labels, and letters

In case you're wondering, Marcellus Washburn is Professor Harold Hill's sidekick in *The Music Man*.

Counterproductive Compatibility Options

The Compatibility tab, shown in Figure 1-9, allows you to change the way Word displays documents so that it more closely resembles an earlier version of Word or WordPerfect. These options don't actually change the contents of your document or the way your documents save. Instead, they just change the way the documents display.

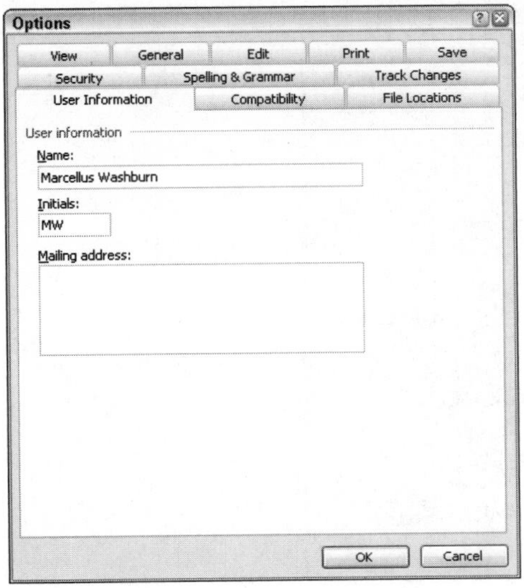

Figure 1-8:
The User
Information
options.

I recommend you stay away from this tab completely. If you must venture here, you find the following options:

✦ **Font Substitution:** This button brings up a dialog box that lets you specify which fonts to display if a document contains a font you don't have on your computer.

✦ **Recommended Options For:** Lets you choose the Word or WordPerfect version for which you want to set the display. Selecting a Word or WordPerfect version from this list changes the combination of options that are selected in the Options list.

✦ **Options:** Lists the compatibility options and indicates which ones are selected. You can specify your own custom combination of options by setting these options however you want.

✦ **Default:** Makes the current selections the default compatibility options.

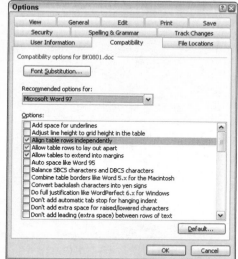

Figure 1-9:
The
Compatibility
options.

Fidgety File Locations Options

The File Locations tab of the Tools➪Options command lets you customize Word by changing the locations of various files that are used. Figure 1-10 shows the File Locations tab.

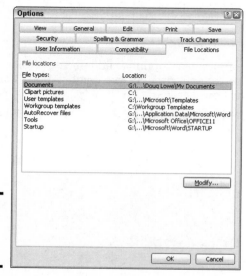

Figure 1-10:
The File
Locations
options.

The File Locations tab consists of a list of files used by Word and a Modify button. To change the location of one of these file types, choose it in the File Types list and then click Modify. You are greeted with a dialog box you can use to choose the drive and directory in which the files are located.

This list gives you the lowdown on the file types:

✦ **Documents:** Changes the default folder for the File⇨Open and File⇨ Save As commands.

✦ **Clipart Pictures:** If you have your own collection of clip art, you may want to modify this file type to make your clip art easier to find.

✦ **User Templates:** You should probably leave this one alone. It tells Word where to create templates.

✦ **Workgroup Templates:** This option lets you set up a secondary location for template files.

✦ **All the rest:** Leave the rest of the options alone.

Secret Security Options

The Security tab, shown in Figure 1-11, lets you set security options, such as passwords.

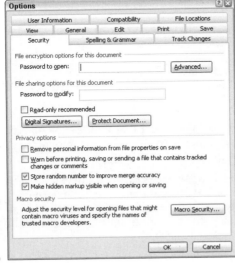

Figure 1-11:
The Security
options.

The following list describes the options you can use to secure the current document. *Note:* These options affect only the current document; they don't affect other documents.

+ **Password to Open:** Specifies a password that must be entered before the document can be opened. When you click OK to close the Options dialog box, you are prompted to enter the password again to make sure you typed it correctly.

   Word doesn't provide any way to recover a forgotten password. If you forget the password, you can't open the document.

+ **Advanced:** Brings up a separate dialog box that lets you specify advanced password options. Use this button only if you work for the CIA.

+ **Password to Modify:** Lets you specify a password that must be entered to save changes to the document. If the user doesn't know the password, he or she must use the Save As command to save changes to a new document. When you click OK to close the Options dialog box, you are prompted to enter the password again to make sure you typed it properly.

+ **Read-Only Recommended:** Displays a prompt whenever the document is opened recommending that the document be opened in read-only mode. This option is a good idea for documents that change infrequently, but that you don't want to go to the trouble of creating passwords for.

+ **Digital Signatures:** Opens the Digital Signatures dialog box, which lets you add a digital certificate to the document to guarantee the document's authenticity.

+ **Protect Document:** Brings up the Protect Document task bar, which I describe in Book VI, Chapter 2.

The Security tab also includes several options that let you limit the amount of personal information that may creep into a Word document. Those options include:

+ **Remove Personal Information from File Properties on Save:** Use this option if you don't want people to see personal information if they snoop around the file properties.

+ **Warn Before Printing, Saving, or Sending a File That Contains Tracked Changes or Comments:** If you send someone a file with tracked changes, that person can easily see text that you deleted or modified. This option issues a gentle reminder that you may want to accept all changes before continuing.

♦ **Store Random Number to Improve Merge Accuracy:** If you want to send a document to several reviewers and later merge the revisions from each reviewer, this option helps Word keep track of the documents.

♦ **Make Hidden Markup Visible When Opening or Saving:** This option displays all comments, revisions, and other types of markup when the document is opened.

Finally, the Security tab also includes a Macro Security button that lets you set security options for working with macros. For more information about macros, refer to Book IX, Chapter 1.

Serious Spelling Options

The Spelling & Grammar tab, shown in Figure 1-12, lets you control the options for the spelling and grammar checker. I describe these options in Book III, Chapter 5, so I won't repeat the description of each option here. *Note:* You can reach these options via Tools⇨Options, or you can click the Options button in the Spelling dialog box during a spell check.

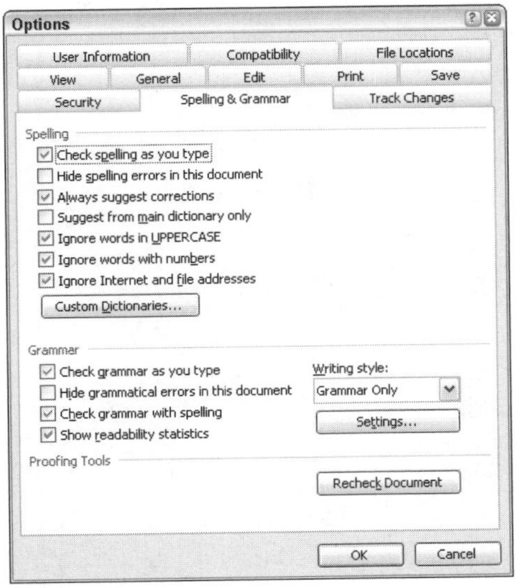

Figure 1-12: The Spelling options.

Book VIII Chapter 1

Opting for Options

Tenacious Track Changes Options

The Track Changes tab, featured in Figure 1-13, lets you change the way tracked changes display. In particular, you can set the formatting used for insertions, deletions, and format changes, and you can change how lines or borders highlight changed lines. You can also specify whether balloons are used for all changes or just for comments, how large the balloons are, and how they display.

For more information about the Track Changes feature, see Book III, Chapter 6.

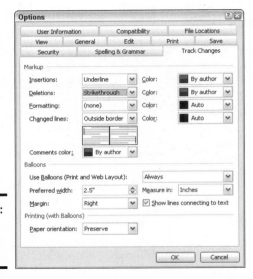

Figure 1-13:
The Track
Changes
options.

Chapter 2: Customizing Toolbars, Menus, and Keyboard Shortcuts

In This Chapter

- ✔ **Making toolbars appear (and disappear!)**
- ✔ **Adding buttons to a toolbar**
- ✔ **Creating a new toolbar**
- ✔ **Messing with menus**
- ✔ **Adding custom keyboard shortcuts**

Hiding down at the bottom of the Tools menu is a potent little Customize command. Lurking within the dialog box that appears when you conjure up this command is the ability to improve the toolbars, menus, and keyboard shortcuts that come with Word. If you routinely apply a Limerick style to samples of fine poetry within your documents, for example, you can add a Limerick button to one of Word's toolbars. Or you can add a Limerick command to the Format menu or define Ctrl+L as a keyboard shortcut for applying the Limerick style. This chapter shows you how.

Please feel free to skip this chapter if you already think that Word is the world's perfect word processor, beyond need for refinement.

Customized toolbars, menus, and keyboard shortcuts are stored along with styles, AutoText, and macros in document templates. Unless you specify otherwise, any customizations you create are stored in the Normal.dot template so that they are available to all documents. If you want, you can store customizations in other templates so that they are available only when you're editing documents attached to those templates. For the complete scoop on templates, see Book I, Chapter 3.

Belly Up to the Button Bar

Martin Luther said, "If you must sin, sin boldly!" The people who designed Word's toolbar buttons were apparently students of Luther because they didn't just throw in a few buttons here and there — they threw in 19 separate toolbars, with something like 98 different buttons. Kind of inspires a song:

Ninety-eight buttons appear on the screen,
Ninety-eight buttons appear,
Tools⇨Customize is a button's demise,
Ninety-seven buttons appear on the screen.

If 98 buttons aren't enough for you, Word keeps a few dozen unused buttons in reserve. You can add these buttons to any of the existing toolbars, or you can create new button bars altogether. And if that's *still* not enough, you can even design your own buttons.

Strictly speaking, the only difference between Word's menu bar and its various toolbars is that the menu bar happens to be filled up with menus, and you can't hide it. In other words, the menu bar is just a special type of toolbar.

Although Word comes configured with just one menu bar and 19 toolbars that are accessed from View⇨Toolbars, you can display a total of 31 toolbars in the Word window. Of course, you wouldn't want to display them all unless you have a 30 inch monitor. Just for fun, Figure 2-1 shows that you can display all the toolbars and still see a few lines of your document. Pretty impressive, eh?

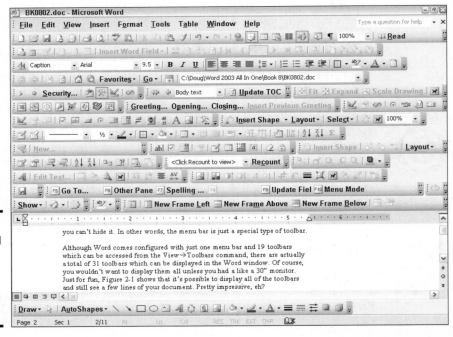

Figure 2-1:
It's cramped
quarters
when all of
Word's
toolbars are
visible.

The best thing about Word's toolbars is that you can completely customize the toolbars that come with Word, and you can add new ones of your own. Microsoft did its best to decide which toolbar buttons are most useful for a widest range of users, and it did a pretty good job, especially with the Standard and Formatting toolbars. Still, you're bound to find several toolbar buttons that you rarely, if ever, use. And if you think for a moment, you can probably come up with a button or two you wish you had.

For example, I almost never use right-justified paragraphs. But I frequently use hanging indents. So I replaced the Align Right button with a custom Hanging Indent button. I even drew my own design for the button image; it took only a minute or two. Now, Word works and looks the way I want it to, not the way Microsoft thinks I want it to work and look.

Making toolbars appear (and disappear!)

If your favorite toolbar is missing, you or someone else may have inadvertently sent it to toolbar exile. To get the toolbar back, follow these steps:

1. **Call up View⇨Toolbars.**

The Toolbars menu appears, as shown in Figure 2-2.

Book VIII
Chapter 2

Customizing
Toolbars, Menus,
and Keyboard
Shortcuts

Figure 2-2:
The
Toolbars
menu.

2. Click the toolbar that you want to display.

A check mark appears in the box and the toolbar displays.

To make a toolbar disappear, repeat the procedure. Choosing an already visible toolbar causes that toolbar to vanish.

Here are a few points to ponder when you display toolbars:

✦ Some toolbars cling to one of the sides of the document window, whereas others are free spirits that wander about the window. Toolbars that cling to one of the edges are called *docked toolbars*. Free ranging toolbars are called *floating toolbars*.

✦ If you don't like the position of a toolbar on-screen, you can move it. To move a docked toolbar, point to the four vertical dots at the left edge of the toolbar, and then click and drag. To move a floating toolbar, drag it by the title.

✦ You can also change the shape of a floating toolbar by dragging one of its edges or corners.

✦ Another way to summon the Toolbars menu is to right-click any visible toolbar.

To make a floating toolbar go away, click the close button in its top-right corner.

Removing toolbar buttons

In case you don't like the buttons that appear on Word's toolbars, you can remove buttons you don't use. You often have to remove some buttons before you add new ones to a toolbar because the toolbars that come with Word are stuffed to the gills with buttons.

Follow these steps to remove a button:

1. Call up Tools⇨Customize.

The Customize dialog box appears, as shown in Figure 2-3.

2. Point to the button you want to remove, and then press and hold down the mouse button and drag the button off the toolbar.

Where you drag the button doesn't matter; just drag it well clear of the toolbar.

3. **Release the mouse button, and the toolbar button is removed.**

   The other buttons on the toolbar hold a little farewell party, and then go on about their business.

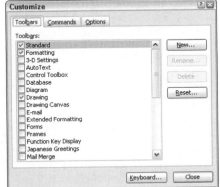

Figure 2-3:
The Customize dialog box with the Toolbars tab showing.

Keep these important points in mind when you remove a button:

+ The Undo command (Ctrl+Z) doesn't cover modifications you make to a toolbar. If you inadvertently delete a toolbar button, however, you can quickly restore the entire toolbar to its pristine condition by using Tools⇨Customize and clicking the Reset button that appears on the Toolbars tab.

+ The Customize command is also available from View⇨Toolbars. And you can get to it by right-clicking any toolbar and choosing the Customize command that appears in the pop-up menu.

Adding a new button to a toolbar

Although View⇨Toolbars lets you access 19 toolbars capable of showing millions of buttons, that's not enough. If you want to add an extra button to a toolbar, follow these steps:

1. **Call up Tools⇨Customize.**

   The Customize dialog box appears (refer to Figure 2-3).

2. **Click the Commands tab.**

   Figure 2-4 shows the Commands tab of the Customize dialog box.

3. Choose the button you want to add from the Category list.

As you scroll through the Categories list, the buttons shown in the Commands section of the dialog box change to indicate which buttons are available for the category. As you examine the categories, you see familiar buttons, such as the New, Open, and Save buttons. But you also find many unfamiliar buttons. These represent Word commands you didn't know existed because they aren't on any of the menus or toolbars by default.

Figure 2-4: The Customize dialog box with the Commands tab showing.

If you're patient enough, you can scroll through the entire Categories list and find four interesting categories hiding out near the bottom of the list: Macros, Fonts, AutoText, and Styles. These options don't present a bunch of predefined buttons you can use. Instead, they let you assign buttons to the specific macros, fonts, AutoText entries, or styles that are available. This commands let you create a toolbar button that runs a macro, applies a font, inserts a specific AutoText entry, or applies a style.

Just above the Macros, Fonts, AutoText, and Style categories is the All Commands category. It lists all the commands available in Word, in alphabetic order.

4. Choose the button you want to add and drag it to the toolbar you want to add the button to, at the location where you want the button added.

As soon as you release the mouse button, the toolbar button is added to the toolbar right where you clicked.

5. Click Close to dismiss the Customize dialog box.

You're finished!

Creating a new toolbar

If you can't find room for a few extra tools in one of the existing toolbars, you can create a new toolbar. Just follow these steps:

1. Call up Tools⇨Customize and click the Toolbars tab.

The Toolbars tab of the Customize dialog box appears. If you must look, refer to Figure 2-3. That's quite a few pages back, though, and you don't really need to see it to continue to the next step.

2. Click New.

A dialog box appears, asking you to type a name for the new toolbar as shown in Figure 2-5.

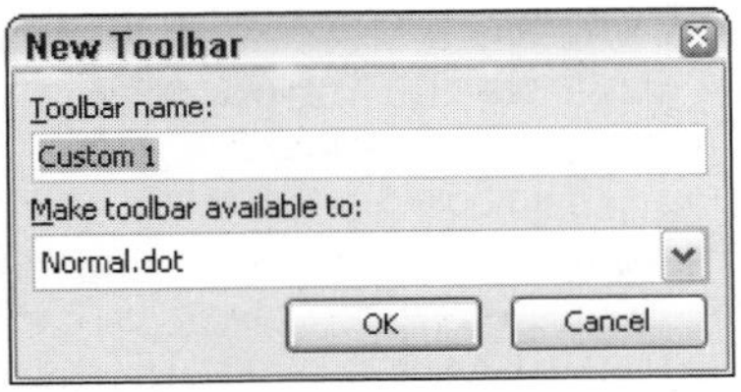

Figure 2-5:
The New
Toolbar
dialog box.

New Toolbar

Toolbar name:

Custom 1

Make toolbar available to:

Normal.dot

OK   Cancel

3. Type a name for the toolbar and then click OK.

Use whatever name you want. When you click OK, Word creates a new toolbar. The new toolbar is devoid of buttons, but you take care of that in the next step.

4. Click the Commands tab in the Customize dialog box and drag whatever buttons you want to the new toolbar.

Refer to the section "Adding a new button to a toolbar" earlier in this chapter for the complete steps for adding buttons.

5. Click Close.

The Customize dialog box vanishes.

6. Move the new toolbar to its final resting place.

Drag it by the edge to wherever you want it to appear on-screen.

7. You're finished.

**Book VIII
Chapter 2**

Customizing
Toolbars, Menus,
and Keyboard
Shortcuts

To delete a toolbar you created, use the Toolbars tab of the Tools⇨Customize command. Choose the toolbar you want to delete, and then click the Delete button. *Note:* Word won't let you delete any of the predefined toolbars that come with Word; you can delete only toolbars you've added yourself.

Creating a custom button

If you can't find a button that meets your needs among the categories of predefined buttons, you can always create a custom button. You can create custom buttons for any of the following:

✦ Any Word command

✦ Macros

✦ Fonts

✦ Styles

✦ AutoText entries

When you create a custom button, you can select one of 42 predefined custom button images, create your own image for the button, or create a text button that shows descriptive text rather than a graphical image.

To create a custom button, follow the same steps as you do to add a predefined button to a toolbar. When you are ready to select the category, choose All Commands, Macros, Fonts, Styles, or AutoText. Then, drag the command, macro, font, style, or AutoText selection to the desired location on the toolbar of your choice. When you release the mouse button, the button is added as a text button. Right-click the new text button, and then choose Change Button Image to display the list of button images shown in Figure 2-6. Finally, click the button image you want to assign to the new button.

Figure 2-6:
Word provides 42 predefined button images for your custom buttons.

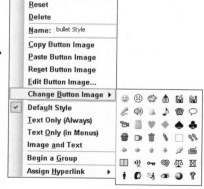

When you create a text button, Word assumes that you want to use the name of the macro, style, font, or AutoText entry as the text button name. You usually have little reason to change Word's proposed name for styles, fonts, or AutoText entries. For macros, you probably want to choose a shorter, more descriptive name. To change the button name, summon Tools➪Customize, and then right-click the button whose name you want to change and type a new name in the Name field.

To use a button image instead of text, summon Tools➪Customize, and then right-click the button and choose Default Style from the pop-up menu. To show both an image and text, right-click the button and choose Image and Text.

Editing button images

If you are creating a custom toolbar button image and you discover that none of the 42 supplied button images is appropriate, you can create your own button by right-clicking the button you want to customize, and then choosing the Edit Button Image command. The dialog box shown in Figure 2-7 displays, which allows you to create any button image you want. You can start with any of the 42 predefined custom buttons and work from there, or you can click the Clear button and start from scratch.

Figure 2-7:
Creating
your own
button
image.

Book VIII
Chapter 2

Customizing
Toolbars, Menus,
and Keyboard
Shortcuts

To paint the button image, click the color you want to paint with and click in the picture area wherever you want to paint. Each square in the picture represents one pixel in the image. As you paint, you can see the effects your actions have on the full-sized version of the button image in the Preview area of the Button Editor dialog box.

The half-gray squares in the Picture area represent pixels that have no color; they allow the background color of the toolbar to show through. When you click a square, it changes to the selected color. Click the square again to change it to transparent.

You can use the four arrow Move buttons to move the entire button image around within the square. These buttons are helpful in case you start drawing your image and realize it isn't quite centered within the button. Just nudge it over a pixel or two by using the Move buttons. You cannot move any portion of the image off the button. If you want to clip a portion of the image, erase the portion you want clipped and use the Move buttons to move the image over.

When you finish editing the picture, click OK.

You can edit the image on any button that's already been placed on a toolbar by calling up Tools⇨Customize, and then right-clicking any visible toolbar button. Select Edit Button Image from the pop-up menu to edit the button. (You can also select Choose Button Image if you want to start over with a new button image.)

Setting toolbar options

Word offers a variety of options that affect the way toolbars display. You can't find these options with Tools⇨Options. Instead, you can find them on the Options tab of the Customize dialog box, as shown in Figure 2-8. Choose Tools⇨Customize, and then click the Options tab.

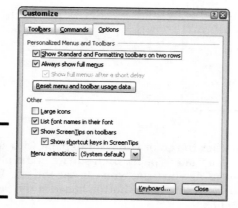

Figure 2-8:
Setting the toolbar options.

The following paragraphs describe what each of these options does:

✦ **Show Standard and Formatting Toolbars on Two Rows:** This option displays the Standard toolbar and the Formatting toolbar on separate rows. If you uncheck this option, these toolbars combine onto a single row to save space.

✦ **Always Show Full Menus:** By default, Word shows only those menu items that it thinks you're likely to use. If you stare at a menu in bewilderment for long enough, Word then displays the additional commands that are initially hidden. Then, Word adjusts the exact mix of menu commands displayed based on which commands you actually use. If you'd rather just see all of the commands without having to wait, check this option.

✦ **Show Full Menus After a Short Delay:** This option causes Word to display the complete menu after a few moments delay. I wouldn't change this option.

✦ **Reset Menu and Toolbar Usage Data:** Click this button to reset the menus to their initial configuration. This button causes Word to forget which commands you frequently use.

✦ **Large Icons:** Displays toolbars with larger icons.

✦ **List Font Names in Their Font:** This option causes the Font drop-down list on the Formatting toolbar to list each font using the font. That way, you can see how each font looks. On slower computers, this option can slow down performance, so uncheck this option if the Font drop-down takes too long to appear when you click it.

✦ **Show ScreenTips on Toolbars:** This option causes Word to display the name of each button when you hover the mouse over the button for a moment.

✦ **Show Shortcut Keys in ScreenTips:** This option adds any assigned shortcut keys to the screen tip.

✦ **Menu Animations:** This option lets you set a cute animation style to the menus. The choices are Default, Random, Unfold, Slide, or Fade.

Messing with Menus

Besides buttons, toolbars can also hold menus. In fact, the standard menu bar is nothing more than a toolbar that contains menus rather than buttons. You can even mix menus and buttons on the same toolbar, as demonstrated by the Drawing toolbar, which has an assortment of buttons for drawing functions in addition to Draw and AutoShapes menus.

What's with the ampersand (&)?

Before I throw you into the depths of customizing Word's menus, I need to warn you that such work exposes you to a little whiff of programmer-speak, in the form of ampersands intermixed with menu and command names. For example, the File menu is written as &File, and the Format menu is written as F&ormat.

Did the Microsoft programmers who wrote Word suddenly develop a twitch in the index finger of their right hands when finishing the Tools⇨Customize command? Not at all. Instead, they decided to use the ampersand as a symbol to indicate which character serves as a menu or command's *hot key* — that is, the key the user can press in combination with the Alt key to invoke the menu or command. The hot key for the File menu is Alt+F because the ampersand precedes the F. For the Format menu, the hot key is Alt+O because the ampersand precedes the O.

Adding a menu command

When most users begin to probe the depths of Word's customization features, they discover that Word includes many commands that are not available from any of its menus. Hundreds of them, in fact. The fact that Microsoft left these commands off the menus should not discourage you from using them. If you find a command that you wish was available via the menus, don't gripe about it, just add it to the menu! Here are the steps:

1. **Choose Tools⇨Customize. When the Customize dialog box appears, click the Commands tab.**

2. **Select the category of the command or other element you want to add to the menu from the Categories list.**

   Don't forget that macros, styles, fonts, and AutoText appear as categories near the bottom of the list.

3. **Select the specific command or other item from the Commands list.**

   Note: The title of this box changes if you select the macros, styles, fonts, or AutoText categories.

4. **Drag the command to the menu where you want to insert the command. Hover the mouse over the menu a moment until the menu appears. Then, continue to drag the command down to the location on the menu where you want the command to appear.**

   When you finally release the mouse button, the command is inserted in the menu.

5. **If you don't like the name assigned to the new command, change the name by right-clicking the new command and typing a new name into the Name field.**

Type an ampersand just before the letter that you want to serve as a hot key for the command. (Don't worry, the ampersand itself doesn't appear on the menu.)

Removing a menu command

The capability to remove commands from menus is just as important as the capability to add commands, not just because it allows you to remove custom commands you've added, but also because it lets you remove built-in commands you never use. Such commands merely take up space on Word's already-crowded menus.

To remove a menu command, call up Tools⇨Customize, right-click the command you want to remove, and choose Delete from the pop-up menu that appears. Poof! The command is banished from the menu.

Rearranging menu commands

You can move a menu command to another location simply by summoning Tools⇨Customize, and then dragging the menu command you want to move to a new location. You can drag a command to a new location on the same menu, or you can drag the command to an entirely different menu.

Using separators

Word's default menus use spacers to group related commands. For example, pull down the File menu and you notice several groups of commands: New/Open/Close, Save/Save As/Save As Web Page/File Search, and so on. The groups are separated from one another with a horizontal line called a *separator,* and you can add or remove separators the same as you can in a normal toolbar. Just right-click the command above which you want to add a separator and choose the Begin a Group command from the pop-up menu that appears. To remove a separator, right-click the command and choose Begin a Group again.

Adding a new menu

Besides adding commands to existing Word menus, Word lets you add completely new menus to hold custom commands. Some good reasons for adding a new menu include

**Book VIII
Chapter 2**

Customizing
Toolbars, Menus,
and Keyboard
Shortcuts

✦ **Creating a menu of commands for features you frequently use that are complicated enough to merit a separate menu:** Word includes a Table menu by default because the Table feature is complicated. You can easily create a separate menu for similarly complicated features, such as Tables of Contents, indexes, and so on.

✦ **Creating a menu to apply the styles you use most:** I do this for my own writing because it is more efficient than wading through the Style list box on the Formatting toolbar, and it's way easier than using the Styles task pane.

✦ **Creating a menu to open commonly accessed documents:** You can create a menu command for a specific document by opening the file you want to add to the menu and then following the steps in the section "Adding a menu command," earlier in this chapter, to add the FileOpenFile command to the menu. To find the FileOpenFile command in the Customize dialog box, choose All Commands for the command category.

You can add your new menu to the standard menu bar or to any other toolbar. To add a new menu, follow these steps:

1. **Choose Tools⇨Customize and click the Commands tab.**

2. **Select the template that you want to add the custom menu to in the Save In list box.**

Pick Normal.dot if you want your menu to always be visible, no matter what document is open.

3. **Scroll all the way to the bottom of the Categories list and click New Menu.**

4. **Drag New Menu from the Commands list to the location on the menu bar or other toolbar where you want to add the new menu.**

A new menu named New Menu is created.

5. **Right-click the new menu and type a name for the menu in the Name field.**

Use an ampersand to indicate the hot key for the menu; for example, type **&Styles** to create a Styles menu.

6. **Drag other commands, styles, AutoText entries, or macros from the Customize dialog box onto the new menu.**

Using the weird way to add menu commands

One of Word's most obscure keyboard shortcuts is Ctrl+Alt+= (the equal sign), which allows you to add custom menu commands without going through the Tools⇨Customize command. To use it, follow these steps:

1. **Make sure that the command you want to add to a menu is available via a keyboard shortcut or a visible toolbar button.**

2. **Press Ctrl+Alt+=.**

   The mouse pointer changes to a big plus sign. You have activated the Add Menu shortcut.

3. **Press the keyboard shortcut for the command that you want to add to the menu or click the appropriate toolbar button.**

   The command is added to the menu that Word thinks is most appropriate for the command.

You can use the shortcut method to add a style or font to the Format menu. Just press Ctrl+Alt+= and select the font or style you want to add to the menu from the drop-down list on the Formatting toolbar.

Unfortunately, you can't tell Word where to insert the menu command when you use the shortcut method. If you want more precise control over how menus and toolbars are customized, you have to use the Tools⇨Customize command.

Creating Custom Keyboard Shortcuts

If you're a keyboard shortcut junkie (as I am), you'll want to create your own keyboard shortcuts. Then, you can assign the styles, macros, and other goodies you use most often to handy keyboard shortcuts.

Follow these steps to assign a new keyboard shortcut:

1. **Call up Tools⇨Customize.**

   The Customize dialog box appears.

2. **Click the Keyboard button.**

   The Customize Keyboard dialog box appears, as shown in Figure 2-9.

**Book VIII
Chapter 2**

**Customizing
Toolbars, Menus,
and Keyboard
Shortcuts**

Figure 2-9:
Creating
custom
keyboard
shortcuts.

3. **Choose the command, style, macro, font, or other item for which you want to create a keyboard shortcut by using the Categories and Commands lists.**

   Spend some time exploring these lists. Lots of useful commands are buried amongst a bunch of strange-looking gobbledygook.

4. **Click in the Press New Shortcut Key field and then type the new keyboard shortcut.**

   When you type the shortcut, Word lets you know whether the key is already assigned to some other command.

5. **Click Assign to assign the keyboard shortcut. Then click the Close button.**

   You're finished! Try the shortcut to see whether it works.

You can also assign a keyboard shortcut to a style. Choose Format⇨Style, click the Modify button, and then click the Shortcut Key button in the Modify Style dialog box. And you can create a shortcut for a symbol by calling up Insert⇨Symbol and clicking the Shortcut Key button.

Resetting keyboard shortcuts

You can erase all of the keyboard shortcuts stored in a template by following these steps:

1. **Call up Tools⇨Customize and click the Keyboard button.**

2. **Select Normal.dot or the attached template in the Save Changes In list box.**

3. **Click the Reset All button.**

4. **When the confirmation dialog box appears, click Yes.**

5. **Click the Close button.**

If you have keyboard shortcuts saved in both Normal.dot and the template attached to the current document, you need to use Reset All for both templates to revert completely to Word's default keyboard shortcuts. And, to make the return to default shortcuts permanent, you must save the template file as well.

Printing your keyboard shortcuts

If you lose track of your custom keyboard shortcuts, you can print a complete list of them for the current document by following these steps:

1. **Open a document that is attached to the template with the keyboard shortcuts you want to print, or open the template itself.**

2. **Call up File⇨Print to display the Print dialog box.**

3. **In the Print What field, select Key Assignments.**

4. **Click OK.**

Keyboard assignments print, starting first with the keyboard assignments derived from the template attached to the document and listing the global keyboard assignments taken from the Normal.dot template. Word's built-in keyboard shortcuts do not print; if they did, the listing would go on for many pages.

**Book VIII
Chapter 2**

**Customizing
Toolbars, Menus,
and Keyboard
Shortcuts**

Chapter 3: Using Voice and Handwriting Features

In This Chapter

✔ Working with the Language toolbar

✔ Training Word to speak your language

✔ Taking dictation

✔ Giving voice commands

✔ Using handwriting recognition

This chapter covers Word's speech and handwriting recognition features. The speech recognition feature lets you enter data and commands into Word by speaking into a microphone. After you set it up and start working, you feel like you're on *Star Trek*. The handwriting feature is designed mostly for computers that have stylus devices, but you can also use it with a mouse if your computer doesn't have a stylus.

Welcoming the Language Toolbar

Word's speech and handwriting recognition features are controlled from a special Language toolbar, shown in Figure 3-1. This toolbar is a little different from the other toolbars in Word. It isn't tied to the Word document window. Instead, it floats freely about the screen and remains ever present. And, you can't summon it via View⇨Toolbars. Instead, you can activate the Language toolbar with Tools⇨Speech.

Figure 3-1:
The
Language
toolbar.

The Language toolbar sports the following buttons:

+ **Microphone:** Turns the speech recognition feature's microphone on or off. When the microphone is on, two additional buttons appear on the toolbar: Voice Command and Dictation.

+ **Tools:** Brings up a menu of helpful speech and handwriting recognition tools, including an Options command that lets you set various speech and handwriting options and a Training command that lets you train Word to recognize your voice.

+ **Handwriting:** Turns the handwriting recognition feature on or off.

+ **On-Screen Keyboard:** Displays an image that resembles a keyboard. You can click the individual keys to type text into your document.

+ **Help:** Displays help information for the speech and handwriting features.

To be honest, the Language toolbar gets in the way if you're not actively using it, so turn it off when you're not working with speech or handwriting features. When you're not using it, you can put it away by right-clicking it and choosing Close the Language Bar.

Using Speech Recognition

Speech recognition lets you dictate text into your documents and issue menu commands by speaking rather than by typing or clicking the mouse. Although it isn't perfect, speech recognition can take dictation with 90 percent or better accuracy if you use the right hardware and configure speech recognition properly.

For speech recognition to work well, you need to have a beefy computer. Microsoft recommends at least a 400MHz Pentium II computer with 128MB or more of RAM for satisfactory speech performance. If you have a slower computer or less than 128MB of RAM, the speech feature works so slowly that you won't want to use it.

You should also invest in a headset microphone. Handheld microphones or boom microphones attached to your monitor do not provide consistent enough sound for speech recognition to reliably figure out what you're saying.

Speech recognition is not installed by default when you install Office 2003 or Word 2003 on your computer. If speech recognition is not installed on your computer, you can install it by firing up Word and choosing Tools⇨Speech. Word notices that speech recognition is not installed and automatically installs it.

Configuring speech recognition

The first time you use speech recognition, you are asked to train it. To train speech recognition, you just read aloud text that appears on-screen, as shown in Figure 3-2. It feels a little strange at first just talking to your computer, but when you get into it, it's kind of fun. Speech recognition listens to your speech, matches it up with what it is expecting you to say, and records the subtle nuances of your voice. As Word recognizes what you're saying, it highlights the text on-screen so that you can see your progress.

The training session takes about 15 minutes.

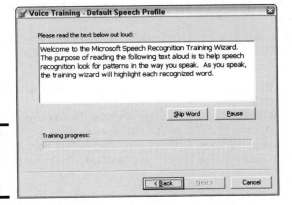

Figure 3-2:
Teaching
Word to
listen.

If, after completing the training session, you find that Word still doesn't recognize a high percentage of your speech, you can send it back to school by choosing Tools⇨Speech, and then choosing Tools⇨Training on the Language toolbar.

Dictation

To dictate text into an Office document, follow these steps:

1. **Position the insertion point where you want to insert the text you dictate.**

2. **Click the Microphone button on the Language toolbar to turn on the microphone.**

   Skip this step if you already turned the microphone on.

3. **Click the Dictation button on the Language toolbar to activate dictation mode.**

4. **In a normal tone of voice, clearly speak the words you want dictated.**

   The words don't appear on-screen at first. Instead, a series of shaded periods appear while speech recognition tries to figure out what you said. In a moment, the words you spoke, or (hopefully) something close, replaces the shaded periods.

   Pause once in a while to let speech recognition catch up. But don't talk slowly. Speech recognition works best when you speak in a normal voice.

5. **When you finish dictating, click the Microphone button to turn off the microphone.**

6. **Correct any dictation mistakes by right-clicking any incorrect words and choosing the correct word from the list of alternatives that appears.**

   Or, just delete the incorrect text and retype the correct text in its place.

Don't forget to turn off the microphone by clicking the Microphone button when you finish dictating. If you leave the microphone on, any stray noises that the microphone picks up — such as a sneeze — find its way into your document. And who knows how speech recognition will translate your sneezes.

To dictate punctuation, just say the name of the punctuation mark you want to use, such as "Period," "Comma," or "Semicolon." For quotation marks, say "Open quote" or "Close quote." To start a new line, say "Enter" or "New Line." To start a new paragraph, say "New Paragraph."

Voice commands

To speak commands to Word, click the Microphone button to turn on the microphone if you have not already done so, and then click the Voice Command button. Then, tell the computer what you want it to do. Or, if you're already in dictation mode, just say "Voice Command."

To use menu commands, just say the name of the menu option. For example, to activate the File menu, say "File." Then, to select the Open command, say "Open."

Although you can speak dictation at a normal pace, you have to speak voice commands a little slower. You have to wait for Word to process each command before you speak the next command.

If Word doesn't recognize a command, a balloon with the message "What was that?" displays in the Language toolbar.

When you are in a dialog box, you can speak the name of a button or other dialog box control to activate the button or control. For example, saying "OK" clicks the OK button. In the Font dialog box, saying "Strikethrough" checks the Strikethrough option.

Here are some additional words you can say to move around in a document or dialog box:

Enter	End
Backspace	Home
Delete	Up
Space	Down
Spacebar	Left
Escape	Right
Cancel (same as Escape)	Page Up
Right-click	Page Down

You can also speak the name of most toolbar buttons to activate them. For example, say "Bold" or "Italic" to apply bold or italic formatting. Say "Font" to open the font list. Then, say the name of the font to select it.

Handwriting Recognition

The handwriting recognition feature is designed to convert handwritten text into real text. Like speech recognition, handwriting recognition isn't 100 percent accurate. But if you got a C+ or better in penmanship, the accuracy is pretty good. Figure 3-3 shows an example of Word recognizing some pretty bad penmanship.

Book VIII
Chapter 3

Using Voice and Handwriting Features

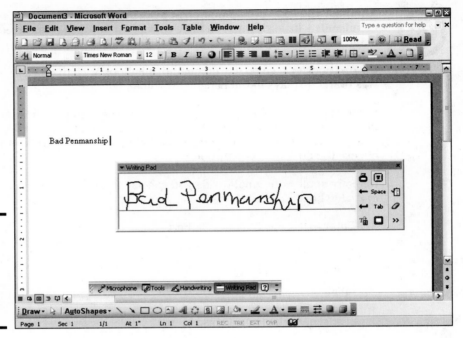

Figure 3-3:
If Word recognizes this, it will probably recognize anything.

Handwriting recognition works best with an input device such as a graphic tablet or a stylus pad, but it can work with a mouse too.

To use handwriting recognition, follow these steps:

1. **Place the insertion point where you want to insert the handwritten text into your document.**

2. **Click the Handwriting button on the Language toolbar, and then choose Writing Pad.**

   If the Language toolbar isn't visible, you can summon it by choosing Tools⇨Speech. Click the Microphone button to turn off voice recognition, and then choose Handwriting⇨Writing Pad.

3. **Write your text in the Writing Pad window.**

   As soon as Word recognizes what you wrote, it inserts the text into the document and erases the text from the Writing Pad window.

4. **When you're done writing, click the Close button in the Writing Pad window.**

If you click the Ink icon in the Writing Pad window (the one that looks like a bottle of ink), Word doesn't attempt to convert your doodlings to text. Instead, it inserts the text as an *ink object*, which is like a little picture that appears inline with your text. If the picture is too small to see, select it and increase its size by using the Font Size drop-down list from the Formatting toolbar, as if the ink object were regular text.

**Book VIII
Chapter 3**

Using Voice and Handwriting Features

Book IX

Programming Word with VBA

Contents at a Glance

Chapter 1: Recording and Using Macros

In This Chapter

✔ **Recording a macro**

✔ **Running a macro**

✔ **Editing a macro**

✔ **Using auto macros**

A *macro* is a sequence of commands or keystrokes that Word records and lets you play back at any time. Macros allow you to create your own customized shortcuts for things you do over and over again. For example, Word comes with built-in keyboard shortcuts to make text bold (Ctrl+B) and to make text italic (Ctrl+I), but no built-in shortcut exists to make text bold and italic all at the same time. To do that, you have to press Ctrl+B and then Ctrl+I. If you do that a million times a day, pretty soon that extra keystroke becomes bothersome. Wouldn't having a shortcut for bold-italic be nice? With Word's macro recorder, you can create one.

This chapter shows you how to record and play back simple macros. It doesn't show you how to create complex macros by using Word's macro programming language, Visual Basic for Applications. That's the topic of the remaining chapters in this book.

Where Do All the Macros Go?

You can store macros in documents or in templates. When you create a macro, you have three choices for where to store the macro:

✦ The current document

✦ The template that's attached to the current document

✦ The Normal.dot template

Note: If the current document is based on Normal.dot, you really have only two choices. When you run a macro, you can pick macros from Normal.dot, the current document's template, the document itself, or the Normal.dot template.

When you create a macro, you need to think about when you are going to want to run the macro. If you need to run the macro only from within a specific document, then create the macro in that document. If you want the macro to be available only to documents based on a particular template, then create the macro in that template. But if you want the macro to always be available no matter what document you are working on, store the macro in Normal.dot.

Actually, you can store macros in a fourth place: in a global template. A global template is a great place to create a library of macros that are available to all of your documents. For more information about using global templates, refer to Book I, Chapter 3. *Note:* To create or edit macros in a global template, you must open the template. After you create macros in a template, you can close the template, attach it as a global template, and then run any macros it contains.

Doing the Macro Recorder Dance

The easiest way to create a macro is to use the *macro recorder,* which is kind of like a videocassette recorder. After you turn on the macro recorder, it follows you around and makes a precise record of everything you do until you turn the recorder off. Well, not really *everything.* The Word macro recorder records only the stuff you do in Word. It doesn't notice when you dribble coffee down your chin or sneeze on the monitor. But when you turn on the recorder, anything you do in Word — whether you're typing text, applying formatting, calling up a command, or filling out a dialog box — is carefully recorded.

Then when you turn off the recorder, you can replay the recorded macro to repeat the exact sequence of steps that Word recorded in the macro.

About the only thing that is *not* recorded by the macro recorder are mouse movements within the document. The macro recorder records buttons or menu choices you click, but if you move around the document with the mouse or select text with the mouse, those actions aren't recorded. As a result, use the keyboard for navigating or selecting text while recording a macro.

To record a macro, follow these 12 steps:

1. **Try to talk yourself out of it.**

Fiddling around with macros can be a bit of a time-waster. Ask yourself whether you really will use the macro after you have gone to the trouble of recording it. If not, go directly to Step 12.

2. **Think about what you're going to do.**

   Think through all the steps you have to follow to accomplish whatever task you want to automate with a macro. To create a macro that makes text bold and italic, for example, all you have to do is press Ctrl+B and then press Ctrl+I. That's a pretty simple macro, but other macros can be much more complex, involving dozens of steps. If necessary, rehearse the steps before you record them as a macro.

3. **Call up Tools⇨Macro⇨Record New Macro.**

   The Record Macro dialog box appears, as shown in Figure 1-1.

Figure 1-1:
The Record
Macro
dialog box.

4. **Type the name of the macro you want to create in the Macro Name text box.**

   The name can be anything you want, but it cannot include spaces, commas, or periods. When you first pop up the Record Macro dialog box, the macro name is set to something like Macro1 or Macro2 (or Macro783 if you've been busy). Surely you can come up with a better name than that. (I know, "Yes, I can . . . and stop calling me Shirley.")

5. **Set the Store Macro In list box to the location where you want to store the macro.**

   The default setting stores the recorded macro in the Normal.dot template so that it is always available. The other choices available in this drop-down list are storing the macro in the document that you were working on when you called up the macro recorder or storing the macro to the template that document is based on.

6. **To make your macro accessible from a toolbar or the keyboard, click the Toolbars or Keyboard button.**

   This step calls up the Customize dialog box, which is ready to add your macro to a toolbar, menu, or keyboard shortcut. Figure 1-2 shows the

Customize Keyboard dialog box that Word displays if you click the Keyboard button. Type the shortcut key combination you want to assign to the macro (in this case, I pressed Atl+Ctrl+B), click the Assign button, and then click the Close button.

Figure 1-2:
The
Customize
Keyboard
dialog box.

For more information about customizing toolbars, menus, or the keyboard, refer to Book VIII, Chapter 2.

7. Click OK to begin recording the macro.

The Record Macro dialog box disappears, and a little macro recorder toolbar appears, as shown in Figure 1-3. You use this toolbar to stop recording the macro.

Figure 1-3:
The Stop
Recording
toolbar.

8. Type the keystrokes and menu commands you want to record in the macro.

To record the BoldItalic macro, for example, press Ctrl+B and then press Ctrl+I.

For more complicated macros, you may have to access menu commands. You can do that by using either the keyboard or the mouse.

9. **If you have to stop recording temporarily, click the Pause button. Click it again to resume recording.**

   You may forget how to do something, for example, especially if you skipped Step 2. If you click the Pause button, you can call up Word's Help command, look up the procedure for whatever it is you forgot, dismiss Help, and click the Pause button again to resume recording.

10. **After you finish recording the macro, click the Stop button.**

    Word adds the macro to the template or document. You're almost done.

11. **Test the macro.**

    If you assigned the macro to a keyboard shortcut, use the shortcut now to see whether the macro works. Otherwise, follow the steps in the later section, "Running a macro."

12. **You're finished.**

    Congratulate yourself.

If the function of the macro isn't obvious from the macro name, type a more elaborate description of the macro in the Record Macro dialog box's Description field. You'll thank yourself later when you forget what the macro does.

Macro Recording Tips

Here are some tips to keep in mind as you record macros:

+ You can call up the Record Macro dialog box directly by double-clicking the letters REC on the status bar at the bottom of the screen. Double-clicking REC saves you from wading through the Tools menu and the Macro dialog box.

+ If the macro doesn't work, you may have made a mistake while recording it. If the macro is short enough, the best thing to do is to record the macro again. If the macro is long and you don't have anything important to do, try editing the macro to expunge the problem. See the section "Editing a Macro" later in this chapter.

+ Macros are normally stored in the global Normal.dot template. To store a macro in the template attached to the current document, change the setting of the Record Macro dialog box's Store Macro In list box.

♦ Do not make any assumptions about where the insertion point will be when you run the macro. If necessary, begin the macro with a positioning command by moving the insertion point to the beginning of the document, the beginning of the line, or the beginning of a word. (Not all macros require a positioning command. But if your macro depends in any way on the position of the insertion point, this step is a must.)

♦ Do not use the mouse to select text or navigate through the document. Word does not record these mouse actions. You can use the mouse to select menu commands or to click toolbar buttons, but not to move the insertion point.

♦ Use Ctrl+Home or Ctrl+End to move to the beginning or end of a document. Do not use repeated PageUp or PageDown keys for this purpose. Three PageUps may get you to the top of your document when you record the macro, but when you run the macro, it may not. Similarly, use Home and End to move to the start or end of a line rather than the left or right arrow keys.

♦ If you use the Find or Replace commands, be sure to move to the beginning of the document first.

♦ Avoid any commands that depend on the contents of a document that's active when you record the macro.

I hate to tell you about unexpected side effects

Sometimes a macro has unexpected side effects. Suppose that rather than record the keystrokes Ctrl+B and Ctrl+I for the BoldItalic macro, you decide to record these steps instead:

1. Call up Format⇨Font.

2. Choose Bold Italic as the font style.

3. Click OK.

The macro seems to work, but sooner or later, you discover that in addition to recording the Bold Italic font style, the macro recorded other character attributes — such as font, size, and effects. If the text to which you applied the

Format⇨Font command when you recorded the macro was 10-point Times New Roman font, any text you apply the macro to is switched to 10-point Times New Roman.

You can avoid these side effects in two ways:

✔ Avoid recording dialog boxes in macros whenever a keyboard shortcut or toolbar button can do the trick. Whenever you record a dialog box in a macro, you record all the dialog box's settings.

✔ Fix the macro later by editing it and removing the extraneous information. See the section "Editing a Macro."

Running a Macro

If you assigned a macro to a toolbar, menu, or keyboard shortcut, you can run the macro by clicking the toolbar button, choosing the menu command, or pressing the keyboard shortcut. If you did not, you can run it by following these steps:

1. **Choose Tools⇨Macro⇨Macros to summon the Macros dialog box shown in Figure 1-4.**

As a shortcut, you can press Alt+F8.

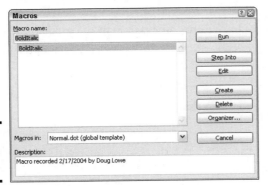

Figure 1-4:
The Macros
dialog box.

2. **If the macro you want to run isn't already selected, select it now. If the macro you want doesn't appear, try changing the Macros In setting.**

The macro may be in a different template.

3. **Click Run.**

Editing a Macro

If you make a mistake while recording a macro, you can abandon the recording and start over. Or, you can finish the recording and edit the macro to correct the mistake. When you edit the macro, the macro's commands appear in a separate window. You can delete or modify erroneous commands, you can insert new commands if you know how, or you can merely study the macro to try to figure out how it works.

When you edit a macro, you are exposed to Visual Basic for Applications. VBA is not as deadly as the Ebola virus, but it can cause severe headaches and nausea if you're not inoculated with the Programmer Vaccine. For more information about VBA and its editor, refer to Chapter 2 of this minibook.

Here are the steps for editing a macro:

1. **Choose Tools⇨Macro⇨Macros.**

The Macros dialog box appears.

2. **Select the macro you want to edit and click the Edit button.**

Word launches the Visual Basic editor, with the macro you selected visible in its own window. See Figure 1-5.

3. **Make whatever changes are necessary to the macro.**

Correct misspelled words, delete extraneous commands, and, if you're brave, add additional commands.

4. **Use File⇨Save Template to save your changes.**

5. **Use File⇨Close to close the macro window.**

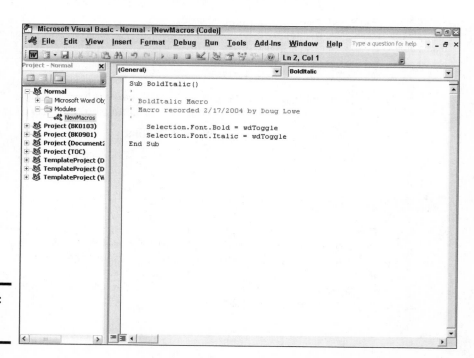

Figure 1-5:
Editing a
macro.

Simple Macro Edits That Don't Require a Ph.D. in VBA

Before you make massive changes to a macro, however, you need a pretty good knowledge of VBA. But you can make certain types of changes without knowing much about VBA at all. Here's a sampling:

✦ **Correct spelling errors.** If you inserted text into a document and misspelled it, don't hesitate to edit the macro to correct the misspellings. Text you insert into a document while recording a macro is included in a `Selection.TypeText` command, like this:

```
Selection.TypeText Text:="This is some simple text."
```

You can correct any spelling mistakes or change the inserted text altogether, provided you take care not to remove either of the quotation marks that appear before and after the text. For example, you can correct the above line to:

```
Selection.TypeText Text:="This is some sample text."
```

✦ **Remove extraneous commands.** If you inadvertently used a command while recording a macro, you can clean up your macro by removing the unnecessary command.

✦ **Remove unwanted dialog box settings.** If you record a dialog box in a macro, Word includes every setting in the dialog box. You can remove the settings that you do not want the macro to change. For example, if you use Format⇨Font to format text with small caps, Word inserts the following commands into the macro:

```
With Selection.Font
    .Name = "Times New Roman"
    .Size = 12
    .Bold = False
    .Italic = False
    .Underline = wdUnderlineNone
    .UnderlineColor = wdColorAutomatic
    .StrikeThrough = False
    .DoubleStrikeThrough = False
    .Outline = False
    .Emboss = False
    .Shadow = False
    .Hidden = False
    .SmallCaps = True
    .AllCaps = False
    .Color = wdColorAutomatic
    .Engrave = False
    .Superscript = False
```

```
                    .Subscript = False
                    .Spacing = 0
                    .Scaling = 100
                    .Position = 0
                    .Kerning = 0
                    .Animation = wdAnimationNone
              End With
```

This command looks complicated at first, but if you study it, you see that it is little more than a list of all the dialog box controls that appear in the Font dialog box. The periods look strange appearing in front of each command arguments as they do, but they are required. You can safely delete the lines that specify those dialog box controls you don't want to use so that the resulting command looks like this:

```
With Selection.Font
        .SmallCaps = True
End With
```

Tip: Actually, with a little more VBA knowledge, you can also remove the With and End With command, and substitute just the following:

```
Selection.Font.SmallCaps = True
```

Using Auto Macros

An *auto macro* is a macro that runs automatically whenever some key event happens, such as when Word starts or when a document closes. Word recognizes auto macros by their names. For example, a macro named AutoNew automatically runs when you create a new document from a template, and a macro named AutoClose automatically runs when you close a document.

The following paragraphs describe the various auto macros available in Word:

✦ **AutoExec:** Runs when Word starts. Store it in the Normal.dot template.

✦ **AutoExit:** Runs when Word exits. Store it in the Normal.dot template.

✦ **AutoNew:** Runs whenever a new document is created using the template that contains the AutoNew macro.

✦ **AutoOpen:** Runs whenever an existing document opens. You can create an AutoOpen macro in the Normal.dot template or in the template that's attached to the document. Or both.

✦ **AutoClose:** Runs whenever an open document closes. This macro can reside in Normal.dot or in the template attached to the document.

Macro security

Computer viruses can exploit Word's auto macro feature to infect your computer. As a result, you need to take some steps to protect yourself from the possibility of being hit by a macro virus. Here are some things you can do:

✔ Set your macro security to at least the Medium setting to protect yourself from malicious macros. To set the macro security, choose Tools⇨Options, click the Security tab, and then click the Macro Security button. Then, choose the security level you're most comfortable with.

✔ Don't open documents from people you don't know or trust, especially documents that arrive as attachments in unsolicited e-mail messages.

✔ Install an antivirus program such as McAfee VirusScan (www.mcafee.com) or Norton AntiVirus (www.norton.com). These programs sniff out and smash all known macro viruses, as well as other more common types of viruses and worms

You can prevent any auto macro from executing by holding down the Shift key while performing the action that otherwise triggers the macro. For example, holding down the Shift key while creating a new document prevents the AutoNew macro from running.

Chapter 2: Programming with VBA

In This Chapter

✔ Using variables, strings, and other VBA elements

✔ Working with objects, properties, and methods

✔ Executing macros with If, While, and Select Case

✔ Displaying information and obtaining input from the user

✔ Working with user-defined subroutines and macros

I cover the basics of recording and playing macros in Chapter 1 of this minibook. Chapter 1 touches on the subject of VBA programming, just enough to whet your appetite and give you the skills needed to create and use the various macros that appear throughout this book. But I reserve the real meat of VBA programming for this chapter. It is here that I show you VBA in-depth so that, with a little practice and a lot of trial and error, you can create VBA macros of your own.

This chapter is admittedly a bit of a whirlwind introduction to VBA programming. If you have absolutely no programming experience, this chapter may seem a bit overwhelming. Don't let the details of VBA bog you down. Study the sample macros that appear in this chapter and in the remaining chapters in this book, experiment a lot, and keep your chin up. You'll catch on soon enough. If you're not sure about how to use Tools⇨Macro⇨Macros to create and edit macros, better review Chapter 1 of this minibook before proceeding.

The Basic Structure of VBA Macros

When you first create a macro by calling up Tools⇨Macro⇨Macros, typing a macro name, and clicking the Create button, Word switches you to the VBA editor and creates a skeleton of a macro for you, like this:

```
Sub BoldItalic()
'
' BoldItalic Macro
' Macro created 2/18/2004 by Doug Lowe
'

End Sub
```

The lines that begin with apostrophes are comments. VBA ignores them completely, but you can use them to remind yourself what the macro does or how it works. Comments can appear on lines all by themselves, or they can appear at the end of a line, like this:

```
Sub BoldItalic()   'The BoldItalic macro
```

The Sub statement and the End statement mark the beginning and end of the macro's main procedure. As you see later, a macro can call upon other procedures or functions that you define elsewhere in your code. However, the simplest macros consist of these lines with some additional VBA statements in between.

For example, the following macro contains two VBA statements, one to make the selected text bold and the other to make it italic:

```
Sub BoldItalic()
    Selection.Font.Bold = wdToggle
    Selection.Font.Italic = wdToggle
End Sub
```

The net effect of this command is to make the selected text both bold and italic.

Well, not quite. Actually, the effect of this macro is to change both the bold and italic attributes of the selected text. If the text isn't already bold or italic, the macro makes it bold and italic. But if the text is already formatted as bold but not italic, the macro turns off the bold attribute but turns on italic. And if no text is selected at all, the macro sets the bold and italic attributes for text you subsequently type.

So here, just a page into this chapter, you already have an example of the Undeniable Truth of VBA programming: Even simple macros sometimes don't work the way you expect them to. The outcome of a macro is usually very much dependent on whether text is selected, how the selected text (if any) is formatted, the view (Normal, Page Layout, or Outline), and many other factors. The moral of the story: *Test everything.*

Basic Elements of VBA

The following sections present a whirlwind tour of some of the basic elements of writing VBA macros.

Rules for writing VBA statements

The normal way to write VBA statements is one per line. You can gang up several statements on a single line by separating the statements with colons, as in this example:

```
Dim i As Integer : i = 100
```

But your macros are easier to read if you stick to one statement per line.

You can indent lines to show the relationships among statements by using tabs or spaces. For example:

```
If Weekday(Now()) = 1 Then
    MsgBox "Time for football!"
End If
```

Spacing *within* a VBA statement generally isn't important. You can omit spaces when different elements of a statement are separated by a comma, colon, or other punctuation. However, don't be surprised if VBA automatically inserts spaces around such elements as you type them.

If you need to continue a statement onto two or more lines, end each line except the last one with an underscore character, like this:

```
MsgBox ("This is a really " _
  & "long message.")
```

The underscore character indicates to Word that the statement continues on the next line, so the successive lines are treated as a single statement.

Comments

Comments are marked with apostrophes. When you use an apostrophe anywhere on a line, VBA completely ignores everything on the line after the apostrophe. This treatment allows you to place comments directly on the lines where they relate:

```
Sub BoldItalic()  ' This macro applies both bold and italic.
    Selection.Font.Bold = wdToggle     'Toggles Bold
    Selection.Font.Italic = wdToggle   'Toggles Italic
End Sub
```

Projects, modules, procedures, and macros

At the simplest level, a macro is a single VBA procedure that you can run from an application such as Word. However, VBA lets you gather procedures together to form modules and projects to help you organize your macros. The following paragraphs describe each of these organizational units:

✦ **Procedure:** A *procedure* is a named collection of VBA statements that's contained between a Sub and End Sub statement.

✦ **Macro:** A *macro* is a specific type of procedure that you can invoke directly from a Word document. You can run a macro from Tools⇨Macro⇨Macros, or by associating it with a customized toolbar button, a keyboard shortcut, or a menu command.

✦ **Module:** A *module* is a named collection of procedures. All Word documents begin with a module named New Macros. When you create a macro from the Macros dialog box, the new macro is created in this module. If you are working with a lot of macros, you can create additional modules to help keep them organized.

✦ **Project:** A *project* is a collection of modules and other Word objects. Every document and template is a project.

Working with Variables and Data

A *variable* is a name assigned to a bit of computer memory that is used to hold a value. Variables are one of the key features of any programming language, and VBA is no exception. Variables play an important role in all but the most trivial VBA macros.

Using assignment statements

You use an assignment statement to assign values to variables. For example:

```
Pi = 3.14159
X = 0
MessageText = "Hello from Planet Earth"
```

In a concession to the 40-year-old legacy of BASIC programming, VBA allows you to preface assignment statements with the word LET:

```
Let Pi = 3.14159
Let x = 0
Let MessageText = "Hello from Planet Earth"
```

The Let keyword is not required, however, and is considered quaint.

Declaring variables

You declare a variable by using a Dim statement, like this:

```
Dim i As Integer
```

This statement declares a variable named i. The type of the variable is Integer.

Variable names can be up to 40 characters, must start with a letter, and can contain only letters, numerals, and the underscore (_). Also, you cannot use any of VBA's reserved words (such as function names), the names of VBA statements, and so on.

You use the As keyword to specify the data type for variables. VBA provides a number of data types you can use for variables. The valid data types are:

✦ Boolean: True or False values.

✦ Byte: Integers from 0 to 255.

✦ Integer: Integers from -32,768 to +32,768.

✦ Long: Large integers. Values can be from approximately -2 billion to +2 billion.

✦ Currency: Decimal numbers with up to 19 digits.

✦ Single: Single-precision floating point numbers, not used often in Word macros.

✦ Double: Double-precision floating point numbers, used even less often in Word macros.

✦ Date: A date or time value.

✦ String: A string, such as "Humpty-Dumpty."

✦ Object: Any object, such as a Word document or a window.

✦ Variant: A generic number or string.

If you omit the data type, Variant is assumed.

Placing your declarations

The normal place to declare variables is within a procedure before you need to use the variable. Some programmers like to place all variable declarations at the start of the procedure, but that isn't necessary. You can declare a variable any time up to the first time you use the variable.

You can also declare variables at the module level. Module-level variables are available to all procedures in the module. Place any module-level variables before the first procedure in the module.

Using static variables

A *static variable* is a variable whose value is preserved between executions of the procedure in which it's declared. You'll find many excellent uses for static variables in Word macros. For example, you may use a static variable to temporarily keep track of text entered by the user, to remember the location in the document where an operation was performed, or to keep track of actions taken since the last time the macro was run.

To create a static variable, use the Static keyword rather than the Dim keyword, like this:

```
Static iCaseCount As Integer
```

You can use static variables only in procedures. You can't create a static variable at the module level.

Using Option Explicit

Unlike in many other programming languages, such as C and Pascal, you do not have to "define" variables before you can use them in VBA. The first time you use a variable in a VBA macro, the variable is automatically defined.

Most experienced programmers consider the fact that you do not have to define variables to be *the* major weakness in BASIC and all of its dialects, including VBA and Visual Basic. The trouble is that you never know when you've misspelled a variable name because if you misspell a variable name, VBA assumes that you want to create a new variable. For example, suppose at the start of a macro you ask the user to enter a string value, and you store the value entered by the user in a variable named InputString. Then, later in the macro, you use the variable in a statement, but misspell it InputStrign. Does VBA point out your error? No. It just assumes that you want to create a new variable named InputStrign. This InputStrign variable is given a default value of "" rather than the value entered by the user.

Such problems are very common in VBA programming. Any time you are faced with a macro that looks like it should work, but doesn't, carefully double-check all your variable names to see whether you misspelled any.

You can avoid the problem of misspelled variable names by adding the following line to the very beginning of your VBA module:

```
Option Explicit
```

This line forces you to declare variables before you use them. Then, if you use a variable that you haven't declared, an error message displays.

Using Strings

Strings are one of the most common data types for macros when working with Word documents. You need to know how to manipulate string data if you hope to accomplish anything meaningful in Word VBA.

For starters, you can create string *literals* — that is, strings which are simply quoted in your macro. To use a string literal, enclose a string value in quotation marks: full-fledged double quotes, not apostrophes. For example:

```
MessageText = "Hi there!"
```

In this example, "Hi there!" is a string literal whose value is assigned to the string variable named MessageText.

You can use an apostrophe within a string literal with no ill effects, as in the following example:

```
MessageText = "Hi y'all"
```

But you cannot include quotes within quotes. For example, the following produces an error:

```
MessageText = "Say, "Cheeseburger!""
```

To see how to create a string value that includes quotation marks, read the following sections on concatenation and string functions.

Concatenation

A technique called *concatenation* allows you to join two or more strings together end to end to make a single, larger string. For example:

```
Entre = "Cheese" & "burger"
```

results in the string "Cheeseburger" being assigned to the Entre variable. The ampersand (&) is used for this purpose. The spaces around the ampersand are optional; if you leave them out, Word adds them in when you run the macro.

Concatenation becomes very useful when combined with string variables and, as you see in a moment, string functions. For example, consider this statement:

```
Message = "Could not deliver message to " & Recipient
```

Here, a literal string value is concatenated with a variable string value. If the value of the Recipient variable is "Jimmy Hoffa," the Message variable is set to "Could not deliver message to Jimmy Hoffa."

The number of concatenations you can string together in a single statement has no limit.

String functions

VBA provides several built-in functions that work on strings. Table 2-1 summarizes these functions. Most of these functions come in handy from time to time.

One of the most commonly used string functions is Chr: It lets you generate any character by specifying its ANSI code number, which ranges from 0 to 255. You can use concatenation along with the Chr function to create strings that contain quotation marks. For example:

```
Message = "Say, " + Chr(34) + "Cheeseburger!" + Chr(34)
```

Here, Chr(34) inserts the quotation marks.

Another commonly used string function is Len: It returns the number of characters in a string. For example:

```
Message="Hello world!"
LengthOfMessage = Len(Message)
```

In this example, the LengthOfMessage variable is assigned the value 12, the number of characters in the string Message. *Note:* The Len function returns a number, not a string.

A final group of string functions you need are those used to clean up string values that may contain unnecessary leading or trailing spaces or unprintable characters. These functions include LTrim(), RTrim(), and

CleanString(). For example, to remove spaces from the beginning and end of a string variable, use this statement:

```
TrimmedString = Trim(InputText)
```

Table 2-1	VBA Functions for Manipulating Strings
Function	*What It Does*
Chr(*value*)	Generates the character that corresponds to the ANSI code *value*. Common uses are Chr(9): Tab Chr(11): New line Chr(13): Carriage return Chr(30): Non-breaking hyphen Chr(32): Space Chr(34): Quotation mark (") Chr(160): Non-breaking space
InStr([*n*,]*string1*, *string2*)	Returns the character position within *string1* at which *string2* begins, or 0 if *string2* is not found in *string1*. If *n* is used, the first *n-1* characters of *string1* are ignored.
LCase(*string*)	Converts *string* to lowercase.
Left(*string*,*n*)	Returns the leftmost *n* characters of *string*.
Len(*string*)	Returns the length of *string*.
LTrim(*string*)	Removes leading spaces from *string*.
Mid(*string*,*x*,*y*)	Returns *y* characters from *string* starting at character *x*.
Right(*string*,*n*)	Returns the rightmost *n* characters of *string*.
RTrim(*string*)	Removes trailing spaces from *string*.
Str(*n*)	Converts the number *n* to a string variable. For example, Str(3.15) becomes the string "3.15".
UCase(*string*)	Converts *string* to uppercase.
Val(*string*)	Returns the numeric value of *string*. For example, Val("3.15") becomes the numeric value 3.15.

Of Objects, Properties, and Methods

VBA is inherently *object oriented*, which means that it deals extensively with programming elements known as *objects*. Simply put (as if that's possible), an object is a named entity that represents some component of a Word document. For example, a Document object represents an entire Word document, while a Selection object represents the text that's currently selected in a document.

Objects have three components:

✦ **Properties:** Define the data that's associated with an object. For example, the Selection object has a Text property that contains the text that's in the selection.

✦ **Methods:** Define actions that the object can perform. For example, the Selection object has a Copy method that copies the selection to the Clipboard.

✦ **Events:** The object notifies you that something noteworthy has happened. For example, a Document object raises a Close event when the document is closed.

Although events can be important in certain types of macros, most macros work with just the properties and methods of various Word objects.

Using objects

The basic trick for working with objects in VBA is that you use the period to separate the name of the object you want to work with from the name of the property or method you want to use. For example, Selection.Text refers to the Text property of the Selection object, and Range.Copy refers to the Copy method of the Range object.

One of the most important points about object oriented programming is that the properties of an object can themselves be other objects that have properties and methods. For example, the Selection object has a Font property, which is itself a Font object. The Font object, in turn, has its own properties, such as Name and Size. So, you can refer to the Name property of the selection's font like this: Selection.Font.Name.

Another key to understanding objects is knowing that you can create variables to refer to them. You specify the type of a variable with the As keyword. For example, the following line declares a variable named f that represents a Font object:

```
Dim f As Font
```

Then, you can assign an object to the variable.

You can't use the normal assignment statement to assign objects, however. Instead, you must use a Set statement, like this:

```
Set f As Selection.Font
```

Here, the Font variable f is set to the object referred to by the Font property of the Selection object.

You can then refer to properties of the object variable in the usual way. For example, f.Name refers to the Name property of the f object.

Learning the object model

Much of the trick to writing VBA macros for Word is learning Word's *object model* — that is, the objects available in a Word macro and the properties and methods available for each type of object. You find out more about Word's object model in Chapter 3 of this minibook.

One way to learn about the object model is to let the VBA editor tell you about it. When you type a period after an object name, the VBA editor pops up a helpful list of the properties and methods available for that object. Then, you can scroll down to the property or method you want to use and press the Tab key to insert it into your macro. This way is one of the best to learn what properties and methods are available for any given object.

Another way to learn about what objects, properties, and methods are available — perhaps the best way — is to record a macro that comes close to accomplishing what you want to do, and then switch to the VBA editor to see what code was generated for the macro. For example, suppose you want to write a macro that marks index entries. If you record a macro, and then press Alt+Shift+X to mark an index entry, Word generates VBA code similar to this:

```
ActiveDocument.Indexes.MarkEntry Range:=Selection.Range, Entry:= _
    "Object model", EntryAutoText:="Object model", CrossReference:="", _
    CrossReferenceAutoText:="", BookmarkName:="", Bold:=False, Italic:=False
```

Here, you can tell that you use the MarkEntry method of ActiveDocument.Indexes to mark an index entry, and that this method takes several arguments: Range, Entry, EntryAutoText, CrossReference, CrossReferenceAutotext, BookmarkName, Bold, and Italic.

Using methods

A method is an action that an object can perform. When you call a method, the object performs the action associated with the method. For example, the following statement copies the contents of the current selection to the Clipboard:

```
Selection.Copy
```

Some methods require *arguments*, which supply data for the method to work with. For example, the `Selection` object's `InsertAfter` method accepts a text string as an argument. The text string contains the text that's inserted after the selection.

To use arguments, simply list the argument values you want to pass to the method, like this:

```
Selection.InsertAfter "Some text"
```

Here, `Selection` is an object, `InsertAfter` is a method, and `"Some text"` is an argument.

If a method requires two or more arguments, separate them with commas, like this:

```
Selection.StartOf wdParagraph, wdExtend
```

In this example, the arguments are called *positional* because Word interprets the meaning of each argument based on the order in which you list them. Word also allows you to pass arguments using argument names, as in this example:

```
Selection.StartOf Unit:=wdParagraph, Extend:=wdExtend
```

Note: When you use methods that require arguments, the VBA editor displays tips that let you know what arguments the method expects.

VBA also allows you to enclose the arguments in parentheses, like this:

```
Selection.InsertAfter("Some text")
```

However, the parentheses aren't required.

Using the With statement

The `With` statement is a special VBA shortcut that lets you refer to an object in several statements without having to refer to the object each time. You simply list the object in the `With` statement. Then, any statement that appears between the `With` and its corresponding `End With` statement and that begins with a period uses the object listed in the `With` statement.

For example, suppose you want to set the `Bold` and `Italic` properties of the `Font` property of the `Selection` object for a document named Temp. You can use these lines:

```
Documents("Temp").ActiveWindow.Selection.Font.Bold = True
Documents("Temp").ActiveWindow.Selection.Font.Italic = True
```

Or, you can place these lines within a With/End With block, like this:

```
With Documents("Temp").ActiveWindow.Selection.Font
    .Bold = True
    .Italic = True
End With
```

Granted, the With statement adds two lines of code. But if the object reference is complicated, it can save you typing even if you need to set only two property values.

Working with collections

A *collection* is a special type of object that holds one or more occurrences of some other object. The Word object model, which I discuss further in the next chapter, has many collections that help organize the various objects used in Word. For example, you can store all the currently open documents in a collection called Documents. And you can access all the paragraphs in a document via a collection called Paragraphs.

All collections have a Count property you can use to determine how many items are in the collection. For example, the following code displays the number of currently open documents:

```
MsgBox "There are currently " & Documents.Count _
    & " documents open."
```

Many collections have an Add method that adds a new item to the collection. In many cases, the Add method creates a new object of the type appropriate for the collection, adds it to the collection, and returns the new object as its return value. For example, the following code creates a new document, and then displays the document's name:

```
Dim d As Document
Set d = Documents.Add
MsgBox "The new document's name is " & d.Name
```

You can access the individual items in a collection by using an index number. For example, the following code displays the name of the first document in the Documents collection:

```
MsgBox Documents(1).Name
```

In many cases, you can use the name of an item instead of an index. For example, this statement closes the document named TempDoc:

```
Documents("TempDoc").Close
```

Note: If no document is named TempDoc, the statement generates an error.

Controlling Your Programs

The simplest macros execute their statements one at a time, in the sequence in which the statements are listed in the macro, until they reach the End Sub statement.

More sophisticated macros need more control over the sequence in which statements are executed. For example, you may need to skip over some statements based on the result of a condition test. Or, you may need to create a loop of statements that repeats itself a given number of times or until a certain condition — such as reaching the end of the document — is met.

The following sections describe the VBA statements that let you control the flow of execution in your macro.

The If statement

Do you remember that Robert Frost poem that begins, "Two roads diverged in a yellow wood. . ."? That poem is an apt description of how the If statement works. The macro is rolling along, executing one statement after another, until it comes to an If statement. The If statement represents a fork in the road, and a choice must be made about which path to take.

Many macros need to make such decisions as they execute. For example, a macro that creates an index entry for text selected by the user has to first determine whether or not the user has indeed selected any text. If so, the macro proceeds to create the index entry. If not, the macro does nothing, or perhaps displays an error message saying something along the lines of, "You didn't select any text!" To handle this decision processing, the macro uses an If statement.

VBA's If statement is remarkably flexible, with several formats to choose from. All these forms involve three basic parts:

♦ A *condition test* that is evaluated to yield a value of True or False.

♦ A *then part*, which supplies one or more statements that execute only if the result of the condition test is True.

♦ An *else part*, which supplies one or more statements that execute only if the result of the condition test is False.

For example, consider these lines that may be used in an index marking macro:

```
If Selection.Type = wdSelectionNormal Then
    ActiveDocument.Indexes.MarkEntry Range:=Selection.Range,
        Entry:="index"
Else
    MsgBox ("Please select something to mark.")
End If
```

Here, the If statement begins with a condition test that checks to see whether the selection is a normal text selection. If so, the ActiveDocument. Indexes.MarkEntry statement executes to insert an index field code. If not, a message box displays.

Note: Each component of the If statement must fall on a separate line, as shown in the preceding example. In other words, you cannot place the statements on the same line as the Then or Else keywords.

The Else part of the If statement is optional. However, End If is not optional: Every If statement must have a corresponding End If. (The only exception to this rule is the single-line If format that I explain in a moment.)

While indenting the statements is not strticly required, using such indentation makes the structure of the If statement much more apparent. Consider the preceding example without any indentation:

```
If Selection.Type = wdSelectionNormal Then
ActiveDocument.Indexes.MarkEntry Range:=Selection.Range,
Entry:="index"
Else
MsgBox ("Please select something to mark.")
End If
```

Now imagine that instead of a single statement between the Then and Else lines, the macro has a dozen, with a dozen more lines between the Else and End If lines. Indentation is the only way to keep track of the overall structure of the If statement.

Nested If statements

You can *nest* If statements — that is, you can include one If statement within the Then or Else part of another. For example:

```
If expression Then
    If expression Then
        statements
    Else
        statements
    End If
Else
    If expression Then
        statements
    Else
        statements
    End If
End If
```

Nesting can be as complex as you want. Just remember that you need an End If for every If. And be certain to use indentation so that each set of matching If, Else, and End If lines are properly aligned.

The ElseIf structure

VBA supports a special type of If structure, using the ElseIf keyword. The ElseIf form is a shorthand notation that allows you to simplify If structures that follow this form:

```
If expression Then
    statements
Else
    If expression Then
        statements
    Else
        If expression Then
            statements
        End If
    End IF
End If
```

Using the ElseIf keyword, you can express the same structure like this:

```
If expression Then
    statements
ElseIf expression Then
    statements
ElseIf expression Then
    statements
End If
```

If that's a little too abstract, consider a macro that displays one of three messages, depending on the day of the week. For Sunday, the macro displays
"Time for Football!" For Saturday, it displays "Time to mow the lawn!!" And
for any other day, it displays "Time to go to work!!!"

Here's how to code this macro using ordinary `If` statements:

```
DayOfWeek=Weekday(Now())
If DayOfWeek = 1 Then
    MsgBox("Time for football!")
Else
    If DayOfWeek = 7 Then
        MsgBox("Time to mow the lawn!!")
    Else
        MsgBox("Time to go to work!!!")
    End IF
End If
```

Notice that the first `Else` clause contains a nested `If` statement. By using
the `ElseIf` keyword, the second `If` statement is subsumed into the first, so
a single `If` statement handles the whole thing:

```
DayOfWeek=Weekday(Now())
If DayOfWeek = 1 Then
    MsgBox("Time for football!")
ElseIf DayOfWeek = 7 Then
    MsgBox("Time to mow the lawn!!")
Else
    MsgBox("Time to go to work!!!")
End If
```

In this example, only one `End If` line is required because it has only one `If`
statement. In other words, the `ElseIf` keyword does not require its own
matching `End If`.

In most cases, a `Select Case` statement implements `If` structures that
require `ElseIf` clauses more easily, which I describe later in this chapter.

The single-line If

VBA also allows you to use a single-line form of the `If` statement, which
looks like this:

```
If condition Then statement [Else statement]
```

To use this form of the `If` statement, the condition, `Then` clause, and `Else`
clause (if any) must all be coded on the same line. For example:

```
If x > 0 Then MsgBox("X is " & x)
```

The preceding example displays the message "X is *n*," where *n* is the value of x. But the message displays only if x is greater than zero.

You can include more than one statement in the `Then` part by separating the statements with colons. But if more than one statement is required, or if an `Else` part is required, I suggest you use the basic multi-line `If` form instead of the single-line form.

For/Next Loops

`For/Next` loops allow you to set up a basic looping structure, in which a series of statements execute over and over again, with the value of a counter variable increased by one each time, until the counter variable reaches a certain value.

As a simple — if not very practical — example, the following snippet inserts the numbers 1 through 100 in the current document, one number on each line:

```
For x = 1 to 100
    Selection.InsertAfter Str(x) & Chr(13)
Next x
```

This `For/Next` loop causes the `Insert` statement it contains to execute 100 times. The first time through, the variable *x* is set to the value 1. The second time, *x* is 2; the third time, 3; and so on, all the way up to 100.

The general form of a `For/Next` loop is:

```
For counter-variable = start To end [Step increment]
    statements...
Next [counter-variable]
```

You can specify any starting and ending value you want for the counter variable. In addition, you can specify an increment value by using the `Step` clause. You can use `Step` to create `For/Next` loops that count by twos, threes, or any other value you want. If you omit `Step`, the default is 1.

The term *iteration* is often used to refer to each execution of a `For/Next` loop. For example, a `For/Next` loop that starts with the line `For x = 1 To 10` iterates ten times.

While/Wend loops

`While/Wend` loops provide a more sophisticated form of looping, in which the loop continues as long as a specified condition remains `True`. The general form is

```
While condition
    statements
Wend
```

The `While` loop starts by evaluating the condition. If it is `True`, the statements in the loop execute. When the `Wend` statement is encountered, the condition is evaluated again. If it is still `True`, the statements in the loop execute again. This cycle continues until the condition evaluates as `False`.

At this point, you really need to know just what it means to say a condition is `True`. In VBA, `False` is defined as the numeric value 0, and any nonzero value is considered to be `True`. For example, consider this `While` loop:

```
x = 5
While x
    Selection.InsertAfter Str(x) & Chr(13)
    x = x - 1
Wend
```

This loop continues to execute as long as *x* is not zero. The moment *x* becomes zero, VBA considers the condition expression to be `False` and the loop terminates. As a result, this `While` loop displays five message boxes, showing the values 5, 4, 3, 2, 1, and then it terminates.

To continue a loop as long as an expression evaluates to `False`, use `Not` as part of the condition test. For example:

```
x = 0
While Not x = 5
    Selection.InsertAfter Str(x) & Chr(13)
    x = x + 1
Wend
```

Here, the loop repeats as long as *x* is not equal to 5.

The Select Case statement

Life would be easy if it consisted entirely of either/or choices. But in the real world, you're often faced with many alternatives to choose from. And so it is in VBA. More than a few VBA functions return more complicated results than a simple yes/no, true/false, 0/1. For example, `Selection.Style.Name` returns the name of the style applied to the current selection. You can use this information to cause your macro to take a different action depending on which style is applied to the selected paragraph.

The `Select Case` statement is designed just for such situations. It lets you test an expression for various values, executing different statements depending on the result. Its general form is

```
Select Case expression
    Case case-condition
        statements
  [ Case case-condition
        statements ]
  [ Case Else
        statements ]
End Select
```

The `Select Case` statement starts by evaluating the expression. Then, it compares the result with the case conditions listed in the `Case` clauses, one at a time. When it finds a match, it executes the statements listed for the `Case` clause that matches, and skips the rest of the `Select Case` statement. If none of the case conditions match, the statements in the `Case Else` clause execute. The key point is that only one of the `Case` clauses is selected for execution.

For each `Case` clause, *values* can be any of the following:

✦ A single value, such as **Case 4.** The `Case` clause is selected if the expression is equal to the value.

✦ A list of expressions, such as **Case 4, 8, 12, 16.** The `Case` clause is selected if the expression equals any of the listed values.

✦ A range of values, separated with the keyword `To`, such as **Case 4 to 8.** The `Case` clause is selected if the expression falls between the two values, inclusively.

✦ The word **Is** followed by a relational comparison, such as **Is > 4.** The relation is tested against the expression, and the `Case` clause is selected if the result of the comparison is `True`.

Here is an example of a `While` loop that includes a `Select Case` statement to count the number of Heading 1, Heading 2, and Heading 3 styles from the current selection to the end of the document:

```
Dim Heading1Count As Integer
Dim Heading2Count As Integer
Dim Heading3Count As Integer
Dim s As Style
While Selection.Move(wdParagraph, 1)
    Select Case Selection.Style.NameLocal
        Case "Heading 1"
            Heading1Count = Heading1Count + 1
        Case "Heading 2"
            Heading2Count = Heading2Count + 1
        Case "Heading 3"
            Heading3Count = Heading3Count + 1
    End Select
Wend
```

In this example, the variables Heading1Count, Heading2Count, and Heading3Count count the number of headings for each level. The Select Case statement evaluates the NameLocal property of the Selection's Style object. Then, the Case clauses check for the values "Heading 1," "Heading 2," and "Heading 3." If the NameLocal property returns one of these three values, 1 is added to the appropriate counter variable.

You can use Case Else to handle any values that aren't specifically mentioned in Case clauses.

User Input and Output

The following sections describe various methods of displaying information and obtaining input from the user.

MsgBox

MsgBox allows you to display a dialog box containing an informative message. MsgBox temporarily halts the macro until the user closes the message dialog box.

The MsgBox command has the following form:

MsgBox *message* [,*buttons* [,*title*]]

message is the text to display in the message, *buttons* is a constant that indicates the type of buttons to display, and *title* is the title displayed in the dialog box title bar.

To display a simple message, use a command such as this:

MsgBox "It's Saturday night!"

This command displays the dialog box shown in Figure 2-1.

Figure 2-1:
A MsgBox
dialog box.

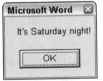

Here's a `MsgBox` call that specifies the type of buttons and a title:

```
MsgBox "It's Saturday night!", vbOKCancel, "Live from New
    York!"
```

Its output is shown in Figure 2-2.

The `button` argument actually controls three things at once: what buttons appear in the dialog box, what icon appears in the dialog box, and which button is the default. Table 2-2 lists the values for these settings. ***Note:*** You can add these constants together to create composite styles. For example, this `MsgBox` statement displays an OK and Cancel button, a Stop symbol, and makes the Cancel button the default:

```
MsgBox "It's Saturday night!", vbOKCancel + vbExclamation +
    vbDefaultButton2, "Live from New York!"
```

Table 2-2	MsgBox Type Values	
Group	*Constant*	*Meaning*
Buttons	`vbOKOnly`	OK only
	`vbOKCancel`	OK and Cancel
	`vbAbortRetryIgnore`	Abort, Retry, and Ignore
	`vbYesNoCancel`	Yes, No, and Cancel
	`vbYesNo`	Yes and No
	`vbRetryCancel`	Retry and Cancel
Icon	`vbCritical`	Critical icon
	`vbQuestion`	A question mark
	`vbExclamation`	An exclamation mark
	`vbInformation`	Information only
Default button	`vbDefaultButton1`	First button (OK, Yes, or Abort)
	`vbDefaultButton2`	Second button (Cancel, No, or Retry)
	`vbDefaultButton3`	Third button (Cancel or Ignore)

`MsgBox` returns a value that indicates which button was clicked, as described in Table 2-3.

Table 2-3	MsgBox Return Values	
Constant	*Numeric Value*	*Which Button Was Pressed*
vbOK	1	OK button
vbCancel	2	Cancel
vbAbort	3	Abort
vbRetry	4	Retry
vbIgnore	5	Ignore
vbYes	6	Yes
vbNo	7	No

InputBox

`InputBox` is a VBA function that displays a dialog box that includes a single text field into which the user can type a response. The user's input is then returned to the macro as the function's return value.

The `InputBox` function accepts three arguments:

InputBox(*prompt* [,*title*] [,*default*]**)**

For example, the following `InputBox` function asks the user to enter a name:

```
Name=InputBox("Type a name:")
```

This example shows how to provide your own title for the input dialog box and display a default choice:

```
Name=InputBox("Type a name:", "The Name Game", UserName)
```

The user's response returns in the `Name` variable. Figure 2-3 shows the dialog box that displays.

Figure 2-3:
An
`InputBox`
dialog box.

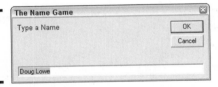

User-Defined Procedures and Functions

Most VBA macros consist of a single procedure. However, VBA lets you create additional procedures and functions that you can call from within the macro's main procedure. Procedures and functions are useful when you have a series of VBA commands or a complex calculation that you need to call upon several times in a macro. By placing these commands in a procedure or function, you can code them once and call upon them as many times as needed.

Using procedures

To create a procedure, use a Sub/End Sub command pair outside the Sub /End Sub command pair for the macro's main procedure. The statements that make up the procedure go between the Sub and End Sub commands, and the Sub command supplies the name of the procedure and any arguments that are passed to the subroutine. For example:

```
Sub SayHello
    BeepMsg "Hello World!"
End Sub

Sub BeepMsg(Message As String)
    Beep
    MsgBox Message
End Sub
```

In this example, the BeepMsg procedure displays a message and sounds a tone to get the user's attention. In the macro's main procedure (called SayHello), you can use BeepMsg as if it were a built-in VBA command.

If you want, you can type the keyword Call before the subroutine name when calling the subroutine. For example:

```
Call BeepMsg "Hello World!"
```

The Call keyword is optional, but some VBA programmers like to use it to help distinguish user-written subroutines from built-in VBA commands.

Using functions

A function is similar to a subroutine, with one crucial difference: A function returns a value. Here's an example:

```
Sub GetAnAnswer
    If GetYesNo("Yes, or no?") Then
        BeepMsg "You said yes."
```

```
        Else
            BeepMsg "You said no."
        End If
End Sub

Sub BeepMsg(Message As String)
        Beep
        MsgBox Message
End Sub

Function GetYesNo(Message As String) As Boolean
        If MsgBox(Message, vbYesNo) = vbYes Then
            GetYesNo = True
        Else
            GetYesNo = False
        End If
End Function
```

Here, the GetYesNo function uses a MsgBox function to display a message box with Yes and No buttons. The return value from the MsgBox function determines which button the user pressed, and the return value of the GetYesNo function is set to True if the user clicked Yes, False if the user clicked No. Back in the Main routine, the GetYesNo function is used in an If statement to display "You said yes" if the user clicks Yes or "You said no" if the user clicks No.

Here, StringVar is passed by value rather than by reference to BeepMsg. As a result, the MsgBox command in Main displays "Original Value" rather than "New Value."

Call-by-value looks peculiar when used with a function call because the parentheses must be doubled. For example:

```
Sub Main
        Prompt = "Yes, or no?"
        Reply = GetYesNo((Prompt))
        MsgBox Prompt
End Sub

Function GetYesNo(Message)
        GetYesNo = MsgBox(Message, 36)
        Message = "New Value"
End Function
```

Here, Prompt is passed by value to the GetYesNo function, so its value is unchanged.

Chapter 3: Working with Word's Object Model

In This Chapter

- ✔ Understanding the basic objects of Word's object model
- ✔ Wrestling with documents, windows, and panes
- ✔ Discovering selections and ranges
- ✔ Creating macros that manipulate text
- ✔ Creating macros that adjust text formatting

Word's *object model* is the programming interface that lets you manipulate Word documents from VBA. The object model consists of a collection of different types of object, such as documents, paragraphs, styles, tables, and so on. Each of these objects has its own properties and methods you can use from VBA. The most difficult aspect of writing Word macros is dealing with this object model, in part because Word's object model is huge. The people at Microsoft who designed Word's object model were not minimalists.

However, after you get your mind around a few basic concepts, such as the difference between selections and ranges, the object model begins to make sense. So, without further ado, this chapter presents an overview of the most commonly used parts of Word's object model.

An Overview of Important Word Objects

Word's object model is far too complex to cover here in a single chapter. All told, the object model has more than 130 types of objects, more than 100 types of collections, and hundreds of methods and properties.

Fortunately, you don't have to know about all the objects, collections, methods, and properties that make up the complete object model to start writing useful VBA macros. To give you an idea for the overall structure of the Word object model, Table 3-1 summarizes the function of the 30 or so most commonly used Word objects and the collections that contain them. You get more details about many of these objects throughout the rest of this chapter.

Please don't let this table overwhelm you. I include it here simply to familiarize you with the name and general purpose of Word's most commonly used objects. Don't feel like you have to memorize it, or give it more than a casual glance for now.

Also, notice that some of the objects listed in this table have a corresponding collection. For example, all of the bookmarks for a document are stored in a Bookmarks collection, with each individual bookmark represented by a single Bookmark object. Not all of the objects in this table have a corresponding collection, however. For example, there is just one Application object, so there's no need for a collection to store this object type.

Table 3-1	Major Objects in the Word Object Model	
Object	*Collection*	*Description*
Application		The Microsoft Word application itself. This object is considered to be the start of the Word object model. Use the Application object to access other top-level objects. For example, use the ActiveDocument property to access the Document object for the current document.
Bookmark	Bookmarks	Used to access bookmarks. You can access the Bookmarks collection via a Document object.
Cell	Cells	Used to access cells in a table. You can access the Cells collection via a Row or Column object. You can also access an individual cell using the Cell method of a Table object.
Column	Columns	Represents a column in a table. You can access the Columns collection via a Table object.
Diagram	Shapes	Represents a diagram. Diagrams are stored along with other shapes in a Shapes collection. You can access the Shapes collection via a Document object.
Document	Documents	Represents a single document. The Documents collection (available via the Application object) contains all of the currently open documents.
Email		Represents the e-mail information for a Document. Accessed via the Email property of a Document object.
Envelope		Represents a document's envelope. Accessed via the Envelope property of a Document object.

Object	Collection	Description
Field	Fields	Represents a field. The Fields collection is accessed via a Document, Range, or Selection object.
Find		Provides the function of the Edit⇨Find command.
Font		Represents a Font object. Accessed via the Font property of a Selection, Range, or Style object.
HeaderFooter	HeaderFooters	Represents a header or footer for a section of a document. The HeaderFooters collection is accessed via the Headers or Footers property of a Section object.
List	Lists	Represents a list in a document. The Lists collection is accessed via a Document object.
Options		Represents the settings in the Tools⇨Options command.
Page	Pages	Represents the pages in a document. The Pages collection is accessed via a Pane object, not a Document object as you may expect. Go figure.
PageSetup		Represents the page setup, including margins and columns. Accessed via a Document or Section object.
Pane	Panes	Represents an open window pane used to view a document. The Panes collection is accessed via a Window object.
Paragraph	Paragraphs	Represents a paragraph. The Paragraphs collection is accessed via a Document, Selection, or Range object.
ParagraphFormat		Represents the format for a Paragraph or Style object.
Range		Represents a range of a document. Many Word objects have a Range property, including Document, Section, Paragraph, and Bookmark.
Replacement		Provides the function of the Edit⇨Replace command.
Row	Rows	Represents a row in a table. The Rows collection is accessed via a Table object.
Section	Sections	Represents a document section. The Sections collection is accessed via a Document object.

(continued)

Table 3-1 *(continued)*

Object	Collection	Description
Selection		Represents the current selection. Accessed via a Selection or Pane object.
Shape	Shapes	Represents a shape. The Shapes collection is accessed via a Document object.
Style	Styles	Represents a style. The Styles collection is accessed via a Document object.
Table	Tables	Represents a table. The Tables collection is accessed via a Document, Range, or Selection object.
Template	Templates	Represents a template. All the available templates (normal template, attached templates, and global templates) are available in the Templates collection, which you can access via the Global object. Use the AttachedTemplate property of a Document object to access the template attached to a document.
TextColumn	TextColumns	Represents a column. The TextColumns collection is accessed via a PageSetup object.
Variable	Variables	Represents a document variable. The Variables collection is accessed via a Document object.
View		Represents the view settings, such as whether paragraph marks or field codes are visible. Accessed via a Window or Pane object.
Window	Windows	Represents an open window. The Application.Windows collection has all open windows. The Windows collection for a Document object has just those windows that are open for the document.

Using the Application Object

The Application object is the starting point for Word's object model. It represents the Word application itself. Here are a few of its more interesting properties:

✦ ActiveDocument: A Document object that represents the active document — that is, the document from which the user ran the macro.

✦ ActiveWindow: A Window object that represents the active window.

◆ Documents: A collection that contains all the currently open documents.

◆ Options: An Options object that represents the current settings for Word. The options are usually set via Tools⇨Options.

◆ ScreenUpdating: Controls whether the screen updates to reflect changes made to the document as a macro runs. Some macros run faster if you set ScreenUpdating to False.

◆ Selection: The text that is currently selected in the active document.

◆ Templates: A Templates collection that contains all the currently available templates.

◆ UserAddress: The user's mailing address.

◆ UserInitials: The user's initials.

◆ UserName: The user's name.

◆ Version: The version of Word being used.

◆ Windows: A collection of Window objects that represents all the currently open windows.

The Application object also has several methods that can be useful. In particular:

◆ CleanString: This method removes non-printable characters from a text string.

◆ GoBack: Moves the insertion point back to previous locations where editing occurred.

◆ GoForward: After using the GoBack method, this method moves forward to previous editing locations.

◆ ListCommands: Creates a new document that lists all of Word's commands along with their keyboard shortcuts.

◆ OnTime: Starts a timer that runs a macro at a specified time.

◆ Quit: Quits Microsoft Word.

◆ Repeat: Repeats the most recent editing action.

◆ Run: Runs another macro.

◆ ScreenRefresh: Updates the screen. This method is useful if you've suppressed screen updating by setting the ScreenUpdating property to False.

◆ ShowClipboard: Shows the Clipboard task pane.

You can use many of the properties and methods of the `Application` object without explicitly specifying `Application`. For example, the following two lines of code are equivalent:

```
Application.Options.AllowFastSave = True
Options.AllowFastSave = True
```

The `Application` object properties and methods you can use without specifying the `Application` object are called *global members*.

Working with Documents

You use the `Document` object to access a document in Word. The `Document` object has many useful properties and methods. Here are a few of the more interesting properties:

- ✦ `Name`: The document's name.
- ✦ `Path`: The disk path for the document.
- ✦ `ReadOnly`: Indicates whether or not the document is read-only.
- ✦ `Saved`: `False` if the document has changed since it was last saved.
- ✦ `Windows`: Returns a `Windows` collection that contains all the windows in which the document is open.
- ✦ `AttachedTemplate`: Returns a `Template` object for the template that's attached to the document.

Here are some of the methods of the `Document` object:

- ✦ `Activate`: Makes the document the active document.
- ✦ `Close`: Closes the document.
- ✦ `PrintOut`: Prints all or part of the document.
- ✦ `Save`: Saves the document. Prompts the user for a name if the document has not been saved before.
- ✦ `SaveAs`: Saves the file using a specified name and path.

Accessing documents

If the document you want to access is the active document — that is, the document from which the user ran the macro — you can just specify `ActiveDocument` to access its properties and methods. For example, the following statement saves the active document:

```
ActiveDocument.Save
```

You can access all the documents that are currently open via the Documents collection. For example, the following code displays a message box that lists the name of each open document:

```
Dim msg As String
Dim d As Document
For Each d In Documents
    msg = msg & d.Name & VbCr
Next
MsgBox msg
```

You can use the Documents collection to access a document by name, like this:

```
Documents("Document1").Save
```

Creating a document

You can create a new document by using the Add method of the Documents collection. The Add method returns the document that was created. The following code creates a new document, and then displays the document's name in a message box:

```
Dim d As Document
Set d = Documents.Add
MsgBox d.Name
```

Note: Creating a document makes the new document the active document. If your macro needs to return to the original active document, it needs to save the active document's name in a string variable, and then use the variable later to return to that document. For example:

```
Dim s As String
s = ActiveDocument.Name
Dim d As Document
Set d = Documents.Add
Documents(s).Activate
```

Here, the active document's name is saved in the string named *s*. Then, a new document is created and the original active document is reactivated.

Opening a document

You may have noticed that the Document object doesn't have an Open method. However, the Documents collection does. The following example opens the document named QuarterlyReport.doc and assigns it to the Document variable named report:

```
Dim report As Document
Set report = Documents.Open("QuarterlyReport.doc")
```

When the `Open` method opens a document, it creates a `Document` object, adds it to the `Documents` collection, and makes the new document the active document. If the document specified by the string argument doesn't exist, an error message displays.

Understanding stories

A Word document actually consists of one or more *stories,* which represent distinct areas of a document. All documents have a *main story* that contains the text displayed within the page margins. In addition, documents can have other stories, such as headers and footers, footnotes and endnotes, text that appears in frames, and comments.

If your macro works only with the contents of the main story, you don't need to worry about stories at all because the main story is the default story of the `Document` object. But if you want to create a macro that manipulates text in another story, such as the footnote story, you have to know how to get to the right story.

To do that, you use the `StoryRanges` collection of the `Documents` object. One of the constants listed in Table 3-2 indexes this collection. For example, the following macro displays the number of paragraphs in the footnotes story:

```
Dim fr As Range
Set fr = ActiveDocument.StoryRanges(wdFootnotesStory)
MsgBox fr.Paragraphs.Count
```

In this example, `wdFootnotesStory` is used as the index for `ActiveDocument.StoryRanges` to get the footnotes story. Then, the `Paragraphs.Count` property displays the number of paragraphs in the story.

Note: The Word object model doesn't have a separate `Story` object. Instead, each item in the `StoryRanges` collection is a `Range` object. I further discuss `Range` objects in the next section.

Table 3-2	Constants for Story Types
Constant	*Description*
wdCommentsStory	Comments made by reviewers
wdEndnoteContinuationNoticeStory	Endnote continuation notices
wdEndnoteContinuationSeparatorStory	Endnote continuation separators

Constant	Description
wdEndnoteSeparatorStory	Endnote separators
wdEndnotesStory	Endnotes
wdEvenPagesFooterStory	Footers for even pages
wdEvenPagesHeaderStory	Headers for even pages
wdFirstPageFooterStory	Footers for the first page
wdFirstPageHeaderStory	Headers for the first page
wdFootnoteContinuationNoticeStory	Footnote continuation notices
wdFootnoteContinuationSeparatorStory	Footnote continuation separators
wdFootnoteSeparatorStory	Footnote separators
wdFootnotesStory	Footnotes
wdMainTextStory	The main text of the document
wdPrimaryFooterStory	Footers
wdPrimaryHeaderStory	Headers
wdTextFrameStory	Text that appears in frames

Understanding Selection and Range Objects

One of the most confusing aspects of Word's object model is that two distinct objects refer to portions of a document: Selection and Range. The Selection and Range objects are similar, with many overlapping features. However, selections can do some things that ranges can't, and vice versa.

In a nutshell, a Selection object refers to a portion of a document that is selected. The selection can be made by the user prior to running the macro, or the macro itself can select text.

Like a selection, a *range* is a portion of a document. However, a range isn't actually selected, so it isn't highlighted in the document window. Ranges allow you to work on document text without drawing attention to the text.

A document can have only one selection at a time, unless the same document is open in two or more windows or window panes. In that case, each window or pane can have its own selection in the document. However, you can create as many ranges for a document as you want. And the ranges can overlap. For example, you can create a Range object that refers to the entire document, another Range object that refers to a particular paragraph within the document, and a third Range object that refers to a single word within that paragraph.

Working with the Selection object

The `Selection` object refers to the portion of the document that is currently selected. If you're writing a macro that manipulates the text selected by the user, you most likely use the `Selection` object. For example, this statement copies the selection to the Clipboard:

```
Selection.Copy
```

And the following code formats the selected text as both bold and italic:

```
Selection.Font.Bold = True
Selection.Font.Italic = True
```

You can access the text that's contained in a selection by using the `Text` property. For example, the following statement displays the selected text in a message box:

```
    MsgBox Selection.Text
```

Getting the right selection

When you refer to a `Selection` object using just the word `Selection`, you're accessing the selection in the currently active document window. This method is the most common way to use a `Selection` object.

However, you can also refer to other `Selection` objects. You can display each open document in more than one window, and you can split each of those windows into two panes. Because you can select text in any window pane, Word's object model lets you access a `Selection` object for each window pane. To access a selection in another document, you use the `Document` object's `ActiveWindow` property, like this:

```
Documents("QuarterlyReport.doc").ActiveWindow.Selection
```

This statement accesses the selection in the active pane of the active window for the QuarterlyReport document.

If the window is split into panes, you can use the `Panes` property to access the selection in either pane. For example, the following code displays a message box that lists the text selected in both panes of the active window:

```
Dim msg As String
msg = ActiveWindow.Panes(1).Selection.Text + VbCr _
    + ActiveWindow.Panes(2).Selection.Text
MsgBox msg
```

Dealing with selection types

A user may make many different types of selections before running your macro. Any macro that works with the Selection object needs to first make sure that the right type of selection is made. You can do that by checking the Type property. For example, this code checks to make sure that the user makes a normal selection before copying the selection to the Clipboard:

```
If Selection.Type = wdSelectionNormal Then
    Selection.Copy
End If
```

The Type property can have any of the constant values listed in Table 3-3.

Table 3-3	Constants for the Selection.Type Property
Constant	**Description**
wdNoSelection	No selection is made.
wdSelectionBlock	A vertical block of text is selected, as when the Alt key is used with the mouse.
wdSelectionColumn	A table column is selected.
wdSelectionFrame	A frame is selected.
wdSelectionInlineShape	An inline shape is selected.
wdSelectionIP	The selection is just an insertion point.
wdSelectionNormal	A normal block of text is selected.
wdSelectionRow	A table row is selected.
wdSelectionShape	A drawing shape is selected.

Working with Range objects

A Range object identifies a portion of a document. It can be as short as a single character or as long as the entire document. Range objects let you access text from within a macro without actually selecting the text on-screen or affecting the text that's currently selected.

Getting ranges

Many objects with the Word object model have a Range property that you can use to create a range that represents a portion of the document. For example, suppose you want to access the first paragraph of the active document as a range. To do so, you can use this code:

```
Dim r As Range
Set r = ActiveDocument.Paragraphs(1).Range
MsgBox r.Text
```

Here, the `Paragraphs` collection accesses the first paragraph in the active document.

The following table lists the objects that have a `Range` property:

Bookmark	HeaderFooter	Selection
Cell	Hyperlink	SmartTag
Comment	InlineShape	Subdocument
Endnote	List	Table
Footnote	Paragraph	TableOfAuthorities
Formfield	Revision	TableOfContents
Frame	Row	TableOfFigures
HeaderFooter	Section	

Notice that among these objects is the `Selection` object. As a result, you can get a `Range` object that corresponds to the current selection like this:

```
Dim r As Range
Set r = Selection.Range
```

Several properties of other objects also return `Range` objects. For example, the `Document` object has a `Content` property that returns a `Range` object representing the entire content of a document. For more ways to get ranges that represent portions of a document, see the section "Accessing text" later in this chapter.

Getting a range from a bookmark

Book III, Chapter 1 explains how you can use bookmarks to assign names to portions of a document. In effect, a bookmark is simply a named range that's saved along with the document. Bookmarks are commonly used in macros because they allow you to refer to a predefined area of text by name. If your macro needs to insert text into a document at predefined locations, bookmarks are the easiest way to do it.

To create a `Range` object for a bookmark, use code similar to this:

```
Dim r As Range
Set r = ActiveDocument.Bookmarks("FromAddress").Range
```

This code is fine if you're certain that the bookmark is always there. If you can't make that guarantee (and you can't, really), check first to make sure the bookmark exists, like this:

```
If ActiveDocument.Bookmarks.Exists("Customer") Then
    Dim r As Range
    Set r = ActiveDocument.Bookmarks("FromAddress").Range
Else
    MsgBox "Missing bookmark!"
End If
```

Here, the `Exists` method of the `Bookmarks` collection determines whether the `Customer` bookmark exists before it is accessed.

Creating a range from scratch

You can also create a `Range` object by using the `Range` method of the `Document` object. Note that I said the `Range` *method,* not the `Range` *property.* The `Range` method of the `Document` object creates a new range for the portion of the document you specify. In the `Range` method, you must provide the starting and ending character position for the range. Here's an example:

```
Dim r As Range
Set r = ActiveDocument.Range(0, 100)
```

Here, a `Range` object that includes the first 100 characters of a document is created.

Selecting a range

The `Range` object has a `Select` method that you can use to make a range the current selection. For example:

```
Dim r As Range
Set r = ActiveDocument.Range(0, 100)
r.Select
```

Here, a `Range` object is created for the first 100 characters of a document. Then, the `Range` object is selected.

Moving Selections and Ranges

The `Selection` and `Range` objects both have a `Start` and `End` property that indicates the character position of the start of the section or range and the position of the end of the section or range. You can set these properties directly to change a selection or range. For example, to collapse the active selection, you can use this code:

```
Selection.End = Selection.Start
```

Note: This statement leaves the insertion point at the start of the selection. If you want to collapse the selection and leave the insertion point at the end of the selection, use this code instead:

```
Selection.Start = Selection.End
```

You can also add or subtract values to the selection Start or End properties. For example, the following code extends the selection by one character:

```
Selection.End = Selection.End + 1
```

Methods for moving the selection

The Selection and Range objects sport several methods that let you move the start or end of the selection or range:

+ Collapse: Makes the Start and End values the same. You can specify a direction as an argument to indicate which direction the selection or range collapses. Specify wdCollapseStart to collapse to the start of the selection or range. Specify wdCollapseEnd to collapse to the end.

+ EndOf and StartOf: Moves the start or end of the selection or range to the start or end of a specified unit. I list the possible unit values, which are used in several other methods as well, in Table 3-4.

+ Expand: Expands the selection to include the next unit.

+ Move: Collapses the selection or range, and then moves the selection or range the specified number of units.

+ MoveStart, MoveEnd: Moves the start or end of the selection or range the specified number of units.

+ MoveStartUntil, MoveEndUntil: Moves the start or end of the selection or range until one of the specified characters is found.

+ MoveStartWhile, MoveEndWhile: Moves the start or end of the selection or range until a character that is not one of the specified characters is found.

+ MoveUntil, MoveWhile: Similar to MoveStartUntil/MoveEndUntil and MoveStartWhile/MoveEndWhile, but collapses the selection or range first.

+ Next and Previous: Moves the selection to the next or previous specified unit.

Table 3-4	Constants for Word Units
Constant	*Description*
wdCharacter	Character
wdWord	Word
wdSentence	Sentence
wdParagraph	Paragraph
wdSection	Section
wdStory	Story
wdCell	Table cell
wdColumn	Column
wdRow	Table row
wdTable	Table

A macro that moves the selection

To illustrate how you can move the selection in a macro, the following example shows a macro that displays a message indicating how many times the font has changed in a selection:

```
Sub CountFontChanges()
    Dim iCount As Integer
    Dim iEnd As Integer
    Dim sFont As String
    Dim r As Range
    Set r = Selection.Range
    iEnd = r.End
    r.Collapse
    sFont = r.Font.Name
    While r.Start < iEnd - 1
        Set r = r.Next(wdCharacter, 1)
        If r.Font.Name <> sFont Then
            iCount = iCount + 1
            sFont = r.Font.Name
        End If
    Wend
    MsgBox "The selected text has " & iCount _
        & " font changes."
End Sub
```

This macro starts by assigning the selection to a Range object named r. It then saves the ending character position of the range in a variable named iEnd, and then collapses the range. Next, it saves the name of the font used for the first character in the selection in a variable named sFont. Then it launches into a While loop that continues until the start of the range reaches the character that was just before the last character of the original selection.

Within the loop, the Next method moves the range to the next character in the document. Then, the font of this character is compared with the previously saved font name. If it's different, the iCount variable is incremented to indicate that the font has changed, and the name of the new font is saved in the sFont variable. When the loop finishes, the message box displays how many times the macro determined that the font changed.

Note: You can accomplish this type of character-by-character movement through a selection or range in many different ways. For example, I could have coded the While loop like this:

```
While r.Start < iEnd - 1
    r.Start = r.Start + 1
    r.End = r.Start + 1
    If r.Font.Name <> sFont Then
        sFont = r.Font.Name
        iCount = iCount + 1
    End If
Wend
```

And, as I discuss in the next section, you can also code this macro by using the Characters collection of the Selection object.

Working with Text

The following sections describe various ways to work with text in a macro.

Accessing text

The Document, Selection, and Range objects have several properties you can use to access the contents of a selection or range. These properties work the same whether you're using a Document, Selection, or Range object. The following paragraphs describe how they work:

✦ Text: Returns a string that contains the text marked by the selection or range.

✦ Characters: Returns a collection of Range objects, each representing one character of the selection or range. *Note:* There is no Character object. Instead, each character is represented by a separate Range object.

✦ Words: Returns a collection of Range objects, each representing one word of the selection or range. As with characters, there is no separate object for words. Instead, each word is represented by a Range object.

✦ Sentences: A collection of Range objects, each representing one sentence of the selection or range. Again, there is no separate object for sentences. Each sentence is represented by a Range object.

✦ Paragraphs: A collection of Paragraphs, each representing one paragraph of the selection or range. Once again, there is no — made you look! Word's object model *does* have a separate Paragraph object. That's because many formatting options, such as line spacing, indentation, and tabs, are applied to paragraphs via the Paragraph object.

✦ Sections: Returns a collection of Section objects, representing the sections in the selection or range.

You can easily implement the CountFontChanges macro that I present earlier in this chapter (in the section "A macro that moves the selection") by using the Characters collection of the Selection object:

```
Sub CountFontChanges()
    Dim iCount As Integer
    Dim sFont As String
    Dim r As Range
    sFont = Selection.Characters(1).Font.Name
    For Each r In Selection.Characters
        If r.Font.Name <> sFont Then
            sFont = r.Font.Name
            iCount = iCount + 1
        End If
    Next
    MsgBox "The selected text has " & iCount _
        & " font changes."
End Sub
```

Here, the For Each loop accesses the characters in the selection one at a time, so the macro doesn't have to keep track of the start and end of the range as it loops.

Inserting text

The Selection and Range objects offer the following methods for inserting text into your document:

✦ InsertAfter: Inserts the specified text after the selection or range. The selection or range expands to include the new text. For example, the following statement inserts text after the selection:

```
Dim s As String
s = "So let it be written, so let it be done."
Selection.InsertAfter(s)
```

+ `InsertBefore`: Inserts the specified text before the selection or range. The selection or range expands to include the new text. Here's an example that writes text before the selection:

```
Selection.InsertBefore("Listen up!")
```

+ `InsertParagraph`: Replaces the selection with an empty paragraph.

+ `InsertParagraphAfter`: Inserts an empty paragraph after the selection or range. The selection or range expands to include the new paragraph.

+ `InsertParagraphBefore`: Inserts an empty paragraph after the selection or range. The selection or range expands to include the new paragraph.

Rather than using the `InsertParagraph` methods, you can also use the special VBA constant `vbCr` to insert a paragraph mark. For example, the following code moves to the end of the current paragraph, and then inserts the text "Listen Up!" as a separate paragraph:

```
Selection.Move (wdParagraph)
Selection.InsertAfter ("Listen up!" & vbCr)
```

You can use a similar constant, `vbTab`, to insert tab characters. For example:

```
Dim s1, s2 As String
s1 = "Hello"
s2 = "There"
Selection.InsertAfter (s1 & vbTab & s2 & vbCr)
```

Here, the words "Hello" and "There" are inserted into the document, separated by a tab.

Deleting text

I had an English teacher in the 10th grade who told us that any book report that contained the words *stupid, dumb,* or *boring* would get an automatic F. Too bad, because I read a lot of books that were stupid, dumb, *and* boring. I probably would have passed the class if only I had a macro that automatically deleted those words from my book reports.

Here's a macro that uses the `Delete` method of a `Range` object to delete those three words from an entire document, and then displays a message to tell you how many words were deleted:

```
Dim iCount As Integer
Dim r As Range
For Each r in ActiveDocument.Words
    Select Case Trim(r.Text)
        Case "stupid", "dumb", "boring"
            r.Delete
            iCount = iCount + 1
    End Select
Next
MsgBox "Deleted " & iCount & " words."
```

Here, any occurrence of the forbidden words is deleted from the document.

Copying, cutting, and pasting

Both the `Selection` object and the `Range` object support the standard copy, cut, and paste operations via the Clipboard. The methods are, not surprisingly:

+ `Copy`: Copies the selection or range to the Clipboard.

+ `Cut`: Cuts the selection or range to the Clipboard.

+ `Paste`: Pastes the contents of the Clipboard into the selection or range. Use the `Collapse` method to collapse the selection or range if you don't want the Clipboard contents to replace the contents of the selection or range.

For example, the following code copies the contents of the first paragraph in the document to the selection:

```
ActiveDocument.Paragraphs(1).Range.Copy
Selection.Collapse
Selection.Paste
```

Note two things about this example: First, I had to use the `Range` property of the paragraph to get to the `Copy` method — because the `Paragraph` object doesn't have a `Copy` method. And second, I collapsed the selection before pasting it so that the macro doesn't overwrite any text.

You don't always have to use the Clipboard to copy text to another location in the document. For example, the following code does the job without involving the Clipboard:

```
Dim r As Range
Set r = ActiveDocument.Paragraphs(1).Range
Selection.Collapse
Selection.InsertAfter (r.Text)
```

Formatting Text

All the options for formatting text are available through objects you can access as properties of the `Selection` or `Range` objects. For example, to make the current selection bold, set `Selection.Font.Bold` to `True`.

The following paragraphs describe the formatting objects you can access via the properties of the `Selection` or `Range` objects:

✦ `Borders`: A collection of `Border` objects that define the borders for the selection or range.

✦ `Font`: A `Font` object that lets you set character formatting. For more information, see the section "Using the Font object" that's coming right up.

✦ `ParagraphFormat`: A `ParagraphFormat` object that controls paragraph formatting, such as line spacing, alignment, and indentation. For more information, see the section "Using the ParagraphFormat object."

Two other formatting properties you may want to use are

✦ `Style`: Sets the name of the style for the selection or paragraph. For example, to set the selected paragraphs back to the Normal style, use this code:

```
Selection.Style = "Normal"
```

✦ `TabStops`: A collection of `TabStop` objects. This collection is available only from a `Paragraph` object. For example, this code accesses the first Tab stop for the first paragraph in a selection:

```
Dim t As TabStop
Set t = Selection.Paragraphs(1).TabStops(1)
```

Using the Font object

The `Font` object gives you access to all of the character formatting options available via the Format⇨Font dialog box. As a result, most of its properties look familiar. Table 3-5 lists the properties you're most likely to use.

Although you must access most of these properties via the `Font` property of a `Selection` or `Range` object, the `Range` object has shortcuts to the `Bold`, `Italic`, and `Underline` properties. Thus, you can set a range to bold, italic, or underline without going through the `Font` object. For example, this statement sets the first sentence of the active document to bold:

```
ActiveDocument.Sentences(1).Bold
```

The Sentences collection is a collection of Range objects, so Sentences(1) returns a Range object for the first sentence in the collection.

Many font properties can be set to True, False, or the special Word constant wdToggle. The wdToggle constant changes the value of the property from whatever its current value is. So if the property is True, wdToggle changes it to False. If it's False, wdToggle changes it to True. This constant mimics the behavior of many formatting shortcut keys, such as Ctrl+B or Ctrl+I.

Table 3-5	Properties of the Font Object
Property	*Description*
Bold	Applies bold formatting
Color	Sets the font color
DoubleStrikeThrough	Applies double-strikethrough formatting
Emboss	Embosses the text
Engrave	Engraves the text
Hidden	Hides the text
Italic	Applies italic formatting
Kerning	Sets the smallest point size at which Word applies kerning
Name	Sets the font name
Outline	Applies outline formatting
Position	Raises or lowers the text by the number of points specified
Shading	Sets shading for the text
Shadow	Applies a shadow effect
SmallCaps	Applies small cap formatting
Strikethrough	Applies strikethrough formatting
Subscript	Applies subscript formatting
Superscript	Applies superscript formatting
Underline	Underlines the text
UnderlineColor	Sets the color for the underline

Using the ParagraphFormat object

The ParagraphFormat object gives you access to all of the paragraph formatting options available via the Format⇨Paragraph dialog box. As a result, most of its properties look familiar. Table 3-6 lists the most commonly used properties of the ParagraphFormat object.

Note: The properties that require a measurement value (such as `FirstLineIndent`) require the measurement in points. There are 72 points in an inch. But if you don't want to do that calculation manually, you can use the `InchesToPoints` function to do the calculation for you. For example, this code sets the `FirstLineIndent` to ¾":

```
With Selection.ParagraphFormat
    .FirstLineIndent = InchesToPoints(0.75)
End With
```

Table 3-6	Properties of the ParagraphFormat Object
Property	*Description*
Alignment	Sets the alignment. The most common values are wdAlignParagraphLeft, wdAlignParagraphCenter, wdAlignParagraphRight, and wdAlignParagraphJustify.
Borders	Sets the borders for the text.
FirstLineIndent	The indentation for the first line, in points.
KeepTogether	Specifies whether the paragraph is kept on one page.
KeepWithNext	Specifies whether the paragraph is on the same page as the next paragraph.
LeftIndent	Specifies the left indent in points.
LineSpacing	Sets the line spacing in points.
LineSpacingRule	Sets the type of line spacing. The options are wdLineSpace1pt5, wdLineSpaceAtLeast, wdLineSpaceDouble, wdLineSpaceExactly, wdLineSpaceMultiple, and wdLineSpaceSingle.
PageBreakBefore	Specifies whether the paragraph begins a new page.
RightIndent	Specifies the right indent in points.
Shading	Sets the shading for the paragraph.
SpaceAfter	Sets the spacing after the paragraph, in points.
SpaceAfterAuto	Specifies whether Word automatically sets the space after.
SpaceBefore	Sets the spacing before the paragraph, in points.
SpaceBeforeAuto	Specifies whether Word automatically sets the space before.
Style	The name of the style for the paragraph.
TabStops	The TabStops collection for the paragraph.

Chapter 4: Creating UserForms

In This Chapter

⌦ Adding a UserForm to a macro project

⌦ Discovering labels and text boxes

⌦ Fiddling with frames

⌦ Carrying on with check boxes and option buttons

⌦ Working with combo boxes

⌦ Creating list boxes that allow multiple selections

This chapter shows you how to create macros that display customized dialog boxes called *UserForms*. A UserForm can collect information from the user, and then perform actions based on the information the user entered. UserForms are the key to creating sophisticated Word macros that mimic the built-in Word wizards. But UserForms aren't just for complicated macros. Sometimes even a simple macro can benefit from a modest UserForm to get a few critical items of data from the user before proceeding.

Understanding UserForms

UserForms let you obtain any kind of information you need from the user in a single interaction. For example, suppose that you need to know a person's name, company, and e-mail address. You could use a series of InputBox statements, such as this:

```
Dim Name, Company, EmailAddress As String
Name=InputBox("Name:", "Info", Name)
Name=InputBox("Address:", "Info", Address)
Name=InputBox("Email Address:", "Info", EmailAddress)
```

But wouldn't simply displaying a single dialog box to get all three items, as shown in Figure 4-1, be more convenient for the user? With UserForms, you can.

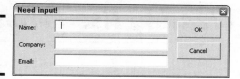

Figure 4-1:
A custom
UserForm.

UserForms are not as powerful as the forms you can create with a full-fledged programming language, such as Visual Basic or C#. However, you can create forms with any of the dialog box controls listed in Table 4-1.

Table 4-1	UserForm Controls	
What It Looks Like	*What It's Called*	*Description*
Name:	Label	Displays text on the form
Type text here.	TextBox	Lets the user enter text
Arial / Arial / Courier New / Symbol	ComboBox	Displays a drop-down list
Times New Roman / Arial / Courier New	ListBox	Displays a scrollable list
Option 1	OptionButton	Used to select one of several alternative settings
Check Here	CheckBox	Supplies a yes/no or on/off setting
Toggle On / Toggle Off	ToggleButton	Yet another way to select yes/no values
Options	Frame	Creates a group of controls
OK	CommandButton	Invokes a sub procedure when clicked
Tab1 / Tab2	TabStrip	Divides a form into multiple tabs
Page1 / Page2	MultiPage	Divides a form into multiple pages

What It Looks Like	What It's Called	Description
	ScrollBar	Displays a scroll bar
	SpinButton	Allows the user to select from a range of values by incrementing or decrementing the value
	Image	Displays a picture

Creating a UserForm

The VBA editor includes a form designer that lets you create UserForms by dragging and dropping controls from a toolbar onto the form. You can then adjust the property settings for each control using the Properties pane. Adjusting the properties is the fun part of creating a UserForm. Figure 4-2 shows a UserForm being created in the form designer.

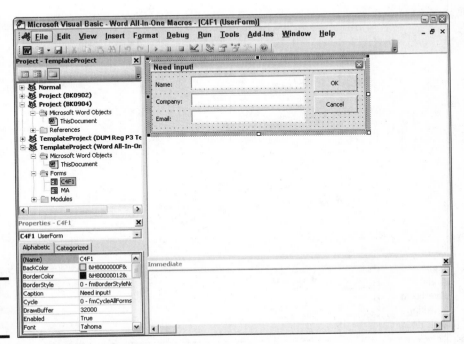

Figure 4-2:
Creating a
UserForm.

To create a UserForm, follow these steps:

1. **Select the project you want to add the UserForm to in Project Explorer.**

   The Project Explorer window appears in the upper-left corner of the VBA editor. Each open document and template is listed as a project. If you want to create a UserForm in the Normal.dot template so that it's available to any document, you can just select Normal in Project Explorer. But if you want to create the UserForm in another template, you must first open that template by choosing File⇨Open. If you simply open a document that's attached to the template, the template is listed in Project Explorer, but you can't access it.

2. **Choose Insert⇨UserForm.**

   A blank UserForm is created, as shown in Figure 4-3.

3. **To add a control to the form, click the control you want to add in the Toolbox, and then click the form where you want to add the control.**

   After you add a control, you can drag it around the form to its final position. And you can resize the control by clicking the control to select it, and then dragging one of its size handles.

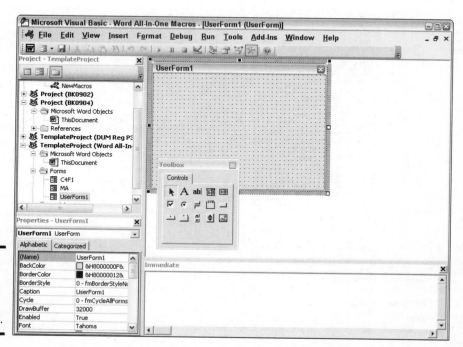

Figure 4-3:
A blank
UserForm
awaiting
your design.

4. **To change a property, select the control you want to change, and then use the Properties window to set the property you want to change.**

   To set a property for the form itself, click the form anywhere outside one of its controls. You find more information about setting properties for form control in the next section.

   You can also use the drop-down list that appears at the top of the Properties window to choose a form or control.

5. **To see how your form will appear when run, click the Run button.**

   Running the form from the VBA editor in this way is useful for making sure the form looks the way you want. When you're satisfied, click the form's Close button to close the form.

6. **Write whatever code is necessary to implement the form's processing requirements.**

   You can write code that executes whenever the user clicks a button by double-clicking the button in the form designer. This action takes you to the VBA editor and creates a Sub procedure that's all set up to run when the user clicks the control.

   You may also want to write code that executes when the form first displays. To do that, switch to the code window by choosing View⇔Code. Then, choose the form from the drop-down list at the top left of the code window and choose Initialize from the drop-down list at the top right of the code window. A Sub procedure automatically runs when the form is initialized. (One common use for the form Initialize procedure is to add items to a drop-down list or list box control.) For more information, see the sections "Using Combo Boxes" and "Using List Boxes" later in this chapter.

Here are a few other points to ponder as you create UserForms:

✦ Be sure to save your work often by clicking the Save button in the VBA editor.

✦ To remove a control from the form, click the control to select it and press the Delete key.

✦ If your form requires several similar controls, create one of them first and adjust its properties the way you want. Then, use good old Copy & Paste to duplicate it. Select the control, press Ctrl+C, and then click the form to select it and press Ctrl+V.

✦ If you inadvertently double-click a control and the code window pops up, you can select and delete the Sub and End Sub statements that are generated. To get back to the form designer, choose View⇔Object.

✦ If the Toolbox disappears on you, you can get it back by choosing View➪ Toolbox.

✦ If you accidentally create the form in the wrong template, you can use the Project Explorer window to drag the form to the correct template.

✦ If you want the form to appear automatically whenever you create a new document based on the template that contains the form, create an AutoNew macro in the template. This macro can then call the form's Show method to show the form. For example:

```
Sub AutoNew()
    UserForm1.Show
End Sub
```

✦ Even if you include an AutoNew macro to automatically call up the form when a new document is created, you may also want to provide another way for the user to access the form after the document opens. For example, you may want to create a macro similar to the preceding AutoNew macro to show the form. Then, you can create a custom toolbar button or menu command to call up the form. For more information about customizing toolbars or menus, see Book VIII, Chapter 2.

Working with Controls

Most of the work of creating macros that use UserForms is setting up the controls that appear on the form. After you add a control to a form, you need to adjust the control's properties. You can do that via the Properties window. First, select the control whose properties you want to adjust. Then, locate the property you want to adjust in the Properties window and specify whatever settings you want to apply.

All controls have several properties in common. In particular:

✦ Name: The name of the control, which is used to access the control from code. Provide a meaningful name for every control that you need to refer to in code. For controls, such as labels, that aren't referred to in code, you can leave the default names (such as Label1) as they are.

When you create a name for a control, beginning the control with a short prefix to indicate the type of control is a good idea. For example, give text boxes names such as txtName and txtEmail, and give buttons names such as btnOK and btnCancel.

✦ Caption: Not all controls have a Caption property, but most do. The Caption property sets the text that the control displays. The default value for the Caption property is the control's name, so you almost certainly want to change it to something more suitable.

✦ `Accelerator`: This property specifies the letter that the user can use along with the Alt key to activate the control without using the mouse. The first occurrence of this letter is underlined in the control's caption. For example, if you specify Proceed for the `Caption` property and "o" for the `Accelerator` property, the caption appears as Pr<u>o</u>ceed on the control.

✦ `TabStop`: Indicates whether the user can move to the control by pressing the Tab key. Controls that accept input usually have this property set to `True`.

✦ `TabIndex`: Specifies the order in which the Tab key cycles through the controls. After you have all the controls set up on a form, you can set the `TabIndex` property of each control to get the tab order right. For example, set the `TabIndex` to 1 for the control you want to be first in the tab order; 2 for the control you want to be second, and so on.

✦ `Enabled`: Indicates whether the control is enabled. If you set this property to `False`, the control is dimmed.

✦ `ControlTip`: This property supplies text that's displayed as a tip if the user hovers the mouse over the control for a few moments. You can use this property to provide additional information about what the control does or what happens if the user clicks the control.

After you have a control's properties set the way you want, you can add code for the control by double-clicking the control. Double-clicking takes you to the code window and creates a `Sub` procedure that executes if the user clicks the control. In most cases, you create a `Sub` procedure only for command button controls. However, you can create a procedure to handle clicks for any control on a UserForm, not just command buttons.

The following sections describe some of the details you need to know to work with the most common types of UserForm controls, such as command buttons, labels, and text boxes.

Using Command Buttons

Command buttons are the workhorses of most UserForms. You usually need to set one property for a command button: the `Caption` property. Use the `Caption` property to specify the text you want to appear on the button. You may also want to set the `Accelerator` property for command buttons.

The hard part of working with command buttons is writing the code that executes when the user clicks the button. To create this code, simply double-click the button in the form designer.

Creating a Cancel button

All forms need a Cancel button that lets the user bail out of the form without doing anything. The click procedure for the Cancel button typically looks like this:

```
Private Sub btnCancel_Click()
    Hide
End Sub
```

The Hide statement is actually a call to the Hide method of the current form, which closes the form and returns the user to the document. You could specify the form name on this statement, but the current form is assumed by default if you don't, so just coding Hide is enough.

The Hide method doesn't stop the macro from running. If your macro needs to do additional work after it closes the form, it can include additional statements after the Hide method call.

Creating an OK button

Most UserForms also contain a button that processes the data that the user enters on the form. This button goes by various names, such as OK or Save, depending on what the form does. In many cases, the code for this button extracts the data the user entered in the form and inserts it into the document, either at the location of the insertion point or at predefined locations marked by bookmarks.

For example, the following code shows the click procedure for the OK button in the form that was shown in Figure 4-1. Here, the information from the three text boxes is inserted into the document after the selection:

```
Private Sub CommandButton1_Click()
    Selection.InsertAfter txtName.Text & vbCr
    Selection.InsertAfter txtCompany.Text & vbCr
    Selection.InsertAfter txtEmail.Text & vbCr
    Selection.Collapse wdCollapseEnd
    Hide
End Sub
```

After the text is inserted, the selection collapses and the form closes.

Suppose you want to insert the text in an area of the document marked by a Customer bookmark rather than in the selection. In that case, you use code similar to this:

```
Private Sub CommandButton1_Click()
    If ActiveDocument.Bookmarks.Exists("Customer") Then
        Dim r As Range
        Set r = ActiveDocument.Bookmarks("Customer").Range
        r.InsertAfter txtName.Text & vbCr
        r.InsertAfter txtCompany.Text & vbCr
        r.InsertAfter txtEmail.Text & vbCr
        Hide
    Else
        MsgBox "Missing bookmark!"
    End If
End Sub
```

Using Labels

Label controls display text on the form. For plain, unexciting labels, just drag a label control from the Toolbox onto the form, set the label's Caption property to the text you want to display, and be done with it. For fancier labels, you can set the following properties via the Properties window:

+ Font: The font used for the Caption text. When you set the Font property in the Properties window, a Font dialog box appears that allows you to choose the font, style (bold, italic), and size.

+ TextAlign: Lets you choose the text alignment: left, centered, or right.

+ SpecialEffect: Lets you apply one of the four special effects shown in Figure 4-4.

+ WordWrap: Indicates whether the text wraps onto multiple lines if the label isn't wide enough to display it all.

Figure 4-4:
Special effects you can apply to label controls.

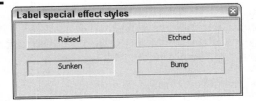

Label special effect styles	
Raised	Etched
Sunken	Bump

Using Text Boxes

Text boxes are the main way to get text input from the user for your macro. The user's input is available via the Text property. The following code assigns the text entered into a text box named `txtCompany` to a variable named `Company`:

```
Company = txtCompany.Text
```

You can also use the `Text` property to assign an initial value to a text box. Then, if the user doesn't change the value, the initial value is retained. You can set the initial text value with an assignment statement such as this example in the form's `Initialize` procedure:

```
txtCompany.Text = "John Wiley & Sons, Inc."
```

Or, you can set the initial value in the Properties window when you design the form.

Text boxes have a few other noteworthy properties:

+ `MaxLength`: Limits the number of characters the user can enter. When the entry exceeds the `MaxLength` limit, anything else the user types is ignored.

+ `MultiLine`: If set to `True`, this property allows the user to enter more than one line of text into the text box. The user must press Shift+Enter to create a new line. You usually want to increase the height of the text box so that the additional lines can display.

+ `PasswordChar`: Allows you to create a password entry field. Instead of displaying the text entered by the user, the password entry field displays the password character. That way, nosey bystanders can't see what the user typed.

Using Frames

A frame control is a container that lets you group controls on a form. A frame not only adds visual structure to the form, but it also helps out when you use option buttons, as I discuss in the next section.

To use a frame control, just drop a frame on your form, and then resize it and position it however you want. Then, you can drop other controls onto the frame.

The only property you're likely to set for a frame control is the `Caption` property, which sets the text displayed in the margin of the frame. You may also want to play with the `SpecialEffect` property if you want to give the frame a non-standard look.

Using Check Boxes and Option Buttons

Check boxes and option buttons allow the user to select options. For example, Figure 4-5 shows a UserForm that gathers information needed to order a pizza. The size of the pizza is selected by a group of option buttons and the toppings are selected by check boxes. (This UserForm also uses frames to provide nice borders around the Size and Toppings sections of the dialog box.)

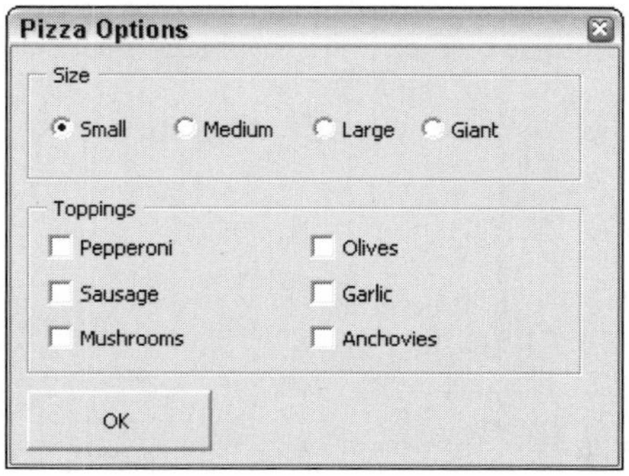

Figure 4-5:
A pizza
order form.

When you create a check box or option button, you use the `Caption` property to set the text that describes the option. Then, in your code, you can use the `Value` property to determine whether the check box is checked or the option is selected.

Grouping option buttons

The main difference between check boxes and option buttons is that check boxes are independent of one another. In contrast, option buttons travel in groups, and a user can select only one button in a group at a time. To indicate which group an option button belongs to, you set the `GroupName` property. If a form has only one group of option buttons, you can leave this property blank. You can also ignore the `GroupName` property if you place each group of option buttons in a separate frame. But if you have two or more groups of option buttons and they're not isolated in frames, you must set this property to indicate which group each option button belongs to.

Testing option button and check box values

You can test the setting of a check box or option button in code by testing the `Value` property for `True` or `False`. For example, here's the code that runs when the user clicks the OK button for the UserForm shown in Figure 4-5:

```
Private Sub btnOK_Click()

    Dim s As String
    s = "Pizza size: "
    If obtnSmall.Value = True Then
        s = s & "Small" & vbCr
    ElseIf obtnMedium.Value = True Then
        s = s & "Medium" & vbCr
    ElseIf obtnLarge.Value = True Then
        s = s & "Large" & vbCr
    ElseIf obtnGiant.Value = True Then
        s = s & "Giant" & vbCr
    End If

    s = s & "Toppings: " & vbCr
    If chkPepperoni.Value = True Then
        s = s & vbTab & "Pepperoni" & vbCr
    End If
    If chkSausage.Value = True Then
        s = s & vbTab & "Sausage" & vbCr
    End If
    If chkMushrooms.Value = True Then
        s = s & vbTab & "Mushrooms" & vbCr
    End If
    If chkOlives.Value = True Then
        s = s & vbTab & "Olives" & vbCr
    End If
    If chkGarlic.Value = True Then
        s = s & vbTab & "Garlic" & vbCr
    End If
    If chkAnchovies.Value = True Then
        s = s & vbTab & "Anchovies" & vbCr
    End If

    Selection.InsertAfter s
    Hide
End Sub
```

In this example, a string variable named s constructs the text that's inserted into the document. First, the option buttons are checked in a series of If/ElseIf statements to determine which size was selected. Then, a series of separate If statements determine which toppings to include in the order.

Suppose you run this form, select a large pizza, and check the Pepperoni, Garlic, and Anchovies check boxes. In that case, the following text is inserted into the document when you click the OK button:

```
Pizza size: Large
Toppings:
    Pepperoni
    Garlic
    Anchovies
```

You'd better be hungry because you'll probably end up eating this one by yourself.

Using Combo Boxes

A combo box displays a drop-down list that lists options from which the user can choose. Depending on how you configure the combo box, the user may also be able to type in a selection if one of the items in the list isn't suitable.

List boxes are similar to combo boxes. I discuss them in the next section, titled (surprisingly enough) "Using list boxes."

When you create a combo box, you can set the `Style` property to indicate what type of combo box you want to create. The choices are `DropDownCombo` and `DropDownList`. `DropDownCombo` allows the user to enter a value in the text box part of the control. `DropDownList` forces the user to choose one of the items from the list.

To use a combo box in a macro, you have to know how to write code to do two things: load the items for the list into the combo box and determine which of the list items the user selected. I describe these coding techniques in the following sections.

Loading items into a combo box

To load items into a combo box, you use the `AddItem` method. The best time to use the `AddItem` method is when the form is initializing. For example, here's an `Initialization` procedure for a form that loads a combo box with items that can be included as toppings on a pizza:

```
Sub UserForm1_Initialize()
    cboSize.AddItem "Small"
    cboSize.AddItem "Medium"
    cboSize.AddItem "Large"
    cboSize.AddItem "Giant"
End Sub
```

And here's a `For Each` loop that loads the names of all the available fonts into a combo box:

```
Dim FontName As Variant
For Each FontName in FontNames
    cboFonts.AddItem FontName
Next
```

Determining which item was selected

To determine which item from a combo box the user selected, use the `Value` property. For example:

```
Dim Size As String
Size = cboSize.Value
```

If, for some reason, you're interested in knowing the index number of the item chosen by the user, use the `ListItem` property instead. However, be aware that unlike most VBA indexes, the `ListItem` value for the first item in the combo box is 0, not 1.

Setting the selected item

In some cases, you want to set the item that's selected in a combo box from VBA. For example, you may want to force the first entry in the combo box to be selected when the form is initialized. You can use the `ListIndex` property to do that. For example:

```
cboSize.ListIndex = 0
```

Here, the first item is selected. (***Remember:*** Combo boxes number their list items beginning with 0, not 1.)

Using List Boxes

A list box is similar to a combo box, but doesn't have the drop-down ability that combo boxes do. Instead, a list box displays one or more items from the list, depending on the vertical size of the list box. If all the items don't fit, a scroll bar appears to allow the user to scroll through the list.

In most cases, list boxes are much less useful than combo boxes. However, list boxes have one feature that combo boxes don't have: the ability to let the user select more than one item from the list. For example, Figure 4-6 shows a form with a list box that lets the user select from a long list of pizza toppings.

To get the effect shown in the list box in Figure 4-6, I set two properties for the list box:

✦ `MultiSelect`: I set this property to `Multi` to allow more than one selection.

✦ `ListStyle`: I set this property to `Option` to display check boxes next to each item in the list.

Figure 4-6:
A pizza
order form
with a list
box and a
combo box.

Loading items into a list box

You load items into a list box just like you load items into a combo box. For
example, here is some of the code from the form Initialize procedure for
the form shown in Figure 4-6:

```
lbToppings.AddItem ("Pepperoni")
lbToppings.AddItem ("Sausage")
lbToppings.AddItem ("Salami")
lbToppings.AddItem ("Linguica")
lbToppings.AddItem ("Pastrami")
lbToppings.AddItem ("Ground Beef")
lbToppings.AddItem ("Chicken")
lbToppings.AddItem ("Canadian Bacon")
```

Dealing with multiple selections

Determining which items are selected in a multi-select list box is tricky. You
need to use three properties of the list box to do this:

✦ ListCount: The number of items in the list.

✦ List(*index*): Retrieves the specified item from the list.

✦ Selected(*index*): Indicates whether or not the specified item was
selected.

Putting these three properties together, the following For/Next loop creates
a string variable named msg that lists all the toppings selected from the
lbToppings list box:

```
Dim s As String
Dim i As Integer
For i = 0 To lbToppings.ListCount - 1
    If lbToppings.Selected(i) = True Then
        s = s & lbToppings.List(i) & vbCr
    End If
Next i
```

The If statement determines whether the item for the current index value is selected. If so, the item is appended to the string.

Index

E

help, creating for, 517–518
overview, 505–507
pre-printed, 518
templates, creating, 507–509
text fields, creating, 511–512
Forms toolbar
buttons, 510–511
creating forms, 508
Formula dialog box, 205
=(Formula) field code, 503
formulas, in tables, 205–207
For/Next loops (VBA), 700
Forward button (Web toolbar), 436
Fraction and Radical Templates button
(Equation Editor toolbar), 420
fractions, formatting with AutoFormat, 273
Frame dialog box, 377–379
frames
creating, 377
formatting, 377
overview, 376
UserForms, adding, 740
Web pages, creating, 471–473
Web pages, editing, 475–476
Web pages, formatting, 473–475
Web pages, hyperlinks and, 476
Web pages, overview, 469–471
Web pages, previewing, 478
Web pages, scroll bars, 475
Web pages, setting as resizable, 475
Web pages, tables of contents and,
476–478
Frames Properties dialog box, formatting
frames (Web pages), 473–475
Frames toolbar
Table of Contents button, 476–478
overview, 471–472
free Web sites, 442
freeform shapes, drawing, 345–347
Frequently Used Programs List, launching
Word, 10
From existing document option (New
Document task pane), 22
Front of the Sheet option (Print dialog
box), 93

FTP (File Transfer Protocol)
documents, opening from, 435
documents, saving to, 435–436
overview, 433
site setup, 434–435
function text type (Equation Editor), 421
functions
strings (VBA), 690–691
user-defined, 706–707

G

General tab (Options dialog box)
options, 628–631
overview, 622
generating indexes, 550–551
Getting Started options (task pane)
overview, 13
recently used files list, 18
GIF files, defined, 320
global templates
activating, 48–49
characteristics, 47
defined, 40
macros, 48
Go Back command, 236–237
Go button (Web toolbar), 437
Go To command, document navigation,
234–235
GoBack method (Application object), 713
GoForward method (Application
object), 713
GoToButton field code, 500
gradient effects, 361–362
grammar checker
options, 292–293, 295
overview, 290–291
readability statistics, 293–294
graphics. *See* drawing; images; pictures
graphs. *See* charts
Greater Than comparison test (mail merge
data), 617
Greater Than or Equal comparison test
(mail merge data), 617

Help system online, 101–102
network places, creating, 428–430
OfficeOnline site (clip art source), 325
Internet Explorer, documents, opening in, 432–433
Internet service providers, overview, 441
Is Blank comparison test (mail merge data), 617
Is Not Blank comparison test (mail merge data), 617
Italic button (Formatting toolbar), 108
italic font, applying, 108
Italic property (Font object), 729

J

JPG files, defined, 320
justify paragraph, 117

K

Keep lines together option (Paragraph dialog box), 121–122
Keep Original Formatting option (table of authorities), 571
Keep Track of Formatting (Options dialog box Edit tab), 633
Keep with next option (Paragraph dialog box), 121–122
KeepTogether property (ParagraphFormat object), 730
KeepWithNext property (ParagraphFormat object), 730
kerning fonts, 112–114
Kerning property (Font object), 729
keyboard
    document navigation, 231–232
    text, deleting, 244
    text, selecting, 242–243
keyboard shortcuts
    case, changing, 251
    closing documents, 18
    column breaks, 183
    copy/cut/paste commands, 245–246
    creating custom, 657–658

deleting all content from documents, 45
Equation Editor, 422–423
exiting Word, 19
fields, 493
fields, locking, unlocking, and unlinking, 499
Find command, 253
footnote window, displaying, 225
Go Back command, 236–237
Go To command, 234
heading styles (predefined), 558
Mark Index Entry dialog box, displaying, 548
Normal paragraph style, reapplying, 145
opening documents, 17, 22
Outline view, 524–525
paragraph alignment and line spacing, 118
predefined heading styles, 152
printing, 15, 89
printing list of, 659
Redo command, 237
Replace command, 259
resetting, 658–659
saving documents, 16, 33
selecting text, 243
Start button, displaying, 10
styles, assigning to, 150–152
table navigation, 195
keystrokes, forms, filling out, 516–517
Keywords field code, 501
keywords (VBA). *See also* statements (VBA)
    As, 687
    Static, 688

L

Label Height field (New Custom laser dialog box), 585
Label Name field (New Custom laser dialog box), 585
Label Options dialog box, 611
Label Width field (New Custom laser dialog box), 585
Labeled Arrow Templates button (Equation Editor toolbar), 420